M000251591

Rethinking the Andes–Amazonia Divide

Rethinking the Andes–Amazonia Divide

A cross-disciplinary exploration

Edited by

Adrian J. Pearce, David G. Beresford-Jones and
Paul Heggarty

First published in 2020 by
UCL Press
University College London
Gower Street
London WC1E 6BT

Available to download free: www.uclpress.co.uk

ISBN: 978-1-78735-747-1 (Hbk)
ISBN: 978-1-78735-741-9 (Pbk)
ISBN: 978-1-78735-735-8 (PDF)
ISBN: 978-1-78735-753-2 (epub)
ISBN: 978-1-78735-759-4 (mobi)
DOI: https://doi.org/10.14324/111.9781787357358

This book is dedicated to John Hemming, who has crossed the Andes–Amazonia divide more than most, both intellectually and on foot, and to the memory of Tom Zuidema, whose chapter here constitutes the final publication in a long and distinguished career.

Contents

Note: Within the text, references to numbered Chapters refer to other chapters in this volume.

List of figures

List of tables

List of contributors

Adrian J. Pearce is Associate Professor of Spanish and Latin American History at University College London. He has worked on Spanish and British colonialism in the Americas, with a focus primarily on politics and economics and on the eighteenth century. On these topics, he published *British Trade with Spanish America, 1763–1808* (2007, Spanish language ed. 2014) and *The Origins of Bourbon Reform in Spanish South America, 1700–1763* (2014). Since 2008, he has been involved with the ongoing interdisciplinary project of which this volume is the latest product, and he also co-edited (with Paul Heggarty) *History and Language in the Andes* (2011). He currently works on the native peoples of the Andes in the nineteenth century and on the Anglo-Argentine Falklands War of 1982. His teaching interests range across Latin American history, from pre-Columbian times to the present, and also include modern Spain.

David G. Beresford-Jones is a fellow of the Heinz Heinen Centre for Advanced Study, University of Bonn, and an affiliated researcher at the McDonald Institute for Archaeological Research at the University of Cambridge. His archaeological research interests are diverse and cover a range of geographical areas and chronological periods, but have in common two main themes: the transition to agriculture and its role in determining past human impacts on ecosystems and landscapes, and the synthesis between different disciplines. To the latter end he has long collaborated with linguists, geneticists and historians of the Andean Region and convened, along with his fellow co-editors of this book, a series of interdisciplinary meetings, including the 'Rethinking the Andes-Amazonia Divide' symposium, held at the Max Planck Institute for Evolutionary Anthropology in Leipzig in June 2014, from which this book emerges.

Paul Heggarty is a senior scientist in the Department of Linguistic and Cultural Evolution at the Max Planck Institute for the Science of Human History in Jena, Germany. His focus is on language (pre)history, aiming to ensure that the perspective from linguistics is better understood outside that field, to contribute towards a more coherent, cross-disciplinary vision of the human past. To that end he works closely with archaeologists, geneticists and historians. Within interests that range worldwide, his specialisms are in the origins of the Indo-European language family, and in the indigenous languages of the Andes, particularly the divergence history of the Quechua and Aymara families. Since 2008 he has convened, along with his fellow co-editors of this book, a series of nine interdisciplinary conferences and symposia on the Andean past. Among those was the symposium 'Rethinking the Andes–Amazonia Divide', from which this book emerges.

Willem F. H. Adelaar is Emeritus Professor of Amerindian Languages and Cultures at Leiden University in the Netherlands. He has conducted field research on different varieties of Quechua and on minor languages of the Andes. He has also worked on the genetic relations of South American languages of the Andes and the Amazonian region and has been involved in international activities addressing the issue of language endangerment. His further areas of expertise include linguistic reconstruction, contact and areal linguistics, oral literature and ethno-history of South American and Mesoamerican peoples, as well as the interface of linguistic studies with archaeological and historical research. His publications include *Tarma Quechua* (1977) and the comprehensive *The Languages of the Andes* (2004), of which he is the main author.

Chiara Barbieri is a molecular anthropologist, specialized in the multidisciplinary study of human past and present diversity. She is a senior researcher at the University of Zurich and a research associate at the Max Planck Institute for the Science of Human History in Jena. She did her PhD at the Max Planck Institute for Evolutionary Anthropology in Leipzig. Her work draws on the parallels between genetics and linguistics, and includes case studies from sub-Saharan Africa, southern Europe, and South America. She is currently focusing on Andean prehistory and on the diffusion of the Quechua language family.

Cristiana Bertazoni holds a PhD in Art History and Theory from the University of Essex (UK). She currently works as invited lecturer at the Department of Anthropology of the Americas at the University of Bonn (Germany) where she is also a member of the Research Group Amazon-Andes. She is a founder member of the Centro de Estudos Mesoamericanos e Andinos at the University of São Paulo (Brazil) where she was one of the coordinators for seven years. She has worked as a postdoctoral researcher for the Museum of Archaeology and Ethnology of the University of São Paulo, as associate research fellow for the University of London and as curatorial assistant for the British Museum. She is one of the editors of the book *História e arqueologia indígena: Tempos Pré-Colombianos e coloniais* (2017). Her interdisciplinary research focuses on the Inca Empire and its connections with Western Amazonian groups during pre-Columbian and colonial times.

José M. Capriles, PhD, is a Bolivian anthropological archaeologist who is broadly interested in the transition from foraging to food-producing communities in the Andean highlands and Amazonian lowlands of central South America. He is presently an assistant professor in the Department of Anthropology at Pennsylvania State University.

Tom D. Dillehay is Rebecca Webb Wilson University Distinguished Professor of Anthropology, Religion, and Culture and Professor of Anthropology and Latin

American Studies in the Department of Anthropology, Vanderbilt University, and Profesor Titular in the Escuela de Arqueologia, Universidad Austral de Chile, Puerto Montt. Known mainly for his outstanding work at the older-than-Clovis site of Monte Verde in Chile, Tom has carried out numerous archaeological and anthropological projects in Peru, Chile, Argentina and other South American countries, and in the United States. His main interests are migration, long-term transformative processes leading to political and economic change, and the interdisciplinary and historical methodologies designed to study those processes. He has been a visiting professor at several universities around the world. He currently directs several interdisciplinary projects focused on long-term human and environmental interaction on the north coast of Peru and on the political and cultural identity of the Mapuche people in Chile. Professor Dillehay is a member of the American Academy of Arts and Sciences.

Lars Fehren-Schmitz is an associate professor in the Department of Anthropology at the University of California, Santa Cruz (UCSC) and co-director of the UCSC Paleogenomics Labs. He received a PhD in Evolutionary Biology and Ecology from the Georg-August-University Goettingen, Germany, and holds an MA in Prehistoric Archaeology from the same institution. His research interests include the genomic population history of Central and South America, the interplay of culture and biology in shaping human genomic diversity, and the evolutionary impact of complex human–environment systems in general.

Rik van Gijn is a lecturer at Leiden University. His research interests focus on South American indigenous languages, with a special interest in western South America. His research topics include descriptive linguistics, (areal) typology, and language contact.

Alexander Herrera Wassilowsky's research builds on the historical ecology approach developed to study strategies of settlement in the eastern Conchucos mountains of his native Peru, and addresses the *longue durée* of identities, interaction and territories across the Andes. Investigations into ancient hydraulic technology over the last two decades have led him to query standard usage of territory and identity in archaeological discourse, on the one hand, and to highlight the potential for climate change adaptation of ancient hydraulic system rehabilitation, on the other. Ongoing research in the Ancash region of Peru and the Pasto – Nariño area of southern Colombia dovetails with curatorial work at Los Andes University, Bogotá, where he teaches archaeology and precolonial art history.

Alf Hornborg is an anthropologist and Professor of Human Ecology at Lund University, Sweden. His PhD thesis in Cultural Anthropology (Uppsala University, 1986) built on a comparative analysis of indigenous kinship terminologies from lowland South America. One of his research interests is the application of world-system perspectives to account for archaeological and linguistic distribution patterns in ancient Amazonia and the Andes. He has also applied a world-system approach to various topics in interdisciplinary fields such as environmental history, political ecology and ecological economics. He is the author of *The Power of the Machine* (2001), *Global Ecology and Unequal Exchange* (2011), *Global Magic* (2016), and *Nature, Society, and Justice in the Anthropocene* (2019). He is also editor of *Rethinking Environmental History* (2007), *The World System and the Earth System* (2007), *Ethnicity in Ancient Amazonia* (2011), and *Ecology and Power* (2012).

Peter Kaulicke is Professor of Archaeology at the Pontifical Catholic University of Peru, where he has taught since 1982. His research foci include Archaic and Formative chronology, funerary contexts and analysis, art and religion, the origins of social complexity, the ethnohistory–archaeology relationship, and the history of archaeological research in Peru. He has excavated at many sites on the coast and in the highlands, such as Uchcumachay, Pandanche, Vicus and Coyungo. He has received several awards and has been guest professor at many universities and research centres in Asia (China, Japan), Africa (Cairo), Europe (France, Spain, Germany), as well as North and South America. He is an Ordinary Member of the German Archaeological Institute and the Institute of Andean Studies, among others. He has been director of the *Boletín de Arqueología PUCP* and is author and/or editor/co-editor of some twenty books and about 200 papers.

Umberto Lombardo is an earth scientist working at the University of Bern. He studies landscape evolution and human–environment interactions in southern Amazonia during the Holocene. His interests include neotectonics, fluvial geomorphology, paleosols, pre-Columbian agriculture and settlement patterns and the region's earliest hunter-gatherer occupations. In particular, over the past five years he has been investigating human presence, anthropogenic landscape modifications and environmental change during the Holocene in the Llanos de Moxos, Bolivian Amazon.

Eduardo Machicado Murillo is the resident field geoarchaeologist at the Cambridge Archaeological Unit, Archaeology Department, University of Cambridge. Originally from Bolivia, he has been part of long-term research projects from the South Titicaca Basin (University of California, Berkeley) to North Eastern Bolivia in the Llanos de Moxos (DAI/KAAK, the German Archaeological Institute's Commission for Archaeology of Non-European Cultures). His most recent work is focused on the micromorphology and geochemistry of raised field agriculture (*camellones*) and pre-Columbian settlement sites in San Ignacio de Moxos.

Brian McCray is a doctoral candidate in the Anthropology Department at Vanderbilt University. His research focuses on interregional connections and boundary processes at the interface of the Andes and Amazon. He has conducted field research in Peru's Amazonas province since 2011.

Pieter Muysken obtained his BA from Yale University (1972) and his PhD from the University of Amsterdam (1977). His main research interests are Andean languages, Creole languages, and language contact. He was awarded the Spinoza

Prize in 1998, a KNAW Academy Chair in 2008, and an ERC Advanced Grant in 2009. His current work focuses on language contact and language history in South America. He is a Member of the Royal Netherlands Academy of Sciences, Academia Europea, and the Max Planck Gesellschaft. He is author of *Bilingual Speech: A Typology of Code-Mixing* (2000), *The Languages of the Andes* (2004, Willem Adelaar, in collaboration with Pieter Muysken) and *Functional Categories* (2008), all from Cambridge University Press.

Patricia J. Netherly is a research associate professor in the Department of Anthropology at Vanderbilt University, USA.

Eduardo Góes Neves is Professor of Brazilian Archaeology at the Museum of Archaeology and Ethnology for the University of Sao Paulo (MAE-USP), Brazil. He has more than 30 years of research experience in the Brazilian Amazon, where he has coordinated different multi-year survey and excavation projects. He is a past president of the Brazilian Archaeological Society (2009–11), a past member of the Board of Directors of the Society for American Archaeology (2011–13), and has served in the Advisory Council of the Wenner-Gren Foundation for Anthropological Research (2011–14). He is also faculty at the Graduate Program of Neotropical Archaeology in the Polytechnic University of Litoral (Guayaquil, Ecuador). He has around 120 publications, including books, reports, peer-reviewed articles and book chapters, and texts for the general public. He has advised 25 masters dissertations and 13 PhD theses, and is currently supervising 10 PhD projects. His current research is a joint Bolivia–Brazil–UK project on the long-term landscape and indigenous history of the Southwestern Amazon.

Heiko Prümers is a senior researcher at the German Archaeological Institute's Commission for Archaeology of Non-European Cultures (DAI/KAAK) at Bonn. He has MA and PhD degrees in Americanist Studies from the Rheinische Friedrich-Wilhelms-Universität, Bonn. His research topics relate to settlement archaeology and pre-Hispanic textiles. He has done fieldwork in Mexico, Ecuador, Peru, and Bolivia. Currently he is part of a joint project of the DAI and the Pontificia Universidad Católica del Ecuador on the formative Machalilla culture of the Ecuadorian coast.

Fabrício R. Santos is full professor at the Federal University of Minas Gerais (UFMG) in Belo Horizonte, Brazil. He is a biologist and geneticist with a PhD in Biochemistry in UFMG (1995), post-doctorates in Human Evolutionary Genetics at Oxford University (1995–7), and at the National Geographic Society and University of Pennsylvania (2008). He is resident professor at the Institute of Advanced Studies (IEAT) of UFMG, former President of the Brazilian Society of Genetics (2014 and 2016), and a member of the Ibero-American Academy of Evolutionary Biology (AIBE). He has published more than 200 peer-reviewed articles, as well as scientific books and chapters. He coordinates a research group focused on natural history and the evolutionary biology of biodiversity and human populations. From

2005 to 2015 he coordinated the Genographic Project in South America, funded by the National Geographic Society, working with indigenous populations from different countries of South America.

André Strauss is a Brazilian bioarchaeologist interested in the deep history of Native Americans. He received his BA (Social Sciences and Geology) and MA (Genetics) from the University of São Paulo (USP) and was a PhD candidate at the Max Planck Institute for Evolutionary Anthropology (Germany) and a fellow at the Konrad Lorenz Institute (Austria). He obtained a PhD in Archaeological Sciences from the Eberhard Karls Universität Tübingen (Germany) and is an assistant professor at the Museum of Archaeology and Ethnology of USP. Currently, he coordinates a multi-disciplinary project on the population history and biocultural adaptation of ancient Native Brazilians based on isotopic analysis, ancient DNA and virtual anthropology. He is the director of archaeological excavations at Lapa do Santo, a Late Pleistocene/Early Holocene site in the Lagoa Santa region. He also works in northern Peru (Lambayeque) on a project aiming to better understand the relationship between long-term adaptive strategies and the emergence of complex societies.

Vera Tyuleneva was born in Saint Petersburg, Russia, and has lived and worked in Cusco since 1999. She graduated in History and Art History from the Saint Petersburg State University and received her Master's degree in Anthropology from the European University at Saint Petersburg. She holds a PhD in History and Andean Studies from the Pontifical Catholic University of Peru (PUCP – Lima). Her main areas of interest include relations between the Andean region and the Amazon lowlands during the late pre-colonial and early colonial period. She has been a professor at the Universidad San Ignacio de Loyola (USIL) International Center for Studies and Research in Cusco since 2013, and its director since 2016.

Darryl Wilkinson is an assistant professor in the Department of Religion at Dartmouth College. He received his PhD in anthropology from Columbia University and has held postdoctoral fellowships at several institutions, including the University of Cambridge and the University of Wisconsin-Madison. His research interests include the archaeology and visual culture of the ancient Americas, the deep history of interactions between Amazonia and the Andes, and the development of new theoretical approaches to infrastructure. He currently directs the Amaybamba Archaeological Project, situated on the eastern slopes of southern Peru (La Convención, Cusco).

Roberto Zariquiey is a Peruvian linguist. He has a PhD in Linguistics from LaTrobe University (Melbourne, Australia); for his thesis, he wrote a reference grammar of Kakataibo, which was granted an honourable mention in the prestigious Panini Award (from the Association for Linguistic Typology). This grammar was published by the Grammar Library of Mouton De Grutier (2018). He has conducted linguistic fieldwork in both the Andes and the Amazon. Most of his current research is dedicated to the documentation and typologically oriented description of Peruvian languages of the Panoan family (a mid-sized Amazonian language family with members in Peru, Brazil and Bolivia), the grammatical structure of obsolescing languages worldwide and the development of computerization of minority languages of Peru. He is currently an associate professor at the Pontificia Universidad Católica del Peru (PUCP), where he directs the Master's degree programme and the Digital Archive of Peruvian Languages.

R. Tom Zuidema was Professor of Anthropology and Latin American and Caribbean Studies at the University of Illinois at Urbana-Champaign. He is renowned for his seminal contributions on Inca social and political organization. His early work consisted of a structural analysis of the Inca *ceque* system. He later extended this approach to other aspects of Andean civilization, notably kinship, the Inca calendar, and the Inca understanding of astronomy. His publications include *The Ceque System of Cuzco* (1964) and *Inca Civilization in Cuzco* (1990). He was born in 1927 in Haarlem in the Netherlands, and died in 2016, during the preparation of this volume.

Introduction to maps and sources

Maps in this book were reproduced by Paul Heggarty from maps provided by chapter authors, by converting them into a GIS (Geographic Information System) database, collated and enriched for South America for the purposes of this book. All data used on the maps are thus geo-referenced – set to actual latitude and longitude coordinates – as precisely as possible. Individual point-locations (such as cities, towns and archaeological sites) are generally exactly pinpointed, by precise known coordinates. Continuous lines or area outlines ('polygons') may be more approximate and inferred, especially for historical, archaeological or language distributions.

In all maps, the coordinate reference system used is the common standard EPSG 4326 – WGS 84. All maps follow a standard layout and design, produced in QGIS 3.8 (open source, available from https://qgis.org) using the layers detailed below under 'Geographical base maps'. The main base geographical data are taken from existing online GIS databases, as identified below. All these base sources are open access, apart from the World Language Mapping System.

Much of the mapping data needed for this book and specific to the archaeology, history, linguistics or ecology of the Andes–Amazonia divide was not available online. Examples include the geographical limits to archaeological horizons in the Andes (Inca, Wari and Tiwanaku); ecological zones, such as the Llanos de Mojos, or the montane forest regions intermediate between the high Andes and Amazonian rainforest; and past distributions of languages now extinct or whose extents are now much reduced. These data have been geo-referenced as points, lines and polygons by Paul Heggarty, using the geo-referencer tool built into QGIS, on the basis of map images provided by the chapter authors. This tool allows original map images to be transformed to the same projection and overlaid as a part-transparent image over the geographical base map, in order to re-draw given geographical features in GIS. The original images supplied by chapter authors were themselves based on various sources, as cited in the caption specific to each map here.

Geographical base maps

The standard layout and design used for all maps in this book is composed of a series of layers of basic geographical data, with respective transparency levels set appropriately to give the best overall result. These base map layers were all sourced from open GIS databases, as follows.

- For **ocean bathymetry**, and for the underlying **base land colour and relief** shading, the data source is the worldwide base-map image file, at a scale of 1:10m, provided within the *Natural Earth* package: [NE2_HR_LC_SR_W_DR.tif] at https://github.com/nvkelso/natural-earth-raster/tree/master/10m_rasters/NE2_HR_LC_SR_W_DR
- **Hill-shading** was added using the 'Shaded Relief Basic' data file within the *Natural Earth* package: [SR_HR.tif] from https://github.com/nvkelso/natural-earth-raster/tree/master/10m_rasters/SR_HR
- For much **higher-resolution** topography (to approximately 30 m at the Equator), **elevation data** were taken from the SRTM (Shuttle Radar Topography Mission) database, using the six 30 × 30° tiles that cover South America, such as [cut_n00w090.tif], from http://srtm.csi.cgiar.org/srtmdata
- **Elevation bands** were shaded using a **colour ramp** custom designed (by Paul Heggarty) for the elevation profiles of the Andes and Amazonia. See the **Elevation band colour ramp** values and corresponding colours (p.xxviii). The maps in Figures 2.4.2 and 2.4.3 use a different custom colour ramp, devised specifically to highlight the Huancabamba Depression through the Andes in northern Peru. This colour ramp uses a simple contrast of green up to 2300 m, and white above 2300 m (and the same hill-shading as on all maps).
- The base data files for **bodies of water** were taken from various files within the 1:10m scale *Natural Earth* 'Quick Start Kit' package of physical data at https://www.naturalearthdata.com/downloads, namely
  - Coastline: from [ne_10m_coastline.shp]
  - Lakes: from [ne_10m_lakes.shp]
  - Major river lines: from [ne_10m_rivers_lake_centerlines_scale_rank.shp].
- Many maps, especially those zoomed in to sub-regions of the continent, required **additional coverage of smaller rivers**. To this end, customized subsets of river-line data were added as appropriate to each map, from the following sources:
  - For the rivers of the Amazon basin: [reseau1511.shp], [lineaire_1km.shp], [lineaire_4km.shp] and [lineaire_10km.shp] from www.ore-hybam.org/index.php/eng/Data/Cartography/Amazon-basin-hydrography
  - For rivers in Peru: [Rio_navegables.shp] and [Rios_Quebradas.shp] from www.diva-gis.org/Data

Point locations: Mountain peaks, cities, settlements, archaeological sites

- The latitude and longitude coordinates of modern cities were taken from the 1:10m scale *Natural Earth* 'Quick Start Kit' package of *cultural* data: [ne_10m_populated_places.shp].
- The latitude and longitude and elevation values for some mountain peaks were taken from the 1:10m scale *Natural Earth* package of *physical* data: [ne_10m_geography_regions_elevation_points.shp].

- For smaller towns and settlements in South America, and other peaks and mountain passes, new entries and their latitude and longitude coordinates were added by Paul Heggarty, from online gazetteer resources.
- For archaeological sites (for example, maps in Figures 2.1.1 and 2.4.1), latitude and longitude coordinates were added from online gazetteer resources and published books and articles.

Geographical/environmental

- The Amazon basin watershed line is taken from the HyBAM database: [amazlm_1608.shp] from www.ore-hybam.org/index.php/eng/Data/Cartography/Amazon-basin-hydrography
- Areas of montane forest (for example, Figure 3.7.1) were geo-referenced from a source map provided by Tom D. Dillehay, Brian McCray and Patricia J. Netherly.
- The area of the Llanos de Moxos (such as in Figures 4.4.1 and 4.4.2) was geo-referenced from a source map provided by Umberto Lombardo and José M. Capriles.

Archaeological/historical

- The outline of the Inca Empire at its greatest established extent was geo-referenced from various source maps, principally those in D'Altroy (2015), and especially from larger-scale maps, such as D'Altroy (2015, 328) and Prümers (Chapter 4.2, this volume) that pinpoint known Inca 'frontier' fortresses.
- The approximate range of Wari (Middle Horizon) influence was geo-referenced from the source map in Beresford-Jones and Heggarty (2012b).
- The approximate range of Tiwanaku (Middle Horizon) influence was geo-referenced from various source maps, particularly Beresford-Jones and Heggarty (2012b) and Isbell (2004).
- The approximate extent of the Chachapoyas culture in north-western Peru was geo-referenced from a source map provided by Tom D. Dillehay, Brian McCray and Patricia J. Netherly.
- Historical province and *audiencia* borders in ('Upper' and 'Lower') Peru were geo-referenced from a source map in Pearce (2001).

Language distributions

Many of the linguistics chapters in this book include maps that illustrate 'present-day' distributions of the indigenous languages of South America. In reality, however, in many regions indigenous languages have been in rapid decline in recent decades, and the areas where they are spoken have continued to shrink. Strictly, then, these 'present-day' distributions often more accurately reflect where it is reliably known that given indigenous languages *were* spoken, at least until *recent* decades. Almost all published maps of Quechua distributions include Chachapoyas Quechua, for example, but recent fieldwork confirms that there are very few active speakers in the region, and none in the younger generations.

The maps of 'present/recent' distributions of language families are based on the following sources.

- The World Language Mapping System (WLMS), from www.worldgeodata-sets.com/language (commercial software, not open source, and at the time of publication taken over by www.ethnologue.com and apparently no longer available for purchase).
- Where the WLMS is incomplete or of uncertain reliability, language distributions were reconfirmed, adjusted or added by being geo-referenced from other sources.
- Additionally, for the three main Amazonian language families, language points were geo-referenced on the basis of the three maps in Dixon and Aikhenvald (1999, 66, 126 and 22) of the distribution of languages in the Arawak, Tupí and Carib families respectively.
- Within Peru, language distributions were further refined by geo-referencing from the *Atlas Lingüístico del Perú* (Chirinos Rivera 2001), particularly for Yanesha and other Arawak languages in the lower eastern slopes of the Andes.

Historical language maps in this book aim to show the distributions of indigenous language families that are either now completely extinct, or much reduced geographically (generally replaced by European languages). These historical databases were geo-referenced on the basis of various historical sources, authored by linguists who have sought to reconstruct these past language distributions as accurately as possible. This is often a difficult task, however, and requires working from limited historical documents in which language identifications may be clear or ambiguous.

- For the Arawak and Carib languages of the Caribbean (Figure 1.2.1), estimated distributions were geo-referenced on the basis of Granberry and Vescelius (2004).
- For languages of the Puquina and Uru lineages in the Altiplano of Bolivia and southernmost Peru, estimated distributions at the end of the sixteenth century (Figures 4.1.1 and 4.2.1) were geo-referenced on the basis of Torero (2002, 465), itself based on reports in Spanish colonial *visitas* from the sixteenth century.

- For the Culle language of central Peru, its estimated distribution in the sixteenth century (Figure 2.5.1) was geo-referenced from a source map supplied by Alexander Herrera, itself drawn up on the basis of Adelaar (1989), Adelaar and Muysken (2004), Cerrón-Palomino (1995) and Torero (1989 and 2002).

Elevation band colour ramp for Andes–Amazonia

Below sea Level = Base map image
1 m+
400 m
500 m
700 m
850 m
1500 m
2500 m
3000 m
3350 m
3650 m
4000 m
4200 m
4400 m
4600 m
4800 m
4850 m
6000 m

© Paul Heggarty.

Introduction. Why Andes–Amazonia? Why cross-disciplinary?

Adrian J. Pearce, David G. Beresford-Jones and Paul Heggarty

Andes–Amazonia: What it means, why it matters

The Andean highlands and Amazonian rainforest run cheek-by-jowl for thousands of miles through South America. Popular perception, at least, would have the Andes as a cradle of civilization, set against Amazonia, where even the Incas feared to tread. But is the 'divide' between them a self-evident, intrinsic definition of opposing Andean and Amazonian worlds – or a simplistic parody?

A case study in environmental determinism

We begin by setting the Andes–Amazonia divide in its broadest possible context and relevance. In the search for big-picture explanations for the human past, arguably the most fundamental controversy of all revolves around environmental determinism. How far might major contrasts in environment shape and even explain aspects of our cultures and the nature of our societies? How much are any such effects mediated through culture, and indeed how much through subsistence and demography, to the extent that those too depend on ecology? This book explores this controversy across the whole range of disciplines in anthropology and (pre) history. And to do so, it focuses on what is arguably the paradigm case of immediate juxtaposition of radically contrasting environments.

Nowhere on earth is there an ecological transformation so extreme and so swift as between the snowline of the high Andes and the tropical rainforest of Amazonia. Crucially, unlike the world's other alpine regions, the Andes straddle the Equator and Tropics. Farming and large populations can thus flourish up to elevations far higher here than anywhere else; yet the Andes also abut directly onto tropical rainforest. From jungle to glacier-hemmed peaks to desert coast, a transect of as little as 200 km makes for a roller-coaster through up to 84 of the world's 103 'life-zones' (Holdridge 1967).

Does this abrupt contrast in environment underlie a divide that goes far deeper, too? Beyond just topography and ecology, does it extend to the people, cultures and societies that inhabit the Andes on the one hand, and Amazonia on the other? If so, how deep does such a divide run back in time, perhaps even to when humans first populated South America, potentially even by separate Andean and Amazonian settlement routes? And how far has it persisted into recent centuries? These are among the central questions that this volume addresses.

This book is no work of environmental determinism, however. It is not theory-driven, and starts out from no fundamentalist presumptions either way. On the contrary, it aspires to serve as a balanced exploration of the reality – or otherwise – of an Andes–Amazonia divide. It is intended as a compendium that reflects the state of the art of collective insights and diverse views within and across the disciplines. From all their various perspectives, the question asked of all 26 contributors was the same. Geography and ecology aside, to what extent is an Andes–Amazonia divide real on any other levels: cultural, historical, archaeological, genetic, linguistic, and so on? Or to turn that around, to what extent is the idea of a divide just a simplistic, self-perpetuating mirage that clouds and distorts what is and was a much more progressive and complex reality?

To the worldwide debate on environmental determinism, this book aspires to bring a novel and significant contribution. For, despite Amazonia and the Andes representing such an extreme case of immediate environmental contrast, the perspective this book offers remains little-known outside South America. Indeed, even within the continent itself, the Andes–Amazonia divide has rarely been addressed head-on, and from all disciplinary viewpoints together. This is, at last, the explicit theme and objective of this book.

This introduction will now set out some important clarifications on our theme that hold in general, for all disciplines. We then go on to set the book in the context of the broader interdisciplinary project out of which this book arises. Later, we outline how the volume is structured before summarizing the core message of each of the 25 chapters, and how each thus fits into the theme and structure of the book.

Reality, myth or scholarly tradition?

The Incas' oft-mentioned reluctance to venture far into Amazonia may, at least in part, reflect experiences of specific military reverses there. But it was accompanied in any case by a good dose of myth about the Amazonian 'other' (see Chapters 5.1 and 5.2) – and in this the Incas were not alone. Similar mythical visions of Amazonia and its peoples endured long into the colonial era, in a Spanish Empire that likewise remained at heart a highland and coastal entity (see Chapters 5.3 and 5.4).

It is an open question how far such myths may in fact have come to overrule the reality of any actual Andes–Amazonia divide, and not just in the perceptions of Incas and Spaniards. Scholars of South America have themselves tended to fall into camps of 'Andeanists' and 'Amazonianists'. Their publications, from Steward's (1946, 1948) seminal *Handbook of South American Indians* onwards, likewise often align with this divide (see Chapter 1.1). To take one publisher and discipline as an example, when Cambridge University Press extended to South America its series of reference works on the languages of the world, it did not take the continent as a whole, but published separate volumes for *The Languages of the Andes* (Adelaar and Muysken 2004) and *The Amazonian Languages* (Dixon and Aikhenvald 1999). Does this follow some real contrast in the languages themselves, their origins or structures? Or is the divide more one of scholarly tradition and niches? (For more on this particular case, see Chapters 1.2 and 3.4.)

It does at least bear thinking about whether the whole concept might in fact be more a reflection on the scholars themselves, and their own preferences, than on the reality of any divide. There can be many reasons (some eminently understandable, others less so) for this split among scholars and publications, irrespective of actual evidence on the ground. Such is the scale and complexity of both regions and their prehistories that either of them already makes for a very large brief to master. Familiarity with and expertise in both demands far more than limiting oneself to either one. Faced with such complexity, there is also a natural pigeon-holing instinct to seek to classify and bring order to it. Stark contrasts in environment can seem ready-made as a neat, straightforward, over-arching criterion, leading to the temptation to (want to) see parallels in culture, too. And there is even a further consideration that one might entertain, particularly in the many disciplines that require extended fieldwork. For scholars are simply different people, and whether intellectually defensible or not, some of us may feel more drawn to and at home in the hotter, wetter lowlands; others in the cooler, crisper highlands.

The divide into camps and publishing trends need not be alike in all disciplines, of course. Quite how it plays out in each one will be taken up in more detail in the first part of this book, in the set of chapters that outline overall perspectives on the Andes–Amazonia divide from a series of different disciplines. It seems clear that it is anthropologists who tend to raise the strongest voices against the concept of a stark divide (as in Chapter 1.4 by Alf Hornborg, Chapter 1.5 by Tom Zuidema, and also Bruce Mannheim during the conference that gave rise to this book). This only highlights another reason why the book should indeed extend to all disciplines – to hear all the alternative perspectives on the 'divide'.

Beyond individual researchers, it is also conceivable that research in the Andes and in Amazonia might follow different prevailing approaches, or even have a rather different disciplinary mix. There can be various reasons for this. There are apparently obvious differences between the Andes and Amazonia in the visibility and preservation of the archaeological record and the practicability of fieldwork, with significant consequences for how that record is interpreted, as discussed further by Beresford-Jones and Machicado Murillo in Chapter 1.1.

Patterns of survival of the indigenous language record, too, make for a further intriguing illustration. South America has a striking diversity of scores of independent language lineages. The survivors are heavily concentrated in (Greater) Amazonia, however, home to some of the most unusual and exceptional languages in the world (such as Pirahã and Hixkaryana). This linguistic diversity corresponds to a large number of distinct ethno-linguistic groups, although each is generally small in demographic scale. Many of these Amazonian groups were all but unknown until the last century, some even until the last few decades. So here, linguistic research goes along with a prominent role for the present-day study of anthropology, ethnography and identity. In the Central Andes, by contrast, precious few language lineages are left, almost all having been replaced by just Quechua and Aymara (or Spanish), with their large speaker populations. Those language families are, however, set amid an extremely rich record in archaeology, and feature in the historical record ever since the 1530s, opening up much more scope for language history and prehistory here.

The differing disciplinary mix in the Andes and in Amazonia seems to carry through into default interpretations of processes in prehistory, too. In the Andes, where archaeology and history so clearly demonstrate large populations, complex societies and state-level organization and power, those known factors have to many scholars seemed natural candidates for explaining patterns in our records of the past here – again, including major language families. Debate on Quechua and Aymara origins focuses less on *whether* expansive complex societies were responsible for their expansions, and more on simply identifying *which* (see the various contributions to Heggarty and Beresford-Jones 2012). Research in Amazonia, however, tends more to eschew explanations of such types, in favour of models of network-like interaction, exchange and convergence instead, as in Hornborg's (2005) 'ethnogenesis' hypothesis for the Arawak family.

Applied specifically to the theme of this book, an Andean perspective of state organization seems compatible, at least, with relatively clear 'frontiers' and contrasts, particularly along a relatively swift and radical environmental transition. Sharp frontiers would seem a less natural fit, however, with the Amazonian inclination to favour models of interaction and convergence. Clearly, we venture this as no more than a general tendency in scholarship that seems discernible in our experience, 'on average' only. Obvious exceptions are to be found in individual scholars working in either region. Moreover, recent years have seen a clear shift, as archaeology has made a stronger case for the prevalence of complex societies and large population sizes in Amazonia too, which in these respects would thus have been not so different from the Andes after all – see Chapter 1.1 on this new archaeological orthodoxy.

When is a divide not a divide? Andes–Amazonia interactions

One other critical consideration that recurs throughout this book is what to make of the concept of a divide if there is nonetheless also contact across it. For whatever arguments may favour a divide, there is also copious evidence of contacts and exchanges between the peoples of the Andes and Amazonia. How can these two concepts be reconciled?

A 'fundamentalist' position might have it that the mere fact of any such contact is enough to disqualify the idea of a divide in the first place. This misconstrues the nature of what is generally intended by the term 'divide', however, which does not necessarily break down at the first instance of contact across it. None of our contributors would deny that contact and exchange went on; the point is how significant they were in relative terms. Were they rather limited and incidental to what in many other, fundamental respects remained a meaningful contrast? Or were they so thoroughgoing and intense as to make for a transition so gradual, over such a wide span of territory, that the concept of a (sharp) divide is more a distortion of reality than a reflection of it?

In genetics, for example, are populations markedly more similar to each other within the Andes and within Amazonia than between the two? Does the same hold true of the relationships between their languages? And of the nature and complexity of their societies, to judge from the archaeological and historical records? Assessing this balance in each discipline is the central task for this book.

Clarifications: 'Andes' and 'Amazonia', geography and culture

Some clarifications are in order on the use of the terms 'Andes' and 'Amazonia'. Both might at first sight seem essentially geographical terms, with more or less established technical definitions. That said, while the Andes are defined primarily by geology, Amazonia is traditionally (and in this book) taken to refer not simply to the entire drainage basin of the Amazon River. Rather, 'Amazonia' is typically used with an additional ecological criterion, to refer only to the (large) part of that drainage basin that is also covered by rainforest (or at least was, before modern deforestation). This qualification is crucial for our purposes here, because of course the Amazon's main tributaries actually rise far in the highlands, at the periphery of its drainage basin but still, by definition, within it. Such elevations far above the rainforest biome fall into the common working definition of the 'Andes', then, and actually outside 'Amazonia', when defined as the tropical rainforest region.

This does not yet complete the clarifications needed, however. In practice, both terms are often used rather loosely, in various ways. For in the lowlands, 'Amazonia' is often tacitly taken to overstep its basic hydrological definition in any case. Beyond the technical northward limit of the Amazon's drainage basin lies that of the Orinoco; but it, too, is covered in part by a continuation of the same rainforest that helps define 'Amazonia'. So if one allows that criterion priority, then a 'Greater Amazonia' would run all the way to the northern limit of the rainforest – before it opens out into the more savannah-like *Llanos* of Colombia and Venezuela. Some justification lies in the continuity of the rainforest biome, across what is hardly the most marked of watersheds here; indeed, the Amazon and Orinoco basins are even linked, most unusually, by the Casiquiare 'distributary' river between them.

Figure 0.1 Overview map of South America showing the Andean cordillera(s), the watershed of the Amazon basin, the established boundary of the Inca Empire in 1532, and selected major geographical features. © Paul Heggarty

'Andes' also tends to be used loosely, but in this case with a reference much narrower than the basic geological one. There is a sense of a prototypical 'Andes' focused on what are geographically just the (north)central latitudes of the mountain range: most classically, Peru and Bolivia, although also extending to Ecuador and southernmost Colombia. So even in a country like Chile, whose very shape is defined by the mountain range, *andino* is nonetheless often assumed by default to refer to regions mostly outside of Chile to its north, so charged is the term with connotations of the indigenous cultures of highland Peru and Bolivia.

Physical environment aside, then, other considerations have long since intruded on how the terms Andes and Amazonia are regularly taken, particularly in the (pre)historical and anthropological disciplines. In practice, both terms are often bound up, explicitly or implicitly, with cultural connotations. Many authors use either or both as names for a 'culture area'. This, indeed, is precisely the crux of this book: to assess whether this vision of the (Central) Andes and Amazonia as contrasting culture areas is valid, and with it, the implication that the primary cultural division in South America follows and 'obeys' the continent's primary contrast in natural environments (see Chapter 3.7 for more on this).

Given that the terms Andes and Amazonia have various possible readings, different authors may not be consistent in how they define or apply them. More generally, the different disciplines, too, can have their own grounds and criteria for what most meaningfully for them counts as 'Andean' or 'Amazonian'. The main families of languages typically identified as 'Amazonian', for instance, extend widely into other neighbouring regions too (for example Arawak, which spread as far as the islands of the Caribbean), although notably for our theme, they hardly impinge on the Andes at all.

Geographically, of course, the Andes and Amazonia cover far from the whole of South America. Alternative two-way 'carve-ups' of the continent do incorporate a divide between them, but also bring in all remaining regions that fall under neither – that is, Western versus Eastern South America, or highland versus lowland South America. These alternatives are not without problems of their own, however; not least that the 'eastern lowlands' end up extended to environments that include the Chaco, Pampas and even Patagonia, while the western slopes of the Andes embrace some of the world's driest deserts and extend down to sea level along the Pacific coast. These are so radically distinct from Amazonia as to undermine the meaningfulness and utility of seeking to define the whole continent by only a two-way contrast in the first place.

In any case, our intention here is to keep this book focused on the core case of the most extreme juxtaposition between the two major environments. So by the 'Andes–Amazonia divide' we refer here essentially just to tropical latitudes, and follow common usage in focusing our 'Andes' on just the central (generally higher and drier) part of the cordillera that borders directly on the tropical rainforest of ('Greater') Amazonia (see for example Denevan 2002, 53; Epps and Michael 2017, 935).

The broader context to this interdisciplinary project

This book does not stand alone; rather, it comes out of a broader interdisciplinary project, ongoing since 2008, that has been based on a series of conferences and has already yielded several publications. This project first grew out of conversations between a linguist (Heggarty) and an archaeologist (Beresford-Jones), then both at the University of Cambridge, which rapidly came to include also a historian

(Pearce, at the University of London). Over the years since, the disciplines involved in the conversation have expanded, to include genetics, anthropology and ethnohistory. In general terms, the project focuses on applying interdisciplinarity to the largest issues in the population prehistory of the Andes, and now also of Amazonia. Conferences in the series have taken place in Cambridge and London in 2008, Lima in 2009, Leipzig (one event in 2011; two in 2014), Jena in 2015, and most recently in Belo Horizonte, Brazil, in 2017. The present book derives from one of the conferences held in Leipzig in 2014 and constitutes the fourth volume in a loose series. The other volumes published to date are:

- *Archaeology and Language in the Andes*. Heggarty and Beresford-Jones (eds.), 2012. Oxford: Oxford University Press.
- *History and Language in the Andes*. Heggarty and Pearce (eds.), 2011. New York: Palgrave Macmillan.
- *Lenguas y sociedades en el antiguo Perú*. Kaulicke, Cerrón-Palomino, Heggarty and Beresford-Jones (eds.), 2010. Lima: PUCP *Boletín de Arqueología* 14.

Both the conferences and the resulting publications have taken an unusual format. Rather than present lengthy papers on relatively narrow topics arising from their particular research interests, invited speakers were tasked by the organizers with presenting the perspective of their discipline as a whole on key issues of concern to all: what do we know about the nature of the Wari Middle Horizon in the Andes, for example; or about the distribution and impact of Inca *mitmaq* colonies; or about Inca relations with Amazonia? Participants were to try to speak from a disciplinary rather than a personal perspective and, in this sense, to be as neutral in their presentations as possible, outlining what their field knew on the topic in question, how it knew it, with what degree of confidence, and so on. Presentations were kept decidedly short, so that the majority of each session was given over to debate and enquiry. Only after the conference and in the light of these discussions did speakers write up their contributions, within a framework set by the editors. The overall aim has been to achieve publications that are very different in character and format from standard conference proceedings, and in which the interdisciplinary focus is core to the structure and the organization of the book, as well as to its contents.

Of course, interdisciplinarity is now generally seen as a Good Thing. This is attested anecdotally in the high proportion of calls for academic jobs that now specify some interdisciplinary focus as a prerequisite for candidacy, as well as in the near-ubiquitous presence on CVs and personal statements of references to work that 'stands at the intersection' of one field and others. But even if many of us now talk the interdisciplinary talk, it is still the case that rather few of us actually walk the interdisciplinary walk. And with good reason: the biggest lesson for the editors of their endeavours of the past decade is just how hard it is truly to cross disciplinary lines. Different disciplines not only employ profoundly different methodologies, and in some cases even perceive particular problems in profoundly different ways, they also speak very different research 'languages'. Among the disciplines represented in this volume, linguistics and genetics in particular deploy a forbidding technical vocabulary, which poses a real practical obstacle to specialists from other fields who seek to penetrate their orthodoxies. Not the least of the challenges when editing books such as this has been the need for every discipline's perspective to be accessible to specialists from other fields, when contributors are also well aware that too much 'dumbing down' of their technical vocabulary will render their work unpalatable to fellow scholars in their own fields. But what are the prospects for the interdisciplinary conversation if it demands as prerequisites an adequate grasp not just of gonosomes, meiosis and phylogenetic analysis, but also of morphophonemic nasal spread and liquid phonemes? Moreover, interdisciplinary work is not only hard to produce, it is hard to consume as well. It falls between the large cracks that still separate the disciplines, even in the very vehicles for publishing their findings.

A further challenge is that to weave together such different disciplines is not trivial. There are no simplistic, one-to-one equations of language = genes = (archaeological) culture, for instance. Our endeavour calls for a far more realistic and sophisticated logic. Archaeology, genetics and linguistics employ radically different datasets that require very different analytical methods. But that also makes their respective records of the past highly complementary to each other, in that they all bear simultaneous traces of the same powerful processes in prehistory – cultural, social, demographic, and so on – that shaped them all. So it is on this level of processes that impacted on past populations and societies, including the languages they spoke, that the disciplines can more meaningfully be linked.

Notwithstanding the challenges, then, we certainly defend the value and the fruits of the exercise. Precisely because the walls between disciplines remain so high, the benefits of scaling them are all the greater. The cross-disciplinary whole – a coherent, holistic vision of the human past – is indeed greater than the sum of its disciplinary parts. It has been a considerable surprise to the editors, over the past ten years, to see just how little we know or understand, as members of given disciplines, of the tools and knowledge of the past that are available to other fields. And it has been an ongoing source of satisfaction, in previous publications as in this one, to witness how the fruits of cross-disciplinary discussions can enrich the research findings of all participants. We trust that these same benefits are evident in this volume, too, as detailed in the Conclusion that rounds off the book.

Structure of this book

This book contains 25 (generally short) chapters, which are organized into five parts.

Part 1, 'Crossing frontiers: Perspectives from the various disciplines', includes those chapters that set out the broad perspective of each discipline on the reality or nature of any putative divide between Andes and Amazonia. The chapters here are titled simply 'Archaeology', 'Linguistics', 'Genetics' and 'Anthropology'. Their purpose is to provide review footings for the other chapters in the volume by setting out the core methodologies, datasets, and interpretative tools available to each discipline, alongside its broad stance towards the 'Andes–Amazonia divide'. Is a divide perceptible to each discipline? In what ways, and on the basis of what data? How confident can we be as to this interpretation, and what reservations might we feel with regard to it? From the start, as will be seen, there develop strikingly differing views on this question among the disciplines represented.

The remaining chapters are collected into Part 2, on 'Deep time and the long chronological perspective'; Part 3, 'Overall patterns – and alternative models'; Part 4, 'Regional case studies from the Altiplano and southern Upper Amazonia'; and Part 5, 'Age of Empires: Inca and Spanish colonial perspectives'. In general terms, the book is thus organized chronologically, from deepest prehistory up to the Spanish colonial period, and with increasing resolution, from the very broadest scale and topics to more detailed case studies and the most recent times. Above all, each of the book's five parts contains chapters written from a range of disciplinary perspectives: primarily archaeological, linguistic, genetic and anthropological for Parts 1 to 4, and ethnohistorical and historical for Part 5. All chapters are brought to bear on the key concern of this volume: to scrutinize the notion of an Andes–Amazonia divide. Taken together, they do this from multiple perspectives and in most chronological and geographical contexts, where Amazonia meets the Andes from the Colombia–Ecuador border in the north to the Altiplano and Gran Chaco in the south.

Chapter summaries

Finally in this Introduction, we summarize the 25 chapters in turn, highlighting the main focus and themes of each, as well as their conclusions and major contributions.

Part 1. Crossing frontiers: Perspectives from the various disciplines

Chapter 1.1, 'Archaeology', by David G. Beresford-Jones and Eduardo Machicado Murillo, provides an overview of the Andes–Amazonia divide from the perspective of archaeology. Emphasizing that perceptions of a divide have long been largely based on history and ethnography rather than archaeology *per se*, the authors trace the development of that discipline in South America to show how new methods have gradually led to a 'new archaeological orthodoxy', particularly for Amazonia. That consensus calls attention to a deep-time flux of cultigens and ideas across the Andes–Amazonia divide, and also to Amazonia's significant environmental diversity, which sustained intensive agriculture and dense human occupations in prehistory. While archaeological evidence continues to suggest that trajectories on either side of the divide proceeded more or less independently, many uncertainties still underlie this new archaeological orthodoxy, so that archaeological data can best be interpreted in the context of the sort of cross-disciplinary synthesis promoted in this book.

In Chapter 1.2, 'Linguistics', Paul Heggarty sets out, for readers from outside linguistics, the basic principles and concepts that are needed to understand any apparent Andes–Amazonia divide in language. The Arawak and Quechua language families, for example, dispersed through thousands of kilometres across highly diverse environments – but both largely balked at trespassing over the transition from Andes to Amazonia. The chapter first explores what such language *families*, and in particular their geographical expansions and migrations, can tell us of the 'divide'. It then switches to the opposing dimension of the linguistic panorama: how languages from multiple different origins can *converge* on each other, albeit to very different degrees of intensity, attesting to the nature and strength of past contacts and interactions between the Andes and Amazonia. Finally, the chapter clears up some common cross-disciplinary confusions, and summarizes the prospects for linguistics – its potential and limitations – to inform on the Andes–Amazonia divide.

In Chapter 1.3, 'Genetics', Lars Fehren-Schmitz discusses the science behind human population genetics and the potential of his discipline to contribute to South American population prehistory. Genetics has made major contributions to Amerindian population history at the broadest scale, of first settlement or early migration routes. But alongside the general problems of working with ancient DNA, there are specific challenges to genetic studies of South Amerindian populations. *Inter alia*, comparative studies between populations here require very high resolution to yield useful results, while the quality of available genetic data also varies for the east and west of the continent and from ancient to modern populations. Nevertheless, genetic studies of cross-cultural interactions at the regional level have already begun to bear fruit. And Fehren-Schmitz concludes that the best scope for future advances lies precisely in the interdisciplinary approach pursued in this book, entailing expertise from both the natural and social sciences.

In Chapter 1.4, 'Anthropology', Alf Hornborg argues that his discipline is especially well placed to rethink Andes–Amazonia relations. This is because, in its 'four-field' conception, anthropology represents 'an attempt to understand various kinds of cultural phenomena holistically'. Specifically, it can interpret the forms of social organization that may have linked the Andes and Amazonia in prehistory, help understand change and continuity in relations over time, and attempt to unite the analyses of other disciplines in a single, integrated perspective. Focusing on long-distance cultural connections across the 'divide', Hornborg then discusses four case studies. He suggests that these case studies indicate a 'recurring pattern' of interaction between Andes and Amazonia, with important societal and linguistic repercussions. He also argues that 'it has been a mistake to assume that Andean polities were necessarily more hierarchical, populous or extensive than their counterparts in Amazonia', an 'illusion' that has dominated European thinking since the conquest.

In Chapter 1.5, 'The Andes–Amazonia culture area', Tom Zuidema notes the common background and similarities in social and ritual systems of peoples far across any putative divide between Amazonia and the Andes, including the Incas, the Tukano of north-western Amazonia, and even the Ge and Bororo of central Brazil, very far indeed from the Andes. He notes striking commonalities, for instance, between the spatial organization of the Inca capital Cuzco and the villages of the Bororo; between the age-class systems of the Ge-speaking Canela and the Inca *panaca* royal dynastic descent groups; and between the roles of ranked male members of those Andean panacas and among the Tukano. Yet these fundamental similarities between cultural models in Amazonia and the Central Andes did not, he argues, derive from direct contact but, rather, through a deep-time cultural continuum that once stretched from the Andes to Central Brazil, which he defines as an 'Andes–Amazonia culture area'.

Part 2. Deep time and the long chronological perspective

In Chapter 2.1, 'Initial east and west connections across South America', Tom Dillehay reviews the archaeological, genetic and craniometric evidence of Andes–Amazonia relations for the earliest time periods, from first settlement to the Middle Holocene. While emphasizing the scarcity of this evidence, Dillehay outlines some broad trends and themes: the earliest inhabitants of the corridors linking Andes and Amazonia were mobile hunter-gatherers, who established exchange networks along accessible routes through which ideas, resources and technologies could spread, crystallizing into more permanent networks during the early to middle Holocene, when tropical lowland crops first appeared in northern Peru and western Ecuador. By this time, foraging societies were becoming increasingly complex and sedentary, thereby generating various forms of down-the-line exchange and 'reliable networks for accessing exotic food crops'. The chapter emphasizes the complexity of movements of people and resources in 'exchange patterns and cultural transmissions', from the Andes to Amazonia and vice versa.

Chapter 2.2, by André Strauss, discusses 'The Andes–Amazonia divide and human morphological diversification in South America'. For readers from other disciplines, Strauss begins by noting that diversity in cranial morphology is not only unusually high in South America from a global perspective, but also that this diversity broadly aligns 'with an east–west division – or approximately, an Andes–Amazonia divide'. Strauss further notes that 'there is in fact a close link between cranial morphology and population history', so that cranial morphology 'can potentially be used as a proxy for ancestry'. On this basis, he argues that 'the east–west contrast defined by the Andes is most certainly implicated' in all or any of the processes hypothesized as having brought about cranial differentiation. Hence, however it is interpreted, the craniometric evidence 'supports the notion that the east–west division that the Andes impose on the continent is crucial to understanding the population structure observed in South America'.

Chapter 2.3, by Paul Heggarty, 'Deep time and first settlement: What, if anything, can linguistics tell us?', reports the linguistic consensus answer: unfortunately, precious little. Language changes too fast, so the linguistic signal progressively 'decays' to become indistinguishable from the background level of resemblances between languages that are inevitable by statistical chance. In South America, linguistic prehistory fades out before we can see back to first settlement. Speculations on long-range language relationships across the Andes–Amazonia divide, once hypothesized in outdated linguistic literature, have long since been abandoned. Population genetics, however, has remained in thrall to one proposed 'ethno-linguistic' framework on first settlement, including a potential early Andes–Amazonia divide, which linguistically is vacuous, and is largely just geographical. References are provided to standard sources debunking these claims and providing instead the established, valid classifications of the languages of the Americas from which geneticists could actually make much more of their data.

In Chapter 2.4, 'Early social complexity in northern Peru and its Amazonian connections', Peter Kaulicke discusses the archaeological evidence from the north of Peru: a region of particular importance for relations between the Andes and Amazonia, since the highlands here are relatively narrow and low, offering natural passage from Amazonia across the Andes to the Pacific coast. Here, faunal and floral associations (including primates, crocodilians and large felines) extended across 250 kilometres from the coast to Amazonia. Evidence for deep-time interactions across this 'Huancabamba corridor' is scarce, but by the Late Archaic, coastal sites such as Ventarrón in the Lambayeque Valley preserve faunal remains such as macaws and monkeys that suggest contacts with the Amazonian lowlands. Thereafter, the archaeological record suggests unfolding connections not only between the coast, northern highlands and Amazonia but also from southern Ecuador to the Bolivian Altiplano, although the precise nature of these contacts requires further research.

In Chapter 2.5, 'Changing Andes–Amazonia dynamics: *El Chuncho* meets *El Inca* at the end of the Marañón corridor', Alexander Herrera discusses the ecological, archaeological, linguistic and ethnohistorical evidence for this key corridor between highlands and eastern lowlands. Unmarked monoliths in the Upper Marañón valley are today identified as the lithified bodies of *chuncho* lowland Indians slain by the mythical *Inca*, and they reflect widespread traditions of violent highland dominance over the lowlands. While for the earliest periods, the archaeological evidence suggests influence through the Marañón corridor from lowlands to highlands, afterwards this 'inter-Andean *yunga*' came to be dominated by highland cultures: initially by Culle-speaking peoples from the Huamachuco region, and later by the Incas themselves. The stone bodies of the fallen *chunchos* of the Upper Marañón therefore mark 'a conceptual boundary in the landscape that may profitably be seen as an indigenous precursor to the Andes–Amazonia divide'.

Part 3. Overall patterns – and alternative models

In Chapter 3.1, 'How real is the Andes–Amazonia divide? An archaeological view from the eastern piedmont', Darryl Wilkinson uses recent work in the Amaybamba valley in southern Peru to argue that the piedmont is more than just a transitional zone between the Andes and Amazonia. Rather, it constitutes a distinct geographical, ecological and cultural region in itself. This is evident not least in the fact that this was perhaps the last major region of South America to be settled permanently, after 1000 BP. This settlement proceeded from the Andes, with an apparently spontaneous first colonization followed by formal incorporation into the Inca Empire. In this archaeological view of the piedmont, the Andes–Amazonia divide was indeed a reality: barely perceptible prior to the Middle Holocene, but unambiguous in later prehistory, as contrasting regional systems emerged with 'the expansion of imperial states in the highlands and of major linguistic-agricultural complexes in the lowlands'.

In Chapter 3.2, 'Genetic diversity patterns in the Andes and Amazonia', Fabrício Santos also detects a divide. For however South Amerindian populations are divided on the basis of their genetics, in all major studies 'Central Andean populations always appear as a clearly distinctive regional group'. These populations are distinguished by greater genetic diversity within local population groups, higher levels of gene flow between these groups, and greater effective population sizes, while inverse patterns are observable in Amazonia. And the consensus is that, rather than reflecting different founder populations at first settlement, this pattern developed only much later, from no earlier than the Middle Holocene. Santos thus joins Wilkinson and others in pointing to the intensive agriculture and hierarchical social and political organization to develop in the Andes over the past few thousand years as creating a divide with Amazonia that had been largely absent prior to that time.

A further contribution from genetics is Chapter 3.3, 'Genetic exchanges in the highland/lowland transitional environments of South America', in which Chiara Barbieri is concerned with the genetics of the peoples of the eastern Andean piedmont itself – a neglected topic. Her chapter both summarizes the results of published studies on four specific populations, from Peru to Argentina, and presents her own wider comparison based on available datasets for South American populations. Overall, Barbieri notes that, in most cases, research reports 'the sharing of genetic motifs with current populations living at high altitude', and that thus 'the global picture … seems to agree on a predominant influence of the Andean highlands'. Her work supports a scenario of the extension of highland influence into the piedmont in recent millennia, perhaps culminating under the Incas. By contrast, it does not suggest much extension of influence beyond the piedmont, into Amazonia itself.

Chapter 3.4, by Paul Heggarty, surveys 'Broad-scale patterns across the languages of the Andes and Amazonia', following the same structure as Chapter 1.2. Firstly, language *families* generally do respect a divide in their expansion histories, although there are some limited counterexamples. The chapter also explores whether some underlying, deeper contrast might explain why the families of the Andes and Amazonia differ in various other respects, too: in the patterning of their distributions, in the size of their speaker populations and in how far back in time their expansion histories go. Secondly, linguistic *convergence* illustrates how languages along the Andes–Amazonia transition clearly did engage in contact, particularly in loanwords, although interactions were more intense within each region than between them. The summing-up inclines to the 'divide' being real, and even rather striking when zooming out to set the Andes–Amazonia case in the broadest possible perspective, of the worldwide linguistic panorama.

Chapter 3.5 is Rik van Gijn and Pieter Muysken's 'Highland–lowland relations: A linguistic view'. This takes a quantitative look at a dataset of over 20 specific aspects of language structure (in sound system, word structure and grammar) across over 70 languages on either side of the Andes–Amazonia divide, from southern Colombia to the Gran Chaco. The results in fact imply *three* main zones: the Andes, northern Upper Amazonia, and southern Upper Amazonia. Another key conclusion is that where (unrelated) languages are seen to have converged on each other in structure, through contacts between their speakers, those influences 'operated mostly in one direction, from the highland languages into the lowland ones'. Languages of the foothills are left structurally more similar to their Andean neighbours than to languages of eastern Amazonia, so rather than any radical, sharp Andes–Amazonia divide, a starker one may lie further east, within Amazonia itself.

In Chapter 3.6, 'Rethinking the role of agriculture and language expansion for ancient Amazonians', Eduardo Góes Neves argues that 'distinctive ecological and geographical contexts' created different economic and political trajectories in the Andes and Amazonia. These do not, however, support outmoded views that saw the Andes as the primary centre for cultural innovation and Amazonia merely as a 'marginal backwater'. Rather, Amazonia's great biological diversity engendered a florescence of equally diverse cultural traditions, evident in stone tools and ceramics. Indeed, ceramic production in South America first arose in lowland tropical environments, and Amazonia's great linguistic diversity similarly reflects this broader cultural diversity. In summary, the 'distinct economic, demographic and political trajectories' that unfolded in the highlands and eastern lowlands were likely determined by contrasts between the 'ecologically diversified and highly productive environments in the lowland tropics' and the very different conditions on the Pacific coast and in the Central Andes.

In Chapter 3.7, 'The Pacific coast and Andean highlands/Amazonia', Tom Dillehay, Brian McCray and Patricia Netherly seek to go beyond the long-standing paradigm of an 'Andean co-tradition' constructed partly in opposition to Amazonia. They consider alternative models for interregional exchange, here treating the

Pacific coast as a 'separate cultural entity' that interacted independently with other regions. They then consider possible alternative 'co-traditions' – those uniting the Andes and western Amazonia, for example, or the north coast of Peru and the eastern *montaña* – or even the notion of a *tri*-tradition, to include coast, highlands and eastern lowlands. (The latter might apply particularly at Chachapoyas, where a 'mixture of highland, lowland and coastal traits' is apparent.) While acknowledging the paucity of archaeological data for highland–lowland relations, the chapter suggests that over time there has been a 'flow of knowledge between eastern, central, and western Andean societies … in multiple directions'.

Part 4. Regional case studies from the Altiplano and southern Upper Amazonia

Part 4 opens with Chapter 4.1, "Linguistic connections between the Altiplano region and the Amazonian lowlands', by Willem Adelaar. The focus is the Puquina language, now extinct but once widely spoken across the Altiplano, and potentially the main language of the region's greatest indigenous 'civilization', Tiwanaku. Even though surviving documentation on Puquina is very limited, Adelaar detects indications of major formative inputs to it from both Amazonia and the Andes. Along with interactions between other highland languages and the adjacent lowlands, Adelaar sketches out a three-stage scenario for the Altiplano: early balanced interaction with Amazonia; then (up to 1500 BP) a significant influx of Amazonian cultural elements; and, finally (from 900 BP), impacts from the Central Andes so powerful that the deeper Amazonian influences were overwritten. This scenario recalls early influential hypotheses in archaeology that pointed to lowland origins for highland civilizations, and sees an Andes–Amazonia 'divide' developing only in later prehistory.

In Chapter 4.2, 'Hypothesized language relationships across the Andes–Amazonia divide: The cases of Uro, Pano-Takana and Mosetén', Roberto Zariquiey focuses on the nature of connections between these language lineages on either side of the highland–lowland divide in Bolivia. He reviews grave methodological flaws in a past claim that Uro and Pano-Takana go back to a common ancestor language, which would have implied some past *expansion* across the divide. Rather, Zariquiey uncovers a weaker but more valid signal of *contacts* across it. These are only faint between Uro and Pano-Takana, but Mosetén, located geographically between them, does show clearer contacts with Uro. This supersedes the claim of a deep language relationship, and thus paints a very different scenario for language prehistory here, and one that is more consistent with the language data, more coherent and more specific. Zariquiey outlines an initial case for a linguistic convergence area from the Southern Andes into Amazonia, as a working hypothesis that merits further exploration.

The remaining chapters in Part 4 are by archaeologists, and begin with Heiko Prümers' Chapter 4.3, 'The Andes as seen from Mojos'. The flat savannahs of the

Llanos de Mojos, covering 150,000 km² in northern Bolivia, ostensibly make an ideal case study for Andes–Amazonia relations, since they boast a particularly well-studied archaeological record. Prümers focuses on the period of dense human presence attested for the region for the last thousand years prior to the European invasions, c. 1500–500 BP. His presentation of the archaeology of the Llanos de Mojos is certainly striking: the evidence for contact between the Llanos and the adjacent Altiplano is limited to tiny quantities of imported materials, of stone or metal. Even for the Inca period, *no* 'Inca-related archaeological evidence … has ever been reported from the region'. For this densely settled region, then, adjoining the highlands, the divide between Andes and Amazonia appears at its sharpest.

Also discussing the Llanos de Mojos are Umberto Lombardo and José Capriles, in Chapter 4.4, 'The archaeological significance of shell middens in the Llanos de Moxos: Between the Andes and Amazonia'. The authors here discuss their discovery of shell middens in the Llanos that apparently attest to human occupation dating back more than ten thousand years. The scarcity of archaeological sites for this early period renders these middens of special interest. Most importantly, the evidence from these middens 'supports the hypothesis of the *independent* emergence of social complexity in the region' (emphasis added). That is to say, the Llanos represented 'a centre of innovation where social complexity emerged, rather than a place that was "invaded" by groups stemming from other regions'. The divide between Andes and Amazonia described for the Llanos de Mojos much later in prehistory in Chapter 4.3, then, was apparently already present in far earlier times.

Part 5. Age of Empires: Inca and Spanish colonial perspectives

The final part of the book opens with Chapter 5.1, 'The Amazonian Indians as viewed by three Andean chroniclers', by Vera Tyuleneva. This chapter pores over some key ethnohistorical accounts written from an Andean perspective in the years following the Spanish conquest, so as to establish Andean attitudes to Amazonia and its inhabitants. Its primary conclusion is unambiguous: the well-known tropes that associate the highlands with civilization and the lowlands with barbarism were already deeply entrenched in the Andes in late prehistory and had probably developed there many centuries prior to European contact. By Inca times, native Amazonians were already firmly associated pejoratively with nudity, idolatry and cannibalism. What seems striking in broader perspective is how closely these Inca attitudes correspond with those held afterwards by the Spanish during colonial times. Indeed, the evidence presented here points to a cultural divide between Andes and Amazonia that bridged the historical watershed of the Conquest itself.

In Chapter 5.2, 'The place of Antisuyu in the discourse of Guamán Poma de Ayala', Cristiana Bertazoni analyses a major source also used by Tyuleneva: the *mestizo* author Guamán Poma's *Nueva Corónica y Buen Gobierno*, which is distinguished by numerous unique illustrations. Both in these illustrations and the text,

Bertazoni encounters many of the same tropes regarding Amazonians already described by Tyuleneva. But Bertazoni then goes further, to argue that despite this 'othering' of the lowlands and their inhabitants, they were nevertheless considered *conceptually* as integral to the empire. This is an important point, for Bertazoni further argues that this essential ambiguity in Inca attitudes to Amazonia was lost with the Spanish conquest. Despite many similarities in Inca and Spanish relations with Amazonia, then, the Conquest nevertheless marked a real shift, and the true 'genesis of a sharp division between Andes and Amazonia' that would only deepen in later centuries.

The final two chapters are by Adrian Pearce, and begin with Chapter 5.3, 'Colonial coda: The Andes–Amazonia frontier under Spanish rule'. Pearce emphasizes that during colonial times, the Andes–Amazonia divide was a phenomenon of real substance. Amazonia presented few real incentives to Spanish settlement, as well as significant disincentives, and so remained marginal to Spanish interests. The heartland of Spanish rule lay in the highlands and on the coast, while Spain's presence in the eastern lowlands was limited. Pearce then charts the huge demographic impact of European colonization on the pre-Columbian demography of both Amazonia and the Andes. He concludes by dwelling on the striking similarities between Spanish colonial and Inca imperial attitudes to Amazonia, and concludes that if these attitudes prevailed in two such different polities, then it was surely their *Andean* character – based on intensive agriculture, large populations and urban civilization – that maintained the divide, even across the transition from indigenous to European rule.

Lastly, and also by Pearce, Chapter 5.4, 'A case study in Andes–Amazonia relations under colonial rule: The Juan Santos Atahualpa rebellion (1742–52)', provides concrete illustration of how the key themes and processes sketched out in the preceding chapter operated in practice. The mid-eighteenth-century episode discussed by Pearce in this chapter appeared to mark a moment of particularly intense interaction between Andes and Amazonia, sparked by a major rebellion among the peoples of the central montaña. On closer inspection, however, this case study rather confirms the limited nature of Spanish interest in Amazonia, along with the limited predisposition of the colonial state to support colonizing or missionizing endeavours there. The Juan Santos rebellion constitutes an 'exception that proves the rule', then: a rare case of vigorous intervention across the frontier during colonial times proved not to be durable, and the general pattern of a clearly defined 'divide' quickly re-established itself.

To close this Introduction, we wish to thank all our contributors, both for their chapter submissions and for their patience over the lengthy gestation of this book.

Part 1
Crossing frontiers: Perspectives from the various disciplines

1.1
Archaeology

David G. Beresford-Jones and Eduardo Machicado Murillo

This chapter provides an overview of the history of an Andes–Amazonia divide from the perspective of archaeology. Strictly speaking, by this we refer to the study of the past through the excavation of archaeological sites and the analysis of ancient arte-facts and other physical remains. Such an emphasis is necessary because so much of the interpretation of prehistory on both sides of the Andes–Amazonia divide has long been made upon *other* lines of evidence, not least analogies drawn from a relatively recent historical past and then projected back in time.

We begin at one extreme of the historical imagination, first sparked by the Old World's encounter in the sixteenth century with the Inca Empire. Here was a manifestly highland power that imposed a political and economic order on such a scale that the early Spanish chroniclers turned to ancient Rome for comparisons. This Andean order was, moreover, sustained by a sophisticated agriculture set amidst an alpine landscape, itself seemingly domesticated into monumental flights of terraces and intricate traceries of irrigation canals.

Though there were a few divergent accounts by conquistadors swept away down the continent's vast eastward draining river systems, the early view of Amazonia through Andean eyes – whether Inca or Spanish – was of an indomita-ble green wilderness inhabited by colourful 'savages' and 'cannibals'. Its relentless environment imposed seemingly self-evident limits on agriculture, demography and social complexity. By the late nineteenth century, Amazonia had come to be regarded as a mostly empty wilderness beyond the course of human history and ripe for 'colonization' by the new South American republics, particularly in the exploitation of rubber. This vision of the Andes–Amazonia divide as the last fron-tier between culture and nature was, however, never much justified by archaeology.

Amazonia's enormity is now acknowledged to encompass a significant diver-sity of environments beyond merely uniform seasonally flooded forest with poor soils. Rather than being everywhere hindered, agriculture's very origins in South America may have been incubated in that diversity. Far from being the passive recipient of Andean influences, some archaeologists would now see the tropi-cal lowlands as the wellspring of the civilization that eventually emerged in the highlands. Arriving at that current orthodoxy, however, will also entail a brief review of its epistemology: the critical issue of how we know what we (think we) know scientifically. For Amazonia sometimes seems transformed in the prevailing academic imagination from one extreme – that of an empty, pristine wilderness fit only to be either conquered, cultured or preserved as a moral imperative – into another, in which its environments seemingly imposed *no* limits, or even much influence, on the populations and societies sustained here during prehistory.

We begin with the briefest sketch of the environmental distinctions that have for so long shaped ideas of divergent trajectories across the so-called divide between the Andes and Amazonia by following a notional transect through the Neotropical realm.

A transect across the Andes–Amazonia divide

Any west–east transect across South America embraces extreme topographical and environmental variations (see Figure 1.1.1).

Rising almost directly out of the Pacific Ocean, the Andes attain altitudes second only to the Himalaya, across a mere few hundred kilometres. Over such a transect the Andean highlands occupy between 200 and 600 km, comprising, for the most part, two parallel longitudinal chains of mountains and high plateaus, bisected by deep intermontane valleys descending roughly south–north into Amazonia. After some 200 km of varied, precipitous piedmont, the remainder of any such transect, more than 80 per cent, is virtually flat for up to 3,000 km to the Atlantic Ocean. The northern and southern peripheries of this Amazon basin are marked by other significant geographical features, including the Orinoco basin, and the Guiana and northern Brazilian highlands. Together they comprise 'Greater Amazonia' (in the sense of Denevan 2002, 53) which totals some 7 million km², more or less equivalent to the area of Western Europe.

The extreme altitudinal variation along the western end of this transect compresses the most ecologically diverse region on earth, across 'horizontally condensed' space (Shimada 1985, xi). No fewer than 84 of Holdridge's (1967) 103 world 'life-zones' are to be found here. The Pacific littoral itself is extremely arid because of a rigidly stratified atmosphere over cold seas driven by the Humboldt Current, yet is traversed by lush riverine oases along the dozens of watercourses that rise in the adjacent Andes. Seasonally inundated with rich alluvium and endowed offshore with the world's richest marine resources, these valleys were the locus of the earliest florescence of large populations and monumental civilization during the third millennium BC, and of a rich succession of coastal cultures thereafter, built upon irrigation agriculture on ever-increasing scales.

The Andean cordilleras themselves are unique among alpine regions because they span tropical latitudes and therefore can sustain life year-round, even at great altitudes. Long before the Inca Empire, large populations and social complexity

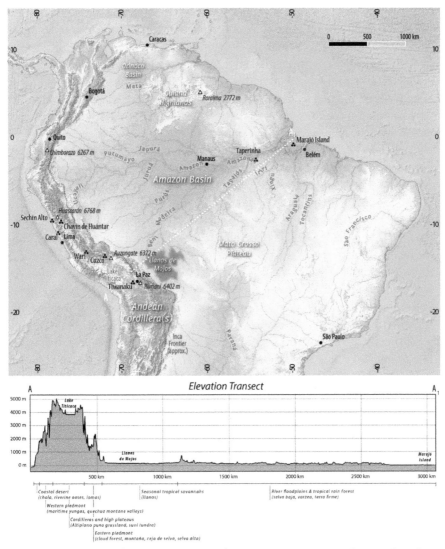

Figure 1.1.1 Map showing a topographic transect across South America along with archaeological sites and ecological zones mentioned in the chapter. © D.G. Beresford-Jones and Paul Heggarty.

flourished in the highlands: around Lake Titicaca, for instance, at 4,000 m on the Bolivian Altiplano during the first millennium AD, sustained by lakeside tuber agriculture and the greatest extent of camelid pasturage in the Andes. Indeed, expansions of people or ideas termed 'horizons' in the archaeological record all arose from highland heartlands, and periodically came to control or otherwise interact with the adjacent lowlands to the west and east.

To the east, the flanks of the Andes descend precipitously, blocking the humidity of the inter-tropical convergence zone over the Amazon basin, which is thereby forced to rise and condense as tremendous seasonal rainfall so that these eastern slopes are lush with montane cloud forest. Geographically, the idea of an Andes–Amazonia divide arises here. For while there was an enduring flux of products and crops across this eastern piedmont, historically at least, its dramatic changes in elevation and ecology imposed physical and adaptive barriers to relationships between highland and lowland populations. In densely vegetated landscapes, rivers offer natural conduits of movement, but across certain Andean gradients navigation upstream can become impossible, as early Spanish expeditions discovered.

Misconceptions of a homogeneous tropical landscape across Amazonia also arise here, whereas any notional transect to the east will embrace many different ecologies. As the many high-energy rivers that drain the eastern slopes emerge onto the Amazonian foreland basin, they transit abruptly to slow meandering systems, depositing their sediment burden in rich alluvial floodplains all along the foot of the Andes. Many now envisage the origins of South American agriculture as lying in the distinctively seasonal tropical savannahs ('Llanos') around the periphery of the Amazon basin. The spread of that agriculture, and indeed later interactions between highlands and eastern lowlands, likely followed the courses of rivers draining the deep intermontane valleys between the various Andean cordilleras, rather than the vertiginous outer flanks of the Andes themselves (Sauer 1952, 117). Transects across northern Peru and Ecuador bring the coast, highlands and eastern lowlands into particularly close proximity. Later, after around AD 800, large tracts of these seasonal wetlands in Bolivia, Ecuador, Guiana and Venezuela were transformed by systems of raised field agriculture to support significant settled populations.

Beyond the piedmont, the rivers bear the different geological signatures of their Andean headwaters into the heart of Amazonia, where they merge into constantly shifting courses across a vast, entirely flat landscape characterized by 'large [vegetation] patterns with gradual transitions and … reduced floristic diversity' (Sauer 1952, 43). Along the banks of these rivers the first European explorers claimed to have seen almost continuous, well-organized settlements, now understood to have been sustained by rich aquatic resources and agriculture along the river floodplains ('varzea'), complemented by more dispersed exploitation of the enormous interior ('terra firme') that makes up the vast majority of the Amazon basin (Denevan 2002, 127).

Finally, at the far eastern extreme of the transect, the combined waters of what is by far the largest river system in the world emerge into the Atlantic across a delta 320 km wide, in which large fluvial islands such as Marajó were home to flourishing complex societies in the centuries after AD 500.

Archaeology in South America

Archaeology emerged in South America, as it did in the Americas generally, from anthropology, much coloured by a presumed continuity between the New World societies that had emerged into history only centuries earlier and their ancient ancestors. This led to the division of the continent into 'culture areas' (or 'co-traditions', see Chapter 3.7), within which peoples inhabiting similar environments were assumed to share aspects of culture in common, eventually crystallized in Steward's (1946, 1948) *Handbook of South American Indians*. The Andes–Amazonia divide ran through the *HSAI*, between volumes, on the one hand, for 'marginal', 'tropical forest' and 'circum-Caribbean *tribes*'; and on the other, for 'Andean *civilizations*', the very titles of which conferred cultural evolutionary privilege on the Andes (Isbell and Silverman 2008).

The recognition by Max Uhle, among others, that stratigraphy recapitulates chronology was the foundation of a specifically archaeological methodology to trace culture history back to long before the relatively recent ethnohistorical past. The pioneers of that archaeology in South America, such as Kroeber, Tello and Bennett, sought the hallmarks of a distinctively *Andean* civilization, including intensive agriculture and herding, large polities sustained by co-opting communal labour, highly developed material cultures and long-distance exchanges promulgated by pilgrimages. Yet many of these hallmarks (later sometimes termed *'lo Andino'*) were, and indeed still are, derived by analogies with the Inca Empire that had been described by Spanish chroniclers (for example, Cobo 1653/1998): that is, from a version of history or ethnography, rather than from archaeology *per se*.

The problem of chronology

Throughout the first half of the twentieth century, archaeologists were concerned to describe and classify into relative chronologies the material remains of the 'cultures' revealed by stratigraphic excavation, periodically integrated across 'horizons'. Most research was invested in the Andean cultural area, as the presumed hearth of civilization, and defined initially by three such pan-regional epochs of cultural unity – Chavín, Wari/Tiwanaku and Inca. These horizons all emanated from highland heartlands, and were interspersed with periods of more fragmented, local cultures, in due course elaborated into a unified archaeological chronology (Rowe 1960, 1967). While a separate and significant trajectory within this Andean culture history was often accorded to its western Pacific coast based upon its rich material culture record (for example, Lanning 1967; Moseley 1974; Bird et al. 1985; Chapter 3.7), the eastern lowlands were more or less excluded from it.

Despite the long-standing prejudices that conceived of only small-scale societies dwelling from time immemorial amidst virgin tropical forest wilderness, and indeed the formidable difficulties of practising archaeology there, chronological schemes were also developed for the tropical lowlands: for the Caribbean area (Cruxent and Rouse 1958–9); and for central Amazonia (Meggers and Evans 1961).

While many refinements and restyling of nomenclature have been proposed, and gaps acknowledged in these 'culture histories' of both sides of the Andes–Amazonia divide, they still provide the essential chronological skeletons for more than six decades of subsequent archaeological work.

From chronology to explanation

By the later part of the twentieth century, however, there was increasing interest in explanations for how and *why* change in the archaeological record had occurred. Although culture history provided the building blocks for such interpretations, facile associations between material cultures, 'peoples' and languages became widely mistrusted. One reason for this was the advent of radiocarbon dating in the 1960s, which forced a reassessment of time depth, slowing perceived rates of transformation so that 'events' became 'processes' in prehistory. Rather than explaining change in the archaeological record though 'migrations of peoples' or 'diffusion of cultures', archaeologists in the latter half of the twentieth century looked to autochthonous processes of population growth, social differentiation and human–environment interactions: not least the advent of agriculture, widely presumed to be the foundation for all subsequent demographic and social transformations and the emergence of complex civilizations (for example, Childe 1951).

Clearly, the densely populated, state-level societies that eventually emerged in the Andean region had depended on sophisticated agricultural systems set amidst the high intermontane valleys and along the fertile riverine oases along the Pacific coast. Yet early research on that coast (for example, Bird et al. 1985), motivated in part by the extraordinary preservation of organic plant, animal and human remains afforded by its arid climate, suggested that the genesis of that Andean civilization had lain not in agriculture but rather in exploiting the ocean's prodigious inshore marine resources (Lanning 1967; Moseley 1974). Certainly, by around 5000 BP, marine resources and floodplain agriculture sustained large-scale sedentary populations building monumental architecture in a number of these valleys, today epitomized by the site of Caral (Shady and Leyva 2003; Dillehay et al. 2012) (see Figure 1.1.1).

Meanwhile, apparently contrasting features of the historical 'tropical forest' and 'marginal' tribes of the eastern lowlands – small, autonomous villages of root crop farmers or mobile hunter-gatherers, respectively (Steward 1946, 1948) – were explained as the outcome of environmental limitations. Meggers (1954, 1957), for instance, proposed Amazonia to be a 'counterfeit paradise', whose abundant vegetation belied poor soil fertility in an extremely wet climate and rendered intensive agriculture impossible. Others presumed that the slash-and-burn that defined contemporary Amazonian agriculture had been impossible before the coming of steel tools and in the general absence of suitable stone sources (for example, Métraux 1959). Such factors were claimed self-evidently to impose limits on demographic growth and social development, and yet were increasingly questioned in subsequent debates about the degree to which human action is conditioned by the environment (Carneiro 1974; Lathrap 1968a and b; Roosevelt 1989, 1991; Balée 1989).

Julio C. Tello (1923) had strongly advocated the highland origin of all the major pan-Andean cultural expansions, but also called attention to supposedly jungle-derived archetypes in the earliest, Andean 'mother culture' of these: the Chavín Early Horizon (see Chapters 1.4, 2.4, 2.5 and 3.7). The geographer Carl Sauer (1952), meanwhile, held that early plant domestication in South America differed from that of 'seed farmers' elsewhere, in its focus on vegetatively propagated starchy root crops, whose origins he envisaged in the highly seasonal wetlands along the western peripheries of Amazonia (see Chapters 2.1, 4.3 and 4.4).

In due course Lathrap (1970, 1977) elaborated these ideas into an influential thesis that, far from being the occasional passive receiver of traits and cultigens from outside habitats, the eastern lowlands had been *foundational* to the Andean trajectory, as movement up the western tributaries of the Amazon had brought sophisticated 'house garden' traditions into the Andes as early as 10,000 BP (see Chapters 1.4, 2.4 and 3.7). Rather than historical Amazonian societies reflecting some unchanging primordial subsistence regime, Lathrap (1970) argued that the history of the tropical forest cultural area had been dynamic: marked by epochs of expansion and agricultural intensification as evidenced by the early historical accounts of large, centrally organized societies living along the Amazon and Solimões rivers (Medina 1934), and increasingly, also by archaeology.

At the same time, mechanisms for intense contacts and interchanges *between* different culture areas were also being proposed, such as Murra's (1985) concept of the 'vertical archipelago' to describe how particular highland ethnic groups established colonies dispersed into lowland ecological tiers, thereby gaining access to a broader range of agricultural products and diversifying subsistence risk (Chapters 2.5 and 3.1). Under such models, rather than hindering movement, the extreme environmental variations along the Andes–Amazonia divide actually *drove* social dynamics between culture areas: interactions eventually written into the institutions of the Inca Empire, and indeed the antecedent pan-Andean horizons (for example, Wilkinson 2018).

Although such systems of 'ecological complementarity' (Salomon 1985, 511) affirm how different environments moulded the different cultural trajectories of their occupants, they also illustrate how the relationships between people and habitat were mediated by culture. This 'cultural ecology' attenuated the environmental determinism of earlier eras as new methodologies revealed recursive, long-term relationships between culture and environment (for example, Denevan 2002; Heckenberger and Neves 2009). Those methods also enabled a more refined perception of the range of lifestyles that lay between mobile hunting and gathering on the one hand, and intensive agriculture on the other; and a better understanding of how combinations of intensive foraging and agriculture along that continuum might sustain sedentary populations and different degrees of social complexity, not least in Amazonia (for example, Dillehay et al. 2012; Roosevelt 2017; Chapters 2.1 and 3.6).

The application of archaeological science

Throughout the twentieth century, developments in methodologies in archaeology and in other related disciplines continued to promote a more rigorous, empirically based approach to field archaeology. By the end of the century these coincided with increasing political stability and economic development through much of South America, greatly facilitating archaeological fieldwork. While such methodological and economic developments have reshaped research across the Andes–Amazonia divide, they have had particular impact on the archaeology of the tropical lowlands.

For the enormous environmental diversity along the Andes–Amazonia transect entails commensurate variation in all those factors that influence the preservation and visibility of the archaeological record, from its moment of deposition to its uncovering and analysis. These 'taphonomic' variations inherent in particular environments enormously skew data recovery and, therefore, greatly influence the empirical basis on which we can make interpretations of the past. Just as the visibility and preservation of the archaeological record of the arid Pacific coast made it an early focus of research, in the highlands a highly visible monumental archaeological record also attracted long investigation, although here organic remains, other than in certain dry cave sites, are poorly preserved. Yet this same high visibility also provoked centuries of destructive depredation of both coastal and highland archaeological records, through looting, initially for precious metals and later to supply antiquities and 'art' markets. Meanwhile, the humid tropical lowlands have long presented specific challenges to both the preservation and visibility of the archaeological record (Meggers 1954), making progress in research here particularly responsive to the application of new methodologies.

From the 1960s onwards, methods from physical geography, earth science, climatology, zoology, ecology and plant sciences were increasingly incorporated into archaeology, not least to reconstruct past environments and to trace the origins and consequences of agriculture. These revealed the hitherto unsuspected extent of human intervention in world environments through time. For South America this included evidence for the dramatic effects of ancient land use practices on many parts of the coast, highlands and tropical lowlands (for example, Denevan 2002, 2003; Beresford-Jones 2011), and a growing suspicion that the 'pristine' New World of historical imagination was no more than a myth (Denevan 1992b), distorted by the catastrophic population collapse that followed first contact with Old World pathogens and subsequent history (Cook 1981; Hemming 1995; Chapter 5.3).

For parts of Amazonia in particular, these new methodologies have revealed greater social complexity and promoted far higher estimates of past populations (Denevan 2003; Heckenberger et al. 2003; Erickson 2006). Soil science has given us a more nuanced understanding of variations in the productivities of tropical soils (cf. Sombroek 1966; Coulter 1972) and, with micromorphology, has identified tracts of black earth ('*terra preta*') as the legacy of ancient human occupations

(Lehman et al. 2003; Woods et al. 2009; Chapter 4.4). Multiple lines of botanical evidence have also been applied to reconstructing past environments and subsistence regimes, ranging from microfossil evidence in the form of pollen, phytoliths and starch grains, to plant macro remains, sometimes preserved more abundantly than commonly assumed in humid tropical environments, through charring (Piperno and Pearsall 1998; Piperno 2011a; Iriarte et al. 2010; Roosevelt 2017). Meanwhile, technological advances in geophysics, GIS systems, LIDAR (Light Detection and Ranging) and lightweight survey tools such as drones have made it possible to discover and record archaeological sites through increasingly accessible, high-resolution, remotely sensed data. In Amazonia this has been inadvertently enabled by massive, ongoing deforestation, revealing previously invisible archaeological records (Heckenberger et al. 2008; Prümers 2014).

Andes–Amazonia: A new archaeological orthodoxy?

While the possibilities opened up by these new methods have influenced archaeology across the Andes–Amazonia divide, it is particularly in Amazonia that they have substantially altered perceptions of prehistory, and made Amazonian archaeology one of the discipline's fastest growing and most prolific research fields in the past decade.

Over the deepest time-depths, archaeological orthodoxy now envisages little difference across the divide in the timing of first human occupation during the Late Pleistocene (Roosevelt et al. 2002; Dillehay 2017; Rademaker et al. 2014; Chapters 2.1 and 4.4), or the subsequent coalescence of various complexes of domesticated plants and animals to form the basis of sedentary, small-scale horticultural lifestyles before 7000 BP (Dillehay et al. 2011; Waters et al. 2014; Roosevelt 2017; Lombardo et al. 2020; Chapters 2.1 and 2.4). Indeed, the Neotropical lowlands are, following Sauer (1952) and through biogeography, now widely claimed as a major cradle of agricultural origins, home to around half of all crops of the Americas (Iriarte 2009; Piperno 2011a), and Amazonia, in particular, the source of 'at least 83 native species … domesticated to some degree' (Clement et al. 2015, 2) – although archaeological evidence of these processes is extremely sparse.

Along the coasts of South America between 6000 and 4000 BP Mesolithic-like lifestyles based on rich aquatic resources sustained increasing social complexity and sedentism (Marquet et al. 2012; Dillehay et al. 2012; Dillehay 2017; Beresford-Jones et al. 2015, 2018); and into its interior along the river levees of the tropical lowlands of Ecuador, Colombia, Brazil, Bolivia and Guyana (Chapters 2.1 and 4.4). In Amazonia sites such as Taperinha (Roosevelt 2017) (see Figure 1.1.1), show the earliest evidence for pottery on the continent around 7000 BP, long before the advent of agriculture (Hoopes 1994; Roosevelt 1995; Lombardo et al. 2013; Chapter 3.6). Since moving plants through different ecologies selects for those genetic factors controlling harvest timing and seed dispersal – ultimately 'domestication' (Vavilov 1992; Lynch 1973) – agriculture's very origins in South America likely lay in deep-time interchanges across the tremendous ecological diversity of the Andes–Amazonia transect. The lowest and narrowest such transect between Amazonia and the Pacific lies through the Huancabamba depression (see Chapter 2.4, Figure 2.4.3), and the archaeological record of southern Ecuador and northern Peru includes the earliest hints of plants being moved beyond their ranges of natural distribution (Piperno 2011a; Dillehay et al. 2011; Chapter 2.1), and indeed of the subsequent unfolding of precocious complex society (Chapter 2.4).

Beginning around 5000 BP, however, significant differences start to emerge in the Late Archaic trajectories on either side of the Andes–Amazonia divide. In certain valleys of the coast of Peru, subsistence regimes underwent transformational intensification through floodplain agriculture of cotton for fishing nets and, increasingly, certain food crops, which precipitated the earliest monumental civilization in South America (Moseley 1974; Shady and Leyva 2003; Chapter 2.4). Similar precocious developments followed immediately thereafter in the highlands (see Chapter 2.4). While archaeologists may debate precisely what kind of societies built monumental sites like Caral on the coast of Peru, there can be little doubt that by the end of the third millennium BC, the Late Archaic archaeological records of the coast and highlands evince population densities and social complexities of a different order of magnitude to any contemporary developments in Amazonia.

These differing trajectories became more marked as the subsequent Formative Period unfolded (for example, Chapter 2.4). This culminated during the first millennium BC with the first truly pan-Andean transformation, the Cupisnique–Chavín Early Horizon, followed by the florescence of diverse, complex and (on the north coast) expansive societies during the Early Intermediate Period to around AD 500. And although the northern periphery of Greater Amazonia also saw the expansion of 'horizons' (as yet poorly understood) along the Caribbean coast and into the Orinoco basin during the Formative (Cruxent and Rouse 1958–9; Roosevelt 2017), the archaeological record of central Amazonia for this time is essentially silent. This 'Amazonian hiatus' (Neves 2008) remains one of the most important unanswered questions of archaeological and palaeoenvironmental research in the basin, not least because, for the centuries immediately thereafter, the new archaeological orthodoxy does envisage rapidly increasing populations and social complexity across Amazonia (Denevan 2003; Heckenberger et al. 2003; Erickson 2006; Chapter 3.6).

On the Andean side of the divide, the Middle Horizon dawned around AD 500, showing what many would regard as the first unequivocal hallmarks of 'state-level' societies in the Andes, including the co-opting of labour for agricultural intensification, roads and military expansion, khipu record-keeping and those other elements that would later define 'Inca' statecraft too (D'Altroy and Schreiber 2004). The Middle Horizon saw the building of urban conglomerations such as Wari and Tiwanaku, today among the largest archaeological sites in South America (see Figure 1.1.1), and some would link this period to the expansions of major Andean language families (Beresford-Jones and Heggarty 2012a; Chapter 3.4).

Evidence suggests that around this time Greater Amazonia too saw significant demographic growth, nucleated along the Amazon and Orinoco floodplains and the Guiana coasts, and sustained by intensive agriculture of root crops and sometimes maize (Heckenberger et al. 2008; Dickau et al. 2012; Roosevelt 2017). When this began remains vaguely defined, sometimes related with putative dates of language family expansions (Clement et al. 2015; Chapter 3.6). Certainly, however, by AD 500 many of those Amazonian societies exhibited features typically taken to connote social complexity: ranging from extended patterns of semi-autonomous villages along the central Amazon (Neves and Petersen 2006) to integrated networks of settlements, sometimes attached to monumental centres, epitomized by sites in Marajó (Roosevelt 1991) or the Llanos de Mojos (Lombardo and Prümers 2010; Chapter 4.3). From around AD 900 there is evidence too for increasingly intensive land-use practices across the lowlands of Bolivia, Ecuador, Colombia and Guyana (Denevan 2002; Rostain 2008). Yet despite increasingly convergent trajectories[1] on either side of the Andes–Amazonia divide at this time, there is little archaeological evidence that they were directly related. For instance, not a single fragment of unequivocally Amazonian material culture has been excavated in the Andes from this period; or vice-versa (Chapter 4.3).

As the Middle Horizon collapsed in the Andes around AD 1000, it was replaced during the Late Intermediate Period once again by expansive large-scale polities along the coast, epitomized by the Chimú Empire, while the now relatively dense populations in the highlands became fragmented into hundreds of small-scale petty chiefdoms engaged in almost constant warfare and competition. One of these, the Inca, would suddenly emerge after 1450 to dominate a vast 4,000 km swathe of the highlands and coast (the Late Horizon, see Figure 1.1.1). During this time in Amazonia, there is also evidence of broader, pan-regional systems (Heckenberger et al. 2008), and for frequent conflict between larger-scale chiefdoms including defensive architecture and buffer zones separating them (Heckenberger et al. 1999; Schaan 2001).

In sum, then, the archaeological record suggests considerable flux across the Andes–Amazonia divide unfolding gradually over the millennia from first occupation of South America to the Late Archaic (c. 5000 BP); gradually increasing *divergence* in largely independent trajectories thereafter, through the Formative and Early Intermediate Periods to around AD 500; followed by increasing *convergence*, again of largely independent trajectories, albeit with ephemeral periods of resonance between the two, before the European conquest. Archaeological consensus also suggests, however, that while on the north coast of Peru or in the south-central highlands, expansionist 'state-level' societies arose from time to time to exert influence across vast geographies (culminating in the Inca Empire), this was never the case in Amazonia (Chapter 3.6).

Conclusions

Twenty-five years of accumulated methodological innovation and archaeological research have made it possible to test the theories of Tello, Lanning, Moseley, Meggers, Lathrap and others. This has forced a critical re-evaluation of many of the preconceptions that lay behind the concept of an Andes–Amazonia divide. Indeed, they have led some to conclude that the idea of that divide is little more than 'a product of colonialism, epidemics, preconceptions and ignorance' (Chapter 1.4).

Certainly, a new archaeological orthodoxy calls far greater attention to the deep-time flux of cultigens, products, people and ideas across the eastern piedmont of the Andes, and to how they shaped significant cultural changes on both sides of the Andes–Amazonia divide. 'To state the obvious, the Amazon basin is a very big place' as Piperno et al. (2015, 1595) put it, and patently, it was not all inimical to intensive agriculture, nor forever sparsely inhabited by small-scale dispersed communities. Long-discounted claims of the ill-fated 1542 Orellana expedition (Medina 1934) of towns for leagues along the banks of the Amazon with 'land as fertile and normal in appearance as our Spain', are today far more credible under this new orthodoxy.

Perhaps the most significant change in our perception, however, has been in how large parts of Amazonia's supposedly pristine landscape and vegetation have in fact been shaped by millennia of significant human occupation, with consequently profound and widespread impacts on its ecology (Erickson 2010; Roosevelt 2013; Clement et al. 2015; Watling et al. 2017; Maezumi et al. 2018; Chapters 3.6 and 4.4). Under the paradigm of 'historical ecology' (Balée 1989), Amazonia's environment, rather than *determining* its cultural trajectories, is envisaged as the *outcome* of them, still exhibiting vestiges of its former 'cultural parkland' condition (Heckenberger et al. 2003), in much the same way as tracts of the Andean highlands and Pacific coast have long been understood to be domesticated landscapes (for example, Denevan 2002).

The implications of this change of perception, however, remain contentious within the discipline. Measuring the distributions of thousands of square kilometres of anthropogenic *terra preta*, raised fields and other earthworks later reclaimed by the tropical forests could provide a proxy for the intensity of past human occupation and impact on Amazonian landscapes. Indeed, some have extrapolated from these indicators to revise estimates for pre-European contact populations of Greater Amazonia to between a 'minimum' of 10 million, and an 'unlikely maximum' of 50 million (Clement et al. 2015, 5). Such figures would be at least equivalent to, or at their upper extremes far greater, than estimates for the population of the Inca Empire (D'Altroy 2015, xv) that extended across much of the Andes at that time.

Estimates of prehistoric populations are, however, notoriously problematic and, across the enormity of Greater Amazonia they are further confounded by very uneven demographic distributions: along the Atlantic coast, in the llanos, and along its riverine levees, as suggested by *terra preta* distributions.

For the Andes and the Pacific coast population, estimates at the moment of European contact have been made by synthesising many *different* lines of evidence; including, *inter alia*, extrapolations from Spanish census data, ecological data, estimates from social organization, disease mortality models and archaeology (Cook 1981; Chapter 5.3). By contrast, using a single proxy of extrapolated anthropogenic *terra preta* distributions to estimate pre-contact Amazonian populations almost certainly conflates many different and weakly established chronologies, perhaps over millennia of occupation.

Indeed, it may be time to rein back on some of the recent hyperbole attending the intensity and chronology of human settlement in Amazonia and to rebalance, somewhat, the pendulum of archaeological perceptions. To see Amazonia as either a largely untouched wilderness, or an extensively transformed landscape, is to set up a false dichotomy with, as Piperno et al. (2017) note, 'an expectation of the latter … likely to be as misleading as the former'. For no-one outside the discipline should fail to understand the serious uncertainties and empirical problems that still underlie many parts of the new archaeological orthodoxy. Roosevelt (2017) offers a useful review of these. Many culture historical sequences, unfashionable but still the backbone of archaeological method, remain poorly studied across the Andes–Amazonia divide. Establishing secure stratigraphy presents many challenges, not least in contexts disturbed by centuries of tropically fecund bioturbation or enormous water throughput. Radiocarbon dating of many archaeological contexts is still scanty and sometimes inconsistent across the immensity of Amazonia, particularly when applied to large-scale, long-term processes of landscape modification. Different classes of plant remains, particularly certain microfossils (for example, Mercader et al. 2018) used to reconstruct past agriculture and land use, each come with particular limitations of taphonomy, identification and comparability. And last, but not least, diverse factors may be implicated in changing environments and thereby confound perceptions of past human impacts, including Holocene climate change (Burbridge et al. 2004; Mayle et al. 2000, 2006; Whitney et al. 2011; Chapter 2.1), natural fires (Cordeiro et al. 2008; Mayle and Power 2008; Urrego et al. 2013), massive avulsions (Lombardo et al. 2015) and tectonics (Lombardo and Veit 2014). There is, for instance, particular debate about how far distributions of plant microfossils or modern botanical inventories over relatively small scales can be extrapolated to determine the intensity of the human imprint beyond the river floodplains, across the *terra firme* hinterlands that make up the vast majority of Amazonia (McMichael et al. 2012; Piperno et al. 2015; Watling et al. 2017; Piperno et al. 2017; Lombardo et al. 2020).

This review began by emphasising just how much long-standing perceptions of an Andes-Amazonia divide were not the consequence of archaeology, *per se*, but rather of Inca and Spanish imperial histories and relatively recent ethnologies. Acknowledging all the problems and limitations just mentioned, the patient accumulation of empirical archaeological evidence, increasingly augmented by the methods of archaeological science, has and will certainly continue to challenge those perceptions. Such evidence, however, alongside that from other disciplines, informs our interpretations over particular, often radically different, scales of spatial and temporal resolution, as illustrated by many of the chapters in this book. So while at certain scales, such as the transitory reverberations across the divide of the Andean horizons or the deep-time protracted introduction and adaption of cultivars across different ecologies, new archaeological evidence seems to render the Andes–Amazonia divide less substantial, at others it seems to establish it more firmly than ever. How else would materials from across the divide connote particular value and exotic status? For this reason, archaeology will always be best used to understand prehistory across the Andes–Amazonia divide in *conjunction* with the other, independent lines of evidence offered by disciplines such as history, genetics and linguistics: this book's *raison d'être*.

1.2
Linguistics

Paul Heggarty

Language lessons on the Andes–Amazonia divide

To other disciplines that seek to understand the human past, it is not always immediately apparent how our languages can have much to say. So the task of this chapter is to set out how linguistics can indeed inform our assessment of the Andes–Amazonia divide. It also aims to forearm non-linguist readers, before they embark on the linguistics chapters in this book. It introduces the main concepts in language prehistory that are relevant to understanding any apparent Andes–Amazonia divide in linguistics, and seeks to head off certain common cross-disciplinary misunderstandings about what those linguistic concepts do or do not really mean for our purposes.

We begin with a foretaste of how languages on either side of the divide can shed light on the (pre)histories of the societies that spoke them through time, the inhabitants of the Andes and of Amazonia. Even from just the broadest overview, striking facts stand out. Arawak, for example, is a family made up of scores of languages that all unquestionably descend from a single common origin. Many lie within the core of the Amazon and Orinoco drainages, but other notable Arawak languages spread much further afield, too (see Figure 1.2.1). Moxo is spoken in the Llanos de Moxos in lowland north Bolivia. Taíno was the first native tongue of the Americas encountered by the Europeans in 1492, and was soon to become extinct from the many Caribbean islands where it had been spoken (although some deportee populations do still speak Garífuna along the continental coast of the Caribbean from Belize to Nicaragua). Other Arawak languages were once spoken even in parts of Paraguay and northern Argentina. In short, Arawak is the most expansive of all language families in South America, spread not just across Amazonia but far beyond. And yet there was one environmental gulf that it would not cross: the Andes–Amazonia divide. No Arawak language is spoken high in the Andes or on the Pacific coast.

In the Andes, meanwhile, the one family that approaches Arawak in the scale and environmental diversity of its expansion is Quechua. Its distribution has long been observed to overlap fairly closely with that of the Inca Empire, although that parallel is a beguiling one that has also led to many superficial and anachronistic presumptions about Quechua's prehistory (see Beresford-Jones and Heggarty 2012b, 4–6). In the one respect most relevant to our theme here, however, the parallel does seem to hold. In pre-Columbian times, at least, Quechua did largely mirror a much-noted characteristic of the Andean societies that speak it: a reluctance to venture into Amazonia.

Indigenous languages can inform the Andes–Amazonia question, then, not least because they can be categorized, on specific linguistic criteria, into larger groupings of languages that go together in some way. One can then explore whether those entities or groupings have, through prehistory, either aligned with the Andes–Amazonia frontier, or crossed it. And for a further perspective on how meaningful any divide might be, one can also assess how far linguistic criteria define either just a single, coherent unit on either side of the divide, or multiple entities fragmented by further dividing lines within each region.

Also, as the structure of this chapter implies, it is not all about language families, like Arawak or Quechua. Families are just one of the *two* main levels – which moreover can crosscut one another – on which languages can be analysed into larger entities. Besides language families, the second level is that of 'linguistic convergence areas'. These are far less well known outside linguistics, and are often confused with families, when in fact for prehistory they mean very different things. A first indication is the contrast already evident between Figure 1.2.1, which maps the main divergent language families in South America, and Figure 1.2.2, which maps the main linguistic convergence areas.

Language families: Origins, expansions, migrations and divergence

So to begin with language families, what does a label like Arawak or Quechua really mean for our purposes here? The key is that any language family attests to a process of geographical expansion through time. By definition, every language family started out as a single ancestral language, from which all its 'daughter' languages descend. Spoken languages are always changing, however, incrementally through the generations. And if by some process of geographical expansion – demographic and/or cultural – a language comes to be spoken in different regions whose populations are no longer in constant contact, then from that point on, different changes can arise in different regions. These changes can affect all levels of language: vocabulary, sound system, grammatical system, and so on. Ultimately, so many changes accumulate, so different from one region to the next, that the original source language ends up effectively diverged into what have become its different 'daughter' languages. What also follows from this natural process of divergence, once a language is widely dispersed, is that the common ancestral 'proto-language' of any

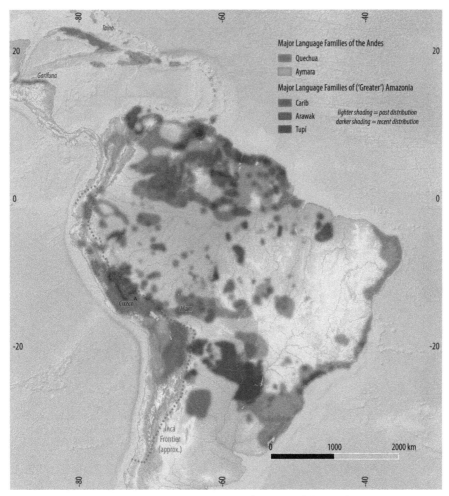

Figure 1.2.1 The main expansive language families of the Andes and Amazonia. © Paul Heggarty. For a closer view along the Andes–Amazonia transition, see Chapter 3.4, Figure 3.4.1.

family must originally have been spoken in just a relatively small region, and its divergence into a family came about in the first place only because of its expansion out of that homeland (see Heggarty and Renfrew 2014a, 23).

For a concrete illustration of how a language family arises by geographical expansion and divergence through time, the classic, historically known example is that of the Romance language family in Europe. In this case, the real-world driver that caused the family to come into being is very clear. The Roman Empire brought much of Europe to speak *Romanice*, 'in the Roman way' – in other words spoken, 'Vulgar' Latin. But once so dispersed, Latin was free to change in different ways in each new region. By today, the 'neo-Latin' spoken in those different regions has become so

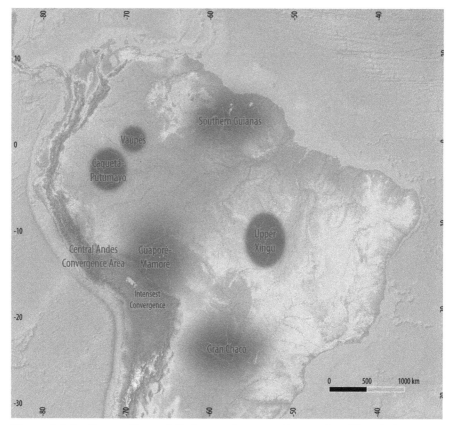

Figure 1.2.2 Zones of especially intense language interaction ('linguistic convergence areas') within South America, based on Beresford-Jones and Heggarty (2012b) for the Andes, and on Epps and Michael (2017) for the lowland languages. © Paul Heggarty. Earlier proposals of a looser convergence area stretching much more widely across most of Amazonia are increasingly challenged: see text, and Chapter 3.5.

divergent as to form the *family* of the various *Romance* languages. Amongst them are Romansch and Romanian, aptly named, but also Italian, French, Spanish, Portuguese and Catalan, and scores of lesser-known sister languages and dialects.

That Arawak is a 'family', then, also means that it is the set of languages that all go back to the same Proto-Arawak source language, but have long since scattered and diverged into significantly different languages, no longer mutually intelligible. Likewise for Quechua. Divergence within Arawak is actually somewhat greater than within Romance, whereas within Quechua it is if anything a little less. Since divergence is cumulative through time, the default implication is that Arawak has been dispersing and diverging for longer than the two millennia since the spread of *Roman(i)ce*, and Quechua for a little less than that. (Linguists have long been dissatisfied with such impressionistic statements, of course, and have tried to put more precise, strictly cross-comparable numbers on degree of linguistic divergence. The nature of language itself, however, continues to pose serious methodological challenges to that goal.)

The key to what any language family means for prehistory, then, is that Romance did *not* 'crystallize' out of some process of <u>con</u>vergence out of some diverse ancient speech already across Europe. On the contrary, Latin spread to *replace* almost all other language lineages previously spoken across much of continental Western Europe (the famous exception being Basque). Romance came about by a process of <u>di</u>vergence, out of Latin, once it had dispersed. Until the rise of ancient Rome, Latin had been spoken only in that city and the province around it, Latium (modern Lazio), whence its very name, *Latin*.

Likewise, Arawak, as a language family, must originally have gone back to a much smaller homeland region, out of which it expanded. So too must Quechua. Each family must thus also have had reasons or 'drivers' for its geographical expansion – although by no means necessarily an empire like Rome, since many other processes can also drive demographic and/or cultural expansions that can take languages with them. Indeed, directly relevant to our theme is whether the expansions of the major language families in the Andes and in Amazonia were driven by similar types of demographic and/or cultural processes, or by very different ones on either side of the 'divide'. If the two regions did indeed have radically different socio-political and demographic histories, then the processes that spread Arawak, for instance, might be expected to be correspondingly different to those that spread Quechua. Arawak may have no good analogues, then, for those late phases of Quechua expansion that seem to result from major, state-directed reconfigurations of Andean demography by the Incas. Certainly, languages do not necessarily require demographic dominance to spread. (That said, the languages of small demographic *elites* have typically fared badly before the modern era, except in particular 'primus inter pares' conditions: see Heggarty 2015, 622–3.) Quechua itself illustrates occasional expansions with precious little demographic trace, and precisely in the exceptional cases where it did spread down from the Andes into some parts of Amazonia, as explored linguistically in Chapter 2.3, and genetically in Chapter 3.3 by Barbieri. For, as in those cases, a particular socio-cultural context can confer utility on a language, making it a target for populations to switch towards. Still, that utility derives not from anything in the language *per se,* but from the scale, power and/or cultural prestige of the populations and cultures that (already) speak it. The language is carried along with a broader cultural package that is doing the expanding.

So it is not as if language families themselves have some innate and somehow 'linguistic' propensity to spread of their own accord. Their distributions stand very much at the *effect* end of a cause-and-effect relationship. Indeed, if language families can attest to the operation of expansive processes in prehistory in the first place – whether demographic and/or socio-cultural – then that is because they are the direct results of those real-world processes (see Heggarty 2015, 600–2; Heggarty and Renfrew 2014a, 19–21). And in all cases, the basic principle remains: whichever particular expansive mechanisms lie behind any given language family, they are still expansive and divergent in nature, not convergent. The fundamental process that creates a family is still one of geographical spread, not convergence *in situ* in some form of network. It necessarily entails at least some migration of speakers, to carry the language lineage to other regions. This holds even if thereafter, in addition, locals may also switch to speaking the language of those incomers, for cultural and/or demographic reasons.

It is also these migrations, their directions, sequence and stages, that determine the structure of the 'family tree' of descent within each family, its branches and sub-branches. Those past processes thus remain encoded in that tree structure, hence the value for prehistory of recovering it by comparative linguistics. (Hence also the discipline's near obsession with sound change laws especially, as the most reliable diagnostic for establishing those trees.) The Quechua of Cuzco and that of Bolivia, for example, share distinctive changes that define them together in the family's far southern (or 'QIIc+') branch. These changes thus effectively prove that the Quechua of the Bolivian Altiplano can be derived from a movement of speakers southwards from the Cuzco region, at a relatively late stage, in the Inca and/or Spanish colonial period – and that the Quechua of Central Peru cannot.

The origins and main dispersals of the major language families of South America lie far back in prehistory; the shallow historical record here catches only their last phases. But this makes comparative/historical linguistics all the more valuable, because the discipline enjoys so many known historical test-cases, like Romance, that it has been able to develop and test its comparative methodology, and confirm the validity of its results against ancient written languages. By now, the same methods can confidently be applied without even requiring a historical record – and in some respects can even partly make up for the lack of one, in regions like South America.

Language families, then, can offer various perspectives on the Andes–Amazonia question. The first lies simply in how they map out across the continent, as we have already seen for Arawak and Quechua. That first illustration can seem unequivocal, in supporting the reality of a divide. On closer inspection, however, it turns out that the constraint not to trespass from the Andes into Amazonia does not hold up entirely, as explored in the 'language families' section of Chapter 3.4. That chapter surveys what else *families* can tell us of the Andes–Amazonia divide in various other respects, too, beyond any such 'trespassing' taboo.

Contact and linguistic areas: Interaction and convergence out of diverse origins

In any case, there is plenty more that language can tell us about the reality or otherwise of an Andes–Amazonia divide, on another level that has nothing to do with families. For relationships of common descent ('families') are only one way of looking at languages. The linguistic panorama includes another quite separate dimension that can cut across language family distributions, and indeed often does. This is only natural, in fact. For while a language *family* is the result of geographical expansion out of a single origin and the ensuing language d̲ivergence, it is hardly as if human societies only ever undergo processes that are expansive and divergent. On the contrary, groups with diverse origins can come into and remain in contact and interaction with each other. Intense and/or long-lasting interactions result in powerful processes of c̲onvergence. These too have their corresponding impacts in language – and most importantly, these impacts are not the same as the signals left by shared origin and divergence.

Languages can in fact display a whole scale of different degrees of intensity of contact effects upon each other (whether reciprocal or predominantly one-way). And for (pre)history, those different degrees of contact effects attest to different corresponding real-world contexts, of ever stronger interaction between the populations and societies that spoke them. For the purposes of this book, then, it is crucial to assess how intense was the level of past interactions between the Andes and Amazonia, as still recorded in their languages.

To start from the weakest indications, individual words may be borrowed from one language into another. Naturally, this happens especially with words for anything that is new to the speakers of one language, but already known and referred to by speakers of another. Just as European languages resorted simply to borrowing in words such as *llama*, *puma* or *coca*, it is natural that when people on one side of the Andes–Amazonia divide needed to refer to species or concepts typical of the other environment, they could simply borrow a word for it from one of the languages of that other environment, particularly an immediately neighbouring language along the divide itself.

Occasional loanwords for species or concepts 'alien' to the borrower language do not prove much more than the most limited interaction, however. On a greater scale are *Wanderwörter*, 'wandering words' that range far and wide, irrespective of language family, so much so that it can even end up unclear which family they actually originated in. For an idea of what these *Wanderwörter* can in principle tell us of the past, consider some well-known, long-range examples across Europe, such as words for *coffee*, *sugar*, *tea*, *potato*, or even *lion*, and mythical concepts such as *dragon*. These words in modern European languages even bear phonetic details indicative of which different external source they were loaned from, or indeed of how and when they were loaned serially from one language to another. (Note how English *café* differs from *coffee*; each tells a separate history. The former attests to French cultural influence in the late nineteenth century, and the latter to how the drink had first reached Europe some three centuries earlier, ultimately from speakers of Arabic, but only through speakers of Turkish as the intermediary traders.) Such *Wanderwörter* make for linguistic traces of the exchange routes of the corresponding real-world products, or the cultural networks through which concepts and mythologies spread. South America offers plenty of intriguing examples, often the names for species, tradable items or cultural concepts (Epps 2017). A natural explanation is that such words spread through exchange networks. A caveat, however, is that far-flung *Wanderwörter* have often tempted unsuspecting scholars to read rather too much into them. They still need not mean anything more than a chain of local networks of 'down-the-line' trade, for example. Loanwords often spread through languages in series, just as *llama* reached Europe not by direct contact with the source language, but via Spanish (hence the *ll-*, even in the English spelling).

So however far they roam, individual loanwords remain only the most superficial form of language convergence, and they may result from limited exchanges involving just a few members of a community. Evidence for much more sustained and widespread interaction lies rather in whole swathes of loanwords that overtake significant proportions of the vocabulary, as with the flood of Norman French loanwords that reshaped much of the vocabulary of English. Even that, however, falls short of the next level up in 'interference' effects between languages, the quantum leap when those go beyond the vocabulary and encroach upon the sound and grammatical systems and structures of the languages involved. An example of such a 'structural' characteristic is how a language orders the components in a basic sentence, as subject-verb-object (svo, as in many European languages), subject-object-verb (sov, in many South American languages), or some other order. (Many other structural characteristics are illustrated by Van Gijn and Muysken in Chapter 3.5.)

Where a language switches to adopt a deep structural characteristic of another language, this typically attests to a past phase of widespread bilingualism, if not multilingualism. Where such a phase ends up with a community switching from its original language to that of another population, then the contact effects can be particularly far-reaching. The generation(s) involved can carry over (unawares) structures from their original native tongue into the new language that they are (thus 'imperfectly') learning. At its most extreme level, the result is the wholesale restructuring of the sound and/or grammatical system of one language on the structural model of another. One such case arose between early forms of Quechua and Aymara, which has a bearing on the Andes–Amazonia question in ways taken up in Chapter 2.3.

Moreover, language interaction need not involve only two languages. Indeed, the scale of the Andes–Amazonia question requires us to zoom out to look at how language convergence phenomena pattern much more widely. At the broad, multilanguage level, linguistics employs a concept that is in many ways the antithesis of a language family, and of the process of separation and divergence by which that arises. On this other dimension, of contact and interaction, the basic concept is instead that of a 'linguistic area', shorthand for 'linguistic *convergence* area'. This denotes a region across which multiple languages share certain structural characteristics, which, however, they did not all originally have, and have come to share only through contact and interaction.

To illustrate this more concretely, we take some of the evidence that Dixon and Aikhenvald (1999, 8–9) invoke to argue that Amazonia is a linguistic convergence area (even if their case is today challenged; see Chapter 3.5 by Van Gijn and Muysken, and Chapter 3.4). Amazonia is home still to scores of languages that are entirely mutually unintelligible and belong to dozens of different lineages with independent origins. Yet despite that, and irrespective of which family they come from, many languages here have (through interaction) come to share certain fundamental characteristics of language structure. Dixon and Aikhenvald (1999) list 15 of these, although here we illustrate only the less technical ones. The sound systems of Amazonian languages generally do not distinguish *r* from *l*, for example (as Chinese also does not, entirely coincidentally), and they typically have five basic vowels (*i, e, a, i, u/o*), as well as nasal vowels (as in Portuguese *São* or French *un bon vin blanc*). Their grammatical systems, meanwhile, have extensive gender systems, but few grammatical cases, and most allow prefixes.

The illustration becomes clearer still when Dixon and Aikhenvald (1999, 9–10) then look to the contrast with the opposing linguistic area of the Andes. Here, languages have converged instead on other structural characteristics, many of them diametrically opposed to the Amazonian ones. That is, their sound systems *do* distinguish *r* from *l*, but have only *three* vowels (*i, a, u*), and *no* nasal vowels. Their grammatical systems have *no* gender, *many* grammatical cases, and do *not* allow prefixes. Quechua and Aymara share all these characteristics, and more, making them very alike in the underlying nature of their sound and grammatical systems. They nonetheless remain utterly unintelligible to each other – inevitably so, because they are not of the same language family.

What defines a linguistic area, then, are effectively characteristics that are shared *not* because of common inheritance. Indeed, by default, a linguistic area spans languages from multiple *different* families and origins. When linguistics employs the term 'areal', then, tacit within that is the concept of (arisen by) convergence out of different origins.

To be clear, however, to avoid any dangerous misunderstandings: what emerges out of such convergence processes is *not* a new 'hybrid' language, and certainly not a *lingua franca*. Convergence can never go so far as to make two unrelated languages somehow become intelligible to each other, let alone identical. A linguistic area is nothing like this: it is merely a collection of unrelated languages, still radically different in countless ways, that have become alike only in certain deep structural features.

On this second main dimension of the linguistic panorama, languages in South America attest to interaction effects of all types, scales and degrees of intensity of interaction, from individual loanwords to full-blown structural remodelling. And there is interaction both between individual pairs of languages and across much wider linguistic convergence areas. For the Andes–Amazonia divide, the question is whether these convergence effects pattern geographically in ways that either respect or disqualify the idea of a divide. And, whether the convergence effects visible *within* the Andes and within Amazonia are far stronger than whatever convergence there has also been *between* the two regions. These are the themes taken up in the third section of Chapter 2.3 – where the overall picture does appear broadly compatible with an Andes–Amazonia divide, albeit with many attendant qualifications – and again in Chapter 3.3.

Confusions and clarifications: Divergent families versus convergent areas

This fundamental contrast between language families and linguistic areas – between divergent *versus* <u>con</u>vergent processes – helps to place the various linguistic contributions to this book in context, and to understand the different perspectives they give on the Andes–Amazonia question. Firstly, the families/areas contrast is the obvious criterion used to structure the overview, in Chapter 3.3, of the broadest-scale patterns in the linguistic panorama with respect to the Andes–Amazonia frontier. Chapter 3.5 (by Van Gijn and Muysken) focuses on linguistic areas, and presents a wide-ranging, quantitative assessment of the degree of convergence in structural characteristics between many languages of the Andes and of Amazonia. Most importantly, it also assesses differences within Amazonia, between languages nearer to and further from the Andes. Chapter 4.1 (by Adelaar), meanwhile, looks at language families, but beyond the clearly established ones that do not significantly cross the Andes–Amazonia divide. It explores instead a hypothesis of an even wider, deeper relationship that would, if true, mean that one Andean language significant in prehistory (Puquina) might in fact have originated in a major lowland family. Chapter 4.2 (by Zariquiey) also looks at a past hypothesis of a 'long-range' family relationship across the divide, only to debunk it. In the process, however, it finds evidence for a potential linguistic convergence area instead, and one that would indeed span the Andes–Amazonia divide.

Linguistics and genetics, classification and admixture

On this fundamental issue of distinguishing divergent language families from linguistic convergence areas, a clarification is needed to address a common misconception across the disciplines, in this case particularly with genetics. This is about what goes by the name of 'language classification'. The defining criterion – tacit and understood in linguistics, and therefore potentially misleading to other disciplines – is direct *descent* of a language, in an unbroken chain of transmission and intelligibility through the generations, even as *modifications* do progressively build up. (Note the model of *descent with modification*: the process is best conceived of in terms of language *lineages*, more analogous to species, rather than in terms of discrete language units, as if they were individual organisms.) So by comparison with genetics, for example, there is nothing on the scale of the roughly 50–50 recombination of all autosomes with each new generation. On this criterion, it is a black-and-white 'yes' that English is of the Germanic family, because it descends in an unbroken chain through the generations from Proto-Germanic. However much 'admixture' later came into it from Norman French, there never was a chain through the generations from English back to Latin. So English does not classify as a Romance language: again, a clear-cut 'no'. Likewise, the classification of the Quechua of Ecuador and Bolivia is entirely clear-cut: both are of the Quechua family, transmitted through the generations from Proto-Quechua. Yes, Ecuador Quechua underwent convergence effects with other indigenous languages of Ecuador, as is perfectly well known to any linguist working on it. But such effects belong on the separate level of convergence; they are not part of the classification proper.

For a very rough analogy with human genetics, in linguistics it is as if it is both necessary and generally fairly easy to detect and exclude all impact of admixture (in autosomes), and as if classification were done entirely on the level of a uniparental marker that gives a clearer phylogeny of descent. Admixture effects are a key part of what we know of languages like Ecuadoran Quechua, but non-linguists should *not* expect to find them within the *classification* as Quechua. They are analysed on a quite separate dimension of contact and convergence effects, 'despite' the ancestry chain back to Proto-Quechua. Indeed, for the purposes of classification they are *confounds*, to be set aside to prevent them clouding the identification of direct descent.

This is hardly to say that contact effects are ignored by linguists – anything but. It is just that they (rightly) need to be kept separate from the task of classification into families. It is in fact a strength of linguistics that it has a developed methodology that generally does allow us to tease apart what is inheritance and divergence from what is contact and convergence. Geneticists would not confuse autosomal and uniparental markers, or assume that either will give the whole signal. Likewise, when comparing with linguistics, the different markers need to be compared independently with the different levels of language data – on convergence effects as well as on family classification – that correspond most closely.

Definitions and circularities?

The Introduction to this book identified how the very terms 'Andean' and 'Amazonian' can end up compressed and stretched, respectively, away from their basic geographical definitions. Linguistics seems particularly guilty of this, on both dimensions of divergent families and convergent areas. And this carries a risk that such malleability might end up in a self-fulfilling definition of a divide.

Perhaps more than in any other discipline, linguists have let their very data source shape their thinking towards a 'Greater' Amazonia. In lowland South America, the main language families spread far beyond Amazonia proper, through the Caribbean and much of Brazil beyond the rainforest. But those wider distributions are then what linguists have effectively taken to define an area of interest. Epps and Michael (2017, 935), for instance, put it thus: 'Amazonia, which we define loosely here as the lowland region drained by the Amazon and Orinoco Rivers and extending to the northern and eastern littorals of the continent'. They then cite other leading linguists of the region who do much the same: Dixon and Aikhenvald (1999, 4) and Rodrigues (2000, 15). This usage extends to the other dimension of a hypothesized Amazonian linguistic convergence area, too. Here, the dangers of circular definitions are even greater. For a language *family* does generally allow for a very clear-cut definition of which languages are or are not its members. Convergence areas, however, typically have a diffuse core-and-periphery structure and are defined by only partial overlaps in a bespoke collection of structural criteria, cherry-picked by researchers. Their exact geographical distributions, then, are much more malleable.

Conversely, and also as foreshadowed in the Introduction to this book, in linguistics as in some other disciplines, 'Andean' tends to be focused by default on just the *central* latitude band of the Andes. Again, this does not just *happen* to be the heartland of the two main families, Quechua and Aymara; rather, they have helped define that focus anyway. This narrow definition of Andean is reinforced on the convergence dimension, too, because Quechua and Aymara are the same two families that constitute the core of the 'Andean' linguistic area. Some of its defining structural characteristics actually begin to be lost even in the northernmost varieties of Quechua, in Ecuador and southern Colombia, through partial assimilation to local languages that are only peripheral, at most, to what is in reality mostly just a *Central* Andean convergence area.

In other words, linguists have conveniently stretched and compressed their Amazonia and Andes in line with known language patterns, in any case. The two regions are defined in part by the ranges across which the major language families have spread, and/or across which certain hand-picked structural characteristics are widely shared – and this in a context of widespread pre-existing conceptions of contrasting 'Andean' and 'Amazonian' realities. The effect can be to make the two regions appear as linguistically self-contained and coherent units that contrast with one another more starkly than they would if one kept to the stricter, geographical senses of the terms Andes and Amazonia (as discussed in the Introduction of this book). The impression can be further heightened because linguists use 'Andean' with a focus on those same central latitudes where the highlands abut onto the Amazon basin proper.

Other disciplines, of course, should also reflect on whether they too have preferred working definitions of Andes and Amazonia that risk turning the divide between them into a self-fulfilling prophesy.

The linguistic perspective: Potential, limitations and prospects

This chapter aspires to have clarified that linguistics has much potential – at least in principle – to help uncover the past, and to inform on the Andes–Amazonia question specifically. There is one great proviso to this, however, that is particularly acute in South America. Before all else, the ability of linguistics to help is premised on having adequate language data in the first place. But documentation is still sorely lacking for many indigenous languages in Amazonia, which are dying out faster than a small band of fieldwork linguists can analyse them. In much of South America, it is already too late, including in the Andes of northern Peru, for example, a graveyard of languages that have vanished all but undocumented. Most of the indigenous linguistic diversity at first European contact is already long extinguished, and it is a race against the clock to record the little that remains. The result is that, for many a language in South America, for now we still have precious few clear answers on the where, when, how and why of its origins and expansions – and in some cases we will simply never be able to know. Similarly, as yet we have little in the way of consistent, large-scale databases of loanword and structural convergence across the continent, although ongoing work suggests improving prospects here, such as Epps (2017) or the database on which Chapter 3.3 is based.

Another general proviso is that for all the strengths of linguistics in its internal methodologies, it is rather less straightforward to step from language family tree diagrams or statistical measures of convergence into the precise real-world contexts in prehistory that they might denote. Linguistics has developed various methods to try to bridge the gap from the prehistories of languages to those of their speakers, but most remain contested. A general exploration for non-linguist readers is Heggarty and Renfrew (2014a). Individual methods are set out in detail in many general works on historical linguistics, such as Campbell (1997), while Heggarty (2015) provides a briefer survey. Other introductions focus on South America in general (such as Heggarty and Renfrew 2014b), on Amazonia (like Epps 2009, and Epps and Michael 2017), or on the Central Andes (for example Heggarty 2007, 2008).

Obviously, the full details of those methods are beyond the scope of this chapter, which has focused instead on providing clarity on just the most basic linguistic concepts and principles that frame any attempt to learn about prehistory from linguistics. On the strength of this, it is hoped that readers from other disciplines are now better placed to approach the linguistics chapters within this book. Chapter 3.4, particularly, will build on the general methodological background set out here, to offer a large-scale summary of what the great language families and linguistic convergence areas of South America mean in practice for the linguistic reality, or otherwise, of an Andes–Amazonia divide.

1.3
Genetics

Lars Fehren-Schmitz

To understand the dynamics of human interaction at the transition of ecological zones so radically different as the Andes and Amazonia, one must look not only to cultural traits and environmental factors, but also the bio-historical archive that mediates between them: humans themselves. From the biological diversity of modern and ancient populations it is possible to infer demography and population relatedness, and thereby reveal the dynamic processes that underlie or accompany cultural interactions between human groups.

Our understanding of the origin and evolution of Native American populations has already gained much from the study of genetic and quasi-genetic markers (for example, cranial and dental morphology), in conjunction with the archaeological record. Up until the 1980s, the field was dominated by the analysis of morphological diversity (which still plays a major role in the scientific debate, see Chapter 2.2, by Strauss). From the 1960s and 1970s onwards, however, genetics began to play a prominent role in studies of Native American diversity, as technological advances made it possible to analyse classical genetic markers such as blood groups and proteins (cf. Salzano and Callegari-Jacques 1988). While those early studies were thus able to identify patterns of genetic relatedness within and between tribal communities, it was not until the advent of modern *molecular* biology in the 1990s – that is, the ability to analyse, directly and in detail, the actual sequence of molecules in our DNA – that genetics was transformed into a far more valuable tool. The molecules in question are the nucleotides or bases arranged in sequence to form the double helix of our DNA. By now, modern indigenous populations in the Americas, especially in South America, have been well characterized at this genetic level. Additionally, since the 2000s, an increasing number of studies have analysed DNA fragments preserved in pre-Columbian human remains – ancient DNA – and thus added a deep-time perspective to our exploration of how genetic diversity developed in the indigenous Americas.

Yet despite the scientific progress made, still little is known of the direct relationships between the populations of the Andes and of Amazonia. Arguably, the potential of genetics to verify or deny the existence of an 'Andes–Amazonia divide' has been inhibited by the mere existence of that idea in the first place, for it has significantly biased the way scientists have approached the study of native South American genetic diversity over the last few decades.

While other contributions in this book (Chapters 3.2, by Santos, and 3.3, by Barbieri) will directly discuss the concept of the Andes–Amazonia divide from a genetic perspective, this chapter aims to set out the basic methodological background, and to discuss both the potential and the limits of genetic research to contribute to the debate.

Genetic markers

In general, population genetic studies refer to two sources of genetic information: mitochondrial DNA (mtDNA) and nuclear DNA (nDNA). The latter refers to the DNA contained within the nucleus of (for example) human cells, organized into chromosomes, of which there are two types: autosomes ('regular' chromosomes, that is, autosomal DNA) and gonosomes (the sex chromosomes: X and Y). Nuclear DNA encodes the majority of the genome and is inherited in line with the Mendelian principle, meaning that two copies of each chromosome (homologous pair = diploid) are found in the nucleus: one copy (haploid) coming from the mother and one from the father. During meiosis – a specialized type of cell division responsible for the formation of sex cells – these two homologous copies of each chromosome become randomly assorted with each other, and each chromosome thus 'recombined', leading to a unique combination of genetic information from both parents in each offspring. The haploid nuclear genome consists of 3.3 billion nucleotides, molecular building blocks consisting of a sugar group, a phosphate group and one of four nitrogenous bases (adenine, guanine, thymine or cytosine) sequentially chained together to form one strand of the DNA molecule. The two strands are connected via hydrogen bonds between the nitrogenous bases, which can only pair with a specific complementary base due to specific molecular characteristics (A with T, C with G). This specific rule of base pairing between the two strands ensures that they carry identical information. It also leads to the use of the term base-pair (or bp) when describing one specific nucleotide position in the genome.

In contrast to the rest of the nuclear genome, the Y-chromosome is found only in male individuals, and so is inherited only from father to son. Since it lacks any homologous chromosome, most of the Y-chromosome does not undergo recombination (the 'non-recombining' proportion of the Y-chromosome, nryDNA), except for a small proportion that is homologous to the X-chromosome (Underhill and Kivisild 2007).

The mitochondrial genome, meanwhile, is a small (only ~16,560 bp), circular, double-stranded molecule found *outside* the nucleus, in the mitochondria of eukaryotic cells. A distinctive characteristic is that each cell contains hundreds to thousands of copies of mtDNA. The mtGenome (or mitogenome) is exclusively maternally inherited, from the mother to children (male or female), so it too lacks recombination, and evolves faster than nuclear DNA (Pakendorf and Stoneking 2005). Both of the uni-parentally inherited markers, mtDNA and nryDNA, are passed unchanged from generation to generation unless mutation occurs, and so make it possible to study the phylogeny of descent of specific maternal and paternal lineages. This characteristic made uni-parental markers the data of choice for population genetic studies for nearly three decades. These studies proved valuable for reconstructing the global spread of *Homo sapiens*, and thus understanding longer-term global patterns of human diversification (Underhill and Kivisild 2007). Analyses of maternally inherited mtDNA and paternally inherited nryDNA from present-day populations have successfully shed light on many aspects of the first colonization of the Americas: source populations, number of migrants, migration dates, routes, etc. (for example, Torroni et al. 2006; Perego et al. 2009; Bisso-Machado et al. 2012). Comparing the data from both genetic markers also makes it possible to analyse sex-specific patterns in mobility and migration (for example, Wilder et al. 2004). Most studies to date on the population history of South America have used uni-parentally inherited markers, as outlined in this book by Santos in Chapter 3.2 and Barbieri in Chapter 3.3.

In contrast to the benefits outlined above, however, mtDNA and nryDNA studies also suffer from major drawbacks compared with analyses of parts of autosomal DNA, or indeed of the whole genome. Firstly, mtDNA, the most widely studied marker, fails to capture any information about the history of males – which may well differ from that of females, because demographic processes can be sex-biased. The converse is true for nryDNA studies. More importantly, a single locus like mtDNA or the Y-chromosome (or two, if both markers are combined) has much less statistical resolution than the nuclear genome. The whole genome of an individual contains information about not just a single ancestral lineage, but about thousands of his or her ancestors, given the modes of inheritance described above. This also means that autosomal DNA makes it possible to study *admixture*: a detailed and more complex analysis of all the ancestral genomic components that contributed to an individual's genome (Pickrell and Reich 2014). Advances in genome sequencing technologies have recently also enabled studies of large numbers of genetic variants from Native American populations (for example, Yang et al. 2010; Reich et al. 2012; Harris et al. 2018; Barbieri et al. 2019). On the other hand, these vast amounts of data demand far more complex 'downstream' processing – particularly statistical and modelling analyses – than do uni-parental markers, which in practice have therefore remained (for now) the dominant type of genetic data used in researching the population history of the Americas.

Ancient DNA

Ancient DNA (aDNA) analysis has proved a valuable tool for studying continuity and discontinuities in prehistoric populations (Pääbo et al. 2004; Kirsanow and Burger 2012; Pickrell and Reich, 2014). It nonetheless also faces some major limitations, including limited success rates in detecting DNA at all in many ancient samples, and the risk of contamination and false positive results.

Ancient DNA refers to DNA molecules potentially preserved in historical or pre-historical biological material. A key determining characteristic of aDNA is not so much the age of the molecules, but an advanced stage of degradation. DNA decay starts immediately after death, triggered by endogenous enzymes that break the molecules down (Lindahl 1993). In the absence of DNA repair mechanisms, additional chemical processes such as oxidation and hydrolysis have far-reaching disruptive effects on the structure and stability of DNA, and can break down the molecules further, modifying the primary sequence information (Pääbo et al. 2004; Hebsgaard et al. 2005; Gilbert et al. 2007). The preservation of DNA traces in ancient specimens is very highly dependent on the burial environment. Major factors are high temperature, high humidity, low pH-values of the soil and exposure to UV radiation (Burger et al. 1999; Hummel 2003; Pinhasi et al. 2015). Even if burial conditions are optimal, and slow down the degradation process, only a very few copies of DNA will be found in ancient sample material, with fragment lengths of mostly less than 150 base pairs (bp) (Kirsanow and Burger 2012). Additionally, the sample material can be contaminated, both by chemical substances that inhibit the biochemical reactions needed to analyse the DNA, and by microbacterial DNA deriving mostly from the wider burial environment. All research strategies therefore must be adapted to the characteristics specific to ancient DNA, and every archaeological site, every skeleton, has to be treated differently, depending on the various factors that have affected it.

Contamination with modern human DNA is another complicating factor. After three decades of research (Hagelberg et al. 2015) and with ever more efficient technologies, ancient DNA researchers have developed effective measures to control for contaminating DNA in the laboratory, or identifying and filtering it out bioinformatically (Hummel 2003; Willerslev and Cooper 2005; Skoglund et al. 2014; Renaud et al. 2015). Nevertheless, samples that are heavily contaminated before entering the laboratory still pose a problem. The lower the amount of endogenous (human) DNA preserved in ancient specimens, the greater the risk of contamination. Contamination with modern human DNA can result from any contact with people involved in processing the sample – from excavation through to lab-work – but can also be found in chemicals, disposable ware and everything else used in storage, transport or in the laboratory (Kirsanow and Burger 2012). Even the smallest traces of contaminating DNA are enough to generate huge complications for the analysis.

Here is where one particular advantage of mtDNA, as noted above, comes to the fore: since it is found in not one but thousands of copies per cell, there is a correspondingly far higher probability that it may be preserved in ancient specimens, relative to nuclear DNA. This, combined with methodological limitations, has meant that to date most ancient DNA studies on pre-Columbian South American populations have focused on the mitochondrial genome, and indeed on only a 400 bp small part of it known as the Hyper-Variable Region (HVR). This specific locus of the mtGenome, also used in modern DNA studies, has allowed researchers to distinguish specific maternal haplotypes. Nonetheless, the overall resolution of this marker is very limited due to its size and the lack of recombination, especially in genetically relatively homogenous populations such as Native Americans.

Technological advances now also allow genome-wide sequencing of ancient DNA. Just during the period in which this chapter was undergoing review and revisions, three new papers reported on ancient genomes from pre-Columbian Central and South American individuals (Lindo et al. 2018; Moreno-Mayar, Vinner et al. 2018; Posth et al. 2018). With a growing number of ancient genomes, the coming years will show how far this new data quality will advance our understanding of Native American population history.

Genetic diversity in South America

Despite the richness of their cultures and of the environments that they inhabit, Native South Americans harbour a relatively low level of genetic diversity compared with other continent-scale regions. Nearly all Native Americans belong to only a small number of identified mitochondrial and Y-chromosome founding haplotypes (Bisso-Machado et al. 2012). Most of their mitochondrial diversity derives from only four major ancestral lineages, the mt-haplogroups labelled A, B, C and D (Torroni et al. 1993). These lineages are widely found throughout the Americas, but there is a great deal of variation in their relative frequencies in different populations and geographic regions. A fifth founding mitochondrial haplogroup, designated X, is found only in indigenous populations of far northern North America (Dornelles et al. 2005). All of these mt-haplogroups are definitively of Asian ancestry, and furthermore, the genetic data indicate that the ancestral source population probably originated in south-central Siberia, from where it migrated to Beringia and then into the New World (Schurr 2004). In the initial founding population, each of these five major matrilineages (mt-haplogroups) was represented by only a few sub-lineages, known as the mt-haplo**types** within each haplo**group**. Studies of modern DNA have identified at least 15 of these founding mt-haplotypes, but that number is rising as studies of complete mitochondrial genomes become more frequent (Perego et al. 2010; Chapter 3.3).

In Y-chromosome DNA, meanwhile, most male Native Americans belong to two principal founding haplogroups, C and Q (in the nomenclature of the

Y-Chromosome Consortium 2002). Most frequent in Native South American males is haplogroup Q1a3a* (formerly Q-M3), at 77 per cent (Bortolini et al. 2003). Within the overall Q1a3a* group are a number of (sub)haplogroups like Q1a3a1, -2 and -3 that are specific to South America (Karafet et al. 2008), and more are being found as more studies focus on Y-chromosome diversity. Haplogroup Q* ancestral to Q1a3a* is the second most frequent group, while C* has been found only in a very few indigenous South American individuals on the northern coast (Bortolini et al. 2003; Bailliet et al. 2009).

The low genetic diversity of Native Americans is also reflected in their nuclear DNA, with much lower heterozygosity – the condition of having two different alleles at a genetic locus – than in populations from other continents. Additionally, Native Americans have fewer distinct alleles per locus than populations in other geographical regions (Wang et al. 2007). The loss of diversity increases along a north–south gradient through the Americas, with the highest levels of heterozygosity observed in North America, and the lowest in South America. The lowest heterozygosity levels of any populations worldwide are found in isolated populations of Amazonia and eastern South America, such as the Suruí and Ache (Wang et al. 2007; Reich et al. 2012). This is generally attributed to a process called genetic drift, a random loss of genetic diversity over time owing to the chance disappearance of particular genes as individuals die or do not reproduce. Genetic drift is largest in small populations (stochastic) and amplified in isolated populations that do not exchange much genetic information with others. More generally, heterozygosity is reduced in eastern compared with western South America (refer to Chapter 3.2 for more detailed information).

It is commonly agreed that these observed patterns of neutral genetic diversity – considering regions of the genome that do not contribute to phenotypes – can be largely attributed to the processes of the initial peopling of the Americas. The genetic data support a scenario with a single founding population of low effective population size, migrating to the Americas from Beringia and rapidly spreading to southern South America (Fagundes et al. 2008; Bodner et al. 2012). It must be emphasized here that effective population size does not refer to the overall census size of a population, but only to those that actively contribute their genetic information to subsequent generations. Thus, the effective population size can be much smaller than the census population size. A recent study analysing genome-wide Single Nucleotide Polymorphisms (SNPs) from 52 Native American populations found evidence for two additional later waves of immigration to the Americas besides the first main wave, but these waves brought the Eskimo-Aleut and Na-Dene populations into northernmost and north-western North America, and did not contribute to the South American gene pool (Reich et al. 2012). The first genome-wide studies of ancient DNA from Native American populations support this hypothesis. Full genomes recently sequenced from a ~12,500-year-old human skeleton found in Montana (Anzick-1) and from the remains of the ~9,000-year-old Kennewick Man found in Washington State show that they share ancestry with most modern Native American populations (Rasmussen et al. 2014, 2015).

However, the findings of two recent ancient DNA studies that sequenced genomes of pre-Columbian individuals contradict the hypothesis of a single wave of genetically homogeneous migrants as the ancestral source of all South Americans (Moreno-Mayar, Vinner et al. 2018; Posth et al. 2018). The patterns of genomic diversity and distribution observed with these ancient individuals – dating from around 10,000 BP to the late pre-Contact period – suggest several waves of diffusion into the continent (Posth et al. 2018). All these ancestral lineages share common ancestry in Beringia or North America, and are differentially related to Anzick-1, indicating an existing degree of genetic population structure early in the peopling of the Americas (Moreno-Mayar et al. 2018; Moreno-Mayar, Vinner et al. 2018).

Two studies of genome-wide diversity in modern Native American populations identified an additional ancestry component in certain Amazonian populations (so far restricted to Suruí and Karitiana). This lineage descends partly from some Native American founding population that carried ancestry more closely related to indigenous Australians, New Guineans and Andaman Islanders than to any present-day Eurasians or Native Americans (Raghavan et al. 2015; Skoglund et al. 2015). Besides these modern indigenous populations, this lineage has so far been observed only in one ~10,000-year-old pre-Columbian individual from Lagoa Santa, Brazil (Moreno-Mayar, Vinner et al. 2018). None of the models formulated to account for this observation have yet provided a satisfactory explanation for when and how that ancestry component arrived in South America. However, this might not be possible to answer based on genetics alone. To understand the complexity of population dynamics in South America we need to avail ourselves of the whole breadth of available sources to generate testable models. In other words, interdisciplinary approaches are indispensable, calling on expertise in archaeology, ecology, linguistics and ethnology. This chapter is thus to be read in conjunction with others in this book that also address first settlement of South America and any very early Andes–Amazonia divide, but from the complementary perspectives of other disciplines: from archaeology (Chapter 2.1), cranial morphology (Chapter 2.2) and linguistics (Chapter 2.3). See also the map in Figure 2.1.1, Chapter 2.1, showing the main find sites in South America from which human ancient DNA has recently been recovered.

A further complication attending the interpretation of genetic data is the massive population decline in the Americas that followed European contact, which led to a second bottleneck, severely reducing genetic diversity among Native Americans (O'Fallon and Fehren-Schmitz 2011). Indicators of this loss of diversity are already being uncovered in studies that compare ancient and modern mtDNA from South America (O'Fallon and Fehren-Schmitz 2011; Llamas et al. 2016). Nonetheless, further comparative studies of ancient and modern diversity, also now in nuclear DNA, are needed if we are fully to understand the complexity and extent of this European impact. Again, for a complementary perspective on a parallel loss of linguistic diversity, see Chapter 1.2, this volume; and for more historical background, see Chapter 5.3.

Genetics and cross-cultural interactions

While at first sight it can seem obvious that genetics has the potential to contribute to questions of cross-cultural and interregional interactions, not least across the Andes–Amazonia divide, there are also limitations. Many modes of human interaction, such as trade, do not necessarily result in gene-flow or reproductive interactions, and thus may not leave any genetic traces. Additionally, without knowledge of the reproductive behaviour of the groups studied, such as marriage patterns (including exogamy, matrilocality versus patrilocality, polygyny, etc.), and indeed of how those may have changed through time, interpretations of observed genetic diversity patterns might be biased. Cultural traits can be inherited in far more complex ways than genetic ones. Whereas genetic information in humans almost entirely follows vertical inheritance, cultural information can be shared horizontally, increasing not only its spatial range but also the speed with which information can be exchanged. On the other hand, the maintenance of cultural variability over time is dependent on demographic structure, such as population size and intergroup exchange, which can be inferred from genetic data (Powell et al. 2009).

Regional studies explicitly designed to be interdisciplinary (for example, Chapter 3.3 by Barbieri) have the potential to overcome these limitations, by considering the full range of different forms of information in their models. Nonetheless, there remain many examples where interpretation of genetic data suffers from over-simplifications of the cultural contexts.

Some studies that have sought to correlate language and genetic diversity in South America illustrate these problems. The interdisciplinary combination of linguistic, archaeological and human biological data has a long tradition in the study of Native American population history. One of the most prominent early examples remains Greenberg's classification of native American language families (which has been generally dismissed), which purported to be based on linguistic data validated by dental and genetic data (Greenberg et al. 1986; Greenberg 1987). But it is not enough just to claim to be following an 'interdisciplinary' approach, when Greenberg's language classification was condemned from first publication, and any apparent matches with genetics are spurious (Bolnick et al. 2004). For a more detailed discussion of why Greenberg's methodology and results are considered invalid, see Heggarty, Chapter 2.3. For those Native American language families that *are* demonstrably real (see Chapters 1.2 and 3.4, and their corresponding maps), attempts have continued to correlate their dispersals and divergence with genetic data. The ongoing development of new technologies and methods in molecular genetics, and increasing data resolution, have provided much more detailed insights into population dynamics and demography. Researchers have sought to understand the complex relationship of language and genetic population structure and diversity on both continental (for example, Hunley et al. 2007; Roewer et al. 2013) and more regional scales (for example, Lewis et al. 2005; Sandoval, Lacerda et al. 2013a; Barbieri et al. 2014), using both uni-parental and autosomal genetic markers. While none of the broad-scale analyses have found congruence between linguistic and genetic structure in South and Central America, some of the regional analyses have found evidence that more local population dynamics do indeed correlate with patterns of language diversity (see Chapters 3.3 and 3.4).

Does this mean that genetics can *only* help us to reveal cross-cultural interactions on regional levels? Fortunately, it does not. Rather, we need to take care that the questions we ask, and the data we employ to answer them, are on the same hierarchical or systemic levels. For example, it may not be possible to address such interactions from an interdisciplinary perspective when using data from different time-depths, such as attempting to understand relatively recent convergence between two language lineages (for example, Aymara and Quechua, within the last few millennia at most) by tracking genetic introgressions using mitochondrial haplogroup data. While their diachronic changes in haplogroup frequencies occurred throughout the pre-Columbian period (Fehren-Schmitz et al. 2014), their general pattern of diversity reflects that of the initial population of the Americas, at a time remove too great to allow comparison on the same systematic level as correspondences between Quechua and Aymara. To address linguistic signals at that level requires forms of genetic data that reflect rather more recent reproductive interactions, such as nuclear DNA that allows us to study admixture patterns (for example, Barbieri et al. 2019). Another approach is to add time-depth to the genetic data by including ancient DNA from human remains that are more or less contemporary with the putative processes of admixture. This can increase the chances of uncovering possible underlying processes in population dynamics, by reducing the potential bias from later, unknown demographic events.

Especially when it comes to considering whether any meaningful Andean–Amazonian divide actually exists and, if so, then on what systematic levels, experimental design can become an issue in itself, especially as regards sampling strategies. As outlined by Santos (Chapter 3.2), many population genetic studies in South America have concentrated on finding explanations for apparent differences in genetic structure observed between the Central Andes and Amazonia. Samples may thus have been selected in the first place in such a way as to presume these different patterns, thereby overlooking potential connections. Additionally, the modern genetic and demographic structure of indigenous populations in Amazonia may no longer reflect that of the pre-Columbian era. As discussed by several authors in this book (notably by Beresford-Jones and Machicado Murillo in Chapter 1.1, and by Hornborg in Chapter 1.4) there is evidence from archaeology and ethnohistory that at certain times in the past, populations in Amazonia were much larger, their social organization was far more complex, and opportunities for intergroup gene-flow were perhaps more intense than has been the case since European contact. More recent historical processes may have transformed the genetic landscape of the region, thereby obscuring our ability to study possible connections with the Andes from modern populations alone. Again, integrating *ancient* DNA data from pre-Columbian Amazonian populations could in principle mitigate such problems, or even overcome them entirely. Preservation of human remains is generally so poor in the environmental conditions in Amazonia, however, there are scarcely enough samples even to start the task. Still, research continues to try to analyse DNA from some of the few extant prehistoric human remains from Amazonia and, if successful, may reveal a completely new picture of the population history of eastern South America. Indeed, genetics needs to recognize that its potential to contribute to the main issues of this book faced a spatio-temporal sampling bias until quite recently. From *modern* populations, up until 2018 we had more genetic data (at least in nuclear DNA) from eastern South America than from the Andes; for pre-Columbian populations, however, the opposite applies. This bias is now beginning to be resolved for modern populations, thanks to the recent publication of large, genome-wide datasets from Andean populations (Barbieri et al. 2019; Gnecchi-Ruscone et al. 2019; Harris et al. 2018). Ancient DNA studies will need to catch up, however, if genetics is to realize its full potential to contribute. Excitingly, the aforementioned genome-wide studies of living populations have confirmed at least limited gene-flow between Amazonia and the Andes. Gnecchi-Ruscone et al. (2019) observe uni-directional gene flow from the Andes to groups in Peruvian Amazonia, contributing about 5 per cent of their ancestry. Barbieri et al. (2019) and Harris et al. (2018) observe that groups from north-west Peruvian Amazonia long-distance show gene-flow with groups from the Andes and especially from the north coast of Peru. While it will take more genomic studies of living and ancient individuals to securely determine the directionality and timing of these gene-flow events, these studies indicate that, at least in some regions, Andean and Amazonian populations have not developed in isolation from each other.

All in all, to properly address fundamental questions in the population history of South America – not least the existence or otherwise of an Andean–Amazonian divide in population genetics – requires a genuinely interdisciplinary approach that entails expertise from both the social and natural sciences. There also remain clear technical limitations, a result of the still poor availability of samples and the generally low genetic diversity of Native American populations. Since all those populations share a relatively recent common ancestry, genetic distinctions between groups are hard to pin down and characterise. But the contributions here by Barbieri (Chapter 3.3) and Santos (Chapter 3.2) show how some of these issues can begin to be overcome. More generally, too, this book can aspire to illustrate how a start can be made in the cross-disciplinary discussion necessary to gain a more complete picture of pre-Columbian population history.

1.4
Anthropology
Alf Hornborg

Recent archaeological research in Amazonia suggests that it has been a mistake to assume that Andean polities were necessarily more hierarchical, populous, or extensive than their counterparts in Amazonia. This illusion has dominated European understandings of South American societies since the sixteenth century, for several reasons:

1. Due to their physical surroundings, Amazonian societies did not construct conspicuous and imperishable architecture, as Andean societies did.[1]
2. The conditions for archaeological research are very different in the two areas: the periodic inundations, shifting riverbeds and humidity in Amazonia leave very little for archaeologists to investigate, particularly in comparison with the arid Pacific coast.
3. Before being documented by Europeans,[2] Amazonian societies were almost obliterated by epidemics introduced by them, whereas Andean societies, while severely decimated, were documented and incorporated into tributary, colonial hierarchies.
4. Europeans perceived the tropical lowlands as unhealthy and obstructive to the development of complex societies.[3]

For these reasons, the illusion of the Andes–Amazonia divide has been entrenched not only as an economic and cultural boundary, but as a boundary between civilization and savagery.[4] In this chapter, however, I shall suggest how an anthropological perspective could revise our understanding of the two regions as radically distinct.

Contemporary anthropology is predominantly concerned with ethnography, and I would like to concede at the outset that twenty-first-century ethnography can by itself make only modest contributions to the data on which we can base a rethinking of the long-term history of the Andes–Amazonia 'divide'. To be sure, modern ethnography can document lively communication between indigenous peoples across this 'divide' along the length of the Andes in recent times, but to draw inferences from such communication for reconstructions of pre-modern conditions would be speculative and open to objection. A reasonable objection, for instance, would be that the modern social organization of this geographical zone is fundamentally different from that of pre-colonial times. To the extent that pre-colonial people had incentives to interact across the Andes–Amazonia divide, such incentives would have been generated by the kinds of societies in which they lived, and would have had little in common with the kinds of incentives prevalent today.

Where anthropology can make an important contribution to rethinking the Andes–Amazonia divide, however, is in how we should conceptualise how pre-colonial societies were organized. Notwithstanding the alternative views presented by other contributors to this volume (for example, Chapters 3.1, 3.2, 3.4, 4.3 and 5.1), anthropologists have indeed found grounds for seeing the notion of a socio-cultural boundary between the Andean highlands and the Amazonian lowlands as a construction of colonialism and its European tradition of territorially bounded nations (Renard-Casevitz et al. 1986; A.-C. Taylor 1999; Dudley 2011). Prior to European conquest, the eastern slopes of the Andes were a zone of lively interaction of different kinds (Lathrap 1973). The interests and influence of the Inca Empire (*Tawantinsuyu*) extended deep into the eastern lowlands, establishing patterns of inter-ethnic cultural and ceremonial exchange while extracting tropical resources such as coca, feathers, resins and dyes (Camino 1977; Lyon 1981; Gade 1999; Pärssinen et al. 2003). The *Antisuyu* quarter was a very significant component of the empire. However, the Spanish conquest of the Andes marginalized the eastern slopes by leaving them outside the main sphere of colonial interest (Dudley 2011; Chapters 5.2 and 5.3). Although exchange across this colonial boundary continued at the local level, the categories of 'Andean highland' and 'Amazonian lowland' were deeply entrenched in the European mind. Not least in the imagination of twentieth-century anthropology, these categories assumed the form of distinct 'culture areas', which allegedly owed their specificity to the influence of different environmental conditions (Steward 1946, 1948; Meggers 1971; Chapter 3.7).

The pre-colonial transformations of Amerindian societies into chiefdoms, states and empires like those encountered by Spaniards in the Andean highlands was geared to the political economy of prestigious and fetishized artefacts such as the *Spondylus* shells imported from coastal Ecuador (Salomon 1986; Hornborg 2014). The Thorny Oyster or *Spondylus* generally occurs naturally not much further south than the Gulf of Guayaquil, but it was in high demand throughout the Andean area for millennia before the Spanish conquest. Whether in the form of intact shells or fashioned into ornaments, beads or powder, it has been discovered in a number of archaeological sites ranging from coastal Peru around 2500 BC to Inca-period sacrifices on high peaks in the southern highlands (Paulsen 1974; Pillsbury 1996; Carter 2011). Ethnohistorical sources indicate that *Spondylus* symbolized fertility and water and that one of its primary uses was as offerings to the gods to ensure good harvests (Salomon and Urioste 1991; Blower 2000). Following a very widespread pattern in pre-modern societies, controlling the imports of distantly derived prestige goods was a source of political power. Access to items derived from *Spondylus* provided the lords of pre-Hispanic Andean theocracies with a means of claiming prestige and honour in proportion to harvests, and thus to establish claims on the labour of their dependent peasants.

Empirical data on pre-colonial interaction across the Andes–Amazonia divide generally derive from archaeology, genetics, linguistics or ethnohistory. Anthropology, however, can offer theoretical models of the kinds of social organization that may have generated such data. Its comparative understanding of various arrangements of kinship, reciprocity, ritual and political economy in a vast spectrum of societies in time and space provides a foundation for reasonable reconstructions of the kinds of social relations that have spanned the highland–lowland divide in different periods. Archaeologists, geneticists, linguists and historians thus often benefit from models of social organization developed in anthropology. Indications of long-distance connections in pre-colonial times – whether traced through art styles, genes, languages or archival records – are best interpreted in terms of such models, as they represent a feasible framework for societal reconstruction. The discipline of anthropology is familiar with diverse forms of non-modern social organization and with their economic foundations in various form of exchange. It is also accustomed to considering social processes from the perspective of identity formation. Shifting fields of 'ethnogenesis' are crucial for understanding the emergence of cultural homogeneities such as the expansion of art styles or the dispersal of languages (cf. Hornborg 2005, 2014).

While the systematic empirical examination of evidence of early Andean–Amazonian connections must be left to archaeologists, geneticists, linguists and historians, anthropologists may thus be helpful in suggesting plausible models of social organization and political economy that might account for the connections. In this context, the strength of anthropology lies more in its interpretative capacity than in its empirical data. From Arthur Posnansky's theory of the ancient diffusion of Tiwanakoid culture throughout South America and beyond to more recent hypotheses of massive pre-colonial migrations and demographic displacements, the feasibility of such models of large-scale social processes can be tested against anthropological theory. Although more or less intuitive recognition of stylistic affinities in material culture among geographically distinct societies has often proven valid, indications of the 'diffusion' of specific traits tell us very little about the societal processes that have generated such affinities. Fritz Graebner's and other diffusionists' criteria for establishing cultural relatedness seem methodologically reasonable but are not concerned with identifying the social mechanisms underlying the dispersal of art styles, iconographies and other features. Similarly, the technically sophisticated mapping of multiple dimensions of the linguistic panorama (language relationships, linguistic diversity, convergence into linguistic areas) in linguistics might sometimes profit from the application of anthropological understandings of recurrent patterns of interaction among actual social groups (cf. Hornborg and Hill 2011). In general, hypotheses of large-scale social processes in pre-colonial times would need to consider the significance, in these societies, of aspects such as identity, ritual and the political economy of long-distance exchange. In other words, they would need to look for the societal incentives to engage in long-distance transfers of people, ideas, artefacts and language.

Another aspect of culture investigated by anthropologists that is useful in understanding Andean–Amazonian connections is the comparative study of cosmology or, as it is currently fashionable to say, ontology. Anthropologists have traced common mythological themes, metaphors and symbolic schemes shared by specific native peoples of both areas (for example, Lévi-Strauss 1973, 344–5 and 1978, 98; Reichel-Dolmatoff 1972), suggesting either common cultural roots or interchange.[5] Occasionally, when there are reasons to posit long-term cultural continuities, ethnography can provide frameworks for interpreting archaeological remains. Such 'ethno-archaeological' approaches to highland–lowland parallels have been applied both to mundane practices and to more abstract cultural phenomena such as belief systems (Reichel-Dolmatoff 1972) or the symbolic schemes organizing social space (Hornborg 1990). At an even more abstract level, fundamental ontological principles adhered to by indigenous peoples in the two regions, and generally presented as clearly distinct (Descola 2013), may be understood as structurally related to each other and to variations in political economy (Hornborg 2015).

The cultural continuities linking Amazonian and Andean societies have intrigued a number of anthropologists working on both sides of the *montaña*, including Lévi-Strauss. To recognize the continuities, we must properly understand the differences. Rather than understand the fundamental difference between Amazonian animism and Andean 'analogism' (Descola 2013) as an essential contrast in worldview or ontology, the challenge for anthropology should be to account for the difference in terms of historical transformations of social organization. Indigenous Andean and Amazonian societies have experienced quite divergent postconquest trajectories. While Andean communities have remained integrated in the large-scale colonial hierarchies that replaced the Inca Empire, Amazonian groups have been more thoroughly victimized by depopulation and societal fragmentation. However, archaeological investigations in various parts of Amazonia indicate that, prior to exposure to European colonialism, the region was home to densely settled and hierarchical polities that may have been comparable to those of the Andes (see also Chapter 1.1). Extensive areas of raised fields, anthropogenic soils and earthworks testify to the pre-colonial existence of complex sedentary societies in various parts of the tropical lowlands (Balée and Erickson 2006; Schaan 2012). Although most of the prestige goods that circulated in and between these polities would have been perishable, there are archaeological indications of long-distance trade in items such as green-stone amulets, shell beads and snuff trays (Boomert 1987; Gassón 2000; Torres 1987). As Santos-Granero (2009, 19) has implied, the contemporary uses of ritual artefacts among indigenous groups in Amazonia may represent fragmented echoes of pre-colonial political economy. The role of such artefacts may have been as significant for ancient Amazonian social organization as *Spondylus* shells were for polities in the pre-Hispanic Andes. If, as Descola (2013) proposes, the 'analogist' ontologies of the Andes (that is, worldviews in which both interior and exterior aspects of reality are radically discontinuous[6]) have emerged to reconcile the myriad differences in stratified pre-modern societies, the distinction between Amazonian animism and Andean analogism should not be seen as a timeless and intrinsic one, but a post-conquest divergence of societies that once belonged to the same continuum.

Finally, and notwithstanding its preoccupation with ethnography, anthropology is not a methodologically specialized discipline like archaeology, genetics, linguistics or history, but – at least in its 'four-field' conception – an attempt to understand various kinds of cultural phenomena holistically, as reflections of social processes generated by specific features of political economy, cosmology, ritual, symbolism and identity formation. To rethink the Andes–Amazonian divide requires precisely such an integrated perspective, which brings together discoveries from various subfields and conceptual tools from the natural sciences, social sciences and humanities.

In sum, anthropology can contribute models for:

1. interpreting the kinds of social organization that may have connected the Andean highlands and Amazonian lowlands in pre-colonial times,
2. understanding the variation and continuities between the two areas with regard to cosmology, mythology and symbolic phenomena in general, and
3. attempting to integrate the discoveries and perspectives of disciplines such as archaeology, linguistics and ethnohistory.

I shall now discuss four specific indications of long-distance cultural connections between prehistoric societies in the Andes and Amazonia, suggesting anthropological frameworks for understanding them. All four examples involve archaeological evidence dated to the first millennium AD or, in the case of Chavín de Huántar, even earlier.

Chavín de Huántar

Lathrap (1971), Burger (1992), and many others have noted that much of the iconography associated with the Early Horizon (900–200 BC) Andean site of Chavín de Huántar, near modern Huaraz, depicts animal species found in the Amazonian lowlands, such as jaguars, anacondas, and caymans. There are also numerous indications that hallucinogenic plants from the lowlands were an important ingredient of ritual conducted at the site (Burger 1992). It thus seems incontrovertible that this ceremonial centre, situated in the highlands near the headwaters of the Marañón River, maintained a lively interaction with lowland societies (but see

Chapter 3.7). At the same time, we must conclude from the distribution of art styles and other evidence that there was regular interaction between the Chavín heartland in Ancash and much of the central Andean coast, notably the Casma River valley and the more distant Paracas peninsula in southern Peru. Ritually important marine shells such as *Spondylus* and *Strombus*, both from coastal Ecuador, were imported in significant quantities to Chavín de Huántar. The supreme deity decorating the New Temple at Chavín de Huántar holds a *Strombus* shell in its right hand and a *Spondylus* shell in its left hand. Cordy-Collins (1978, 3) and Burger (1992, 174 and 236, n. 22) have proposed ethno-archaeological affinities with contemporary ritual among the Kogi of Colombia, in which gastropod and bivalve shells are similarly associated with the right hand and the left hand and are used to represent male and female principles (cf. Hornborg 1990, 87, n. 22). A cache of twenty *Strombus* shell trumpets discovered at Chavín de Huántar testifies to the ritual significance of this long-distance import. The site undoubtedly served as the hub of a vast sphere of long-distance exchange and interaction reaching from the Pacific coast to the tropical lowlands east of the Andes (Rodriguez Kembel and Rick 2004; Contreras 2011). Its position as a 'middleman' or 'gateway' community granted it special opportunities to control and accumulate symbolic-cum-economic capital in the form of tropical products coveted by coastal populations and, conversely, coastal products coveted by Amazonian societies. Although the trade in exotic goods was recursively connected to its prestigious position, it would obviously be inappropriate to think of the 'capital accumulation' occurring in Chavín de Huántar in terms of modern profits from trade. We may safely assume that there was no generalized medium of exchange that could have been hoarded as profit but, drawing on anthropological understandings of non-modern economies, we can postulate alternative means of accumulation. We can assume that some of the various prestige goods imported to Chavín de Huántar, such as hallucinogens and symbolically potent shells, were fundamental to the ritual activities conducted there, and that these activities were in turn fundamental to reproducing the claims of ritual specialists on the labour and resources of the other participants, whether local populations or pilgrims from remote parts of the Chavín domain. The participants' relations to these ritual specialists were probably represented in terms of familiar idioms of kinship, reciprocity and ethnicity. Through ritual, the exotic imports could thus be converted into yet more ceremonial infrastructure, such as the complex architecture of the temples at Chavín de Huántar,[7] as well as irrigated agricultural land (so-called landesque capital; cf. Håkansson and Widgren 2014), agricultural produce, or other exotic imports. Controlling the movement of prestige goods, in other words, was recursively connected to controlling labour and agricultural surplus. Political economy was geared to the symbolic evaluation and redistribution of *Spondylus* shells and the cosmology and phenomenology of hallucinogenic ritual. Similar interfusions of what modern people distinguish as the 'economic' and the 'symbolic' continued to characterize the metabolism of Andean societies until they were conquered by the Spaniards in the sixteenth century.

San Agustín

As Torres (1987, 52, 85–6), and others have observed, there are compelling stylistic similarities between stone statues from San Agustín, in the highlands of southern Colombia, and stone figurines attributed to the Kondurí culture on the lower Amazon. These sculptures from San Agustín and Kondurí feature a feline alter-ego crouched on top of a fanged human figure. Several details of the carvings are so similar that they suggest direct emulation, which would mean that stone carvers had travelled the vast distance of over a thousand miles that separates the two areas. Considering the relative ease of river traffic in the Amazon, and the location of San Agustín near the headwaters of the Japurá-Caquetá River, this is a distinct possibility, but we need to consider what incentives there might have been for such long-distance journeys. As in the case of Chavín de Huántar, the clue may lie in the trade in psycho-active tropical plants. There is overwhelming ethnographical and ethnohistorical evidence from both the highlands and the Amazon lowlands of a very widespread association between shamanism, beliefs in were-jaguars, and the ritual use of hallucinogenic snuffs prepared from the seeds of *Anadenanthera* (Reichel-Dolmatoff 1972). This is not only a persuasive explanation of the feline imagery at San Agustín – and at Chavín de Huántar – but is also corroborated by the Kondurí figurines. These portable lithic figurines were likely mortars for preparing *Anadenanthera* snuff (McEwan 2001,194–5). Moreover, snuff trays encountered over vast areas of Amazonia as well as in the southern Andean highlands – even as far as San Pedro de Atacama in Chile – are frequently decorated with the same image of a feline alter-ego (Torres 1987). There appears to be ample evidence to suggest that the shamanic use of *Anadenanthera* snuff, were-jaguar mythology, and ritual paraphernalia such as snuff trays and mortars comprised a very widespread cultural complex over much of South America on both sides of the highland–lowland divide. Like Chavín de Huántar, the ceremonial centre of San Agustín may have shared the ritual use of *Anadenanthera* with societies along riverine trade routes extending deep into Amazonia.

The 'geoglyphs' of the Upper Purús

Some of the ceremonial arenas discovered underneath the tropical rainforest of Acre, Brazil (Schaan, Ranzi and Damasceno Barbosa 2010; Schaan 2012; Saunaluoma 2013), bear a strong formal resemblance to the plazas of highland ceremonial centres such as Tiwanaku in the Titicaca Basin. Although the geographical environments and available building materials are very different, it seems that people in both areas struggled to materialize conceptions of a quadrangular ceremonial space for public events. The Tequinho site, for instance, seems inspired by cosmological principles – a geometrically perfect square, a marked central axis, multiple walls and moats – that are very similar to those that organized the construction of the plazas of Tiwanaku.[8] To assess whether it is at all reasonable to suggest cultural affinities between the upper Purús and the Titicaca Basin, we can mention other circumstances that might strengthen the hypothesis. First, populations in the two areas in the first millennium may have been linguistically related. The builders of the so-called 'geoglyphs' of Acre were probably related to the builders of earthworks in the Llanos de Mojos, and their descendants in both areas are still Arawak-speakers. Meanwhile, the first-millennium population of the Titicaca Basin – the builders of quadrangular ceremonial centres such as Chiripa, Pucara and Tiwanaku – may have spoken Pukina, an extinct language distantly related to Arawak and currently preserved in a number of toponyms throughout the former domain of Tiwanaku, ranging from the area east of the Titicaca Basin to the Arequipa area near the Pacific Coast (Adelaar and Muysken 2004, 351–3; Torero 2002; Chapter 4.1).[9] Second, early societies of the Titicaca Basin such as Tiwanaku are believed to have maintained trade along the Beni River with the Arawakan chiefdoms of the Llanos de Mojos and further into the tropical lowlands. A central element of this trade may have been hallucinogenic plants (Browman 1978) and the paraphernalia associated with their use (Torres 1987). This trade across the highland–lowland divide undoubtedly contributed to the interchange of ideas and even iconography between the two areas. Common to the Titicaca Basin and the Llanos de Mojos, for instance, are extensive areas of raised fields, a method for intense cultivation of periodically inundated marshlands which may have been inspired through prehistoric contacts (but see Chapter 4.3 for a contrary view). The long-distance trade connections may also have been responsible for some of the stylistic affinities that Posnansky interpreted as indications of the 'diffusion' of Tiwanaku 'high culture' into the lowlands. It is not difficult to imagine how lowland purveyors of tropical herbs, having visited ceremonial centres in the Titicaca Basin, may have been inspired to reproduce similar plazas in the rainforests along the upper Purús.

The Kallawaya

The burial of a 'medicine-man' at the highland site of Niño Korin, Bolivia, dated between the fourth and the eighth century but thought to be an ancestor of the modern Kallawaya, contained herbs from the tropical lowlands as well as items decorated with Tiwanaku iconography (Wassén 1972). In their esoteric ceremonial practices, modern Kallawaya shamans preserve some words from the extinct Pukina language (Stark 1972; Chapter 4.1). This ceremonial language combines elements of a Pukina lexicon with a Quechua grammar, some features of which appear to derive from the Mantaro Basin (Stark 1972). The travelling Kallawaya healers and herbalists represent a tradition going back at least to the Middle Horizon (AD 600–1000). In purveying tropical plants great distances along the eastern slopes of the Andes, the Kallawaya may have contributed to the spread of Tiwanakoid iconography in the Middle Horizon (Isbell 1988, 181). The longevity of these traditions is confirmed by the linguistic affiliations with pre-Inca Quechua from the Mantaro Basin and Pukina from the Titicaca Basin (Stark 1972). The Kallawaya were widely respected for their medicinal knowledge, even among the Inca, and are mentioned by Guamán Poma as accompanying Huayna Cápac in his conquest of Ecuador (Torero 1984, 379). The Inca elite may have shared with the Kallawaya an ancient ethno-linguistic heritage from Tiwanaku, as it has been suggested that they used Pukina as a 'secret language' among themselves (Cerrón-Palomino 2012). Although they have now shifted completely to Quechua in common speech, the Kallawaya may in the sixteenth century have exemplified a type of sub-Andean, frequently Arawak-related ethnolinguistic group specialized in trading tropical plants and other Amazonian products to populations in the highlands. Judging from the evidence suggested by our earlier examples, they would have had counterparts all along the eastern slopes of the Andes, from Colombia to Bolivia.

These four brief deliberations on data and inferences from archaeology, linguistics and ethnohistory suggesting interaction across the Andes–Amazonian divide add up to a recurrent pattern. Megalithic highland ceremonial centres in the Early and Middle Horizons such as San Agustín, Chavín de Huántar, and Tiwanaku all relied on imports of psycho-active plants from the tropical lowlands, conveyed along tributaries of the Amazon by ethnic groups inhabiting those lowlands or the *montaña* zone along the eastern slope of the Andes. The highland centres were governed by means of ritual specialists and the control and redistribution of exotic imports. The extensive interaction spheres dominated by each of these centres may have been integrated by a particular *lingua franca* to facilitate exchange and to establish a sense of common ethno-linguistic identity. This may in part explain the widespread dispersion of language families such as Quechua.[10]

Conclusion

A reasonable assumption about the political geography of pre-colonial South America is that at the beginning of the second millennium AD both the Andean highlands and the Amazon basin were home to several extensive, complex societies.[11] Rather than defining their boundaries in distinct, territorial terms, these societies were organized as overlapping networks of ethno-linguistically affiliated communities, the political economy of which was in part dependent on the long-distance exchange of symbolically important valuables. Even if the lords of Amazonian chiefdoms could not boast stone masonry, the volume of labour at their disposal and their military strength may have been closer to those of Andean polities than we have previously understood. The Andes–Amazonia divide, we would conclude, is largely a product of colonialism, epidemics and ignorance.

1.5
The Andes–Amazonia culture area

R. Tom Zuidema[1]

In this chapter I do not intend to point out the obvious contrasts between the Andean mountains and Amazonian lowlands and the peoples living there, nor will I enter into a history of contact between the two areas. Instead, I wish to stress their common background and the essential similarities between their cultural systems, both social and ritual. I will address the issue primarily with regard to the Central Andes, as unified under the Inca Empire, and peoples living far to their east, in particular the Ge and Bororo of Central Brazil and the Tukano of north-western Amazonia. An additional and practical reason for this choice is that those peoples have become particularly well known to us.

I see the problem at hand also in wider terms, however. When studying general anthropology and reading ethnographies from all over the world, it struck me that theoretical approaches to studying them showed differences not only between continental areas but also between the cultures within each continent. For instance, Australian systems of kinship and social organization, in their explicit forms, occur almost uniquely in their own continent. Aside from Australia, South America is the most isolated of the continents, and Andean civilization arose independently, more so than any other. Popular arguments for this independent character include the claims that Andean civilization never developed the wheel or writing. But currently of more interest may be, for instance, to emphasise the exclusively South American character of Andean kinship systems and nomenclatures (Lounsbury 1986; Zuidema 1977). The same idea was developed, albeit in a more restricted and specific way, by J.P.B. de Josselin de Jong (1983) for the Indonesian archipelago, and further applied by others, in particular Van Wouden (1968, 1983). Here I will consider basic social and ritual systems in the Andes, alongside those for Ge, Bororo and Tukano peoples (Zuidema 1965).

The villages of the Ge people, of which I take as an example one of the Canela villages (also called Eastern Timbira) in eastern Brazil, are characterized by four fundamental properties:

1. matrilocal family houses, arranged in a circle
2. the use of the central plaza by males
3. plaza moieties and six (primarily male) plaza groups, in two moieties of three
4. four active male age-classes, plus two inactive ones.

In addition to these, a final, fifth property is that each of the foregoing organizations also has a two-way division, but without them becoming exogamous moieties (though the idea of exogamy is known of in a ritual way). The houses in the village circle play hardly any formal role in the other organizations, though such connections are found in cultures further towards the Andes – that is, in other Ge cultures, the Bororo, and peoples of lowland Bolivia. In the Canela system, succession is conferred by inheriting personal names, in particular for membership in the plaza organizations. For men this is passed on matrilineally to a sister's son, and for women patrilineally to a brother's daughter. Such a custom of name succession is also mentioned for the Aymara around Lake Titicaca (Bertonio 1984). Elsewhere, however, plaza groups may become related to the matrilineal houses on the village circle. I return to this issue below, and a very explicit example, also from the Bororo.

Let us turn now to the Canela age-class system, which bears a formal similarity to that of the plaza groups yet serves a totally different and opposing function (Nimuendajú 1946). We are dealing here with a theoretical problem of great importance, and one which was echoed in a similar function in Inca society.

When youths begin to form a new age-class of men aged 20–29 years, such as the one on the east side in the year 1920, the age-class residing there moves into the position of the 40–49 age-class. At that point there is no movement on the west side. Ten years later, youths enter on the west side, with the same result for the age-class 20 years older (30–39): they move into the position of the 50–59 age-class.

Table 1.5.1 Canela age-classes (20–, 30–, 40–, 50–) in their East and West moieties. Note the places within the structure for youths (–20) and old men (60–). © The estate of R. Tom Zuidema.

years 1920, 1940		years 1910, 1930	
West	East	West	East
10–20		10–20	
30–40	20–30	20–30	30–40
60–		60–	
50–60	40–50	40–50	50–60

So the moieties are in fact in a way endogamous in their relations to each other. Their role is totally different from the plaza groups, for example, although in cultures further to the west, nearer the Andes, the ritual action of moieties and plaza groups may become integrated with each other in certain ways. But in part this growth may also have been a misunderstanding on the part of ethnographers. While kin groups clearly highlight lineage continuity through multiple generations, age-class systems, too, can establish temporal contrasts between longer, regular time-spans, including generations. These contrasts were a significant feature of Canela and Inca concepts of the past. In fact, Nimuendajú mentions examples of how the Canela remembered historical events back to the beginning of the nineteenth century, by reference to successive 40-year cycles. I will argue below that this was also a feature of the Inca age-class system, and over even longer periods.

As for the Bororo, their village organization bears a remarkable similarity – all villages following exactly the same schema and group names – to that of Cuzco, the Inca capital (Fabian 1992). Where in Bororo villages houses are connected through paths that all lead to the men's house, in Cuzco (and in Inca provinces, towns or villages) these paths became the *ceque* directions leading from the central temple of the Sun, the *Coricancha* (house of the Sun), out to the horizon, and documenting the locations of *huacas,* each one worshipped by a different family on a different day. There is also an impressive coincidence in the number of groups in the Bororo and Inca systems, save for one difference. In Cuzco there are two moieties, four quarters (*suyu*), and nine ceques in each suyu (that is, three groups of three ceques each) – with the exception that in the lowest ranked suyu, some ceques were each split into two minor ones. In a Bororo village there are two moieties, four quarters, but only two (not three) lineages in each quarter, although each lineage is again divided into three sub-lineages. It is noteworthy that there were more houses in the lowest quarter than in the other quarters, a feature similar to the Cuzco system (and some other Peruvian cases). Despite the great similarity of the Bororo model to that of Cuzco, there is no reason to suggest that Inca culture, or any similar pre-Inca culture, had spread to Bororo territory, either by conquest or any other long-term domination. It seems that we must simply accept that there existed a fundamental similarity between cultural models in Central Brazil and in the Central Andes.

Let me now pay attention to the parallels between two other distinctive features of Bororo and Andean cultures. Perhaps because the Bororo moved various ritual features from the plaza to the houses in the village circle, some of the contrasts between lineages and age-classes have become less marked over time. Recent reports on Bororo rituals and the myths that belong to each lineage no longer mention age-classes. Nonetheless, according to Fabian (1998), who conducted a specific study of social and temporal organization, calendars and astronomy in a Bororo village, older people still remembered the role of age-classes, and references to them are found in the myths belonging to various lineages.

This first problem may be related to a second one, which played an important role in the Andes as well as in Bororo society. Bororo moieties are exogamous. Both are also divided into quarters. The two hereditary village chiefs each belong to the leading lineage of a different quarter in the higher-ranked moiety. They have the unique prerogative of marrying endogamously, each within his quarter. Here we are dealing with a problem of political hierarchy that was all-important in Cuzco, too, as the capital of Inca society and empire, and which still leaves traces to this day.

It is well known that the Inca king could marry his own sister. In fact, we have here a hierarchical system where people of higher ranks marry ever closer relatives, within more endogamous groups (Zuidema 1990). However, men of higher rank were also allowed to marry, exogamously, further secondary spouses, thus building up larger political networks. These two features influenced social and political situations that can still hold today, in relationships between moieties, for instance. In Inca Cuzco, there was a well-described ranking difference between the city's two moieties, in which Inca high nobility belonged, endogamously, to the upper moiety. Nonetheless, our first and best-informed chronicler, Juan de Betanzos, claims to the contrary that Inca moieties in the Cuzco province were exogamous; he is, in fact, the only chronicler to make such an explicit claim. The issue is of even more interest in that Polo de Ondegardo, an equally well-informed early chronicler, explicitly states and concludes that people of one of the Cuzco moieties could not possess and inherit land in the other moiety, thus implying that these moieties were endogamous, contrary to Betanzos (Zuidema 2013). The apparent contrast is resolved when one realizes that Betanzos was referring to secondary marriages, and Polo to primary ones. Similar problems are still important today. Moieties in local communities are frequently claimed to be strictly endogamous. In one village where I have conducted fieldwork (Sarhua, in the Ayacucho department), one family belonging to the upper moiety claimed Inca descent and was said to engage in more endogamous marriages than was permitted to other families.

So far, I have introduced only in rather general terms the formal similarities between the Ge-Bororo and Andean social and ritual systems. Let me now move on to more precise descriptions of two mutual, complementary models within the Inca age-class system. In particular, I will stress how the second of these models shows great similarity to the Canela model. This leads me to argue also for a basic similarity with the Tukano social system.

The first model is one mentioned by various chroniclers of Inca culture, in which adults were grouped into five age-classes, of five years each. Other sources mention that there could be a further, sixth age-class, either as an introductory or as an exiting class. In one source, the Huarochirí manuscript, the model is described also as a hierarchy of five or six brothers and as many sisters (G. Taylor 1999), with the fourth child nonetheless being called 'youngest'. Such a model is still a popular conception of a 'complete' family – with the fourth child called 'youngest', and two extra children – in Andean society today (from my own fieldwork

Table 1.5.2 Age-class system for Inca *acllas*, with six groups presented in an alternating hierarchical descending sequence. © The estate of R. Tom Zuidema.

Age-class 1: 20–25 years	Age-class 3: 30–35 years
Age-class 2: 25–30 years	Age-class 4: 35–40 years
Age-class 5: 40–50 years	Age-class 6: 50–60 years

in Ayacucho: Zuidema 1990). The chronicler Guamán Poma de Ayala gives us a detailed description of the age-class system of the Inca *acllas*, 'chosen' virgins (Guamán Poma de Ayala 1987/1615; Zuidema 1990; on Guamán Poma, see Chapters 5.1 and 5.2). Since I have analysed elsewhere the very intricate but consistent information that Guamán Poma provides, I will here limit myself to some relevant conclusions. First, the author mentions the age-classes in a kind of alternating hierarchical descending sequence (1, 3, 2, 4, 5, 6) that I present as follows:

The three younger, higher-ranked aclla age-classes (1, 2, 3) were assigned to ranked sacred places, while the older three (4, 5, 6) were ranked as weavers. Since ranks 1 and 3 represent a clear inside–outside opposition (worship of the sun in the city's supposedly central temple of the sun, as opposed to worship of *Huanacauri* mountain on the flanks of the Cuzco valley), I assume that the opposition holds also for the two columns. There is a close correspondence with the Canela age-class model.

The second model concerns the ten ranked sons – or probably better, ten groups of sons – of the Inca, called *panaca*, five panacas belonging to the upper moiety and five to the lower one. While later sources would seriously distort the essence of the system in order to serve Spanish interests, here I follow both the earliest description, derived from our most trustworthy and knowledgeable source (Las Casas 1967), and the one that remained closest to the pre-Hispanic value of the panaca system (Santo Tomás 1995). One later but still trustworthy reference, however, also implies a sixth position of younger sons in each moiety who had not yet entered into the system (Cobo 1636/1964; Zuidema 2011). In line with the ten panacas, the Cuzco valley was itself divided into ten ranked administrative sections, called *chapa*. All bordered on the river *Huatanay*, flowing west to east, with the five *Hanan* sections arrayed in sequence to the north of the river, and the five *Hurin* sections south of it. Each chapa and its inhabitants was governed by a panaca member. Each panaca was also in charge of the rituals of one particular month in the Inca calendar. In conclusion, we are clearly dealing here with the age-class system in its highest and most elaborate form. It was also thus the instrument perhaps best expressed in Inca rituals, Inca religion, Inca ideas about the past and Inca art.

Let me give two examples. First is a description of the role of the panacas at the close of the highest state rituals in the two royal months around the time of the summer solstice (December). Each panaca offered and sacrificed a llama to a different deity, according to its rank. By weaving together a complete picture out of many sources, we can conclude that the first panaca, in Hanan as well as in Hurin, made offering to the Sun, the second to Thunder, the third to Viracocha (in whom the Spaniards recognized a creator god), and the fourth and fifth either to the Moon or to the Earth. What we have here is a hierarchy, particularly of the first three gods. Other well-informed chroniclers also make special mention of this religious hierarchy, which moreover conforms very closely with that set out by Guamán Poma in describing the aclla age-classes.

The second example concerns a beautiful Inca tunic, possibly from early colonial times, showing a row of six Inca crowns (*mascapaycha*). The lower parts consisted of a fringe of red wool, which (according to one chronicler) represented blood dripping from decapitated enemy heads. One of the fringes, however, is of yellow wool, to reflect that it belonged to a person of lower rank, a crown prince, who had not yet killed an enemy. Above the fringe are represented five, not six, decapitated heads, to recognize that they correspond only to the red mascapaychas. In this case we can conclude that the five mascapaychas corresponded to five panacas, and to one other group, explicitly recognized as not being ruled by a panaca in its corresponding month.

One last remarkable property of the panaca system leads me now to close with a direct comparison to an important political concept that unifies the exogamous groups in various political units of Tukano peoples living along headwaters of the Amazon in north-west Amazonia. Given that the social systems of these peoples are very similar to each other, the observations of various anthropologists can be discussed together as part of one and the same system. The male members of one family, as well as those within any one exogamous group, are distinguished from each other as 'brothers' of five different ranks and functions. In the following schema I set this structure alongside the ranks in the Andean panaca system (Zuidema 2011).

Although the sequences of functions are not exactly the same in both lists, and at least one function, the fourth, is different, the correspondence is nonetheless remarkable, and even more so given that in Tukano opinion the dancers and singers are most similar to western priests. The correspondence between both orders is further supported when one takes into account the mythical origin of the Tukano peoples all living along the same tributary of the Amazon. They were

Table 1.5.3   Andean panaca rankings and Tukano male ranks/functions.
© The estate of R. Tom Zuidema.

Rank	Inca status/function	Tukano status/function
1	Sun; government	Chief
2	Thunder; warfare	Dancers, singers
3	Viracocha; priests	Warriors
4	(Villagers?)	Shamans
5	Servants	Servants

said to be descended from the same ancestor who had travelled upriver from the Amazon. Along that tributary, the first to go ashore and settle was the brother who was to become the chief. Further and further upstream the other four brothers disembarked in the ordained sequence, to become founders of their respective villages. The process also applies over generations, however. Thus when someone from the third village, for instance, that of the warriors, would later visit someone from the first village, he would address the latter as 'grandson' and not as 'younger brother' (nor as 'older brother' as we might expect). Even though the five founders had started out as 'brothers', the distinctions between them in time came to be expressed in terms of generations, and inversely to their age rank.

The structural similarity is clear, between the five Tukano brother groups and the five panacas in each Cuzco moiety – who likewise could be referred to by the Inca himself either in an ascending or descending hierarchy. It is also striking that both hierarchies were laid out along a river, even if in the Tukano case the descending hierarchy goes upstream and in the Inca case downstream (along the Huatanay). An essential point is that time distinctions, not only in the past but also in the future, were in both cases made through age-groups. These were primarily age-classes of brothers or of sisters, but also generations, and in the Inca case could span periods much longer still (Ossio 2015; Zuidema 1964, 1995).

The Tukano peoples lived closer to the Andes than the Bororo, but aside from the illustration just given it is difficult to find other examples of similarity between the Tukano and Inca cultures. It is also difficult to argue for historical contacts between the peoples of the Andes and those of eastern Bolivia and Brazil. On the other hand, given the designedly circular forms of pre-Tiahuanaco settlements like Pucara and Chiripa, both on the Altiplano near Lake Titicaca, one might consider that there had once stretched a cultural continuum from the Andes to central Brazil. Ceque systems like that of Cuzco, and age-class systems, had an importance far wider and more profound than is perhaps recognized in modern studies of Andean culture. They were still vital when the Spanish chroniclers reported them, and retain their influence today, even if the study of other matters seems more urgent. And although I have been able here to give examples of continuity only between the Andean and Amazonian culture areas, that continuity probably held much more widely across the South American continent. Age-class systems were a major element of Andean as well as Amazonian cultures, and should be studied intensively, perhaps also with a view to establishing contacts across any putative Andes–Amazonia divide.

Part 2
Deep time and the long chronological perspective

2.1
Initial east and west connections across South America

Tom D. Dillehay[1]

Both the archaeological and genetic evidence reveals that humans migrating from North America colonized South America (Dillehay 2009; Meltzer 2009). The latest archaeological data suggests that the earliest populations moved along several probable entry and dispersal routes: down the Pacific coastline, down the spine and throughout the lateral valleys of the Andes, and along the Caribbean and Atlantic sides of the continent, with occasional movement into the deeper interior environments (see Figure. 2.1.1; Rothhammer and Dillehay 2009).

The evidence also indicates that people had arrived in South America by at least 15,000 years ago (all ages are calibrated). The presently available radiocarbon dates for sites across the continent do not suggest a particular dispersal rate; nor do they necessarily imply the initial appearance of people in each region. Instead, they indicate a record of demographic growth. Although sparse, the genetic and human skeletal records also document human demography and, along with the archaeology, suggest some of the conditions and complexities of that growth. Collectively, the data suggest that dispersal was a slow, prolonged, complex process with multiple colonizations of many different regions, probably with some environments (for example, high Andes, dense humid forests) never fully settled on a permanent basis due to less productive resources or difficult climatic conditions, at least during the Terminal Pleistocene period (~15,000–10,000 cal BP). Others, such as the coastlines and major river valleys, appear to have continuously supported human populations since the outset of human entry. This essay briefly discusses current evidence for the demographic relationships and cultural transmissions among different culture areas in the north and central Andes and the eastern tropical lowlands from approximately 14,000 to 5,000 years ago. The focus is primarily on the intervening corridors between these two broad regions, which currently have a paucity of reliable early archaeological, skeletal and genetic evidence. In order to understand the types of contacts and relationships that might have occurred

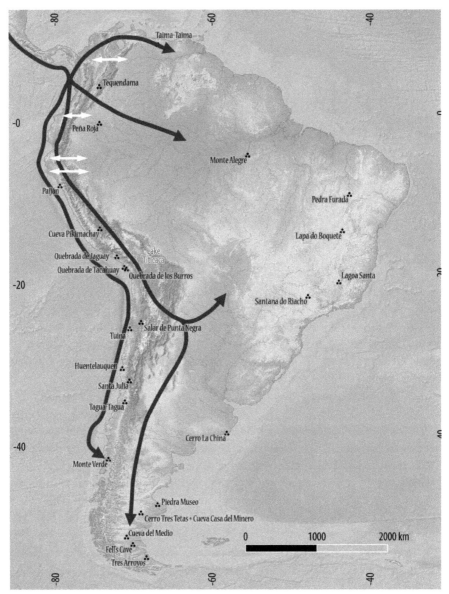

Figure 2.1.1 Map of South America showing the location of major terminal Pleistocene sites, probable early migration routes (grey arrows), and areas of the northern Andes where the mountains are low and narrow (white arrows), which presumably facilitates passage across them. © Tom D. Dillehay and Paul Heggarty.

during this early period, this chapter aims to project from the better-known records of adjacent regions to hypothesize the long-term relationships within and across these corridors.

Terminal Pleistocene and Early Holocene: ~15,000–8000 cal BP

While culture areas changed over time and were certainly different in the terminal Pleistocene, the continent was also ecologically different than it is today (Clapperton 1993; cf. Netherly 2011a). Geography and biota, which were changing dramatically in some environments during this period in response to the glacial and interglacial periods in parts of the Andes, would have shaped some human movement into some areas, especially through mountain passes from one side of the continent to the other. As a result of major environmental and climatic changes, some plant and animal communities were altered considerably throughout this period. For instance, the tropical rainforest of the Amazon basin was generally less dense and characterized by patchy parklands and savannahs. The middle Holocene climatic information (~8000–4000 cal BP) demonstrates a greater stability and more modern-day environments than the earlier periods (Bush et al. 2011; Mayle and Power 2008), but due to gradual population increases in hunter-gatherer and incipient farming communities over time, minor changes such as prolonged local droughts or excessive flooding during El Nino years probably had major effects on the distribution of sites, their size and duration of occupation, and ultimately their preservation and archaeological visibility. For instance, long-term drought may force some local groups to migrate to more productive areas or to stay for shorter periods of time in one locale, either creating a brief hiatus in the local archaeological record or resulting in smaller campsites with less cultural debris left behind, respectively.

Some forms of hunter-gatherer social and economic behaviour are inferred from a few documented archaeological site locations, sizes, and internal features (for example, León Canales 2007; Schmidt Dias and Bueno 2014). But the fundamental archaeological data provide only insights into certain aspects of the economy and technology of these people and suggestive hints as to how they might have interacted with each other and with their environments. In this regard, site distribution, preservation and visibility are major factors that shape the current archaeological and human skeletal evidence available for reconstructing the early prehistory of the continent. But in many regions, such as the Amazon basin and the high mountain valleys of the northern and central Andes, this evidence is very scarce. For instance, what is known of the late Pleistocene of the northern half of the continent is derived from a handful of reliably ^{14}C-dated archaeological sites, and most of these are along the Pacific coastal plains of Peru and north Chile, in the major river valleys of the western and central Andes, and in parts of far eastern Brazil (Léon Canales 2007; Dillehay 2000; Lourdeau 2015; Schmidt Dias and Bueno 2014; and see also Chapter 4.4 for Llanos de Mojos, Bolivia). Unfortunately, those areas most crucial for understanding early east–west contacts and especially the later cultural transmission of ideas and goods between the Andes and the eastern lowland tropics are the least known. Specifically, these are the far western fringes of the Amazon basin, the northern rim of the continent (today where

Venezuela and the Guyanas are located), the western tropics of Colombia, Ecuador and northern Peru that front the Pacific Ocean, and the lower eastern slopes and foothills of the Andes from Colombia to north-west Argentina. The existing data suggesting connections among these regions primarily come from genetic affiliations based on present-day blood groups of living Native Americans and on human skeletons from a few archaeological skeletons of the early Holocene period (for example, Barbieri et al. 2014; Rothhammer and Dillehay 2009) as well as the presence of a few diagnostic projectile points and other stone tools.

A problem with early diagnostic lithic assemblages, however, is that the more widespread projectile point classifications are often ill-defined, overlapping, and in some cases – such as the Fishtail and stemmed Paijan point types (Figure 2.1.2) – vary appreciably in spatial extent and duration.

The present distribution patterns of these and other point types reflect more information about sampling biases than technological trends. Given that the Fishtail point, for example, was one of several early contemporary types, potentially recognizable patterns distinguishing its regional technological traditions should be detected in subsistence and settlement, site distributions, and typology wherever such traditions existed. But they are little understood in most regions and presently non-existent in the intervening corridors between the Andes and the Amazon. The problem is that so few sites have been excavated

Figure 2.1.2   Fishtail projectile points from northern Peru dated around 11,200 BP (Dillehay 2011: courtesy of G. Maggard).

and analysed in detail, not only across the continent but especially in the inter-vening regions, that hardly any data are available on chronology, genetic, tech-nological, subsistence and settlement patterns. Moreover, point styles and other diagnostics do not represent people and their movements and relationships. Nor do they provide geographical vectors or causes and effects of human movements and contacts. At best, they reveal temporal and spatial markers, the diffusion of technological styles.

Furthermore, as yet, Fishtail and other diagnostic artefact types have not been documented in the Amazon basin and the corridors between the east and west (although most major drainages run west to east in these corridors), but given their ubiquity in neighbouring areas such as semi-tropical northern Uruguay and south-east Brazil around 10,500 BP (for example, Suárez 2015), it is likely only a matter of time before they are found in these areas. Their presence would help fill temporal and spatial lacunae as well as inform us of early techno-environmental adaptations. Unifacial lithic industries across the northern half of the continent are also significant. Although ubiquitous in many regions, they are not as diagnostic as projectile points and generally provide less information about early technolo-gies, economies, and lifestyles in general. An exception may be the limace, an elon-gated, multi-purpose unifacial tool present throughout many regions, suggesting it spread early during the transition from the Pleistocene to the Holocene period (for example, Lourdeau 2015). Again, little is known about the conditions and types of sites associated with the diffusion of this and other tool types and, above all, of the specific kinds of societies producing them and of their demographic and subsist-ence patterns.

We can thus only surmise that the first people in the intervening corridors were generalized hunters and gatherers whose mobility allowed them to adapt to changing environmental challenges at the end of the Pleistocene and the begin-ning of the Holocene period. Perhaps once certain levels of demographic density were reached in the early to middle Holocene, exchange networks were estab-lished along accessible routes of movement and communication, probably large river basins, through which certain ideas, resources (for example, food crops), and technologies spread. These developments were probably more consistent and accentuated in more productive environments such as the coastlines, lacustrine and riverine systems, and some of the richer forest habitats (for example, season-ally dry forests).

Incipient farming

It is becoming clear that the consistent use of several productive environments such as the seasonally dry tropical forests in the north-west Andes and in parts of the Amazon basin played an important role in the appearance of early hunter-gatherer social and economic complexity. For instance, recent genetic and archaeological studies inform us that the wild ancestors of many staple crops are native to the varied seasonally dry forests in the northern Neotropics of the continent, in Colombia, Ecuador and the north-west Amazon (Piperno 2007, 2011a). More so than projectile point styles and genetic linkages, it is perhaps food crops that best suggest human movement across the northern half of South America and/or systematic short-distance, down-the-line exchange of ideas and goods from one group to another during the Terminal Pleistocene to the middle Holocene period (~8000–4000 cal BP). More systematic long-distance exchange is probably less likely during this period because socio-economic networks would have required a certain density of the human population across several contiguous environments and less mobility among them in order to have established and sustained semi-permanent to permanent nodes of contact and exchange. It is thus more likely that ideas and goods spread during the terminal Pleistocene and early Holocene as a result of the migration of people, and those people in contact with a few more territorially based groups in richer environments. More permanent exchange networks probably developed during the early to middle Holocene period, also the time when exotic crops from the tropical lowlands, such as squash, peanuts, and chilli peppers, began to appear in the distant areas such as regions of western Ecuador and northern Peru (Pearsall 2003; Piperno 2011a; Piperno and Dillehay 2008).

For this early period, there is only scant evidence of plant foods that survive in the archaeological record. In localities where organic remains are preserved, there is good macro-botanical evidence (for example, burned seeds) of the cultivation of squash (*Cucurbita moschata*) in Colombia, Ecuador and Peru by at least 10,000 BP (Piperno 2011a) and the use of palm nuts (*Arecaceae* sp.) and other plants in Colombia by 9200 BP (Gnecco and Mora 1997). At the end of the Pleistocene, when climate conditions were generally warmer and more stable, current evidence indicates that intentional plant manipulation was underway in a few areas, but primarily in the Neotropics of north-west South America (Pearsall 2003; Piperno 2007, 2011a; Piperno and Dillehay 2008). Much of this manipulation can probably be attributed to the mobility of early hunters and gatherers, either through deliberate migration from one habitat to another or simply opportunistic exchange between groups occasionally coming into contact with one another.

The only early known Terminal Pleistocene site in the high-altitude corridor between the Andes and the eastern lowlands is Manachaqui Cave in the Chachapoyas area, which has calibrated ^{14}C dates between 12,200 and 11,900 cal BP. These dates are associated with stemmed point types similar to the Paijan style on the north coast of Peru and in highland Ecuador and with Manachaqui and other points possibly of types representing early lithic styles from the eastern slopes of the northern Andean. As Church notes, 'great stylistic variability suggest that more than one transient population used the cave' (Church and von Hagen 2008, 907–8).

Genetic and craniometric evidence

Although not directly pertinent to the Terminal Pleistocene period, the continent-wide bioanthropological information on interregional human contact and movement is inferred from genetic and craniometric studies. Several studies of genetic variation among living Native South Americans (cf. Wang et al. 2007; Lewis et al. 2007; Nakatsuka et al. 2020) have suggested east-to-west differences in genetic diversity, showing that eastern Brazilian populations had slightly lower levels of heterozygosity. (This pattern was also observed earlier with Y-chromosome markers [Tarazona-Santos et al. 2001; Llamas et al. 2016]). If Brazil and the Amazon basin generally exhibit the lowest levels of genetic variation, this might suggest an initial colonization of western South America and perhaps a subsequent peopling of the eastern part by western subgroups, even though both were probably derived from the same founder population. There also might have been two or more migrations inhabiting these regions at different times, but from the same founder group. These patterns are only suggestive at this time because there are sampling problems with these studies; in short, more data are needed from more regions to confirm these and other patterns.

We also must keep in mind that the current genetic record is based on a very small sample of ancient skeletal material, most of which is derived from early to middle Holocene skeletons. These later remains do not represent the first Americans; they are descendants removed by at least 450 generations, during which time many processes could have altered the genetic record. This is not to say that these records do not reflect some early genetic and morphological traits. Rather, they are useful for suggesting some of the continuous and transformational processes of demographic exchange among different east and west groups over extended time and space, and how these processes might have added or reduced variation in the sampled populations.

The possibility of two distinct and chronologically separate populations entering South America also is suggested in the early to middle Holocene skeletons, where more narrow and long, prognathic faces generally occur in the west and more short and wide, orthognathic faces generally are in the east (Neves et al. 2007; González-José et al. 2008). These regional differences generally agree with the genetic evidence, which also suggests some differences between the east and west. It is not known whether this pattern is best explained by genetic drift, by the division of a single founder population after people first entered the continent (that is, the founder effects in two different colonizing groups splitting east and west), by geographic isolation, or by selection. Geographical barriers of the Andes and the Amazon basin may have contributed to some skeletal differences and to discontinuous and continuous connections, as well as regional population dynamics and socio-cultural patterns. Variation in the early skull forms could also be indicative of climatic adaptations more than genetic signals, or of gene drift and adaptations to local evolution after the first people arrived and then spread out over the continent. Whatever the reasons may be, the data reveal some variation in early crania morphology, and like the genetic data, only suggest at this time the possibility that separate migrations took place into or within the continent perhaps from different source areas, or that the first immigrants were already heterogeneous at the time of entry and dispersal from east to west or vice versa, or that there was simultaneous entry into both sides of the continent.

The archaeological record of the early Holocene (~10,000–8000 cal BP) generally agrees with the patterns produced by the genetic and cranial studies, suggesting that the east and west sides of the continent have different chronologies of human dispersal, albeit also connected both in early times and continuously connected throughout prehistory. Yet, during this early period, there is no combined archaeological, genetic, and skeletal evidence to suggest a continuous one-way direction of genes, ideas, peoples or goods between the east and west. If anything, the movements are two-way or multiple ways through time and space. As mentioned above, patterns drawn from the current evidence probably relate more to sampling biases than to widespread demographic and cultural trends.

Early to Middle Holocene

Between ~10,000 and 8000 BP, there is a more complete archaeological record to draw from for reconstructing past contacts and relationships. Early Holocene foragers continued many of the patterns that characterized the previous period, although there were changes in the social, demographic, and economic organization. In the Andes, from ~10,000 to 7000 BP, there is evidence for more socially complex foragers practising a broad-spectrum economy that included gardening and food production, living in semi-permanent to permanent households (Lavallée 2000; Dillehay 2011). In the tropical lowlands mixed economies of foragers are evidenced at several early sites (Bueno et al. 2013; Lourdeau 2015; Kipnis 1998). There also is archaeological evidence that early Holocene groups began to become less mobile, aggregate, establish more permanent camps and manipulate environments to their benefit along major rivers, in coastal bays and near active springs. Examples are in the north-eastern lowland tropics at sites like Peña Roja in Colombia (Gnecco and Mora 1997), possibly in the eastern Amazon basin (Roosevelt et al. 1996), at several sites of the Nanchoc Valley in northern Peru (Dillehay 2011), and at the Las Vegas II site in south-west Ecuador (Stothert et al. 2003). These and other sites were more localized, as indicated by the presence of local lithic raw material and by various floral and faunal foods indigenous to the local environments. The populations occupying these sites also established more permanent settlement nodes and probably places of down-the-line exchange of plant foods and other items. This becomes more evident after 8000–6500 BP when more exotic crops begin to appear in the archaeological record of sites such as Las Vegas II in south-west Ecuador, at Paredones and Huaca Prieta on the desert coast of north

Peru (Dillehay et al. 2012), and slightly later at a few Chinchorro sites on the hyper-arid north coast of Chile (Marquet et al. 2012), environments far distant from the wet tropics where most of these crops were likely first domesticated.

More specifically, some of the major species exchanged long distances during this period are manioc, sweet potato, peanuts, squash, avocado, palm, potato, common and lima beans, quinoa, chilli peppers, maize, cotton, coca, tobacco, and others (Piperno 2011a), many of which were likely derived from the western Amazon basin. Squash from Colombia and peanuts from south-eastern Bolivia moved into northern Peru by 10,000 and 9000 BP, respectively. Manioc from the eastern tropical lowlands occurs there by about 7000 BP; it is present in central Panama at about 7600 BP. Chilli peppers were dispersed from western Amazonia by at least 9000 BP. Maize from Mexico spread into lower Central America by 7600 BP and moved into Colombia by 7000 BP and Peru by 6500 BP (for example, Chapter 3.6). These and other plant foods suggest north to south, south to north, and east to west long-distance movements of crops, most probably originally from the eastern Andean valleys or western Amazonia. But these developments were not taking place everywhere, as evidenced by our study of numerous sites in multiple ecological zones in the Nanchoc and nearby valleys (Dillehay 2011).

The introduction of non-native plants into regions on the western side of the Andes suggests that the maintenance of widespread interregional communication channels probably fulfilled the important adaptive and economic task of keeping up reliable networks for accessing exotic food crops. Furthermore, the configuration of these routes, whether along major rivers, coastlines, and/or mountain passes, would have required the maintenance of contact points and interaction spheres along major lowland rivers and on either side of the Andes and up and down the Pacific coast. Not known is whether this contact was direct by long-distance exchange, indirect by down-the-line exchange, or both. It can be surmised that most of these crops were probably diffused throughout a vast geographic network of social and economic interaction along down-the-line exchange routes as well as some migration that connected the tropical lowlands both east and west of the Andes and the coasts of Colombia, Ecuador, Peru and Chile. It is important to keep in mind that the tropical forests of western Colombia down to northern Peru could have provided many of the same plant foods and other items (for example, bird feathers, jaguars, harpy eagles) found on the eastern side of the Andes. One must remember that southern Ecuador and northern Peru, as well as other geographical areas in Colombia and northern Ecuador (see Figure 2.1.1), represent the narrow-est and lowest areas of the Andean mountain chain (Chapter 2.4). The eastern side of northern Peru is where the Marañón River flows down into the Amazon basin. Yet, on the other hand, even the opposite type of terrain – high and wide moun-tains such as those in the south-central Andes – may not have been much of a geo-graphic impediment to long-distance exchange because tropical bird feathers and seeds are present in tombs of the late Chinchorro culture around 5,500 years ago

(Rivera 1974). It is possible that these items were obtained via north-to-south down-the-line exchange along the Pacific coast.

Epilogue

It seems that we often forget the long-term persistence of widely ranging, highly mobile foragers and hunter-gatherers during the long time span from the Terminal Pleistocene to the middle Holocene, and specifically their continued presence alongside and beyond areas later inhabited by early farmers, fishers and pastoralists, and the continued role they played in dispersing ideas, people, economic plants and other resources. As part of this persistence, the unevenness with which early stone tool industries and the first cultigens spread throughout the continent provided opportunities for foragers and non-foragers to strike a variety of early, short- and perhaps long-distance down-the-line exchanges with each other across multiple ecological zones stretching from the Pacific coast to the Amazon basin. Whatever the cause and effect of these contacts and movements, they must have been multi-directional, forming mosaics of many different types of early exchange patterns and cultural transmissions from north to south, south to north, and especially from the Andes to Amazonia and from Amazonia to the Andes and the Pacific coast among many different kinds of societies. These and other transformations provided some of the earliest demographic and economic foundations for the subsequent development of early Andean and Amazonian civilizations.

2.2
The Andes–Amazonia divide and human morphological diversification in South America

André Strauss[1]

The morphology of the cranium is the result of a complex process involving the interaction of genes and the environment. It is, therefore, potentially capable of tracking the impact of migration, drift, selection, climate, diet and subsistence strategy in the differentiation of human populations across time. It is not surprising, therefore, that the study of diversity in cranial morphology among Native Americans, past and present, has been central to debates on when the New World was first settled, and by whom. Within recent South America, differences in cranial morphology (cultural deformation discounted) broadly align with an east–west division – approximately, an Andes–Amazonia divide. The picture is not quite as clear-cut as may first appear, however, and there is as yet no agreement on which of various hypotheses offers the best explanation for this pattern.

In truth, the evidence so far available from cranial morphology is relatively scarce, and it has often been invoked to support opposing models for first settlement of the Americas. There is nonetheless overall agreement that early Americans shared a morphological pattern (effectively, a cranium shape) distinct from that seen among most Native Americans of late and recent periods. This distinctive pattern, dubbed 'Paleoamerican morphology', is known from several sites across South America (green circles in the map of Figure 2.2.1): in East-Central Brazil at Santana do Riacho (Neves et al. 2003); in Northeast Brazil at Toca das Onças (Hubbe et al. 2004) and Serra da Capivara (Hubbe et al. 2007); in Southern Brazil at Capelinha (Neves et al. 2005) and in the interior of Rio Grande do Sul (Neves et al. 2004); at Sabana de Bogotá in Colombia (Neves et al. 2007); in the rock shelter of Lauricocha (Fehren-Schmitz et al. 2015) and the sites associated with the Paiján tradition in Peru, in the Pampas region of Argentina (Pucciarelli et al. 2010) and at the very southern tip of the continent in Palli Aike (Neves et al. 1999).

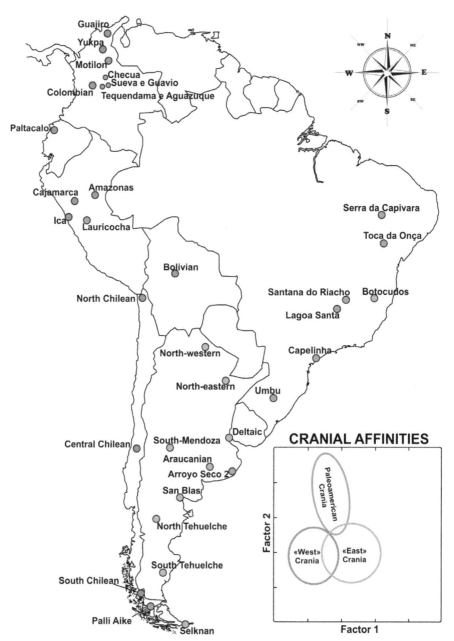

Figure 2.2.1 Map showing the approximate location of archaeological sites presenting crania with a Paleoamerican morphology (green circles), and of the recent populations identified by Pucciarelli et al. (2006) as presenting cranial morphology typical of the 'east' (blue circles) and of the 'west' (red circles). © Chiara Barbieri. In the lower right corner, the bivariate plot of the canonical variate analysis by Pucciarelli et al. (2006) over 30 linear measurements of the cranium shows the three distinct cranial morphological patterns in the continent.

Since the nineteenth century it has been noted that early South Americans (and to a certain degree early North Americans too) differ significantly from their late and recent counterparts in cranial morphology. Among present-day Amerindians, meanwhile, morphological diversity was commonly assumed to be low. Hrdlicka's concept of an American homotype (Fewkes 1912, 11), according to which indigenous groups in the New World were physically similar to each other, associated with a putative linguistic homogeneity embracing the entire continent, favoured the view of a 'biologically homogenous megapopulation' (Pucciarelli et al. 2006). Following initial observations by Neumann (1942, 1952) and Bass (1964), however, recent studies on late/recent Native South American populations (Ross et al. 2002, 2008; Sardi et al. 2005; Pucciarelli et al. 2006; Perez et al. 2009; Hubbe et al. 2014) have revealed greater diversity, indicating that cranial morphology in South America varies significantly not just over time but also between contemporary populations.

Similarly, most linguistic studies now strongly contradict the hypothesis of homogeneity and depict South America as the most diverse of all continents as far as native language lineages are concerned (Nichols 1990; Campbell 1997; Nettle 1999). Nettle (1999), for example, proposes a simulation model in which high linguistic diversity would be a consequence of rapid group fission and relative isolation once people arrived in the unoccupied South American lowlands.

As for genetic data, the general picture remains one of overall homogeneity and of a single founding population for all Amerindians (Reich et al. 2012; but see Skoglund et al. 2015). It has also been recognized, however, that although there is little genetic diversity *within* any given population group in South America, the differences *between* some groups can actually be rather high (see also Chapters 1.3 and 3.2). Wang et al. (2007, 2052), for example, report that in eastern South America 14.7 per cent of the total genetic variance is found between populations while the remaining variance is found within populations. This proportion is almost twice as high as in other continents and points to significant processes of between-group genetic differentiation in South America.

This high diversity in cranial morphology among recent South American groups is all the more interesting given how starkly it contrasts with the pattern in genetics, where diversity generally decreases with distance from Africa (Cavalli-Sforza et al. 1994; Prugnolle et al. 2005; Wang et al. 2007). Of all continents, it is the Americas whose native populations present the lowest genetic diversity within any one population group (Chapter 1.3). Similar patterns have been reported for

---

(cont.)
Sample size ranged from 8 to 42 crania per population totalizing 500 individuals. Differences between Eastern, Western and Paleoamericans are statistically significant (Between-group Wilk's $\lambda = 0.322$; $F = 12.7$). The colour coding is the same as above. For details see the original publication (Pucciarelli et al. 2006).

worldwide diversity in cranial morphology (Manica et al. 2007; Betti et al. 2009). Nonetheless, this largely refers just to low *average* within-group diversity and is a function of serial founder effects and range expansion as populations migrated out of Africa. On the other hand, differences *between* population groups are actually high in South America compared to other regions of the world. As Howells puts it: 'intraregional heterogeneity is greatest in Polynesia and the Americas, the two regions we can certify as the latest to be occupied. This goes counter to any expectation that such recency would be expressed in cranial homogeneity' (Howells 1989, 83).

In South America, therefore, genetics and morphology are still to be reconciled. In part, this might be related to the east–west divide imposed in the continent by the Andes. On a continental scale, this has been shown to be an important axis along which differences in cranial morphology broadly align (Pucciarelli et al. 2006). In a study based on 485 non-deformed South American crania, a strong relationship was identified between geographical origin (east or west) and cranial morphology, with populations in the east (blue circles in Figure 2.1.1) being characterized by longer and wider posterior neurocranium, and a smaller auricular region, than those in the west (red circles in Figure 2.1.1).

In the context of this volume, however, it is important to stress that the east–west division described by Pucciarelli et al. (2006) is not completely analogous to any putative Andes–Amazonia divide. In fact, truly Amazonian populations are all but absent from their analyses. The only exception is a single series of eight crania from the Peruvian Amazon. And this group actually clusters with crania of Andean morphology – not unexpectedly, given its relative geographical proximity to those populations. The general paucity of skeletal remains from Amazonia has traditionally been attributed to acidic soils precluding their preservation. Although this must certainly be taken into account, there are other important factors too, not least the vast scale of the region and the relatively recent beginnings of systematic research there. This gap in the archaeological record will certainly be filled, at least to some extent, over coming decades, as research in the region continues to expand and intensify. At this point, however, the study by Pucciarelli et al. (2006) remains the best and only attempt to understand how any 'east–west' division has impacted cranial morphology.

Different hypotheses have been postulated to explain the high level of morphological diversity among recent Amerindians. One possible explanation sees this as the result of a late survival of so-called Paleoamerican morphology into recent times. The non-Asiatic morphology of the Pericus in Baja California (González-José et al. 2003) and of the Botocudos in central Brazil (Strauss et al. 2015) has been understood in this context. However, recent genetic studies have found exclusively Amerindian ancestry for those groups (Rasmussen et al. 2014; Raghavan et al. 2015). Moreover, such a hypothesis presumes the existence of 'two main biological components' in the settlement of the continent (Neves and Hubbe 2005), a scenario not accepted by all scholars and which leaves little room for *in situ* processes of morphological differentiation.

An alternative hypothesis proposes that this high morphological diversity of recent Amerindians is mainly the result of intense drift, given the small population sizes of the founder groups. Powell (2005), for instance, presents a scenario favouring microevolution within the New World to explain the marked differences in cranial morphology between early and late or modern Native Americans. This is based on assumptions that the first Americans exhibited an especially high degree of genetic diversity, and that this highly variable source population was then subject to strong genetic drift, mainly due to group fission keeping population sizes small, factors that together would explain the morphological diversity of late Native Americans. This scenario, however, is based on the scant early material available in North America, a limiting factor also confronted by Jantz and Owsley (2001).

Sardi et al. (2005) suggest a similar scenario. Recognizing that late or modern Native South Americans display very different cranial patterns, they do not dismiss the possibility that the morphological pattern of late Holocene populations was generated *in situ* from the early pattern by local stochastic processes of differentiation. In their opinion, however, the local differentiation scenario would be feasible only if Early South Americans had displayed an uncommonly high degree of biological diversity, which has not been properly evaluated to date. A similar scenario has been proposed to reconcile the contrasting degrees of diversity in genetics (low) and in cranial morphology (high) observed across the continent. According to González-José et al. this unexpected combination would be explained if, in the early stages of settlement, the population of the continent was highly diverse morphologically, and maintained continuous gene-flow with Asia (González-José et al. 2008; Azevedo et al. 2011).

A third line of reasoning sees diversity in cranial morphology as a product of non-genetic shape changes during the growth of each individual during its youth (that is, developmental plasticity), under the influence of different environments and/or subsistence strategies. Some authors have suggested that the Amerindian morphology could be the result of adaptation to regular plant cultivation and consumption from the Middle Holocene onwards, either as a result of reduced mechanical stress during mastication (Perez and Monteiro 2009; Perez et al. 2011), or as a result of nutritional differences in diet itself, that is, carbohydrate and protein intake (Menéndez et al. 2014). In a change from past thinking on this, however (Boas 1912; Carlson and Van Gerven 1977), current research has shown that although plastic responses do have localized influence on cranial morphology, this is very limited in the cranium as a whole and across samples taken on a broad geographical scale (Sparks and Jantz 2002; González-José et al. 2005b; Paschetta et al. 2010).

To evaluate these alternative hypotheses fully requires an understanding of the evolutionary nature of cranial morphology. Contrary to standard thinking for most of the twentieth century, there is in fact a close link between cranial morphology and population history (Roseman and Weaver 2007). This association was first recognized by studies demonstrating that craniometric traits, like many other phenotypic traits, are in fact heritable, although some cranial traits more so than others (Carson 2006; Sherwood et al. 2008; Martínez-Abadías et al. 2009). Cranial morphology does, therefore, present a genetic base and can potentially be used as a proxy for ancestry (Cheverud 1988; Roseman and Weaver 2004). This perception has made it possible to extrapolate certain concepts from population genetics and apply them to cranial morphology (Sherwood et al. 2008). As well as statistics such as F_{ST}, a measure of inter population differentiation (Williams-Blangero and Blangero 1989; Relethford 1994; Relethford and Harpending 1994), there are also now techniques for inferring how far natural selection and/or stochastic evolutionary processes can influence cranial morphology (Ackermann and Cheverud 2004). Together, these advances have significantly improved prospects for exploring how diversity in cranial morphology patterns on a global scale, so that it can be compared and contrasted with neutral genetic markers, the markers of ancestry par excellence.

The patterns of global variation in cranial morphology (Relethford 1994, 2002) are very similar to those observed for neutral genetic markers (Lewontin, 1972; Bowcock et al. 1991; Barbujani et al. 1997; Rosenberg et al. 2002): differences between groups account for around 15 per cent of total worldwide variation. Neutral genetic markers (Ramachandran et al. 2005; Liu et al. 2006) and cranial morphology (Manica et al. 2007) both show declining diversity with distance from Africa. Moreover, the genetic architecture that determines cranial morphology appears to be governed, at least to a certain extent, by what is known as an additive polygenetic system (Martínez-Abadías et al. 2009). This means that when two different populations intermix, their hybrid offspring will have cranial morphology intermediate between them, so that it remains possible to recover their population history.

It is important to stress, however, that all evidence in favour of a neutral evolutionary basis for the diversity in cranial morphology among modern human populations seems to hold only across wide geographical ranges. In more localized studies, it has been suggested that selection or environmental plasticity has a more determining role in morphological differentiation (Relethford 2004). Specific studies have shown that some craniometric measurements and anatomical regions may be under long-term selection, in response to climatic conditions, especially in populations adapted to extreme cold (Beals et al. 1984; Hubbe et al. 2009). Significant correlations have also been reported between specific craniometric measurements and environmental factors such as altitude (Guglielmino-Matessi et al. 1979; Rothhammer and Silva 1990) and life-style (Carlson and Van Gerven 1977; González-José et al. 2005b; Paschetta et al. 2010). These may have played a role in how crania became so differentiated across South America and have been taken by some to argue in favour of cranium shape being highly responsive to local environmental conditions.

Whichever of these theories proves to be the best explanation for variation in cranial morphology across South America, the east–west contrast defined by the Andes is most certainly implicated in the differentiation process. For scenarios that emphasize stochastic processes (Powell 2005; Sardi et al. 2005; González-José et al. 2008; Azevedo et al. 2011), the Andes are relevant as a potential barrier to gene flow, creating two semi-independent evolutionary universes within the sub-continent (see also Chapter 3.2). For those who would stress instead the dual input of distinct biological stocks during the initial colonization phase (Neves and Hubbe 2005), the east–west divide could represent different ecological corridors each favoured by the distinctive 'waves' as different dispersal routes. Or, if one favours the importance of developmental plasticity in determining how crania became differentiated across South America, it was ecology and historical contingency that created profound differences in subsistence strategies and diets on both sides of the Andes.

At this point is not possible to discern which of these provides the best explanation, but the craniometric evidence, though scarce, supports the notion that the east–west division that the Andes impose on the continent is crucial to understanding the population structure observed in South America. In future, as more skeletons are retrieved from Amazonia and the corresponding genetic data are made available, we may come to better understand the processes behind the intriguing pattern of cranial differentiation observed across the continent. In particular, we stand to gain a clearer picture of the reality, scale and detail of the apparent Andes–Amazonia divide, and a clearer understanding of how, why and when it came about.

2.3
Deep time and first settlement: What, if anything, can linguistics tell us?

Paul Heggarty

1. Deep time and first settlement

Chapters 1.3 and 3.4 in this book survey what linguistics can and does usefully say on the Andes–Amazonia divide. This chapter bears a sober message also on what it *can't*. It is equally needed, however – and we shall shortly see why – for the avoidance of any doubts across the disciplines, on this touchstone of misconceptions between them.

This chapter's starting point is the same contrast on which Chapters 1.3 and 3.4 are structured: the opposing concepts of a language family, diverging out of a single origin, and a linguistic area, formed by languages converging (partially!) 'out of different origins'. Yet that formulation already raises a nagging question: 'But didn't *all* human languages ultimately start from the same origin, perhaps even long before human expansion out of Africa?' In South America particularly, is it not possible that only a small founder population originally crossed the isthmus of Panama, speaking just one language? In that case, there would originally have been no linguistic divide along the Andes–Amazonia frontier. Or does linguistics tell us that multiple different 'ethno-linguistic' groups entered South America and dispersed by different routes through the continent, establishing a linguistic Andes–Amazonia divide from the very first?

All of this is in fact quite possible. But linguistics – despite many speculative attempts and claims – is simply not able to bear on the first settlement of even this last of the continents to be colonized by *homo sapiens*. There is no real linguistic foundation to the speculative claims, schemas and deep-time 'language' entities that have sometimes been entertained. They are not some 'best guess' that we can go on at this level, even if 'controversial'. They offer nothing valid to go on at all. So one could just simply end the discussion here, were it not for a grave and ongoing interdisciplinary problem.

For over three decades now, many researchers outside linguistics, notably in genetics, *have* listened to one siren song of a purportedly linguistic framework on first settlement, and within it a potential early Andes–Amazonia divide. Greenberg's (1987) *Language in the Americas* interprets certain language data as constituting evidence that all languages of South America (and most of North and Central America) can be proven to descend from a single source, 'Proto-Amerind'. For the Andes–Amazonia question in particular, within Greenberg's purported 'Amerind' family are also his purported sub-branches, which risk being taken to support such a divide. One of those branches, indeed, he names specifically 'Andean'.

From the first, linguists have retorted, and repeatedly demonstrated, that Greenberg's 'data' provide no such *evidence* at all, as we shall see in the next part of this chapter. Linguists, then, immediately saw through the methodological deception of Greenberg's 'mass comparison' approach – or 'megalo-comparison', as Matisoff (1990) dubbed it. Frustratingly, though, many scholars in other disciplines did succumb to the temptation of a grandiose, 'big picture' pigeon-holing of all indigenous populations of the Americas, not least where it provided helpful myths upon which they could build. In genetics particularly, broad-scale publications on the indigenous Americas still routinely identify and group their genetic samples by Greenberg's constructs. Even high-profile recent papers as Reich et al. (2012), Rasmussen et al. (2014) and Moreno-Mayar, Potter et al. (2018), all published in *Nature*, use Greenberg's purported 'Andean', 'Equatorial-Tucanoan', 'Northern Amerind' and 'Central Amerind' categories, for example.

These are not the big-picture reference points that many geneticists imagine, but mere faces in the fire. They are subjective interpretations proposed by one scholar, and decried as vacuous by the rest of the discipline. Even these second-tier branches in Greenberg's schema are not valid language families. What coherence they may have is on a different level, obvious from the very names Greenberg gave them. *Andean, Equatorial, Northern, Central* – these are essentially just *geographical* groupings. For the challenge of working out whether linguistics aligns with the Andes–Amazonia divide, the first two are especially circular: purported linguistic entities, but actually geographical ones. If geneticists, then, find parallels in their own data, that is no support for the linguistic claims, but for the known relationship frequently found between genetics and *geography*. It is frustrating how many genetics papers could actually make considerably *more* of their findings, if only they switched to standard, meaningful language classifications, such as Campbell (1997) for the Americas, or the worldwide *Glottolog* freely available online (Hammarström et al. 2019: https://glottolog.org). It goes without saying that there is no trace of Greenberg's chimeras in those standard classifications.

But how come linguistics can say so little of deep time? Chapter 1.2 set out how the discipline can be particularly valuable in South America, where the historical record is so shallow. That is because well beyond just the five centuries or so of history here, linguistics works at its highest level of detail and confidence back a few millennia more. What dictates this timeframe, over which linguistics is most applicable, are the typical natural rates of *change* in language. Change, and thus language divergence, happen fast enough that they give high resolution over this timescale of just a few millennia. One cannot have it both ways, however. For that natural rate is so fast that after much longer periods, so many changes have built up that one can no longer see through them all to whatever the original, deepest linguistic signal may have been.

All disciplines and individual methods can have their limits. Much of the archaeological discussion in this book mentions the paucity of the Early Holocene archaeological record across the Andes–Amazonia divide, particularly in Amazonia (see Chapters 1.1 and 2.1). Radiocarbon dating offers a more specific methodological analogy. For ultimately the decay of carbon-14 isotope leaves so little left that by 50,000 BP the method comes up against its intrinsic limits. In comparative linguistics, even though different aspects of language change at different paces, beyond a certain time-depth limit, *none* of the signals that can firmly establish *family relatedness* survives enough.

The natural pace of language change – and thus signal 'decay' – is so fast that any surviving traces of an ultimate common origin progressively fade. An absolute cut-off date is hard to pin down, for it depends on a number of variables, but the contexts in South America are very far from the ideal. Unlike in Eurasia, where ancient texts gave a head start of up to four millennia into the past, in South America no (decipherable) ancient writing existed that could take back the starting point for the decay of the linguistic signal here. And the crucial comparative data needed have been decimated by the irrecoverable extinction of so many indigenous language lineages after 1492 (see Dixon and Aikhenvald 1999, 19), driven not least by the pandemics unleashed by Old World pathogens, with their devastating demographic consequences (Chapter 1.1). Estimates therefore vary, but there is consensus that certainly by a time-depth of ten millennia or so, so little trace is left of whatever deep origins a language may have had that the signal starts to become indistinguishable from the background level of resemblances between languages that are inevitable by statistical chance. Even in South America, and even assuming the most recent timeframe postulated for first settlement, that lies already significantly beyond this ceiling on the ability of linguistics to recover the past. So there is no real prospect of recovering anything much of linguistic patterns at the time of the first peopling of the Andes or of Amazonia. In fact, as noted in Chapter 3.4, it turns out that linguistics has not been able to establish any language families in South America that might approach ten millennia. The families that are detected here began to diverge much more recently, and Chapter 3.4 finds a significant contrast between the Andes and Amazonia in just how recently.

We can now return to our original puzzle: 'But didn't *all* human languages ultimately start from the same origin?' All that is missing is just a key qualification to any language classification. This qualification is so intrinsic to historical linguistics that it is generally just left tacit – but with understandably misleading consequences for other disciplines. Linguistic texts (including the various chapters here) normally simply state that given languages are not related to each other, and that their lineages are independent of each other in origin. The tacit, missing qualification is that they are unrelated and independent *as far back as linguistic methodology can detect relationships of common descent at all*. Such statements are understood to hold for all practical intents and purposes, or more precisely, for any attempt to use linguistics to contribute to understanding prehistory. To that end, 'unrelated' means only that two languages (or families) do not go back to the same origin at least *within* the last ten millennia or so. For otherwise, that relationship should be detectable – although in South America the visibility limit may be even shallower here, given the unfavourable contexts described above.

Full details on the inapplicability of linguistics to the question of first settlement of the Americas can be found in Goddard and Campbell (1994). Wider discussions oriented for non-linguists are Heggarty and Renfrew (2014a, 25–8), or specifically for South America, Heggarty and Renfrew (2014b, 1347–51).

Beyond the question of first settlement, this chapter has three remaining tasks. Section 2 below justifies the rejection of the methodology behind Greenberg's 'Amerind', 'Andean', 'Equatorial' and such like. The lessons there then serve also in section 3, to row back from various other speculative, deep-time claims for deep relationships of common language origin, specifically across the Andes–Amazonia divide. Finally, section 4 looks at attempts to uncover deep language relationships through correspondences not in specific sounds and meanings, but in more general and abstract characteristics of language structure. Again, we explore the limitations that necessarily attend those ambitions.

2. What is so wrong with Greenberg's 'Amerind', 'Andean' and 'Equatorial'?

For disciplines other than linguistics, it can be disconcerting to see the vehemence with which linguists have rejected Greenberg's 'Amerind', especially when it so temptingly offers the deep-time, big-picture perspective that suits others' deep-time research purposes so well. What could really be so invalid with the method Greenberg employed? Does it not appear, on the surface at least, reminiscent of how historical linguists usually seem to establish language relatedness: by comparing words from different languages in similar meanings? And if enough words look sufficiently similar, then do they not demonstrate that those languages are related? Didn't Greenberg just take this to a new level, the entire continental scale of the Americas, daring to perceive links that narrower, regionalized studies had simply failed to notice until then?

That beguiling sell has been unmasked by a rollcall of prominent figures in comparative and historical linguistics, ever since Greenberg's *Language in the Americas* first appeared. Outside linguistics, however, their publications remain less known than Greenberg's work itself. So this section will attempt to warn off unsuspecting disciplines in the terms perhaps clearest to them, by setting out just how invalid is Greenberg's entire methodology. (It is not at all, of course, how historical linguistics actually goes about establishing relationships of linguistic descent.)

For a start, there is immediate methodological concern with Greenberg's cavalier approach to the data. He reassures that 'the method of multilateral comparison is so powerful that it will give reliable results even with the poorest of materials' (Greenberg 1987, 29). In fact, so great is the power of the method that it can *always* be made to give positive results, that is, to find large numbers of 'matches' between any desired language families in the world (see below). Greenberg took this 'power', moreover, specifically to exonerate using 'the poorest of materials'. As Adelaar (1989, 252) observes of the data quality for Quechua, for example: 'the number of erroneous forms probably exceeds that of the correct forms'. It can even be unclear which languages the 'data' are supposedly from. Experts in Quechua are rightly bemused by Greenberg's multiple references to a so-called 'Huanacucho' dialect. As Adelaar (1989, 252) puts it: 'Is this to be interpreted as the Ayacucho dialect, spoken by more than a million people and not mentioned even once ... or is it the undocumented (and probably hypothetical) Huamachuco dialect ...?'

We focus here only on the single most basic methodological issue, which can be seen grossly in statistical terms. Necessarily, lookalike words can just happen. Spanish *mucho* and English *much* do not in fact come from the same source, and they resemble each other purely by chance. They are evidence of nothing, in this case. So in order to use apparent similarities in sound and meaning to prove that languages are related, it is crucial to exclude statistically that they could be lookalikes just by chance. (One also needs to exclude other sources of lookalikes: sound symbolism like *shush*, near-universal nursery words like *mama* and, above all, loanwords. Greenberg makes no real attempt to exclude any of these.)

This, indeed, is where lies the most fundamental error of all in Greenberg's 'multilateral comparison' methodology. For in the name of big-picture scale, Greenberg so relaxes the criteria for a match, on all levels, that the statistical effect, far from excluding chance, is exactly the opposite: opening the floodgates so widely that 'matches' are statistically *guaranteed*. His 'method' is a machine for generating false positives, as follows.

Firstly, matches are drawn not between individual pairs of languages A and B, but between any two languages within large pools of languages. For 'Amerind', the pool effectively extends to the vast majority of indigenous languages in the Americas. Moreover, the small subsets of languages in which 'matches' are reported vary hugely from word to word. This multiplies enormously the probability of finding lookalikes by chance.

Secondly, on the level of sound, the criteria are likewise far too lax. As Goddard (1987, 657) points out, for Greenberg 'acceptable similarity ... is often a match of only a single consonant', citing examples such as *mye:w* 'road' matched with *ma* 'go', or *-sit-* with *ʔas* for 'foot'. Greenberg abandons any requirement for regular, recurrent patterns, makes free recourse to misleading spellings, and in any case, as Adelaar (1989, 252) observes, 'most examples are erroneous (e.g. Quechua *ruk* "to see" …, presumably meant to represent the verb *riku*-)'. Again, this methodological laxity hugely raises the probability of chance lookalikes.

Thirdly, on the level of meaning, comparison is made not between one word in language A and one in language B, but between potentially dozens of words with even the faintest semantic connection (and across any of hundreds of languages). Greenberg reports 'matches' between words that mean variously *night, excrement* and *grass*; or between *back, wing, shoulder, hand, buttocks* and *behind* (Goddard 1987, 657). If the desired sound string in *bitter* in one language is not found in *bitter* in another language, then a match is accepted also with sounds in *to rot, sour, sweet, ripe, spleen* or *gall*, while sounds in *body* can match with any of *belly, heart, skin, meat, be greasy, fat, deer*, and so on (Campbell 1988, 600). This too multiplies the pool of possible words for any match, and with it the probability of finding lookalikes by chance.

Under these criteria, pronouncing 'matches' becomes utterly subjective, and turns into a self-fulfilling prophesy. Critics have repeatedly shown how the combined result of these relaxed criteria is that multilateral comparison can produce 'matches' between any languages selected at random (see Campbell 1988, for example, on Finnish with Greenberg's 'Penutian'). Or for a new illustration, take some colour terms in English and compare them with Cuzco Quechua: /ɹɛd/ with /puka/; /gɹiːn/ with /q'umiɾ/; and /jɛləʊ/ with /q'iʎu/. None appear to match (and they are indeed all unrelated). But if we relax all our criteria, then we can instead propose 'matches' between Ayacucho ('Huanacucho'?) Quechua *jellu* (in Spanish spelling) and *yellow*, between *(j)omer* and *emer(ald)*, and even between *(p)uca* and *ochre*. If this seems fanciful nonsense, then of course it is – and it matches the impression one has as an informed linguist perusing much of the supposed 'data' in Greenberg's *Language in the Americas*.

In short, wherever one might wish to find false positives, multilateral comparison can oblige. There is a great deal more that is wrong, invalid and beguiling in Greenberg's approach than can be said here. (And there is far more to the methodology of historical linguistics than just comparing across languages the phonetic forms of their words for the same meanings.) Further dismantling of Greenberg's chimera of a big-picture linguistic prehistory of the Americas can be found, *inter alia*, in Campbell (1988), Adelaar (1989), Matisoff (1990), McMahon and McMahon (1995) and Campbell and Poser (2008).

3. Other linguistic misreadings on an Andes–Amazonia divide

Here is also the place to forewarn of certain other, not dissimilar dangers for the linguistic assessment of an Andes–Amazonia divide. In older linguistic literature, one finds a series of speculative hypotheses that would link individual languages (or families) from different sides of that divide, in claiming to detect between them a signal of a deep, long-range relationship of common descent. One such suggestion is that the Uro family of the Andes, for instance, is related to the Pano family of Amazonia (Fabre 1995). Chapter 4.2 in this book takes up that particular speculation, based on similarly lax methodological criteria to Greenberg, and illustrates, in the detail of that case too, just how poor the methodology behind it really is.

In other cases, supposed shared linguistic origins between the Andes and Amazonia result from a straight misunderstanding between the disciplines, a confusion across the fundamental contrast in linguistics between language divergence and convergence (see Chapters 1.3 and 3.4). Hornborg (2005, 605, endnote 49), for instance, reports that 'Torero (2002, 488–92) suggests that Puquina … and Uru … both share an Arawakan derivation'. But Puquina and Uru are not related to each other in any case, so they cannot be derived in common from Arawak. And what Torero actually refers to here is just contact and convergence, not common 'derivation' or origin in Arawak. (On the Puquina case, see also Chapter 4.1.) Linguists themselves, like Torero in this case, sometimes muddy the waters, by talking loosely in terms of a 'contact relationship', when the ambiguous term 'relationship' is best reserved uniquely for common ancestry within a language family.

Many a misconception about language relationships goes back to this same general error. Certain linguistic parallels are often misread as evidence of a supposed deep-time language family and divergence event, when the linguistic signal concerned in fact results from and attests to <u>con</u>vergence processes instead, often much more recent. One such discredited claim is that by Büttner (1983) for a supposed 'Quechumara' *family* uniting Quechua and Aymara, when the parallels he identifies were actually the result of intense convergence (Mannheim 1991; Torero 2002). Yet despite two decades of dismissal by linguists of the Andes, when Diamond and Bellwood (2003, Figure 3) applied to South America the hypothesis that major world language *families* were spread by farming, they nonetheless invoked the chimera 'Quechumara' *non*-family as if in support.

Claims for such 'deep' relationships pepper the older linguistic literature, particularly during and around the 1960s. At that time, enthusiasm remained fresh for staking bold, far-reaching claims upon all too superficial comparisons of just minimal lists of words. The consensus methodology of comparative linguistics had not yet been applied to many indigenous language families of South America (even for Quechua, not until the mid-1960s). As those rigorous analyses did gather pace over subsequent decades, almost all of the old claims duly fell by the wayside. Very few hypotheses of common descent of languages of the Andes and of Amazonia are even entertained today, and only where a more solid case has been made for a potential connection. See Chapter 4.1 for a case-study.

Only one significant case *has* been made with a methodology that is fairly orthodox: by Rodrigues (2009), for a hypothetical 'Jê–Tupi–Carib'. But the data invoked are extremely sparse, and this proposal remains firmly outside standard classification. Tellingly, older speculative proposals had claimed to relate Tupí to Arawak instead, and Jê and Carib to Panoan. So mutual incompatibility alone entails that a majority of such claims must inevitably be wrong – if not indeed all of them. And for our purposes, even if Rodrigues were right, this would only reinforce the Andes–Amazonia divide, for even his vast 'Jê–Tupi–Carib' would obey it.

4. Alternative linguistic signals on deep prehistory?

We remain with the limitation, then, that beyond a threshold of ten millennia or so, we cannot trace language relationships back any further through sound-to-meaning correspondences. But might some other type of language take their place, to push back the threshold deeper into prehistory? In particular, one current in linguistics looks hopefully to structural characteristics – of the type discussed in Chapter 1.2. As an example, how does a language put together the basic components in a sentence, particularly the main v̲erb, its s̲ubject and o̲bject? English follows the order svo, but most languages in South America use sov (https://sails.clld.org/parameters/NP2#5). Such fundamental contrasts in how languages structure their grammatical systems have long been taken to define fundamental 'types' of language, as in some sense intrinsic, deep-seated characteristics of a language. With that, might they also be unusually stable over long time-periods, and thus potential indicators of language relationships deeper than even ten millennia or so?

Nichols (1992) marked the first major attempt to identify which structural features might be so stable. More systematic and wider-scale research is now possible thanks to major comparative databases such as the *World Atlas of Language Structures Online* (Dryer and Haspelmath 2013b, http://wals.info), the *South American Indigenous Language Structures* database (SAILS) (Muysken, Hammarström, Krasnoukhova et al. 2014, the data source for Chapter 3.4), and the *GramBank* database now nearing completion (Harald Hammarström, personal communication). For all their value for research in linguistic typology, however, the aspiration to use these databases to demonstrate deep language relationships still faces existential challenges. Each abstract, structural criterion allows of only a small set of possible answers, often just two: does a language have nasal vowels or not, for example, or does it put the adjective before a noun, or after? With so few options to choose from, hundreds if not thousands of languages around the world, irrespective of whether they are related or not, necessarily share the values they have on such criteria. These characteristics thus offer little statistical power to exclude chance as an explanation for the parallels. Moreover, many structural characteristics are not fully independent of each other in any case, further reducing their diagnostic power.

Recall too, from Chapter 1.2, that many structural features are well known to pattern geographically. That is, they are susceptible to convergence between neighbouring languages, irrespective of whether they are related to each other or not. Attempts are made to try to 'control for geography' statistically, to hone down to parallels that might result from deep relatedness instead, but they generally fail to convince. Indeed, the search for the methodological holy grail of structural characteristics that are deeply stable is proving increasingly frustrating, even to its followers. Many of the candidates in fact turn out to be considerably *less* stable than even sound-to-meaning correspondences in core vocabulary (Greenhill et al. 2017). Meanwhile, there are good grounds to consider 'deep' features actually to be positively unreliable as indicators of language relatedness. Stable they may be, but in almost the opposite sense. When speakers switch to another language, not least of a totally different family, the 'deepest' characteristics of their original native tongue can be precisely the ones they retain. That is, they carry those characteristics over into how they speak the new language that they are ('imperfectly') learning. Far from keeping in step with deep relatedness, then, these characteristics intrude into un̲related languages (see Heggarty 2017, 169–71). South America itself provides plenty of examples. Many languages distinguish two forms of the pronoun *we*. Cuzco Quechua, for instance, uses *nuqayku̲* for *I + you* (inclusive *we*), but *nuqakuna̲* for *I + other(s), not̲ you* (exclusive *we*). This structural characteristic is precisely the one that Nichols (1992, 209) ranks as the 'most stable' of all those she analyses worldwide. Yet within even the shallow Quechua family, while Cuzco Quechua does make a distinction, Ecuador Quechua does not.

In short, no deep-time language relationship has ever been proven on the basis of structural characteristics. Nor, given the considerations above, is it ever likely to be. The optimism for 'deep' characteristics always comes back up against the reality, that it falls foul of the basic opposition that has always defined and demarcated comparative linguistics into two complementary fields (Heggarty 2017, 140–3). Historical linguistics employs those concrete, sound-based forms of language data that *are* amenable to proving language relationships. Language universals and typology studies the more abstract, structural characteristics that have so much to say on aspects of language *other* than relatedness. New structural databases like SAILS are a great advance in many ways, as we shall see for our Andes–Amazonia question in Chapter 3.4. But they are unlikely to prove any new, deep families on either side of the Andes–Amazonia divide, or spanning it.

2.4
Early social complexity in northern Peru and its Amazonian connections

Peter Kaulicke

This chapter aims to summarise the main ecological and socio-cultural factors in a region where archaeological research had long been largely neglected in favour of other more southerly regions, where early complexity is currently assumed to have originated. The region concerned falls essentially within the modern departments of Piura, Cajamarca, Lambayeque and Amazonas in northern Peru. The main topics addressed are the particular ecological background in this region and its relevance for early connections between Pacific coast and Amazon basin, as well as cultural and technological transfers.

Ecological distinctiveness

The Piura department is home to the broadest section of the Peruvian coastal strip, more than 100 km wide, compared with only about 20 km to the south. Here is also the narrowest and lowest part of the Andean highlands, known as the Huancabamba deflection (Reynel et al. 2013, 175–8, Figures 15–17). This deflection is formed by the Huancabamba river as it joins the Chamaya river. As it turns northwards, the Chamaya widens before joining the main Marañón. Another relatively large river valley is the Quebrada Jaén, which meets the Marañón at Bellavista. From there to the north the Marañón forms, together with the Chinchipe and Utcubamba rivers, a large flood plain (about 25 km by 4 km) at c. 400 m. The Utcubamba forms a connected flood plain of its own, nurtured by the numerous smaller rivers that join it near the modern town of Bagua. The northern part of this region is the gateway to the Amazonian lowlands (see Figure 2.4.1).

The coast here abuts onto three transition zones in the Pacific Ocean, ranging from temperate waters to the south, through a transition between temperate and tropical in the centre, to a tropical sea to the north. The region hosts a suite of some 17 ecological landscapes from west to east (More Cahuapaza et al.

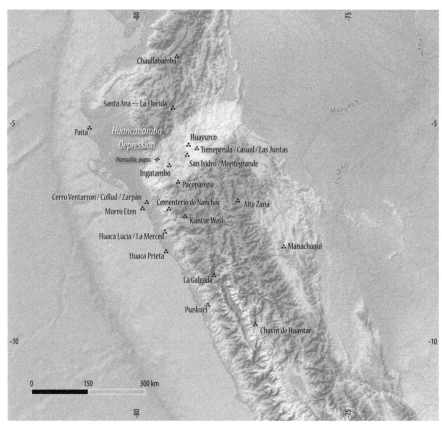

Figure 2.4.1   Archaeological sites mentioned in the chapter, and the
Huancabamba Depression. © Peter Kaulicke and Paul Heggarty.

2014): islands, mangrove relics, wetlands, various types of dry forest on the coast
and lower slopes, in the highlands and in inter-Andean valleys, highland shrubs,
humid cloud forests, and high grasslands (*páramo*). While many of these have
been severely reduced by various anthropogenic impacts, they still maintain a
bewildering array of endemic plants and animals, some of which are characteristic also of the eastern Andean slopes. So there are primates (*Allouata palliata*,
Cebus albifrons), peccaries (*Pecari tajacu*), ocelots (*Leopardus pardalis*), jaguars
(*Panthera onca*) and *Boa constrictors* living in the tropical Pacific forest in the
Tumbes region, as well as crocodiles (*Cocodrylus acutus*) in the mangrove environments (Reynel et al. 2013, 103–4), and most of them are also to be found in
the dry forests of Piura. Wild cats like the jaguar, puma (*Puma concolor*), jaguarundi (*Herpailurus yaguarondi*), ocelot, oncilla (*Leopardus tigrinus*) and margay
(*Leopardus wiedii*) are sympatric in this region and once lived from sea level to
high altitudes (Sunquist and Sunquist 2002). In other woodlands, such as the
humid cloud forests, similar animals are also to be found in the more easterly

Amazonian regions, including the mountain tapir (*Tapirus pinchaque*), spectacled bear (*Tremarctus ornatus*), sloths (*Choloepus hoffmanni*) and primates (*Alouatta seniculus, Cebus albifrons*). Extraordinarily high numbers of bird species and vascular plants (Reynel et al. 2013; Barthlott et al. 2005) contribute to the extremely high ecological diversity of this region.

While there are many endemisms, this short list indicates that even the evidently impoverished modern fauna and flora here share elements with the eastern edge of the Andes and with Amazonia, over a distance of less than 250 km from coast to the Amazon lowlands. There is also the extraordinary phenomenon of coastal dry forests penetrating into the highlands as far as the Marañón basin, while at higher altitudes Amazonia-like forests reach the headwaters of the coastal rivers (see Figures 2.4.2 and 2.4.3). This situation differs markedly from central and southern Peru, from the Jequetepeque southwards, where the coast–highland connections are more restricted without known direct eastern counterparts, with the exception of the Huánuco basin in the central eastern Andes (for climate changes during the Pleistocene and early and middle Holocene, see Weng et al. 2006; Netherly 2011a; Lodeho 2012).

The archaeological evidence

As mentioned above, this northern region has not been the object of intensive archaeological research until recently. Aside from some sporadic early efforts, only since the 1970s has the region come into closer focus. In what follows, I consider an archaeological timeframe from the Final Pleistocene and Final Formative (late Holocene, c. 14,000 BP) up to 2200 BP.

Evidence dating to the Final Pleistocene is restricted to slightly more southerly coastal environments in the Chicama (Chauchat 1992; Briceño Rosario 2010), Zaña, and Jequetepeque valleys, where it is known as the 'El Palto' phase (13,800 to 9800 BP) (Dillehay 2011, 15), although sporadic finds are also known from coastal Piura (Chauchat and Zevallos Quiñones 1980), the Cajamarca highlands (Cárdich 1994; Narváez 2007; Lodeho 2012) and the eastern Andes (Manachaqui) (Church 1996; Lodeho 2012). The absence of any evidence in other areas, including the Amazonian lowlands in the Bagua region and in the inter-Andean valleys, should not be imputed to the absence of human occupation but, rather, to a lack of research.

The following early Holocene occupations on the coast and in the adjacent highlands are collectively known as 'Paijanian' (or Early and Late Paijan sub-phase) (13,000 to 9800 BP) (Dillehay 2011; Briceño Rosario 2010, 2011; Lodeho 2012; Maggard 2013). While broad-spectrum hunting and gathering is prevalent, there is some indication of semi-sedentism and possibly some incipient horticulture during the late Paiján, as evidenced by a cultigen (*Cucurbita moschata*) found from about 10,000 BP in dry grass and forest micro-environments (Maggard and Dillehay 2011).

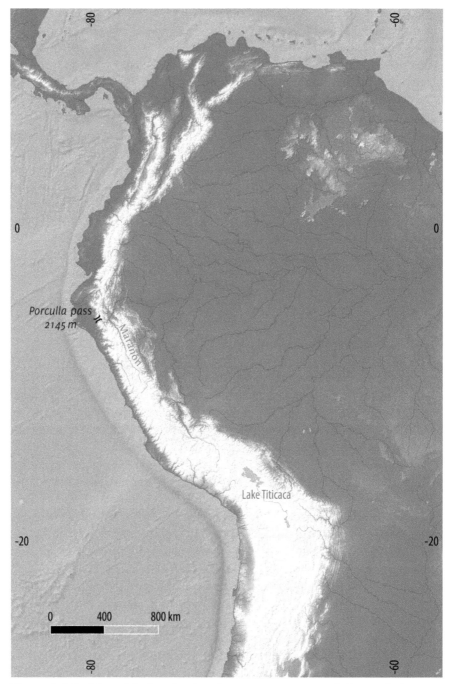

Figure 2.4.2 Map with elevation bands set to contrast areas below and above 2,300 m, to reveal the Huancabamba Depression in northern Peru. © Paul Heggarty.

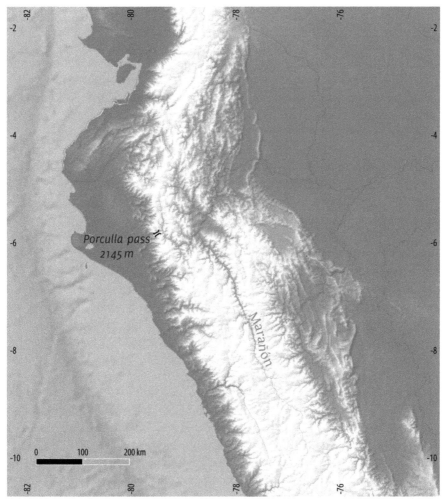

Figure 2.4.3 Map with elevation bands set to contrast areas below and above 2,300 m, to reveal the Huancabamba Depression in northern Peru (closer view). © Paul Heggarty.

In the Zaña valley the following phase is of particular importance, as it relates to the earliest evidence of cultigens in the Central Andes. In the 'Las Pircas' phase (9800 to 7800 BP), clusters of small sites with hut structures, associated gardens and middens (with signs of possible anthropophagic practices) are found in what was, up until the nineteenth century, humid forest. Fauna typical of this habitat include tropical insects, boas and jaguarundi. Garden furrows contained quartz crystals, ammonite fossils, a jaguarundi bone and stingray spines, probably as garden magic. Manioc (*Manihot* sp.), peanuts (*Arachis hypogaea*), a quinoa-like chenopod, beans (*Phaseolus* sp.) and the pacae fruit tree (*Inga* sp.) seem to have been cultivated here (Rossen 2011). Piperno (2011b) relates these plants with those from sites of similar age in Panama and the Colombian Amazon. While faunal evidence shows connections with the coast, these plants hint instead at long-distance contacts to the north-east (see Chapter 2.1). The Huancabamba corridor could have served as a convenient entry route, though contemporaneous sites are not known from the eastern part of that corridor or from further to the east. In Piperno's words: 'Our first farmers were *smaller-scale horticulturists* growing a variety of seed, root, and tree crops in small – often home garden-plots; they continued to hunt, gather and fish while living in small household clusters … Today in the tropical forest it is still easy to find examples of people who practise similar kinds of horticulture while hunting and fishing, and who derive many of their calories from cultivated and domesticated foodstuffs' (Piperno 2011b, 282).

The following 'Tierra Blanca' phase (7800 to 5000 BP) in the Zaña valley saw the appearance of new technologies, burial practices, increased food production, water management, and mound building (Stackelbeck and Dillehay 2011). Houses, previously circular, were now rectangular instead. Alongside the earlier cultigens, coca (*Erythroxylum coca novogratense*) was now grown, a plant which in wild form appears on the slopes of the eastern Andes, while cotton (*Gossypium barbadense*) was domesticated on the coast. The Cementerio de Nanchoc (CA-09-04), which dates from the late Las Pircas to the end of Tierra Blanca phase (Dillehay et al. 2011), consists of two low mounds, built in three stages, and a workshop. This is a very early example of public architecture used and maintained by local residents over extended time periods. Huaca Prieta in the Chicama valley also shows early mound building between about 7500 and 6540 BP. Here too this marks the starting point of successive building phases up to about 4000 BP (Dillehay et al. 2011). While Nanchoc lies in a dry forest environment, Huaca Prieta forms part of a complex of wetland, semi-arid lowlands and coastal estuarine and marine settings. Here the earliest grown plants are squash (*Cucurbita moschata*), lima bean (*Phaseolus vulgaris*) and avocado (*Persea americana*), to which were added, from 7000 to 6000 BP, chilli pepper, gourds, maize and a long lists of others, including those mentioned above for the Zaña valley sites.

In our region of interest, richer data are known from the Final Archaic (Late Preceramic). Between 4500 and 4000 BP several mounds with monumental architecture (ceremonial centres) are known from Cerro Ventarrón (Alva Meneses 2012), in the Lambayeque valley, Ingatambo in the Huancabamba valley (Yamamoto 2010, 2012), Pacopampa (Pandanche) (Kaulicke 1982), Santa Ana (La Florida) in the Ecuadorian upper Chinchipe area (Valdez 2008), and Montegrande in the city of Jaen (Olivera 2014) (see map in Yamamoto 2012, Figure 3). Three of these are of particular importance: Cerro Ventarrón, Santa Ana (La Florida) and Montegrande.

Cerro Ventarrón stands in the Reque river valley, to the south of modern Chiclayo and about 20 km north of the Zaña valley. The course of the Reque connects to the important ceremonial center of Pacopampa in the highland cloud forest, which in turn is close to the Huancabamba valley and Ingatambo (about 40 km distant) (see map in Yamamoto 2012, Figure 2). The shore is also nearby, only 22 km away (see Alva 2012). Cerro Ventarrón thus occupies a central location, enhanced by impressive natural rock formations relevant to a ritualized landscape into which the architecture is incorporated, and which gave the site its name (Alva Meneses 2012, 16–17). It consists of a single complex of monumental architecture in the plain and on the nearby slopes of Cerro Ventarrón, with a series of contemporaneous compounds that together cover a total area of approximately 30 ha. The main section is a platform building integrated into an isolated rock formation, in an area originally covered by dry forest and wetlands. It measures about 150 by 60 m and was built in five main phases, with superimposed buildings characterized by platforms, stairways, enclosures on the top level, and aggregated smaller buildings in a south-west to north-east orientation. The enclosures are decorated with reliefs and/or paintings of zoomorphic motifs interpreted as opossum, fish (phase 1), a deer hunt (phase 2) and other, geometric designs. Offerings in the form of caches left in some of the enclosures give interesting hints at contacts with other regions. Thus a decorated pectoral in crescent shape in the central enclosure of building phase 2 is made of the pearl oyster *Pinctata mazatlanica*, found only in tropical waters. A shell trumpet (*Tricornis peruviana*) also from tropical Pacific waters was found in the same enclosure. Finally, as a closing ritual from the same context, a burial of macaw (*Ara arauna*) or guacamayo hints at contacts with the Amazonian lowlands. The bird was adorned with a necklace of green stone pendants. In phase 3 another burial of a monkey (*Cebus albifrons*) and an otter (*Lontra felina*) relate these offerings to both the tropical forest and ocean shore. Other deposits are probably evidence of feasting with large amounts of burnt fish bones of various species from both the ocean and river, ducks and other aquatic birds, deer and jaguarundi, as well as chilli pepper, squash, beans, avocado, lúcuma, and small amounts of maize (Alva Meneses 2012; see Vásquez and Rosales Tham 2014). This impressive architectural and contextual evidence suggest widespread connections and evident ritualized power at an early stage of cultural development. The presence of animals treated in such special ways not only hints at connections with the Amazonian east, but also that they may have been kept as pets (macaw, monkey, and perhaps jaguarundi). A burial of a macaw was also found at San Isidro, an early site in Jaen (Olivera 2014, Figure 119).

Santa Ana (La Florida) Palanda is a site of about 1 ha in the upper Chinchipe valley, at about 1050 m. It consists of a large sunken circular plaza and circular houses to the northeast and southwest (5 to 12 m in diameter). To the east of the plaza stands an 80 m² circular structure with containing walls forming a spiral. The presence of a structure on top, and of hearths and elite burial contexts, have led to this being identified as a temple. All the buildings were made of river cobbles topped with *bahareque* walls, and all date to c. 4500 BP. Several funerary contexts were found in the centre of the 'temple' structure, in the form of a chamber at a depth of 2.3 m which contained a *Strombus* conch-shell trumpet, a necklace of turquoise pendants and hundreds of small pearls of the same material, eight pottery vessels, three polished and decorated stone bowls, a small lithic mortar, and hundreds of pearls of turquoise and pseudo-malachite at a deeper level. Guffroy (2008, 892) quotes for this tomb a ^{14}C date of 3700 BP (uncalibrated), which would make it a younger intrusion. Four associated burial structures, with similar but unspecified objects, complete the funerary area (Valdez 2008, 2014; Valdez et al. 2005). Valdez (2008, 880) compares the designs on some of the stone bowls with textile motifs from Huaca Prieta and La Galgada in northern Peru.

A similar circular structure was excavated at Montegrande in the modern town of Jaén, though no ^{14}C dates are yet available and most of the human burials are probably later (Olivera 2014), with ceramic sequences spanning the Early to Late Formative. A similar elite context is still missing, and the accompanying spectacular objects from Palanda were not found. Despite these limiting factors, both sites should be connected culturally and chronologically.

Other sites are less well known because they have been covered by later architecture, but they do often show a remarkable continuity of occupation: Ingatambo (4500 to 2550 BP) (Yamamoto 2010), Pacopampa (with Pandanche) (4400 to 2000 BP) (Kaulicke 1982; Seki et al. 2010). Further to the south, Kuntur Wasi (with Cerro Blanco 5000 to 2050 BP) (Onuki 1995; Inokuchi 2010) boasts a similar occupation span. The densities and complexities of these sites seem to differ through time and space, however. Early Formative sites in the region thus seem to be scarce and relatively small, although this might be a false impression due to the lack of systematic surveys and excavations. But ceramics similar to those from Pandanche are to be found at Ingatambo, in the Bagua region and in the Huallaga basin (Manachaqui near the Marañón basin, Church 1996; Church and von Hagen 2008) suggesting long-distance contacts, particularly within the eastern and north-eastern Andes. Further south, meanwhile, from the Casma to the Jequetepeque valleys, the situation is much more involved, with the Casma valley characterized by complex and monumental architecture, and the Jequetepeque valley hosting another dense occupation including minor centres, that have been relatively well studied (for a synthesis see Kaulicke 2010b, 394–6).

The situation changes during the Middle and Late Formative (c. 3200 to 2500 BP), when monumental architecture and (ceremonial) centres appear across the whole area. In the Lambayeque valley several sites are known, such as Collud and Zarpán (Alva Meneses 2012), Huaca Lucía and La Merced (Shimada et al. 1983) in dry forest environments, as well as Morro Eten (Elera Arévalo 1980) and others near the shore, which take the form of large cemeteries. Meanwhile, earlier sites such as the abandoned Cerro Ventarrón were used intensively for funerary purposes (Alva Meneses 2012). The ground plans with central monumental staircases repeat a pattern known from the Cupisnique area to the south and east (Pacopampa). Collud has a monumental staircase and a well-preserved polychrome mural with Cupisnique-like motifs, and burial contexts with ceramics from the Middle and Late Formative, unfortunately not yet dated by ^{14}C. Further material from looted contexts between the Jequetepeque and Lambayeque rivers has been published by Alva (1986). This pottery is rather varied, but its distribution patterns have not been studied seriously. Little is known about the exchange of ceramics within the region of primary interest to the present volume, although there is some evidence of long-distance connections to the Bagua region during the Late Formative (Elera Arévalo 1980, Figures 44–7). Elite burials are known from Piura to Jequetepeque, but only those from Kuntur Wasi have been excavated scientifically (Kuntur Wasi phase, Late Formative). These are of great importance as they reveal long-distance contacts with modern Bolivia (El Sapo sodalite mine near La Paz), while silver ornaments and some of the ceramic vessels suggest contact with Chaullabamba (south highland Ecuador) (Tellenbach 1998, 119–20, Plates 177–9). Elite burials seem to have been looted in the Bagua region (also with gold sodalite pearls, Olivera 1998, 111, Figure 9; for gold objects, see Alva 1992, 62–4, Plates 32–4), and show stylistic parallels with the Jequetepeque valley. Apparently, many similar tombs were found in the Lambayeque valley (Lothrop 1941 [Chongoyape]; Alva Meneses 2012, Figure 34 [Zarpán]).

Further north a sharp difference is noted between the archaeological records of the lower and upper Piura Valley. For the lower reaches no monumental architecture is reported, and ceramics are distinct from those further up the valley, known as the Paita tradition (Lanning 1963), although pottery of this tradition was nonetheless widely distributed. It is found in Ñañañique (upper Piura, see below), Catamayo, the Loja province of highland Ecuador (Guffroy 1987, 2008), and probably in Bagua (Shady 1971, 1987, 1999). In the upper Piura valley, several sites with monumental architecture date from the Middle to Late Formative (c. 3150 to 2450 BP; for site locations see Guffroy 1994, Figure 2.4). The best-known and probably most extensive of these is Cerro Ñañañique in the modern town of Chulucanas. A later component is La Encantada (c. 2400 to 2200 BP). Three superimposed platforms were built at the foot of the Ñañañique hill, with significant buildings on top in Late Formative times (Panecillo) (c. 7000 m^2). The major structure (47 by 35 m) is a symmetrically arranged room complex with small staircases and columns with *kincha* walls. The architecture seems to be stimulated by southern models, for example at Santa Lucía in the Lambayeque valley, but is notably more modest. Also of importance are burnt human remains, often mixed with midden. Anthropophagy in ceremonial (feasting) contexts thus cannot be excluded. Ceramics are abundant and classified into a bewildering number of local and imported styles (Guffroy 1994, 251–412; Kaulicke 1998). These have a wide distribution from Jequetepeque to coastal and highland Ecuador and the Bagua-Jaén region (Kaulicke 1998, Figure 36; see Guffroy 2008). The imported styles are from Paita (Paita C–D); hollow figurines are similar to those from Pacopampa (Morales 1999, Figure 4). Polychrome styles are also found in Pacopampa and the Bagua-Jaén region. Numerous pieces show clear influence of the Cupisnique styles to the south.

An important contribution to the archaeological evidence known within the Huancabamba deflection region was made by Yamamoto, who defined a sequence at Ingatambo and localized another 60 sites of Middle and Late Formative age along the middle course of the Huancabamba river, distributed in clusters over some 50 km (Yamamoto 2010, 2012). He distinguished three phases (Huancabamba – see above, Pomahuaca and Ingatambo), and sub-phases within them. Particularly important is Ingatambo I (ca 2900 to 2700 BP), with imported and emulated Cupisnique ceramics and a distinctive (albeit Cupisnique-emulated) polychrome style. This style is apparently more popular in the Jaén and Bagua regions (Shady 1971, 1999; Shady and Rosas 1979; Olivera 2014), and looted specimens include spectacular stirrup-spout bottles (see Olivera 1998, Figures 10–13). The polychrome style is also present in highland Ecuador (Catamayo, Guffroy 1987) as well as in Pacopampa.

Other than the Montegrande site, the Jaén basin is known for a relatively large number of sites that are not very thoroughly documented or published. Huayurco has been known since the 1960s (Rojas 1969) and has recently been re-excavated (Clasby and Meneses Bartra 2012). It became famous for finds of many stone bowls and plates, probably a workshop, a shell trumpet, a necklace and a Cupisnique-style ceramic bottle that probably dates to the Middle Formative; the recent excavations, meanwhile, are mostly later (Final Formative). Stone bowls and other lithic objects were found at San Isidro, amid architecture similar to Final Formative Huayurco, although there are also polychrome vessels that hint at buried architecture of Middle to Late Formative age, the likely association for the stone objects (Olivera 2014, 116, Figure 95). In the Bagua region, Olivera excavated at several sites with monumental architecture (Tomependa, Casual, Las Juntas) which show polychrome murals (Olivera 1998, 2014) different from either coastal or highland patterns. The ceramics, however, share the distinctive polychrome style and other incised decorative techniques. This seems to show that long sequences, akin to those described from the coast and the highlands, are also present in the Jaén-Bagua region.

Discussion

This long but still incomplete and somewhat patchy list permits some speculative generalizations. First, much of the entire area was occupied ever since first human colonization, although better documentation is limited to the coast and adjacent western Andes. This holds true also for very early occupation of the Amazonian lowlands (see Neves 2008). In the early Holocene, early domestication and sedentism remain limited to the upper Zaña valley in forested environments. Sites there provide evidence of cultigens of exotic origin that hint at contacts with the Eastern Andes and Amazon lowlands, even if archaeological evidence from those regions remains scarce and is of little help in understanding the nature of these putative contacts. At the heart of early social cohesion and growing social complexity may have been ceremonialism, as shown by the use of domesticated or wild plants and animals in the context of early mound building both on the coast and in humid or dry forest environments. At about 4500 BP, the formerly rather shadowy networks were reinforced and extended. Cerro Ventarrón and many other sites to the south boasted rather ostentatious ritualized architecture, feasting, and socially enhanced individuals adorned with exotic decorated objects. Some of the latter hint at contacts with the east; possible pets from those regions stand as further evidence. In this period, complex sites and mound-building are known from the Chinchipe and Jaén regions too. Although smaller here, and with different kinds of architecture, they do reveal surprisingly complex funerary customs with spectacular stone recipients and turquoise ornaments. These are similar to what much later become known from the Amazon lowlands as muriquitãs. These sites share with highland and coastal sites finds of shell trumpets and shell ornaments (necklaces or pectorals) from tropical seas. They also reveal stone recipients that in more or less contemporaneous coastal sites take the form of often highly decorated mortars (for example, San Juanito [Chapdelaine and Gagné 2015], Punkurí [Samaniego 2007]), also associated with ceremonial buildings and burials with greenstone appliqués such as at Santa Ana. All this hints at societies with shared values and the regular circulation of prestige commodities against a background of horticulture, fishing, hunting and gathering. The Jaén and Bagua region probably participated in this political-ritual economy network, although concrete evidence remains scarce.

The latter region's flair for distinctiveness seems to have been maintained in its later monumental architecture and decoration, while pottery gives some clues as to distribution ranges. While certain forms (bottles and bowls) are similar across wide areas, decoration styles are more locally restricted. From the south to Piura, motifs are related to Cupisnique figurative canons, which are adapted or imported in the north and the north-east. Particularly important is a rather spectacular polychrome style that seems to have its centre in Jaén-Bagua, but is distributed over a wide area including Piura, the Ecuadorian highlands and the Cajamarca humid forest environment. Yamamoto maps this dense network during the Late Formative (Yamamoto 2012, Figure 5). The Jaén-Bagua region is relevant also for the production of stone bowls, widely distributed during the Middle and Late Formative, but again one needs to highlight the richly decorated stone bowls (some of the same form as at Jaén-Bagua) and beakers from Jequetepeque to the Lambayeque over the same time-span (for example, the famous Limoncarro bowl, see Salazar-Burger and Burger 1996, Plate 11; Alva Meneses 2012 [Collud], Figure 30). In the Ofrendas gallery at Chavín de Huántar, stone objects from both traditions are present (compare Lumbreras 1993, Plates 85.671 and 85.672 with Olivera 2014, Figures 223–6).

Conclusions

If the Jaén-Bagua region was so closely bound into such wide-ranging networks, then, what does that entail for the question of connections with the nearby Amazonian lowlands? Lathrap (1970) postulated that the Central Amazon should be considered the origin of his tropical forest culture, although Neves (2008, 363) notes a hiatus of occupation of almost 5,000 years' duration in precisely this area. He suggests that 'human occupation surged only after current tropical climatic and ecological conditions were reached about 1000 BC' (Neves 2008, 364). This time estimate corresponds quite closely to the flourishing of the Jaén-Bagua societies, even if much remains to be done to get a clearer picture. The proximity to the Amazonian lowlands would suggest that the western and north-western Amazon basin is a better candidate for early contacts with the Andes than is the Central Amazon, although probably not as a principal founder of Andean cultures as envisaged by Lathrap, but rather as an early part of a large interaction sphere which I refer to as the Cupisnique sphere (Kaulicke 2011). Last but not least, Amazonian fauna and flora must have been well known by Archaic and Formative coastal and highland societies. This is contrary to the generalized belief that these are only based on memories of a distant mythical Amazonian homeland that provided models for 'Chavín' art, as has become all but a truism among many Peruvianists ever since Tello (see Morales 2011).

2.5

Changing Andes–Amazonia dynamics: *El Chuncho* meets *El Inca* at the end of the Marañón corridor

Alexander Herrera Wassilowsky

Oral traditions from the upper Marañón valley are remarkably explicit about the boundary between the *Inca,* the civilized pre-Christian people of the high Andes, and the lowland *Chuncho*. The former are often portrayed as mighty giants (cf. Molinié 2004) and the latter as the savage, effeminate and cannibalistic other from the forested eastern Andean piedmont and lowlands (for example, Steward 1946; Dean 2001). My first encounter with this boundary was at twilight in July 2000, well past Yauya and en route to archaeological excavations near the confluence of the Marañón and Yanamayo rivers (departments of Áncash and Huánuco). At the bottom of Quebrada Maribamba we spotted from afar a large, flat, rounded rock resembling the muscular back of a giant lying face down in the river. Inquiries about the striking rock formation quickly led to its name: *Chunchuwanunga*, '[the place where] the *chunchu* dies'. He was slain by *El Inca,* who performed the feat from *Inkawarakayuqjirka* across the valley, 'the mountain [from which the] Inca wields his Sling'.

To investigate this mythical slaying of an Amazonian Indian in the upper Marañón landscape, 3,000 metres above sea level, I returned to upper Marañón in 2011, but could not find *Chunchuwanunga*. It appeared to have been buried by a massive landslide, but a knowledgeable local guide from Queroyoc Village had no hesitation in taking me to *Chunchurumi* '*Chunchu* stone', also killed by *El Inca*. Like the former rock, this monolith is found uncarved and unpainted, with no associated structure or surface find to indicate any particular significance to the archaeologist, an unmarked grave (Figure 2.5.1).

As elsewhere across the central Andes Quechua oral traditions anchor a primordial time of highland dominance that toponyms situate in the towering geological landscape. The *Inca* not only appears to have killed several *Chuncho*, he rested at *Inkajamanan*, the limestone quarry at *Uchpaqotu* was his ashtray, at the

Figure 2.5.1 Landscape features marking the endpoint of the upper Marañón corridor: (a) *Chunchurumi*; (b) *Inkawarakayuqjirka*. © Alexander Herrera Wassilowsky.

site of Inkasaltanán, south of Piscobamba he jumped and turned into andesite at *Inkawarakayuqjirka* (Figure 2.5.1).

The place in the landscape of the *Chuncho*'s dead bodies correlates with a treble boundary. First, a stark ecological transition in the rain shadow of the Cordillera Oriental and a geological shift from Andesitic to Limestone formations whose interplay is the origin of the erratic block at *Chunchurumi*. Narrow gallery forests line the hot and deeply entrenched floor of the Marañón and its tributaries and stand separated from the core area of Andean agro-pastoralism by arid and very steep slopes of thorny shrub and scree that are notoriously dangerous to traverse, rarely less than one days' walk (c. 2,000–3,000 m). Secondly, it marks a technological boundary at the lowermost end of integrated mid- and upper slope *Kichwa* and *Suni* irrigation farming systems. The areas of agricultural production in the inter-Andean *Yunga* ecozone dotted along the valley floor gallery forests are often very small hydraulically independent pockets that draw water from seasonal streams or springs. One of these is Yangón brine spring, a day on foot from *Chunchumi*, at the confluence of the Yanamayo and Marañón rivers (see below). The suffix '–gón' means 'water' in the Culli, K'uli or Culle language of northern Peru (Adelaar 1989; Adelaar and Muysken 2004; Torero 2002), a poorly documented language spoken across part of the northern highlands of Peru in the sixteenth and seventeenth centuries that coexisted with Quechua over long periods in the pre-colonial past (Adelaar 1989, 88). The toponyms of valley bottom archaeological sites in central Conchucos, such as Yangón and Pogtán, are also the southernmost Culle place names identified in the central Andes suggesting a third, linguistic and possibly cultural boundary between speakers of the Culle and Quechua languages.

In this chapter, I examine the nature and development of this boundary between Amazonia and the Andes, located between c. 2,000 and 3,000 metres above sea level in the inter-Andean highland setting of the Marañón valley. My review of ecological, historical, linguistic and archaeological perspectives from the region goes back in time from oral history to ethnohistory and linguistics to consider how archaeological evidence from the lower Yanamayo basin may inform the spread of the Culle language in the upper Marañón (Adelaar 1989; Adelaar and Muysken 2004, 173, 401). I hope to show that the trope of violent highland dominance across an ecological juncture was enshrined in oral histories in both Quechua and Culle, and that it masks a deep and ongoing history of reciprocal relations between lowland and highland dwellers (Renard-Casevitz et al. 1988). I will argue that *El Inca*'s violent place making belies the fluid dynamics and deep history of changing social, political and material interactions of people across ecological gradients. For millennia these have revolved around the circulation of knowledge and of commodities such as salt, stone axes, ceramics, textiles and metal implements from the Andes to Amazonia – while in the other direction came wax, feathers, wood, seeds and other plant parts, as well as ritual knowledge and healing practices. While always one of reciprocal interdependence the balance changed through time and archaeological investigations suggest that, in the deep past, it was the lowlands that were the dominant source of influences impacting on the highlands. Ultimately the balance switched in favour of the highlands and it is the aim of this chapter to try and characterize this transition.

The Marañón corridor

Along with the Ucayali to the south and the Putumayo and Rio Negro to the north, the Marañón River is one of the principal tributaries of the Amazon, with a basin of 31,920 km² and a mean discharge at the confluence of 751 m³ per second (INRENA-PNUD 1995). It has carved its upper course between the central and eastern ranges of the Andes, following a geological fault line that runs from south to north for over 400 km, roughly parallel to the Santa and Huallaga rivers (Figure 2.5.2).

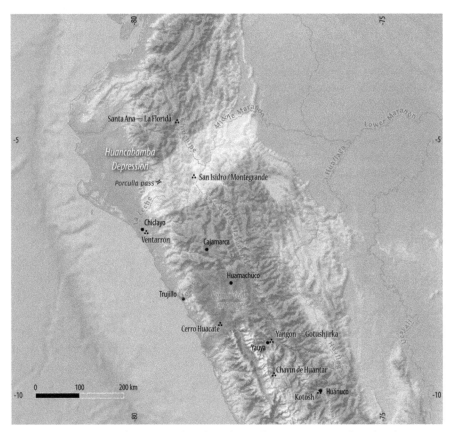

Figure 2.5.2 Map of places and archaeological sites mentioned in the chapter, also showing the Huancabamba Depression and the hypothesized distribution of the (now extinct) Culle language in the sixteenth century. © Alexander Herrera Wassilowsky and Paul Heggarty.

This deeply incised canyon also marks the present political frontier between the Peruvian departments of Ancash and Huánuco to the south, and Cajamarca and Amazonas to the north. Where the Huancabamba Depression interrupts the central cordillera the Marañón River changes course and its middle and lower sections drain eastward into the Amazon basin.

As has long been noted (for example, Hocquenghem 1990; Chapter 2.4), the Huancabamba Depression (6° S) offers passes through the central Andes such as Porcula at 2,145 m that are substantially lower than those to the north and south. Lowland areas west and east of the Piura, Cajamarca northern and Lambayeque highlands not only stand relatively close to each other. They are also ecologically similar, making this a preferred area for east–west species interaction between the Pacific and Amazon basins, as well as human transit. Further south, however, the torrent of the upper Marañón, as well as the steep flanks and prevailing aridity of its canyon, mark a major physical barrier to east–west travel, adding to the c. 150 km of glaciated peaks crowning the central Cordillera Blanca. Here, the main route between Amazonia and the Andes is from north to south, following the canyon of the upper Marañón. Such routes along the gradually rising inter-Andean valleys may been seen as friendlier for long-distance displacements than the steep and cold passes across the rugged central and eastern cordilleras. It is these narrow strips of deeply entrenched riverine terraces covered by gallery forests along the valley floor of the Marañón and its tributaries that I will refer to as the Marañón corridor.

When waters recede, in the dry season, the long beaches that form along the riverbank can greatly facilitate north–south travel over considerable distances, especially when aided by balsa wood rafts. The rain shadow cast by its deep and narrow entrenchment means precipitation is negligible, but seasonal runoff and springs occasionally provide water for gravity irrigation, as mentioned above. This can still be difficult to harness because the waters cascade so powerfully, but long strips and patches of relic fields attest to an intensive occupation that continued into the colonial period and, to varying degrees, into the present. Places at which the entrenched rivers of the Marañón corridor may be crossed using bridges or rafts are strategic points, particularly where they stand near the oases dotted along the valley floor.

Present-day vegetation cover in the Marañón corridor indicates a long history of anthropogenic impacts. Agricultural pockets on the valley floor were carved out of the deciduous gallery forests and thorny scrub dominated by acacias, *Bombacacea* and *Pati (Ceiba* spp.) trees that thrive in the hot and arid *Yunga* canyons below c. 2,300 m. Small, isolated stands of native fruit trees in well-watered, frost-free sections of particular ravines, including *chirimoya*, *pacae* and *lúcuma*, strongly suggest fruit tree farming in the past, and large, exclusive stands of *Tara* (*Caesalpina tinctoria*) in the steep, arid slopes above (c. 2,300–3,000 m) may also be a result of human alterations (cf. Luteyn and Churchill 2000). Dating these landscape modifications is as yet impossible, however, but past agroforestry in the Marañón corridor seems more closely aligned with lowland forest management practices (for example, Peters 2000) than with highland Inca *Alnus* agroforestry, as suggested on the basis of pollen studies from the Cusco region (Chepstow-Lusty and Winfield 2000).

Having outlined the nature of the physical and ecological transition between Andes and Amazonia in the Marañón corridor, I now turn to survey the sequence and directions of structured interregional interactions or influences along it, both upstream and downstream, chronologically. Since the more recent periods are better understood I start with ethnohistory, before venturing back to earlier times from an archaeological perspective.

Ethnohistory of multilingual interaction

Reviewers of colonial accounts of Inca drives into the eastern lowlands have singled out the mid-fifteenth century case of Huancoayllo or Anco Huallo, a Chanca or Huanca captain of Capac (Topa Inca) Yupanqui who chose to abandon the conquest of Chinchaysuyu and to banish himself from the Inca realm (Saignes 1985; Chapters 5.1 and 5.2). With his followers he is said to have entered the forested eastern *Anti* region from Huánuco heading towards Chachapoyas and reportedly settling on the shores of an unnamed lake (1985, 69). Citing Sarmiento de Gamboa and Cabello de Valboa, Rostworowski de Diez Canseco (1999, 116) sees in these accounts *prima facie* evidence of Chanca desertion. Their migration, or escape, followed a descending movement, north- and eastward from the south-central Andes, a pattern of eastward movement and colonization followed by many later highland migrants during the colonial period, including 8,000 malcontent Indians from Chucuito and a handful of disgruntled Spaniards (Renard-Casevitz et al. 1988, 121).

Before turning to colonial sources to ask if highland populations were pushing into inter- and trans-Andean *Yunga* areas before the Inca expansion, and query archaeology to find out whether the direction of thrust should be seen as integral to the *longue durée* of Andean history or responds to a historically more restricted *conjuncture*, it seems pertinent to mention oral accounts of the origins of the Quichua-speaking Inga people of southern Colombia. Located in the Andean foothills of northwest Amazonia, Sibundoy Valley is home to Inga (Quichua) and Kamëntsá speaking people (Bonilla 1968; Friedemann and Arocha 1982; Ramírez de Jara 1996). A large lake, drained in the 1970s, figures prominently as the source of the Amazon River in maps of the late sixteenth and early seventeenth century, including Ortelius' *Peruviae Auriferae Regionis Typus* (1592) and *America Noviter Delineata* (c. 1637–40) by Joost de Hondt (Jodocus Hondius). It may seem tempting to hypothesize that Huancoayllo's people travelled over 2,000 km to settle on the shores of Sibundoy Lake but this is unlikely. The presence of agricultural terraces in Sibundoy has been suggested to indicate Inca influence (Patiño 2016) but there is yet insufficient archaeological evidence to assert or date the presence of precolonial migrant settlers (Ramírez de Jara 1996). Living oral traditions of the Inga, however, are unequivocal in distinguishing two ancestral migrations, from the Pasto plateau east- and downwards and a northwest *ascending* movement from lowlands to highlands undertaken up the Napo River. The former echoes the highland pre-eminence in ethnohistoric sources and the oral account cited at the outset, a predominant pattern of highland–lowland interactions in the fifteenth and sixteenth centuries that largely continues today. The latter echoes other, more recent and less well-known historic migrations within northwest Amazonia, such as the sixteenth- and eighteenth-century movements of Abijiras, Auca, Encabellados and Pariana (Renard-Casevitz et al. 1988, 271, Map 30).

Colonial census accounts reflecting indigenous negotiation strategies against the *encomienda* system and prior to the forced resettlement policies under Viceroy Francisco de Toledo, such as the 1562 *Visita de León de Huánuco* (Murra 1972, 1978, 1985), have been pivotal to the study of Andean modes of socio-economic organization across space. Following Murra, political articulation of dispersed production zones across complementary ecological settings in a vertical landscape was achieved through webs of reciprocity and redistribution extending from core areas of ethnic settlement in the highlands to enclaves or islands on the high punas or in the low-lying inter-Andean piedmont. Entrusted with production of complementary goods including cotton, ají, peanuts and fruits as well as pigments, feathers and salt, people designated as migrants or colonists to distant places, seasonally or permanently, were undoubtedly exposed to multilingual situations and crucial to language dispersal.

But since when have highlanders been pushing into the hot and arid inter-Andean *Yunga*? Historical documents pertaining to the construction of *obraje* mills in Conchucos in 1572 (León Gómez 2003, 460; 2018) tend to confirm the suggestion that Inca enclaves in the Conchucos *Yunga* were settled by highland *mitmaq* colonists, including people displaced from as far as *Cuntisuyu*, most probably by force (Herrera 2003, 2005). Mention of a *pachaca* named Cullos tends to confirm the presence of an earlier population of Culle speakers in the Marañón corridor, as suggested by Torero and Adelaar. Yet Culle is not a lowland language. Rather it is closely associated with the cult of Catequil, ancestor hero of Huamachuco who had a main shrine and a network of secondary shrines, referred to as 'wives', 'daughters' and 'sons' (San Pedro 1992/1560[?]; Topic 1992, 1998; Topic et al. 2002). The creation myth recorded by Augustinian Friars in Huamachuco ends with Catequil driving his mother's brothers from the highlands, a people referred to as Guachemines. He then digs up a new people created by the supreme deity Ataguju at Guacat. John Topic's (1998) reconstruction of the sacred landscape of Catequil locates this *pacarina* place of ethnic origin at the confluence of the Santa and Tablachaca rivers, on the present border of Conchucos, Huaylas and Huamachuco, while 'Guachemin' is shown as a recurrent toponym of hills and ravines descending to the Moche Valley. '[T]hese [toponyms] probably commemorate the places where the Guachemines were driven out of the province ... the creation myth [also] defined the territory of Huamachuco as ecologically *sierra* and the people as ethnically *serranos* and contrasts them to people adapted to life on the seacoast.' (Topic 1998, 113).

A further indication that highland pressure on the inter-Andean *Yunga* precedes Quechua expansion into the region is given by Cristóbal de Albornoz '*Instrucción para descubrir todas las guacas del Pirú y sus camayos y haziendas*' (1967/1582[?]) and the Augustinian friars' Huamachuco chronicle (San Pedro 1992/1560[?]. Albornoz uses the Quechua name of *Guaracayoc (Warakayuq)* as an alternative for the Huamachuco pacarina, whereas San Pedro names it as one of the nine principal waka shrines of Catequil (cf. Topic 1992). It seems probable that *Guaracayoc* and *[Inka]warakuyjirka* denote the same place in the sacred landscape associated with the cult of Catequil.

The presence of a major *waka* of Catquil at the south end of the Marañón corridor and the Inca conquest of the area seem to support the spread of Culle as earlier than that of Quechua. Moreover, it appears that the violent, frontier-setting myth may be earlier too. The proposed transformation of Catequil into *El Inca* at *Warakayuqjirka* may be interpreted to suggest two successive waves of advance, violent attempts to extend the reach of highland centres and appropriate lowland enclaves through selective migration. The later wave may be hypothesized as contemporary with the peak of Inca expansionism during the fifteenth century, when the Culle-speaking others came to be subdued. In light of the above, it seems tempting to suggest that Culle-speaking populations were reduced to the valley bottom and became in later mythology the very same *Chuncho* – at *Chunchurumi* and *Chunchuwanunga* – that Catequil had vanquished before from *Warakayuq*. What follows will thus review the archaeological evidence of Inca colonization in eastern Chinchaysuyu and turn to archaeological study of settlement strategies, in search of plausible material correlates of Quechua and Culle language dispersals, as well as the primeval *Chuncho* twice slain by *El Inca* and Catequil.

Archaeology beyond *El Inca* and Catequil

Archaeological survey and excavations in the upper, westernmost edge of Amazonia are rare in comparison with the central Andes. Work in the Huallaga and Chinchipe basins has yielded significant results for the early rise of social complexity (Valdez 2008, 2014; Valdez et al. 2005; Olivera 2014; Chapter 2.4), while studies in the upper Marañón (Mantha 2006; Mantha and Malca Cardosa 2017; Herrera 2003, 2005, in prep. A) shed light on later Andean prehistory and will be drawn upon liberally in what follows.

At the juncture of the Yanamayo and Marañón valleys the overall spatial and temporal distribution of later productive, domestic and mortuary architecture tends to correlate well with the aforementioned ethnohistoric accounts, and the trope of highland dominance. Inca sites line the main *Puna* road of Chinchaysuyu from Huari to Tambo Real, near Yauya, where it descended to a hanging bridge over the Yanamayo (Ccente and Román 2006; Herrera 2005; cf. Caja and Diáz 2009). A secondary eastern road along the entrenched valley floor connected the bridge with several small farming enclaves, the brine spring at Yangón and the balsa raft crossing over the Marañón at Pogtán. Salt is a rare resource in the Andean piedmont, so it is not surprising that Yangón, deep down on the Yanamayo valley floor, was repeatedly terraced for salt production through evaporation.

Inca occupation appears exclusive to the farming enclave of Warupampa, made possible by changes to the water catchment from a spring across the ecological boundary outlined above, several kilometres steeply upslope. The path from the hanging bridge over the Yanamayo leads to a two room Inca *kancha* complex with a rock *ushnu* at the centre of a small plaza (c. 240 m²). A special room with a split floor double jamb access overlooks a narrow stretch of the upstream valley bottom path from atop a massive boulder forcing a bend in the Yanamayo River, upstream of the salt source. The orthodox layout and shallow depth of Inca occupation deposits are consistent with the resettlement of *mitmaq* from Chachapoyas, Condesuyos or elsewhere in Tawantinsuyu, as reported in the 1572 *obraje* list mentioned above. Different types of contemporary domestic architecture raise the possibility of different groups of settlers. Square dwellings next to the bridge at Platanal and the hilltop site of Pirkajirka may suggest a distinct group of people was entrusted with places of control. The rectangular domestic structures east of Quebrada Maribamba may point to a different group of *mitmaq* terrace farmers. Such ethnically distinct colonists would have most probably not spoken Culle.

Farming terrace walls excavated below the Inca *kancha*, show that construction of the Inca enclave restructured an earlier agricultural landscape. Pre-Inca occupation farming in the string of Yunga enclaves comprising the Marañón corridor depended upon small springs and seasonal runoff channels to provide irrigation water to sets of low, square farming terraces along the riverbanks. Public architecture in Yunga valley bottom pockets includes distinct rectangular patio group enclosures with rooms on the lower river terraces (c. AD 800–1500) and enclosures that are circular to oval in plan on the upper river terraces (c. AD 200–800). As 'stages' for ritual activity such buildings are often associated with ancestor veneration, but also with interaction between ethnic groups. Following Rostworowski's model for Andean ethnicity (1991), unity of origin and beliefs, dress and socio-political unity went hand-in-hand with a common language or dialect. At Yangón two pairs of *chullpa* mortuary structures flanked the upriver and upvalley entrance juncture to the brine spring east of the small perennial stream descending from Huagllauquio. The need to materially assert an ancestral presence collectively suggests a mortuary and ceremonially diverse population.

Excavations in contemporary monumental enclosures high above the valley bottom, on the nearby prominent hilltop of Gotushjirka (3,200 m), have revealed abundant evidence of ritual feasting. Elsewhere (Herrera 2006) I have suggested that circular *kancha* enclosures may have served to host periodic gatherings of distinct mortuary and ceremonial communities that shared roots with the north Andean Recuay tradition (c. 200 BC–AD 800) long hypothesized by Terence Grieder (1978) as borne by Culle speakers. Such an interpretation would fit well with a top-down model, in line with pre-Inca verticality. Yet if highland colonization of the inter Andean *Yunga* as a process dates back to the turn of the millennium, the possible predominance of influences from lowlands to highlands must be sought in earlier periods. As we shall see, direct evidence is elusive, but exploration of archaeological research in this light takes us back to the spread of farming.

Construction of enclosed plazas and groups of rooms centred around patios is a tradition widespread across the northern highlands from the Late Formative through to the Inca Period. Yet these open stages associated with public ritual stand in contrast to an earlier tradition of enclosed public architecture associated with the first sedentary occupation and farming in inter-Andean *Yunga* settings by the Initial Formative (3500–1700 BC). The Mito architectural tradition (Bonnier 1997a, 1997b; Fung de Pineda 1988) is characterized by small chambers with elaborate hearths, often with rounded corners or split-level floors, and was first described for the Huallaga Valley (Izumi and Sono 1963; Izumi and Terada 1972; Izumi et al. 1972). Its presence has also been attested in the Callejón de Huaylas (Burger 1985; Burger and Salazar-Burger 1985, 1986; Herrera in prep. A), the upper Marañón basin (Bonnier and Rozenberg 1988; Bonnier 1997a; Herrera in prep. B), and the Tablachaca Valley (Grieder and Bueno 1985; Grieder et al. 1988).

The religious tradition associated with Mito architecture is known as Kotosh (Burger and Salazar-Burger 1985, 1986; cf. Siveroni 2006) and overlaps in time with the development of Chavín de Huántar (Contreras 2010). This suggests that the lowland linkages evident in ritual iconography and practice were forged early, probably during the Initial Formative (or 'Late Preceramic'). In this sense, the Mito tradition may be seen as the culmination of large-scale and low-intensity phenomena, driven by developments in the lowlands that hark back to the first human settlement, the development of horticulture and the spread of dry- and irrigation farming. While there is little evidence to relate these phenomena causally, or indeed with language spread, they do co-occur in inter-Andean ecological settings linked directly to Amazonia, such as the upper Apurímac, Huallaga and Marañón basins.

The notion of the tropical lowlands of Amazonia and the upper reaches of the Amazon as an ancient cultural hearth is enshrined in the writings of Donald Lathrap (1970, 1973, 1977) and many of his students. His 'Out of the Amazon' thesis drew heavily on the work of Julio César Tello, who famously, but wrongly, proclaimed Chavín as the Mother Culture of Andean civilization (1960). Their works have long led scholars to study shared, indeed interdependent ritual practices and paraphernalia as well as the associated iconography of the middle to late Formative (1200–400 BC) (Kano 1979; Zeidler 1988; Burger 1984; Lumbreras 1993; Chapter 1.4). There is still discussion regarding the biological origins of motifs prevalent in Chavín art and whether these represented reptiles, felines, birds and plants that make implicit or explicit reference to the Pacific coast, the Andean highlands, or the Amazonian lowlands (for example, Kaulicke 1994, 454–76; Chapters 2.4 and 3.7). This debate is important since one of the key Amazonian inputs to the highlands is of course that many food plants cultivated in the Andes including achira (*Canna edulis),* manioc (*Manihot esculenta*), peanut (*Arachis hypogea*) and, possibly, yacón (*Polymnia sanchifolia*) are thought to have been domesticated in Amazonia (Clement 1999; Clement et al. 2010; National Research Council 1989; Piperno and Pearsall 1998; Chapter 2.1). There were also many non-domesticates widely recognized as important for ritual, such as achiote (*Bixa orellana*), coca (*Erythroxylum* spp.; for example, Chapter 3.1), ishpingo (*Ocotea floribunda*), vilca seeds (*Anadenanthera Colubrina;* for example, Chapter 1.4) and the yagé or ayahuasca (*Banisteriopsis caapi*) vine.

Interaction across the torrents of dangerous rivers is perhaps more characteristic of the main Yunga enclaves still settled along the upper Marañón than of precocious farming or tending of any of the above plants but achira, manioc and peanut are all farmed in the lower Yanamayo. Evidence of yacón, peanut and cotton has also been found in excavations at Yangón but the finds are relatively late, and it is difficult to suggest a date for introduction of these cultivars. The architectural evidence of irrigation and farming technology may be taken as a proxy to suggest them as old as the earliest extant architecture. It may well be much earlier than the second century BC, however. Dating the stands of *Ochromia* spp., or balsa wood, and the manufacture of rafts to cross the Marañón River and its tributaries provides a particularly intriguing challenge.

Having reached the Formative period in our search for the *Chuncho* it seems fitting to review Chavín iconography of the Yauya stela, largest known Chavín style carving outside the famous ceremonial centre (Tello 1923; Espejo Nuñez 1964; Burger 2002; Herrera 1998). There is no indication of a ceremonial centre in the Yauya area comparable to Chavín and the three fragments found in the area of Montengayuq and Weqrukucha may suggest the piece broke *en route* northwards after being quarried or pillaged from Chavín (Herrera 1998). The stela prominently depicts an opposing symmetrical pair of fierce segmented beings with feline and reptilian attributes as well as huge circular eyes. Its association with fish led Lathrap (1971) to dub it 'Master of the Fish' but its iconography may also be interpreted as depicting four stages in the development of a dual supernatural emanating from the central axis (Herrera 1998).

Excavations at nearby Gotushjirka tend to confirm that Chavín style iconography had little impact in the Yanamayo Valley, even though it is only 70 km north of Chavín. A major break in the ceramic sequence is apparent after a hitherto unknown Formative style, characterized by a combination of incision, punctation and painting prevalent in the earliest deposits. Similarities with incised and painted wares from the upper Huallaga and middle Marañón may suggest a shared culture in this area – supporting Tello's hypothesized Marañón Culture – but much remains unclear about the deeper prehistory of the Yanamayo Marañón juncture.

Archaeologists working closer to the Huancabamba depression near the middle Marañón at sites such as Monte Grande, Tomependa and San Ignacio (Olivera 1998, 2014) and in the northern Marañon basin, Santa Ana (La Florida) Palanda (Valdez 2008, 2014; Valdez et al. 2005), have tended to stress lowland influence for the precocious monumental architecture found in this area. In their view early lowland pre-eminence in interregional dynamics came to be superseded by increasing highland dominance, within a reciprocal framework of interdependence (for example, Chapter 2.4).

Yet as more and more of the Initial Formative (3500–1700 BC) monumental sites have been investigated along the northern and central Pacific coast (for example, Alva Meneses 2012; Shady Solis and Leyva 2003; Chu Barrera 2008) some scholars have tended to stress coastal pre-eminence in regional developments following a general west to east pattern of dispersal of culture. It seems fitting to end this review by pointing to the three-way spatial metaphor manifest in the conspicuous deposition (c. 3200 BC) of marine molluscs, large felines and parrots at the centre of the main plaza at Ventarrón (Alva Meneses 2012) animals brought together from very distant and very distinct habitats.

Cultural pulsations at the endpoint of the upper Marañón corridor

In this chapter I have sought to explore the history of a violent myth of highland dominance enshrined in the landscape and expressed in oral traditions. Geology, topography, ecology and history were considered in addressing the development of structured relations underlying the reciprocal interactions that constitute a social boundary in the upper Marañón. *El Inca*'s violent making of place as evidenced by Quechua toponyms masks a deep history of changing social, political and material interactions between people across ecological gradients. I have aimed to show this boundary as fluid and historically contingent, a multi-layered cultural construct defined by structured interactions that played a key role in the construction of social identities (Zubrow 2005). Clearly the *Inca* and the *Chuncho* needed each other in this sense. The archaeological evidence for the *Chuncho*'s presence in this area has proved elusive, despite the seemingly obvious linkages suggested by the spread of cultigens developed in Amazonia.

It may seem tempting to relate the lithified *Chunchu* to the Culle-speaking populations of the sixteenth century as a distinct population, but the warriors' sling was probably wielded by Catequil himself first. Rather than, or additional to, referencing historical contingencies, the slain *Chuncho*'s place appears to mark a conceptual boundary in the landscape that may profitably be seen as an indigenous precursor to the Andes–Amazonia divide and interdependence, the result of long histories of negotiations about cooperation, rights to resources or simply access, as well as ethnic, linguistic and political difference. Addressing the development of multi-ethnic, multi-lingual enclaves appears a suitable way to address the bridging of such 'divides'.

Part 3
Overall patterns – and alternative models

3.1

How real is the Andes–Amazonia divide? An archaeological view from the eastern piedmont

Darryl Wilkinson

Introduction

It is understandable that the contrast between the Andes and Amazonia tends to dominate our large-scale perceptions of South American geography. After all, highland–lowland interactions are a topic of global scholarly interest, and the Andes–Amazonia divide offers one of the most dramatic (if sometimes stereotyped) cases. In this chapter I wish to make three points about this great divide. The first is that the divergences between these two regions are real; from the point of view of archaeology, often quite stark. Yet even if we accept the validity of such contrasts, they can sometimes lead us to overlook the distinctiveness of the spaces in between – that are neither up nor down, so to speak. Thus my second argument is that the piedmont zone of the eastern Andes needs to be considered as a separate place, distinct from either Amazonia or the highlands proper.[1] As a 'transitional' ecozone, we can understand the piedmont as exhibiting an admixture of highland and lowland characteristics; but this still captures only a part of the complex reality. Indeed, the piedmont also demonstrates a variety of attributes that are unique to itself – which are, in other words, neither typically Amazonian nor typically Andean. However, this raises the question of what exactly *is* 'typical' with respect to these two regions. My third point, then, is that such transitional areas are not only interesting in their own right, but also provide an ideal vantage point from which to examine the nature of the wider Andes–Amazonia divide. By this I mean that when we stand where these two 'worlds' meet, what makes them so distinctive is brought into clearer focus.

In what follows I will discuss these themes in greater detail, drawing primarily on archaeological evidence from my own fieldwork in the Amaybamba Valley (Peru). From the outset I should therefore acknowledge that my arguments largely reflect my research experiences in one particular piedmont region. Unfortunately, no-one is yet in a position to provide an overall summary of the archaeology of the entire Andean piedmont, because so little work has been carried out there (and even less has been published). In comparison with the Andean highlands and coast, and in some respects even with Amazonia, the piedmont remains largely unknown in archaeological terms (cf. Chapter 2.5). Yet, as will become clear, many of the issues I raise are by no means unique to somewhere like the Amaybamba Valley and impinge upon the issue of the Andes–Amazonia relationship more generally.

Before proceeding it is also useful to provide a basic definition of the word 'piedmont', since there are multiple terms used in South America to describe this region that are almost, but not quite, synonyms (for example, *montaña, selva alta, yungas, ceja de selva*). In the basic etymological sense of the word, the piedmont covers all the foothills of the Andes east of the Cordillera Blanca. But as a coherent cultural zone, I take it to be the mountainous region of the eastern Andes where the *valley floors* range between approximately 2,500 m and 1,000 m in elevation.[2] Some specialists in the region might find my definition here to be rather restricted. For example, the upper limit of the piedmont is often taken to be the tree-line (around 3,800 m); for some, the lower limit can stretch all the way down to the Amazonian plains at around 300 m (for example, Lathrap 1970). Whereas most scholars define the piedmont first in terms of its (non-human) ecology, and only consider its 'cultural' facets after the fact, my definition instead emphasizes the region's human ecology. Thus the 1,000 m line is important because below this elevation most of the major west–east running rivers of the Andes become sufficiently deep and wide to be routinely navigable in canoes. This change might not have mattered all that much in terms of plant and animal biogeography, but its significance to the human inhabitants was enormous. The Andes generally lacks navigable rivers, which tends to make waterborne transport impractical, whereas the extensive river systems of Amazonia were the primary highways for moving goods and people of all kinds, especially in bulk quantities. In the piedmont then, anything moving across the Andes–Amazonia frontier had to transfer between these very distinct terrestrial and aquatic networks. Whereas the absence of navigable waterways determines the lower limit of the piedmont, the upper limit (around 2,500 m) reflects the ecological viability of several key domesticated species. Andean camelids generally do not extend below 2,300 m (Stahl 2008), nor potatoes below 2,000 m (Hawkes 1990) – while coca and manioc are typically only cultivable up to 2,300 m (Isendahl 2011; Plowman 1985, 12).

So in terms of human ecology, aside from the issue of river navigability, the greatest divergences between Amazonia and the Andes lay in their rather distinct sets of animal and plant domesticates. By the late prehistoric period in particular – roughly the millennium prior to the Spanish conquest in AD 1532 – we can think of the Andean highlands as a zone with an agricultural regime reliant on two staple cultigens: maize and potatoes. The importance of maize lay not only in the calories it provided, but also as the main crop that was used to produce *chicha* (a fermented maize drink). The significance of state-produced alcoholic beverages in underpinning the labour politics of the later Andean empires (especially the Incas) is difficult to underestimate (Bray 2003; Goldstein 2003; Morris 1979). Effectively, taxes were paid to the prehistoric state in form of labour, which were reciprocated via elite-sponsored feasts during which large quantities of alcohol were consumed. In addition, much of the Andes also exhibited a mixed agro-pastoral economy, particularly in the high plains of the Altiplano to the south where it sometimes even verged on specialized mobile pastoralism (Capriles 2014). The two domesticated animals of greatest importance were the llama and the alpaca, which provided a source of dietary protein – although the secondary products derived from these species were likely even more significant. For instance, woollen textiles were a key means of facilitating human adaptation to the cold climates of the high-altitude regions, while the use of llamas as pack animals was an important development in promoting long-distance exchange networks in the southern highlands (Nielsen 2009). Although not one of the 'classic' secondary products described by Sherratt (1981, 1983), we should also bear in mind that in an environment often deficient in wood sources, camelid dung would have been a critical fuel source.

In many respects, Amazonia was quite different. Historically, the most important Amazonian cultigen was manioc, although maize, squashes and plantains were all significant too. But like maize in the highlands, the value of manioc went far beyond its role as a source of bare calories – in the sense that manioc beer has long been the social lubricant *par excellence* of the neotropical lowlands. In Amazonia, the consumption of manioc beer is central to exchange encounters, and indeed to social and ritual occasions of all kinds (for example, Killick 2009; Uzendoski 2004; Walker 2012). Whereas alcohol in the highlands became central to state-controlled practices of labour extraction, in late prehistoric Amazonia, alcohol was more important in furthering long-distance trading relationships between far-flung communities. Moreover, Amazonia lacked any equivalent to the Andean reliance on domesticated animals, with higher levels of consumption of wild fauna, and virtually no exploitation of secondary products (for example, wool). Yet despite its lack of domesticated animals, Amazonia saw considerable human intervention in the agricultural productivity of its landscapes during late prehistory (Erickson 2006; Chapter 3.6). The consequence of centuries of accumulated household organic waste, Amazonian Dark Earths (ADE) are a type of highly fertile anthropogenic soil that was an increasingly prominent feature of farming zones in the lowland tropics during the millennium prior to European colonization (Clement et al. 2015; Chapters 1.1 and 4.4); something for which there is no direct Andean equivalent. Terracing, a rather different phenomenon, was the primary means by which Andeans sought to modify the quality of soils.[3]

So far, I have admittedly been dealing in broad generalities, which is not to deny that considerable internal variations existed within the Andes and Amazonia. But when working at a sufficiently grand scale of analysis, it is possible to draw valid contrasts between an overarching Amazonian pattern and an Andean pattern.

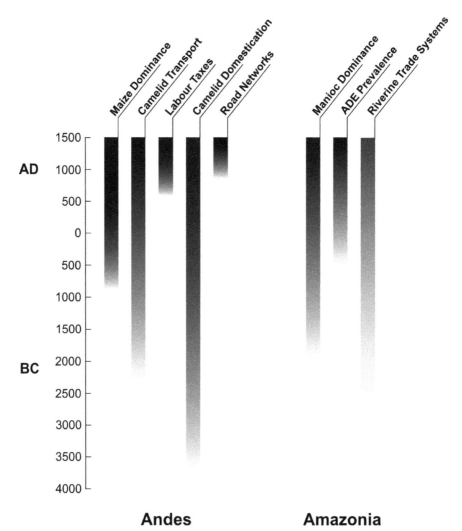

Andes   **Amazonia**

Figure 3.1.1 Chronological chart showing the time-depth of the major archaeological divergences between Amazonia and the Andes prior to c. AD 1500. © Darryl Wilkinson.

These patterns were far from 'timeless', however. Indeed, the later the prehistoric period, the greater the extent to which both Amazonia and the Andes show evidence of being integrated into contrasting regional systems with distinctive characteristics – largely a product of the expansion of imperial states in the highlands and of major linguistic-agricultural complexes in the lowlands. In Figure 3.1.1, I have represented the approximate time-depth of the main archaeological factors differentiating Amazonia from the Andes.

It is clear that, although the initial divergence begins with camelid domestication some 6,000 years ago, most of the other factors only come into play much later in prehistory. For instance, if one were to compare the Andes and Amazonia during the first six millennia following their initial colonization by *Homo sapiens*, these contrasts would be far less pronounced, or in some cases absent altogether. Indeed, for the early Holocene the only significant difference between the regions would have perhaps been altitude-related adaptations. Even then, it is worth noting that the highest Andes (areas above 4,000 m) only became permanently (that is, non-seasonally) occupied by humans following the domestication of camelids (Capriles et al. 2016). Llamas and alpacas were essentially machines for converting wind-swept high-altitude grasslands into food and fuel for human consumption, thereby turning a previously marginal zone into a highly productive one. Thus in terms of human ecology, the Andes–Amazonia divide emerges and becomes increasingly pronounced over time; rather than reflecting any primordial distinction between the two regions (cf. Chapter 1.1).

Migration and disease

Although most archaeological work on prehistoric migrations in South America has focused on earlier agricultural and linguistic expansions, there is evidence that the Late Intermediate Period (c. AD 1000–1450; hereafter the LIP) saw a signifi-cant penetration of highland groups down into the upper piedmont. For example, in central Peru there are signs of considerable genetic (Barbieri et al. 2014) and linguistic (Adelaar 2006) interactions between Quechua speakers and piedmont-dwelling Arawaks. The time depth of these interactions is not entirely clear, although they appear to predate the Inca expansion. In southern Peru, the phe-nomenon of late pre-Inca expansions of highland settlers into the piedmont valleys is also well supported by archaeological evidence, at least in regions where any has been gathered. Consider the area around the Vilcabamba, Amaybamba, upper Urubamba and upper Apurímac valleys, which represents the most intensively sur-veyed region of the Peruvian piedmont. Throughout this region, comprising some 15,000 km², the absence of pre-LIP archaeological remains is striking – whether measured in terms of sites, or even a lack of isolated scatters of lithic and ceramic artefacts. This contrasts markedly with the situation during the LIP, where we see an explosion of new sites across the landscape after c. AD 1000. Thus far, 178 sites with an LIP date have been identified (see Figure 3.1.2).

All of these take the form of small settlements with rustic stone-built archi-tecture. It therefore appears that during the LIP, this broader landscape was transformed into one occupied by densely packed networks of small agricultural villages. Of course, this does not mean the region was 'uninhabited' prior to the LIP, and presumably small numbers of hunter-gatherers would have been present.

If such data are truly representative of other piedmont zones, it suggests that the eastern slopes were only permanently settled during the final centuries of the pre-colonial era. This situation is markedly different from the Andes and Amazonia,

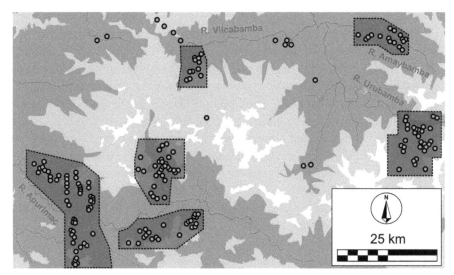

Figure 3.1.2 Map of the Apurimac, Vilcabamba, Amaybamba and Urubamba valleys (south-eastern Peru), showing the locations of known LIP sites. Polygons indicate regions of intensive survey, as opposed to general reconnaissance.
© Darryl Wilkinson, based on Bauer et al. (2015), Drew (1984), Kendall (1984), Lee (2000), Saintenoy (2016), Von Kaupp and Carrasco (2010) and Wilkinson (2013).

which both saw several millennia of agricultural occupation prior to the arrival of Europeans. Although it is true that recent excavations have confirmed the presence of Middle Horizon (that is, Wari) outposts in the piedmont (Fonseca Santa Cruz and Bauer 2013), the evidence for settlement predating AD 1000 is still extraordinarily sparse. To my mind, this relatively sudden appearance of large numbers of LIP villages in the piedmont represents a largely unrecognized, yet highly significant, migration phase in South American prehistory. The fact that the permanent human settlement of the piedmont was so conspicuously late is also one of the region's most distinctive characteristics.

The reasons underlying the downslope migrations of the Late Intermediate Period are unclear, and undoubtedly complex. But one potential stimulus was the long-term population growth in the highlands due to increasingly intensified maize cultivation (Finucane 2009) – perhaps the terminal phase of a farming-language dispersal of Quechua speakers (see Beresford-Jones and Heggarty 2012b). The eastern piedmont was also a prime source of coca leaf, a crop of increasing value to Andean highlanders throughout the late prehistoric and colonial periods. There is ethnohistorical evidence that the highland elites of the LIP established agricultural colonies in the nearby piedmont regions in order to secure regular access to coca (LeVine 1979), a phenomenon that has received archaeological corroboration in Hastorf's (1987) identification of preserved coca endocarps from two pre-Inca elite contexts in the upper Mantaro Valley dating to AD 1300–1460. This phenomenon, whereby communities establish colonies across multiple ecozones in order to exploit a more diverse range of species, is referred to as a 'vertical archipelago'; a model originally developed by John Murra (1972) and one of the most influential paradigms for interpreting ancient Andean economic formations.

That said, more 'political' factors might have been at play too, in the sense that not all people would have necessarily welcomed the emergence of the great highland empires of late prehistory. Andean dissidents have long sought out the lowlands as a space of refuge from highland authorities; from the neo-Incas led by Manco Inca in the 1500s to Juan Santos Atahualpa's indigenous rebellion in the mid-1700s. And I doubt that the tradition of highlanders fleeing to the lowlands to evade state power only began in the colonial period. Taxes are seldom popular in any time or place, so the exaction of (often steep) labour levies under the imperial states of late prehistory may have induced some communities to move to lower elevations in search of greater autonomy. Andean archaeologists have devoted considerable effort to assessing the verticality model, on the grounds that it is well attested in the ethnohistorical record. Yet so far as I am aware, the possibility that prehistoric highland populations moved into the lowlands as an *escape strategy* has received virtually no archaeological consideration, despite this being a phenomenon that is equally well documented.

Whatever the causes, one consequence of the LIP migrations into the piedmont was more frequent encounters between Andeans and lowland diseases against which they had little biological resistance. The introduction of new pathogens to human populations with limited immunity was a key aspect of the 'Columbian Exchange' that was associated with the European invasions of the Americas (with the waves of new diseases often spreading faster than the colonists themselves). But prior to the colonial era the main location of such pathogenic encounters was the eastern piedmont (albeit on a much smaller scale), since in South America the distribution of many diseases is strongly correlated with altitude. In terms of disease ecology, Amazonian and Andean populations have undergone considerable divergence since our species' initial colonization of the Americas – a fact brought into sharp relief during late prehistory when highland populations sought to settle the eastern piedmont for the first time.

In this context, the most significant illness of the pre-colonial Americas was Mucocutaneous Leishmaniasis, caused by the protozoan pathogen *Leishmania braziliensis braziliensis* and infecting humans through the bite of a sandfly vector. The sandfly's habitat is the lowland forests of the neotropics, and the disease is thus endemic to much of Amazonia. The major symptom is the development of skin lesions, which in severe cases can lead to extensive necrosis of the facial tissues, and even death. Early colonial documents clearly show that Quechua-speaking populations in the highlands were aware of Leishmaniasis and associated it with travel in the forested lowlands (Gade 1979), while indigenous lowland populations do not seem to have suffered from the disease to the same extent, likely the result of having developed greater genetic resistance. Modern epidemiological research corroborates the view that highlanders are much more susceptible to Leishmaniasis than are lowland populations. For example, one study in the Bolivian Amazon concluded that for individuals between the ages of 5 and 20 years, the risk of developing Leishmaniasis was three times greater for highland migrants as compared to native lowlanders. And for highland-born children under 5 years old, the risk was 10 times greater (Alcais et al. 1997).

In the Amaybamba Valley there is archaeological evidence for a significant Late Intermediate Period occupation comprised of highland migrants. The evidence that they were migrants is seen primarily in their material culture, with both houses and ceramics showing strong similarities to those of LIP communities in the adjacent uplands. The mortuary architecture of the Amaybamba also bears a close similarity to that of the northern side of the Vilcanota (Urubamba) Valley in the highlands, with multiple cave burials, and a mixture of rectilinear and circular aboveground sepulchres (Covey 2006). All this is relevant to the current discussion because the Amaybamba LIP communities would thus have been non-natives moving into a low-lying zone where Leishmaniasis was endemic. Looking at the settlement pattern of these communities – as per the data obtained from the archaeological survey – it appears that the Amaybamba LIP groups were aware of this disease threat, and deliberately sought to avoid it (see Figure 3.1.3).

In particular, no LIP settlement in the valley is located below 2,150 m, while the local upper limit for Leishmaniasis is approximately 2,000 m (Gade 2016, 109–11). This would have been somewhat inconvenient for the communities involved, given that there is very little cultivable land in the Amaybamba, with the exception of the valley floor itself.[4] In other words, by settling the upper slopes, they were creating a significant distance between themselves and the places where they would have had to grow their crops. Most conspicuously, they only settled the valley floor in the upper portions of the drainage where it lay above 2,150 m. They completely avoided the lower stretches of the valley floor, despite these being much wider and thus more amenable to agriculture.

Thus there is a bipartite vertical settlement pattern in the LIP sites of the Amaybamba, consisting of (1) the residential and mortuary zone (2,150–2,700 m) and (2) the primary cultivation zone (1,600–2,100 m). This distinctive settlement pattern might be seen as representing an adaptation specific to the piedmont, a product of the fact that the region was home to populations – of both humans and protozoa – with limited prior exposure to each other. Encounters with unfamiliar pathogens are not unusual when colonizing new regions; but as the last major area of South America to receive permanent agricultural settlement, this situation would have been somewhat unique to the piedmont by late prehistoric times.

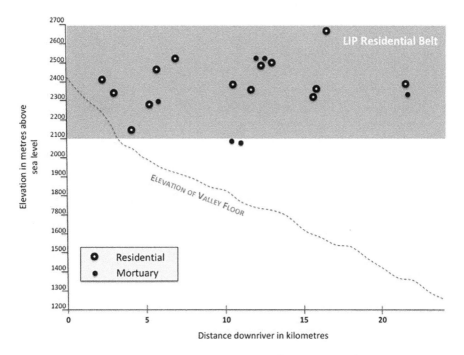

Figure 3.1.3 Diagram showing the elevations of Late Intermediate Period archaeological sites in the Amaybamba Valley, in relation to the valley floor. © Darryl Wilkinson.

Exchange, production and subsistence in the piedmont zone

The Incas' occupation of the Amaybamba dominated the valley floor rather than the surrounding hillsides, making it markedly different to that of the preceding LIP. According to the available documentary evidence, the Incas populated the Amaybamba with 1,000 *mitimaes* (or *mitmaqkuna*) in order to cultivate coca (Rostworowski 1993, 149; cf. other sources in Chapter 5.1). *Mitimaes* were involuntary colonists, typically sent to a particular region to maximize the production of a specific good. Their relations with the Incas were often more direct, bypassing the system of provincial organization that involved intermediary local elites (called *curacas*). Although the institution served a variety of purposes, many *mitimaes* were involved in the production of goods over which the Incas sought to maintain a theoretical monopoly, such as precious metals. Coca leaf was one such good, hence the dominance of *mitimaes* in the coca fields of the eastern piedmont (D'Altroy and Earle 1985, 196).

All this speaks to a general Inca pattern, not one peculiar to the Amaybamba. In the highlands, the dominant labour system was one based on the *mit'a* (that is, taxes paid in labour, not in kind; similar to the *corvée* system of feudal Europe). In the piedmont, however, it was predominantly the *mitimaes* who laboured for the state. To be clear, colonies of *mitimaes* were established in the highlands too; the difference being that under the Incas the piedmont increasingly moved towards a labour extraction system based exclusively on *mitimaes*. And again, Amazonia was different from either. Amazonian communities seem to have given substantial tribute to the Incas, but not through institutionalized labour systems. Instead, lowland goods flowed into the highlands either as gifts,[5] or in many cases (at least according to the Spanish chronicles) as plunder obtained in military adventures (Pärssinen 1992). The particular kinds of valuables that were exchanged across long distances also serve to distinguish the piedmont, Amazonia and the Andes. In Amazonia, the major prestige goods exported to other regions generally took the form of wild animal products, chiefly the feathers of tropical birds. In the highlands, the key goods exported included metals, obsidian and fine ceramics. Yet for the piedmont, the main high-value export had always been coca leaf – a species of domesticated flora rather than a wild animal or mineral product. Although coca is often described as a 'lowland' cultigen, it is more precisely understood as a crop of the piedmont (see Plowman 1985). Modern eradication programs targeting the cocaine economy have pushed many coca fields down into areas below 1,000 m, where they are less susceptible to interference from highland-centred governments, but in the past the crop was often grown as high as 2,200 m.

Turning to the means by which such products were actually moved, the river systems of the piedmont are similar to those of the highlands in that they are generally non-navigable. As noted earlier, most of the major highland–lowland river drainages only become safe for canoe traffic below 1,000 m, and even then, only in the dry season, since the waters are less violent. As such, the piedmont lay outside the extensive waterborne exchange networks of prehistoric Amazonia. However, it was much more directly incorporated into the transport networks of the highlands. The terrestrial transport networks of the Andes reached their pre-colonial apogee in the imperial highways (or Qhapaq Ñan) of the Incas; and as a rule this system included the eastern piedmont, but did not reach beyond into the Amazonian plains (see Chacaltana et al. 2017). In this respect the Amaybamba Valley was no exception. The late prehistoric roads of the region speak to the impressive levels of infrastructure investment that the Incas directed towards the piedmont, as well as across the highlands. The main Inca road along the Amaybamba, for instance, had a typical width of between 2 and 2.8 m, and was paved with stone for at least 3.6 km along the valley floor. But the archaeological evidence from the Amaybamba also indicates considerable integration of the piedmont into terrestrial exchange networks *prior* to the imperial era. Excavations at the LIP site of Pistipata, for example, have produced evidence of pre-Inca exchange relations with the sierra in the form of copper-based artefacts and waste from obsidian tool manufacture – excavated from contexts that were radiocarbon dated to AD 1409–47 and AD 1310–1421 (calibrated) respectively. The presence of obsidian is particularly relevant because the nearest known sources are 200 km away (see Figure 3.1.4).

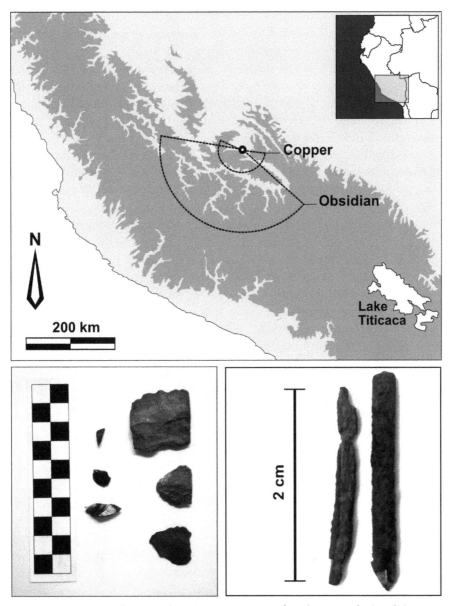

Figure 3.1.4 Map showing the minimum extent of trade networks involving the site of Pistipata with respect to highland copper and obsidian sources. Images of lithic artefacts, including obsidian debitage (bottom left) and copper-based artefacts (bottom right) excavated from Unit 01 at Pistipata. Map and photos © Darryl Wilkinson.

The extension of the Inca highway network into the Amaybamba clearly did not initiate long-distance links between the piedmont and the highlands; it formalized and intensified trade networks already in existence.

With even the basic culture-history of the piedmont still largely unknown, very little research has yet been carried out on late prehistoric subsistence strategies in the region. The floor of the Amaybamba Valley ranges from 2,550 m to 1,100 m, so in theory both maize and manioc would have been viable staples in the region. It is therefore interesting to what extent it might reflect an 'Andean' or 'Amazonian' subsistence pattern. Carbonized maize was excavated from a sub-floor deposit in one of the residential structures at the LIP site of Pistipata, confirming that it was at least present. As for the Inca period, there are legal documents from the mid-1500s that refer to the pre-conquest royal estates of the Amaybamba, indicating that the main crops being grown there were coca leaf and maize (Aparicio Vega 1999). The valley's population effectively collapsed in the aftermath of the Spanish conquest (Wilkinson 2013, 34–7), so this likely reflects the dominant crop regime under the Incas as well. It is worth noting here that the *mitimaes* who cultivated the coca for the Inca State were theoretically self-sufficient once established in their new home, so it would make sense that they had to grow maize for their own sustenance, alongside the coca leaf that they produced for export to the highlands. The archaeological survey of Inca sites in the Amaybamba has also furnished ceramics typically associated with the consumption of fermented maize, including in one instance the remains of a stand for a large *aríbalo* of the kind used to hold maize beer during feasts. Before and after the Inca annexation then, the Amaybamba region appears to have been integrated more with the world of maize consumption (in both solid and liquid forms) than the lowland sphere of manioc consumption. Although such distinctions obviously do relate to subsistence matters, I should emphasize that the divide here is as much a cultural one as anything else. Maize is widely cultivated in Amazonia, and manioc is commonly grown in the Andean coastal valleys. But in the Andean highlands, a social occasion without maize beer is something of a contradiction in terms, while the same might be said for manioc beer across much of the forested lowlands. Thus the fact that the Amaybamba was part of the maize-consuming world probably tells us more about the wider social networks in which it participated, rather than any local ecological constraints.

On the topic of subsistence, one final point is worth making with regard to the presence and absence of Andean camelids in the piedmont. Due to the poor preservation of bone in the acidic soils of the eastern Andes, the primary archaeological indicator of camelid exploitation is corral structures. Several sites with corral structures were identified in the survey of the Amaybamba Valley, but all were of Inca (or possibly colonial) cultural affiliation, while none were associated with the earlier LIP occupation (Wilkinson 2013). The eastern piedmont is not a particularly hospitable environment for Andean camelids, since it generally lacks suitable pasturelands (at least without extensive burning of the landscape). Also, diseases such as Toxoplasmosis (*Toxoplasma gondii*) seem to infect Andean came-lids with considerably greater frequency in warmer climates (Chávez-Velásquez et al. 2014). Interestingly, the aforementioned presence of corrals at Inca sites in the Amaybamba appears to have been related not to subsistence or wool produc-tion, but to long-distance transport. Instead of being distributed across a range of potential grazing zones, the Inca corrals are largely concentrated in a single site (Qochapata), which appears to have been a centre for loading pack-llamas with coca leaf, to be transported to the highlands following each harvest cycle (Wilkinson 2013, 359–78). There is thus little evidence that the Amaybamba section of the piedmont was ever integrated into the agro-pastoral subsistence systems of the highlands, and instead it seems to have tended towards more exclu-sively agricultural/horticultural strategies, likely supplemented by fishing. In this respect, it reflects a more typically 'Amazonian' pattern, even after it had been incorporated into the Inca Empire.

Conclusions

In sum, there are various respects in which a piedmont region such as the Amaybamba can be seen as exhibiting archaeological patterns that are either typi-cally Amazonian or Andean. Yet in other cases, we can identify characteristics that are unique to the piedmont itself, reflecting neither highland nor lowland norms (cf. Chapter 3.7). Table 3.1.1 presents my (simplified) synopsis of this argument. It remains an open question as to how far the patterns identified here will hold true for other piedmont valleys. That said, many of the elements I have discussed are hardly unique to the Amaybamba. For instance, factors such as highlanders' lack of immunity to Leishmaniasis, the unsuitability of the piedmont for domesticated camelids, the lack of navigable rivers above 1,000 m and the importance of coca leaf as a crop best suited to intermediate elevations *should* all pertain, in one form or another, across the entire piedmont zone. Whether local conditions produced strategies or outcomes that differ from those seen in the Amaybamba remains to be seen. My arguments are therefore best thought of as a model to be tested through future research in comparable regions, rather than a conclusive account.

As I have also suggested, the piedmont provides a privileged window onto the nature of the Andes–Amazonia divide more generally. Phenomena are often clear-est at their boundaries, and in this respect the large-scale patterns that typified the human ecology of prehistoric South America are no exception. It is in the pied-mont, where both the Amazonian and Andean worlds meet, that their divergences are made most apparent. A good example of this is seen in the 'choice' between manioc or maize in a transitional region like the Amaybamba. On purely ecological grounds both crops were equally viable, but only the latter appears to have been cultivated to any significant degree. The reason for this was that by late prehis-tory, manioc and maize had become far more than just a basic source of calories.

Table 3.1.1 Table indicating the areas in which the piedmont reflects Amazonian patterns (dark grey), highland Andean patterns (light grey) and piedmont-specific patterns (white).

	Amazonia	Piedmont	Andean highlands
Resource extraction under the Incas	Tribute through gift-giving or plunder	Formal labour extraction (through *mitimaes*)	Formal labour extraction (through *mit'a*)
Primary prestige goods for export	Wild faunal products (esp. bird feathers)	Domesticated floral products (esp. coca leaf)	Mineral resources (i.e. metal and lithic materials) and finished ceramics
Pathogenic context	High levels of pathogens, high immunity	High levels of pathogens, low immunity	Low levels of pathogens, low immunity
Transport systems	Riverine transport	Terrestrial transport	Terrestrial transport
Staple crop + alcohol	Manioc, manioc beer	Maize, maize beer	Maize, maize beer
Linguistic affiliation	Amazonian languages	(Highland) Andean languages	(Highland) Andean languages
Subsistence economy	Agricultural	Agricultural	Agro-pastoral

They had also come to underpin two contrasting social networks – a highland one based on terrestrial transport systems and state-controlled labour systems, and a lowland one based on riverine transport systems and far-flung trading diasporas. The fact that the Amaybamba could be part of one of these spheres (but not both) is a testimony to the stark reality of the Andes–Amazonia divide during the final centuries before European contact. If nothing else then, I hope to have offered a convincing case that the piedmont – as the space that both separates the Andes and Amazonia and links them together – is one deserving of considerably more study than it has hitherto received. And not just because it is a place that merits examination in its own right (although it certainly does), but because it was the hinge upon which many of the interregional networks of the late prehistoric and colonial periods turned.

3.2

Genetic diversity patterns in the Andes and Amazonia

Fabrício R. Santos[1]

Reconstructing the human past is a complex multidisciplinary task that only makes sense if independent types of evidence are integrated into a consensual and coherent history.

In scientific historical surveys, genetics can be used to reveal genealogical connections between individuals and populations, to assess their past demography and to trace movements of ancestors through time and space (among other applications). In these historical genetic studies, population dynamics and structure are key aspects for understanding the distribution of the present-day genetic diversity of indigenous South Americans, which was shaped by a complex set of evolutionary events involving ancestral populations.

Historical genetics of Native Americans

Genetic analyses of genotypes (DNA inherited from parents) have been used since the 1980s to reconstruct the (pre)history of Native Americans. Available genetic evidence largely supports a common Asian ancestry of Native Americans and Northeast Asians until the Late Pleistocene, <26,000 BP (Santos et al. 1999; González-José et al. 2008; Bodner et al. 2012; Rasmussen et al. 2015). Only a much more limited data set, however, has been applied to the study of indigenous groups of South America specifically (Tarazona-Santos et al. 2001; Jota et al. 2011; Battaglia et al. 2013). The first Native Americans were likely derived from a population living in Beringia at ~18,000 BP (González-José et al. 2008; Rasmussen et al. 2015), which spread through the entire length of the American continent in perhaps less than 2,000 years, initially along the Pacific coastline (Bodner et al. 2012). At the end of this epic journey, South America was first settled around 14,000 BP (Ruiz-Narváez et al. 2005; Rothhammer and Dillehay 2009; Bodner et al. 2012; Rasmussen et al. 2015). Even though South America was the last continental landmass reached by *Homo sapiens*, it displayed among the richest diversity of peoples and cultures worldwide (Salzano and Callegari-Jacques 1988), exemplified by the innumerable indigenous languages spoken in pre-Columbian times (Rodrigues 2005).

Although much effort has been expended on understanding the first peopling of the Americas, the indigenous history of South America still requires many detailed studies to be performed by geneticists, archaeologists, physical anthropologists, linguists and other historical scientists. A common view describes South American Indians as derived from North American groups who arrived through the Isthmus of Panama at the end of the Pleistocene (Rothhammer and Dillehay 2009). However, much debate still centres on the timing of the arrival of the first South Amerindians (Bodner et al. 2012) and the dynamics of subsequent flows of migrants from North America (Ruiz-Narváez et al. 2005). Within South America, the spread of ancestral peoples to colonize various landscapes and biomes, which resulted in many biologically and culturally diverse indigenous groups, has also been extensively discussed (Salzano and Callegari-Jacques 1988). These and many other questions on the origins of Native Americans were raised as soon as the first European chroniclers arrived in the New World, as brilliantly illustrated in the sixteenth-century work of Fray José de Acosta (Acosta 1590).

Pre-Columbian demography and population dynamics of South America

European conquistadors reported divergent demographic scenarios across different regions of the Americas, with modern estimates for the total native population in 1492 ranging from 8.4 to 112.5 million people (Thornton 2005). In almost all published population estimates for pre-Columbian South America, the Andes present much the highest population *density*, with estimates varying from three to 37 million inhabitants, that is, up to three times more people than all remaining areas of the continent combined (Dobyns 1966; Denevan 1976). (Notwithstanding recent upward revisions of estimates of population *size* in Amazonia [Chapter 1.1], the contrast in *density* remains.) The high population density in the central part of the Andes, from southern Colombia to northern Chile, was associated, at the time of first contact with Europeans, with the domains of the Inca empire or *Tawantinsuyu*, the most complex indigenous society found in South America in the sixteenth century (Denevan 1976; D'Altroy 2015). Currently, in the highlands of the Central Andes there remain abundant speakers of indigenous languages, mainly of the Quechua and Aymara families, notably in Ecuador, Peru and Bolivia (as mapped in Figure 1.2.1, Chapter 1.2), where speakers sum up to about 8.5 million (Howard 2011).

Motivated by earlier historical reports, some genetic studies focused on the likely consequences of demographic differences between Andeans and other populations in South America (Luiselli et al. 2000; Rodríguez-Delfín et al. 2001;

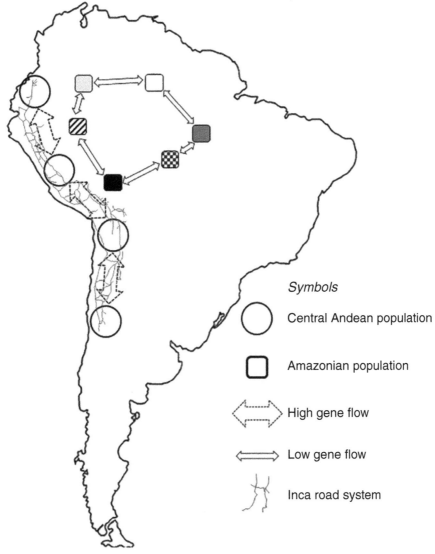

Figure 3.2.1 Population dynamics model of the pre-Columbian settlement of South America. © Fabrício R. Santos.

Tarazona-Santos et al. 2001; Fuselli et al. 2003). This resulted in a model of how populations evolved during the pre-Columbian settlement of South America (Tarazona-Santos et al. 2001) which predicted that indigenous populations from the Central Andes (Quechua- and Aymara-speakers) and from 'lowland' areas should fit two contrasting patterns of genetic drift and gene-flow (see Figure 3.2.1).

In the Central Andes, Quechua- and Aymara speakers displayed greater genetic diversity within each local population group, and a higher gene-flow (migration of individuals and genes) between such groups. Lowland population groups, particularly in Amazonia and in the Central Brazilian Plateau, by contrast, had less genetic diversity within each group (showing more impact of genetic drift, and low effective population sizes), and there was less gene-flow between groups. (For explanations of all technical terminology from genetics used in this chapter – for example, genetic drift, effective population size, autosomal markers, and so on – see Chapter 1.3.) The genetic pattern of the Central Andes was confirmed in a study using many autosomal markers, which also revealed a large repository of genetic diversity among Quechua-speaking populations (Scliar et al. 2012). Another genomic study (Yang et al. 2010) identified the same divide between Amazonia and the Andes, but the authors suggested that it was caused by an early separation of the source populations during initial settlement of South America. This ancient split is not supported by more recent studies, however (Sandoval, Lacerda et al. 2013; Battaglia et al. 2013; Roewer et al. 2013). Besides, a genomic study using a Bayesian dating method (Scliar et al. 2014) has estimated that the population split between Andean Quechua-speakers and Amazonian Shimaa (Machiguenga, Arawak language family) dates to no earlier than 5300 BP. Although the authors suggest an Andean origin for Shimaa, another likely explanation for this shared ancestry would be that some Andean highlanders have an ancient Amazonian origin.

At the phenotypic level, analyses of the cranial morphology of late pre-Columbian South Amerindians (Pucciarelli et al. 2006; see also Chapter 2.2) have also detected a divide between highland and lowland populations. In fact, the genetic model of population evolution (Tarazona-Santos et al. 2001) also predicts that phenotypes should be more homogeneous throughout the Andes, and quite heterogeneous among Amazonian populations. However, Pucciarelli et al. (2006) found no differences in intra-population diversity between the two regions, likely due to the multifactorial inheritance and quantitative nature of skull shape variation, which may also be subject to selection. Indeed, quantitative variation and trait differentiation have been shown to correlate only weakly with effective population size (Wood et al. 2015).

The particular population dynamics of pre-Columbian South America, as detected in genotypes and phenotypes, have often been attributed to historical and present-day differences between the populations of those areas, in both demography and gene-flow patterns. These genetic differences correlate with cultural aspects, such as the advanced agriculture and social complexity observed in the Central Andes, when compared to lowland groups (Tarazona-Santos et al. 2001). (If that cultural contrast is challenged, as by recent revised thinking on social complexity and demographic scale in Amazonia – see Chapter 1.1 – then the correlation is weakened.) Indeed, population (and language family) expansions have frequently been associated with the spread of first farmers worldwide (Diamond and Bellwood 2003) and in South America (Heggarty and Renfrew 2014b). Genetic studies of indigenous populations worldwide (Gignoux et al. 2011) and in the Americas (Regueiro et al. 2013) also show a remarkable increase in population size over the last 10,000 years.

The high population densities observed in the pre-Columbian Central Andes may have been intensified by the development of an ecologically flexible and thereby mobile agricultural package based on maize (Heggarty and Beresford-Jones 2010). Interestingly, a clear divide has also been identified between strains of maize developed in the Andes and Amazonia, in a genetic study of current indigenous and archaeological maize samples (Freitas and Bustamante 2013). This study suggested an initial introduction and further divergence of maize strains at about 5000 BP in the Andes, and 2000 BP in the Amazonia. Furthermore, a genetic study of a human paternal lineage (a Y-chromosome variant – see Chapter 1.3) originating around 5000 BP in northern Peru indicates a recent secondary human dispersal path from north to south through the Central Andes (Jota et al. 2011), which echoes the spread of maize through the Andean highlands (Vigouroux et al. 2008).

Pre-Columbian Amazonia was home to some large urban complexes (Heckenberger et al. 2003), and here too agriculture was practised by many indigenous groups, including those speaking languages of the Tupí and Arawak families (Clement et al. 2015; see Figure 1.2.1 in Chapter 1.2). However, in the Central Andes farming was remarkably advanced, which supported the emergence of many complex societies and the largest pre-Columbian cities found in South America in the sixteenth century (Lumbreras 1974). The *relatively* homogeneous cultural landscape found in the Central Andes, where some domestic plants and animals were bred to adapt to high altitude (from 1,000 to 4,200 metres above sea level), may also have been an important factor in the establishment of complex societies here. A hierarchically organized society, with advanced farming technology adapted to a high-altitude landscape along the Central Andes, would be expected to display a high inter-population gene flow and to maintain large effective population sizes. These past dynamics of pre-Columbian peoples would result in cultural homogenization along the Central Andes (when compared to Amazonia), facilitated by the use of the pre-Columbian road networks, known under the Incas as the *Qhapaq Ñan*, and which totalled c. 23,000 km in the sixteenth century (see Figure 3.2.1 and Lumbreras 2004). In contrast, Amazonia and other lowland biomes of South America present much higher cultural and genetic differentiation between indigenous groups (Tarazona-Santos et al. 2001; Wang et al. 2007; Cabana et al. 2014), where populations tend to remain isolated and to differentiate due to environmental conditions or life-styles more dependent on foraging. Much of the human diversity found in South America can also be explained by a fission-fusion model of indigenous populations (Neel and Salzano 1967), where tribal splits and subsequent isolation and drift could explain observable differences, particularly among Amazonian groups.

As for the big-picture pattern of genetic contrasts across South America, different studies give very contrasting results. A large study with 678 microsatellite loci found a much larger divergence among native groups in eastern South America than in other indigenous populations worldwide (Wang et al. 2007). In another broad genomic study, Reich et al. (2012) used an admixture graph method (AG) to identify three different groups of indigenous populations in South America: in the Andes, Chaco and eastern South America (Amazonia and the Central Brazilian Plateau). Furthermore, they observed low intra-population diversity and high inter-population divergence among indigenous populations of eastern South America. South-eastern South America, which includes the Chaco, Pampas and Patagonia, was identified by Callegari-Jacques et al. (2011) as a third distinctive component of the population structure in the continent, besides the Andes and Amazonia. In other words, even though results presented by different genetic studies (Callegari-Jacques et al. 2011; Reich et al. 2012; Roewer et al. 2013) do not at all agree on a single divide among South American indigenous groups by broad geographic regions, the populations of the Central Andes do always appear as a clearly distinctive regional group.

Cultural influences on population dynamics and history

As discussed above, pre-Columbian population groups in the Central Andes and Amazonia present contrasting general patterns of gene-flow and effective population sizes, which appear to be associated with environmental and cultural differences between these regions. However, widespread cultural heterogeneity can be observed, particularly in Amazonia, ranging from groups with a lifestyle based entirely on hunting and foraging to horticulturalists and farmers, and from nomadic to semi-sedentary populations. Even in the Central Andes, surrounded by complex farming societies, speakers of Uru languages (Adelaar and Muysken 2004) were still practising a foraging life-style associated with lakes and rivers in the Andean Altiplano until as recently as colonial times (Wachtel 1986; and see Figure 4.1.1 in Chapter 4.1). Indeed, a genetic study (Sandoval, Lacerda et al. 2013) was able to identify that Uru populations (the Uros in Peru, and the Uru-Chipaya and Uru-Poopó groups in Bolivia) are clearly differentiated from neighbouring groups in the Altiplano who speak Quechua and Aymara. This suggests that the ancestors of Uru groups derive from population sources different to those of likely more recent farming groups.

On the Central Brazilian Plateau, on the fringes of the Amazonian rainforest, are many Jê-speaking groups. The Xavante, Kayapó and Panará, for example, although practising some rudimentary agriculture by the time of contact in the twentieth century, lived as typical foragers (Neel et al. 1964). In a seminal publication by Neel and Salzano (1967) based on a study of the Xavante, a fission-fusion model was used to explain a pattern of population dynamics that resulted in groups splitting into endogamous tribes, which may have then evolved in relative independence for a while, or fused with another tribe. This dynamic could result in a rapid evolution of genes and morphological characters, as evidenced by the Xavante, who show a rapid phenotypic divergence in skull shape when compared to other closely related indigenous groups, probably in response to culture-mediated processes (Hünemeier et al. 2012a).

Among lowland populations, demic expansions (the geographical dispersal of growing populations) were frequently associated with farming-dependent societies in South America, such as speakers of Arawak, Carib and Tupí languages (Diamond and Bellwood 2003; see Figure 1.2.1, in Chapter 1.2). A genetic study of the range expansion of Tupí populations revealed a typical isolation-by-distance pattern, while Jê speakers, who are mainly foragers, dispersed in a non-linear pattern (Ramallo et al. 2013). This agrees with the different population structure outcomes expected between foragers (Jê, etc.) and farmers (Tupí, Arawak, etc.), where the latter will be largely impacted by past demographic expansion and dispersal. The more dependent a population is on foraging, the less its dispersal is accompanied by demographic expansion, and each group tends to differentiate without significant gene-flow.

Although demic fusions appear to be common among tribes of the same ethnic group (Neel and Salzano 1967), different languages and cultural practices would tend to prevent fusion between distinct ethnic groups in Amazonia (Hünemeier et al. 2012a) – although see below and Chapter 3.4 on the linguistic exogamy of the Vaupés region. This could be a major cause for the general differences in population dynamics observed between lowland areas and the Central Andes. However, populations with different levels of dependence on agriculture, heterogeneous social organizations and cultural practices, and who have experienced past fission and fusion events, should present a strikingly complex dynamic of demic evolution, particularly in Amazonia.

A genetic divide between indigenous populations of the Andes and Amazonia

In the Central Andes, settlement was dominated by many overlapping cultures succeeding each other ever since the Late Preceramic period (~4500 BP), exemplified by the ancient sites of Caral and Kotosh in Peru. With the establishment of agriculture-based societies between 4000 and 2000 BP, the highlands came to be dominated by farming, which eventually gave rise to the most complex indigenous societies of South America (Heggarty and Beresford-Jones 2010). In the genetic pattern as currently observed, the peopling of the Central Andes fits a demic diffusion model, as first suggested for the Neolithic transition in Europe (Ammerman and Cavalli-Sforza 1984). In this model, a massive movement of people would be connected with the spread of new technologies (agriculture), eventually assimilating all local forager societies – as may be the case of populations who spoke the now almost 'extinct' Uru-languages (Sandoval, Lacerda et al. 2013). Since extensive archaeological data

(Stanish 2001) point to a more likely origin on the Pacific coast for the complex societies later found in the Andean highlands, a demic diffusion of farmers could also explain the assimilation of other former highland forager populations who share a recent (<5000 BP) ancestry with current Amazonians (Scliar et al. 2014).

The pre-Columbian occupation of Amazonia presents a much more complex scenario, with a larger diversity of ethnic groups, cultural practices and languages, associated with higher genetic differentiation between those groups, and relatively lower diversity within each group. Given past fission and fusion events, and heterogeneous demographic outcomes for populations with different levels of farming technology and social structures, the evolutionary dynamics of populations suggests this area has been inhabited by a complex human metapopulation (Morris and Mukherjee 2006), within which many dynamic demes have been constantly changing in size, going extinct and re-colonizing other areas through time and space. Because culture (language, farming, rituals, beliefs, and so on) is so important to how humans adapt to new environments, it may be that density-dependent habitat selection (Fretwell and Lucas 1969) played a significant role in shaping the diversification of Amazonian peoples in pre-Columbian times. Indeed, niche construction by hunter-gatherer and farmer populations (Rowley-Conwy and Layton 2011; Hünemeier et al. 2012b) may have been important in shaping local adaptations that drove the expansion and dispersal of different indigenous groups throughout Amazonia. Other environmental and cultural aspects can also be expected to play important roles in this dynamic, such as the upper Rio Negro cultural alliance in north-western Amazonia, between Brazil and Colombia (Epps and Stenzel 2013). In the upper Rio Negro (Vaupés) region, alliances involving at least 600 years of marriage practices between indigenous groups, speaking many different languages from two independent families, have created a multi-ethnic system across an area of 250,000 km², occupied by humans since 3200 BP (Neves 1998). In contrast to the remaining areas of Amazonia, this region is expected to have developed a large and complex population made up of many patrilineal clans and tribes linked by gene-flow, due to the exchange of wives between speakers of languages of the Arawak and Tukano families.

Much of the genetic difference observed between indigenous populations in the Central Andes and in Amazonia can be accounted for by their contrasting histories of gene-flow, demic expansion and dispersal. That said, although these contrasting patterns can be recognized between the two regions, within each there is also significant heterogeneity of (biological) populations and cultural relationships, changing through time and space. Besides, there are three sets of indications that this 'divide' is of course not entirely abrupt or absolute: reports of historical gene-flow between indigenous groups from the Andes and Amazonia (Sandoval, Lacerda et al. 2013; Cabana et al. 2014; Barbieri et al. 2014); the existence of outlier groups in each region (Sandoval, Lacerda et al. 2013); and the absence of clear geographical and linguistic associations with genetic diversity (Callegari-Jacques et al. 2011; Reich et al. 2012; Roewer et al. 2013). More recently, some large studies including complete genomes of modern (Gnecchi-Ruscone et al. 2019) and ancient (Moreno-Mayar, Vinner et al. 2018) Native Americans indicate a complex demographic scenario for the occupation of South America, with multiple dispersal events between South and Central America giving rise to indigenous populations of Andes and Amazonia (and other non-Andeans). Future studies in population genetics should significantly enrich our understanding of the origin and diversification of the indigenous populations of South America, who still bear direct cultural and genealogical connections to their pre-Columbian ancestors.

3.3
Genetic exchanges in the highland/ lowland transitional environments of South America

Chiara Barbieri

Introduction

Geneticists have often evoked the contrast between the Andean and Amazonian environments to explain the major patterns in the genetic structure of South America. Major differences, as already described in Chapters 1.3 and 3.2, revolve around the ratio between the diversity within a given population, and around the diversity between different populations. In the Central Andes, populations are characterized by high genetic similarity to each other, but high genetic diversity between the individuals within a population; populations from the Amazon basin, meanwhile, are characterized by high differentiation between each other but low diversity across the individuals within a population. These contrasts have been interpreted in the light of different social dynamics playing out in the two environments: small isolated populations in the Amazon basin, and larger populations connected by gene-flow in the Andes (Tarazona-Santos et al. 2001; Fuselli et al. 2003; Wang et al. 2007; Dillehay 2009; Sandoval et al. 2016). Genetic contrasts between populations of the Andes and Amazonia include also a different composition of characteristic genetic lineages, such as uniparental haplogroups (on which see Chapter 1.3, and the review in Bisso-Machado et al. 2012). These differences have been critical to demographic studies, which have proposed separate routes for the first settlement of the continent (Keyeux et al. 2002; Yang et al. 2010). Finally, genomic differences between populations of high and low altitude play a fundamental role in functional studies on how environmental constraints may have driven selection for specific biological adaptations (Beall 2014).

Few genetic studies, however, have addressed the circumstances of contact and exchange in regions transitional between the two major environments of Andes and Amazonia, which constitute the focus of this chapter. It presents four genetic case-studies on the effect of contact and exchange between different ecological and cultural domains, highlighting limitations imposed by the respective population samples available and by the different genetic data chosen for the analyses.

Demographic studies that include genetic profiles of native populations have been focusing above all on uniparental markers, the DNA markers that are inherited on either the maternal (mitochondrial DNA, or mtDNA) or the paternal (Y-chromosome DNA) side (Chapter 1.3). Due to their transmission pattern they are suitable for reconstructing genealogies, and they are regarded as the gold standard for investigating phylogeography (that is, the distribution of phylogenetic lineages in specific regions of the world) and human migration and contact (Underhill et al. 2001; Pakendorf and Stoneking 2005; Torroni et al. 2006; Kundu and Ghosh 2015). For these markers, a large amount of data are available for inter-population comparisons. As a downside, when looking at the mtDNA or Y-chromosome we are limiting ourselves to a small fraction of the total DNA information carried by each individual, and we are considering only one ancestry line among the many that an individual bears. Deeper resolution is achievable with the use of autosomal data, which is still more demanding in terms of monetary and labour costs. As explained in Chapter 1.3 of this book, with the term autosomal we consider all the genetic material of our chromosomes (except the sex chromosomes) that is not transmitted solely on either the maternal or paternal side, but by virtually all our ancestors. Autosomal genomic data are more informative for fine-scale demographic reconstructions, but published data are still very few and far between for the populations of the Americas (Bustamante et al. 2011; Wall et al. 2011). Recent publications are improving the genomic coverage of the continent, revealing new sources of genetic diversity (Raghavan et al. 2015; Skoglund et al. 2015; Harris et al. 2018; Gnecchi-Ruscone et al. 2019).

The first two recent studies I examine here have made use of high-resolution autosomal data (SNP chip data). While the first employs a dataset that consists of only two populations, it is targeted towards research questions very much in line with the theme of this section. The second draws on a larger dataset, although oriented primarily to research questions on functional adaptation. Broader comparative datasets are included in the third and fourth case studies, based on mtDNA and Y-chromosome data. This chapter also includes a novel targeted comparative analysis that yields further insights into the questions already debated in the four case studies proposed. In its conclusions, it recapitulates the emerging major trends in the genetic make-up of populations inhabiting these transitional environments.

Autosomal data: A fine-grain resolution

A single Andean origin for Arawakan speakers of central Peru

The first case-study, based on autosomal data, looks into the origins of the Shimaa, a small population living in the transitional environment of the eastern slopes of the Andes (or *Yungas* in some interpretations of that term) in central Peru. The Shimaa speak Machiguenga, a language of the Arawak family, and present cultural features typically found in neighbouring Amazonian regions (on Arawak and its distribution, see Figure 1.2.1 in Chapter 1.2, and Chapter 3.4). Scliar et al. (2014) compare the diversity within fragments of autosomal DNA across ten Shimaa individuals and 11 Quechua speakers from Tayacaja, 300 km to the west, chosen to represent a population from the highlands. The authors apply Bayesian statistical analysis and model-testing to explore the nature of the relationship between the two populations. The results provide strong support for a split between the two populations that would have taken place not more than 5,300 years ago. The authors conclude by suggesting that the ancestors of the Shimaa were a small group who separated from a wider Andean population: this inference is based on the lower diversity of the Shimaa individuals, who harbour only a subset of the genetic variants found in the Quechua sample. The authors therefore evoke a scenario in which the Shimaa migrated from the Andes to the lower slopes towards Amazonia and underwent a cultural/linguistic shift after coming into contact with Arawak speakers. Unfortunately, the lack of any other comparative autosomal data prevents the authors from evaluating the contact dynamics of the Andes–Amazonia transition zone more widely; in fact, with just two samples available, only one divergence model could be tested. It would be crucial to test an alternative model where the Shimaa diverged from an Amazonian population, but this would require additional data from neighbouring regions, and from other Arawak speakers in particular.

Extremely high altitude influences genetic differentiation

The second case-study, again based on high-resolution autosomal data, focuses on functional adaptation. The Andes make for a good scenario for testing the effects of natural selection, given the increasingly hostile environment at higher altitudes. To survive at extreme elevations, humans developed a number of biological adaptations to hypobaric hypoxia (see review in Beall 2014). Yet altitudes above 4,000 m appear to have been settled from the late Pleistocene onwards (Rademaker et al. 2014), giving thousands of years for adaptations to high altitude to develop.

Studies on functional genetics suggest that highlanders are in part genetically differentiated from lowlanders. Eichstaedt et al. (2014), for example, found traces of selection on genetic markers associated with cardiac reinforcement when comparing two neighbouring populations of north-west Argentina: the Wichí of the Gran Chaco who live below 1,000 m, and the so-called 'Colla' who live in the highlands above 3,500 m. (This present-day population that goes by the name 'Colla' is not to be confused with the ethnic group immediately west and south of Lake Titicaca during the rise of the Incas.) This example serves as a useful reminder of the role played by factors other than demography (in this case, high-altitude environments) in shaping human genetic diversity.

In a second study, Eichstaedt et al. (2015) analyse whether a population living at intermediate altitudes might also be affected by moderate levels of hypoxia. The Calchaquíes of north-west Argentina live at 2,300 m in a region intermediate between the Altiplano and the Chaco: this region served as a migration corridor during late Inca expansion. Both studies from Eichstaedt and colleagues compare autosomal SNP data from their target populations with other available South American populations. These are taken from the public databases of HGDP-CEPH and from Reich et al. (2012) and Mao et al. (2007), for a total of 19 populations; eight of these, however, have fewer than ten individuals each, making it difficult to represent the genetic make-up of the whole target population. In the population analysis by Eichstaedt and colleagues, the Calchaquíes present an ancestry component commonly found in the neighbouring 'Colla', as well as in other (Quechua- and Aymara-speaking) populations of Peru and Bolivia. The Wichí, meanwhile, present an ancestral component widely found in other populations of the Gran Chaco, such as the Toba and, to a lesser extent, the Guaraní. The marked genetic difference between the Calchaquíes, who appear similar to other Andean highlanders, and the Gran Chaco populations, who all harbour (albeit at varying percentages) an ancestral component exclusive to their region, was not unexpected (Frank 2008). The Calchaquíes were also interacting intensely with populations from higher altitudes, as Inca allies and colonists were moved into this territory from various regions including the Titicaca basin (Lorandi and Boixadós 1988). Finally, the Calchaquíes present a subset of the genetic adaptations to high altitude found in the Argentine 'Colla', although the origin of this genetic signal is difficult to assess: it could be a mild response to environmental stress, or simply the result of gene flow from intermarriage with the 'Colla'.

Uniparental markers: Larger comparative datasets

Turning to uniparental markers (mtDNA and Y-chromosome), there are certainly more South American populations for which we have data, especially in the Andes (Bisso-Machado et al. 2012). Only recently, however, have studies begun to abandon a compartmentalized 'Andes or Amazonia' vision, to focus on exchanges *between* the two environments, that is, both the contribution of Andean genetic lineages to Amazonia and vice versa (see Chapter 1.3). New colonization routes have been proposed to account for the distribution and phylogeny of certain characteristic maternal and paternal lineages (Perego et al. 2010, 2012; Bodner et al. 2012; Saint Pierre et al. 2012a, 2012b). In some cases, the migration hypotheses are justified by historically attested population movements that offer plausible explanations for the patterns observed today (Bodner et al. 2012), but more often these phylogeographic studies are focused on the genealogy of specific lineages, rather than on the prehistory of specific populations.

Here I report on two case-studies based on uniparental markers, which investigate the origin and demographic history of two populations who live(d) in transitional environments, geographically close to those covered in the autosomal studies above. These are the ancient populations of the Quebrada de Humahuaca in north-west Argentina, and the present-day Yanesha, another Arawak-speaking population in the Andes–Amazonia transition in central Peru.

A window into the past: aDNA from Argentina shows maternal (but not paternal) connections with the Gran Chaco

Mendisco et al. (2014) analysed mtDNA and Y-chromosome data from archaeological remains found in the Quebrada de Humahuaca (Jujuy province) and in the neighbouring Calchaquí valley (Salta province). Ancient DNA (aDNA, see Chapter 1.3) was obtained from teeth dated AD 1000–1450, corresponding to the Regional Development Period (RDP). The Quebrada de Humahuaca is a valley in a strategic location between the Andean highlands (the Bolivian Altiplano and Argentinean Puna) and the eastern edges of the lowland forests and the Chaco. The region has been inhabited for at least 10,000 years and has long been characterized by a significant level of cultural, economic and social interactions, with relatively highly developed societies and dense populations (Nielsen 2001). The relationships between the ancient population of the Quebrada de Humahuaca and other ancient and present-day South American populations were explored through both the maternal (mtDNA) and paternal (Y-chromosome) lines. The mtDNA profile of the Quebrada de Humahuaca shows a high percentage of haplogroup A2, a lineage otherwise frequent in populations of *northern* South America, in the Guianas, and in some scattered populations of the Amazon basin (Bisso-Machado et al. 2012). This high frequency is unusual for this region, found neither in surrounding contemporary populations nor in ancient Andean samples. In fact, ancient and contemporary Andean highland samples are instead characterized by high frequencies of haplogroup B2 (Bisso-Machado et al. 2012; Fehren-Schmitz et al. 2014). Other analyses are also possible from mtDNA: not just comparing haplogroup frequencies per population, but analysing parts of the mtDNA sequence, which allows for finer resolution. The Quebrada de Humahuaca female-line mtDNA profile is overall genetically intermediate between the Andean and Gran Chaco population clusters (the latter represented by the Wichí and Guaraní), possibly suggesting a mix of the two genetic components.

For the Y-chromosome, meanwhile, a set of STR (Short Tandem Repeat) markers was analysed and compared to similar data retrieved from the literature. In this male-line STR data, the Quebrada de Humahuaca profile is closer to that found in populations speaking languages of the Aymara, Quechua, Guaraní and (formerly) Uro linguistic lineages (for the latter, see Chapter 4.1). The authors therefore conclude that the pre-Hispanic populations of the transitional region of the Quebrada de Humahuaca may have evolved locally without a significant genetic contribution from preceding or contemporary highland Andean cultures. Nevertheless, some exchanges could have occurred on the maternal side, towards the Gran Chaco, as a consequence of patrilocal exogamy (that is, the tendency for men to remain in their home region while women from elsewhere 'marry in' to it).

Layers of genetic and linguistic contact in Arawak speakers of central Peru

Our fourth and final case-study here addresses the origin of the Yanesha, a population in the Selva Central of Peru (provinces of Junín and Pasco), on the eastern slopes of the Andes (Barbieri et al. 2014). The Yanesha speak an Arawak language, like the Machiguenga in the first case-study by Scliar et al. (2014). The Yaneshas' form of Arawak, however, betrays especially heavy influence from Quechua, and indeed certain other language sources. In other words, their Arawak base language has been impacted by a series of different contact strata. The single most significant impact was from the Yaru dialect of central Quechua, spoken in neighbouring areas of the highlands. Other sources of borrowing are southern Quechua, nearby Amazonian languages and other unidentified languages (Adelaar 2006). These contacts affected aspects of the sound system, grammar, and above all the lexicon, in the form of a large number of loanwords. The home territory of the Yanesha, situated along a trade route towards the Cerro de la Sal (for which see Chapter 5.4) already established before the Incas (Lumbreras 1974), may have been marked by conspicuous population movements influencing the linguistic and genetic diversity of the Yanesha. For more on the Yanesha or Amuesha language, see Chapter 3.4.

To understand the origins of the Yanesha and the genetic impact of these several waves of contact over the centuries, samples were collected from communities at different altitude levels, in the high selva (*selva alta*), from altitudes between 1,200 m and 1,800 m, and in the intermediate selva (*selva media*) at c. 300 m, for a total of 214 individuals. Both uniparental markers were analysed, to compare the genetic profile of the Yanesha against the rest of the continent, in particular the neighbouring Andean and Amazon populations. The Y-chromosome comparative dataset includes 62 populations, the mtDNA dataset 77 populations.

A first observation is that for both uniparental markers, genetic diversity between individuals is higher than the average across the other South American populations analysed. The high diversity values indicate that the Yanesha populations were not particularly isolated, and/or had a large effective population size (proportional to a lower likelihood of marrying a relative). This could indicate that the Yanesha were part of an exchange network that introduced a degree of geneflow from other populations. In further pairwise comparisons with other South American populations, it became clear that the mtDNA dataset does not have enough resolution to be able to pinpoint any single major source of genetic contribution. The maternal profile of the Yanesha appears not particularly distinct, but similar to other South American populations from the Andes, Amazonia and the north of the sub-continent.

The most informative results come from individual genetic profiles (haplotypes) composed of 15 Y-chromosome STRs. The haplotypes of individuals belonging to different populations were compared. Assuming that identical haplotypes are shared by genealogically related individuals (who inherited the haplotype from a common ancestor, not too many generations ago), then the share of identical haplotypes between individuals of two populations will be proportional to the strength of recent contact and intermarriage (in this case, of male lineages, in these Y-chromosome data). As the generations succeed each other after the contact period, there is a higher chance of accumulating mutations, which would make the haplotypes look increasingly different. Of the two Yanesha populations, the high selva Yanesha share more haplotypes with other populations than do the intermediate selva Yanesha. This may reflect an environmental factor: the intermediate selva villages are more densely surrounded by forest, and possibly less accessible from the exchange routes.

It is also possible to plot onto a map of South America the frequencies of identical and similar haplotypes in the source populations that potentially exchanged these haplotypes with the Yanesha. Notably, the main source of contact is found in areas that once fell within the southern half of the Inca Empire (from 1472 or earlier): from the shores of Lake Titicaca as far as central-western Bolivia. This pattern does not seem to be paralleled in the female line, however, so this predominantly male gene-flow might be best explained by movements of male traders (the result of deep-time processes of exchange), and/or military forces (associated in some way with the Inca Empire: short-lived but with apparently dramatic impacts upon populations). The results do not, however, allow us to detect any specific gene-flow from the population that had the most powerful contact impact on their language, namely Yaru Quechua-speakers from central Peru. This may be attributed to two factors: a) that our database lacks populations suitably representative of Yaru speakers (the closest geographic proxy would be the sample of Quechua speakers from Huancavelica), or b) more recent contact masking the earlier inputs from the Yaru. A third scenario would simply imply that the linguistic contact was not accompanied by any substantial gene-flow.

The genetic composition of the Yanesha, then, would appear to result from intense exchanges with Andean populations. The genetic data alone neither support nor refute a potential Amazonian origin for the Yanesha population, but that is inferred from the nature of the Yanesha language as Arawak in origin, with later strata of contact influence from highland languages (Adelaar 2006). On the other hand, an Amazonian genetic component was not contemplated for the Shimaa, a population similarly living in the eastern Andean slopes and speaking an Arawakan language of Amazonian origin. In the first case-study above, in fact, the authors exclude any Amazonian genetic input to this population, which would thus have to have completely shifted language and culture away from their Andean genetic origins (Scliar et al. 2014). Comparisons obtained from autosomal data and a reduced comparative dataset are probably not exhaustive for testing the dual Andean–Amazonian component in these transitional environments of the Andean eastern slopes. Would the Shimaa share the same genetic profile of their linguistic neighbours the Yanesha, if one looked at their uniparental markers?

Additional Y-chromosome comparisons shed light on the genetic make-up of populations living in the highlands/lowlands transitional environment

To clarify the factors that could have contributed to the genetic make-up of the Shimaa, and of other populations from transitional environments, I have performed further comparisons using the one genetic marker that can provide both maximum availability of comparative population data and a satisfactory level of resolution. STR markers are positions on the Y-chromosome characterized by a high mutation rate between generations, and which are thus highly variable. Roewer et al. (2013) reports STR data for 17 loci in a wide set of South American populations. This dataset, merged with other available population data, proved to be highly informative for the Yanesha case-study (Barbieri et al. 2014). The time-depth of isolation and contact reachable with such comparisons was formally tested with Bayesian simulations (Barbieri et al. 2017). I have therefore used the most updated dataset from Barbieri et al. (2017) and compared patterns of haplotypes shared with the chosen target populations. Comparisons of the amounts of shared haplotypes within pairs of populations were evaluated on two levels: haplotypes that are either identical or very similar, and which therefore reflect divergence times within the last 100 years; and less similar haplotypes, with divergence times calculated to fall within the last 500 years.[1] For further technical details on the genetic data and analyses followed, see Barbieri et al. (2017).

The results in Figure 3.3.1 show the amount of very similar haplotypes (those that could be derived from a common ancestor within approximately 100 years, or 3 to 4 generations) and of less similar haplotypes (an approximate divergence time range of 500 years) for various populations: high selva Yanesha (A and B), Machiguenga (C and D), Quebrada de Humahuaca (E) and Llanos de Moxos (F).

The Machiguenga populations analysed in Mazières et al. (2008) and Sandoval, Lacerda et al. (2013) were considered as a linguistic proxy for the Shimaa, who also speak a Machiguenga language. These population samples share very similar haplotypes (and therefore recent common ancestors) with the neighbouring Quechua speakers of Cuzco, the Aymara and Quechua speakers of Lake Titicaca, and the Quechua speakers of Potosí, as well as with the Yanesha populations with whom they share the same Arawak language lineage (C). The paternal ancestry of the Arawakan Machiguenga is therefore similar to that of the

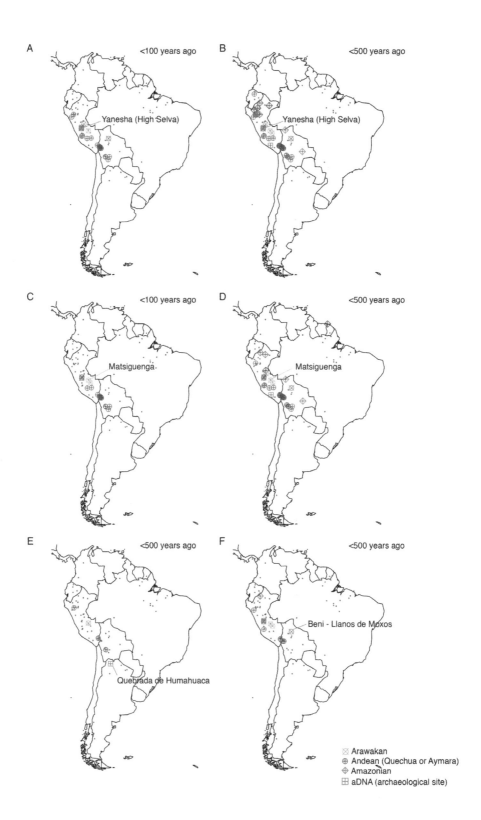

A   <100 years ago

Yanesha (High Selva)

B   <500 years ago

Yanesha (High Selva)

C   <100 years ago

Matsiguenga

D   <500 years ago

Matsiguenga

E   <500 years ago

Quebrada de Humahuaca

F   <500 years ago

Beni - Llanos de Moxos

⊠ Arawakan
⊕ Andean (Quechua or Aymara)
◈ Amazonian
⊞ aDNA (archaeological site)

Arawakan Yanesha, with gene-flow from the highlands until even more recent times. At a deeper timescale, however, the Machiguenga share similar haplotypes with populations of the Llanos de Moxos in Bolivia, and with the Kalina of French Guiana (D), as well as with Quechua speakers of the Amazonian regions of north-eastern Peru. Another point of difference with the Yanesha is that the Machiguenga have very low genetic diversity (that is, the Machiguenga individuals share very similar haplotypes between each other). Low genetic variance (as a measure of diversity) is correlated with a high degree of isolation, which prevents the genetic component from being admixed and thus prevents its diversity being enriched by introduced non-local haplotypes. The value of internal diversity (here calculated as haplotype variance) is only 0.36 and 0.24 in the two Machiguenga samples, while it reaches 0.67–0.70 in the Yanesha and in the ancient Quebrada de Humahuaca sample. The low values of the Machiguenga are more compatible with those found in prototypical isolated Amazonian populations, as explained at the beginning of this chapter, while the Yanesha and the Quebrada de Humahuaca seem more in line with levels of mobility and exchange found in the Central Andes. See also Figure 3.2.1, in Chapter 3.2, and a list of diversity values for different populations in Supplementary Table 2 in Barbieri et al. (2014).

In the next target population in this analysis, the ancient sample from Quebrada de Humahuaca, we do not see any haplotypes shared with living populations over the last 100 years, as expected given the time elapsed since the death of the individuals recovered from the site. With a deeper time frame, less similar haplotypes are found shared in present-day Quechua-speakers from Taquile and Amantaní islands in Lake Titicaca, and in Aymara-speakers from Pampa Aullagas (Bolivia), as well as in a population from Amazonia (Yine) and in the northern Andes (near Chachapoyas) (E). No similarities are found with the other ancient DNA samples included in the analysis, from the site of Tompullo. So while a connection with the ancestors of living Andean populations seems plausible, the evidence is sporadic at best, and historical contact appears difficult to reconstruct.

←———

Figure 3.3.1 Chronological chart showing the time-depth of the major archaeological divergences between Amazonia and the Andes prior to c. AD 1500. Maps indicate the populations in the South American dataset that share haplotypes with the selected target populations, within approximate timeframes of 100 and 500 years. The small dots locate each of the populations included in the comparative dataset (for details, see Barbieri et al. 2017). On each map, the target population is indicated with a line. Maps A and B: sharing patterns for the high selva Yanesha. Maps C and D: sharing patterns for the Machiguenga (averaged between the two samples available from Mazières et al. 2008 and Sandoval et al. 2013b). Map E: sharing patterns for the ancient DNA from Quebrada de Humahuaca. Map F: sharing patterns for the Llanos de Moxos, Beni department. Map built in R with dedicated packages (Becker et al. 2018). © Chiara Barbieri.

Finally, further comparisons are shown for a sample from the Llanos de Moxos (Beni department, Bolivia: Chapters 4.3 and 4.4), to add a perspective from another transitional environment: the Bolivian piedmont. This sample, analysed by Cárdenas et al. (2015), consists of a mix of individuals from various rural localities with good representation of the province of Moxos, where the Moxo languages of the Arawak family are spoken (Aikhenvald 1999). Interestingly, this Moxos population shares identical or very similar haplotypes only with the Yanesha population (data not shown) and less similar haplotypes with a set of populations slightly different to those plotted in B and D: Aymara- and Quechua-speakers from the shores of Lake Titicaca, but also people from Cajamarca in northern Peru, and above all with the Yanesha and Machiguenga. It is tempting to suggest a genetic connection between Arawak speakers of the eastern slopes of the central Andes (such as Yanesha and Machiguenga) and the Bolivian lowlands of the Moxos, which would be in line with the (controversial) hypothesis that the Arawak language family originated in the western Amazon basin (Walker and Ribeiro 2011), and that its expansion was associated with that of domesticated manioc in southern Amazonia, again where it reaches into Bolivia (Olsen and Schaal 2001). Nevertheless, these speculations are difficult to prove without a more complete dataset, which would need to include other populations representative of Amazonian Arawak speakers.

Overall genetic trends in the Andes–Amazon transition, and conclusion

In conclusion, genetic data support various different structures between Andean and Amazonian populations, with both uniparental markers and autosomal data showing different ancestral components and different patterns of diversity (Tarazona-Santos et al. 2001; Fuselli et al. 2003; Bisso-Machado et al. 2012; Barbieri et al. 2014; Eichstaedt et al. 2014). Many factors played a role in building the Andes–Amazonia genetic divide: demographic, historical, but also environmental, as shown by Eichstaedt et al. (2014, 2015); see also Chapters 2.2 and 3.2. Nevertheless, the dynamics between these two major regions have only recently begun to be addressed from a genomic perspective (Gnecchi-Ruscone et al. 2019).

Population contact can translate into gene-flow, the direction of which generally comes from the culturally dominant population. In most of the recent case studies reviewed, the authors reported the sharing of genetic motifs with current populations living at high altitude: the global picture therefore seems to agree on a predominant influence of the Andean highlands. This happens in particular with the Calchaquí of north-west Argentina (Eichstaedt et al. 2015), but also with the two Arawakan populations on the eastern slopes of the Central Andes, the Yanesha and the Machiguenga, who received a major paternal contribution from the southern highlands (from Lake Titicaca to Potosí), plausibly when these regions all came under the Inca Empire. For the Shimaa Machiguenga, Scliar et al. (2014) propose an exclusively Andean origin and a subsequent complete linguistic/cultural shift to Arawak; this scenario may not hold once more neighbouring populations from both highlands and lowlands are included in their models. In the above section, for instance, I suggest evidence for possible connections with the Bolivian piedmont which merit further inquiry.

Other regional patterns of exchange are also detected: the ancient population of the valley of Quebrada de Humahuaca, in north-west Argentina, shows a maternal contribution from the Gran Chaco, in line with a patrilocal marriage practice. Finally, the patterns of sharing between the Llanos de Moxos, the Yanesha and the Machiguenga reveal the possibility of a connection between Arawakan speakers of the Andes–Amazonia divide and the lowland fringe of the Andes.

Our perspective is strongly biased towards the data available: the choice of populations sampled, and the choice of genetic data analysed. In some cases, the results are non-informative (for example, the maternal ancestry of the Yanesha looks very similar to the one found in the majority of the South American populations analysed, see Barbieri et al. 2014). With the latest publications releasing further fine-scale genetic data (full mtDNA genomes, high-resolution Y-chromosome SNP and STR data, and, in particular, high-coverage autosomal data), and more coverage of case-study populations, we will be able to shed further light on population dynamics across the Andes–Amazonia transition.

3.4

Broad-scale patterns across the languages of the Andes and Amazonia

Paul Heggarty

1. Themes and structure

This chapter provides an overview of the broadest-scale perspectives that linguistics can offer on our theme of an Andes–Amazonia divide. It follows the same contrast as in Chapter 1.2, between two fundamental and opposing linguistic concepts, each with their corresponding signals of the human past. Section 2 looks at language families, created by and attesting to past processes of geographical expansion and divergence. Section 3 looks at linguistic convergence, attesting to processes of interaction between past societies. Section 4 concludes by stepping back to a final, broadest, worldwide perspective on the validity of a divide between the languages of the Andes and of Amazonia.

2. Language families: Expansions and divergence

Respecting or bridging the Andes–Amazonia divide?

As already explored at the start of Chapter 1.2, the most far-dispersed language family in South America is Arawak. Although considered quintessentially Amazonian, it nonetheless ranges far beyond Amazonia proper. This only makes it all the more telling, then, that the one environmental frontier that it did balk at was that between Amazonia and the Andes (see section 3 below, for the borderline case of Yanesha, spoken up to 1,800 m in central Peru). But what of the other three main language families of lowland South America? The Tupí family was similarly very expansive within Amazonia and beyond, along the coast of Brazil and into the Chaco. It includes notably the Guaraní language, spoken particularly in Paraguay and *lowland* Bolivia. But like Arawak, Tupí has not significantly crossed the frontier into the Andes (see Figure 3.4.1). The next main family, Carib, is likewise spoken

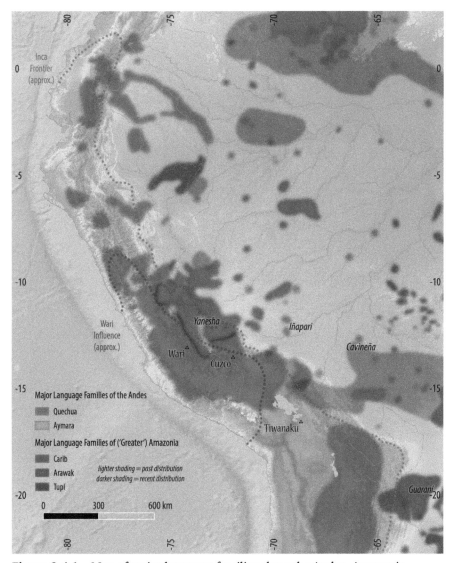

Figure 3.4.1 Map of major language families along the Andes–Amazonia transition. © Paul Heggarty.

almost exclusively in the lowlands, except for a few forms that spread to somewhat higher elevations in northern Colombia. Brazil does count one other main indigenous family, Jê (or 'Macro-Jê', in various hypotheses that extend it to a few other individual languages), but it is of less relevance here since it is mostly distributed outside the Amazonian rainforest itself, to its south-west.

Greater Amazonia does host many more language families, scattered over geographical scales that are relatively smaller, although still of the order of 500–1,000 km for families like Pano, Tacanan and Tukanoan, for example (see

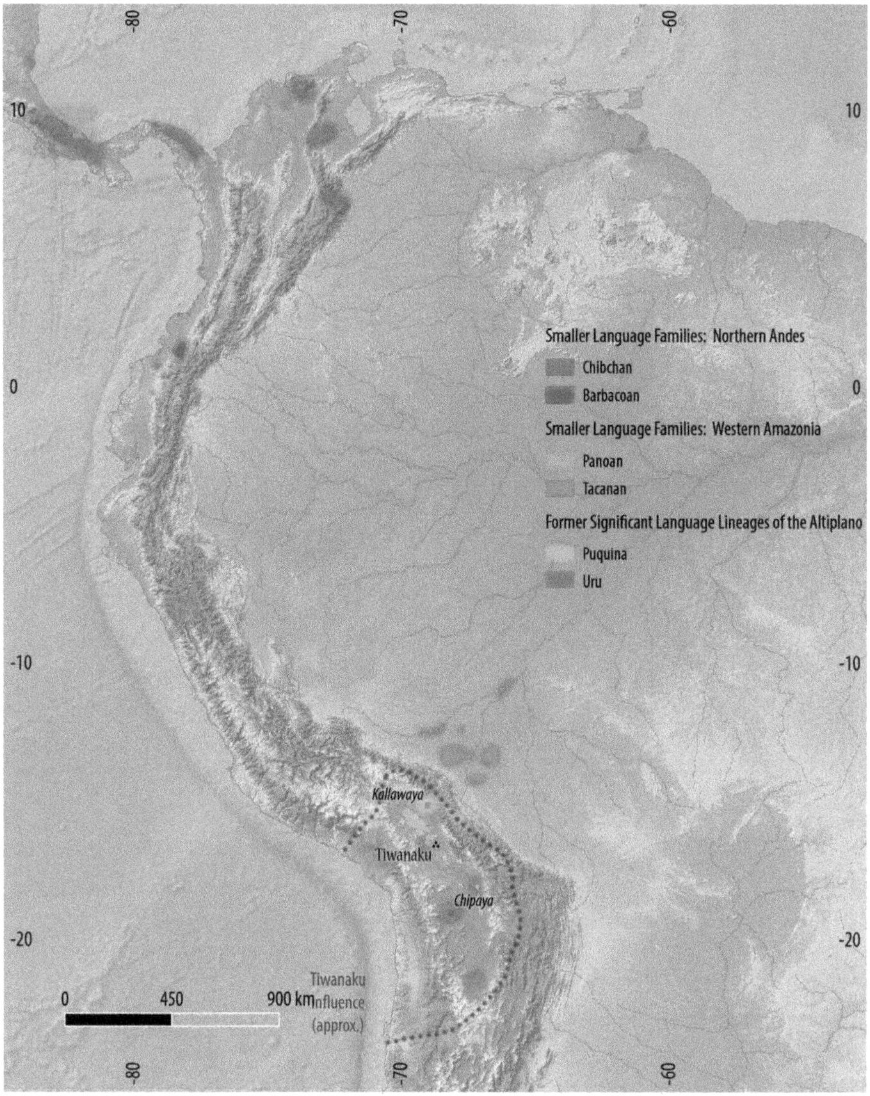
-80
-70
-60
10
10
Smaller Language Families: Northern Andes
Chibchan
Barbacoan
Smaller Language Families: Western Amazonia
Panoan
Tacanan
Former Significant Language Lineages of the Altiplano
Puquina
Uru
0
0
-10
-10
Kallawaya
Tiwanaku
Chipaya
-20
-20
Tiwanaku
Influence
(approx.)
0
450
900 km
-80
-70
-60

Figure 3.4.2 Map of smaller language families of the Andes and western Amazonia. © Paul Heggarty.

Figure 3.4.2). Despite that, and despite their presence up to the very westernmost edges of Amazonia, again no languages of these families are found in the neighbouring Andes. In Ecuador, the highlands do at least host occasional placenames, as well as loanwords and some structural features in the local forms of Quechua, that have been hypothesized to derive from languages originating in Amazonia. It is not excluded, then, that some Amazonian families may once have had some presence higher into the Andes than today. Most of the indications are limited and tenuous, however, and only further research may confirm or disconfirm them convincingly. Our knowledge of the pre-Quechua languages of highland Ecuador is very patchy (Adelaar and Muysken 2004, 392–7), and the strongest case that can be made is for a wider past distribution here of the Barbacoan family. That survives today in southern Colombia and northern Ecuador, and not just in highland but also in lowland regions – although tellingly, in the lowlands of the coastal, Pacific side of the Andes, not in the Amazonian Oriente.

It was noted in Chapter 1.2 that by far the most widespread language family of the highlands, likewise, does generally respect the Andes–Amazonia divide, from the other side. Quechua spread very much north–south, along the Andes, rather than east–west (see Figure 3.4.1). So too did the Inca Empire, but the superficial correlation is deeply misleading if interpreted as causation – that is, as if the language distribution were only a result of Inca rule. This is clear from the profound mismatch in chronology. The initial expansion and divergence phases of the Quechua family go back many centuries before the Incas (Beresford-Jones and Heggarty 2012b). Tawantinsuyu seems to have been (in part) responsible only for the main two Quechua expansions beyond Peru itself, northwards into highland Ecuador and south-eastwards (beyond Aymara) into highland Bolivia. Far-flung as they were, these movements were still constrained to the highlands, and so do indeed mirror the Incas' reluctance to venture deep into the lowlands (Chapter 5.1). Moreover, these late Quechua expansions were further driven by Spanish colonial rule, again broadly respecting the Andes–Amazonia frontier (Chapter 5.3). In short, if a causation is sought for the rough correlation in geographical scope between the distributions of Quechua and of the Inca Empire, then it is not so much that the latter shaped the former, but that both were shaped by the same underlying context: the Andes–Amazonia divide.

Yet although Quechua remains quintessentially a highland family, there is one significant exception to this, in the northernmost part of its range. In Ecuador, forms of Quechua are spoken not just in the highlands but in the lowlands of the *Oriente*, too. Moreover, from there Quechua is also distributed downstream along the Napo and other parallel-flowing rivers into north-eastern Peru, to add to a scatter of further enclaves in the Amazonian provinces of San Martín and Loreto. This does not contradict the Incas' reluctance to enter Amazonia, however, because these lowland Quechua-speaking areas seem to have become established only later, during the Spanish colonial period. In fact, set against the general weakness of the Spanish footprint in the lowlands (Chapter 5.3), it is language that here turns out to provide a rare indication of an undeniable and striking cultural spread from the Andes into Amazonia.

Ironically, though, the mechanism that spread this indigenous language lineage was one of the very few real agents of *European* influence on the lowlands: missionary activity by Jesuits and Franciscans (Chapter 5.3). In particular, the *reducciones* policy gathered together diverse Amazonian populations who had no common language. To fulfil that role, and not least to provide a language through which to evangelize, European missionaries 'seeded' Quechua in these new mission communities, by bringing in speakers from the nearby highlands. The choice of Quechua was largely for the Europeans' own convenience, since it was the *lingua franca* that they were already using to communicate with and evangelize indigenous populations in the highlands (some of whom also retained their own diverse native tongues until well into the colonial era). The northernmost of all forms of Quechua, the 'Inga' variety in southern Colombia, is also spoken down into the Amazonian lowlands, and its origins remain somewhat unclear.

Much more recently, the last few decades have also seen some spill-over of highland languages, as speakers of them have migrated down from the Andes to claim new land for farming in Amazonia. Their languages have few prospects of ever becoming entrenched there, of course, as Spanish now spreads at the expense of all indigenous languages. In pre-Columbian times, though, there is no good evidence for any significant Quechua presence in Amazonia.

The other significant language family in the highlands, Aymara, likewise seems to observe the 'divide', just like all four major Amazonian ones. So, in sum, the distributions of all major language families do seem to support the reality of an Andes–Amazonia frontier. The only possible caveat is that there is at least a hypothesis, albeit tentative, that one notable Andean language, Puquina, may in fact have very deep roots in Amazonia, and be distantly related to Arawak. The potential significance is clear for the Andes–Amazonia divide – although it should be noted that there is controversy not just on the claim itself, but on whether the issue can ever really be settled, given how little we actually know of the now extinct Puquina. The case is taken up in more detail in Chapter 4.1.

Language families can also contribute other valuable perspectives on the Andes–Amazonia divide, besides ostensibly observing some taboo on trespassing across it. For the families on either side present quite distinct panoramas on other levels, too: in the patterns of their geographical distributions, in the size of their speaker populations and in how far back in time their expansion histories go. We now take each of these in turn.

Geographical patterns

In Amazonia, each of the three main families – Arawak, Tupí and Carib – is curiously scattered and splintered across its whole extent, interspersed piecemeal with members of the other two, and with languages of many smaller families, as well as language isolates (Epps 2009). In the Andes, by contrast, Quechua occupies just a few large blocks of continuous territory (Cerrón-Palomino 2003): the *Zona Continua* from northern Ancash to Lake Titicaca (breaking up only now as the language cedes to Spanish); in the Ecuadoran highlands and into the Oriente; and in the southern and eastern highlands of Bolivia. Only in northern Peru, where it never appears to have been widely established, is Quechua found scattered in just small, isolated enclaves (Cañaris, Inkawasi, Cajamarca and Chachapoyas). As shown in Figure 3.4.1, one of the few breaks in the geography of Quechua is filled by another broad, continuous distribution, that of the other widespread Andean language family, Aymara (which formerly extended further across the southern highlands of Peru, where Quechua then replaced it). In short, the Andes–Amazonia frontier seems to mark a curious contrast also in how language families are distributed on either side: respectively, in large, coherent and exclusive blocks of territory, or scattered and splintered amongst each other.

Demography, forced migrations and genetics

A second major dimension of difference is demography. To judge from most recent census figures, Quechua counts c. 6–7 million speakers, Aymara about 1.9 million (Howard 2011). Arawak, by contrast, has only 750,000 speakers, Carib far fewer (Simons and Fennig 2018). Only Tupí has a similar demographic scale to Quechua, and much less evenly distributed, because the single language Guaraní accounts for the vast majority of the family's speakers. Obviously, such was the demographic cataclysm provoked by the advent of the Europeans and their pathogens, and such has been the scale of shift from indigenous languages to European ones, that modern population figures are not good indicators of past demography. That said, they do at least remain compatible with the traditional assumption that the intensive farming and complex societies of the Andes had come to support higher populations and densities than in Amazonia, and that would also have applied to their respective language families. The latest archaeological thinking in Amazonia, of course, would have us revise population figures for pre-Columbian Amazonia upwards by a huge factor (see Chapter 1.1). This is not for linguistics to judge, although it does leave to be explained the mismatch in the sizes of modern populations speaking indigenous languages of Amazonia and of the Andes.

On another aspect of demography, at least some of the main expansion phases of Quechua were clearly driven by very significant forced population movements, as historically reported under the regimes of Spanish colonialism (such as the Potosí draft) and the Incas (*mit'a, yanakuna,* imperial armies). Even the Jesuit and Franciscan missions that led to Quechua's footholds in Amazonia were in part forced population movements, if on a smaller scale. This brings us to a critical proviso, however, when inferring 'migrations' from branching structures in language family trees: it does not always have to be people who move *en masse.* As the New Archaeology would have it, ideas and culture can move, too. People can largely stay put, but switch to another language that itself is doing the expanding and 'migrating'. To be precise, a minimum number of speakers must move, but in particular circumstances (especially underlying linguistic diversity: see Heggarty 2015, 622–3) they need not be a demographic majority – as when European missionaries 'seeded' Quechua into their Amazonian *reducciones* through just a few native-speaker highlanders.

Taken together, these observations are all at least compatible with another potential contrast between the Andes and Amazonia. The major language families of the Andes seem to have been driven at least in good part by demographic processes, shaped in turn by agricultural productivity and state-led interventions to that end (including forced migrations). On the traditional view that such state structures were less prevalent in Amazonia, then the main families there may have been spread more by cultural processes than by demographic ones. Again, though, that view is now directly challenged by the 'new archaeological orthodoxy' (Chapter 1.1) that no longer sees pre-Columbian Amazonia as so different from the Andes in these respects after all.

Languages can in fact bear certain tell-tale characteristics that tend to betray that a language lineage was at some point ('imperfectly') learnt by a population that had originally spoken other languages. There are a few such features, for example, in the Quechua spoken in enclaves in Peruvian and Ecuadoran Amazonia (and to an extent also in highland Ecuador). Some scope for interpretation still remains with such characteristics, however, so it is all the more valuable to combine the linguistics with an independent, complementary data source specifically on matters demographic, namely genetics. The key is not to assume any one-to-one link between language lineages and genetic ones, of course, but on the contrary to compare and contrast where they do match with where they do not – that is, where a language spread mostly by demographic or by cultural expansion, respectively. Ultimately, it should in principle be possible for linguistics and genetics, working intelligently together, to tease these apart, to confirm or refute this further potential contrast between the Andes and Amazonia: in the dominant mode of language family expansions in each, demographic versus cultural. In practice, both disciplines need first to achieve the data coverage and resolution necessary (see also Chapter 1.3), but the potential is already clear from existing illustrations on more localized scales, some already focused on the Andes–Amazonia divide, as explored here in Chapter 3.3.

Time depth

Finally, a third dimension is of scale not in geography or demography, but in time. Every language family has its own chronology, from whenever the geographical expansion began that took that family's ancestral proto-language beyond its homeland, to set the divergence clock ticking in different regions. Since changes and differences accumulate through time, in principle the greater the divergence between the languages within a family, the longer that family must have been diverging. But while a *relative* sequence of divergent branching and 'migration' events is often clear, putting narrow, *absolute* dates on them is near impossible. Language change is anything but clockwork, and not remotely akin to the natural laws of radiocarbon decay. Various methods have been proposed, and most found wanting. Arguably the most promising – Bayesian phylogenetic dating – is nonetheless highly controversial, and limited in South

America, where the lack of a deep written record robs the method of the deep-time calibrations that it needs in order to work most reliably. (For more on these methods, see Heggarty 2014.)

At present we remain stuck with largely impressionistic estimates, within very wide confidence limits (and no firm quantitative estimate of those, either). Yet even such broad ranges are enough to show a clear contrast across the Andes–Amazonia divide. The main expansive families in the Andes are relatively shallow in time-depth: Quechua is generally considered less diverse than Romance (whose divergence dates back only to the Roman Empire), and is thus normally assumed to have spread only within the last 1,500 years or so. Aymara is of a similar order (or only slightly older, on some dubious measures). The major Amazonian families, meanwhile, are generally taken to have begun spreading and diverging at least twice as far back in prehistory. Kaufman and Golla (2000, 52) report estimates of 3700 BP for Carib, 4500 BP for Arawak, and 5500–6000 BP for Tupí. Such figures are to be taken with a very large dose of salt: few linguists would dare commit even to the digit for the millennia (Heggarty and Renfrew 2014b). Nonetheless, in line also with impressionistic comparisons of the diversity within each family, the default assumption is that major language families trace their expansions back far earlier in Amazonia than they do in the Andes.

To put that more explicitly in terms of what it means for prehistory, we have here something of a reversal of traditional visions on the contrast between these two regions. For in order for any language to begin diverging into a family at all requires some powerful expansive process on a large geographical scale. Conditions to foster such expansions would seem to have arisen in Amazonia long *before* they did in the Andes, then – to judge from the time-depths of the surviving language families, at least. The only other possibility would be if late developments in the Central Andes had overwritten all traces of some much earlier language expansion(s), just as Quechua has overwritten much of the earlier Aymara spread, and as Spanish is now replacing both. It is unlikely that we will ever be able to rule this out, although in those parts of the Andes where we do have indications of the earlier linguistic panorama, such as in northern Peru, they support a picture of high diversity rather than any large, early families.

There are, of course, some claims to reach wider and deeper in time: the putative 'macro-families' that pepper outdated linguistic literature (especially around the 1960s). Chapter 2.3 explains why they lack any methodological support, are disregarded by orthodox linguistics, and are therefore not considered here.

Bringing it together: Homelands and origins

So if the main language families in Amazonia and in the Andes differ simultaneously in patterning, demography, expansion mode and time-depth, is there any broader, deeper explanation that brings all of these dimensions together? There is something of an Andes–Amazonia divide at least in how scholars have tried to explain how, when and why these families came to exist in the first place – by spreading at the expense of other languages.

In Amazonia, much is made of the role of rivers, perhaps understandably so. Firstly, as conduits for easy mobility, rivers have been invoked especially to explain the Arawak family and its distribution. For Hornborg (2005), Arawak was spread across a water-borne trade network, and thus mostly by cultural processes and adoption, rather than by some major population expansion and migration, and without needing any expansive 'state' society behind it. (Rivers have also been suggested as conduits for the contrasting process of language convergence, but the evidence seems poor: see van Gijn et al. (2017).) Secondly, rivers were crucial to subsistence regimes that came to rely on farming the rich alluvial soils along *várzea* floodplains. This would have led farming groups to spread primarily along major rivers (Denevan 2002), leaving hunter-gatherers pushed back into the *terra firme* forest interior. Certainly, that is where most language isolates are found today, not (yet) displaced by the main expansive families. The distribution of those families would thus be more logical and consistent than the patchwork it might first appear. Hypotheses on the homelands of the major lowland families have also inclined towards regions at the upper, western reaches of the Amazon basin (Epps 2009). Some have even ventured that it is simply easier to move long distances downstream rather than upstream. More substantially, the main connection drawn has been with the periphery of Amazonia as where several important food plants began to be farmed, spreading outwards (and downstream) from there (Dixon and Aikhenvald 1999).

In the Andes, homelands for the major language families and explanations for their expansions have typically been sought and framed in very different terms: by explicit association with complex societies and their signatures in the archaeological record (Torero 1972, 91–9; Torero 1984; Cerrón-Palomino 2003). Initial assumptions (outside linguistics) were that all Quechua was the work of the Incas spreading out of Cuzco, and that Tiwanaku spread Aymara. Those were based on present-day language distributions and have rightly been abandoned as anachronistic. But they have been replaced by hypotheses that effectively just redirect the associations to other complex societies and languages. Notably, the (pre-Inca) Wari Middle Horizon in Peru is linked by different scholars to the early expansions of either Aymara or Quechua, or both (see Heggarty and Beresford-Jones 2012), while its contemporary polity in the Altiplano, Tiwanaku, is now associated with spreading the Puquina language, now extinct (see Chapter 4.1, and Cerrón-Palomino 2013).

The first beginnings of agriculture play no significant role here, since they long pre-date any of the language family expansions that can be identified in the Andes. Rather, at their shallow time-depths, any potential role of subsistence factors would necessarily have been mediated by complex societies in any case, not least given their ability to command large labour-forces for major public works that could intensify agricultural productivity. Rather than enlisting natural river courses as in Amazonia, in the Andes some explanations for language expansions have even invoked how humans *modified* the landscape by road networks, terracing and irrigation (Beresford-Jones and Heggarty 2012b). Those could permit population growth and spread languages through demographic pressure, as well as cultural prestige and utility, to explain also the larger populations that speak Andean as opposed to Amazonian languages. Relatively denser populations and state-like structures of control also seem a better explanation for the larger, continuous expanses of territory speaking languages of the same family (although even in the Andes that pattern was still not fully consolidated until late colonial times).

All of this can seem fairly logical, although clearly framed within a pre-existing view of supposed basic contrasts in the nature of human societies, their scale and complexity, on either side of the Andes–Amazonia divide. Sceptics might wonder whether this is something of a self-fulfilling prophesy, then. Or it might alternatively be challenged by the latest thinking in Amazonian archaeology that there was no great contrast with the Andes after all. To make either case, though, would nonetheless require alternative explanations for why the major language families on either side of that divide should have come to contrast with each other on multiple dimensions, as well as being so reluctant to venture across it.

3. Language contact and convergence

We now switch to the very different dimension of linguistic evidence of interaction and convergence. We follow the scale of increasing intensity of such interactions set out in Chapter 1.2, beginning with the relatively superficial level of loanwords.

Loanwords

Within either the Andes or Amazonia there are many clear loanwords and striking long-range *Wanderwörter*. In Amazonia, Epps (2017) explores various *Wanderwörter* in flora, fauna and cultural terms, such as *coca*, *parrot* and *knife*. In the highlands, the Chipaya language of the Uru family is laced with loanwords from Aymara, and even Mapudungun in Patagonia shares with Quechua occasional words such as *challwa* (fish*)* (Golluscio et al. 2009; see http://wold.clld.org/word/7211254370820389). And Quechua and Aymara themselves have exchanged far more than occasional words – up to a quarter of their entire vocabularies, in both directions (Cerrón-Palomino 2008).

There are certainly also loanwords that have crossed the Andes–Amazonia divide. Various lowland languages have taken their (higher) numerals from languages of the Andes, for example. The now extinct Chamicuro language (of the Arawak family), in the Amazonian lowlands of northern Peru, takes its numerals above four from Quechua (see https://mpi-lingweb.shh.mpg.de/numeral/Chamicuro.htm). In the Cavineña language of the Tacanan family in northern lowland Bolivia, the source language of numerals above two is, more unexpectedly, Aymara (which had itself originally borrowed some of the higher numbers from

Quechua). Further north, Haynie et al. (2014) map variants of the word *purutu* (beans), suggesting that it originated in Quechua and spread to lowland languages, albeit also through regional Spanish. In reverse, where highland languages have names for Amazonian species and artefacts, it is no surprise that many were borrowed in from lowland languages.

Isolated loanwords between individual language pairs are not much to go on, however. To make well-grounded, generalizable inferences calls for a widespread, systematic survey of exchanges in lexicon across the Andes–Amazonia divide, and a principled approach to interpreting what any patterns found would mean for other disciplines too. Research such as that by Epps (2017) shows the potential for Amazonia, but it has not yet been extended to the Andes – a symptom of the ongoing divide in research itself. Only once comprehensive language databases do span this divide will we really be able to judge whether the loanwords that are widespread *within* each region are or are not paralleled by as many that *did* dare to cross the Andes–Amazonia divide.

Structural convergence

Moving on to deeper interaction effects that extend beyond the lexicon into the sound and grammatical systems of the languages affected, South America is home to 'linguistic convergence areas' (see Chapter 1.3), on different levels of scale and intensity. Epps and Michael (2017) survey multiple localized pockets of intense linguistic convergence in the lowlands, such as the Upper Xingú region and the spectacular case of linguistic exogamy (where there is a convention *against* marrying somebody of the same native language) in the Vaupés region. In the Andean Altiplano, meanwhile, there is localized and especially intense convergence between the southern varieties of Aymara and Quechua. And this comes on top of a phase of convergence also between the early stages of the entire Quechua and Aymara lineages. This is frequently presented as having brought about the wholesale restructuring of one language on the model of the other (although without consensus on which language played which role). Muysken (2012a) surveys multiple levels of interaction between Andean languages, and the various real-world contact scenarios that they imply.

Zooming out geographically, Quechua–Aymara interaction is actually taken as the core of a wider convergence area in which other Andean languages also participate. Torero (2002, section 6) summarizes the structural characteristics that he takes to define this linguistic area, often termed simply 'Andean'. Like many convergence areas, this one too shows a core-and-periphery pattern. As one moves away from the Central Andes, northwards or southwards, languages tend to share in progressively fewer of the structural characteristics found in the Quechua–Aymara core. Even Quechua itself, for example, lost a few of the core Central Andean characteristics when it spread far north into Ecuador. Similar proposals have been made for a broad 'Amazonian' linguistic convergence area, notably by Derbyshire

(1987, 311) and by Dixon and Aikhenvald (1999, 7–10), who provide lists of the shared structural characteristics that they see as defining it.

That only brings us to the usual question, however: what of convergence *between* the Andes and Amazonia? None of the localized convergence zones spans the Andes–Amazonia divide. As for the macro-areas, Dixon and Aikhenvald (1999) go so far as to contrast explicitly their 'Amazonian' structural characteristics with opposing ones that they deem typically 'Andean'. Their presentation has not gone unchallenged, however. Others have objected that not all of Dixon and Aikhenvald's criteria really hold so widely across the languages of Amazonia anyway (see Chapter 3.5; Epps and Michael 2017), and that there is in fact a significant east–west shift in structural characteristics within Amazonia itself. Rival proposals see the major division through the continent as one that would put western Amazonia if anything together with the Andes, and opposed to eastern South America as a whole (see Chapter 3.5 by Van Gijn and Muysken, and Van Gijn et al. 2017). An intermediate view is that both dividing lines have support in different selections of structural characteristics, which together give a three-way division of Andes *versus* western Amazonia *versus* eastern Amazonia. As that suggests, the question is not one that can be resolved by cherry-picking individual characteristics that favour one definition of convergence zones or another. Again, it requires large-scale linguistic databases right across South America, as a basis for more comprehensive, objective and quantified analyses of how the data pattern across the continent. Chapter 3.5 here is founded on precisely such an approach by the authors, which they focus here on our Andes–Amazonia question. Also highly recommended is the balanced overview by Epps and Michael (2017).

Case studies of convergence along the Andes–Amazonia divide

A further interesting perspective is to be had from languages that represent borderline cases. The Yanesha language (also known as Amuesha) is variously described by Adelaar (2006) as an Arawak language 'of the Peruvian Amazon' or 'spoken in the Andean foothills of Central Peru', and within the Arawak family is deemed to belong to a 'Pre-Andine' branch. Notwithstanding its Amazonian (Arawak) origins, then, Yanesha has encroached somewhat into the highlands, formerly up to elevations of c. 1,800 metres, even if still within cloud-forest. A key motivation may have been to control access to the *Cerro de la Sal* (Salt Mountain), an important source for the salt trade to Amazonia. (As an aside, it would be intriguing to survey, right along the eastern slopes of the Andes, the exact altitudes at which indigenous languages considered Andean tend to give way to those considered Amazonian.)

The theme of Adelaar's (2006) paper is the clear impact of Quechua on this 'Amazonian' language. That might in itself be taken as Yanesha invalidating the idea of a sharp divide. That said, the interest is precisely because Adelaar sees Yanesha as an *exception* to a more general rule, of the only 'incidental borrowings that affected other Andean and Amazonian languages' across the frontier. And even this exception has its limits. Recall that loanwords in the vocabulary reflect only a more superficial level of interaction than is needed to create the much more far-reaching convergence in language structure between Quechua and Aymara, for example. At that deeper level, Adelaar is clear that 'Quechua impact on Amuesha grammar' was 'very limited when compared with the rather spectacular lexical influx'.

In such cases of contact across the 'frontier', the complementary perspective of human genetics can be all the more informative. Yanesha-speakers do show some Andean admixture, particularly on the male side, but overall they remain genetically more Amazonian than Andean (see Chapter 3.3 by Barbieri, and Barbieri et al. 2014). The linguistic and genetic data concord, then, in diagnosing the Yanesha case as one of contact with highland populations and their languages.

On one view, the case of Yanesha, like the Quechua enclaves in Amazonia, illustrates that in language the Andes–Amazonia divide is by no means complete and hermetic. Nonetheless, both cases also show how in certain respects, deep-seated contrasts continue to show through. In the case of the Yanesha, the interactions were certainly not far-reaching enough to obscure that their genetic and linguistic ancestries both remain dominantly and manifestly Amazonian. Speakers of Quechua in Ecuadoran and Peruvian Amazonia also retain their predominantly Amazonian genetic lineage (Sandoval et al. 2016; Barbieri et al. 2017), but in this case European missionaries did force a mismatch by bringing them to switch to a linguistic lineage that is Andean. Even here, though, there are qualifications. For the Quechua that did become established in the lowlands did so at the 'cost' of some degree of assimilation to linguistic characteristics typical of Amazonia, eroding – at least to some extent – their 'Andean' structural profile. Those characteristics, carried over into the originally highland Quechua, mark an enduring substrate from local, Amazonian languages.

4. On balance

It was noted in Chapter 1.3 that the very terms 'Andean' and 'Amazonian' as used by linguists were to an extent circular and self-fulfilling, in that the distributions of the main families and convergence patterns have had at least some role in shaping the common linguistic reading of those terms in the first place. That point nonetheless needs to be set in context, by stepping back to an even broader observation. For whichever other regions they do or do not extend to, the linguistic 'Andes' and 'Amazonia' do nonetheless coincide at least with the swift geographical transition from the high Central Andes to the Amazon basin proper. What is more, the linguistic definitions align with each other on both of the basic dimensions of language prehistory that have structured this chapter. The significance of this can only be fully appreciated in a global perspective. For elsewhere worldwide, divergent language families and convergent linguistic areas conspicuously do *not* allow of a single common geographical schema or frontier to divide them into great blocks. The paradigm case is Tibeto-Burman, a single family but whose member languages have converged on either the 'Sinosphere' or the 'Indosphere' type of structural profile (Matisoff 1991, 485–6). That some Tibeto-Burman languages could go one way, and others the other way, is precisely because this one family is dispersed across both sides of the dividing line between those convergence areas. The same goes for languages of the Austro-Asiatic family, across the same convergence frontier. Similarly in Africa, the main areal convergence zones patently do *not* align with the distributions of the major language families, but crosscut them (Güldemann 2018). Obviously, the powerful processes that shaped the prehistory of human populations and societies have left their clear linguistic effects in South America too. Here, however, those formative processes, divergent *as well as* convergent, do all appear to have respected the same double frontier: an Andes–Amazonia divide.

3.5

Highland–lowland relations: A linguistic view

Rik van Gijn and Pieter Muysken

Introduction

It has long been the prevalent view in ethno-history, archaeology and linguistics that the Andean and Amazonian cultural spheres form separate worlds, with little interaction between them. Some scholars, however, most notably in anthropology, have voiced different opinions, as expressed particularly in Chapters 1.4 and 1.5 in this volume, and in the extensive discussion of these contrasting visions in the introduction to this book. Among the best-known analyses suggesting that the separation between highland and lowland cultures was not always as evident as it appears to be today is that of Renard-Casevitz et al. (1988). Based on ethno-historical and (to a lesser extent) archaeological evidence, they argue that a lively trade existed in pre-Columbian times. In their view, the gradual decline of highland–lowland interactions is connected to the disintegration of the Wari cultural complex and the subsequent turbulent period in the lowlands, where local feuds and migrations had rendered the lowland polities less reliable allies for highland peoples. From then on, highland expeditions into the lowlands (and vice versa) slowly decreased in number, but in fact contacts persisted until well into the Inca era. Highland–lowland interactions probably took place predominantly in different directions in different periods. Earlier on, lowland groups possibly helped shape highland cultures. A case in point is the role that Arawakan cultures possibly played in the creation of complex highland societies, as in the case of Tiyawanaku, which through one of its main languages, Puquina, may be linked to the so-called Arawakan matrix (Santos-Granero 2002) although the evidence for this is indirect (for more detail, see Chapters 4.1 and 4.3 for an archaeological perspective). Later on, in the centuries preceding and following the Spanish conquest, highland cultures influenced the lowlands. Linguistic evidence for this comes in the form of Quechua varieties spoken in the lowlands, and the loanwords from Quechua into many languages of the eastern slopes and Amazonia proper.

Here we adopt the methods of linguistic typology, which means that we systematically compare features across languages, rather than primarily looking at family relationships (see Chapters 1.2 and 2.3 for more on this general distinction within linguistics, and what it means for interpretations for prehistory). The study of language structure (that is, the grammatical 'architecture' of languages)[1] has lagged somewhat behind other disciplines in recognizing the more intricate and gradual transition between the highlands and lowlands; a number of linguistic overviews of the area are based on the presumption of a sharp distinction (Torero 2002; Adelaar 2008, 2012a; Derbyshire and Pullum 1986; Dixon and Aikhenvald 1999). This distinction has the virtue of clarity, but it is ultimately not very helpful as it is too simplistic. There is now a large literature on the broad outlines of the geographical distribution of grammatical characteristics of South American languages, which suggests a rather different picture. Generally speaking, the following broad conclusions can be drawn.

1. There is wide typological diversity among the languages of the continent. However, it has been repeatedly observed that a number of grammatical characteristics are shared by many South American languages over large geographical areas, and across language families (see for example, Van Gijn 2012, 2014a, 2016, for studies of such widely shared individual features). In a global study based on the data provided in Dryer and Haspelmath (2013a, 2013b), Dediu and Levinson (2012) conclude that the language families of South America are somewhat more similar to each other than those of other continents, in that they seem to share partial profiles.[2]

2. There is a central Andean cluster (termed CAC here), encompassing the two language families most widely diffused in the Andes, namely Quechuan and Aymaran. Morphological and phonological evidence would suggest that Aymaran was the original model (Adelaar 2012a; Muysken 2012b), given that it appears more irregular and complex than Quechuan. Puquina and Uru-Chipaya are also influenced by this cluster, but show features of their own, while Mochica on the north coast of Peru, for example, was very different (Kerke and Muysken 2014).

3. More broadly, several families in the western part of South America, such as Barbacoan (with languages spoken in western Ecuador and south-western Colombia) and Jivaroan (with languages spoken in northern Peru), vaguely resemble the languages in the CAC (Muysken et al. 2014b).

4. Languages in the foothills may tend more towards the CAC profile or to an Amazonian profile, but most show a mixed signal in their structural characteristics (Van Gijn 2014b).

5. In terms of grammatical language profiles, there is indeed a broad east–west division in South America (Krasnoukhova 2012, 2014; Birchall 2014a, 2014b). In these studies, the dividing line between the two regions does not, however, coincide with that between the Andes and their foothills with Amazonia. Where broad generalizations can be made, the foothill languages

resemble their Andean neighbours structurally more than the more easterly Amazonian languages.

6. Overall, the languages in the western part of the continent show less diversity than those in the east (Muysken, Hammarström, Krasnoukhova et al. 2014), broadly speaking. The similarities of the languages in the west may be leftovers from very old relationships, too deep to be detectable by orthodox methods of recovering shared descent (see Chapter 2.3), or may result either from long-standing interaction zones, or from recent convergence due to ethnic reshuffling in the wake of the European invasions.

In this chapter we zoom in on the transition area between the Andes and Amazonia: the upper Amazon area. This is defined here as a broad strip of land between the Andes to the west and Amazonia to the east, and roughly between the Putumayo River that separates present-day Ecuador from Colombia in the north, and the savannahs of the Gran Chaco in Paraguay and northern Argentina in the south (see Figure 3.5.1).

Structural features are shared or differ between the languages of the highlands and lowlands in a complex and multi-layered network; to represent it fully will ultimately require the concerted effort of specialists from several subdisciplines. Dixon and Aikhenvald (1999, 10) mention that 'there is no sharp boundary between the Amazonian and Andean linguistic areas: they tend to flow into each other'.[3] The goal of this chapter is to come to a more refined picture of how these areas 'flow into each other', by focusing on how specific structural features are distributed geographically across the languages of the upper Amazon and adjacent areas in Amazonia and the Andes, building on an approach developed by Van Gijn (2014b). In particular, we will be concerned with the role of elevation differences in shaping the distributional patterns. In the next part of this chapter we introduce the language sample and the choice of linguistic features; following this we discuss the patterns that emerge and what these mean. In further work we will also try to explore the region through a fine-grained analysis of the individual river systems, but this chapter presents a more global exploration, building on Van Gijn (2014b).

Approach

The upper Amazon is characterized by the many rivers that rise in the Andes and come together further eastwards to form the great Amazon River. The sediments of this abundance of rivers, in combination with the differences in elevation between the Andean slopes and Amazonian lowlands, create a landscape of great ecological diversity, which is matched by the cultural-linguistic diversity in the region. The western part of South America is among the linguistically most diverse zones in the world in the diversity of independent language lineages (Dahl et al. 2011).

For specific parts of the eastern slopes it is also structurally highly diverse (Dahl 2008).[4] In particular, both the northern edge of the upper Amazon, in Ecuador and northern Peru, and the southern edge in Bolivia, are extremely diverse.

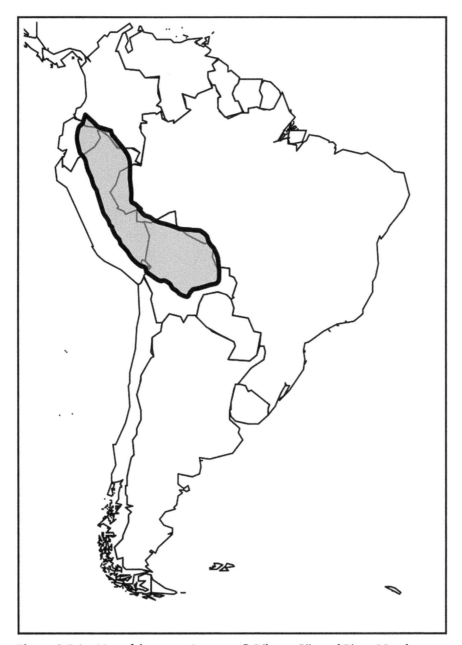

Figure 3.5.1 Map of the upper Amazon. © Rik van Gijn and Pieter Muysken.

Sample

Given this diversity, and because we are especially interested in local patterns, we have sampled as densely as possible, wherever languages are well documented enough for us to include them. We have also included languages spoken in the adjacent parts of Amazonia and the Andes, to gain a more complete picture. The sample is presented in Figure 3.5.2 and Table 3.5.1 (affiliations and locations are based on Hammarström et al. 2015).

A reviewer correctly notes that the locations of specific languages have changed over time, and that taking present location as a point of reference may thus

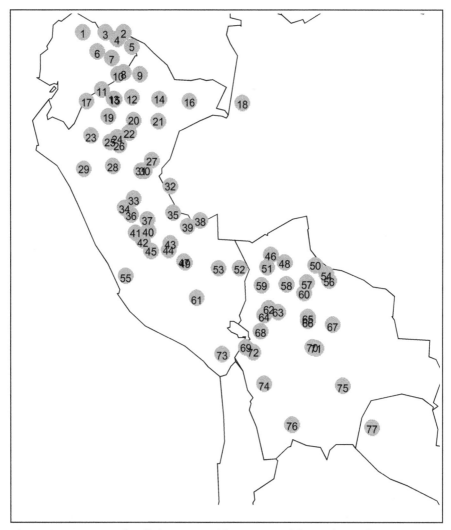

Figure 3.5.2 Map of well-documented languages of the Andes and upper Amazonia covered in this study. © Rik van Gijn and Pieter Muysken.

Table 3.5.1 Sample languages, affiliations, ISO codes, and main sources.
© Rik van Gijn and Pieter Muysken, based on Hammarström et al. 2015.

No.	Name	Affiliation	ISO	Main source(s)
1	Imbabura Q	Quechuan[a]	qvi	Cole (1982)
2	Siona	Tucanoan	snn	Bruil (2014)
3	Cofán	Isolate	con	Borman (1962); Fischer and Van Lier (2011); Tobar (1995)
4	Napo Q	Quechuan	qvo	Mercier and Marcos (1979)
5	Secoya	Tucanoan	sey	Johnson and Levinsohn (1990)
6	Tena Quechua	Quechuan	quw	fieldwork notes Muysken for Arajuno
7	Waorani	Isolate	auc	Peeke (1973, 1991); Saint and Pike (1962)
8	N Pastaza Q	Quechuan	qvz	Nuckolls (2010)
9	Arabela	Zaparoan	arl	Rich (1999)
10	Záparo	Zaparoan	zro	Peeke (1991)
11	Achuar	Jivaroan	acu	Fast and Fast (1981, 1996)
12	Taushiro	Isolate	trr	Alicea Ortiz (1975a, 1975b)
13	Andoa	Zaparoan	anb	Peeke and Sargent (1959)
14	Iquito	Zaparoan	iqu	Eastman and Eastman (1963)
15	S Pastaza Q	Quechuan	qup	Landerman (1973)
16	Yagua	Peba-Yaguan	yad	Payne (1985, 1986)
17	Shuar	Jivaroan	jiv	Saad (2012)
18	Omagua	Tupian	omg	Michael and O'Hagan (2016)
19	Candoshi Shapra	Isolate	cbu	Anderson and Wise (1963)
20	Urarina	Isolate	ura	Olawsky (2006)
21	Kokama	Tupian	cod	Vallejos Yopán (2011)
22	Chamicuro	Arawakan	ccc	Parker (2010)
23	Aguaruna	Jivaroan	agr	Overall (2007)
24	Jebero	Cahuapanan	jeb	Valenzuela (2012)
25	Chayahuita	Cahuapanan	cbt	Rojas Berscia (2015)
26	Muniche	Isolate	myr	Michael et al. (2009, 2013); Michael p.c.
27	Capanahua	Panoan	kaq	Loos (1969); Loos and Loos (2003)
28	San Martin Q	Quechuan	qvs	Coombs et al. (1976)
29	Cajamarca Q	Quechuan	qvc	Quesada (1976)

Table 3.5.1 Continued

No.	Name	Affiliation	ISO	Main source(s)
30	Shipibo	Panoan	shp	Valenzuela (2003)
31	Panobo	Panoan	pno	Gomes (2010)
32	Shanenawa	Panoan	swo	Cândido (2004)
33	Cashibo	Panoan	cbr	Zariquiey Biondi (2011)
34	Cholón	Hibito-Cholon	cht	Alexander-Bakkerus (2005)
35	Ucayali-Yurúa Ash	Arawakan	cpb	García Salazar (1993)
36	Huallaga Q	Quechuan	qub	Weber (1989)
37	Ajy Apurucayali	Arawakan	cpc	Payne (1981)
38	Yaminahua	Panoan	yaa	Faust and Loos (2002)
39	Amahuaca	Panoan	amc	Osborn (1948); Hyde (1980); Sparing-Chávez (2012)
40	Pichis Ash	Arawakan	cpu	Payne (1989)
41	Yanesha	Arawakan	ame	Duff-Tripp (1997)
42	Ashéninka	Arawakan	prq	Mihas (2010)
43	Yine	Arawakan	pib	Hanson (2010)
44	Caquinte	Arawakan	cot	Swift (1988)
45	Nomatsiguenga	Arawakan	not	Shaver (1996)
46	Ese ejja	Tacanan	ese	Vuillermet (2012); Vuillermet p.c.
47	Nanti	Arawakan	cox	Michael (2008)
48	Chácobo	Panoan	cao	Córdoba et al. (2012)
49	Machiguenga	Arawakan	mcb	Snell (1978, 1998)
50	Itene	Chapacuran	ite	Angenot-de-Lima (2002)
51	Araona	Tacanan	aro	Emkow (2006, 2012)
52	Iñapari	Arawakan	inp	Parker (1995)
53	Amarakaeri	Harakmbut	amr	Helberg Chávez (1984)
54	Itonama	Isolate	ito	Crevels (2012a)
55	Jaqaru	Aymaran	jqr	Hardman (1983, 2000)
56	Baure	Arawakan	brg	Danielsen (2007)
57	Cayubaba	Isolate	cyb	Crevels and Muysken (2012)
58	Cavineña	Tacanan	cav	Guillaume (2008)
59	Tacana	Tacanan	tna	Ottaviano and Ottaviano (1965)
60	Movima	Isolate	mzp	Haude (2006)
61	Cuzco Q	Quechuan	quz	Lefebvre and Muysken (1988); Cusihuamán Gutiérrez (2001)
62	Mosetén	Mosetenan	cas	Sakel (2004)

Table 3.5.1 Continued

No.	Name	Affiliation	ISO	Main source(s)
63	Reyesano	Tacanan	rey	Guillaume (2012)
64	Leco	Isolate	lec	Kerke (2009)
65	Ignaciano	Arawakan	ign	Ott and Ott (1983); Olza Zubiri et al. (2004)
66	Trinitario	Arawakan	trn	Rose (2014)
67	Sirionó	Tupian	srq	Firestone (1965); Priest and Priest (1965); Gasparini (2012, p.c.)
68	Callawaya	Mixed	caw	Muysken (2009)
69	Uru	Uru-Chipaya	ure	Hannss (2008)
70	Yurakaré	Isolate	yuz	Van Gijn (2006)
71	Yuki	Tupian	yuq	Villafañe (2004)
72	Aymara	Aymaran	ayr	Hardman (2001)
73	Southern Aymara	Aymaran	ayc	Coler-Thayer (2010)
74	Chipaya	Uru-Chipaya	cap	Cerrón-Palomino (2006)
75	Canichana	Isolate	caz	Crevels (2012b)
76	Bolivian Q	Quechuan	quh	Plaza (2009)
77	East Bolivian Guaraní	Tupian	gui	Dietrich (1986)

[a]We use the ending *–an* to refer to language families, such as Quechuan and Tucanoan. Q stands for Quechua.

present an incorrect picture. There have been attempts, such as Eriksen (2011), to map the precise locations of all languages at the time of contact with the Spanish and Portuguese invaders. We have chosen to use present locations for several reasons. First, the information available for the contact period is not always complete. Second, that is also just a snapshot of a specific moment. Ethnicities would have been moving constantly in the pre-Columbian past as well, and we cannot say what was the relevant precise moment for changes to have taken place. Needless to say, however, more focused micro-studies of sub-regions of the area surveyed here are urgently needed, with the largest possible time-depth, taking demographic, ecological, cultural, archaeological and ethno-historical data into account. Such studies may help explain specific sub-patterns within the overall patterns we focus on in this chapter.

Features studied

The methodology used in this chapter analyses a list of individual properties of language structure (in the sound system, word structure, and sentence syntax). Each property is 'coded' as a binary opposition, that is, either present or absent in each individual language in our sample – or in some cases, as a three-way opposition. The codes are assigned by analysing published language descriptions, and in exceptional cases on our own field notes. Most sources are modern comprehensive grammars (for example, Sakel 2004; Overall 2007; Guillaume 2008; Zariquiey Biondi 2011), but in a few cases we had to resort to older and/or less comprehensive descriptions. Sometimes this coding is fairly straightforward, as in 'does language X have a central high vowel?', but sometimes it is fairly complex, as in 'does the adjective follow or precede the noun?'. The reason is that all languages have vowels, but not all have adjectives in exactly the same way, and adjectives may precede *and* follow the noun, as in Spanish (for example, *un gran amigo* but *una casa grande)*. The data are sometimes hard to interpret, then; also, data are sometimes simply lacking.

Any study that is based on comparing structural features has to select those features on the basis of a certain rationale. The underlying principle in this chapter is to consider features that have already been proposed by various authors as either typical of Amazonia or of the Andes, and therefore attesting to convergent processes at play right across each region. This approach, and the justification of the features, is discussed more extensively in Van Gijn (2014b), so for this chapter we confine ourselves to mentioning the sources and briefly describing the features.

Table 3.5.2 describes the linguistic overview studies of the Andean and Amazonian regions that are the sources consulted in drawing up our list of features. It lists the source reference in the first column, an abbreviation code by which we refer to those publications hereafter, a brief description of the feature, and the macro-area (Andean or Amazonian) to which it applies. Table 3.5.3 lists the 23 structural features coded for all languages in our sample.

Results and discussion

Figure 3.5.2 summarizes the degrees of difference between all languages with respect to all features in this section of the chapter in the form of a Neighbour-Net graph (Bryant and Moulton 2004).[5] The three best represented families are additionally indicated by a square (Quechuan), circle (Arawakan), or a rhombus (Panoan). The languages taken together roughly divide into three groups, which can be characterized areally:

1. An Andean subgroup, which contains all the Quechuan and Aymaran languages, as well as – more distantly – the Uru-Chipaya languages, the Tacanan languages, Jebero (Cahuapanan), and the isolates Candoshi and Leco.
2. A northern upper Amazon subgroup, bringing together all Panoan, Jivaroan and Tucanoan languages in our sample, the northern Tupí-Guaraní languages Kokama and Omagua, the other Cahuapanan language Chayahuita, and the northern (semi-)isolates Cofán, Waorani, Taushiro, Yagua and Urarina. Two

Table 3.5.2   Survey of linguistic studies of the Andean and Amazonian areas.
© Rik van Gijn and Pieter Muysken.

Source	Code	Description	Area
Büttner (1983)	B	Comparison of languages from the central Andes in lexis, and in broad typological features in phonology and language structure.	AND
Derbyshire and Pullum (1986)	DP	Survey of a number of morphosyntactic 'areal typological similarities', based on a sample of 20 languages.	AMZ
Derbyshire (1987)	D	Report based on a sample of 40 languages, which reconfirms some of the Amazonian features mentioned in DP.	AMZ
Payne (1990)	P1	Survey of morphological characteristics for a sample of selected Amazonian languages.	AMZ
Dixon and Aikhenvald (1999)	DA	List of features encountered across families in the whole of Amazonia.	AMZ
Payne (2001)	P2	Review of Dixon and Aikhenvald which criticizes their list of Amazonian features and proposes a number of additional ones.	AMZ
Torero (2002)	T	List of 40 features for the central Andean area, ranging from northern Peru to north-east Argentina and Chile; includes proto-languages and extinct language data; also includes some data from languages of the foothills.	AND
Adelaar (2012a; 2012b)	A	Overview of the language situation in the central Andes, focusing on structural and lexical traits of the Aymaran and Quechuan language families.	AND

unexpected languages in the 'northern' cluster are Amarakaeri (Harakmbut) and Mosetén (Mosetenan).[6]

3. A southern upper Amazon subgroup, with all Arawakan languages, the southern Tupí-Guaraní languages Sorionó, Yuki and east Bolivian Guaraní, Chapacuran Itene, and the southern and central (semi-)isolates Cholón, Itonama, Cayubaba, Movima, Yurakaré and Canichana. Surprising languages in the southern cluster are Zaparoan Arabela and Záparo, and the isolate Muniche.

The general picture that emerges is one of areal contact-induced convergence effects, as well as genealogical relatedness in language families. Contact effects can arguably account for the closeness of Tacanan languages to Uru-Chipaya languages, as well as that of Urarina, Leco and Jebero to the Quechuan and Aymaran

Table 3.5.3 Linguistic features studied in this chapter. © Rik van Gijn and Pieter Muysken.

	Feature	amz	and
1	Phonemic central high vowel	Y	N
2	Phonemic mid vowels	Y	N
3	Phonemic nasal vowels	Y	N
4	Phonemic palatal nasal consonant	N	Y
5	Phonemic velar-uvular opposition for stops	N	Y
6	Phonemic retroflex affricates	N	Y
7	More phonemic affricates than fricatives	Y	N
8	Single liquid phoneme	Y	N
9	Proportion of consonants permitted in syllable coda	A	C[a]
10	Presence of morphophonemic nasal spread	Y	N
11	Presence of phonemic glottalized stops	N	Y
12	Presence of phonemic aspirated stops	N	Y
13	Presence of prefixes	Y	N
14	Identical markers of possessor and of core verbal arguments	Y	N
15	Elaborate case-marking system	A	C[b]
16	Presence of core case markers (ERG, ABS, NOM, ACC)	N	Y
17	Accusative alignment in simple clauses	N	Y
18	Dependent marking for possession	N	Y
19	Presence of noun class or gender systems	Y	N
20	Object before subject in basic main clause constituent order	Y	N
21	Basic adjective-noun order within the noun phrase	N	Y
22	Presence of indigenous numerals higher than 9[c]	N	Y
23	Presence of an ideophone word class	Y	N

[a] Three-way distinction based on the percentage of phoneme consonants that can occur in coda position, ranging from 0 to 100, divided into three groups: A: 0–30, B: 31–60, C: 61–100.
[b] Three-way distinction (A) small set of case markers or no case marking (0–4), (B) medium set of case markers (5–6), large set of case markers (>6)
[c] Not counting obvious loans from Spanish, Portuguese, Quechua, or Aymara.

languages. The split of the Tupí-Guaraní languages between northern (Kokama, Omagua) and southern (Sirionó, Yuki, East Bolivian Guaraní) is also suggestive of contact effects, as is the presence of the southern and northern isolate languages in the southern and northern clusters, respectively. Areal effects seem nonetheless outweighed by language genealogy (inherited structures from a common ancestor), across most major families – Arawakan (except Chamicuro [ccc]), Panoan, Quechuan, but also smaller families like Jivaroan [jiv, agr, acu] and Aymaran [jqr, ayr, ayc] – since each of these clusters relatively homogeneously.

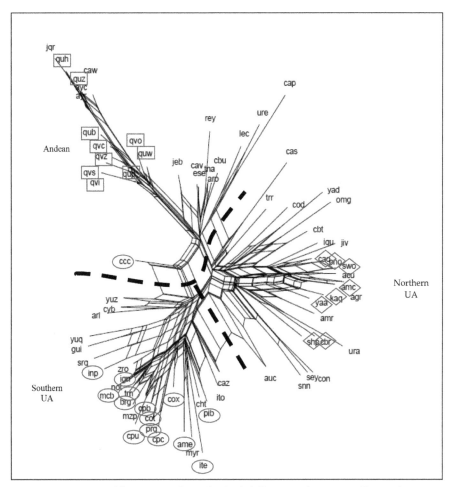

Figure 3.5.3 Neighbour-Net of typological differences between all sample languages (all features). © Rik van Gijn and Pieter Muysken.

The areal effects suggested by Figure 3.5.3 call for a closer look. In the remainder of this chapter, we concentrate on the distribution of individual features: in phonology (that is, the sound system – see section on 'phonological features', below), morphology (that is, word structure, see 'morphological features'), syntax (that is, clause structure, see 'syntactic features') and lexis ('lexical features').

Phonological features

Figure 3.5.4 shows the approximate geographical distributions of the four features to do with vowels. The x-axis in each of the plots shows latitude from south (left) to north (right); the y-axis shows elevation from low (bottom) to high (top).

The first vowel feature is whether each language has a central high vowel – a sound intermediate between Spanish /i/ and /u/. As can be seen, the central high vowel is

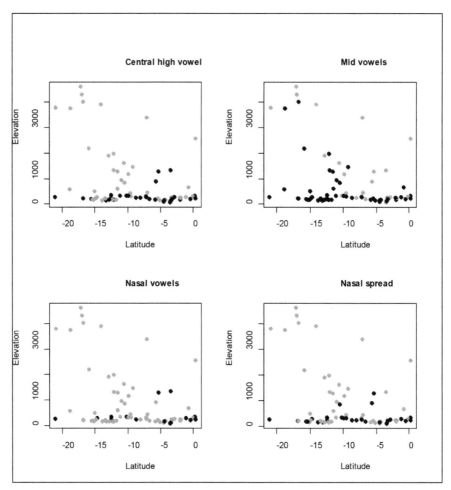

Figure 3.5.4 Distribution of four vowel features by latitude and elevation in the languages of the Andes and upper Amazonia. © Rik van Gijn and Pieter Muysken.

clearly a lowland feature: all the black dots, for languages that do have the feature in question, are at low elevations; the dots for the highland languages, meanwhile, are all grey, showing that they do not have this feature. The central high vowel is found over the entire north–south span of the upper Amazon (though it is slightly less frequent in the south). The three languages spoken at slightly higher altitudes and that also have a central high vowel are Chayahuita (of the Cahuapanan family), and Shuar and Aguaruna (both languages of the Jivaroan family; the third Jivaroan language in the sample, Achuar in the lowlands, also has a high central vowel). Both the Cahuapanan and Jivaroan territories stretch from higher altitudes eastwards to lower altitudes. Nonetheless, there are also many lowland languages that do not have the central high vowel. Interestingly, although it is assumed that proto-Arawakan did have a central high vowel (Aikhenvald 1999, 76), most modern Arawakan languages in the sample do not (Baure, Ignaciano, Trinitario, Ashéninka, Nomatsiguenga, Ucayali Yurúa Ashéninka, Nanti, Machiguenga, Yanesha'), implying that it must have been lost, perhaps under the influence of highland contact.[7] Furthermore, the central high vowel is not found in any of the Tacanan languages, suggesting that their common ancestor did not have it either. Alternatively – given the putative deep genealogical connection with the Panoan languages, which do generally have the high central vowel – this phoneme was perhaps lost before the Tacanan languages dispersed.

Mid vowels are pronounced with the tongue at a mid height in the mouth, for example, /e/- and /o/-type vowels, rather than 'high' /i/ and /u/, or 'low' /a/. In the upper Amazon, mid vowels show a less clear-cut pattern by elevation: they seem almost omnipresent in the lowlands, but are certainly found at higher altitudes as well, notably in the Uru-Chipaya languages, in some of the higher Campan Arawakan languages (Nanti, Matchiguenga, Nomatsiguenga, Ashéninka Perené, Pichis Ashéninka, Caquinte),[8] and in some of the (semi-)isolates spoken at higher altitudes (Kallawaya, Cholón, Leco, Canichana). Tena Quechua, one of the lowland Quechuan languages, has also developed phonemic mid vowels (unlike most highland Quechua varieties). This distribution suggests an important role for genealogy, since there are very few clear examples of mid vowels being acquired (other than in unadapted loanwords), while they were perhaps lost (and both low and high vowels were retained) in some of the Arawakan languages, such as Yanesha and Ajyíninka Apurucayali. The same important role for genealogy can be observed in the lowlands of the central upper Amazon, where Panoan languages generally do not have mid vowels.

Phonemic nasal vowels (Figure 3.5.5) are independent vowels of the same general type as those pronounced in French *un bon vin blanc* (where the written <n> is no longer pronounced as a consonant n at all), or written with a tilde as in Portuguese *São Paulo*. Nasal spread refers to a more automatic process in some languages, where one or more of the vowels in a word acquires a nasal pronunciation automatically, if that word also contains a nasal consonant (*n*, *m*, and so on). Taking these together (that is, whether phonemic or not), nasal vowels seem to be a clear lowland feature in the sense that they are hardly ever found in the highlands (except in Jivaroan languages) – although that does not mean that they are omnipresent in the lowlands. In particular, phonemic nasal vowels seem relatively rare, and concentrated mostly in the northern upper Amazon, which thus potentially constitutes a minor areal pattern spanning the Tucanoan languages Secoya and Siona and the isolates Cofán and Waorani, concentrated along the Aguarico River (the northernmost group on Figure 3.5.5).
Nasal spread is more common, and may follow areal patterns, expanding along rivers: the Aguarico/Napo in the north, Marañón in northern Peru, Ucayali in central Peru, and the Mamoré in Bolivia (see Figure 3.5.6).

To summarize, the central high vowel and nasal vowels seem to be lowland features, and the range of the latter especially (phonemic or not) seems to have

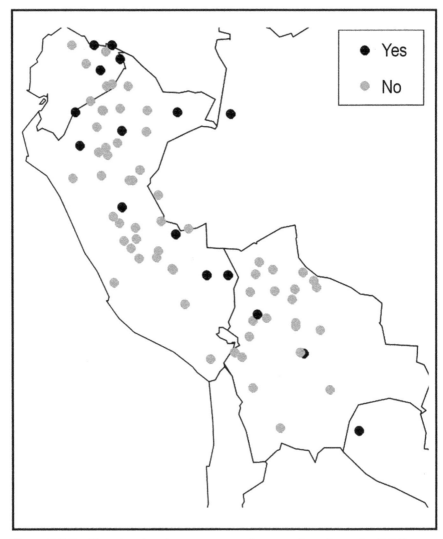

Figure 3.5.5 Map showing the presence or absence of nasal vowels. © Rik van Gijn and Pieter Muysken.

been expanding, possibly through contact. The presence of mid vowels seems to be determined mainly by language affiliation, but their absence may be a contact effect, especially in some of the Campan languages.

Moving on to the consonant features, Figure 3.5.7 shows the geographical distributions of the presence of:

1. a phonemic palatal nasal (the sound spelt <ñ> in Spanish, and <nh> in Portuguese);
2. a retroflex affricate (that is, a sound of the type spelt <ch> in Spanish and English, but pronounced retroflex, with the tongue curled back);

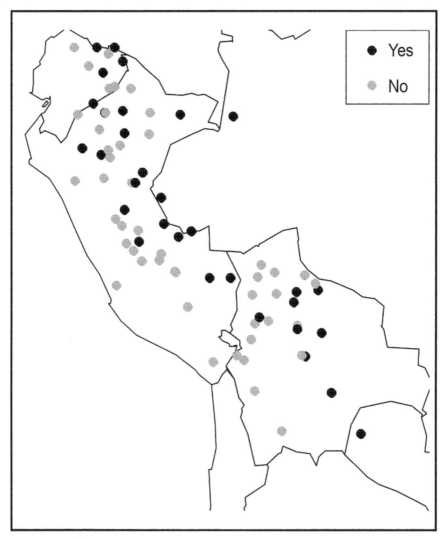

Figure 3.5.6 Map showing the presence or absence of nasal spread. © Rik van Gijn and Pieter Muysken.

3. more affricate than fricative phonemes (that is, more sounds of the type spelt <ch>, <dg> or <ts> in English, than of the type spelt <sh>, <z>, <s>, <th>, <f>, etc.);
4. only a single liquid phoneme (that is, not both *r* and *l* sounds, but just one, undifferentiated *r/l*).

The distribution of the palatal nasal may have areal dimensions, as it occurs in the Aguarico, Santiago and Marañón areas, as well as in the upper Ucayali, Madre de Dios, and part of the Mamoré. More broadly speaking, and especially in the central

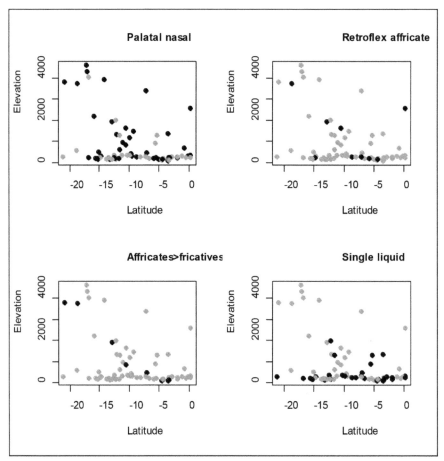

Figure 3.5.7 Distribution of the presence or absence of a palatal nasal by latitude and elevation in the languages of the Andes and upper Amazonia. © Rik van Gijn and Pieter Muysken.

upper Amazon, languages closer to the Andes more often have a phonemic palatal nasal than those further east, which again may point towards highland–lowland interactions (see Figure 3.5.8).

The retroflex affricate and cases of affricates outnumbering fricative phonemes, are rare in the entire area, as well as in the adjacent Andean languages. They do not seem to be particularly associated with either the highlands or lowlands, nor with particular river systems or sub-areas in the upper Amazon.[9] In fact, it is rather surprising to find the retroflex affricate in so many lowland languages (Urarina, Muniche, Cashibo, Shipibo, Reyesano), and to find affricates outnumbering fricatives in highland languages (Bolivian Quechua, Chipaya, Jaqaru). Just a single liquid phoneme, meanwhile, seems to be a lowland rather than a highland feature, although it is also found in some scattered lowland languages, with potential diffusion areas in northern Peru and central Bolivia in particular.

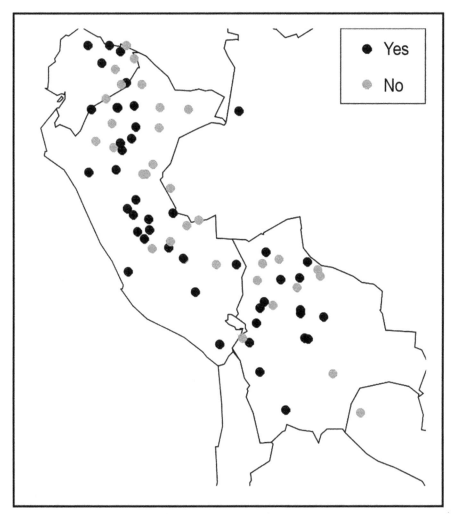

Figure 3.5.8 Distribution of four consonantal features by latitude and elevation.
© Rik van Gijn and Pieter Muysken.

These consonant features, in other words, do not pattern clearly by elevation; the palatal nasal and a single liquid phoneme show distributions that may be connected to river-based expansions.

Figure 3.5.9 shows three features related to the pronunciations of stop (or 'plosive') consonants (that is, those of the type /p/, /t/, /k/ and /b/, /d/, /g/). All three stop features have been associated, in published areal studies, with the Andes, or perhaps more narrowly with the Quechuan and Aymaran families. These features are whether a language has distinctions between:

1. velar versus uvular stops, that is, the contrast between sounds spelt <k> and <q> respectively, in modern indigenous orthographies for Quechua

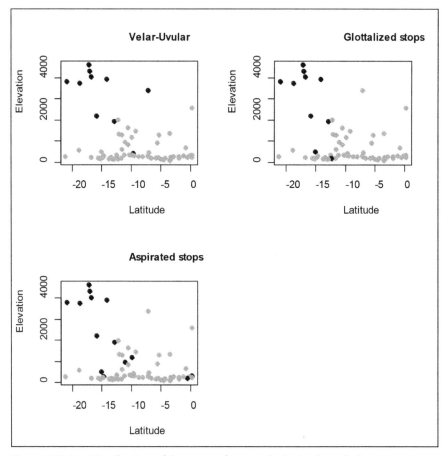

Figure 3.5.9 Distribution of three stop features by latitude and elevation.
© Rik van Gijn and Pieter Muysken.

and Aymara (for example, the k in *piki* and the q in *llaqta*, in the name of the well-known archaeological site of Pik̲illaqta, 'flea town');

2. normal versus glottalized stops (the latter spelt with an apostrophe, for example, in P'isaq);
3. normal versus aspirated stops (the latter spelt with a following <h>, for example, *khipu*).

All three stop features are fully present in the Bolivian and south Peruvian high-lands (in the Quechuan,[10] Aymaran and Uru-Chipaya families), but glottalized and aspirated stops are lacking in the more northerly Quechuan varieties of Imbabura, San Martín, Napo and Cajamarca Quechua. The velar-uvular distinction has also been lost in Imbabura, Napo and San Martín Quechuas. Leco (an isolate) also has glottalized as well as aspirated stops, undoubtedly under the influence of a Southern Quechuan and/or Aymaran language. Itene (Chapacuran)

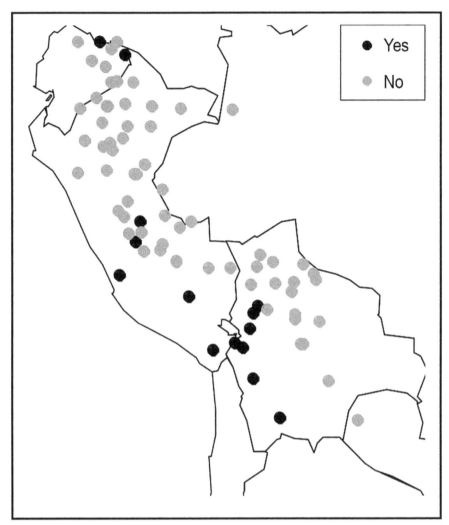

Figure 3.5.10 Map showing the presence or absence of aspirated stops.
© Rik van Gijn and Pieter Muysken.

has pre-glottalized stops, which seem unrelated to the Andean type of glottalized stops, given both the geographical distance and their contrasting phonetic realizations. Secoya (Tucanoan), Mosetén (Mosetenan), Cofán (isolate), the Arawakan languages Ashéninka Perené and Ajyíninka Apurucayali, as well as the isolate Leco, are all lowland languages that do have aspirated stops. There are two regions in particular – around Lake Titicaca, and also in central Peru – that seem to be diffusion areas for aspirated stops (Figure 3.5.10): they came into Quechua from Aymara, and seemed to have expanded eastward into the lowlands.

There is some leakage of these typical Andean stop features into languages of the foothills. In particular, aspirated stops seem to have diffused to languages

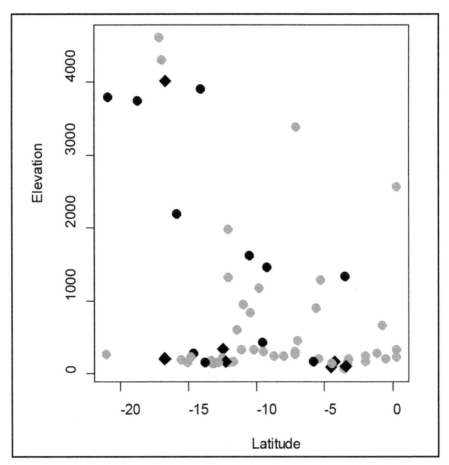

Figure 3.5.11 Distribution of closed syllables by latitude and elevation.
© Rik van Gijn and Pieter Muysken.

spoken at lower altitudes. At the same time, many northern Quechua varieties in Ecuador (although not Imbabura) surprisingly do have the aspirated/non-aspirated distinction in stops (but not the glottalized/non-glottalized contrast), possibly due to Cuzco Quechua adstrate or superstrate[11] in the Inca period.

As a final illustrative feature in phonology, Figure 3.5.11 looks at closed syllables, that is, those that do not end in a vowel, but have a consonant immediately following it. Specifically, Figure 3.5.11 asks what proportion of the consonant phonemes in a language are permitted in (underlying) coda position, that is, at the end of a syllable, after the vowel (for example, the two /n/ sounds in English Lo*n*do*n*). The grey circles are languages with the most restrictions, those that allow less than a third of their consonants to stand in coda position. The black circles are languages with the least restrictions, allowing over two-thirds of consonants in codas; and the black diamonds are the intermediate cases. Of the highland languages, southern and central Quechuan varieties generally do allow many of their consonants to stand in the syllable coda, as do Uru-Chipaya languages (although with slightly more restrictions in Uru). Aymaran languages, however, have more restrictions, at least underlyingly (that is, before suffix combination rules allow some vowels to be dropped), as do the northern Quechuan languages. Other languages at mid-elevations that put few restrictions on the coda are Yanesha', Shuar, Callawaya and Cholón. Lowland languages with few to intermediate restrictions on the coda are Amarakaeri, Mosetén, Yurakaré, Candoshi, Itene, Muniche, Movima, Yagua and Kokama. The foothill languages Mosetén and Yurakaré, as well as the languages at mid-elevations, may have been influenced by Andean languages.

Morphological features

An important typological characteristic of Andean languages is that they tend to be exclusively suffixing, whereas many Amazonian languages have (person) prefixes. Figure 3.5.12 indicates that although prefixes certainly tend to become less

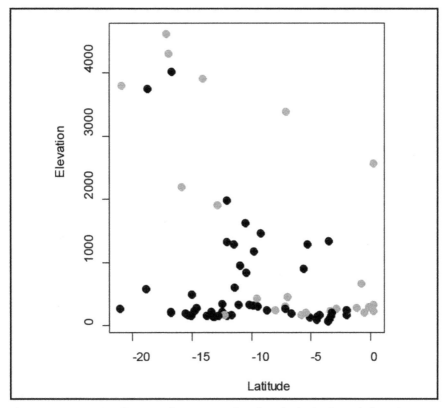

Figure 3.5.12 Distribution of presence of prefixes by latitude and elevation.
© Rik van Gijn and Pieter Muysken.

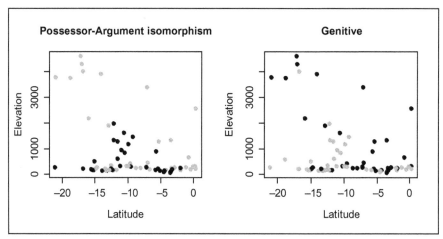

Figure 3.5.13 Distributions of possession-related features by latitude and elevation. © Rik van Gijn and Pieter Muysken.

common as one moves to higher elevations, the transition is not abrupt. Moreover, the far north of the upper Amazon lowlands seems to form a mini-area of exclusively suffixing languages.

The two languages spoken at higher elevations that do have prefixes are the related languages Uru and Chipaya, and both have only a marginal inventory of prefixes. The prefix system probably used to be more elaborate, involving referential (object) prefixes (Cerrón-Palomino 2006, 78–9; Hannss 2008, 133–4), so its current marginal status suggests that contact-induced influence from Quechuan and Aymaran languages has led to this decline in prefixes. The languages spoken at intermediate elevations and that do have prefixes are generally of the Aymaran and Jivaroan families, as well as a number of isolates (Cholón, Canichana, Leco). In the lowlands, the Panoan languages generally have very few or no prefixes, and there are also a few languages lacking prefixes in the northern Napo-Aguarico river system, including Quechuan languages (Imbabura, Napo, northern Pastaza), Tucanoan languages (Siona, Secoya), and isolates (Cofán, Waorani).

Figure 3.5.13 shows two aspects of how languages mark possession. The left-hand chart shows whether languages have bound possessive pronouns (like *my, your, his* in English, but attached to the verb) that are (nearly) identical (isomorphic) to the bound pronouns used for one of the verbal arguments (*very* roughly: is a possessor noun marked in the same way as either a subject or object noun?). This is an Amazonian characteristic, in that the black dots for languages that do show that isomorphism cluster mostly at lower elevations. The right-hand chart shows a more Andean feature, with black dots dominant at higher elevations: does the language have a genitive case marker?

In spite of some black dots at higher altitudes in the left-hand chart, possessor-subject/object isomorphism seems to be fundamentally a lowland rather than highland feature,[12] since the black dots towards the top of the graph are mostly Arawakan languages (maintaining a feature typical of that family), as well as some of the higher-altitude (near) isolates and representatives of small families like Cholón, Leco and Chayahuita.

The genitive shows almost a mirror image, partly reflecting a more general contrast in languages' structural systems (head-marking versus dependent-marking). Quechuan and Aymaran languages do have a genitive marker (they actually use double marking). The grey dot conspicuous at high altitude is Uru: it does in fact have possessive dependent (case) marking, but only on pronouns (Hannss 2008, 186–7), whereas the diagnostic feature we study is focused on nouns. Nevertheless, possessive case marking may have been more widespread in Uru in the past, pronominal case marking being a remnant of that more encompassing system. Jivaroan languages also have genitive markers, as does Chayahuita. Arawakan languages generally do not, an exception being Yanesha'. Of the lowland languages, those of the Panoan family generally do have a genitive marker (this seems to be a genealogical predisposition) as do those of the Tacanan family. A number of other lowland languages (Mosetén, Chamicuro, Yagua, Iquito, Candoshi and others) also have genitives, so this cannot justifiably be called a highland feature per se. Genitive markers do seem to be relatively rare in the southern upper Amazon, though.

Figure 3.5.14 shows two further features reported in the literature as typically Andean: core case markers (that is, case markers for the obligatory arguments of a verb) on the left-hand side and accusative alignment (a system such as exists in English, where the subject of an intransitive clause – with a single obligatory argument – for example, 'I' in *I walk* – behaves in the same way as the subject of a transitive clause – with two obligatory arguments – for example, 'I' in *I hit him*), in simple main clauses. There do seem to be plenty of lowland languages,

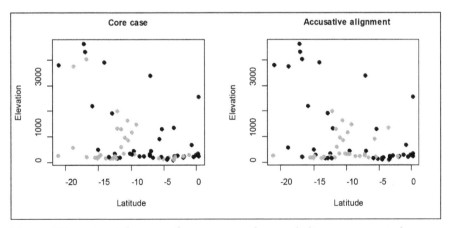

Figure 3.5.14 Distributions of core case markers and alignment pattern by latitude and elevation. © Rik van Gijn and Pieter Muysken.

however, that also have core case markers. Often these are ergative case markers (in the Tacanan and Panoan families), but accusative case markers certainly occur too (in Jivaroan and Tucanoan). Nonetheless, generally speaking, object case markers in lowland languages seem less 'structural', in that they are often subject to conditions, leading to differential object marking (for example, only animate objects are case-marked, see Van Gijn, 2019). The Uru-Chipaya languages do not have core case.

Accusative alignment is found throughout the higher Andes, as well as in some languages at lower altitudes (for example, Amarakaeri, Leco, Yurakaré, Canichana) and especially in the northern upper Amazon (for example, Aguaruna, Waorani, Cofán, Siona, Secoya, Candoshi). The Arawakan family has split S systems, while Tacanan and Panoan have ergative systems.

A final morphological parameter is the number of case markers in a language. Dixon and Aikhenvald (1999) claim that lowland languages generally have small case inventories, but for our sample this seems true mainly for Arawakan and most Tupian languages, as well as for a few (near-)isolates (for example, Movima, Iquito, Itonama, Muniche and Canichana). Otherwise, many lowland languages have extensive case inventories (see Figure 3.5.15). So although it is true that highland languages have extensive case inventories, so too do many lowland languages.

Syntactic features

In languages worldwide, there is an overwhelming universal preference for word orders in which A (transitive subject) comes before O (object) (Dryer and Haspelmath 2013a, 2013b). Exceptionally, however, deviant word orders with O before A have been claimed as areal patterns in parts of central Amazonia (Derbyshire and Pullum 1986). As can be seen in Figure 3.5.16, O before A orders are nonetheless decidedly rare in the upper Amazon. Only Urarina, Itene, Arabela, Sirionó, Yuki, and Reyesano were classified as having O before A.[13] Although it is true that these are all lowland languages, it seems a stretch to consider this an areal feature, given that these languages are so few and far apart.

The order adjective–noun is typical of Andean languages, as corroborated by Figure 3.5.16. However, Figure 3.5.16 also shows that this order is common in the lowlands of the upper Amazon, too. In fact, from a distributional point of view, a number of diffusion areas can be identified, as shown in Figure 3.5.17, where the northern Napo-Aguarico-Pastaza area in Ecuador, as well as the Marañón and the Madre de Dios, contain various languages spoken in contiguous areas that all have adjective–noun order.

To summarize, O before A order is uncommon in general and does not seem to follow any areal pattern. Adjective before noun order is found throughout the Andes, as well as in a number of adjacent areas in Ecuador, northern Peru, and Bolivia.

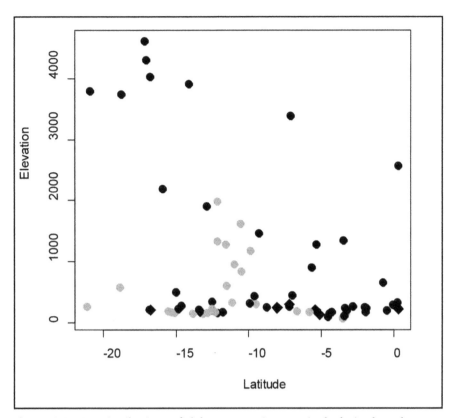

Figure 3.5.15 Distributions of elaborate case inventories by latitude and elevation. © Rik van Gijn and Pieter Muysken.

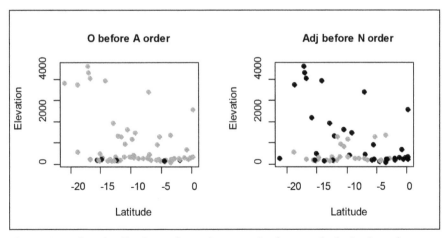

Figure 3.5.16 Distributions of constituent order features by latitude and elevation. © Rik van Gijn and Pieter Muysken.

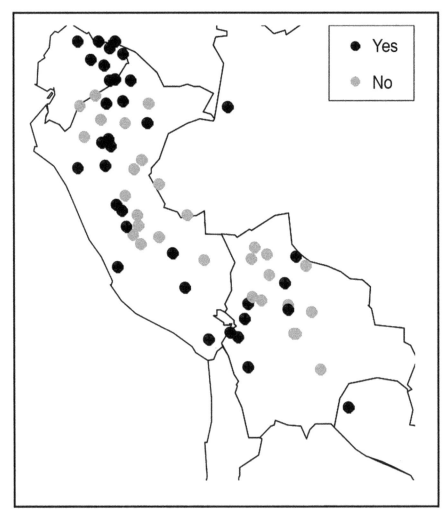

Figure 3.5.17 Map showing adjective-noun order. © Rik van Gijn and Pieter Muysken.

Lexical features

Figure 3.5.18 shows the distribution of three features related to the lexicon: whether languages categorise their nouns into classes or genders; whether they have (native) words for high numerals; and whether they have a clearly distinct word-class of ideophones that behave differently to other nouns.

Noun class or gender systems can be found in Arawakan languages in central Peru, but also in a number of Guaporé-Mamoré isolate languages (Cayubaba, Movima, Itonama, Mosetén), and in north-eastern Peru and Ecuador (Yagua, Muniche, Chayahuita, Omagua, Arabela, Záparo, Cofán, Secoya, Siona). None of the traditional Andean families (Quechuan, Aymaran, Uru-Chipaya) has a noun class system.

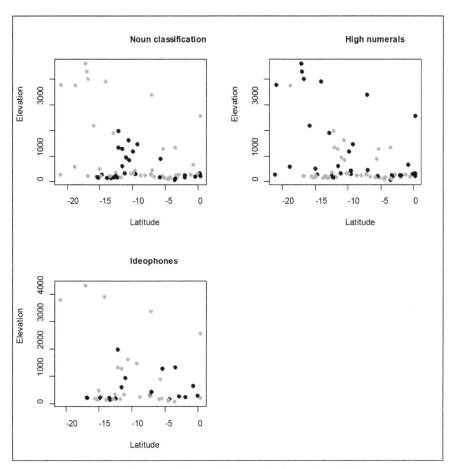

Figure 3.5.18 Distributions of lexical features by latitude and elevation.
© Rik van Gijn and Pieter Muysken.

While Andean languages generally have elaborate numeral systems, Amazonian languages have a reputation for having very small native numeral systems, often no more than just the first two or three numbers. The plot in Figure 3.5.18 counts only native numerals, to the extent that we can establish which words have been borrowed from other sources. That some larger indigenous numeral systems can be found in the lowlands is partly due to Quechuan languages that are intrusive here (southern and northern Pastaza, Napo, Huallaga, San Martín and Tena varieties of Quechua). Nonetheless, a few other (semi-)lowland languages do seem to have native conventionalized numeral systems that go beyond nine: for example, Itene, Taushiro, Mosetén, Cofán, Yine[14], Leco, Cholón.[15] Chipaya has replaced its native numerals above four with Aymaran numerals. Quechuan/Aymaran influence on numeral systems can be observed in several other upper Amazon languages, for example, Urarina, Kokama, Shipibo-Konibo, Yanesha', Cavineña and Chayahuita. Many other lowland languages use Spanish numerals for the higher numbers.

It is hard to say anything general about ideophones. There are many fewer dots than in other graphs, because from the sources available it is often unclear whether a language does not have ideophones. And even with the languages for which a coding decision was taken, there were different degrees of confidence. The general picture seems to be that highland languages lack ideophones, and that they are more common, though not ubiquitous, in the lowlands. Nuckolls has discovered extensive use of ideophones in (lowland) Pastaza Quechua (2001, 71), and has argued that this feature is common in the area where this is spoken, but we know of no systematic survey in this respect, and descriptions are not complete.

Results and discussion

We have surveyed the distribution of selected features in phonology, morphology, syntax and lexis in over 70 languages in the central Andes and adjacent parts of the Amazon. In this final section we return to Dixon and Aikhenvald's (1999) comment that the Amazonian and Andean areas fade into each other, and come to a rather more precise and detailed picture. Table 3.5.4 briefly evaluates the features studied here. Figure 3.5.19 organizes the features in terms of strongly highland (top left) to strongly lowland (bottom right), with the features in bold showing evidence of diffusion from the highlands toward the lowlands; the features between brackets are those that show less clear patterns as a result of low representation of a feature or feature value.

From Table 3.5.4 and Figure 3.5.19 we can conclude that a few features, notably phonological ones, pattern quite clearly along a highland-lowland divide: the vowel features are concentrated in the lowlands, whereas the stop features are predominantly restricted to the highlands. Other lowland features include the presence of prefixes (or rather, the lack of them seems to be a highland feature), isomorphism of markers for possessor and verbal argument, and gender/noun class systems. Other than in phonology, there seem to be few features clearly restricted to the highlands. Accusative alignment is found in the lowlands too, especially in the north, although accusative case-markers in the lowlands do generally seem subject to more conditions than in the highlands. Adjective–noun order is also found in many lowland languages, possibly due to contact in several sub-areas of the upper Amazon. Higher numerals are perhaps the most strongly Andean feature, and Aymaran and Quechuan languages have certainly influenced lowland languages in this respect, for a good many of them have adopted Quechuan or Aymaran numerals. Other reportedly typical highland or lowland features turned out to be either very rare in the sample in any case (retroflex affricates, more affricates than fricatives, O before S order), or common in both highlands and lowlands (palatal nasal, closed syllables, elaborate case inventories, core case marking, genitive marking).

The contact-induced diffusion of more abstract, grammatical features can be indicative of several different contact scenarios (Thomason and Kaufman 1988; Thomason 2001; Muysken 2010):

Table 3.5.4 Summary of linguistic features and their distributions by latitude and elevation. © Rik van Gijn and Pieter Muysken.

	Feature	Distribution pattern
1	Phonemic central high vowel	**Uniquely lowland feature**
2	Phonemic mid vowels	**Lowland feature**
3	Phonemic nasal vowels	**Uniquely lowland feature**, but fairly rare
4	Phonemic palatal nasal consonant	Widespread
5	Phonemic velar-uvular opposition for stops	**Highland feature**
6	Phonemic retroflex affricates	Rare in the sample
7	More phonemic affricates than fricatives	Rare in the sample
8	Single phonemic liquid phoneme	Mostly lowland
9	Permissibility of closed syllables	No clear pattern
10	Presence of morphophonemic nasal spread	**Uniquely lowland feature**
11	Presence of phonemic glottalized stops (Peru, Bolivia)	**Highland feature**
12	Presence of phonemic aspirated stops (Peru, Bolivia)	Mostly highland, some dispersal
13	Presence of prefixes	**Lowland feature**
14	Isomorphism of possessor and core verbal argument person markers	**Lowland feature**
15	Elaborate case marking system	No clear pattern
16	Presence of core case markers (erg, abs, nom, acc)	Widespread
17	Accusative alignment in simple clauses	Mainly highland and northern Upper Amazon lowlands
18	Dependent marking for possession	Fairly common throughout
19	Presence of classifier or gender systems	**Lowland feature**
20	O before S basic main clause constituent order	Rare in the sample
21	Basic adjective-noun order within NP	Highland, with potential diffusion into lowland areas
22	Indigenous numerals higher than nine	Highland and some lowland languages have complex numerals
23	Ideophone word class	Data limited, mostly lowland

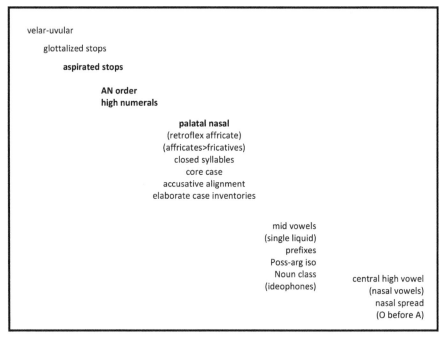

velar-uvular

  glottalized stops

    aspirated stops

      AN order
      high numerals

          palatal nasal
        (retroflex affricate)
      (affricates>fricatives)
      closed syllables
      core case
    accusative alignment
  elaborate case inventories

            mid vowels
          (single liquid)
           prefixes
          Poss-arg iso
         Noun class   central high vowel
        (ideophones)   (nasal vowels)
                    nasal spread
                    (O before A)

Figure 3.5.19   Classification of features as predominantly highland to predominantly lowland, and intermediate positions. © Rik van Gijn and Pieter Muysken.

1. Long-term and intensive contact with borrowing. In this case there should also be plenty of evidence of loanwords, which does not seem to be the case for either the lowland or highland languages.
2. Processes involving imperfect second language learning, for instance by (large) groups of immigrants who marry into a society. If this incoming group is numerous or prestigious enough, the variety they speak (which will include some of the abstract characteristics of the original language of the immigrants) can exert influence in the variety of the group as a whole.
3. Extensive multilingualism, where two (or more) linguistic systems stored in the brains of individuals may influence each other, becoming more alike, especially at an abstract level. If the situation of multilingualism is extensive enough and persists over time, this may lead to languages converging at the societal level (see for example, Matras 2011).

Scenario 1, above, seems unlikely because the amount of loanwords from highland languages in lowland languages and vice versa is limited (see also Bowern et al. 2011), although a definite answer to this matter requires a systematic investigation of lexica across the languages of the Andes and upper Amazon. Scenario 2 would require detailed and densely sampled genetic evidence to show great levels of admixture in upper Amazon groups, which, to our knowledge, is not available at this point. Scenario 3 ideally requires the attestation of multilingual communicative practices. In the absence of such evidence, only indirect evidence, from archaeology, ethnology, and possibly geography can be brought to bear to make the case for scenario 3.

One striking conclusion that is suggested by the data discussed in this chapter, and visualized in Figure 3.5.19 is that if some of these distributions are indeed due to language contact, then the general picture suggests that such contact influences have operated mostly in one direction, from the highland languages into the lowland ones, rather than vice versa.

A non-contact-based account for the shared features between groups of languages is a deep-time genealogical link between them. Some linguists have claimed that grammatical features of languages tend to be highly stable (less changeable) through time (for example, Dunn et al. 2005). If particular grammatical characteristics tend to be very stable over time, they may be indicative of deep genetic links that cannot be recovered using more traditional methods. It is difficult to evaluate this claim, since linguists are still discussing the relative stability of individual linguistic features and the time depth they may represent, and no consensus seems as yet to be in sight (see Chapter 2.3).

From these considerations it becomes clear that a study such as this can only be preliminary, for several reasons. First of all, for many of the smaller languages, particularly in the northern part of our domain of research, the sources are fragmentary. Language data are coded on the basis of descriptions often written by missionary linguists with varying amounts of linguistic training, and the descriptions are far from systematic, making it difficult to be sure that one is coding reliably and consistently across all the different languages covered. In addition, only a limited set of features were included in our study.

Second, our study does not take a full historical perspective, as noted above, in at least two respects. We have not tried to establish, for each language family and its representatives, what the most likely original feature specifications may have been for that family as a whole. More historical research is certainly needed on the various families in this region. Furthermore, ethno-historical sources need to be taken into account in order to tell whether the current distribution of languages reflects their original distribution. It almost certainly does not. A good example of the type of study needed would be Wise (2014), who sketches the relationships between a number of languages on the eastern slopes of Peru, including Yanesha', Chamicuro, Cholón, Candoshi, and languages of the Jivaroan and Quechuan families. She establishes one cluster centred around the Jivaroan languages, but also including Candoshi, Shawi and Shiwilu, Chamicuro, Munichi, and Chachapoyas Quechua. The other cluster involves Campan languages, and Panao and Yaru Quechua. Wise notes that Yanesha' shares many features with languages in the northern cluster, which may point to population movements, possibly as late as the colonial period.

Third, many of the phenomena considered here will gain further significance from a geographically wider perspective, as in the work of González (2015) on the phonological features of the Chaco, within a wider South American context, and in papers by Lev Michael's group (Chang and Michael 2014; Michael et al. 2014).

As better language descriptions become increasingly available, along with modern techniques for analysing complex datasets, together these should allow for more sophisticated analyses of the complex patterns of interaction in the highland-lowland area. Such studies can also be backed up by historical-comparative work on individual families (which has so far lagged behind these structural comparisons), and by closer collaboration with ethno-historians, anthropologists, geneticists and archaeologists. All of this opens up promising perspectives for further research.

We hope that the data presented here will mark a step forward in the debate on the extensive linguistic areas of the Andes and Amazonia, and the interactions between them. In particular, we have tried to go beyond just presenting anecdotal evidence, by being as systematic as possible. Future work will hopefully flesh out the dynamics that lie behind the distributions of linguistic features that are found here.

3.6
Rethinking the role of agriculture and language expansion for ancient Amazonians

Eduardo Góes Neves

It is today increasingly accepted that by the early sixteenth century, when Europeans first reached the area, the Amazon basin was filled with people, (Heckenberger and Neves 2009; Roosevelt 2013) and that the current composition of Amazonian biomes derives at least partially from past pre-Columbian indigenous agency (Balée 2013; Ter Steege et al. 2013; Levis et al. 2017). Yet there remains much uncertainty about the patterns of social and political organization of the people settled along the major Amazonian floodplain and the uplands of the basin at that time – and, indeed, in the deeper past. In the 1990s, scholars proposed that some of these societies, such as those of Marajó Island at the mouth of the Amazon, were strongly hierarchical and stratified, with economies based on the intensive cultivation of crops such as maize (Roosevelt 1991). However, as research has continued in these areas and elsewhere, the role of agriculture as the major productive activity of ancient Amazonian societies has begun to be questioned, because of a lack of evidence for the intensive cultivation of crops such as manioc and maize, in sites mostly along the main course of the Amazon (Fernandes Caromano et al 2013; Hermenegildo et al. 2017; Meggers 2001; Neves 2008; Schaan 2008). On the other hand, evidence from areas upstream, far from the main Amazon channel, suggests a broad and diversified pattern of social economic organization for Amazonia more widely. Such evidence includes investment in constructing earthworks and mounds in the coastal plains of French Guiana (Rostain 2013), the upper Acre basin (Pärssinen et al. 2009; Saunaluoma and Schaan 2012; Saunaluoma 2012; Saunaluoma et al. 2018), and the Llanos de Mojos of Eastern Bolivia (Carson et al. 2014; Erickson 2000a; Prümers and Jaimes Betancourt 2014a); and the creation of a road network establishing a loose, low-density urban pattern in the upper Xingú (Heckenberger 2005; Heckenberger et al. 2008).

Such a wide array of new data demonstrates that there was no single economic and political pattern for ancient Amazonians. This marks a significant departure from how the debate was conducted over much of the second half of the twentieth century by authors such as Lathrap (1968 a and b) or Meggers

(1997), in which discussion revolved around refinements to the so-called 'tropical forest pattern', originally defined by Robert Lowie (1948). Notwithstanding the importance of these contributions, the realization that Amazonian societies were economically and politically much more diversified in the past makes sense when one examines the similarly varied patterns of language diversity found among current Amazonian indigenous societies (for example, Chapter 3.4). For the Amazon and Orinoco basins, there are more than 300 languages included in over 50 'genealogical units': language families or isolates for which no relationship to any other language has been demonstrated (Epps and Salanova 2013, 1). Many of these languages are disappearing at a fast pace. Across the world, scholars have argued that, up to the beginnings of the European expansion into the Americas, Africa, Asia and Oceania in the modern era, there was some correlation between past subsistence patterns and the distribution of major or hypothesized language families (Ammerman and Cavalli-Sforza 1984; Renfrew 1987), in a history that in some cases may go back to the beginnings of agriculture. Briefly, they suggest that such ancient economic patterns relate to the initial adoption of agriculture and the population growth that followed, leading to the demographic and geographic expansion of certain groups speaking genealogically related languages from an initially localized homeland. Such farming language dispersal processes may, for instance, lie behind the expansion of languages of the Indo-European family into both Europe and India (Renfrew 1987), as well as that of Austronesian languages in Polynesia (Bellwood 2005). In Amazonia, quite to the contrary, the lack of any single economic package may be one of the underlying reasons for the significant degree of language diversity found there. Indeed, with the exception of the Arawak and Tupí families[1] most of the other language families of the Amazon seem to have a localized distribution within particular areas of the basin, sometimes in a positive correlation with distinct geographical areas, such as, for instance, Carib languages and the areas around the Guiana Plateau.

These ideas will be briefly discussed in this chapter. Its underlying thesis is that despite the genetic, botanical and archaeological evidence showing that ancient Amazonian and Andean societies were connected throughout their histories (Valdez 2008; Chapter 2.4), the sharply distinctive ecological and geographical contexts – on the one hand, the markedly circumscribed valleys of the dry Pacific coast and Central Andean highlands; on the other hand, the extensive floodplains and uncircumscribed and ecologically diversified tropical Amazonian lowlands – created at the outset conditions for very distinct economic and political trajectories to emerge in the long-run (cf. Chapters 1.1 and 3.1).

The recognition that highland and lowland societies were politically different is hardly new, and it sustained comparative research in South American archaeology in the twentieth century (Steward 1948; Chapter 1.1). The main difference from traditional approaches in the hypothesis presented here is that the opposition between highlands and lowlands has traditionally been constructed from a perspective that accorded the former the role of centre of cultural innovation for the whole continent, whereas the latter was relegated to the status of recipient of such innovations. I will try to briefly show that despite the evidence of mostly political differences in the histories of ancient highland and lowland societies, there is nothing in the archaeological record that supports the notion the tropical lowlands were marginal backwaters in the deep history of South America. By political differences I mean to say that the state never evolved in the Amazon as it did in the Andes at least from the Middle Horizon onwards.

Likewise, I will try also to show that the picture of language and cultural diversity currently found among native Amazonians is probably the outcome of a long-term process of occupation and management of productive environments in the lowland tropics that started at the very outset of the human occupation of South America and that favoured, in the long run, the development of localized and territorial economic strategies which were inimical to demographic expansions. The chronological focus of the chapter rests mostly within the Middle Holocene, that is, from c. 8000–4000 years BP because it is at that time that such economic strategies initially unfolded (Watling et al. 2018; Neves and Heckenberger 2019).

Distinct long-term perspectives on the highlands and lowlands of South America

One of the fascinating aspects of South American archaeology is the fact that most, if not all, indigenous populations that settled the continent by 1492 had a common genetic background, but displayed a wide array of patterns of social and political organization (Skoglund and Reich 2016). South American societies by the late fifteenth century displayed probably all forms of political organization known to social scientists, and likely other forms still waiting to be described and understood. This is remarkable when one considers that the continent remained basically isolated throughout the Holocene. Isolation here does not mean that South America was closed to external influences: maize, a Mesoamerican crop, was introduced quite early from its centre of origin in Mesoamerica (Piperno 2011a), and by c. 4,500 years ago was cultivated far to the south, near the mouth of the River Plate in what is now Uruguay (Iriarte et al. 2004). Likewise, tobacco, a South American domesticate, spread all the way north to the Saint Lawrence basin by the late 1400s. And sweet potato, another South American domesticate, was cultivated in Polynesia and Melanesia before the onset of European colonization of the Pacific.

Isolation, in the context of the discussion presented here, is meant simply to point to the fact that there were no major demographic or military movements into South America from other continents, as happened many times over in Europe, but also in Africa and the Pacific. In this sense, in general, current patterns of indigenous language distribution in South America (despite the brutal losses brought by European colonization) reflect local histories. The deep contrast to be observed when one compares the relatively smaller number of languages and language families recorded in the highlands, with the relatively larger number of languages, language families, and language isolates found in the lowlands, is therefore note-worthy, as much as it may have partially resulted from depopulation in the colonial era or from language loss continuing into more recent times. Moreover, it is inter-esting to see how the highland/lowland barrier applies to language distribution patterns too: the varieties of Quechua spoken in the lowlands, for instance, result from recent colonization of these areas by Andean settlers, and then local adoption of Quechua (for example, Chapter 3.4).

The high level of language diversity in Amazonia is also remarkable given the fact that there are no major physical barriers isolating local populations, such as the mountain ranges found in other hotspots of language diversity (like the Caucasus or New Guinea). Forty-odd years ago, Meggers (1977) proposed that language diversity in Amazonia would be compatible with the general pattern of biological diversity found there as well, a matter that has puzzled naturalists since the nine-teenth century. To explain this diversity, botanists have proposed that past climate change created *refugia* of forests isolated by expanses of drier savannahs (Meggers 1977). This so-called 'refuge theory' has been intensively discussed and tested in the years since, and it is probably not the only way to explain the emergence of biological diversity in tropical America. Meggers was correct, however, when she proposed that there was some form of positive correlation between the intertwined history of the emergence of biological and cultural diversity in Amazonia. The arguments presented here will build also on that hypothesis.

The integration of language phylogenies and histories with the archaeologi-cal record is notoriously difficult, and it becomes ever more so as one moves fur-ther back into the past. Despite such shortcomings, the archaeological record of the early to middle Holocene in Amazonia shows a picture of cultural diversity that seems too closely compatible with the pattern of language diversity found there today for this parallel to be ignored. In other words, in the Amazon there seems to be a coherent, consistent and long-term picture of diversification that could be as old as human settlement there. It is thus important to examine some of the archae-ological evidence for this, before moving on to presenting some hypotheses that might explain it. Let us look initially at the context of early ceramic production in South America.

A brief review of the contexts of early occupation and ceramic production in the Amazon and other tropical areas of lowland South America

Human occupation of the tropical lowlands is as old as in other parts of the conti-nent (Dillehay 2008; Roosevelt et al. 2002). But despite such antiquity, there is no single cultural tradition that can be linked with these early occupations, at least from the examination of the lithics produced by the early settlers (cf. Chapter 2.1). Thus, in the upper Guaporé basin, the Abrigo do Sol rock shelter yielded dates between 14,700 and 8930 BP (Meggers and Miller 2003), associated with a diversified unifacial lithic assemblage belonging to the so-called Dourados complex. At Pedra Pintada cave, on the lower Amazon, close to the Taperinha shell mound, Roosevelt (Roosevelt et al. 1996) has found bifacial lithic artefacts dating back to c. 11,200 BP. Further west, in the middle Caquetá river in Colombian Amazonia, the open-air sites of Peña Roja and San Isidro produced unifacial lithics dating back to c. 9000 BP (Gnecco and Mora 1997). In the Carajás hills of eastern Amazonia, a distinct unifacial lithic tradition found in rock shelters has been dated to c. 8800 years BP (Magalhães 2018). In the upper Madeira basin, south-western Amazonia, there is a long record of the production of unifacial artefacts and flaked axes that also goes back to the early Holocene (Meggers and Miller 2003). There are other examples, such as bifacial lithic industries in the Guiana plateau (Rostain 2013) or central Amazonia in the early Holocene (Neves 2013), but the main point is that of cultural diversity from the onset of human occupation (see Figure 3.6.1).

The same perspective is valid when one looks at the evidence for early ceramic production. One of the interesting aspects of New World archaeology in recent decades has been the quiet realization that the initial centres of ceramic production are located mainly away from the supposed centres of plant domestication

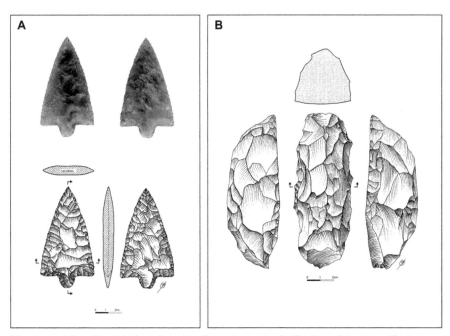

Figure 3.6.1 Chert bifacial projectile point and silicified sandstone unifacial artefact dated to c. 6500 BC, Dona Stella site, Central Amazonia. Late Pleistocene and Early Holocene lithic industries from Amazonia displayed a wide array of technological and formal variability without a single unifying founding tradition. Drawings by Marcos Castro, Central Amazonia Project.

and the emergence of stratified societies across the continent. Among these early centres, in North America there are a series of shell mounds located in the coastal and lagoon areas of Florida and Georgia in the United States, with dates up to 7,000 years ago (Anderson and Sassaman 2012). In South America, the picture is perhaps even more interesting: there are at least four initial production centres, all located along an arc that spans distinct tropical environments: coastal plains, dry tropical forests, estuaries and mangroves: from the Guayas basin in Ecuador in the west, all the way to the mouth of the Amazon in the east, by way of what today are the Caribbean coasts of Colombia and Surinam.

In Ecuador, early complexes include Valdivia, on the Santa Elena peninsula, in the dry forest zone of the Pacific coast, with dates of over 5500 BP (Marcos 2015). In Colombia, early pottery is found at San Jacinto and Puerto Hormiga on the lower Magdalena River, with dates back to 6000 BP in San Jacinto (Oyuela-Caycedo 1995). On the Atlantic coast east of the mouth of the Amazon there are shell-tempered Mina ceramics, associated with shell mounds and open-air sites in a region currently covered by mangroves (Roosevelt 1995; Silveira et al. 2011). Finally, there are Taperinha ceramics, the earliest in South America, found at the eponymous freshwater shell mound located in the lower Amazon, downstream from the present-day city of Santarém, dating back to c. 7000 BP (Roosevelt 1995; Roosevelt et al. 1991). Other early ceramics associated with shell mound contexts are found at Monte Castelo, in south-western Amazonia (Pugliese et al. 2019) (see Figure 3.6.2).

Most of the authors who work with such early ceramics agree that these early complexes were probably unrelated to each other, and that ceramic production in South America began independently in different centres, all in lowland tropical environments (Roosevelt 1995; Oyuela-Caycedo 1995; but see Meggers 1997 for a different perspective). Even the recent findings by Valdez (2008) and Olivera (2014), of ancient ceramics in western Amazonia, dated to about 4200 BP and with remarkable similarities to the later styles of Chorrera and Cupinisque, have parallels in transitional contexts between the Andes and Amazonia, in the *ceja de selva* (Chapter 2.4). Such evidence should be strong enough to refute the hypotheses – more political than scientific – that would relegate the tropics to a marginal context within the cultural history of South America (Evans and Meggers 1968; Meggers and Evans 1957). More interesting, however, is that such early contexts of ceramic production seem to be divorced from the early adoption of agriculture.

Ceramics without agriculture in the lowland tropics

When comparing the processes of domestication of plants and animals, as well as the emergence of institutionalized social inequality in the New and Old Worlds, some contrasts are remarkable. Perhaps the most striking of these is the wide chronological gap between the first evidence for the domestication of plants and

Figure 3.6.2   Ceramic fragments from the Bacabal tradition dated to c. 2200 BC, Monte Castelo site, Southwestern Amazonia. Bacabal tradition ceramics are part of a host of different and apparently unrelated early ceramic complexes found across Amazonia from the fifth to the third millennium BC. Photo by Eduardo Góes Neves.

for the emergence of urban life or even villages in the Americas. In places like Mexico and Ecuador, evidence of early plant domestication is clearly associated with groups that had diversified economies based on hunting, fishing and gathering – as well as on the consumption of plant domesticates – in lifestyles that were maintained for millennia (Piperno 2011a). In the Americas, early plant domestication, and especially the incorporation of domesticated plants into the diet of a given population, seems to have been primarily a process of selection, and not the result of an adaptive imperative, as is indicated by Hastorf (2006) for the contexts of Peru's Pacific coast. It is plausible, therefore, that in the New World there was no adaptive pressure for a rapid adoption of agriculture, just as there was very little pressure to domesticate animals (Stahl 2015).

The example of maize (*Zea mays*) is illustrative in this sense. Maize was domesticated in Mesoamerica, in the Balsas River region, at least 7,000 years ago (Piperno 2011a), and spread rapidly across the continent, reaching (among other places) Ecuador 6,000 years ago (Piperno 2011a), south-western Amazonia around the same time (Kistler et al. 2018) and the distant shores of Uruguay about 4,500 years ago (Iriarte et al. 2004). It is clear that the mere presence of maize among these populations, so distant from each other, does not indicate that they were exclusively farmers, but once again, opportunistic and generalist groups that displayed consumption patterns based on the management and cultivation of natural and wild resources. It is worth noting in this regard that by 1492, the Amerindian plants that were most widespread across the continent were maize and tobacco, whose uses in many cases – aside maybe from parts of the Andes, Mesoamerica and the Mississippi – were associated more with recreational or religious consumption than purely with food consumption (cf. Chapter 3.1). Such data from the New World show that the very distinction between 'natural' and 'wild' in such cases results more from an intellectual heritage forged in other contexts and based on other experiences, than from a faithful reflection of Amerindian classification categories (Fausto and Neves 2018).

In the case of the oldest ceramics of the Americas, perhaps the best study of the associated productive contexts has been made by Oyuela-Caycedo and Bonzani (2005) in San Jacinto, near the Caribbean coast of Colombia. Large surface excavations led to the discovery of preserved food-processing structures, formed of cavities lined with clay and in some cases with fire-cracked rocks disassociated spatially from the places where ceramics were found. This lack of association suggests that the initial ceramics at San Jacinto were not linked to food processing, but rather to the consumption of beverages at festive events. Likewise in Amazonia, data obtained from the shell mounds of Mina phase sites and Taperinha do not support the hypothesis that these were early farmers, even if eventually remains of domesticated plants are found in their midst. On the other hand, on the dry Pacific coast of Central Peru, at sites such as Caral with early monumental architecture and plant cultivation going back to c. 5500 BP, there is no evidence of ceramics (for example, Chapter 1.1).

Such data seem to support the hypothesis that, at least in South America, it is possible to view early ceramic production and the adoption of agriculture as distinct processes, as is also becoming recognizable in parts of the Old World, such as northern Eurasia (Jordan and Zvelebil 2009).

Conclusion

If future work confirms the dissociation between the beginnings of ceramic production and of agriculture in Amazonia and other areas of the Americas, perhaps we will reach the point of rejecting the widespread use of categories such as 'archaic' and 'formative' as evolutionist categories for the Americas. Such concepts were proposed to replace in the New World concepts apparently successful when applied in the Old, such as 'Mesolithic' and 'Neolithic' (Willey and Phillips 1958).

The Amazon basin is a vast area, still poorly known to archaeology. But research undertaken in recent years has contributed to establishing a unique scenario for its past human occupation. The interesting results include the confirmation of a picture of cultural diversity that may go back to the early Holocene, and the dissociation between the early adoption of ceramics and the practice of agriculture, even where domesticates are present in the archaeological record. To these observations must be added the mounting evidence that the dense societies that settled along the main Amazon floodplain and its tributaries, at the core of the basin, based their productive activities in part on cultivating domesticates such as maize, but mostly on the management of tree crops, such as various palms and Brazil nuts, among many others (Neves 2013; Moraes 2015; Shock et al. 2014).

A large-scale inventory of trees in the Amazon basin has revealed that out of the estimated 16,000 tree species found there, just 227, or 1.4 per cent, account for half of all individual trees. Moreover, many of the 227 species found are economically and symbolically important for contemporary indigenous and peasant societies (Levis et al. 2017; Ter Steege at al. 2013), adding to the mounting evidence that Amazonian environments have been strongly managed in the past (Clement et al. 2015). Most of these tree species, however, are technically 'non-domesticates', although highly managed in the past and the present, to the point of being considered tree crops. Similar patterns are being uncovered by research showing the prevalence of 'polyculture agroforestry' over 4,500 years in the lower Tapajós in eastern Amazonia (Maezumi et al. 2018). There, data from lake coring, archaeological excavations, soil profiles and modern vegetation inventories show a consistent pattern of cultivation of annual crops, including root crops and maize, combined with long-term tree management leading to the emergence of the hyperdominant pattern verified in the botanical record. Finally, archaeobotanical work done in south-western Amazonia show a pattern of management and replacement of bamboo-dominated forests by palm-dominated forests over several centuries during the construction of geometric earth structures (Watling et al. 2017). Palms are exceptionally important sources of raw materials and food and it is likely that such pattern of replacement of one type of forest by other, or of extensive palm cultivation in forests, also documented ethnographically among the Waorani of western Amazonia (Rival 2002), could have been prevalent elsewhere in the Amazonian past (see Figure 3.6.3).

Going back to the central argument of this chapter, it is important to consider the role of polyculture agroforestry over the millennia in the making of the large language diversity found in Amazonia. David Harris proposed that:

> the nutritional potential and expansion capacity of EASs (early agricultural systems) were strongly influenced by the presence or absence of domestic herd animals, cereals, pulses (herbaceous legumes), tree and root crops … Tree crops are nutritionally valuable, especially as a source of vegetable oils, but because they are long-lived perennials their cultivation has been inimical to agricultural expansion. So too has been the cultivation of carbohydrate-yielding root crops, which is commonly complemented with protein obtained by fishing and hunting. (Harris 2002, 31–2)

Such an argument applies to the evidence presented here. If the combination of long-term tree cultivation and short term annuals or root crop cultivation was

Figure 3.6.3 Contemporary house garden standing on the top of archaeological site, Parintins, Lower Amazonia. Among the plants cultivated are maize, squash, chives, chilli peppers, and papaya. In the background is a stand of mucajá palms. Archaeological data show that house gardens such as this were cultivated at least since the Middle Holocene in Southwestern Amazonia. Photo by Eduardo Góes Neves.

indeed inimical to agricultural expansion, as proposed by Harris, it is to be expected that, over millennia, the operation of such agroforestry systems would contribute to the emergence of a rich mosaic of distinct languages with the relatively localized distribution typical of Amazonia. These agroforestry practices would in turn contribute to the emergence of the ecological patterns found today in the region. If true, then such forests need to be understood as historical heritage, and as repositories of ancient knowledges and practices, as much as biological heritage. The exception to this was the large demographic expansion of speakers of Tupí and Arawakan languages, a topic long discussed in lowland South American anthropology (Lathrap 1970; Heckenberger 2002), but Tupí and Arawak are but two of the 50 'genealogical units' – language families or isolates – found in Amazonia (Epps and Salanova 2013, 1).

The deep history of language diversity in Amazonia, then, like so much else, needs to be understood in the context of the long-term occupation of ecologically diversified and highly productive environments in the lowland tropics. This is a major difference to either the arid Pacific coast or the circumscribed valleys of the Central Andes. Although welded from the same basic shared ancestral cultural (Urton 1996) and genetic (Skoglund and Reich 2016) backgrounds, highland and lowland societies eventually unfolded distinct economic, demographic, and political trajectories over time. The state never developed in the lowlands and it is likely that plant cultivation there evolved in distinct ways as well. These processes were deeply intertwined but their discussion lies beyond the scope of this chapter. However, as new data emerges from Amazonia, it is becoming clearer that past and contemporary native populations there devised ways to live which were favourable to the emergence of biological and cultural diversity; and this in itself may be a lesson worth learning.

3.7
The Pacific coast and Andean highlands/ Amazonia

Tom D. Dillehay, Brian McCray and Patricia J. Netherly

Introduction

During the 2014 Leipzig conference 'Rethinking the Andes–Amazonia "divide"', archaeologists, linguists, bio-anthropologists and ethno-historians came together to discuss the historical connections between these two vast geographic and cultural areas. It became clear during our discussions that many participants implicitly assumed that if the historical relations between the Andean highlands, including the eastern slopes or the *montaña* or *ceja de selva*, and the flat, western Amazon basin could be understood, then generally speaking, by extension, so could any linkages between Amazonia and the narrow desert Pacific coast of Peru. Traditionally, archaeologists have treated the coastal strip and the highlands as a dynamic core area, with montaña and western Amazonian societies generally perceived as peripheral participants.

Although fallen from use today, scholars have historically thought of the coastal strip and the highlands of the Central Andes as an interactive 'co-tradition'. This emphasis on coastal and highland relations began formally when Bennett pointed out the need for a culture-time-space unit in archaeological-historical interpretation, for which he proposed the term coastal and highland 'co-tradition'. This was 'the over-all unit of culture history of an area within which the component cultures have been interrelated over a period of time' (Bennett 1948, 1). The co-tradition model focused on the idea that interaction among all these various societies through space and time created a major unit of analysis. Despite its implicit use today, this unit still dominates Central Andean archaeology.

As discussed below, such an approach is understandable, given that the majority of archaeological research in the Andes has focused on the coast and the highlands, and that so little is known about the eastern montaña and the western Amazon basin. Other chapters in this volume examine this traditional approach from the perspective of different disciplines. In this brief chapter, we explore an alternate viewpoint, one that, for the sake of argument, treats the coast as a separate cultural entity interacting independently with different geographic areas, as opposed to an Andean highland and Amazonian co-tradition. This heuristic perspective allows us to play with different possible interpretative scenarios and to begin to ask some different questions about cultural transmission and interregional interaction from east to west and vice-versa across the Andes.

The Central Andes

Three basic types of physical environments characterize the Central Andes: western desert, mountain and mountain valleys and eastern tropical lowlands. On the west are the tropical lowlands of the Pacific coast and the wet and seasonally dry tropical forest on the slopes of the Andes of Colombia, Ecuador and extreme northern Peru. To the immediate south is the arid coastal strip and western highlands of Peru and north Chile, one of the great deserts of the world. Life would be impossible here without the river valleys that cross the deserts from east to west. These valleys appear as a succession of narrow green oases amid stretches of arid land. They vary greatly in size though the larger ones are in northern Peru. Once the population had increased, the rivers imposed either unity or conflict on the coastal inhabitants. The western littoral provides immediate access to some of the world's richest marine resources. A short distance inland rise the foothills and higher grassland and often forested valleys of the Andes. Immediately east of the Andes are the forested tropical slopes of the montaña and the adjacent flat, seasonally flooded lowlands of western Amazonia (see Figures 3.7.1 to 3.7.3).

This brief description of the Central Andes gives the impression of a conveniently divided continent from north to south and from east to west, defined by mountains and connected by river valleys (see Figure 3.7.4).

The Andean mountains offer compacted and vertically positioned environments, with the coastal strip and tropical lowlands horizontally extending spaces. Yet, within each of these spaces are hundreds of distinct ecologies forming mosaics of adjacent environments, each offering a different mixture of resources, different resource procurement strategies and different cultures with different histories.

Although archaeologists geographically separate these spaces, addressing them as distinct coastal, highland and eastern montaña and lowland or as Amazonian environments with different culture areas, they also view them as different, sometimes overlapping, spheres of cultural interaction over time, characterized by demographic movements, contacts, exchange networks, cultural transmission and dominant/subordinate relations of power. Archaeological thinking on these variable types of relationships has included a myriad of interpretative concepts, including transhumance (Lynch 1973), trade caravans (Browman 1975; Núñez and Dillehay 1979), colonization (cf. Mayer 2002), *lo andino* (for example, Jamieson 2005), diaspora (Skar 1994), co-tradition (Bennett 1948), verticality (Murra 1972), horizontality (Shimada 1982) and others, all of which have focused

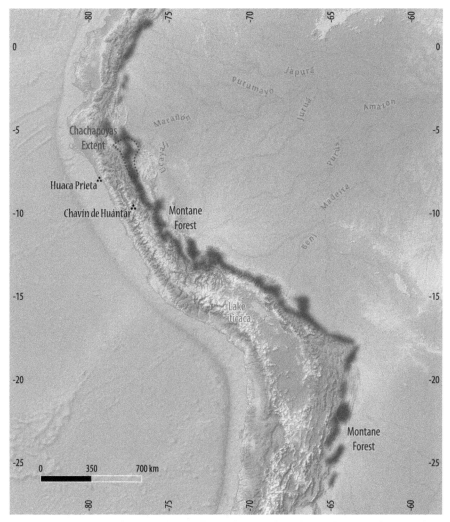

Figure 3.7.1 Map showing the ecological and cultural distributions discussed in the text, particularly the tropical montane forest (*montaña*) zones along the transition between the Andes and Amazonia, and the Chachapoyas culture centred on one such zone. © Tom D. Dillehay, Brian McCray, Patricia J. Netherly and Paul Heggarty.

on the common themes of mobility, political economy and cultural transmission. Most of these concepts, however, and the archaeological and historical data of the Central Andes in general, have been interpreted as the encroachment of highland Andean cultural values and technologies primarily onto the coast and secondarily into Amazonia. Only occasionally has reference been made either to montaña and lowland Amazonian traits appearing in the highlands and beyond down to the Pacific coast (for example, Lathrap 1971; Tello 1960), or to the reverse, that is,

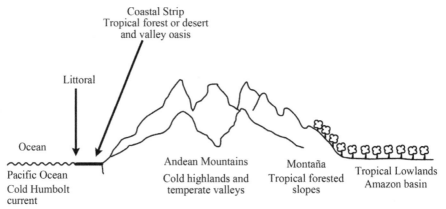

Figure 3.7.2 Schematic cross-section from the Pacific coast through the Andean highlands to the western tropical lowlands of the Amazon basin. © Tom D. Dillehay, Brian McCray and Patricia J. Netherly.

Figure 3.7.3 Eastern montaña of southern Peru and northern Bolivia. Photo by the authors.

coastal influence into the highlands and beyond down into the eastern lowlands (see Chapter 2.4).

Most archaeologists have viewed the later, more complex societies of the Andean highlands (for example, Chavin, Wari, Tiwanaku, Inca) as integral to these

Figure 3.7.4 Highland river valley in northern Peru. Photo by the authors.

encroachments because their archaeological records suggest that they had the ideas, resources, energy and people to hegemonically explore and influence, if not even in some cases directly control, distant lowlands to both the east and west. In the eastern montaña of the Andes and the western fringe of the Amazon basin proper of Peru, an area collectively referred to as the montaña (in the sense used by Raymond 1988), their relative power and influence is much less clear-cut, in part because so little archaeology has been done in this region. The general perception is that montaña and western Amazonian societies were mobile, egalitarian, less complex and thus less capable of engaging in long-term, productive and influential interregional exchange relationships (Kojan 2002). As a result, the *montaña* has generally been seen as peripheral to major cultural centres on the coast and in the Andean highlands (Lyon 1981) as well as to late pre-Hispanic Amazonian centres of population farther to the east (Reeve 1994; Chapter 3.1).

Yet, on the other hand, there also has been a long tradition in Andean stud-ies to classify any iconography depicting felines, raptorial birds and serpents as eastern montaña and Amazonian influence (for example, Tello 1960; Lathrap 1971; Raymond 1988), especially during the Early Horizon or Chavin period. Most archaeologists presume that any tropical traits in the highlands and on the coast of Peru were derived from the eastern side of the Andes, which may not always be correct because many of the same traits are found in the tropical environments and cultures of the coast and western Andean slopes of Colombia, Ecuador and north-ern and central Peru (cf. Chapter 2.4).

In summary, there has been a strong tendency in Andean studies to over-dichotomize, to construct differences and to essentialize broad interregional contacts and movements in terms of uni- or bi-directional influences, with most thought given to mutually serving coastal and highland relations, Bennett's co-tradition, and to give relations with the eastern montaña and Amazonian lowlands much less attention. It is granted that the vast majority of research has been carried out in the highlands and on the coast, presenting a much smaller archaeological base to work with in the montaña and western Amazonia. Nonetheless, conceptual models need to consider the possibility of other types of co-, tri- or other- traditions, such as a combined highland and eastern lowland co-tradition that might have influenced the coast. (It is recognized here that the concept of co-tradition has fallen out of use in recent decades, but we employ it heuristically for the sake of our discussion.) Any movement of people, ideas and goods from the eastern montaña and Amazonian lowlands to the coast had to have passed through the highlands, most likely producing a hybridity of cultural traits and values from both the highlands and the montaña. These movements most likely travelled through the lowest elevations of the highlands, especially in southern Ecuador and northern Peru where the mountain ranges are low and narrow (see Chapters 2.4 and 2.5).

Furthermore, often forgotten in broad-sweeping discussions of co- and other-traditions (for example, highland Andean and Amazonian, coastal and western tropical areas of Ecuador and Peru) are the intra-regional interactions that occurred within small, diverse, little known or presently undefined archaeological societies situated within these wider geographic settings (cf. Cárdenas-Arroyo and Bray 1998; Lathrap 1970; Raymond 1976). If more local and regional archaeological data were available, further divisions would be possible because in some areas there is growing evidence to suggest significant sub-areal cultural differences within the littoral (that is, intertidal zone and shoreline, shoreline and inland lagoons), coastal strip (grassy plains and extended foothills of the Andes), interior coastal valleys, highland puna and tundra, and eastern montaña, each with different geographic vectors and scales of contact and influence. Each of these areas and sub-areas is not merely a copycat following a dominant outside model, or an unthinking institutionalization of ideas imposed by expanding emergent societies or later states.

The reaction of some of these sub-areas was probably very different from each other. For instance, those of the Pacific maritime littoral culture of Peru were not purely coastal or Andean where agriculture probably was first practiced (Dillehay 2017). Some littoral areas, such as the lower Chicama Valley, were mainly associated with the exploitation of marine resources, at least at the outset of human colonization and during a long Holocene process of settling in that lasted until agriculture was introduced around 7,000 to 8,000 years ago. It was not until the lower valley began to establish permanent exchange networks with inland coastal areas (for example, in Norte Chico) and an intensified agricultural economy co-existed with a maritime one that it blended littoral maritime and coastal and highland agricultural economies. The same could probably be said for other sub-areas geographically situated within these broader environments, but culturally located within their own social and institutional setting and not yet transformed into a wider Andean society, whether it was coastal, highland or eastern montaña and Amazonian. On the other hand, some marginal sub-areas may never have become fully 'Andean' (meaning coastal and/or highland influenced) and simply remained in a process of becoming Andean. The point is that in the Andes, archaeologists have given little thought to the mosaic nature of local societies and cultures and how they acted independently of neighbouring areas, state control and interregional relations, to establish their own identities and trajectories (Dillehay et al. 2006). It is these concerns and different types of Andean co- and possibly other-traditions that are the main topics of discussion in this chapter.

Traditional approaches to interregionalism

The greater concern with coast–highland connections in the Central Andes is the result of more archaeological work in and information on these regions since the early 1900s. This emphasis may represent a historical and archaeological reality, that is, in pre-Hispanic times there always was a stronger presence of highland Formative and subsequent state societies on the Peruvian coast (see Figure 3.7.5).

This pattern may be explained by the rivers descending from the western Andean slopes that were used to irrigate the coastal desert valleys and by the establishment of strong mutual exchange networks that probably facilitated and channelled the movement of highlanders to the coast. Furthermore, in the highlands, as well as parts of the coastal valleys, interactions were stimulated by the spread of camelids, trade caravans and expansive religious networks (Browman 1989; Dillehay and Núñez 1988; Núñez and Dillehay 1995; cf. Chapter 3.1). When considering interregional human movement and exchange in the Andes, we should also keep in mind that the little-explored great rivers of the Andes lie on the eastern, not the western slopes. Though the upper reaches of the easterly descending Amazon and its tributaries are largely non-navigable in the montaña, these important transport and communication routes must have facilitated more movement and exchange through time than we have yet to realize. With the exception of a few large rivers in southern Ecuador and extreme northern Peru, none of the other Peruvian coastal rivers are navigable. So one of the most common forms of human communication and transportation in history – by river – was greatly reduced, or simply not possible here.

An important dimension is geographic. In Peru, contact between Amazonia and the Andean valleys is controlled by valleys whose rivers flow northward to the Amazon. Many of these valleys are deep and serve to bring the warm Amazonian flora far inside the highland region. It is also important to understand that there

Figure 3.7.5   Coastal desert of southern Peru, with the western slopes of the
Andes in the background. Photo by the authors.

are discrete geographic areas where contact is much easier. As noted later,
Chachapoyas is one, but there was another in the Balsas to Olmos transect across
the lower Andes of northern Peru. Drainages to the north in the Huancabamba/
Loja region are other possibilities, particularly the San Isidro/Puyango/Tumbes
drainages and the Catamayo–La Chira, which enters Piura in north coastal Peru
(cf. Chapter 2.4). The same can be said for southern Ecuador. More careful archaeology, directed toward recovering household and community religious practices,
recovering the paraphernalia of offerings and small informal shrines, will no doubt
increase our understanding of the ontology and its ties to the Amazon.

A different perspective on Andean and Amazonian interactions comes from
the non-tropical southern Andes where the proto-Mapuche and Mapuche cultures
had Amazonian connections, as revealed in archaeological, linguistic and genetic
records. This region is especially significant, because the closest tropical forest
is 2,500 km to the north, in southern Bolivia and northwest Argentina. Latcham
(1928), Menghin (1962), Dillehay et al. (2007) and others have recognized the
influence of tropical or southern Amazonian design motifs in late pre-Hispanic
Mapuche pottery. It is not known whether these contacts were indirect or direct,
or when they were made. Today, *machi* shamans report that until the late 1800s,
special Mapuche healers crossed the Andes and travelled to southern Bolivia and
northwest Argentina where they conferred with shamans.

In summary, as noted above, we should be considering other cultural and environmental categories that may reveal other types of co- or other-traditions through time. For instance, can we speak of an Andean highland and a western Amazonian co-tradition or a north coastal Peru and eastern montaña co-tradition (cf. Chapter 3.1)? Within such a possible connection, could some coastal areas have been separated historically and culturally from these two regions in some places, especially before large irrigation canals connected the western Andean slopes and the coastal plains? Are there places where we can recognize a possible co- or tri-tradition, which would include the coast and its littoral, the highlands and the eastern lowlands? The likeliest such area is the narrow and low mountain ranges that separate the *páramo* Andes in southern Ecuador from the *puna* Andes in northern Peru, and thus connect the arid coast, together with the western coastal and montaña tropics to its north, to the Andean slopes of northern Peru and the adjacent eastern tropics (for example, Guffroy 2008; Chapter 2.4). Are there other areas and geographical vectors of movement and exchange that have not yet been hypothesized or identified empirically in local and regional archaeologies, such as areas in north-western South America and in the southern cone of South America?

The eastern montaña and tropical lowlands

Curiously, the eastern montaña and tropical lowlands once held a more prominent role in interpreting the origins of, and influences on, coastal and highland Andean society. For example, the Peruvian archaeologist Julio C. Tello pointed to the eastern tropical lowlands as the source for much of the iconography at the highland Formative site of Chavin de Huantar, where tropical animals dominated the artwork. In fact, Tello proposed that the roots of Chavin and Andean culture were in Amazonia (Tello 1960). Despite Tello and later scholars such as Lathrap, Roe, Raymond, DeBoer and others who focused on the lowland tropics, we do not have much empirical data for highland and eastern lowland relations over time, although the Formative period is still better understood than the later cultural periods (Burger 1992; Guffroy 2008; Shady and Rosas 1979). Furthermore, most archaeological effort in the eastern lowlands and Andean Formative periods has gone into investigating a handful of what are considered primary traits – architecture, food crops and iconography. The most significant and shared aspect is pottery style, and particularly iconographic motifs shared among emerging complex societies, not merely materialization but the probable adoption of ideological symbols and technologies from the montaña or eastern lowlands (for example, Lathrap 1970, 1971). It also has been and still is a tradition in Central Andean archaeology to classify any iconography depicting felines, raptorial birds and serpents as having origins in the montaña and eastern tropical lowlands (see Chapters 1.4 and 2.4).

More explicit consideration of contact and cultural transmission between the highlands and eastern tropical lowlands once involved intense debates about whether Amazonian culture influenced Andean culture (for example, Lathrap 1970; Sauer 1952; Tello 1960) or the reverse (for example, Meggers and Evans 1957). As noted above, these debates relied heavily on the interpretation of iconography, pottery styles and exotic goods. Within these debates, the Formative phases of Andean civilization initially appeared as multiple but distinct coastal and highland traditions of social and economic complexity, developing independently but also in tandem as a result of comparable socio-evolutionary processes made widespread by extensive long-distance contacts with the tropical lowlands, wherever that may have been. At the time and still today, there was and is not enough solid, well-dated archaeological evidence from the eastern Andean montaña and the western Amazon basin to resolve these debates.

Moreover, these debates have generally presented a simplistic version of interaction between the highland Andes and the eastern lowlands (see Koschmieder 2012; Narváez Vargas 2013; Ruiz Barcellos 2011). This has begun to change over the past two decades, however, with connections between each region being treated more explicitly (Barbieri et al. 2014). As a result, the differences between them have been reified, magnified and redefined, especially with regard to models of long-distance exchange and interregional connections in the Amazonian lowlands (for example, Heckenberger 2008; Hornborg and Hill 2011). Two exchange models are now postulated to explain interregional linkages: lowland groups specialized in riverine trade, and others engaged in exchange partnerships between individual and lineage-based groups along interfluves of the eastern montaña (A.-C. Taylor 1999, 199). As a result of these and other models (Heckenberger 2011; Hornborg 2005; McEwan et al. 2001; Neves 2001; Pärssinen and Korpisaari 2003; Walker 2012), archaeologists are reconsidering the role of specific areas and sub-areas within broader and different spheres of interaction, and especially riverine models of movement and exchange, which to date have received little attention from archaeologists as strategies of cultural transmission outside navigable valleys. Where attention has been given to specific areas and to their possible ties to adjacent regions, there have been some new, often conflicting, thoughts on the nature and origin of local cultures (for example, Chapters 2.5 and 3.1). For instance, one such area is Chachapoyas, located on the mountainous slopes or montaña of north-eastern Peru, where the archaeologists view the pre-Hispanic polity either as 'Andean' (for example, Narváez Vargas 2013), 'Amazonian' (for example, Koschmieder 2012), or an autochthonous development (for example, Church 1996).

As more archaeological research is carried out in more regions from the montaña to the littoral and western coastal strip, the data will probably show that technological and symbolic transfers resulted from many different waves of innovations flowing from east to west, west to east, north to south and south to north. These data will also probably reveal many different combinations of artefacts and technologies, developing through interaction with different types of societies in multiple directions and through local or self-generated reconstruction and accommodation as they interacted with more widely spread societies in the past, changing themselves according to their own local structures.

In summary, although archaeologists generally have viewed all coastal, highland and montaña culture areas as essentially Andean, all three regions over time were home to many separate areal and sub-areal cultures, none especially widespread or dominant over the others until perhaps late Formative times (1000–500 BC), implying a prehistory markedly different from each other but also blended or hybridized in some ways, especially in terms of certain architectural and iconographic features (cf. Chapters 2.4 and 3.1). That is, if we could access the historical truth, it likely would show that the dissected environment of the Central Andes and peripheral areas contained many different cultures and societies that comprised shifting social, residential, ethnic and other groups through space and time, mixed with different groups, and the pattern more than not with never a single group occupying a territory for a prolonged period of time. The story is probably one of demographic movement and technological and symbolic transfers always complicating matters. This does not necessarily imply the absence of stable cultures and linguistic territories, but simply different culture areas.

The gateway corridor: Eastern Andean montaña and western Amazon

Many of the connecting areas of the eastern Andean montaña and tropical lowlands remain primarily uninvestigated and yet provide significant opportunities for exploring the development and nature of interaction between them and overlapping cultural and political influences. Throughout the Preceramic and early Formative periods, the lowland societies bordering the eastern montaña must have played a critical role in the movement of goods, people and ideas between the more distant higher Central Andes and the western Amazon basin (Church 1994, 1996; Shady 1974; Shady and Rosas 1979), whether that movement went east or west or likely both ways. This movement is perhaps best attested by the presence of various food crops in the highlands and on the coast that probably had their origin in Neotropical lowland forests and savannahs (Piperno and Pearsall 1998). There is also the issue of iconographic influence from one zone to another. As mentioned above, many Andeanists and Amazonianists once claimed that all carnivorous elements (that is, felines, snakes, caimans, harpy eagle) in early Andean iconography were derived from the eastern montaña or Amazonian lowlands. But some could also have been derived from the tropical areas on the western slopes of the Andes from Colombia, Ecuador and northern Peru, where tropical forests and similar plants and animals once existed or exist today (Piperno and Pearsall 1998). North to south movement along the Pacific littoral probably would have facilitated such contacts more rapidly and directly.

Although the early archaeological record from the eastern montaña and the western fringe of the Amazon basin is generally little known, some insight into the types of different relationships that perhaps once existed between them in earlier times can be gained by brief consideration of the later and better known archaeological and archival records. The heartland of interaction between the east and west was the eastern slopes of the Andes, which to date has received little archaeological attention except in areas such as Chachapoyas in north-eastern Peru and more recently the eastern slopes of Ecuador. (Moreover, most of the archaeology in Chachapoyas has concentrated on elaborate architecture and tombs of the late pre-Inca and Inca periods, and not the earlier periods.) Unlike other culture areas, Chachapoyas is located in the narrow and low Andean corridor between the Amazon basin and the coast. It is thus in some ways exceptional, and not truly representative of other interregional interaction areas in the Andes, such as the wider mountainous areas of central Peru, Bolivia and north Chile.

We know that in late pre-Hispanic and early colonial times, a wide range of goods were exchanged between the western Amazon basin and the Andes via the Chachapoyas area, as seen in early documents, ethnographies and archaeological studies (Espinoza Soriano 1967; Garcilaso de la Vega 1609/1985; Guamán Poma de Ayala 1615/1987; Salomon 1986; Schjellerup 1997, 2003). For example, local goods exchanged from Chachapoyas were human resources, gold, coca, cotton and ceramics (Church 1996; Church and Von Hagen 2008; Schjellerup 1997). Exchanged goods from the highlands included ceramics, metal figurines, metal and stone tools, and beads (Church 1996; Church and Von Hagen 2008; Hastings 1987; Salomon 1986). Commodities from the coast included *Spondylus* shells (Church 1996; Guengerich 2012). Amazonian items included ceramics, cinnamon, coca, slaves, clothing, medicinal plants, herbs, honey, beeswax, cacao, wild vanilla, cotton, vegetal dyes, animals, animal pelts, hardwood *chonta* palm and feathers (Church 1996; Church and Von Hagen 2008; Salomon 1986). Evidence of exchange goods from the Pacific coast and Andean highlands passing through the Chachapoyas area is also reported in ceramics, faunal remains, shells, lithics and iconography (Church 1996; Church and Von Hagen 2008; Ruiz Estrada 2009; Schjellerup 1997, 2003). We also know that some Amazonian trade goods reached coastal Peru, as evidenced by the presence of tropical food crops, feathers, medicinal plants and other items at Formative and later sites. In late pre-Hispanic and early Colonial times, *mitmaq* groups from the north coast of Peru were documented in the Cajamarca and Utcubamba areas of the north central and eastern montaña of Peru, respectively (cf. Reichlen and Reichlen 1949, 1950; Netherly 1977, 89–100).

Exchange routes and strategies that people in Chachapoyas may have used in mediating exchange between the Andes and Amazonia remain mostly unknown. The early historic accounts of interregional trade describe periodic communal gatherings for exchange between lowland and highland groups at locations along the lower Andean and montaña interface. The early Spanish referred to these gatherings as marketplaces, though they were not formalized to the same extent as those in Mesoamerica (Lyon 1981; Oberem 1974, 1980; Salomon 1986; Schjellerup 2003; A.-C. Taylor 1999). Strategies of interregional exchange that did not involve communal gatherings were also possible, including long-distance traders such as *mindalaes* and barter fairs, such as those described in Ecuador (Salomon 1987), or people traveling to lowland religious specialists for curing and thus trading while there (A.-C. Taylor 1999, 198).

The motivations that drove South American peoples to seek and to use goods and knowledge from outside their own area are not known. Clearly there can be no definite answer to such a question and no clear understanding of the diachronic relationships between the east and the west, given variations in motivation from region to region and between social groups within any society and culture over time. More inclusive models of culture contact and interregional interaction should view earlier cultural change as developing through both direct and indirect interactions that pertained to varying levels of social complexity. The dynamics of social complexity in overlapping zones of interaction such as Chachapoyas are considered here as resulting from cultural changes that are perhaps best understood as processes that involved a combination of local developments and extra-local traditions adopted and adapted through continuous culture contact. The development of later centralized authorities in such systems, such as the strong Inca presence in Chachapoyas, has been addressed most commonly with migration, diffusion, acculturation and world-systems approaches to interregional interaction and state expansion, that highlight asymmetrical power relations and core-periphery relationships. Archaeology now needs to clarify how local production was organized in places like Chachapoyas and to determine which commodities groups exchanged in order to reconstruct power relationships in the political economy of interaction.

Despite the paucity of data, we also can determine from places like Chachapoyas that interregional interaction incorporated a variety of different but often overlapping forms such as exchange, emulation, colonization and military conquest. Furthermore, if any region perhaps comes close to a tri-tradition, it may be areas of the Andes such as Chachapoyas where the mountain ranges are narrow and where there are mixtures of highland, lowland and coastal traits. Accordingly, the montaña and Andean interface or corridor in this area was well suited to the exploration of cultural transformations, particularly those relating to the rise of centralized political authorities and their contemporary interactions with states in neighbouring cultural spheres in the central and eastern Andean highlands.

Lastly, given the presence of a few Chimu and perhaps other coastal traits, such as ceramic forms and motif styles, in Chachapoyas, this area is one of the few known where the montaña and the highlands form a stronger cultural bond with the coast, similar to those cases documented for certain coastal and highland areas (Reichlen and Reichlen 1949, 1950). Surely, there are other areas of the eastern Andes, perhaps from north-west Argentina and transects across Ecuador and northern Peru, that reveal similar patterns.

Discussion

In the opening paragraphs, we stated our two goals here: (1) to consider alternative possibilities of combined interregional exchange across and beyond the Andes to the east and the west, specifically in this case highland and eastern montaña and western Amazonian influence on the coast, and (2) the need for greater recognition of local diversity independent of wider interregional influences from the major cultural areas and later more complex societies. The periods and places in the Andes most intensively studied by archaeologists are Formative and later state societies (the co-tradition model). Whether it be Huari, Tiwanaku, Chimu, Inca or modern cultures and globalization, we are dealing with the complex interplay between local context and global content, rather than arguing for the primacy of one over the other. However, most archaeologists still treat the Andean past as the inevitable appropriation of local populations by more complex and expansive societies, but this was not always the case. In commenting briefly on these and other issues here, we have created many more questions than we have answered.

Current thinking on coastal, highland and Amazonian relations should consider more the premise that people were in contact with other regional populations at the outset of human dispersion during the late Pleistocene and early Holocene period. Convention once dictated that later social complexities in the montaña and western Amazon basin, beyond small groups of hunters and gatherers, took hold only when more advanced agriculturalists arrived from the Andes with more ideologically and perhaps agriculturally advanced lowland groups moving into the highlands. Some of the more recent data obtained from the eastern montaña have changed this thinking and now present a cultural landscape with more complex societies based on the management of forest and riverine resources (Hornborg and Eriksen 2011; Kracke 1993; Schaan 2012). As more research is carried out in the montaña and western Amazon basin these and other findings will surely change our thinking even more.

In considering the likelihood of influences between Amazonia and the coast, several pitfalls should be avoided. The first is the expectation that contacts or influences will be uniform through time and space – always moving from east to west, for example. If, as seems clear, during the late Pleistocene and early Holocene there were repeated long-distance contacts between the two regions, involving down-the-line exchange or movement of particular individuals over long distances (Lathrap 1973), the nature of influences on the coastal societies and cultures certainly changed over time. The reason for these changes may lie in a shift from the identification of early cultivars and the technology of production, which is feasible archaeologically, to an ontology perhaps initially infused with Amazonian religious concepts, which may be difficult to verify archaeologically. That is, there seems to have been a strong influence of religious imagery and art styles infused with Amazonian concepts represented by plants and animals of the tropical forest, stronger in some places and weaker and more diffuse in others (Lathrap 1974; Morales 1979).

However, through time this ontology may have become more archaeologically invisible as it was expressed in folk practice. A clue to the nature of a possible shift is found in Dillehay's analysis of the ontology of the populations at Huaca Prieta on the north coast of Peru over four millennia (Dillehay 2017). It is probable that the mechanism of diffusion lay with the travels of shamans or healing specialists for training and vision quests. Ethnographic information obtained by Dillehay (2017) in the Chicama Valley, where the Huaca Prieta mound is located, reveals that *curandero* or shamanic folk practices associated with tropical areas farther north in Chiclayo and Piura still continue today. These folk level religious specialists travel to Salas in Incahuasi in the highlands of Lambayeque, northern Peru, where they work with specialists who surely are in contact with others in Amazonia. More concretely, as noted earlier, the Mapuche shamans of southern Chile once undertook long journeys over the Andes and north along the eastern front of the cordillera in Argentina to reach the valleys of southernmost Amazonia where they engaged in training and vision quests (Dillehay et al. 2007). Thus we see that at the level of contemporary folk practice the influence of Amazonia continues.

Furthermore, the interactions between different Andean and Amazonian societies did not always consist of common Andean or Amazonian content, a lexicon of goods or knowledge. Instead, it likely was a common set of broader, even non-Andean and non-Amazonian or hybrid formats and structures that mediated between more or less different degrees of 'being Andean' or 'being Amazonian' (for example, marginal lowland cultures along the eastern flanks of the Andes; northern and southern Andes as well). That is, this interaction was something more than a flow of goods and ideas, or of the meanings attached to them, or even the political, economic and social channels along which those goods, ideas and meanings flowed. Furthermore, the connections between interacting groups were probably created by widespread forms of Andean, Amazonian and non-Andean and non-Amazonian contexts, all of which may have influenced decisions over what to produce and to consume. These contexts probably followed both Andean and Amazonian geographic channels that placed diversity in a recognizable frame, so to speak, and scaled it along a limited number of possible outcomes and dimensions, whether those were conquests, commensal feasts, physical conflicts, alliances, etc., all facing dissimilarities, similarities, and submerging others. As yet, these outcomes and dimensions have not been fully identified and incorporated into Andean and Amazonian archaeological studies.

In any of the regional archaeologies of overlapping interaction spheres in the Central Andes, from the littoral to the montaña and western Amazon basin, the material correlates of some social, economic, political, or ritual activities show evidence of external influence, while those of other activities may not, even though change may still signify evolving local conditions during certain cultural periods. Furthermore, it is to be expected that in such contexts the intermixing of the external with the local and traditional may result in an adaptation of both that produced something entirely new and different, especially along the interfacing corridors between the highlands and the montaña.

In the future, in order to better understand the processes of culture contact and transmission between the coastal and highland Andes and the montaña and western Amazonian lowlands we need to think more in terms of demographic processes rather than the migration of one or a few groups settling into a new area or just the diffusion of ideas across multiple groups. The time and space distances across the continent are too great to consider single populations, cultures and unidirectional exchanges. We should also consider several interrelated processes to attempt to explain east and west connections and cultural transmissions: diaspora, socialization, hybridization, conversion, and so forth. Furthermore, the local network of sites and the connective characteristics of both the eastern and western river valleys are well suited to the application of network analysis in archaeology. In investigating both local and interregional interactions, current thinking about network analysis would perhaps provide a model for exploring nodal relationships between varying types of social groups based on large, multicomponent datasets, to reveal very subtle or even tangential associations.

To conclude, the flow of knowledge between eastern, central and western Andean societies had to have gone in multiple directions. The diffusion of cultural constructs from all sides must have served to provoke advances or delays in cultural transmission and change or have made manifest lacunae in any one cultural domain. The confrontation with something unknown – be this of a social, ritual, technological, political, economic or aesthetic kind – may or may not have struck a cultural resonance with any one group at any one time. If something that presented itself found a resonance among a sufficient number of people in a group, such as a new ideology and its symbols, or exotic cultigens, then it may have been borrowed, transformed to fit local perceptions (recontextualized) and become part of a local discourse; in short, conventionalized. Thus, exotic artefacts, words, practices, crops or ideas would have been absorbed selectively and for different reasons, making for continuous inter-societal flows of knowledge that may not always be archaeologically visible. Lacunae, in this sense, are probably present in all systems of eastern and western cultures of the Central Andes. Social anthropologists have repeatedly warned against drawing conclusions from the comparison of cultures, preferring to interpret the context in which change actually occurs. Unfortunately, we do not yet archaeologically know very much about the specific contexts within which socio-cultural changes took place between eastern and western societies in South America, or what they imply in regard to cultural transmissions and legacies.

Part 4
Regional case studies from the Altiplano and southern Upper Amazonia

4.1
Linguistic connections between the Altiplano region and the Amazonian lowlands

Willem F. H. Adelaar

Introduction

Linguistic evidence points to sporadic but occasionally intense past contacts between the Bolivian and Peruvian Altiplano, on the one hand, and the adjacent eastern slopes of the Andes and the Amazonian lowlands, on the other. In colonial and late precolonial (Inca) times there was an influx of loanwords (especially cultural, trade and administrative terms) from highland languages into the eastern slopes and lowland regions; for earlier periods, however, a more balanced interchange can be discerned. In this chapter we present evidence of such early influence from Amazonian and eastern slopes languages upon languages spoken in the highlands. Particular attention will be given to the Puquina language, which appears to have played an important role in the area dominated by the Tiahuanaco civilization centred on the Bolivian Altiplano (c. AD 500–1100).

Divided between the modern states of Bolivia and Peru, the Altiplano exhibits a relatively straightforward picture so far as the distribution of its two major indigenous language groups, Aymara and Quechua, is concerned. Both are widely distributed and used by considerable numbers of speakers. Aymara (or Southern Aymara, following the terminology in Cerrón-Palomino 2000) is mainly spoken immediately southwards and eastwards of Lake Titicaca, including on the outskirts of the *de facto* Bolivian capital La Paz and the environs of the archaeological site of Tiahuanaco. Quechua, in some of its southern varieties (Puno Quechua and northern Bolivian Quechua, both belonging to the Quechua IIC branch in the dialect classification of Torero 1964), is found along the western side of the lake and on the islands of Taquile and Amantaní. Around the northern shores of Lake Titicaca, the two languages find themselves in competition, although the province of Huancané in Peru and the lakeshores in Bolivia are predominantly Aymara-speaking (Albó 1995).

From convincing linguistic and historical data, as we shall shortly see, it is clear that in spite of their present dominance the Aymara and Quechua language families do not have a very long history in the Altiplano. Their origin lies further north, in central Peru, from where they must have spread south-eastwards sometime between the Late Intermediate Period and the Independence Era (c. AD 1300 to 1800). Initially, Aymara spread throughout much of the Bolivian highlands, replacing local languages that had been spoken there since earlier periods (Bouysse-Cassagne 1975; Torero 1987, 2002, 386–8; Cerrón-Palomino 2000, 294 and 2013, 311–12; Adelaar and Muysken 2004, 263–4). Quechua became generalized here more recently still, and may have owed part of its success to its eventual adoption by ethnic groups who had initially managed to defend their linguistic identity against the impact of Aymarization.[1] Nevertheless, it may be a mistake to assume that the arrival of Aymara- and Quechua-speaking groups corresponded to separate consecutive demographic incursions. More likely, the Aymara- and Quechua-speaking communities were linked by traditional kinship ties and political bonds harking back to the time when they shared the same geographical space in central Peru, and the division between the two language communities may have been accentuated by a difference in economic activities such as agriculture and (agro)pastoralism (cf. Urton 2012).

The conclusion that the introduction of Aymara and Quechua on the Altiplano was a relatively recent event is based on the observation that the internal linguistic differentiation of both language families is limited and shallow within this region, but much wider outside it. A longer presence in the area would predict that a more fundamental dialectal diversity would have emerged here. On a different level, both language families share a complex history of intense language contact, often referred to as 'convergence', which may have occurred in a geographical setting where the two ancestor languages co-existed in a dominant position without the significant presence or interaction of other languages (cf. Adelaar 2012b; Muysken 2012b). A location in the central Peruvian highlands somewhere between Ayacucho and Huaraz, including the upper reaches of some valleys on the Pacific versant of the Andes, would meet such conditions, rather than the Altiplano region, where remnants of non-related pre-existent languages are clearly discernible.

Languages of the Altiplano before the introduction of Aymara and Quechua: Uru-Chipaya and Puquina

The only local languages that have partly survived the incursion of Aymara- and Quechua-speaking groups until today belong to the Uru-Chipaya language family (also referred to as *Uruquilla* in historical sources).[2] The Chipaya language is still actively spoken in Santa Ana de Chipaya, a community in the Bolivian province of Carangas near the Chilean border (Cerrón-Palomino 2006; Cerrón-Palomino and Ballón Aguirre 2011). Remnants of the Uru-Chipaya family are also found among the Uru lake dwellers on the south-eastern shores of Lake Titicaca, although no fluent speakers remain (Hannss 2009). The Uru-Chipaya languages clearly exhibit an earlier linguistic layer than that represented by Aymara and Quechua. However, there is no certainty as to the exact extent of the past distribution of Uru-Chipaya over the area (see Figure 4.1.1). Historical documentation suggests that these languages were also spoken in present-day Peru, in Zepita on the southern shore of Lake Titicaca (cf. Torero 1987) and until the early twentieth century in the locality of Ch'imu, near Puno (Cerrón-Palomino et al. 2016). Although the speakers of Uru-Chipaya have often been associated with a distinct subsistence lifestyle of fishing and foraging in the lakes and watercourses of the Altiplano, not likely to have been able to support large populations, there is no

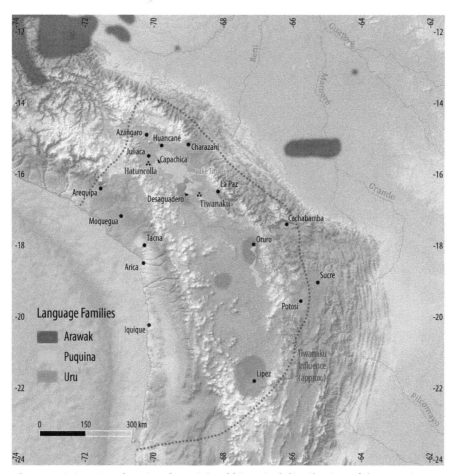

Figure 4.1.1 Map showing the minimal historical distribution of the Puquina and Uru language lineages at the end of the sixteenth century; also shown are the nearest contemporary languages of the Arawak family, and the surviving Chipaya language within the Uru family. © Willem F.H. Adelaar and Paul Heggarty.

reason to assume that they could not have occupied a relatively larger, agrarian domain before they were displaced or assimilated by Aymara speakers. The presence in Uru-Chipaya of agrarian and agro-pastoral vocabulary not derived from either Quechua or Aymara points in such a direction (cf. Cerrón-Palomino and Ballón Aguirre 2011).

A language that certainly did occupy an important position in the Altiplano before the arrival of Aymara and Quechua speakers was *Puquina*. During the early colonial period Puquina was considered to be one of the three 'General Languages' of the Peruvian (ex-Inca) domain (Bouysse-Cassagne 1975, 321). It rapidly became obsolescent and disappeared towards the end of the nineteenth century, although the exact date and circumstances of its eventual extinction are not known. According to colonial accounts, the Puquina language had been codified in a grammar written at the end of the sixteenth century by the Jesuit priest Alonso de Bárzana. Sadly, no copies of this grammar have survived, and the Puquina language remains inadequately documented (cf. Torero 1987, 2002, 408–56; Adelaar and Van de Kerke 2009; Cerrón-Palomino 2013, 59–82).

The only surviving Puquina texts of any significance are included in a manual of religious instruction with versions in several different languages: the *Rituale seu Manuale Peruanum*, published by Luis Jerónimo de Oré in 1607. The Puquina version of the texts in this manuscript is roughly a translation of the Quechua texts in the same publication and in many respects is of poor quality. It is inconsistently spelt and contains several remarkable errors of translation, which call into question the linguistic skills and proficiency in Quechua of the translator (cf. Adelaar and Van de Kerke 2009, 127). Some sections of the Puquina texts do not seem to match the Quechua and Spanish versions and are therefore difficult to analyse or even translate. Nevertheless, some of the characteristics of the Puquina language can be reconstructed on the basis of Oré's Puquina texts, although the resulting picture remains frustratingly incomplete and fragmentary.

The exact distribution of the Puquina language in the period of early European contact is difficult to assess. A colonial document, published by Bouysse-Cassagne (1975) and referred to as the *Copia de curatos* by Torero (1987) in a detailed analysis of its contents, contains an inventory of locations in upper Peru (today Bolivia) that required missionary guidance in the Puquina language. It suggests that around AD 1600, Puquina-speaking territory was highly fragmented and comprised specific areas along the north-western, northern and eastern shores of Lake Titicaca, as well as a limited area between present-day Sucre and Potosí. Puquina was furthermore spoken on the islands beyond the Bay of Puno (Amantaní, Taquile), north-east of Lake Titicaca in the provinces of Larecaja and Umasuyos (Torero 1987, 345), and in an area south-east of the city of Arequipa extending into the Peruvian departments of Moquegua and Tacna and possibly parts of northern Chile (see Figure 4.1.1). Many of these areas are now Aymara or Quechua-speaking, suggesting that Puquina speakers shifted to these languages in late Inca times and thereafter, during the Spanish colonial occupation.

Historical accounts, attributed to the Inca and their descendants concerning their relations with the Colla, whose capital Hatuncolla was located near the modern town of Juliaca (cf. Julien 1983), contain passages that suggest a Puquina identity for the Colla people (Cabello Valboa 1586/1951, Guamán Poma de Ayala 1615/1936). In spite of an alleged antagonism between the Puquina- and Aymara-speaking peoples, the Aymara language of the Altiplano includes a number of Puquina loanwords that suggest that the language of the Aymara-speaking communities of the Altiplano was influenced by a Puquina substratum. Examples include Aymara *imilla* 'girl', associated with the Puquina word for 'mother' <imi>[3]; *layqa* 'witch' from Puquina <reega>; and possibly also *kʰiti* 'who' from Puquina <qui> 'what' followed by the Aymara interrogative affix *ti*. It follows that the Puquina linguistic community may very well have constituted a geographical continuum covering large stretches of the Altiplano before it was occupied by languages originating in central Peru.

Part of the Puquina vocabulary has also been preserved in a professional secret language practised by the so-called *Callahuaya* (or Kallawaya in contemporary spelling) healers, who are established in a number of native communities near the Bolivian provincial capital Charazani (north of Lake Titicaca, not far from the border with Peru), and whose daily language is a local variety of Quechua (see Chapter 1.4). Although the Callahuaya vocabulary is partly of Puquina origin, its grammatical form and structure mainly coincide with that of Quechua. The lexical database of the Puquina language is limited to some two hundred words, and unfortunately it is not possible to safely expand that by drawing on data from Callahuaya (of which we have a vocabulary several times larger), because the latter has also assimilated lexical elements from heterogeneous sources, many of which can no longer be identified. Furthermore, the formation of the Callahuaya language may date to the colonial period or even the early Independence period, when Puquina was already moribund and when probably only fragments of its lexicon could still be remembered. It stands to reason that at least some Callahuaya lexical items were adopted from hitherto unidentified sources after Puquina itself had disappeared.

Nonetheless, there are cases in which Callahuaya words of possible Puquina origin are found in place names, which do make it possible to establish lexical equivalences between the two languages with a reasonable degree of accuracy. For instance, the Callahuaya word for 'water', *mimi*, may have been identical to the word for 'water' in Puquina because it is found in toponyms such as *mimilaque*, the name of a river in the Moquegua area, which must have been Puquina-speaking until colonial times (see below). On the other hand, no word for 'water' was recorded in the written sources for Puquina, and there is no absolute proof that *mimi* did indeed refer to 'water' in Puquina (rather than to 'river' or 'marsh', for instance).

As illustrated in the above example, toponymy can be an important source for obtaining additional data on Puquina. Typical Puquina place names may end in *-baya*, *-coa* ('sanctuary') or *-laque*, and other endings proper to that language.

Even though the meanings of some of these endings remain obscure, such place names can provide an indication of Puquina's geographical distribution during the final stages of its existence. As indicated above, there is an area with an exceptionally dense concentration of Puquina toponyms in the Peruvian department of Moquegua, which also harbours a number of archaeological sites in which typical Tiahuanaco artefacts have been found.[4] These findings indicate that Moquegua was an area of intense colonization for the Tiahuanaco socio-political entity during the Middle Horizon (c. AD 750–1100), while the local toponymy strongly suggests that Puquina was the language used in these Tiahuanaco colonies. It therefore makes sense to assume that Puquina was one of the principal languages in use in Tiahuanaco, notwithstanding the fact that the present-day population there speaks Aymara. Today's communities in Moquegua are divided between speakers of Aymara, Quechua and Spanish.

Puquina toponymy is also to be found on the islands of Amantaní and Taquile in Lake Titicaca, on the peninsula of Capachica on the western shore, and, in general, in areas west and north of the lake. In most of these places Puquina has been replaced by Quechua, and occasionally also by Aymara. Notwithstanding the presence of so many Puquina placenames in the Titicaca basin, it remains difficult to reconstruct the exact linguistic distribution of Puquina as it once must have existed.

The Arawak 'connection' with Puquina

Fortunately, the linguistic affiliation of Puquina is not entirely opaque, unlike that of other Andean languages or language families (including Aymara and Quechua). In some of its formal and structural features, Puquina exhibits significant similarities with languages of the Arawak family, which is distributed over large parts of lowland South America. In other structural or typological aspects, it resembles more characteristically Andean languages such as Quechua. In other words, Puquina has the appearance of a linguistic hybrid, a combination of both Amazonian and Andean characteristics.

The Arawak characteristics in Puquina are detectable most notably in its nominal morphology (that is, the internal structure of noun-based words). Both in structure and in form this is rather similar to the nominal morphology of Arawak languages spoken in the lowlands of Bolivia and southern Peru. Since this type of morphology is also characteristic of the Arawak family in general and is not otherwise found in the Andes, a possible Arawak connection offers the most likely explanation (see also Torero 1992, 177–8). As in many Arawak languages, personal possession in Puquina (*my, your, his/her*) is indicated by means of proclitic (prefix-like) elements that function as possessive pronouns in particular grammatical contexts (1) and are related in form to the corresponding personal pronouns (2):

(1) **no**   'my'   **po**   'your'   **chu**[5]   'his/her'

(2) **ni** 'I'[6]   **pi** 'you'   **chu** 'he/she'

These forms can be compared to elements with similar functions in Arawak languages of the neighbouring lowlands. The similarities are striking. In *Baure*, an Arawak language spoken in the Mojos region in the Bolivian lowlands, singular personal possession is also indicated by means of proclitic elements (Danielsen 2007, 317–19). Except for the feminine 3rd person possessive ('her'), these elements show affinity with corresponding Puquina forms (3). The corresponding personal pronouns are formed on the basis of the same roots, by adding an element *-ti'* (4).

(3) **ni-** 'my'   **pi-** 'your'   **ro-** 'his'   **ri-** 'her'

(4) **nti'** 'I'   **piti'** 'you'   **roti'** 'he'   **riti'** 'she'.

Another Arawak language of the lowlands adjacent to the Altiplano, *Iñapari*, of Madre de Dios in the southern Peruvian Amazon, uses possessive prefixes to express personal reference (Parker 1995). These are also partly similar in form to the Puquina personal pronouns and proclitic forms. The Iñapari form that is closest to the Puquina 3rd person pronoun is the feminine 3rd person possessive prefix *ru-*, which formally corresponds with its masculine equivalent *ro-* in Baure (probably due to a functional metathesis in the latter language).[7]

(5) **nu-** 'my'   **pi-** 'you'   **ru-** 'her'

While acknowledging some variation in the vowels, the *n-/p-* pattern for 1st and 2nd person singular is typical of the Arawak language family and is not found in any Andean language besides Puquina. This pronominal pattern is widely distributed within the Arawak family, so the connection need not come necessarily from one of the Arawak languages spoken in the lowlands immediately adjacent to Puquina, but also conceivably from a geographically more distant Arawak language. It should be observed that the distinction between masculine and feminine gender in the 3rd person is not found in Puquina, from where it may have disappeared under the areal pressure of Andean languages which predominantly lack grammatical gender.[8]

For a fuller perspective, though, it is important to acknowledge that in other respects, Puquina exhibits no particularly close parallels with the Arawak languages, whether those of the adjacent lowlands or further afield. Other than for the suffix referring to 2nd person subject <-pi> (~ <-ui>), which can be identified with the corresponding pronoun of Arawak origin (see above), the general structure of finite verbs, for example, is suffixing and agglutinative in Puquina, as in the Andean languages Aymara and Quechua. Another typically Andean feature of the Puquina language is the use of an inverse marker, to change a personal reference suffix from marking the subject to marking the object (6, 7).

(6) **oreguescanch**
ore-ge-s-k-anč
speak-FUT-INV-1st pers-DECL
'You/he/she will tell me.'
(Adelaar and Van de Kerke 2009, 137)

In example (6), the function of the inverse suffix -s- is to indicate that the personal reference affix <-c> [k][9] refers to a (direct or indirect) *object* 'me', rather than to the *subject* of the verb 'I' as it normally does. Likewise in (7), the inverse suffix -s- changes <-pi> 'you' from the subject to the object of the verb.

(7) **ñus baptizaspi**
ñu-s baptisa-s-pi-i
who-ERG baptize-INV-2nd pers-INT[10]
'Who baptized you?'
(Adelaar and Van de Kerke 2009, 130)

Meanwhile, in example (6), the identity of the subject remains undetermined and has to be inferred from the context. This use of inverse markers in the personal reference system is also found in Andean languages such as Quechua and Mapudungun (cf. Adelaar 2009). It may have been adopted by Puquina under the areal pressure of one of its neighbouring languages. Compare the use of Puquina <-s-> to that of the Quechua inverse marker -su-, which has a similar function as <-s-> in Puquina (8, 9).

(8) **willa-nki**
tell-2nd pers.FUT
'You will tell him/her.'

(9) **willa-su-nki**
tell-INV-2nd pers.FUT
'He/she will tell you.'

To return to characteristics that appear to connect Puquina to the Arawak languages, we could mention that a suffix derived from a free pronoun (in this case, 2nd person -pi) can directly be attached to the past participle of a verb (marked with the ending <-(s)so> [so]), without the insertion of a verb 'to be'. The resulting form refers to a permanent condition of the subject. Note that the pronominal suffix -pi appears in its weakened form <-u(i)> [w(i)] (10). This situation – in which a pronominal affix with subject function is directly attached to a nominal form without the intermediary of a verb 'to be' (or any device replacing it) – is common in the Arawak languages but unusual in Andean languages.[11]

(10) **casarassoui**
    kasara-SO-pi-i[12]
    marry-PART-2nd pers-INT
    'Are you married?'
    (Adelaar and Van de Kerke 2009, 140)

This picture would not be complete unless complemented by *lexical* evidence connecting Puquina to the Arawak language family. Unfortunately, there are very few
Puquina words that can effectively be used to this end, given the limited nature
of the Puquina lexicon that has been preserved. Since the only source consists of
religious instructions, most of the basic vocabulary required to identify possible
relatedness to other language families is missing. This small amount of vocabulary
would moreover have to be systematically compared to a wide array of Arawak
languages, none of which has emerged so far as particularly close to Puquina. In
the absence of any established link between Puquina and a specific subgroup of
the Arawak family, the possibility remains that any similarities discovered are due
to chance. Nonetheless, some interesting lexical parallels have emerged, such as
words for 'sun' and 'moon' that are widespread across languages of the Arawak
family and seem to correlate with words for 'day' and 'night' in Puquina. Compare,
for instance, Puquina <camen ~gamen> 'day' with Waura *kami* 'sun', and Puquina
<quisin>[13] 'night' with Waura *keši* 'moon' (data from Torero 1987 and Payne
1991). For several more suggestions see Torero (1992, 177–8).

   So in sum, what are the origins of Puquina, and what is the exact nature of its
connection with Arawak? In linguistics, this question is normally seen in terms of
a standard opposition set out here already in Chapter 1.2 by Heggarty. That is, are
Puquina and Arawak related to each other within a deep language family, *diverging* out of a common original language lineage? Or are they entirely separate lineages with independent origins, but which came into powerful contact with each
other, such that Puquina *converged* to a significant extent on some of the structures
of Arawak languages? In fact, the Puquina case is one that is difficult to resolve
definitively in such clear-cut terms, given how limited are the data that survive on
Puquina, and that they contain conflicting indications in support of one analysis or
the other. Or rather, as foreshadowed above, the data presented here seem to point
to a third, hybrid analysis, of what is effectively a 'merger' between two language
types: an Andean type reminiscent of Aymara and Quechua, and an Amazonian
lowland type that can be identified with the Arawak language family. This is consistent with a scenario in which an Amazonian group migrated to the Altiplano
highlands, where an earlier population of Andean background would have been
assimilated or displaced. For the time being, it is not possible to assign a date to
this assumed Arawak incursion into the Altiplano, but considering that Puquina
was almost certainly connected with the Tiahuanaco civilization, it would have
occurred before AD 500 at the latest.

Linguistic parallels between Uru-Chipaya and the adjacent Amazonian lowlands

In addition to the Arawak influence on Puquina, lexical similarities have been found between Uru-Chipaya and several linguistic isolates (languages not identifiably related to any others) spoken in the Bolivian lowlands to the north and north-east of the Altiplano. Puquina does not seem to play a role in these lexical connections, although this impression may be due to its poor state of documentation.

To look at a few examples of such loanwords, a characteristic term that appears in Uru-Chipaya and several lowland languages is a word for 'maize' (cf. Adelaar 1987). It appears as *tara* in Chipaya (Métraux 1936), as *tyãrã?* in Mosetén (Sakel 2004, 145), as *ta* in Leco (Kerke 2009, 290), and as *ta* or *tay* in Apolista, an extinct Arawak language (Créqui-Montfort and Rivet 1913). Possibly related forms are found in Itonama, Movima and (Arawak) Trinitario (Pache et al. 2016). Note that although the Aymara and Quechua terms for 'maize' are very different, an etymological relation of Uru-Chipaya *tara* with Quechua *sara* cannot be totally excluded (cf. Métraux 1936).

The word for dog, *paku*, is another case in point. It is found in (Uchumataqo) Uru and in Chipaya and with some variation in a range of lowland languages including Itonama, Movima and Trinitario (Pache et al. 2016). Surprisingly, such a non-cultural term as the word for 'people', 'human being', *suñi, šuñi* or *šoñi* (Cerrón-Palomino 2006, 68) has been recorded in the Uru-Chipayan languages, in Mosetén (*soñi?*, Sakel 2004, 167), and in Yuracaré (*šunñe*, Van Gijn 2006, 116). See Chapter 4.2, for a fuller exploration of the nature of any linguistic connections between Uru and the lowland languages.

These lexical similarities are significant because they appear to pre-date both the predominance of Puquina and the incursion of Aymara and Quechua. Instead, they may point to a relatively early stage of vertical interaction between highlands and lowlands. Alternatively, it is also possible that some of the lowland languages at issue, especially Leco and Mosetén, were originally spoken on the Altiplano but survived in the lowlands and on the eastern Andean slopes after being displaced by the successive incursions. Since we hardly have any reliable data on languages (other than Uru-Chipaya) spoken on the Altiplano before the generalization of Puquina and the penetration of Aymara and Quechua, such a scenario does not seem far-fetched. For the moment, it is safe to assume that the lexical similarities in question are due to borrowing, although it is difficult to determine in which direction such borrowing would have operated.

Other chapters within this book offer further, complementary perspectives from different disciplines in this same region of the Altiplano and the adjacent lowlands, not least on Uru-speaking populations and their origins. Chapter 4.3 by Prümers gives an archaeological perspective, while Chapters 3.2 by Santos and Chapter 3.3 by Barbieri both include genetic analyses of human population histories across this part of the Andes–Amazonia divide.

Conclusion

It appears from the above that Puquina, with its clear Amazonian admixture, is the best candidate for having been the language of official communication in Tiahuanaco. This does not mean, however, that it would have been the only language in use in the Middle Horizon Tiahuanaco realm. Other local languages may have been in use as well, such as Uru-Chipaya (Uruquilla)-related languages, possible modern lowland languages about to be displaced and probable extinct languages of which we have no knowledge or documentation at all. Furthermore, Tiahuanaco, as an influential religious centre of considerable cultural and political reach, likely hosted foreign residents as envoys, traders, religious specialists, artisans, and so on. There can be little doubt that representatives of ethnic groups located further north, likely to have been speakers of Quechua and Aymara, would have resided in Tiahuanaco for shorter or longer periods. So these languages would already have been more or less familiar to the Tiahuanaco people and leadership.

From a strictly linguistic viewpoint, then, we might distinguish three successive stages in the development of relationships between the Altiplano and Amazonia. First a stage of balanced interaction was reached between highlands and lowlands, involving local highland peoples, such as the Uru-Chipaya speakers, and several small ethnic groups settled in the eastern slopes of the Andes overlooking the Amazonian lowlands. In the second stage, an important influx of Amazonian (Arawak) cultural elements was instrumental in the genesis of Altiplano highland cultures, including Tiahuanaco, and the formation of the Puquina language. The final stage, after the demise of Tiahuanaco around AD 1100 (Janusek 2008), saw a massive incursion from the central Andes, unchecked by any significant resistance from local polities. This is confirmed by the limited dialectal diversification within modern Altiplano Aymara, indicative of how recent this central Andean incursion must have been. In this final stage, the linguistic interaction between the Altiplano and adjacent lowlands becomes predominantly unidirectional, from highlands to lowlands – as illustrated, for instance, by the borrowing of Aymara numerals into Tacanan languages such as Cavineña (cf. Marks 2012).

The scenario outlined above illustrates the importance of further systematic research of the local languages that still survive on the eastern slopes and foothills of the Andes adjacent to the Altiplano. These languages should not be approached as just a few more examples of Amazonian diversity but also, and primarily, from the perspective of a possible Andean background and history. This is not an easy task, given the dramatic loss of linguistic diversity among Andean societies from the time of Inca rule onwards, but it may serve as a useful working hypothesis that can contribute to linguistic reconstruction and to a better understanding of Andean–Amazonian interaction through the centuries.[14]

4.2

Hypothesized language relationships across the Andes–Amazonia divide: The cases of Uro, Pano-Takana and Mosetén

Roberto Zariquiey

Introduction

This chapter focuses on a region that stretches from the Altiplano of Bolivia and southernmost Peru into the adjacent lowlands of most of northern Bolivia. I look anew at past claims for putative relationships of common descent between certain language families of this region, that would straddle the Andes–Amazonia divide. I review serious methodological weaknesses behind those claims, but do also uncover a weaker but much more valid remaining signal, and one that is indicative instead of *contacts* between language lineages across the divide (rather than expansion across both areas from a single common origin – see Chapter 1.2). I outline an initial case for a convergent 'linguistic area' (see Chapter 1.2) across the Andes–Amazonia divide, from Lake Titicaca and the Altiplano far into lowland Bolivia – with all that that entails in terms of interactions between the societies and populations of this region.

Hypotheses abound on alleged relationships of common descent between various languages of Amazonia and of the Andes (see Chapter 2.3; 'Background on claimed 'long-range' language relationships', below). If confirmed, such relationships would necessarily stand as evidence undermining any definitive, exceptionless divide between those two regions, at least on this important cultural and ethnic level. Many of these hypotheses, however, are themselves undermined by clear weaknesses in their comparative linguistic methodology. Nonetheless, even if such relationships cannot be proven, there are clear similarities in wordforms and constructions between some Andean and Amazonian languages, which raise interesting questions about the possible exchanges that populations from these two regions established in prehistoric times.

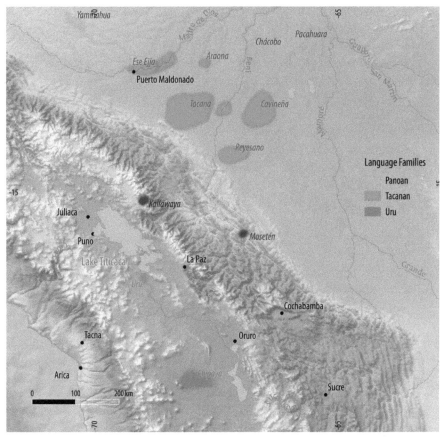

Figure 4.2.1 Approximate current location of the languages discussed in this paper, coloured by language family/lineage. © Roberto Zariquiey and Paul Heggarty.

Scholars in disciplines outside linguistics are understandably perplexed as to what to make of the claims for language relationships across the Andes–Amazonia divide, and the strength of the objections to them (Chapter 2.3). This chapter aspires to bring some more cross-disciplinary clarity, by means of discussing an illustrative case-study across that divide. It also aspires to contribute to the linguistic debate on the alleged lexical similarities between the Uro and Pano language families, of the Andes and Amazonia respectively: see Figure 4.2.1, where Uro languages are shown in purple, and Pano in green.

These similarities were first posited by Fabre (1995), but a relationship of common descent between Uro and Pano is extremely unlikely, and Fabre himself sees the similarities he found as evidence not of that but only of contact between these Andean and Amazonian populations. If Fabre's hypothesis is valid, we still need to understand more specifically what type of contacts these populations may have established. This further step may be of interest for archaeological and anthropological research in the region and may enrich our understanding of the Andes–Amazon divide.

In this chapter, I first set out a careful revision of the data and results presented by Fabre and argue that:

1. the treatment of the data in Fabre's paper is problematic;
2. the sense of a high degree of lexical correspondences between Uro and Pano is illusory;
3. there are nonetheless certainly a few lexical correspondences that are of interest;
4. these correspondences are in fact so few that they are suggestive only of a short and/or indirect contact between Uro and Pano;
5. we need instead to look at other languages, notably Mosetén, to find a potential bridge between languages of the Andes and Amazonia in this region.

All of the above leads on to some further considerations, and to the most far-reaching proposal to be set out in this chapter. Central here is to bring into the picture one of the main indigenous languages spoken in a region that lies *between* where Uro and Pano are (and were) spoken: Mosetén. Again, see the map in Figure 4.2.1 for the respective locations of these three language lineages, where Mosetén is clearly intermediate between Uro and Pano. It is Mosetén, as we will see, that turns out to be the potential bridge between languages of the Andes and Amazonia in this region. Also directly relevant is that since Fabre (1995), increasing support has emerged (for example, Valenzuela and Zariquiey 2015) for Pano in fact forming part of a wider language family along with the Takanan languages – which are those that duly complete the geographical sequence from the highland Uro through Mosetén and Takanan to Pano.

So after the assessment that the linguistic evidence inclines towards a scenario in which contact between Uro and Pano may well have been only indirect, this chapter goes on to highlight some intriguing similarities between Uro and Mosetén, and then in turn between Mosetén and Pano, which require further attention. That is, once Mosetén is brought into consideration, then the similarities between Uro and Pano may be more easily explained, and particularly when the Takanan languages are also considered. Indeed, overall, the data discussed here seem to point towards an appealing explanation in terms of a linguistic convergence area stretching from the southern Andes into neighbouring regions of Amazonia, which may merit further study.

To begin with, some further details are in order on the languages to be discussed here. Uro languages were spoken along the 'Aquatic Axis' of the Altiplano in Peru and Bolivia: the western shores of Lake Titicaca, the Desaguadero River and Lake Poopó. The only extant language of the family is Chipaya (Cerrón-Palomino 2006). Pano, meanwhile, is a middle-sized Amazonian language family with approximately 17 extant languages spoken in Peru, Brazil and Bolivia. The Pano language(s) still spoken in Bolivia are Chakobo and Pakawara. Pano languages are likely related to Takanan (Valenzuela and Zariquiey 2015), which is a small Amazonian language family with only five extant languages, most of them spoken in northern Bolivia and one also in south-eastern Peru (Valenzuela and Guillaume 2017). Mosetén is a linguistic isolate (that is, not identifiably related to any other known language) spoken in Bolivian Amazonia (Sakel 2004). Bolivian Pano languages, as well as Takanan languages and Mosetén, are spoken in the Beni River basin. Figure 4.2.1 maps the approximate locations of the Bolivian Pano languages Chakobo and Pakawara; the Takanan languages Ese Ejja, Cavineña, Takana and Reyesano; Mosetén; Uro and Chipaya; and Kallawalla. Further details on all language families can be consulted at http://glottolog.org, under the respective GlottoCodes for Uro (uruc1242), Pano (pano1256), Takanan (taca1255) and Mosetén (mose1249), for example.

The present chapter is structured as follows. In the following section, I critically examine Fabre's (1995) study on the relations between Uro and Pano-Takanan. Next, I explore some interesting correspondences between Uro, Mosetén and Pano. In the final section I draw conclusions on what these data on language contacts entail for the question of an Andes–Amazonia divide, and I indicate potentially profitable avenues for future research.

Fabre's (1995) study

Background on claimed 'long-range' language relationships

The idea of a possible relationship between the Pano and Takanan languages (both Amazonian families) is relatively old, suggested as early as 1886 by Armentia (quoted in Navarro 1903, 172). In 1933, Schuller was the first scholar to attempt to actually demonstrate such a relationship. Later, Key (1968) and Girard (1971) proposed more detailed 'Proto-Pano-Takana' reconstructions, and until recently the relationship of common descent between Pano and Takanan has been widely accepted.[1]

Some scholars have proposed further links between the lowland Pano-Takanan and other language families. Indeed, such proposals are far from rare in the literature. Greenberg's (1960) 'Gê-Pano-Carib' included his 'Macro-Panoan' group, which, in turn, comprised Takanan-Pano, Mosetén, Mataco, Lule, Vilela, Mascoy, Charrúa and Guaycuru-Opaie. More conservatively, Suárez (1969) proposed a relationship between Pano-Takanan and Mosetén. Pano languages have even been claimed to be related to Meso-American languages: Wistrand-Robinson (1991) postulated a relationship between Pano and Uto-Aztecan (see below for similar claims regarding Uro languages). Most relevant to the discussion in this chapter, of course, are proposals such as Swadesh's (1959) 'Quechuachon', which hypothesized that Pano-Takanan is related not just to the lowland Mosetén (and to the Patagonian language Chon), but also to the *highland* families Quechua, Aymara and Uro.

Other studies have likewise argued that Uro, too, is related to families other than Pano and Takanan. Olson (1965), for instance, hypothesized that Uro was related to Maya. Note that there has also been some confusion over the identities of the Uro and Puquina languages. Speakers of Uro themselves claimed that their language was 'Puquina' (Métraux 1935, 89; Lehmann 1929), and some scholars have taken this as evidence that the two were the same linguistic entity (cf. Créqui-Montfort and Rivet 1925, 1926, 1927: 'la langue uro ou puquina'). The equation of 'Puquina' with 'Uro', however, has been shown to be mistaken since the work of Torero (1987): the data unquestionably show two very different languages, not one. In this connection, it is important to mention that Puquina has itself been claimed to be related to Arawak, the most widespread language family of lowland South America – another potential linguistic connection across the Andes–Amazonia divide, covered here by Adelaar in Chapter 4.1.

In this wider context of multiple claims for long-distance relationships, Fabre (1995) discusses alleged lexical correspondences that might putatively support a connection between Pano and Uro. Although he misleadingly uses the term 'cognate' for those correspondences (see 'A short note on methodology', below), Fabre himself concludes that they are likely to be the result of contact, and not descent from a common proto-language.

A short note on methodology

Since Greenberg's (1987) book, where he set out his hypothesis of a vast 'Amerind' language macro-family, there has been a great deal of criticism not only of the concept of Amerind itself, but also of Greenberg's methodology in seeking to construct it. Basically, Greenberg's approach, known as 'multilateral comparison' (see also Greenberg 1996), attempts to determine possible relationships between languages by superficially comparing large lexical databases, without searching for the regular sound correspondences that orthodox historical linguistics considers necessary to establish firm relationships of common descent between languages. In Greenberg's methodology, lexical evidence is claimed to be enough to postulate such relationships. These ideas have been widely criticized and Greenberg demonstrated to be wrong with regard to many of his claims. For instance, Campbell (1997, 327) observes that: 'In general, considering Greenberg's claims about the power of his method of multilateral comparison, his assertion that "the validity of Amerind as a whole is more secure than that of any of its stocks" (1987, 59) may raise some eyebrows, since his eleven member branches are themselves proposals of very distant relationship, none of which has any general acceptance' (see also Campbell 1991). For more extensive discussion of the methodological flaws in Greenberg's methodology, see Chapter 2.3.

Although Fabre's study does not explicitly state so, it is clear from the treatment of the lexical data included that his methodology is close to the procedures proposed by Greenberg in 1987. Firstly, in order to determine whether two words are 'cognates', Fabre does not look for any kind of phonological correspondence with parallel sound alternations attested also in other lexical entries. He seems to follow nothing more than an intuitive approach and, in some cases, it is only necessary that two words referring to the same or a similar meaning share a single consonant in order to be considered related. In fact, as discussed in the next section, most of Fabre's alleged Uro-Pano 'cognates' do not stand up to any more rigorous analysis. A second respect in which Fabre's study is close to Greenberg's methodology is in how the sample used for the comparisons is drawn up. Fabre freely compares lexical entries drawn from different levels (reconstructed words attributed to proto-languages and words from any one language within either of the families compared). In Fabre's study, it is enough to find a putative lexical correspondence between any two languages, one from each family, in order to claim that there is a 'cognate' between those entire families. Orthodox historical linguistics would apply the comparative method in a far more rigorous way, and preferably compare lexemes reliably reconstructed to the respective proto-language of each family. Thirdly, Fabre's study relies exclusively on lexical data. There is no attempt to explore and compare phonological or structural features of the languages. One final point that deserves attention is the misleading and confused use of the term 'cognate' in Fabre's study, where it is used as a synonym of a 'loanword' from another language – when the accepted use of the term in historical linguistics is to refer on the contrary to words inherited directly from a common ancestor language.

Results

Fabre's (1995) study compares Uro languages to all of the following language families and linguistic isolates: Pano, Aymara, Takanan, Mosetén, Leco, (Kallawaya) Puquina and Arawak. Of these, the author then excludes the languages given in Table 4.2.1, because he finds no or only very few exclusive 'cognates' between them and Uro. Note that Table 4.2.2 includes Mosetén – to which I will return, in the following section. Fabre's study therefore focused on the lexical correspondences

Table 4.2.1   Languages and language families excluded from Fabre's study.

Language	Number of 'cognates' with Uro-Chipaya
Mosetén	1
Leco	2
Kallawaya–Puquina	3
Arawak	0

Table 4.2.2 Languages and language families included in Fabre's study.

Language	Number of 'cognates' with Uro	% of corpus
Pano	19	14.1
Aymara	16	11.9
Takanan	11	8.2
Pano and Takanan	15	11.1
Aymara and Pano-Takanan	17	12.6
Aymara and Pano	7	5.2
Aymara and Takanan	2	1.5

between Uro and the three remaining language families: Aymara, Pano and Takanan. Fabre's results are shown in Table 4.2.2.

Worth emphasizing is that according to Fabre's data, Uro has more lexical correspondences with Pano than with Aymara. This is hard to believe in the light of the strong and well-established contact between Aymara and Uro, and the well-documented influence of the former over the latter (see for instance Cerrón-Palomino 2006). Whatever figures emerge from a comparison such as that carried out by Fabre, one would expect Aymara to be the family with the highest lexical overlap with Uro.

If one combines cases in Fabre of exclusive 'cognates' between Pano and Uro with 'cognates' between Pano, Uro and any of the other languages included, we reach 46.7 per cent. That is, almost half of the 135 words in Fabre's list show, according to the author, a lexical resemblance between Pano and Uro. Thanks to Fabre's paper including as an appendix the database of words he used in his comparisons, one can easily see the breakdown of the data and test the validity of these results.

I have conducted re-evaluation of all the 'cognates' alleged to exist between Pano and Uro, and, although they are based mainly on the same data, my results differ from Fabre's conclusions. In my judgement, most of Fabre's alleged 'cognates' do not stand up to more rigorous analysis. See the cases offered in Table 4.2.3 for exemplification (orthography as in the original).

It is important to mention that Fabre is not totally clear about the sources of his lists. It is unclear if Fabre's 'Uro-Chipaya' data come from Chipaya, the only extant language of the Uro language family, or from Uro, for which some lexical data were documented before it went extinct. In any case, Fabre's 'Uro-Chipaya' forms are not reconstructed proto-forms for the family. Likewise for Fabre's Pano data: many come from specific Pano languages and are not proto-forms either. It is clear that what Fabre considers to be Proto-Pano forms (preceded by <*> in Fabre's lists) were taken from Shell (1965). Yet Shell never claimed to have reconstructed Proto-Pano. She is careful to use the label 'Reconstructed Pano', rather than Proto-Pano, for her reconstruction. The reason for this caution is that she was

Table 4.2.3 Examples of unconvincing 'cognates' between Pano and Uro.

Uro	Pano	Gloss
cakwa	*'išcan ('many')[a]	'big'
cis	*caca ('type of fish')	'fish'
osa	ri-sakí (Chakobo)[b]	'nose'
šiñi	*ašci[c]	'egg'
šqiši	*šakata	'skin'
paqu	kapa (Kashinawá) 'squirrel'	'dog'
puk	*raita	'two'

[a] The sequence <šc> in Shell's reconstruction does not stand as a possible reconstruction. A more appealing proposal would be simply <c>.
[b] Note that the likely Proto-Pano form must have been only *ri
[c] The sequence <šc> in Shell's reconstruction does not stand as a possible reconstruction. A more appealing proposal would be simply <c>.
* = a proposed 'Reconstructed Pano' form, on the basis of reflexes in more than one language of the Pano family.
Where forms are found only in a single Pano language, that language's name is given in brackets ( ).

aware that her language sample was incomplete since she did not include northern Pano languages. Furthermore, 'Reconstructed Pano' evinces some analytical problems that make some of Shell's proposals problematic in various respects. Crucially, some of the alleged similarities between Pano and Uro are based on forms that may be considered errors in Shell's study (see footnotes to table 4.2.3).

None of the alleged lexical correlations in Table 4.2.3 stands up to careful scrutiny. Let us examine each one in turn. In the first example, <cakwa>/*<'išca> 'big', the sequence is shared, but is the first syllable of the Uro word, and the second of the Pano word. Although not necessarily a problem in itself, the lexical relationship is undermined by the realization that in fact the Pano word means something different: 'many' instead of 'big'. In the second example, <cis>/*<caca> 'fish', we also find some degree of semantic difference in that the Pano form refers to one specific type of fish, and the words in question only share a single consonant <c> (/ts/). Even harder to accept is the third example, since the more likely Proto-Pano form for 'nose' is *ri and the corresponding lexeme in Uro-Chipaya is <osa>. The forms for 'egg', <šiñi>/*<ašci>, are also unlikely to be related considering that the s in the Pano form (as also in 'skin') comes from a problematic analysis in Shell (1965), and their formal resemblance is otherwise minimal. For 'dog', the words compared are Uro <paqu> and Kashinawa <kapa>, which do share the syllable <pa>, yet the latter means 'squirrel', not 'dog'. (There are other terms for '(wild) dog' among Pano languages, among which we find *kaman* and *kamun*.) The last example in Table 4.2.3 is equally indicative: the words for 'two' offered by Fabre are simply not similar at all.

The problems identified in the examples in Table 4.2.3 are similar to those revealed in any careful scrutiny of most studies that claim to identify distant language relationships of this sort. This in itself does not necessarily mean that such relationships do not exist, but it does question the idea that they can be demonstrated by resorting exclusively to linguistic evidence of the sort typically used to make such claims, rather than to the methodology of the orthodox 'comparative method' in historical linguistics. Furthermore, the search for correspondences between distinct language families has all too often assumed that any that are found can directly be taken as evidence of a shared origin. Yet the existence of such correspondences may alternatively be evidence only of contact, of course. In fact, there are eight cases in Fabre's corpus that do exhibit a relatively plausible lexical correspondence between Pano and Uro. That is, we find 5.9 per cent shared words between the two families and not 46.7 per cent, but the existence of this 5.9 per cent is still interesting and requires explanation. These cases are listed in Table 4.2.4 (orthography as in the original).

A percentage of 5.9 per cent seems far more plausible than 46.7 per cent for a possible relationship of any sort between Uro and Pano. A rate of 46.7 per cent would be expected only for languages for which it is obvious at first sight that they are closely related even within the same family – certainly not the case for Uro and Pano. As noted above, we would expect that due to intense contact (ongoing in the case of the Chipaya language), Uro should exhibit a higher degree of lexical similarity with Aymara than with Pano. In this sense, Fabre's (1995) result are clearly counter-intuitive and are indeed the result of the application of a problematic methodology. Fabre (1995) is illustrative of the grave problems that Greenberg's

Table 4.2.4 Cases of possible 'cognates' between Pano and Uro-Chipaya.

Uro	Pano	Gloss
yuske	*'išca[a]	'many'
khi	ki (Kashinawa)[b]	'say'
nii	ni- (Shipibo)[c]	'this'
šon	*šanu	'woman'
qalu	kadu (Kashinawa)[d]	'firewood'
-kis	-ki (Kashinawa)[e]	'in, locative'
'ciki	cii (Shipibo)[f]	'light, fire'
šoñi	*oni[g]	'man'

[a] The sequence sc in Shell's reconstruction does not stand as a possible reconstruction. A more appealing proposal would be simply c.
[b] the form ki ~ ik 'say' is likely to be Proto-Pano.
[c] The form is in fact ni and is likely to be Proto-Pano.
[d] The likely Proto-Pano form is *karu.
[e] A likely Proto-Pano form.
[f] A likely Proto-Pano form.
[g] The Proto-Pano form is *honi.
* Indicates a proposed 'Reconstructed Pano' form, on the basis of reflexes in more than one language of the Pano family.
Where forms are found only in a single Pano language, that language's name is given in brackets ( ).

methodology poses for any attempt to study distant relationships between different language families.

So although a handful of lexical correspondences do exist between Pano and Uro-Chipaya, it seems that any claim for *high* lexical similarity between them is simply mistaken. In fact, the corpus used by Fabre reveals that Uro shows greater true similarity with Aymara instead, precisely as expected. The 5.93 per cent of possible shared lexicon between Uro and Pano still requires, of course, an explanation, and the most likely scenario is some sort of contact. Fabre (1995) assumes a similar explanation for the alleged much higher degree of lexical correspondence that he believes he has found between Uro and Pano, and he concludes that 'the cognates are due to areal diffusion'. Note that, as already noted, Fabre's use of the term 'cognate' is idiosyncratic, since the term is reserved in linguistics for cases where similarity goes back to inheritance and *not* to contact. The correct term for lexical similarities that derive from contact is of course simply 'loanwords'. In any case, 46.7 per cent or 5.9 per cent of loanwords presuppose two totally different contact scenarios. The former would imply a long-term and intense contact between the two families; the latter more likely correlates with only short-term and possibly indirect contact.

Our critical revision of Fabre's (1995) study, then, supports his idea that there was some sort of contact between Pano and Uro, but paints a totally different scenario, in which the interactions between these two language lineages were likely only indirect. At this point, the role of another Amazonian language Mosetén (also known as Chimané-Mosetén) becomes central to the scenario. Crucially, the geographic location of Mosetén makes it a likely intermediary between Uro and southern Panoan languages (see Figure 4.2.1) and, as shown in the next section, Fabre's (1995) data do in fact reveal a significant lexical similarity between Uro and Mosetén, underestimated in Fabre's own study. It is Mosetén, then, that turns out to be the potential bridge between languages of the Andes and Amazonia.

From Uro through Mosetén to Pano? Possible linguistic contacts across the Andes–Amazonia divide

Fabre (1995) claims that the data do not suggest any relevant relationship between Mosetén and Uro-Chipaya: 'I have discarded the following languages, spoken in the same general area, from further comparison: (1) Mosetén-Chimane, which showed on the basis of the longer list of 135 glosses only one possible exclusive cognate between Uru-Chipaya and Mosetén' (Fabre 1995, 55). However, my own revision of Fabre's corpus in fact turns up not one but nine possible cases of shared lexicon between the two families. In my view, there is no theoretical or methodological reason to exclude these nine cases. Of these nine cases, at least six seem highly plausible. The discovery of salient lexical similarities between Mosetén and Uro is not new in the literature. Suárez (1977), for instance, claims that 'several of the pairs of cognates identified between Mosetén and Uru-Chipaya are intriguing'. In my view, at least four of the cases in Suárez's data ranks as convincing. Table 4.2.5 lists the six most plausible candidate cases for shared lexicon between Mosetén and Uro in Fabre's (1995) corpus, and the four most convincing given by Suárez (1977). Together these entail that Uro has more salient lexical similarity with Mosetén than with Pano.

The correspondences in Table 4.2.5 are of a different order to Fabre's, far closer phonologically, and far more likely to convince historical linguists. This is above all because they also lead us to posit systematic phonological correspondences between the two language lineages. A quick review of the data published by Fabre and by Suárez not only allows us to postulate the ten cases of likely correspondences in Table 4.2.5, but also to propose three systematic phonological correspondences between these two families, given in Table 4.2.6. As Suárez (1977) remarks, this systematicity is indeed intriguing.

The presence of such systematic correspondences is to be analysed, if not as evidence of a relationship of common origin, then as a clear indicator of an old and to some extent systematic contact between these two language lineages, on opposing sides of the Andes–Amazonia divide. The 'contact-induced' interpretation is all the more plausible based on the scarce data that we have studied, given the reduced number of phonological correspondences – only three – and the fact at least two of those three have counter-examples, and are thus irregular. The lack of regularity in phonological correspondences of the sort listed here has often been interpreted as pointing to contact, rather than to common descent, since the irregularities could be most easily explained if these were loanwords borrowed at different stages in time, with different patterns of phonological adaptation, and/or in different directions.

Given these correspondences between Mosetén and Uro, the other half to the equation is of course what correspondences Mosetén may also show with Pano. This requires more study and will be crucial to providing a more solid basis to the hypothesis of a possible contact area from Uro through Mosetén to Pano. In this respect, one can already point to an intriguing inventory of morphosyntactic features that bring Mosetén close to Pano languages. For instance, in Mosetén some morphological paradigms treat transitive and intransitive verbs differently (Sakel 2004, 181ff), reminiscent of how the morphological distinction between transitive and intransitive verbs is a central feature of Pano languages. Mosetén also exhibits vestiges of what seems to have been a more productive process of verb serialization (Sakel 2004, 249), again as is the case in Pano languages. Furthermore, the Mosetén interrogative word *jäen* (Sakel 2004, 124) shows some formal similarity with *hawe*, which seems likely to have been an old interrogative form in Pano.

Additionally, Uro-Chipaya, Mosetén and Pano all exhibit switch-reference and large inventories of oblique cases. And within those oblique cases, some further morphological similarities are found. All three families exhibit similar comitative markers, for instance: *tan(a)* in Uro-Chipaya, *-tom* in Mosetén, and *-betan* in

Table 4.2.5 Cases of shared lexicon between Mosetén and Uro.

	Uro	Mosetén	Gloss
1	thuñi	itzuñ	'sun'
2	khoci	cosc	'bone'
3	khu	co	'nose'
4	šoñi	šoñi	'man'
5	cihñi	ojñi 'water'	'rain'
6	masi	mas	'stone'
7	cañi	sañ	'leaf' (Suárez)
8	khursi	khondi	'tail' (Suárez)
9	cii	sis	'know' (Suárez)
10	yoka	ak	'ground' (Suárez)

Table 4.2.6 Systematic phonological correspondences between Mosetén and Uro.

Uro	Mosetén	Example occurrences
i#[a] (that is, word ends in *i*)	ø# (that is, word ends without a vowel)	1, 2, 3, 6, 7; but also contrast 4, 5, 8
Kh	c	2, 3; but contrast 8
C	s	7, 9

[a] # = 'word-finally'.

Pano. All three likewise have a locative marker of similar form: *kin(a)/-kiz(i)* in Uro-Chipaya, *-khan* in Mosetén, and *-kin* in Pano. A more careful morphosyntactic comparison needs to be carried out and may well reveal more typological and formal similarities between these three language lineages. Fabre's lexical data do also show at least one instance of a correspondence between the three lineages: all share a similar form for 'person' (which, interestingly, is a known *Wanderwort* from Romance into multiple Germanic languages in Europe too; Paul Heggarty, personal communication).

It is important to stress at this point that a relationship of common origin between Pano and Takanan languages is extremely likely (Valenzuela and Zariquiey 2015) and that Rivet (1910) documents Pano languages that were formerly spoken near the Madre de Dios and Beni Rivers, a relevant region for the hypothesis proposed here. A more comprehensive exploration of the hypothesis would surely benefit from incorporating the extinct Pano languages documented by Rivet, as well as Takanan languages, and indeed the Yurakaré language. A wider comparative study of this sort would seem to hold out promising prospects.

Conclusions

This chapter has sought to revise, based on previously published data, some of the conclusions drawn by Fabre in his 1995 paper. I have sought to show that the degree of lexical overlap between Pano and Uro is far lower than proposed by Fabre, although there do remain a handful of undeniable lexical similarities between these two families. Such lexical similarities are merely possible indicators of indirect contact, however, nothing more.

This chapter has also attempted to highlight that, contrary to Fabre's interpretation, Uro shows in fact a higher degree of lexical correspondences with Mosetén. What makes the case for possible contacts between Uro and Mosetén all the more interesting is that, as shown in Table 4.2.6, there are some systematic phonological correspondences. These data seem to suggest a relatively old and more systematic type of contact between Uro and Mosetén. Thus, with Fabre, I see contact as the most plausible explanation for the similarities between Uro and Pano, but also for the correspondences reported here between Uro and Mosetén. I propose, however, that the contact scenarios were clearly different in both cases.

One final finding here concerns those cases in which the similarities between Mosetén and Uro also reach Pano. The lexical and morphological similarities listed here point to the possibility of a linguistic contact zone that spanned languages of both the Andes and Amazonia. These similarities are strong enough to advocate the idea of a 'Southern Andes to Amazonia' linguistic convergence area as a working hypothesis that certainly merits further exploration and future research may prove true. From Figure 4.2.1 it is clear that between Mosetén and the current location of the southernmost Pano languages is a solid presence of Takanan languages. Given their current distribution, one would expect Takanan languages to have been part of the potential linguistic area hypothesized here. The Takanan data presented by Fabre do hint in that direction, but his Takanan data also still need to be carefully revised, as I have done here for the question of the Uro-Pano relationship. This contact situation may also have included other languages of the area, and I consider that the Yurakare linguistic isolate may be a good candidate.

In my judgement, the available data do not support claims that Uro has a relationship of common origin either with Pano or with Mosetén. This chapter does report, however, certain clear lexical and morphosyntactic similarities, which require explanation. It does seem, then, that Uro, Mosetén and Pano were involved in some form of contact(s), still to be elucidated, across the Andes–Amazonia 'divide'.

4.3
The Andes as seen from Mojos

Heiko Prümers

This chapter explores relations between the Andes and Amazonia as implied by an ideal case study, that of the Llanos de Mojos in Bolivia. For the Llanos de Mojos boast one of the best studied archaeological records of any region of the eastern lowlands of South America. As far back as the early twentieth century, Nordenskiöld was already considering this topic in almost all of his publications on the history and archaeology of the Llanos de Mojos. His views are clear, as exemplified by the following statement:

> Highland culture has not spread into any part of the lowlands of eastern Bolivia. It is most likely that the Indians of the lowlands borrowed one thing or another from those of the highlands, that there occurred from time to time some limited cultural exchanges, as will no doubt be confirmed by future research. Nevertheless, it is safe to say that the Indians of the eastern lowlands of Bolivia remained entirely independent of the powerful highland culture. (Nordenskiöld 1910, 807; author's translation)

Naturally, much more archaeological research has been conducted in the Llanos de Mojos since the days of Nordenskiöld's pioneering work.

To begin with, the Llanos de Mojos need to be defined as a geographical unit, dominated by regularly inundated savannahs (see Figure 4.3.1).

To the west these savannahs run up against the foothills of the Andes, and to the east against the wooded hills of the westernmost outcrops of the Brazilian shield. To the north the limits are the Beni and Guaporé rivers, while the southern limit is defined by the confluence of the Rio Grande with the Chapare. The whole area covers 150,000 km², and although archaeological sites are known of right across it, reliable archaeological data are confined to certain areas and time-periods.

The great majority of the archaeological contexts known from the Llanos de Mojos belong to cultures that flourished during the last thousand years before the Spanish conquest (AD 500–1500). Recent research, however, points to an occupation as far back as the early Holocene (between 8000 and 2000 BC) (see Lombardo

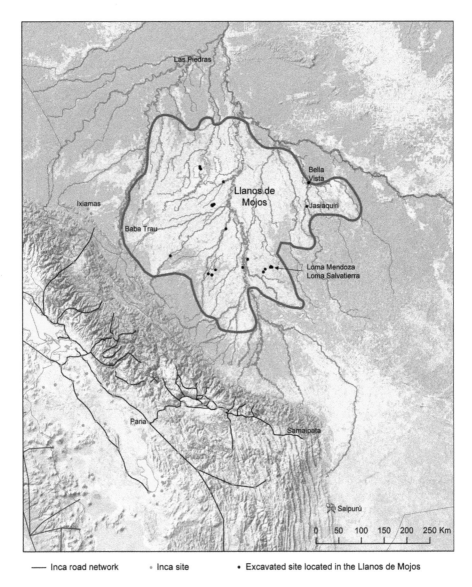

———— Inca road network   • Inca site   • Excavated site located in the Llanos de Mojos

Figure 4.3.1   Map of the Llanos de Moxos with excavated sites; Inca sites and roads outside the Llanos de Moxos also shown. © Heiko Prümers.

et al. 2013; Capriles et al. 2019; Chapter 4.4) and the region does seem to have played an important role in the domestication of plants (see Lombardo et al. 2020). Manioc (*Manihot esculenta*), peanut (*Arachis hypogaea*), chilli pepper (*Capsicum baccatum*) and squash (*Cucurbita maxima*) all possibly dispersed out of an origin in this region as domesticates (Piperno 2011a, S459, Figure 1B). Since manioc and peanut appear in the Zaña Valley on the western slope of the northern Peruvian Andes as early as 7000 BC (Dillehay 2013, 286; Chapters 2.1 and 2.4), some contacts or interactions between the Llanos de Mojos and the Andean world must have existed from far back in prehistory.

It remains little understood why there is such a gap in the archaeological evidence between the sparse early Holocene occupation and the massive presence of different archaeological cultures from c. AD 500 onwards. The fact that there are similar types of hiatus in various regions of Amazonia (Neves 2008, 363–4) suggests that the gap might reflect a real event in which the region was indeed abandoned.

The Llanos de Mojos were densely settled by sedentary agriculturists during late pre-Hispanic times (AD 500–1400), as evidenced by various forms of earthworks for water management and agriculture (channels, dams and ridged fields; see Denevan 1966; Erickson 1980, 2010; Walker 2004, 2018) as well as by settlements continuously occupied for almost a millennium (Dougherty and Calandra 1982; Prümers 2013, 2015; Prümers and Jaimes Betancourt 2014a). Among the earthworks the raised fields are the best studied, and the fact that similar ones are to be found in the highland basin of Lake Titicaca has been mentioned repeatedly in the literature. However, claims that they could indicate contact between the two areas have been missing, with good cause (although see Chapter 1.4, for a contrary view). The fact alone that raised fields can be found all over the world (see Rostain 2013, 26–9) and were constructed in each region at different moments in history demonstrates that their presence (and absence) is not to be related with 'culture contact', but with specific geographical and climatic conditions (see McKey et al. 2014; McKey and Rostain 2016).

The sub-regions of the Llanos de Mojos show marked differences in their ceramic inventories, reflecting different archaeological cultures. Investigation of these regional cultures is still in its infancy and most data available come from just two areas east of the Mamoré river. The first is the Casarabe region, the focal point of the largest habitation mounds known in the Llanos de Mojos. The second is the Baures region, home to settlements established on natural levees protected by complex systems of ditches. I shall first summarize what can be said about those cultures to date, and then turn to the lack of evidence for Inca presence in the Llanos de Mojos.

Evidence from the Casarabe region

More than 100 sites with mounds have been registered in the Casarabe region (Lombardo and Prümers 2010, 1877). They date to c. AD 500–1400 and are therefore contemporaneous with Tiahuanaco and later regional cultures in the Bolivian highlands and inter-Andean valleys.

The Casarabe mounds, ranging in size from 1 to 20 ha and up to 20 m high, are pyramidal structures built on artificial terraces in the middle of their sites. In some cases, polygonal causeways enclose the sites, so their size can be determined precisely. In the Loma Salvatierra, the enclosed area was 21 ha (see Figure 4.3.2),

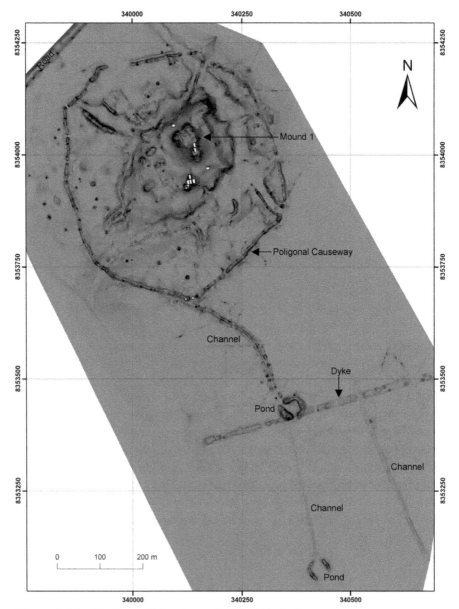

Figure 4.3.2 The Loma Salvatierra site. © Heiko Prümers.

but at another site with two polygonal causeways, the inner one enclosed 75 ha and the outer one 300 ha.

Although the size of these sites alone is surprising considering their Amazonian setting, what makes them especially peculiar is the recurrent pattern of planned architecture discernible in their layout. This layout does not compare to anything known so far from South America and thus points to an autonomous development.

The same can be inferred from an analysis of the ceramics excavated at settlements with monumental architecture in the Casarabe region. More than 40,000 diagnostic ceramic sherds have been analysed by Jaimes Betancourt (2012a, 2012b), and not a single piece shows evidence of influences from the Andean region. On the contrary, 'the ceramic material analysed has its own traits and belongs to exclusively Amazonian traditions. Neither stylistic attributes nor technical characteristics of highland ceramics were found' (Jaimes Betancourt 2012b, 182). Of course, just two sites do not in any way constitute a reliable sample, so I should mention that over 50 other archaeological sites with monumental architecture in the Casarabe region have been surveyed by various archaeological projects – including our own – and test excavations have been conducted at 10 of these.[1] The results of all this research confirm Jaimes Betancourt's conclusions, as cited above. They thus refute earlier assessments by Nordenskiöld (1917) and Howard (1947) of possible relationships with ceramics of the Mizque valley, interpretations already disputed by Bennett (1936, 396), but still cited in recent publications (Orellana Halkyer et al. 2014, 589).

There is, nonetheless, at least some evidence for contacts with cultures outside the region, in the form of artefacts made of 'exotic materials' such as stone and metal. Stone is not naturally available in the alluvial deposits of the central Llanos de Mojos, so every piece of stone here must be an import. Stone axes are quite common in private collections and among exhibits in local museums (in Trinidad, San Ignacio de Mojos, or Santa Ana de Yacuma). There are marked differences in the material and shape of these objects, which frequently show traces of prolonged use, sometimes resulting in asymmetric shapes and reduced sizes. Some of these 'axes' seem to have been (re-)used as pendants.

During our excavations at the Loma Mendoza and Loma Salvatierra sites we found 46 stone artefacts and one raw stone. The latter weighed approximately 2 kg, accounting for more than half the total weight of all the stones recovered. To judge from their weight alone, then, a single person could have brought all of these stones into the sites on a single occasion. They were recovered from different contexts, however, spanning the whole period of the sites' occupation. Furthermore, the objects are made of different types of stone (three distinct kinds of sandstone, white quartz, basalt, granite, amazonite and sodalite) indicative of different geographical origins. The amazonite probably came from Brazil and the white quartz from the Iténez region. The objects made of sandstone, granite and basalt could have come either from Chiquitania or from the Andes. The only artefacts that certainly came from the Bolivian highlands are a number of sodalite beads. Cerro de Sapo in the Cochabamba Department has been identified as the unique source of pre-Columbian artefacts made of sodalite found right across the central and southern Andes (Ruppert 1982, 1983), and signs of pre-Hispanic mining have been reported at the site itself (Ahlfeld and Wegner 1931). It is highly probable, then, that the sodalite beads found at Loma Salvatierra also came from Cerro de Sapo, although no chemical analyses have yet been performed.

Metal objects were especially rare at sites in the Casarabe region. Nordenskiöld (1913) found no metal objects in the three mounds that he studied, nor were any found during excavations at Loma Alta de Casarabe (Dougherty and Calandra 1982) or at Loma Mendoza (Prümers 2004). Only at the Salvatierra site were personal adornments found that were made of copper and bronze, and most came from a single grave, radiocarbon dated to c. AD 670–770.[2] This grave was found at the centre of a smaller platform south of the main pyramidal building, and was probably the first in a series of burials in that platform. Everything points to the person in the central tomb having belonged to a dominant class, especially the assemblage of personal adornments found with him (Prümers 2009, 109–13). Among these were three copper discs, that had been part of a headdress, and ear-plugs. They were plain, without any trace of decoration. The biggest disc, with a diameter of 7 cm and a weight of 37.3g, had been perforated near the edge by brute force (see Figure 4.3.3). This detail illustrates that metal objects were unfamiliar, and so argues strongly against the possibility that the discs were cast at the site.

All metal objects from the Salvatierra site have been analysed by energy-dispersive X-ray fluorescence (XRF) spectrometry (Maldonado et al. 2010). The results showed that the three discs were of almost pure copper, while a small folded metal object found in the same grave, in the oral cavity of the dead, was of arsenic bronze. Interestingly, some minor metal fragments found in disturbed contexts near the surface at the top of the main pyramidal building were made of tin bronze, or in one case copper-arsenic-nickel alloy (Table 4.3.1). This might indicate that trade routes had changed over time, such that metal was then obtained from different sources.

0   1   2 cm

Figure 4.3.3   Perforated copper disc from Loma Salvatierra. © Heiko Prümers.

Table 4.3.1 Chemical composition of the metal samples from Loma Salvatierra. © Heiko Prümers.

#	Context	Cu %	Sn %	Fe %	As %	Ag %	Co %	Ni %	Zn %	Pb %	Bi %	Sb %	Te %
1	1005	99.9	<0.05	<0.02	0.01	0.002	<0.005	0.03	<0.2	0.02	<0.01	0.035	<0.005
2	1005	99.9	<0.05	<0.02	0.01	<0.002	0.005	0.02	<0.2	0.02	<0.01	0.033	<0.005
3	1005	99.5	<0.05	<0.02	0.12	<0.002	0.006	0.06	<0.2	0.02	<0.01	0.212	<0.005
4	1005	78.4	<0.05	0.12	20.8	0.554	<0.005	<0.01	<0.2	<0.01	<0.01	<0.005	<0.005
5	4018	80.1	17.8	1.71	0.13	0.008	<0.005	0.08	<0.2	0.05	<0.01	0.077	<0.005
6	301	95.2	<0.05	<0.02	2.73	0.003	0.017	1.92	<0.2	0.01	<0.01	0.089	<0.005
7	301	85.3	12.6	0.21	1.88	0.002	<0.005	0.01	<0.2	<0.01	<0.01	0.017	<0.005
8	301	75.7	20.5	2.53	1.07	0.011	0.006	0.03	<0.2	0.03	<0.01	0.022	<0.005

Evidence from the Baures region

Settlements on natural levees surrounded by ditches are typical of the Baures region. No site has yet been identified as having a succession of overlying occupations, and until recently there was general agreement that these sites date to the latest pre-Hispanic and early colonial times (Dougherty and Calandra 1985a, 47–51; Erickson et al. 2008, 16–17). This view has recently been challenged, however, by new evidence for two earlier occupations radiocarbon dated to cal AD 350–550 and 600–850 (Jaimes Betancourt 2016; Jaimes Betancourt and Prümers 2015; Prümers and Jaimes Betancourt 2017). There is still a gap between these earlier occupations and the later one, dated to cal AD 1300–1500, but continued occupation of the levees should now be entertained as a plausible new working hypothesis. Such occupation would probably have been limited to small settlements that were displaced from time to time within the limited area offered by the individual levees.

Sites delimited by ditches have been reported from other regions of southwest Amazonia, such as the upper Xingú (for example, Heckenberger 2009, 2011), Acre state (for example, Saunaluoma and Schaan 2012; Saunaluoma et al. 2018), and the northernmost lowlands in Bolivia (Arellano López 2002; Arnold and Prettol 1988). A form of shared tradition has been postulated for these sites (Erickson 2008, 170; Mann 2008), but supporting evidence is still rather poor.

Within the Baures region, two distinct ecological settings have resulted in two different settlement patterns. The southern part is flat and exposed to regular flooding, so dispersed natural levees of varying size determined where settlements were established. In contrast, the northern reaches belong to the western outcrops of the Brazilian shield, and are hilly and well drained, so that settlements could be established almost anywhere, and indeed some of them are actually found side by side. As in the Casarabe region, the density and size of pre-Hispanic settlements in the Baures region, especially near the modern village of Bella Vista, is astonishing. In an area of 200 km² mapped with LIDAR, some 20 sites have been documented, among them seven with an enclosed area surpassing 200 ha (Prümers 2014). The sites are often separated by no more than a small depression, and they are within a five-minute walk of each other. No archaeological data are yet available for most of these sites, however, so their chronology and cultural affiliations remain to be determined.

Nevertheless, it is worth noting that among the abundant ceramic material from the sites excavated near the village of Bella Vista and at the Jasiaquiri levee, there are no pieces that show any traits indicating influences from the Andes. On the contrary, vessel forms, decoration technique and the use of *cauixí* as temper all point to a purely Amazonian tradition and a close connection with ceramics from the Guaporé region to the east (Jaimes Betancourt 2014). No 'exotic' materials were found in the excavations, and they are likewise absent from private collections of pre-Hispanic material in the Baures region. Artefacts made of stone are rare, and without specific analysis it is impossible to say where the material they are made of may have come from.

In summary, the archaeological evidence from Baures, just like that known for the Casarabe, San Ignacio, and Santa Ana regions, continues to firmly support Nordenskiöld's observation (1913) that the lowlands of eastern Bolivia were almost completely independent of Andean cultures. This situation might have changed during the final expansion of Inca state, but evidence is still scarce.

Where did all the Incas go?

If the narration of Diego Felipe de Alcaya in his *Cronica cierta* (1636/2011) is as correct as its title claims, then Mango Ynca successfully entered the lowlands of what is today Bolivia with 8,000 warriors and established some sort of Inca colony in a mountainous region located about 500 km ('100 leagues') north-east of the town of Santa Cruz de la Sierra. He then sent his son Guaynaapoc to Cuzco, who arrived there just after the Spaniards had captured Atahuallpa. So he returned to Paytiti accompanied by 'up to 20,000 Indians'. Thus reunited, the 'Lowland Inca' ensured their peaceful reign over 'innumerable provinces of different nations', and 'in the same way as Cuzco was the head in this realm, in that grand kingdom it is now the Paytiti called Mojos' (Alcaya 1636/2011, 245).

Although the Llanos de Mojos are flat and therefore differ considerably from the description of Paytiti given by Alcaya, the region has repeatedly been identified with the 'Paititi' or 'tierra rica' of the chronicles. This is not surprising, given that other chronicles give different descriptions that allow for many different interpretations (see texts in Combès and Tyuleneva 2011; Renard-Casevitz et al. 1988, 101–7; Chapter 5.1). But if the Llanos de Mojos were identical with Paititi, there should be some Inca-related archaeological evidence. None has ever been reported from the region. Negative evidence is of course always a weak argument, but in this case it should at least be borne in mind. Surveys have been conducted along the Orthon river (Arellano López 2002), on the shores of Lake Rogaguado (Echevarría 2008; Tyuleneva 2010, 35–83), along the Apere river (Erickson 2000b; Tyuleneva 2010, 73–81), the Yacuma and Rapulo rivers (Walker 2008a, 2011a), near Exaltación (Tyuleneva 2010, 30–3), Santa Ana de Yacuma (Walker 2004), San Borja (Erickson and Faldín 1978), and San Ignacio (Michel López 1993), and not a single object of Inca provenance has ever been reported. This is all the more surprising since the Quipucamayos[3] maintained that the Inca had conquered 'the Moxos' with gifts. Furthermore, Inca sites and material culture certainly have been encountered on the western and northern borders of the Llanos de Mojos. Several Inca sites have been identified along the Beni river (Álvarez 2002). Unfortunately, little can be said about them, since only the Las Piedras site, at the confluence of the rivers Beni and Madre de Dios, has yet been investigated to any extent (Siiriäinen and Korpisaari 2002, 2003; Siiriäinen and Pärssinen 2001; Pärssinen et al. 2003).

At Las Piedras, only a few ceramic sherds of Classic Inca style have been found, and the stone architecture is unspecific. Nevertheless, other findings of probable Inca provenance have been reported from the area of Riberalta (Siiriäinen and Pärssinen 2001, 64–5), making the interpretation of the Las Piedras site as an Inca fortress more convincing. Even the bronze plate from Northwestern Argentine, known to have been found in 1921 near Riberalta and published as 'Placa del Beni' (Posnansky 1957, 127, Pl. LXXX.A; Ponce Sanginés 1994; Roos 1994), might serve as an additional argument. A recent study of the few known pieces of this highly diagnostic group of objects (Cruz 2011), has convincingly argued for an association with late pre-Inca or Inca times. The same study also demonstrates that the metal plates of this specific group, found in Bolivia and Peru, all came from Inca sites.

Taken together, such evidence clearly indicates Inca presence at Las Piedras. But what kind of presence? According to Alcaya, almost 30,000 Inca settlers entered the lowlands to colonize Paititi, so the scarce evidence from Las Piedras would most plausibly fit with just a temporary military camp. If so, where did the Incas go on to from here?

As shown by Combès (2008, 2011b), an extensive and well-established trade network in silver and gold objects connected ethnic groups between the Guapay river and the Pantanal, and from there southwards to groups along the Paraguay river. One of the sources of the metal, the 'Cerro de Saipurú', had been occupied by the Incas, and recent surveys near the modern village of Saipurú have succeeded in identifying two Inca settlements and the location of the mines (Cruz 2015; Cruz and Guillot 2009). Interestingly, with the exception of Alcaya's *Crónica cierta*, early colonial chronicles make no mention of these mines, which is why Combès (2009, 2011b) has argued that Alcaya's depiction of Paititi should not be rejected out of hand.

Perhaps past researchers have just not looked far enough, because the possibility of Inca incursion into regions so distant from the Andean foothills seemed altogether too fantastic. Cruz and Guillot have now begun to do so, proposing that Inca sites should be sought in the Serrania de San Fernando, the Pantanal, and the Serra dos Paresis of Mato Grosso (Cruz and Guillot 2009, 11; see also Levillier 1976 and Combès 2011b).

To close, then, let me take on the role of a sixteenth-century informant, and state that the *tierra rica* is still far off, and that in all certainty, *Paititi* lies 'over there'.

4.4
The archaeological significance of shell middens in the Llanos de Moxos: Between the Andes and Amazonia

Umberto Lombardo and José M. Capriles[1]

Introduction

The origin of complex societies in Amazonia in relation to the Andes has been one of the most debated topics in South American prehistory. The hypothesis that has driven much of the debate is known as the 'standard model' of Amazonian prehistory (Viveiros de Castro 1996), and suggests that social complexity could not have emerged spontaneously in Amazonia because of the harsh environment. Thus, complex pre-Columbian societies in Amazonia were thought to have been short-lived results of migrations from the Andean highlands, as any attempts to settle in the tropical forest environment by more highly evolved cultures would inevitably have ended in the decline of those cultures into small, nomadic groups (Meggers 1954). Also, the emergence of the pan-Andean ideological system associated with Chavín, often regarded as the mother culture of Andean civilization, was thought to have been rooted in the tropical lowlands of South America. This was due to the pervasive iconographic presence of jaguars, harpy eagles, alligators, snakes, and other animals typically associated with Amazonia (Lathrap 1977).

Although a growing body of research now favours the idea that Andean and Amazonian cultures developed independently (Heckenberger et al. 2007; Neves 2008; Quilter 2014), there are still many unresolved questions regarding the antiquity, direction, and strength of the interaction between Amazonian and Andean societies (Dillehay 2013; Stahl 2004). A particularly important issue is the sudden appearance of complex societies in Amazonia after 2500 BC. The Llanos de Moxos, located near the southern border of the Andes with Amazonia, may prove essential to the debate over if, whether and when cultures from the highlands entered and settled in Amazonia.

This chapter briefly reviews the recent discovery of shell middens dated between 10,600 and 4,000 years ago in the Bolivian Llanos de Moxos, and discusses the implications of these findings for understanding the early peopling, the origins of agriculture, and the emergence of social complexity in south-western Amazonia, and overall, the links between the Andes and Amazonia.

The Llanos de Moxos

During the last millennium before the arrival of the Spaniards, south-western Amazonia was home to important pre-Columbian agricultural societies. The Llanos de Moxos are a large, seasonally flooded savannah situated between the Andes and deeper Amazonia. The region hosts an impressive collection of pre-Columbian earthworks, including monumental mounds, raised fields, ring ditches, fish weirs, canals and causeways (Erickson 2008; Lombardo et al. 2011; Lombardo and Prümers 2010; Prümers and Jaimes Betancourt 2014a; Walker 2008a; Chapter 4.3). The states of Acre and Rondonia in Brazil also host significant evidence of pre-Columbian cultures, although without so diverse a range of earthworks. Taken together, these are the so-called 'geoglyphs', geometric ditches and ridges that probably enclosed ancient villages (Pärssinen et al. 2009), and the oldest dated sites of *terra preta de indios* (Miller 1992 cited in Neves et al. 2003). *Terra preta de indios,* also known as Amazonian Dark Earths, are anthropogenic soils enriched in organic matter, charcoal, nutrients, and fragments of pottery, which resulted from long term occupation of generally nutrient-poor upland soils of the Amazon basin during pre-Columbian times (Arroyo-Kalin 2014; Neves et al. 2003). Finally, south-western Amazonia is also one of the most linguistically diverse regions in the world, home to over 50 languages from eight different lineages and 11 isolates (Crevels and van der Voort 2008; Chapters 3.4 and 3.6), suggesting that many different pre-Columbian societies occupied the area.

'Andes–Amazonia' contacts and influence have often been suggested based on the geographic proximity between Tiwanaku and the Llanos de Moxos (situated less than 300 km apart), the adoption of raised field agriculture in both regions, and the presence of stone axes and even stone monoliths in the lowlands (Hornborg 2005; Ponce Sanginés 1981; Walker 2008b). Although archaeological research in the region has intensified in recent years, we still know very little about the origins of these societies. It is not yet clear, for instance, when the Llanos de Moxos were first occupied by humans; nor how these early populations made the transition towards increasing social and economic complexity; nor how those trajectories were influenced by external forces such as environmental change; nor when and how agriculture here began and spread. The recent discovery of the earliest known archaeological sites in south-west Amazonia, dating back to the early and middle Holocene (Lombardo et al. 2013; Miller 2009; Schmitz et al. 2009;

Chapters 2.1 and 3.6) can help tackle these questions. It is these earliest sites that we report on here.

Older than we realized: Forest islands and shell middens in south-western Amazonia

There are a number of reasons why, notwithstanding a century of archaeological research (Prümers and Jaimes Betancourt 2014a; Chapter 4.3), no early human occupation was reported in the Llanos de Moxos until very recently. Perhaps the most important is that most of the early archaeological sites in the region were later buried by fluvial alluvium c. 4,000 years ago (Lombardo et al. 2013, 2018). The central and southern Llanos de Moxos form part of the southern Amazonian foreland basin of the Andes where sediments eroded from the mountains are constantly deposited by rivers (Lombardo 2014). Also, because the region lacks any stone outcrops, people could not build using stone or make lithic projectile points or other stone tools, but had to use organic materials instead, which decay too fast in Amazonia for sites to be discovered easily. Nevertheless, thanks to a combination of palaeo-environmental and geoarchaeological surveys, including remote sensing, coring and sediment analysis, we have recently identified and dated four early human occupations in the eastern Llanos de Moxos, and test-excavated three of them (Capriles et al. 2019).

The early Llanos de Moxos sites are found underneath what are known as Forest Islands, alias *Islas de Monte* in Bolivia and *Ilhas* or *Aterros* in Brazil. *Islas de Monte* are conspicuous patches of forest that grow on slightly elevated platforms surrounded by savannah (see Figure 4.4.1).

They normally cover less than one hectare and are less than a metre high. Archaeological findings had already suggested that during the late Holocene (roughly between 2,000 and 500 years ago) almost all *Islas de Monte* here were in some way used by pre-Columbian peoples (Erickson 2006; Langstroth Plotkin 1996). Quite how they originated, however, remains controversial. While some authors consider many *Islas de Monte* to be natural formations, mostly the remains of old fluvial levees (Hanagarth 1993; Langstroth Plotkin 1996), others believe that the great majority were actually built by complex societies during that same period of the late Holocene (Erickson 2006).

That is, hitherto these forest island sites had been thought to be associated with human activity only during the last two millennia. The most significant new finding is that a series of forest islands in south-west Amazonia are now revealing evidence of human presence dating back 10,600 years. These early sites are shell middens (Lombardo et al. 2013; Miller 2009; Capriles et al. 2019), that is, prehistoric waste dumps made up of shells intentionally accumulated by humans (Balbo et al. 2011).

Figure 4.4.1 Forest island *Isla del Tesoro* in the south-eastern Llanos de Moxos.
© Umberto Lombardo and José M. Capriles.

Shell middens are found worldwide, mostly along oceanic coastlines, but also along several inland river systems (Claassen 1998). In South America, there are hundreds of shell middens along the Atlantic coast of south-eastern Brazil. Locally known as *sambaquis*, they are often several metres high (Wagner et al. 2011). Smaller shell middens are also common in southern Argentina, where they are known as *concheros* or *conchales* (Briz Godino et al. 2011). Shell middens have also been reported along the Pacific coast, sometimes associated with seasonal oases known locally as *lomas,* but more often with springs and good sources for collecting shellfish (Beresford-Jones et al. 2015; Kennett et al. 2002; Lanning 1967; Latorre et al. 2017). Most of these shell middens date from the early and middle Holocene (between 10,000 and 3,500 years ago) often predating the introduction of cultigens and irrigation agriculture (and see Chapter 3.6 for a discussion of the association between shell middens and early ceramics). In fact, the emergence of social complexity in the Andes has been often associated with the resources provided by coastal environments (Moseley 1974; Quilter et al. 1991; Chapter 1.1). Interestingly enough, some shell middens near the Pacific coast were also associated with the exploitation of inland resources including land snails (see Beresford-Jones et al. 2015).

The shell middens our team has discovered in south-west Amazonia consist of inland deposits formed by the accumulation of fresh-water snails. *Isla del Tesoro,* excavated in 2012 (see Figures 4.4.1 and 4.4.2), is made up primarily of apple snail (*Pomacea* spp.) shells. The earthen platform that forms the forest island is about 4 metres in diameter, stands one metre above the savannah, and descends a metre and half beneath it. The site is surrounded by a depression, which at the end of the rainy season forms a ring of water that encloses the site. A surrounding moat-like ditch is a feature commonly associated with forest islands in Bolivia (Erickson 2008). Like other early Holocene sites, *Isla del Tesoro* at first sight resembles one of the many earthworks that date instead to the late Holocene, millennia later. Archaeological excavations at *Isla del Tesoro* have confirmed its anthropogenic origin, by unearthing dense shell deposits, faunal remains, burnt earth and two human skeletons buried within the shell midden (Lombardo and Capriles 2013). Radiocarbon dates indicate that the site was occupied between 10,500 and 4200 BP (all dates BP herein are calibrated radiocarbon ages BP). The shell midden formed synchronously with a palaeosol (buried soil) that abuts onto it (see Figure 4.4.2). Both the midden and palaeosol were later buried, c. 4,000 years ago, by alluvium deposited by the Grande River (Lombardo et al. 2012). The site was abandoned during this period of environmental instability, and reoccupied c. 2,500 years later (Lombardo et al. 2013).

Another three sites have been investigated in the Llanos de Moxos that also attest to human occupation in the early and middle Holocene (see Figure 4.4.3). We have excavated human burials at two other sites, *Isla San Pablo* and *Isla La Chacra*, although fewer shells were found in these sites suggesting that different sites could have been used in different seasons and for different purposes (Capriles et al. 2019). For instance, snails are most easily collected in the late dry season but hunter-gatherers, being highly mobile, could have exploited different niches at the same time. In addition to the middens in Bolivia, two other early sites have been found in Brazil: in the state of Rondonia, on the eastern bank of the Guaporé River (Miller 2009; Hilbert et al. 2017), and on the banks of the Paraguai River (Schmitz et al. 2009). Both are about 8,000 years old.

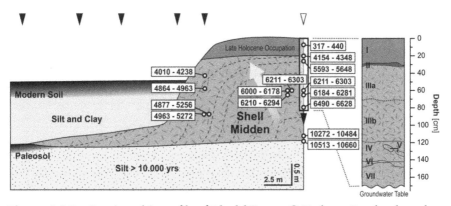

Figure 4.4.2   Stratigraphic profile of *Isla del Tesoro*. © Umberto Lombardo and José M. Capriles.

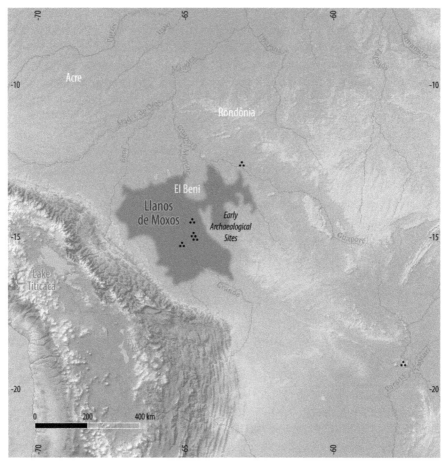

Figure 4.4.3 Map of the Llanos de Moxos, showing the locations of the early and mid-Holocene archaeological sites described in the chapter. © Umberto Lombardo, José M. Capriles and Paul Heggarty.

The discovery of 10,000-year-old shell-midden sites in the Llanos de Moxos, as well as in western Brazil, suggests the presence of humans in the region several thousand years earlier than previously known. Therefore, it would seem that knowledge of these sites may contribute to the discussion about the nature of the long relationship between the Andes and Amazonia, including aspects such as the peopling of South America, the emergence of social complexity, and changing human-environment interactions.

The peopling of inland South America

The earliest archaeological sites in South America have been found along the Pacific and Atlantic coasts (see Borrero 2015; Dillehay 2008). Although the initial peopling of the continent might have followed the coasts, there has been a research bias that has impeded the identification of earlier inland settlements (Capriles and Albarracin-Jordan 2013). At the geographical centre of South America, the shell middens of south-west Amazonia stand between the geographical barrier of the Andes and several thousand kilometres of tropical lowlands. The earliest radiocarbon ages from *Isla del Tesoro* go back to c. 10,600 BP, demonstrating that humans had already occupied the region by the beginning of the Holocene.

Least-cost path analyses have previously suggested that inland routes could have been explored by humans early on, particularly along river systems (Anderson and Gillam 2000). The discovery of the Llanos de Moxos shell middens seems to support this assertion. In contrast to the generalist and highly mobile foraging strategy that might have characterized the earliest human explorers, the shell middens suggest that by the early Holocene, foragers in south-west Amazonia were following increasingly specialized subsistence strategies (cf. Chapter 2.1). The sites studied suggest a pattern of economic reliance on specific resources such as apple snails, wild game and fish, as well as cyclical mobility involving repeated visits to particular sites. In fact, the deep, stratified middens bear evidence of progressive growth over several thousand years as well as their symbolic importance as resting places for human burials (see Figure 4.4.2). We hope that studies of ancient DNA from the bones and teeth retrieved from these sites might greatly further our understanding of the early peopling of South America.

The early Holocene anthropogenic landscape

In a land characterized by minimal topographic relief and seasonal floods, the shell middens of the early and middle Holocene could effectively represent the very first earthworks in the Llanos de Moxos. Besides the four early Holocene sites dated thus far (see Figure 4.4.3), it is likely that many more early sites exist across the vast area of the Llanos de Moxos. For instance, in a recent survey of forest islands in an area of 200 km² near Isla San Pablo, another nine potential sites were found (Zihlmann 2016). Although these have not yet been dated, their stratigraphy is similar to the shell-midden sites already studied, suggesting that they too are early archaeological sites. It seems that the pattern of early human settlement we have identified was more widespread than first anticipated, and that the cultural landscape of south-west Amazonia is much older than has previously been realized. By accumulating snails and other trash remains, early foragers here began to modify their landscape, enhancing its heterogeneity and setting in motion a positive feedback loop of seasonal re-occupation of the same sites. In turn, the activities of these early populations probably contributed to changing the environment itself, by the use of fire. The amount of charcoal, burnt earth, burnt shells and bones found in these sites indicates that fire was used very frequently. Palaeoclimatic data suggests that from 8000 to 4000 BP the climate in south-western Amazonia was drier than today, and the landscape dominated by savannah and dry forest (Carson et al. 2014; Lombardo et al. 2018), more susceptible to natural fires. The discovery of these early sites in what today is part of Amazonia is therefore important for reconstructing human environmental disturbance throughout the Holocene. In Amazonia, lake-core charcoal records of the Holocene show great temporal and spatial variability (Mayle and Power 2008; Urrego et al. 2009), hardly compatible with climate forcing alone. The discovery of early and mid-Holocene archaeological sites supports the hypothesis that this variability could be due in part to human activity (Mayle and Power 2008).

Domestication and the origins of agriculture in Amazonia

Our limited knowledge of the early peopling of Amazonia goes together with a lack of data about plant domestication in the Americas (Piperno and Pearsall 1998). Genetic studies suggest that of all the domesticated cultigens of the Americas, about half seem to have originated in the Amazon basin (Clement 1999), including cassava (or manioc, *Manihot esculenta*), the third most important staple food in the tropics today. Recent studies based on plant genetics indicate that the wild ancestor of domesticated cassava is probably *M. esculenta* ssp. *flabellifolia* (Olsen 2004), which today occurs naturally in the Brazilian states of Mato Grosso, Rondonia and Acre, as well as in neighbouring areas of north-eastern Bolivia (Olsen and Schaal 2001). South-west Amazonia has also been proposed as a possible area for the domestication of the peanut (*Arachis hypogaea*), jack bean (*Canavalia plagiosperma*), two species of chilli pepper (*Capsicum baccatum* and *C. pubescens*) (Piperno 2011a), and the peach palm (*Bactris gasipaes*) (Clement et al. 2010), the only palm domesticated in the Americas.

As yet, however, there are no archaeological data to support these deductions, which are based only on molecular and bio-geographical evidence, mostly because so few early archaeological sites are known in the region (cf. Chapter 1.1). This creates something of a paradox, because the earliest archaeological evidence for some of these crops comes from sites far outside Amazonia (for example, Dillehay et al. 2007; Iriarte 2009; Chapters 2.1 and 2.4). Cassava, for instance, has been found in Colombia dated to 5539–5351 BP, in coastal Chile at 5260–5000 BP, and in coastal Peru at 8500 BP (Piperno 2011a). Moreover, chilli pepper and peanut probably spread in association with cassava (Pickersgill 2007). For these plants to have spread throughout South America during the mid-Holocene, they must have been domesticated earlier.

Arroyo-Kalin (2010) has noted that the starch grains used as archaeological evidence to infer the early domestication of cassava do not in fact necessarily discriminate between wild relatives and the cultigen, so the interpretation of domestication may not be reliable. He argues that cassava may have been domesticated during the mid- to late Holocene, possibly in association with *terra preta* sites. The Llanos de Moxos shell middens offer an ideal depositional context for sampling food residues. Moreover, isotope analysis of dietary staples and human bones, as well as micro-botanical analysis of starch grains and phytoliths within the teeth calculus from burials, may shed light on key questions about the first cultigens in the Americas.

In addition to plant domesticates, south-west Amazonia also offers significant evidence of the domestication of the Muscovy duck (*Cairina moschata*) (Stahl 2005). Preliminary morphological comparisons from specimens found in archaeological sites in eastern Bolivia provide empirical evidence that this species was already being managed, at least, during the late Holocene (Von den Driesch and Hutterer 2012). Yet even though Muscovy duck bones have been found at an increasing number of late Holocene archaeological sites from western Amazonia, it remains uncertain exactly where and when humans began managing this species (Stahl et al. 2006).

The emergence of social complexity in south-western Amazonia

Moving on to the last 2,000 years, the presence of extensive pre-Columbian earthworks, sophisticated pottery, differential burials, and evidence of long-distance trade, attest that complex societies already existed in south-west Amazonia by AD 400 (Erickson 2006; Lombardo and Prümers 2010; Pärssinen et al. 2009; Prümers and Jaimes Betancourt 2014a). Social complexity is here understood as the combination of subsistence intensification, political integration and social stratification following population growth (Johnson and Earle 2000).

Thus far, the limited archaeological evidence available from the Llanos de Moxos has suggested that at least some of these cultures came from outside the region. For instance, similarities in pottery and language have been suggested as evidence that some of the Llanos de Moxos cultures originated in central Amazonia (Michel López and Lémuz Aguirre 1992; Walker 2011b). On the other hand, the uniqueness of some pottery styles found in the Llanos de Moxos (Jaimes Betancourt 2013); the fact that some of the languages spoken here do not seem to have any relation with languages spoken elsewhere (Crevels and van der Voort 2008); as well as the peculiarity of some of the earthworks found (Lombardo et al. 2011), suggest that the Llanos de Moxos was a centre of innovation where social complexity emerged, rather than a recipient place that was 'invaded' by groups stemming from other regions.

The identification, dating and description of early foraging practices in the Llanos de Moxos and along the Guaporé and Paraguai Rivers is important for understanding the period before social complexity emerged in south-west Amazonia. The discovery of early shell middens in the Llanos de Moxos supports the hypothesis of the independent emergence of social complexity in the region. However, some level of social interaction between the Andes and Amazonia cannot be ruled out. Given the finding of copper ornaments in a burial in *Loma Salvatierra* (Prümers and Jaimes Betancourt 2014a) suggesting the existence of trade, and the proximity between the two regions, it is likely that some experimentation with domestication and exchange of plants did occur. As research carried out by Dillehay (2013) on the north coast of Peru implies, people throughout South America might have been experimenting with a variety of cultigens for a very long time (see also Kistler et al. 2018; Chapters 2.1 and 2.4).

Demographic pressure has been identified as a key element for triggering the processes that lead to social complexity (Smith et al. 2012). In the Llanos de Moxos, a demographic surge in the mid-Holocene could have led to increasing pressure on wild resources, explaining the recourse to low-return resources such as apple snails. This could eventually have led to increasing reliance on cultivated plants, and at length to the emergence of institutionalized social inequality during the late Holocene. Given that the two shell middens we have excavated also contain human burials, one might speculate that these sites could effectively have functioned as territorial markers legitimized by social memory and ancestor veneration (see Hastorf 2003).

An intriguing question on the relationship between the shell middens of the early and mid-Holocene (10,600–4000 BP) and the complex societies of the late Holocene (AD 400–1500) emerges from the time gap of 2,500 years that separates these occupations. It is still not fully understood why the sites we have so far investigated were abandoned after 4,000 BP, but in the case of *Isla del Tesoro*, we believe that it was caused by a change of course of the Grande River, which flooded the area and covered the site with a 1.5-metre-thick layer of sediments (Lombardo et al. 2012). It is certainly possible that a synergy between environmental instability and population migrations led to the abandonment of the shell midden mode of life in the Llanos de Moxos. The time gap observed between the hunter-gatherer occupation of the early and middle Holocene and the complex societies of the late Holocene in the Llanos de Moxos coincides with important innovations such as the adoption of ceramics, and of maize as a staple cultigen. Interestingly enough, this time gap also coincides with the emergence and consolidation of a number of regional 'formative' polities in the Andes, including Chavín (cf. Chapter 2.4). Unfortunately, we are still far away from understanding the exact processes that were involved in shaping these cultural changes. Further research is needed to delimit the area that was affected by the mid- to late Holocene environmental change, and to identify new sites outside this area that bear a continuous archaeological record, such as the shell midden in Rondonia recently investigated by Neves (personal communication).

Part 5

Age of Empires: Inca and Spanish colonial perspectives

5.1

The Amazonian Indians as viewed by three Andean chroniclers

Vera Tyuleneva
(Translated by Adrian Pearce from the Spanish original)

A few years after the conquest, when the first Spanish expeditions began to push into the Amazon forests on the trail of abundant and enticing 'noticias ricas' (news of rich lands), their imagination had already been piqued by certain notions as to what they would find in this mysterious and inhospitable region. These ideas drew in part on the expectations and preconceptions brought from the Old World, but mostly they came from local sources. In most of the early Peruvian chronicles, the first images of the Amazonian Indians came only through the filter of the Andean perspective.

In 1981, Renard-Casevitz remarked that the view of the *montaña* (high jungle of the Eastern Andean slopes) and the Amazonian lowlands from the Andes is always a view from the top down, from 'civilization' to 'barbarism'. This perspective was developed over many centuries during the pre-Columbian era by the close links and opaque frontiers between the two regions, by exchange and migration, as well as by conflict, rivalry and prejudice. The limited success of the Inca state in its eastward expansion – simply compare the size of the empire from north to south, as opposed to its obvious narrowness from east to west – and the difficulties in defining and controlling the jungle peripheries turned the Amazonian Indian into the principal bearer of the stamp of 'otherness', indomitable and to be feared, respected in some regards, dismissed and mocked in others.

All the Peruvian chronicles that discuss the natives of the montaña and the lowland plains bear to a greater or lesser extent this stamp of Andean prejudices. To analyse them in the most illustrative and concise way, I here take three canonical texts: the *Nueva Corónica* by Guamán Poma de Ayala, the *Comentarios Reales* by Garcilaso de la Vega, and the *Relación de antigüedades* of Joan de Santa Cruz Pachacuti Yamqui. (For further discussion of Guamán Poma, see Chapter 5.2 by Bertazoni.) Of course, this selection of texts is somewhat arbitrary and might be challenged on a number of grounds. For example, it might be noted that Garcilaso de la Vega's writings are more riddled with European clichés than those of many Spanish authors, despite his blood relation to the land of his birth. It could also be argued that another chronicler, Juan de Betanzos, had a more immediate and prolonged contact with noble circles in Cuzco. Nevertheless, to set ourselves a task achievable within the constraints of this brief chapter, we shall limit ourselves to these three sources.

Of course, 'the Andes' constitute no uniform or undifferentiated mass. Each of the authors discussed here came from a different social and geographical context: Garcilaso from the native and *mestizo* nobility in Cuzco, Guamán Poma from the Yarovilca ethnic group of Huánuco, and Pachacuti Yamqui from the province of Canas and Canchis. This necessarily entails differences in their respective backgrounds and view-points. In addition, it should be remembered that the 'Andean perspective', in its pure state, is mediated in these documents by several decades of drastic cultural change, and that what we trace here is in truth only its remote echoes.

So far as is known, none of our three authors was particularly familiar with Amazonia. This is readily substantiated in the case of Guamán Poma by reference to his celebrated mapamundi, in which the eastern regions are compressed into a narrow strip of thick jungle inhabited, among other creatures, by unicorns and winged dragons, and through which meanders the solitary and unrealistic Marañón river (Guamán Poma de Ayala 1615/2008, ff.983–4 [1001–2]; mapamundi reproduced in Chapter 5.2).[1] Pachacuti Yamqui, in a passage devoted to female warriors (a clearly Amazonian motif), includes Coquimbo, Chile and Tucumán among the neighbouring provinces, opening up an enormous geographical panorama (Pachacuti c. 1613/1993, f.29r). The most learned of the three, Garcilaso (who may have travelled in his youth to the coca fields of Cosñipata, in Amazonian lowlands near Cuzco) makes a typical mistake when he supposes that the Madre de Dios (Amarumayu) is a tributary of the River Plate. None of the three, in describing the jungle 'savages', gives evidence of having had direct contact with them.

'Nations' and 'provinces'

Firstly, let us consider the proper nouns (ethnonyms and 'provincial' names) associated with the eastern regions by each of our chroniclers. Among the most frequently recurring terms are *Anti*, *Chuncho* and *Chiriguana*. We know that in historical sources devoted to given regions of Amazonia, these names have more specific meanings: the *Antis* are generally Arawak-speaking groups (Machiguenga and Asháninka, among others) of the upper Madre de Dios, the Urubamba, the lower Apurimac and their tributaries (Renard-Casevitz et al. 1988, 81–99). The *Chunchos* generally inhabit the lower Madre de Dios, the left bank of the Beni river, and Apolobamba; most of them were speakers of Tacanan languages (see

Tyuleneva 2012, 49; Ferrié 2018). The *Chiriguanas* are the Guaraní who raided along the south-eastern frontiers of Tahuantinsuyu (Combès 2010, 129–138). In our three authors, however, these terms are used generically, with neither ethnic sensibility nor any very clearly defined territories.

Anti or *Ande* is the vaguest and most general term. Since it was used to denominate one of the four *suyus* or 'quarters' of the Inca Empire, it was often applied by Peruvian chroniclers to the whole of the population of this 'Antisuyu'. To add to the confusion, it was later used to refer to the entire mountain range of western South America, which thus became the 'Andes' that we know today. Thus, the Andes–Amazonia duality present in the colonial texts now seems inverted to us: in their formulations of highlands/Andes, or Cuzco/Andes, or Peru/Andes, the term 'Andes' in fact refers to the *Amazonian* region. In principle, Antisuyu formed part of the Inca state. In practice, when the chroniclers tell of Inca expeditions against the *Antis/Andes*, it is understood that they are referring to vastly greater territories, whose limits extend eastwards beyond the visible horizon (see Guamán Poma de Ayala 1615/2008, f.103, f.154 [156], f.269 [271], f.292 [294], f.323 [325], ff.983–4 [1001–2]; Pachacuti c. 1613/1993, f.23r, f.27v, f.29r; Garcilaso 1609/ 1985, book 4, chap. XVI; book 7, chap. XIII–XIV).

In Guamán Poma, *Chuncho* seems to be synonymous with *Anti/Ande*, and in many passages the two names are used together (Guamán Poma de Ayala 1615/ 2008, f.103, f.323 [325], f.439 [441], f.461 [463], f.1073 [1083]). On one occasion, a hybrid term is even coined: *Andesuyo-Chuncho* (f.154 [156]). In his mapamundi, the 'warlike Indians called *Anti Suyo Chunchos*' occupy a peripheral region between the known world and the jungles inhabited by monsters and wild beasts (ff.983–4 [1001–2]). For Garcilaso, by contrast, the warlike *Chuncho* inhabitants of the lower section of the Madre de Dios appear to be a sub-group of the *Antis* (book 7, chap. XIV).

All three chroniclers mention the *Chiriguana*. Guamán Poma calls them *Chiriuanais* and counts them among the tribes of the montaña (f.873 [887], f.901 [915]), although he places them not in Antisuyu but in Collasuyu (f.271 [273], f.325 [327]). Pachacuti Yamqui only mentions them in passing (f.39v). Garcilaso, who devotes greatest attention to them, classifies them among the *Antis* and sets them to the east of Charcas, in 'very bad lands', 'of very little use'. He presents them as the model and maximum expression of barbarity: 'the natives were most savage, worse than the wild beasts'. Their name was evoked to frighten small children (book 7, chap. XVII). Not entirely without gratification, Garcilaso compiles a long list of examples of their bestial behaviour: they had neither laws nor 'good customs'; they built neither villages nor houses; 'they went naked'; they practised incest between close relatives; they ate human flesh and drank human blood, and preferred human flesh to that of animals; they attacked neighbouring villages and killed all their captives so as to eat them; they ate their own dead; they had no religion; and they buried their dead (or rather, the bones left over from their feasts) in crevices in the crags or hollows in the trees. As we shall see, many of these reprehensible characteristics were often attributed to Amazonian natives in general.

Anti, Chuncho and Chiriguana as generic terms for the Indians of the eastern regions are not, of course, exclusive to the texts of Guamán Poma, Pachacuti Yamqui and Garcilaso de la Vega. They are found in most of the documents that, in one way or another, seek to sketch out a portrait of Amazonia as seen from the Andes. Let us now consider some of the more concrete names used by each of our authors.

Both Pachacuti Yamqui (f.27v, f.29r) and Guamán Poma (f.176 [178], f.323 [325], f.784 [798], f.901 [915], f.982 [1000], ff.983–4 [1001–2], f.1032 [1040], f.1064 [1074], f.1073 [1083], f.1074 [1084]), two chroniclers known for their fluency in Quechua, repeatedly use the term Guarmi Auca/Uarmi Auca, which can be literally translated as 'woman warrior(s)'. Pachacuti Yamqui includes a passage referring to 'a province solely of women' (f.27v), and then adds that Inca troops conquered the land of the Guarmi Aucas 'where they left a group of men to serve as stud [para que servieran de garañones]' (f.29r).

Guamán Poma does not comment explicitly on the meaning of the term Uarmi Auca, but in his chapter on fiestas in Antisuyu, he describes the dance of this name, performed by men dressed up as women: 'dancing in a circle holding hands, they make merry and have their fiesta and dance Uarmi Auca, all the men dressed like women with their feathers' (f.323 [325]). These, doubtless, are the famous 'Amazons' or 'women without husbands', who feature on every respectable list of South American geographical myths (see for example Levillier 1976).

In Guamán Poma (but not Pachacuti Yamqui), the name Uarmi Auca is closely associated with another term that morphs between a proper name and an ethnonym: Ancauallo. Often, the two terms appear together, with no comma to separate them, and seem to refer to the same group. The mapamundi describes them as 'warlike Indians who were not conquered by the Incas, called Uarmiauca Anquuallo' (this distinguishes them from the Antis/Chunchos who were subjects of the Incas). They inhabit 'another sierra towards the Northern Sea', a hypothetical range that extended along the whole Atlantic coast, beyond the woods with unicorns and dragons, clearly beyond tangible geographical space (ff.983–4 [1001–2]).

Ancauallo (or Hanco Huallu) Chanca is quite a popular figure in the Andean chronicles, most of which place him in the time of the war between the Incas and the Chancas, and immediately thereafter. This is the case with Pachacuti Yamqui (ff.18r–20v) and Garcilaso (book 5, chap. XXVI; for the versions by other authors, see also Nir 2008). Generally, Ancauallo is a Chanca chief or captain, who makes a temporary alliance with the Incas after the war, but ultimately opts for independence and flees with his people towards undefined eastern regions. Some authors identify these regions with Chachapoyas, while others seem to point further to the south. Guamán Poma and Pachacuti Yamqui convert Ancauallo's name into an ethnonym that includes all of his fugitive subjects (see Pachacuti, f.20v: 'The Ancoallos go deep into the montaña carrying their idol').

In Guamán Poma, Ancauallo Changa is a semi-mythical figure from the time of Manco Capac, and emerges from a lake with fifty billion Indians,[2] with ambitions to 'become Inca' (in what is probably a metamorphosis of the motif of the Chanca invasion itself), and is finally killed by the true Inca. The numerous subjects of Ancouallo, taking his name as their ethnonym, 'withdrew to the montaña and passed over to the other part of the Northern Sea, in the lands and sierra beyond the montaña, a cold and hard territory where they remain to this day, and they are pagan Indians' (f.85).

The linked pair formed by the names *Ancouallo* and *Uarmi Auca* in the chronicle of Guamán Poma is not easy to explain. At first glance, they could be interpreted simply as the names of two neighbouring groups. But on several occasions, the two are so intimately united that they seem rather to be two parts of the same ethnonym. If we recall the 'stud men' that, according to Pachacuti Yamqui, the Inca army left behind among the *Guarmi Aucas*, and also if (getting ahead of ourselves for a moment) we reference the Inca expedition to the *Musus*, described by Garcilaso, when the Inca soldiers receive *Musu* women as wives, then a recurrent pattern emerges based on the formation of Andean enclaves in the lowlands out of a masculine element of Andean or newcomer origin and a local, feminine counterpart. Perhaps the *Ancouallo–Uarmi Auca* duo provides a further example of this pattern, albeit a rather sketchy one.

It is worth pausing to consider the ritual dance called *Uarmi Auca*, described by Guamán Poma as the most representative of the Antisuyu festivals: 'the fiesta of the Andesuyos from Cuzco to the montaña and the other part towards the Northern Sea is sierra [sic]. They sing and dance Uarmi Auca, Ancauallo. There are many pagan people, the Antis and Chunchus sing and dance' (f.323 [325]). Although we cannot be sure whether this author saw the dance with his own eyes, it seems clear from the context that this is no imaginary fiesta from the impossibly remote lands of the *Uarmi Auca*, but rather the tradition of another group of *Antis*, nearer to the highlands, who personify the *Uarmi Auca*. The description has an accompanying drawing (f. 322 [324]) which bears the annotation 'Curipata anti'. This name might offer a clue as to the specific location in which the dance was held – Coripata, in the Bolivian *yungas*? – though in the times of the chronicler, Coripata must have been a relatively common toponym. The custom of representing ethnic groups from distant regions through dance, with masks and costumes, persists to this day in Paucartambo (which, it might be noted, formed part of the highland extension of Antisuyu), and in many other places in the Peruvian highlands. It is possible that Guamán Poma's notion of the *Uarmi Auca* was formed precisely on the basis of this dance and the interpretation accorded to it.

Today, a widespread theory would have it that the legend of the 'Amazons' of South America, who feature in colonial texts, was simply imported to the local context from the classical tradition of the Old World. But the evident popularity of the Quechua expression *Guarmi Auca*, and above all the existence of a dance with the same name, might be taken as evidence of the indigenous roots of this geographical legend. It appears that the tribe of warrior women provoked abundant comment in the Andes even before the arrival of the Europeans.

Turning our attention to Pachacuti Yamqui's *Relación*, in addition to the *Guarmi Aucas*, we find a series of other jungle 'nations' and 'provinces' mentioned in the context of Inca incursions into the eastern regions (see also Tyuleneva 2011). Among them are the Opatiri and Manare, both of which names Renard-Casevitz identifies with the Arawak and related groups of the upper Madre de Dios, Urubamba, and Apurimac (Renard-Casevitz et al. 1988, 81–99).

But the most striking 'province' of all those listed by Pachacuti Yamqui is that of *Escay Oyas* ('two faces' in Quechua): '[the Inca expedition] encountered a great kingdom, called Escay Oya, a rich land, and its people far more warlike than any of the nations here, who it is said feed on human flesh. And they know how to shoot poisonous and venomous [arrows] like people who make pacts with devils, and they are great bowmen, with whom two very hard battles were fought'. Pachacuti also mentions in passing that 'this province is called Dorado' (f.28r). This latter detail brings to mind one of so many versions of the 'news of rich lands' that circulated in the Andes at the time, raising hopes and drawing hundreds of dreamers beyond the world of maps. Renard-Casevitz, giving Pachacuti Yamqui's text a more tangible and concrete orientation, identifies its *Escay Oya* with the *Iscaycingas* (two-noses) of other chronicles, and places them on the river Ene (Renard-Casevitz et al. 1988, 89).

Garcilaso demonstrates familiarity with the geography of the upper Madre de Dios (the details of which he notes with considerable accuracy in sections devoted to the conquest of the coca-producing valleys by Inca Roca: book 4, chap. XVI), though his knowledge of the rest of the eastern regions is sketchy at best. His most extensive reference to Amazonia is structured around the Inca expedition to the *Musus* or *Mojos*. Throughout the colonial period this name, the widespread use of which seems to date from the expedition of Pedro Anzúrez to the river Tuichi in 1538–9 (Tyuleneva 2015), was applied to widely dispersed locations and became one of the most sought-after of the shifting goals of the treasure-hunters. Its application to the savannahs of the Mamoré (Llanos de Mojos) is probably a late phenomenon (see Combès 2012; Tyuleneva 2012, 188–98).

Garcilaso's 'province' of the *Musus/Mojos*, 'a land with many warlike people, fertile in its own way', supposedly lay 200 leagues from Cuzco in a little-defined region. It was reached via the Amarumayu (Madre de Dios), which for Garcilaso united all the great rivers of southern South America, and in turn joined (according to him) the River Plate. The Incas reached the *Musus* exhausted, their ranks thinned after conflicts with the *Chunchos* of the river banks (a clear distinction is made here between the *Chunchos* and the *Musus*). The *Musus* 'rejoiced to receive the friendship of the Incas and to embrace their idolatry, laws, and customs, for they seemed good to them, and they promised to govern themselves by them and to worship the Sun as their principal god. But they did not wish to submit to the Inca as vassals, since he had not conquered them and subjected them by arms ... The Musus gave them their daughters as wives and rejoiced in the relationship they thus formed, and today hold them in great veneration and are ruled by them in peace and war'. It is an idyllic portrait, in line with the general tenor of the *Comentarios*, in which the main goal of the well-meaning Incas was 'to raise [the Amazonian 'nations'] out of the barbarous and inhuman customs they had, and to bring them knowledge of their father the Sun' (book 7, chap. XIV).

Characteristics of Amazonians as seen from the Andes

We turn next to considering those general characteristics attributed to all the natives of Amazonia by our three authors.

Nudity, body decoration, use of feathers

Nudity is among the most typical and obvious attributes that distinguish the 'savages' of Antisuyu from the 'political nations' of the Andean highlands. In four of the six of Guamán Poma's drawings that show the inhabitants of Antisuyu, they appear naked or semi-naked (f.155, f.175 [177], f.291 [293], f.322 [324]), and in the written text of the *Corónica* this aspect is also reiterated several times (f. 323 [325], f.334 [336], f.948 [962]). By contrast, Guamán Poma's *Ancauallos* 'have clothes like the Indians of this kingdom', apparently due to their 'civilized' Andean origins (f.323 [325]). The section devoted to the noble lady of Antisuyu, Capac Mallquima, reads: 'this said lady, though they are well made and very beautiful, whiter than a Spanish lady, nevertheless they wear [only] bunches of grass, and some of them stripped naked, for this is their caste and nature, both men and women' (f.176 [178]). Guamán Poma is unique among the three chroniclers in remarking upon the physical appearance of the *Antis*, emphasizing their light complexion with some admiration ('they are very white, like the Spanish', f.901 [915]). It is not possible to say with certainty whether degree of whiteness as an aesthetic criterion existed in the Andes prior to the Spanish conquest, or if it responds to an imported scale of prestige. Garcilaso also mentions the nudity of the *Chunchos*: 'because that land and region are very hot, they went about naked, with only loincloths' (book 7, chap. XIV).

Other common motifs in descriptions of the appearance of the *Antis* and the *Chunchos* include body paint: 'they are stained and smeared all over their bodies with *mantor* [annato, a reddish pigment]' (Guamán Poma de Ayala 1615/2008, f.176 [178]); 'their faces, arms and legs are coloured with red ochre, and their whole bodies, with different colours' (Garcilaso 1609/1985, book 7, chap. XIV); and feather adornments: 'they wore great feathered headdresses, of parrot and macaw' (Garcilaso 1609/1985, book 7, chap. XIV). Guamán Poma includes impressive feather headdresses and adornments in his drawings showing the *Anti* captain Capac Apo Ninarua (f.167 [169]; image reproduced in Chapter 5.2) and the dancers of the *Uarmi Auca* (f.322 [324]), and writes of 'feather costumes' in funeral rites in Antisuyu (f.292 [294]).

Worship of jaguars and snakes, and other aspects of religion

As well as what was understood as the inferiority and barbarism of the appearance of Amazonians, a further series of stereotypes referred to their spiritual barbarity. Andean beliefs, regarded as 'enlightened', are set in opposition to the 'savage' Amazonian cults. All three chroniclers were good Catholics, and for these writers, Christian norms were the basic reference point and measure of all things. Inca religion, on this scale, occupied an intermediate level; for Garcilaso, it sat not far from the monotheistic standard, to which he sought at any cost to compare his own simplified version of the cult of the sun and the worship of the supposed creator god. Meanwhile, the spiritual universe of the hapless *Antis* lay sunk in the most brutal form of paganism.

Garcilaso does not go into any great detail, limiting himself to a dismissive comment on the 'animals, sticks and stones, and other vile things' worshipped by the *Musus* (book 7, chap. XIV). Pachacuti Yamqui accuses the *Escay Oya* people of 'having pacts with demons' (f.28r). Guamán Poma pays the greatest attention to the topic of religion and beliefs: 'they worship the jaguar, the otorongo, and the amaro, the snake, the serpent, they worship out of fear, not because these things are *uacas* or idols, but because they are fierce animals that eat people, they think that if they worship them they will not be eaten' (f.269 [271]). In Pachacuti Yamqui's *Relación*, when the Incas undertake the first conquest of Antisuyu beyond the Paucartambo cordillera, they encounter a 'fearsome snake, which they say ate many people'; it is defeated by an eagle (f.23r). The serpent figures as a symbol of the Antis, while the eagle protects the Inca army.

Guamán Poma relates how Inca Roca and his son, Otorongo Achachi, both members of Inca royalty who nevertheless had close blood ties with Antisuyu, possessed the ability to turn themselves into jaguars: 'they say that [Inca Roca] could turn into a jaguar, and his son as well, and that is how he conquered any *Chuncho*' (f.103, see also ff.155–4 [156]). Another object of veneration among the *Antis* mentioned by Guamán Poma is the coca leaf (f.269 [271]). In his account, it was precisely Inca Roca and his son who introduced the use of coca among the Incas, importing it from Antisuyu (f.103, f.154 [156]). Garcilaso similarly relates the reign of Inca Roca to the establishment of the coca fields of the valleys of the upper Madre de Dios (book 4, chap. XVI), but fails to mention the ceremonial use of the plant among the *Antis*.

Guamán Poma describes funerary rites in Antisuyu thus: 'As soon as [the deceased] takes his last breath, they dress him in certain feather costumes they make, and they remove the feathers, and strip him and wash him, and they begin to butcher him, and they take the bones and the Indians carry them off, and neither the men nor the women weep, and they place them in a tree they call *uitaca*, where the worms have made a hole, they place them there and they seal it all very well. And from that moment, they never see him again in all their lives, nor do they remember him, and neither do they know any other ceremony like the Indians of the highlands' (f.292 [294]; see also Chapter 5.2). Though Guamán Poma was a true and faithful Catholic, his voice here betrays a discreet reproach, not only for the custom of cannibalizing the bodies, but for the absence of laments and ceremonial and for the fact that the deceased is never to be seen again. From the context it is clear that a dignified, respectful treatment of the dead consists of a burial with grave goods, accompanied by a given set of rituals, with periodic subsequent acts of homage and care.

Warlike behaviour

Despite their 'beastlike' customs, the natives of Antisuyu are presented as valiant warriors and honourable adversaries, which helps to justify the repeated failure of Inca military undertakings in the east. Guamán Poma attributes warlike qualities both to the *Ancouallos* (f.85, f.982 [1000]) and to the *Antis-Chunchos* (ff.983–4 [1001–2]), emphasizing that, in contrast to many docile Andean groups, the 'Indians of the montaña' often presented violent resistance to the Spaniards (f.1068 [1078]). As mentioned, Pachacuti Yamqui writes of the province of the *Escay Oyas*: 'the people there [are] far more warlike than any of the nations here' (f.28r). Garcilaso tells of the exhausting battles that the Inca expedition had to fight on its way to the *Musus*, and describes their province itself as 'a land peopled by many warlike folk', whose inhabitants refuse to submit to the military might of Tahuantinsuyu (book 7, chap. XIV).

The three chroniclers, like many other authors, comment on the skill of the Amazonian natives with bow and arrow, a warlike art quite different from Andean tactics and weapons. Guamán Poma portrays both Otorongo Achachi, the Inca prince with jungle allegiances (f.155), and the captain of Antisuyu Capac Apo Ninarua (f.167 [169]), with a bow and arrows (illustrations reproduced in Chapter 5.2). He also states that the dressed-up dancers of the *Uarmi Auca* carried arrows while they danced (f.323 [325]). The *Escay Oyas* of Pachacuti Yamqui are 'great bowmen' (f.28r). The *Chunchos* of Garcilaso carry 'bows and arrows as weapons of war, which are what all the nations of the Antis use most often' (book 7, chap. XIV). To this traditional Amazonian weapon, Pachacuti Yamqui adds the ability to 'shoot poisonous and venomous [arrows]' (f.28r).

Cannibalism

Cannibalism is the most notorious and scandalous feature of life among the Indians of the montaña, and what definitively sets them apart from the 'political' Andean societies. Garcilaso emphasizes cannibalism only in the above-mentioned case, of the *Chiriguanas*, but not when he writes of the *Anti*, the *Chuncho*, or the *Musu*. Pachacuti Yamqui gives us but a terse note to the effect that the *Escay Oyas* tribe 'feeds on human flesh' (f.28r). By contrast, Guamán Poma devotes two passages to this matter. In his chapter on funerary customs among the *Antis*, he describes their mortuary cannibalism: 'since they are Indians of the montaña who eat human flesh, and so the deceased has barely expired when they begin to eat him, so that they leave no flesh but only bones' (f.292 [294]). On campaign in Quito, the army of Huayna Capac took with it several *Anti* warriors, including the celebrated Capac Apo Ninarua, 'only so they could eat the rebel Indians, and thus these people ate many chiefs' (f.167–8 [169–70]). As a punishment for serious offences, noble Andean women 'are given to the Anti Indians to be eaten, and they eat them alive' (f.312 [314]). Tupac Yupanqui, Guamán Poma's favourite Inca emperor, 'had with him the chiefs of the naked Chuncho Indians, who eat human flesh, for the memory and greatness of the world' (f.948 [962]). A common moniker for the Amazonian natives in the *'Corónica'* is 'Anti runa micoc', that is: 'man-eating Anti' (f.323 [325]).

Inhospitable lands and natural riches

The natural environment that framed the savage lives of the *Antis/Chunchos* was a sphere of extremes and contradictions, where the greatest challenges to human life were juxtaposed with fabulous riches. Garcilaso states that in the Antisuyu there were both rich provinces ('one of the best' was that of the *Musus*), and completely inhospitable and even scarcely penetrable ones 'because of the great mountains, lakes, swamps and marshes' (book 7, chap. XIII). It seems that Garcilaso himself visited the 'mountain called Cañac-huay, which drops almost vertically five leagues, and makes one nervous and fearful simply to see it', on the way down from the Paucartambo cordillera towards the Cosñipata valleys (book 4, chap. XVI). Guamán Poma states that towards the rich land of the *Ancauallo* 'it is impossible to pass through, because in the rivers there are lizards and serpents and poisonous snakes, lions, jaguars, ounces, and many other animals, and hard and mountainous lands' (f.982 [1000]).

In all three chronicles the echoes of 'news of rich lands' resonate powerfully, which might suggest a pre-Columbian origin for the Andean belief in the existence of populous and prosperous lands to the east. Guamán Poma speaks wonders of the unattainable province of the *Ancouallo Uarmi Aucas*: 'It is said there are many Indians with a great many costumes and lineages … and that there is much gold and silver and much land and cattle, and the land is fertile' (f.85); similar comments are scattered throughout his work (f.168 [170], f.176 [178], f.982 [1000]).

Pachacuti Yamqui states that the province of the *Escay Oyas* is that which was called Dorado, and so concealed great mineral riches (f.28r). The Inca expedition to the *Guarmi Aucas*, described in the same document, brought back 'a great quantity of the finest gold to Cuzco. And so the Inca, having seen so much good quality gold brought back, had sheets of gold made to serve as tapestries in Coricancha' (the main temple of the Sun: f.29r). The motif of Amazonian gold used to adorn Coricancha is also present in the chronicle of Betanzos (see Tyuleneva 2011). Another anecdote related to the riches of the eastern regions and recounted by Pachacuti Yamqui tells of the arrival in Cuzco from the 'Andes of Opatari' of 300 'Andes Indians, all loaded with gold in dust and nuggets'.

Behind these repeated references to precious metals undoubtedly lay the real riches of the gold-bearing jungle regions of the Madre de Dios, Carabaya, Apolobamba, and Larecaja. But in other cases the notion of wealth extended beyond gold and silver alone. For example, Garcilaso's province of the *Musus* was rich and attractive not because it possessed highly prized minerals, which are not even mentioned, but because it was fertile and populated.

Andean enclaves in Amazonia

Finally, a prominent aspect present in the three texts is the notion of Andean enclaves established in Amazonia. In Guamán Poma, the enclave is that of the *Chancas Ancouallo*, in a rich but inaccessible land on the edges of the continent, who form a curious union with the *Uarmi Aucas*, the women warriors; in Pachacuti Yamqui, the reference is to the 'stud' Incas who remain behind among the *Guarmi Aucas*, in a land also associated with riches; in Garcilaso's *Comentarios*, it was the remnants of the Inca army lodged in the fertile province of the *Musus* and married to women of the region. It requires little effort to see common traits in all three accounts.

We know that the legend of the 'fugitive Incas' remained current for many decades after the Spanish conquest and that in part it was based on traditions regarding the kingdom of Vilcabamba. However, close study of the three versions described here might lead us to suppose that the motif of the Andean colony in the lowlands precedes the arrival of the Europeans and dates to pre-Columbian times. It might also be surmised that before the 'fugitive Incas' there were the 'fugitive Chancas'; or perhaps both versions coexisted in parallel.

Conclusion

Self-evidently, to reconstruct solidly and consistently the concepts regarding Amazonia that prevailed in the Andes in Inca times represents an impossible task.

What is possible is to capture the reflections of these concepts scattered throughout the colonial sources. And many of the more persistent stereotypes remain alive and well even today.

In recent decades, there has been a growing tendency to erase regional frontiers, to seek routes of connection instead of dividing lines, and continuity instead of rupture. Conflicts, contradictions, prejudices, and opposing views are part of this continuity. They are an undeniable manifestation of diversity, and the logical fruit of contacts and interactions.

5.2
The place of Antisuyu in the discourse of Guamán Poma de Ayala

Cristiana Bertazoni

This chapter explores the place occupied by Antisuyu within the Inca worldview through the lens of one of our best sources of information for this topic – the c. 1615 manuscript *El Primer Nueva Corónica y Buen Gobierno*, by Felipe Guamán Poma de Ayala. That chronicle stands out among colonial manuscripts written by native Andeans by virtue of the multitude of images integral to the text, that make for a unique document combining alphabetical and visual elements to describe both the Inca and early colonial periods. It was written in Spanish in the form of a letter to King Philip III of Spain, with some parts in Quechua (as well as minor additions in other Andean languages) and includes around 400 drawings. Guamán Poma's work represented the first generation of writing from what is now Latin America and is characterized by a strong critique of Spanish rule in the Andes and of abuses against the native population. For further discussion of this author, see Chapter 5.1.

Of central importance to the present book, *Nueva Corónica* offers us an almost uniquely native interpretation and an invaluable record of a period when the position of Antisuyu in Andean history was shifting decisively. As we will see, Antisuyu occupied a rather ambiguous place within the Inca worldview. On the one hand, conceptually, it was seen as an integral part of the empire, one of its four *suyus* or quarters. As one of those quarters, and connected symbolically with Chinchaysuyu, the most important region according to the Inca system, the empire itself could hardly be conceived of without Antisuyu. Yet, on the other hand, the peoples, fauna and flora, and even the landscape of Antisuyu are described in Guamán Poma in ways that stand in opposition to the ideals of Andean civilization. For the Incas, as reflected through Guamán Poma, the Anti Indians are repeatedly described as uncivilized infidels who practiced anthropophagy and whose ceremonies, architecture and language were rudimentary in comparison with those of the Incas. In my conclusions, I will argue that this ambiguity in Inca attitudes towards Antisuyu became obscured under Spanish rule, during which the negative traits associated with native Amazonians persisted, while the conceptual integration of the region into the Spanish Empire was lost, thus further reinforcing the image of Andes and Amazonia as two different universes.

Needless to say, Guamán Poma's views of the Antisuyu, as presented in his manuscript, tell us much more about himself and his time than about the western Amazonian Indians themselves. The aim of this chapter is by no means to use the manuscript in order to evoke, reinforce or deny any particular image of Amazonian Indians as constructed by Guamán Poma, but rather as a way to better understand the complex historical context – through the eyes (and position) of the native chronicler – which produced and projected such perceptions of Amazonian Indians during early colonial times.

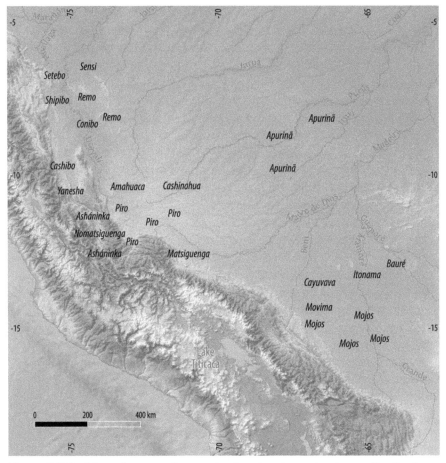

Figure 5.2.1 Map of western Amazonia, showing the approximate distribution of ethno-linguistic groups in late colonial times. © Cristiana Bertazoni and Paul Heggarty.

Antisuyu as conceptually integral to the Inca Empire

When the Incas rose to power after the thirteenth century, according to Guamán Poma's and other chronicles, they reshaped the Andes and founded their empire of Tahuantinsuyu: in Quechua, 'the four quarters united' (Chinchaysuyu, Collasuyu, Condesuyu and Antisuyu). Under this structure of a fourfold kingdom, the region now known as western Amazonia fell within Antisuyu, and all its ethnic groups were lumped together under the generic term Antis. When the tenth Inca emperor, Tupac Inca Yupanqui, took power in c. 1472, extensive parts of Chinchaysuyu, Collasuyu and Condesuyu had already been incorporated into Tahuantinsuyu, while Antisuyu was still predominantly free from Inca control. After extending the borders of the empire in what is now Ecuador, Tupac Inca dedicated himself to the conquest of Antisuyu (Cieza de León 1553/1984; Capac Ayllu 1569/2004; Betanzos 1576/1996; Garcilaso de la Vega 1609/1985; Pachacuti Yamqui 1613/1993; Guamán Poma de Ayala 1615/1980). Following several incursions, the Incas managed to establish important alliances with ethnic groups living in western Amazonia.[1] However, they never managed to conquer Antisuyu fully, and most of the groups they succeeded in subjugating operated more under indirect power and gift-giving strategies rather than on full subscription to the Inca redistributive system (Santos-Granero 1992; Renard-Casevitz et al. 1988).

We start by analysing one of the most interesting images in the Nueva Corónica, the two-page *Mapamundi del Reino de las Indias* (Figure 5.2.2). This map ingeniously combines two very different ways of representing the world: the Inca tradition, characterized by the division of Tahuantinsuyu into four parts, and the European one, evident in the addition to the map of the areas beyond the Andean world (Brotherston 1992, 29), and also in the use of gridlines as representations of latitude and longitude (though in Guamán Poma's map these lines are merely illustrative). Although Guamán Poma assimilated several elements of European cartography and integrated them into his Mapamundi, his outlook was on the whole autochthonous (Wachtel 1973, 177): for instance, his map displays a 90° anticlockwise rotation from the Western convention, and the Inca capital Cuzco is placed at the centre (instead of Lima).

In this Cuzco-centric image of the world, the West is represented by Chinchaysuyu, the East by Collasuyu, the South by Condesuyu, and the North by Antisuyu. The social structure of the Incas was based on a system of complementary oppositions where the world was divided into two parts: *hanansaya* (upper part) and *hurinsaya* (lower part). In the text that accompanies Guamán Poma's Mapamundi, we can clearly observe an internal hierarchy presiding over the four quarters of Tahuantinsuyu, where Chinchaysuyu and Antisuyu represent Hanan Cuzco, and Collasuyu and Condesuyu represent Hurin Cuzco:

> We must know that all the kingdom had four kings, four parts. Chinchaysuyo on the right hand side, where the sun sets. Towards the *montaña* until the

Figure 5.2.2 Mapamundi del Reino de las Indias. Reproduced by kind permission of the Royal Library, Copenhagen, GKS 2232 quarto: Guamán Poma, Nueva corónica y buen gobierno (1615), pp. 983–4 [1001–2]. Drawing 344.

> Northern Sea, Andesuyo, where the sun rises, on the left hand side, until Chile, Collaysuyo; until the Southern Sea, Condesuyo. These so called four parts became two parts: Incas hanan Cuzco where the sun sets Chinchaysuyu; hurin Cuzco where the sun rises; Collasuyu on the left hand side. And thus the head and court of the kingdom, the great city of Cuzco, falls in the middle (Guamán Poma de Ayala 1615/1980, 913).[2]

In the division of the Inca world, Chinchaysuyu represented the most important and privileged quarter. In this system, every suyu had its corresponding or opposing quarter, which in the case of Chinchaysuyu was represented by Antisuyu; a dichotomy that epitomizes, respectively, culture and order opposing barbarism and nature (Wachtel 1973, 180). Although the Antisuyu occupies the position of hanan in the fourfold system, then, it becomes hurin in relation to Chinchaysuyu.

Nevertheless, a key point is that, as Adorno has emphasized:

> … the superiority/inferiority dichotomy does not signify absolute values, but rather articulates a system of oppositions and a hierarchy of preferences, the systematic, complementary quality of terms in opposition is central to this consideration, and the concept of opposition is substantive because it is structural. (Adorno 1988, 91)

Whether in the position of hanan or hurin, Antisuyu thus was an essential part of Tahuantinsuyu, one whose presence was vital in order for the Inca cosmic system to be complete (Wachtel 1973). The two *suyus* were like natural oppositions, such as male/female, high/low, dry/wet, civilized/uncivilized, organized/chaotic. In summary, they were two contraries that were fundamentally complementary to each other. Without one, the other could not exist (Zuidema 1964).

Although there were likely Inca ideological differentiations made between themselves and the tropical forest peoples, then, the Antisuyu had an especially important place in the dualist cosmogony of the Incas. Several aspects of Inca mythology and iconography indicate that the Antisuyu represented a complementary and hierarchically ordered element of identity, within an encompassing model suggesting an opposition between a superior, male, Andean half, and a feminine, inferior, and threatening lowland half (A.-C. Taylor 1999, 202).

'Othering' the peoples and landscape of Antisuyu

Despite this conceptual integration of Antisuyu into the empire, Inca views of the peoples and landscape of western Amazonia, as reflected by Guamán Poma, placed them very much as an 'other', constructed in contrast to the Andean ideal. Amazonia and its dwellers occupied an ambivalent position within the Inca cosmological system. It represented a land rich in resources as well as in shamanic powers, home of fierce warriors. But it also represented the dwelling place of uncivilized inhabitants who resisted submission to Andean civilization as seen from the Inca imperialistic point of view. In this section, I analyse some chapters of Guamán Poma's manuscript in order to explore these issues, with an emphasis on the Inca captains and queens (collas) associated with Antisuyu, as well as the rites and ceremonies held both in Amazonia and throughout Tahuantinsuyu.

In the *Mapamundi del Reino de las Indias*, Guamán Poma populated each quarter of his map with a named couple. Each couple appears appropriately dressed alongside their respective coats of arms, the only exception being the Antisuyu-dwelling couple who appear naked. Apo Ninarva, the Anti native in the Mapamundi, displays some feathers over his head, and his coat of arms (which can barely be seen among trees and animals) is similar to the one shown some pages earlier when Guamán Poma describes him in more detail as the Antisuyu's thirteenth captain (Figure 5.2.4). On the map, the author further populates the sky, the two seas and, interestingly, the barrier of trees at the upper part (where Antisuyu is located) with several creatures. Looking closely from west to east at the barrier of trees one finds a mixture of real and imaginary animals.

During the Renaissance and Baroque periods, maps were seen as small geographical encyclopaedias, and many depicted the fauna and flora as well as the inhabitants of the regions they described. In well-explored areas, cartographers depicted real animals; however, when the regions described were not well known, imaginary beings, such as mermaids, were commonly depicted (Peeri 1998). As mentioned above, Guamán Poma was relatively familiar with maps produced in the tradition of European cartography and he reproduced some of it in his Mapamundi. Considering that his ultimate reader was the king of Spain to whom his letter/manuscript was addressed, it makes sense that the author added in his map elements that could be easily identified and understood by his main reader. In this context, one could argue that the addition by Guamán Poma of imaginary animals where Antisuyu is located indicates that this was an unknown and wild territory, where Amazonian inhabitants, fauna and flora all formed part of the same category. Furthermore, in the Mapamundi, Chinchaysuyu, Collasuyu and Condesuyu are depicted as spaces where everything was orderly, under control and man-tamed. However, in Antisuyu, nature was still uncultivated, waiting to be conquered and domesticated. Cities and buildings were present in all the three suyus, where their inhabitants wear clothes and each man holds their personal bar. None of these elements can be sighted in the Antisuyu quarter. And uniquely, in the case of the Antisuyu, Guamán Poma annotates his Mapamundi with additional written information.[3] It is as though the author wished to offer the reader extra details about this unknown wild territory.

Although it is not entirely clear, Guamán Poma seems to imply that some parts of the Antisuyu were subject to Inca power. However, he also suggests that half of the northern part of the empire (Antisuyu, on this map) was not conquered by the Incas and was inhabited by fertile and warlike Chiriguano Indians. Here, the author again highlights the inhospitable character of the region as well as the dangerous aspects of its fauna that, according to him, prevented the Incas from crossing it:

> Half of the kingdom as far as the Northern Sea is not conquered, even less so the Indians of Chile and the Arawak and Mosquito Indians near the kingdom of Guinea, almost all of whom were subject to the Inca kings. Where there is most wealth of gold is among the Indians from the montaña and in the other part of the sierra of the Guarmi Auca, Anqu Uallo Indians, there is wealth of silver. And they are fertile, warlike Indians like the Chiriguanays. But it is not possible to cross to these lands because in the rivers there are lizards and poisonous snakes and serpents, lions, tigers, jaguars and many other animals and it is a rough and mountainous land; with trickery the Incas conquered those people from the montaña. (Guamán Poma de Ayala 1615/1980, 913)

Capacs: Inca captains

In Guamán Poma's history of Tahuantinsuyu, there were fifteen Inca captains (*capacs*), and in his manuscript, every captain has his own pictorial representation accompanied by a brief description. Each captain is distinct in his own way; however, the two capacs sent by the Incas to conquer the Antisuyu are depicted and described in substantially different terms from the others. In the case of Otorongo Achachi[4] Apo Camac Inga, the sixth capac, the distinction lies in the very particular way he is represented: as an anthropo-zoomorphic figure with the body of a jaguar and a half-human face (Figure 5.2.3). Guamán Poma writes that Otorongo Achachi was the son of Inca Roca (the sixth Inca emperor) and in order to conquer Antisuyu he transformed himself into a jaguar, also having a child by a *chuncho* (Amazonian) woman.

As suggested by Adorno (1988, 89), Guamán Poma's arrangement of icons in space respects a logic that is true to autochthonous values of symbolic representation, thus providing an additional level of pictorial meaning. Following this logic, the left-hand side (from our viewpoint) represents hanan, while the right hand represents hurin. Otorongo is thus placed in the hanan position, while the Anti occupies the hurin position. Within this logic, this image can be read as that of a 'superior' Otorongo victoriously conquering the 'inferior' Anti, as the location of the vanquished is occupied by the Amazonian Indian: an example of Inca imperial ideology reflected in the discourse of Guamán Poma (for related ideas, see Chapter 2.5). The Anti Indian in this drawing can barely be seen because the powerful Otorongo Achachi takes centre stage, while the Amazonian is depicted naked at the far right. The accompanying text tells us that it was Otorongo Achachi's power of transforming himself into a jaguar that enabled him to conquer Antisuyu, the chunchos, and all the montaña (Guamán Poma de Ayala 1615/1980, 133). Capac Apo Ninarva, meanwhile, the thirteenth captain, was sent by Huayna Capac (the eleventh emperor) once again to conquer Antisuyu. In Guamán Poma's drawing, he exudes power and regality (Figure 5.2.4). He wears an exquisite costume and a round feather diadem which is composed of seven feathers above his head, 10 on his right-hand side, and finally, 12 on his left-hand side, making 22 lateral plus 7 (a total of 29).[5] To his left, on the ground, is a coat-of-arms topped by a crown (with seven feathers), with a jaguar in the upper part and a snake in the lower.[6]

With all other capacs discussed in the Nueva Corónica, then, Guamán Poma focuses on their personalities, qualities and/or faults. But in the case of the two Antisuyu captains, he includes neither a personal profile, nor a list of the places they conquered. Instead the author writes about the Anti Indians in general, with recurrent emphasis on the words that the chronicler repeats throughout his manuscript every time he describes the Antis: naked, infidels, rebellious, cannibals and bellicose.

Collas: Inca queens

Guamán Poma also discusses the Inca wives, or *collas*, of whom the lady of Antisuyu, Capac Mallqvima, is the second. In comparison with the other three collas, the author portrays the lady of Antisuyu in a completely different way (Figure 5.2.5). Capac Mallqvima stands in a jungle-like environment where she occupies a central position, with a bird by her left side and a monkey on her right. Again, just as with the Antisuyu capacs, Guamán Poma does not follow the same structure as with

Figure 5.2.3 The sixth captain, Otorongo Achachi Inka or Camac Inka, *apu*. Reproduced by kind permission of the Royal Library, Copenhagen, GKS 2232 quarto: Guamán Poma, Nueva corónica y buen gobierno (1615), p. 155. Drawing 56.

Figure 5.2.4 The thirteenth captain, Ninarua, *qhapaq apu*, powerful lord.
Reproduced by kind permission of the Royal Library, Copenhagen, GKS 2232
quarto: Guamán Poma, Nueva corónica y buen gobierno (1615), p. 169.
Drawing 63.

Figure 5.2.5 The second lady of Antisuyu Mallquima, *qhapaq*. Reproduced by kind permission of the Royal Library, Copenhagen, GKS 2232 quarto: Guamán Poma, Nueva corónica y buen gobierno (1615), pp. 175–7. Drawing 67.

the other collas when presenting Capac Mallqvima. In the accompanying passage about Mallqvima, Guamán Poma gives us important clues to understand how he classified people living under the Inca Empire. The words in (our) italics might indicate that these specific Anti Indians, by wearing few clothes if any, belonged to a different kind of people, more in harmony with nature, according to Guamán Poma's interpretation:

> These ladies, although they have good figures and are very beautiful, with skin fairer than a Spanish woman, yet *they wear few clothes and some go nude, for this is their type and nature, both men and women, and they eat human flesh* … They smear their bodies all over with mantor [annato, a reddish pigment made from the seeds of the achiote tree, *Bixa orellana*] and they live in the montaña and have still not been conquered. And the montaña is so vast that it cannot be conquered … And there are many other ladies in every village of the montaña; in the other part, there are many people and lands abounding in riches, where there are pagan Indians called Anca Huallo, Huarmi Auca, where it is said there is much gold and silver. (Guamán Poma de Ayala 1615/ 1980, 155)

Also significant in the pages devoted to Capac Mallqvima is her close interaction with a monkey. Guamán Poma's choice of a monkey rather than any other creature could imply that the author associated Anti Indians with primates, a sort of half-human, semi-developed creature which had not yet fully made its way towards humankind or civilization. It was not rare for Antis to be associated with monkeys; the Spanish chronicler Cieza de León even wrote that in Antisuyu, men had sexual intercourse with female monkeys, producing half-human, half-monkey offspring (see Santos-Granero 1992, 264).

Rituals and celebrations

Guamán Poma goes on to describe the festivities of Tahuantinsuyu, where celebrations accompanied by music and dances were common practice and took place many times during the year according to the Inca calendar. On these occasions, men and women would dance, taking turns in their choreographed singing performances (Figure 5.2.6). However, in Antisuyu, men dressed like women (thus transcending gender roles), and their music was far from being as complex as that of the other suyus, their songs consisting of only two words, caya and cayaya:

> The Antis and the Chuncho people sing and dance like this: 'caya, caya, cayaya caya, caya, cayaya caya, cayaya caya'. To this rhythm they sing and dance, saying whatever they want in their language. The women answer, singing 'cayaya caya, cayaya caya', and they play a flute which they call *pipo*. To the sound of this flute they celebrate; they do a circle dance holding hands. All

Figure 5.2.6 Celebrations of the Antisuyu. Reproduced by kind permission of the Royal Library, Copenhagen, GKS 2232 quarto: Guamán Poma, Nueva corónica y buen gobierno (1615), p. 322 [324]. Drawing 126.

the men dressed as women with their arrows dance huarmi auca. (Guamán Poma de Ayala 1615/1980, 297–8)

Guamán Poma further describes how people from the four quarters of the empire and from Cuzco conducted their funerals (Figure 5.2.7). He focuses first on Cuzco: Inca burials and rituals in Cuzco were elaborately respectful towards the dead, and included the sacrifice of the Inca's wives and servants. Guamán Poma further describes the ways that people from Chinchaysuyu, Collasuyu and Condesuyu staged their funerals: similarly to the Incas, they would feed the dead regularly, even years after their death, place valuable gifts in their graves, mourn for days on end, dress the deceased in beautiful garments, and display the lifeless body in a procession-like ceremony before the burial (and subsequent reburials). The same, however, did not hold true for the funerary rituals of the Antis. The Antis only cried for a day, and soon held a festival (*carnesería*) at which they ate the dead person:

> It is said that they cry for a day and hold a great celebration. During the celebration they cry and sing their songs. And they do not have ceremonies like the Indians of the sierra … since they are Indians of the montaña who eat human flesh. And so, as soon as the person dies, they start to eat them so that they leave no flesh, but just bones. As soon as the person stops breathing, they dress the body in feathered clothes that they make for them, and they remove the feathers and undress the body and wash it and start to cut it into pieces. (Guamán Poma de Ayala 1615/1980, 267)

After the feast, the bones of the dead were placed inside a tree, where they would then remain. Guamán Poma stresses that, in contrast to the other parts of Tahuantinsuyu, where people honoured their *mallquis* (mummified ancestors) annually, the Antis conducted no further ceremonies in honour of their ancestors:

> They take the bones and the Indians carry them off, and neither the men nor the women weep, and they place them in a tree they call *uitaca*, where the worms have made a hole, they place them there and they seal it all very well. And from that moment, they never see him again in all their lives, nor do they remember him, and neither do they know any other ceremony like the Indians of the highlands, who even put gold, silver, and coca in the mouth of the deceased. They bury them with their silver *ojotas* [sandals]. (Guamán Poma de Ayala 1615/1980, 267; for further discussion of this, see Chapter 5.1)

Reverence, worship and care of mallquis were central to Inca and Andean religion (Urton 1999, 10). For the Incas, periodic burial rituals represented the junction and disjunction between past and present and were an essential part of the

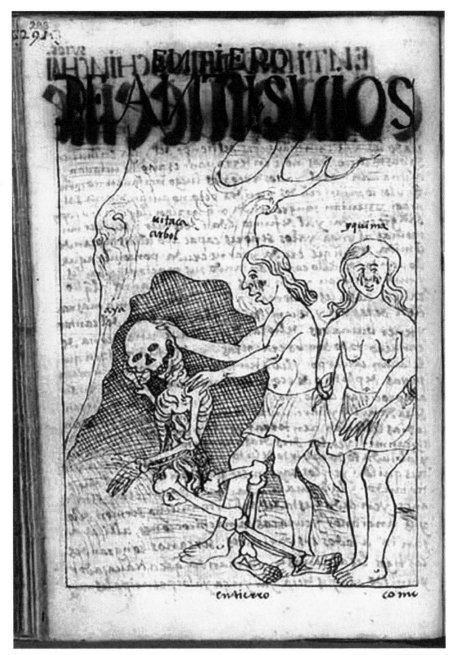

Figure 5.2.7 Burials of the Antisuyu. Reproduced by kind permission of the Royal Library, Copenhagen, GKS 2232 quarto: Guamán Poma, Nueva corónica y buen gobierno (1615), p. 291 [293]. Drawing 114.

historical process (Wachtel 1973). As seen from an Inca or Andean perspective, by eating their ancestors the Antis were disrupting the cosmic order and breaking the on-going communication and interaction between the living and dead.

Discussion and final considerations

In the chapters studied here, it becomes clear that the inhabitants of Amazonia are presented by Guamán Poma as notably different from those of other quarters of Tahuantinsuyu, both in the way the author describes them and in the way he depicts them in his illustrations. In the Nueva Corónica, Antisuyu emerges as a land of 'incompleteness' where the Antis lacked a series of elements required to participate in civilization according to Inca precepts: a complex language, architecture, appropriate rituals, clothes and so forth. In this imperial Inca-centric view, the Antisuyu is presented as a land that was still to be explored; the Antis were still to be assimilated into the fourfold kingdom, where they would ascend from their supposedly rudimentary stage towards the realms of Inca sophistication.

Nevertheless, and despite such an 'inferior' position within the Inca system, the Antisuyu was paradoxically also a fundamental part of the empire. Without it, following the logic of complementary opposition (hanan/hurin) that structured the core of Inca philosophy, Tahuantinsuyu would not be complete. The Antisuyu, or at least part of it, was highly desired by the Incas to be fully incorporated under their rule. However, it also turned out to be the region which the Incas struggled the most to subjugate, mainly due to the resistance of the Antis. As suggested elsewhere, it was possibly because the Antisuyu was the quarter in which the empire thrived the least that the Incas invested the most in ideological discourse, through a variety of media, in order to project an imperial discourse of superiority over its people (Bertazoni 2014, 2007b, and see the parallels in Chapters 5.3 and 5.4).

Although Guamán Poma is well known for his critique of the Incas, in some specific parts of the Nueva Corónica his discourse seems to intertwine with theirs, and even to reflect and reproduce Inca imperial ideology (Brotherston 1992, 254). Moreover, because so much of Inca life was embedded in pre-Inca Andean traditions, it would be difficult to draw a line regarding which elements in Guamán Poma are purely Inca or more broadly Andean. The author seems to embody an amalgamation of traditions; and this is manifest in his manuscript when locating Antisuyu within the Inca system. The history of the Andes as presented by Guamán Poma is multi-layered, as he merges Andean, Inca, and Christian perspectives. Similarly, the position of Antisuyu in Guamán Poma's discourse changes according to the different viewpoints adopted by the author. As an Andean, Guamán Poma reconciles well the dichotomy of Antisuyu as a different but fundamental part of Tahuantinsuyu, following the logic of complementary opposition. However, as a Christian and an informant of the Spanish king, Guamán Poma reinforces and exacerbates the supposedly uncivilized condition of the Antis by emphasizing their nature as infidels and cannibals, transgressors of several taboos.

With the Spanish invasion and the advent of colonial rule in the Andes, this ambivalent position of the Antisuyu within the Inca system was gradually replaced by a history of sharp divisions. Under the new colonial order, Antisuyu was no longer a fundamental part of an integrated kingdom (Chapter 5.3). On the contrary, it became part of a radical discourse that can be understood as the genesis of a sharp division between Andes and Amazonia. The Spaniards failed to grasp the system of complementary opposition between Incas and Antis – a misunderstanding which would echo for centuries, reverberating to a certain degree among modern academics who, influenced by Cuzco-centric colonial ethnohistorical sources, have perpetuated a vision of the Antis as marginal tribes in comparison with the civilized people of the Andes (Taylor 1992). As a result, the supposedly civilized Andean peoples were given precedence over the allegedly anarchical Indians living in the lowlands. The Antis were then pushed to a peripheral position within Andean history due to a series of misconceptions regarding their ontology and society, agency and history.

In the same way that in the sixteenth century, the Spaniards justified the colonization and Christianization of Peru by arguing that the native Indians needed to be civilized and brought to the Catholic faith, the Incas had similar strategies for the conquest of the Antisuyu. However, in the case of the Incas, they established alliances with some Anti groups and Antisuyu was a constituent part of Tahuantinsuyu's cosmology. With the advent of the Spaniards in Peru, these long-established ties gradually faded, and led to a process of almost complete divorce, further isolating the peoples of the lowlands from those of the highlands. The image of Antisuyu as no man's land and of the Antis as savages was then exaggerated and reinforced by the Spaniards, who exploited such an ideological discourse when trying to colonize and convert Amazonian Indians.

The genesis of the conceptualization of Andes and Amazonia as two different cultural areas did not begin during Inca times and probably goes far back in previous pre-Columbian periods with the emergence and expansion of the first centralized socio-political formations in the Andean region (Santos-Granero 2005, 85). Despite the antiquity of such differentiation, it was a relationship marked by alliance and war, cooperation and resistance, negotiation and conflict as well as by inclusion and exclusion. Guamán Poma's manuscript is a key document that tells us much about the shifting position of the Antisuyu both during Inca and early colonial times: a key turning point, fundamental to a better understanding of the complex and intricate history of the Andes–Amazonia divide.

***

Acknowledgements: I would like to thank the editors for the invitation to participate in this volume as well as for their valuable comments and suggestions on the chapter. I also thank Heiko Prümers.

5.3

Colonial coda: The Andes–Amazonia frontier under Spanish rule

Adrian J. Pearce

Introduction

This chapter is framed as a 'colonial coda', since the majority of contributions to this book focus on the pre-Columbian period. Most authors, of whatever discipline, are concerned with relations between Andes and Amazonia in pre-history, rather than in the centuries subsequent to the European invasions of South America in the early 1500s. By focusing on the three centuries that followed those invasions, I hope to demonstrate that study of the colonial period can make valuable contributions to the broader debates addressed in this volume. On the one hand, I argue that the nature of the Andes–Amazonia frontier during colonial times can shed intriguing light on its precedents in the pre-European era. On the other, pre-historians will recognize the need to take into account the ways their own source materials (particularly modern genetic or linguistic data) might have been disturbed or transformed by the dramatic demographic processes inherent to colonial times.

To these ends, the chapter is divided into three sections. The first is devoted to the character of the frontier between Spanish Peru[1] and Amazonia, with an emphasis on its relative substance or 'firmness'. Second, the nature of the Spanish presence in the Amazonian lowlands is discussed, based primarily on the presence of evangelizing missions. And third, demographic trends and population movements, both on either side of and across the frontier, are set out in brief summary. The conclusions then emphasize what seem to be the parallels between Spanish and Inca relations with Amazonia and ponder what these parallels might mean. Finally, this chapter provides a broad theoretical and thematic framework, which is illustrated through the case study presented in its companion, Chapter 5.4; both should be read alongside each other.

A firm frontier

The first point to emphasize is that whatever the picture in prehistory – and other chapters in this book suggest just how complex that picture was – the frontier between the Andes and Amazonia was real enough under Spanish rule. It is possible to trace the eastern border of effective Spanish occupation and control in Peru with some precision, since for the main, it followed the line of the upper *montaña* – the easternmost slopes of the Andes, steep, wet and heavily forested. That is to say, Spain's writ ran as far as the upper montaña, with the highlands and coast to the west considered the colonial heartlands. Beyond, the European presence was often either limited, or indeed negligible, in lowland territories that were in no sense regarded as core to the colony (see Figures 5.3.1 and 5.3.2). This frontier was taken as a fact, even when not too much should be made of the 'de la Frontera' suffixed to the formal names of Chachapoyas or Huamanga (in the latter case with specific reference to the 'Neo-Inca state' at Vilcabamba: Stern 1993, 28). The Spanish colonial frontier is the more easily recognized because the eastern boundaries of Spanish Peru matched those of the Inca Empire quite closely. That is to say, the Spanish inherited the empire of the Incas, up to its own established frontiers, and they seem to have faced similar ecological and/or sociological obstacles in extending their rule beyond them. Even where European influence did extend beyond the montaña, it did so in regions where the Incas too seem to have established some presence; whether through relatively easy access from the highlands (as in the case of Moyobamba and Maynas in the north), or some specific stimulus such as gold deposits (as possibly in the Llanos de Moxos in the south: D'Altroy 2002, 260–1; though see Chapter 4.3).

The question, however, is *why* Spanish Peru remained for the most part within a frontier set to the east by the upper montaña, with little presence in the lowlands beyond. Traditional explanations tend towards the general or vague, even when they contain much that is of substance: the obstacles to intensive agriculture or animal husbandry of the kind practiced in the highlands, the impact of tropical diseases, or even the difficulty of movement through the Amazonian forests. Ultimately, it may be helpful to emphasize that Spanish settlement in the Americas was a rational and not a random phenomenon, one that responded to specific incentives and stimuli. The presence, absence, or combination of these incentives directly determined the course and chronology of the Spanish expansion. The key factors, in roughly descending order of importance, were: abundant native populations capable of providing a labour force and tax base, deposits of precious metals, the inherent quality of the land for agricultural and livestock production, and strategic considerations (of control and defence of key territories) (Elliott 1987b; Restall and Lane 2011, part 2; Livi Bacci 2008).[2] In what became the colonial heartlands, most of these factors operated simultaneously; but where even one of them was present, it could draw the Spaniards into regions that lay outside the areas of dense native settlement or which had been neglected by the great indigenous empires. Thus, the north of Mexico, beyond the Mesoamerican

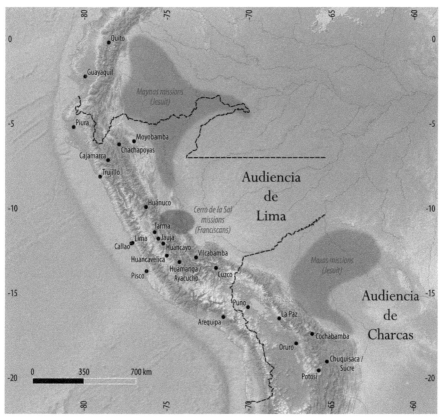

Figure 5.3.1 Map showing the towns of colonial Peru and Amazonian mission districts. © Adrian J. Pearce and Paul Heggarty. The Spanish founded numerous towns across the Andean highlands and coast, but none in the Amazonian lowlands. The only persistent Spanish presence in the lowlands came in the form of missions; these covered vast regions but had negligible European populations. Maps showing the theoretical boundaries of the Viceroyalty of Peru are thus misleading in terms of effective occupation beyond the upper *montaña*. Modern towns in the lowlands such as Iquitos represent later foundations, albeit sometimes with origins in colonial missions.

frontier, was settled because a string of silver strikes was made there from the 1540s onwards (Knight 2002, 62–72). Such regions might include lowland forest lands not dissimilar to the upper Amazon; the Chocó on the Pacific coast of modern Colombia was conquered and settled for its gold fields, the richest in Spanish America (Williams 2004). But most of Amazonia, certainly after the mid-1500s, offered *none* of these incentives, while also presenting major disincentives, in the powerful armed resistance of its indigenous inhabitants, or the presence of lowland diseases and especially of leishmaniasis (for which see Chapter 3.1)

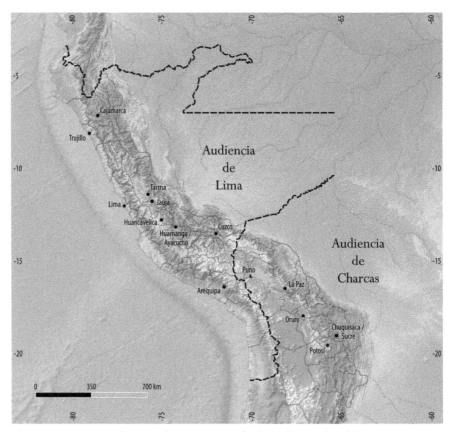

Figure 5.3.2 Map showing the provinces of colonial Peru. © Adrian J. Pearce and Paul Heggarty. The Viceroyalty was organized into several dozen provinces, each with its own governor and magistrate (*corregidor*) and 'secular' ecclesiastical establishment. All of these provinces were concentrated in the highlands and on the coast; there were none beyond the upper *montaña*, in the Amazonian lowlands.

This, then, is what established and maintained the colonial frontier between Andes and Amazonia, which changed little throughout the colonial centuries (or indeed until the late nineteenth century). In 1573, the most powerful of the Spanish monarchs, Philip II, actually prohibited further conquests by his subjects in the Americas – 'from now on, Spain recognized a frontier to its American domains' (Kamen 1997, 150; Lorandi 2005, 104–5) – and decreed that further expansion would only be permitted at the hands of missionaries. This decree rather crowned the process of imperial expansion than put a halt to it, since it recognized implicitly that by this date, Spain had already occupied all the American territory that was truly of interest to it – as Amazonia was not. All of this, of course, has little to do with the border between Spanish Peru and Portuguese Brazil, which is a separate question entirely. That border had been set before 1500 in far eastern South America, by the Treaty of Tordesillas. Over the centuries, the Portuguese pushed westwards, deep into the Amazon basin, until they approached the Spanish lands (Hemming 1995, 2008). Even so, the formal border between Spanish and Portuguese America was not redrawn until after 1750 (Herzog 2015, part 1), while the modern borders between Brazil and the Andean republics were fixed only in the late nineteenth and early twentieth centuries. Even today, those borders lie far to the east of the colonial (and geographical) Andes–Amazonia frontier. It may nevertheless be relevant to underline that the major push towards that frontier during colonial times came not from the Andean polity (Spanish Peru) but from the 'Amazonian' one (Portuguese Brazil). The Portuguese did have an incentive for such expansion – first native slave labour for coastal plantations, later precious metals – and during colonial times they acquired long experience of travel and subsistence in the forests.

Missionary marchlands

In this context, the primary Spanish presence in Amazonia beyond the upper mon-taña was a religious one, in the form of missions. The nature of missions as frontier institutions in Spanish America may not be widely understood, though it has been the subject of historical research for more than a century. A pioneering article by Herbert Bolton set out the essential aspects: missions were 'characteristically and definedly frontier institutions'; their primary purpose was religious, but they served the needs of both church and state; they might be supported financially by Spain, but were expected to be largely self-sustaining; and they provided a defensive cor-don at the very limits of the empire (Bolton 1917). Bolton's conclusions have stood the test of time, so that missions are regarded in the literature as 'one of Spain's most effective colonial institutions along the fringes of empire' (Elliott 1987a, 73).

Missions were founded and run not by the mainstream church with its epis-copal hierarchy (counter-intuitively termed the 'secular' church), but rather by the 'regular' orders (that obeyed a monastic rule or *regula*). There were many such orders, but those most active in the upper Amazon were the Franciscans and especially the Jesuits. East of the Peruvian Andes, three main missionary fields were established: the central region around the Cerro de la Sal, east of Tarma, administered by Franciscans, and Maynas in the north and Moxos and Chiquitos in the south, which were Jesuit. These mission regions were established relatively late: for example, the Jesuits entered Maynas in the 1630s and Moxos half a century later. Missions consisted of settlements centred on a church with an adjoining open space and housing and agricultural land clustered around. They were typically founded on the banks of the major rivers, with a native population often brought together from different ethnic groups scattered throughout wide hinterlands. Due to this concentration of population, they were sometimes referred to as *reducciones*, though it should be emphasized that they were very different in socio-economic structure and demographic impact to the homonymous institution in the highlands.

The concentration of native peoples in missions was at once a pragmatic response to indigenous population collapse and dispersion, a strategic impediment to resistance, and a tool for ethnogenesis. Native peoples agreed to live in missions for different reasons at different times, although key motives included protection from Spanish colonists or Portuguese slavers, and access to trade goods (for the Moxos missions, see Radding 2005). Mission populations could be large – by 1700, the Jesuit missions in Maynas had a nominal population of 160,000, spread among several dozen settlements – though they tended to decline sharply as a result of repeated epidemics. The demographic and linguistic impact of the missions is discussed in the following section, but it should be emphasized that numbers of Europeans were never more than miniscule for such vast regions. In 1680, there were just four Jesuits in the whole of the Maynas territory; a century later, only a dozen Franciscans served the same region (Weber 2005, 118). The non-indigenous demographic input was higher, however, when Andean auxiliaries and occasional Spanish troops are factored in.

Missionary objectives stood in an awkward relation to those of the colonial state. Thus, 'Jesuit colonization in Paraguay and Moxos stood aside from the Spanish colonial state and its Church ally, and this was deliberate' (Lynch 2012, 48). The orders were the most wayward branch of the church, with their own organization and ethos, and relations between them and both the state and the secular church were often tense. The result was that the real initiative behind missions came from the orders rather than the state, and that the support of the state for the missions was limited and, to some extent, contingent. The state certainly seconded the purely evangelizing goals of the orders, and it provided financial subsidies for missions such as those of the Franciscans at the Cerro de la Sal. It also sometimes provided a military escort to missionaries, regarding the missions (with good reason) as a marchland: an outer frontier of influence between the colonial heartlands and the 'wild' Indians and encroaching Portuguese beyond. Nevertheless, the real stake of the Spanish state in Amazonia beyond the upper montaña remained weak, and its support might be tempered or withdrawn altogether if circumstances so dictated. Detailed illustration of just such a withdrawal may be found in Chapter 5.4 of this book; but the most dramatic example was the outright expulsion of the Jesuits from Spain and its empire in 1767, when their ultramontanism (primary loyalty to the Pope) was perceived to outweigh the benefits of their presence in both colonies and metropolis. The expulsion of the Jesuits was 'a great setback for missionary expansion'; the missions were reassigned either to the secular clergy or to other orders, and in many cases the initiative was lost altogether (Lynch 2012, 94; Weber 2005, 109–16). The peremptory expulsion in this way of the most important Spanish presence in the upper Amazon only emphasizes the limited nature of colonial interest in the region.

The small numbers of missions and the limited support they received should nevertheless not obscure their major cultural as well as demographic impact, particularly in Maynas where they were strongest. This lasting impact was evident in the spatial and residential organization of indigenous settlements, or in kinship and demographic structures (including the abandonment of polygyny and adoption of early male marriage). Even in native communities in the region today, 'some politico-ritual institutions ... are directly inherited from the mission', which also brought about changes in dress, so that 'by the end of the eighteenth century, there were almost no longer any naked Indians in the upper Amazon region' (for these questions, see A.-C. Taylor 1999, 225–6). The cultivation of new crops and the prevalence of some kinds of specialized production (of curare or salt) are also Jesuit legacies. A specific impact of interest to linguists was the introduction of Quechua, again particularly in Maynas. Quechua was adopted by the Jesuits as a vehicle for evangelization and a lingua franca for the different groups coexisting in the missions, and as a result, it took root outside its homeland, along the Napo, the Marañón, the lower Huallaga, and the Ucayali. In this way, a quintessentially highland, Andean language entered Amazonia, with the missions providing the mechanism that left Quechua's only meaningful presence there (see also Chapter 3.4). The Jesuits used the Moxo language in a similar way in the Llanos de Moxos (A.-C. Taylor 1999, 225–9; Santos-Granero 1992, 161–2, 170–2), though since Moxo is an Arawak language, this brought no disturbance of the linguistic Andes–Amazonia frontier, in the way that the introduction of Quechua in Maynas did.

Missions were intended to be self-sufficient in agricultural and broader economic terms, and they produced all the food and almost all the basic goods they required. With the introduction of new crops and livestock and of European processes for their production, they also brought innovative economic practices to Amazonia. They were dependent on Spanish Peru only for a limited range of material and religious goods they could not themselves produce, including iron tools, wine or paper. To procure these goods, they depended either on subsidies from their orders or their own surplus production of lowland produce, such as wax or palm products. Small expeditions led by friars accompanied by native auxiliaries left the missions annually by canoe and on foot for the highlands, taking many months to complete the round trip (Santos-Granero 1992, 171–2). These expeditions constituted a rare and modest mechanism for regular communication and material exchange between the highlands and the tropical lowlands, whose significance far outweighed their limited scale. Iron tools in particular were key to this exchange, since native Amazonians recognized the great utility of such implements and made every effort to acquire them. Access to metal goods was one motive why indigenous peoples went to the missions at all, and groups downstream with the easiest access to them gained a mercantile (and occasionally military) ascendency over peoples more distant from the sources of supply, that might transform their status and conditions (Santos-Granero 1992, 162). The missions thus constituted a bridge to deeper Amazonia, as well as a barrier to it, compensating in part for the loss of the more fluid relations across the frontier that, as we shall see, colonial rule may have come to disrupt.

Demographic transformations: The Andes, Amazonia and the frontier

Throughout eastern South America, Spanish rule brought about sweeping and catastrophic demographic change. The most comprehensive study is that of Noble David Cook, who estimates a total indigenous population for Peru of perhaps 9,000,000 c. 1520, on the eve of the conquest era. By 1620, just a century later, this figure had fallen to 670,000, a collapse of more than 90 per cent (Cook 1981, 111–14, 246). The estimate of 9,000,000 c. 1520 is based on the meticulous comparison of different kinds of evidence, from ecological carrying capacity, to archaeology, depopulation ratios, post-contact disease mortality models, and census projections, among others. The fall over the century to 1620 came about primarily due to the impact of Old World diseases, though also because of chronic and generalized violence (for which see Assadourian 1994). In contrast to other regions, including Mexico, Peru's native population then long remained depressed, due primarily to repeated epidemics, and began to recover only from c. 1730 (Pearce 2001). The post-conquest population bottleneck in the Andes, then, lasted for more than a century. Within these overarching figures, there was naturally considerable regional variation. On the Peruvian coast, native populations all but disappeared in the south and centre, but remained dense in the north, in Lambayeque or Piura, presumably as the result of different patterns of Spanish settlement and perhaps regional ecologies. In the sierra, the lower and more accessible northern highlands were particularly hard-hit, while the centre and south proved more resilient. Cook's estimates have proven accurate when tested by archaeological survey, for example in the Mantaro valley (Terence N. D'Altroy, personal communication, 2014). Despite the severity of the collapse, however, it should be emphasized that indigenous people remained a majority in Peru throughout the period of Spanish rule, at least in the formal (and primarily *fiscal*) classification of the colonial state. Indeed, on these terms, the country's native population only finally dropped below 50 per cent at some point between 1900 and 1920 (Thurner 1997, 91, n. 59).

Some recent genetics papers appear to indicate a much lower decline in Andean populations after the conquest. One such study, for example, inferring population declines in the highlands from ancient and modern DNA, 'found the decline in effective population size to be 27% … We also simulated DNA sequence data immediately before the collapse between the Rio Uncallane and the Aymara using a truncated model and found a reduction in average heterozygosity of 23%'. The authors further explicitly note that 'this is a modest decline compared to archaeological and historical estimates, which reached upward of 90% of the total population' (Lindo et al. 2018, 6). It should be emphasized, however, that historical evidence for a larger collapse, while by no means uncontroversial, is reasonably robust and has accumulated over many years. Spanish colonial census records become much more abundant from the mid-sixteenth century, by which point they trace a steep decline that had clearly already been in progress for some decades.

Moreover, there is of course no straightforward correlation between effective population (Ne) and the census population. The former in particular is affected by migration, and as we shall see, mass migration transformed indigenous populations in the Andes during colonial times. The recent evidence from genetics is intriguing, then, but it does not as yet necessarily challenge traditional estimates of a catastrophic decline.

For Amazonia, traditional models suggest an impact that was again drastic, albeit not quite to the same degree as in the Andes. Thus, lower population densities, the absence of major urban centres, and lesser contact with Europeans would have mitigated the spread of disease. William Denevan, for example, indicated an overall population decline of a little over 70 per cent for floodplains, lowland savannahs (including the Llanos de Moxos) and upland forests (such as the central montaña), primarily in the first hundred years (Denevan 1992a, 212, 218, 222); significantly lower than Cook's estimates for the highlands and coast. Demographic trends in the region following the conquest are much less well-known than for the Andes, however, precisely because the European presence there was so limited. The scale of any decline would necessarily reflect the population of Amazonia at first contact, which many specialists now argue was far higher than traditional models allow (Chapters 1.1 and 1.4). For the present purposes, I would emphasize that any model for Amazonian population densities must account for the lack of Spanish interest in permanent colonization and settlement there, for which large native populations elsewhere constituted the primary motive. Three alternatives suggest themselves: Amazonian populations were indeed lower than Andean ones, as traditionally thought; those populations were higher than has been supposed, but the demographic collapse and wider impact of the conquest there was of the same order as or even *stronger* than in the highlands, for reasons as yet undetected; or, socio-economic organization in Amazonia was somehow fundamentally different and, together with different ecological and immunological conditions, deterred Spanish settlement even despite large populations overall. Whatever the true picture, the demographic impact is still likely to have been enormous. Other regions of the Americas besides Amazonia experienced sharp demographic declines even in the absence of significant European populations (the Mississippi valley is a further major example).

The demographic impact of European colonization naturally went far beyond collapse; in both Andes and Amazonia, it also entailed the wholesale reconfiguration of population distributions and settlement patterns. Two processes are observable: the concentration of populations into smaller numbers of larger settlements internally to regions, and the movement of populations across much greater distances (from one region to others). In the Andes, the primary example of the former process was the forced resettlement of some 1,400,000 Indians into new European-style towns or *reducciones*, a process at its peak in the 1570s. *Reducción*, then, sought to concentrate the dispersed rural population of Inca times into a small number of urban centres established within each region (Mumford 2012; Zuloaga

Rada 2012, chap. 4). The movement of populations entirely from one region to another, meanwhile, began with the turbulence of the conquest era and the ensuing 'Spanish civil wars', when Indians were conscripted en masse into rival armies, and *yanaconaje* – the personal service of natives deracinated from home communities – expanded exponentially. It continued into the mature colonial period, notably through the great forced labour drafts or *mitas*, particularly those that served the mining towns of Potosí and Huancavelica. At its peak, *mita* brought some 13,000 forced labourers to Potosí per year, from provinces up to several hundred miles distant, a figure that excludes the families that accompanied many migrants (Cole 1985; Bakewell 1984, chap. 3). Over three centuries, the mining mitas contributed to large-scale migrations, perhaps sufficient in the case of Huancavelica to change permanently the variant of Quechua spoken in the province (Pearce and Heggarty 2011; Itier 2016). They also swelled the so-called *forastero* population, of Indians no longer native to their communities of residence, as Indians sought exemption from *mita* by migrating to provinces not subject to the draft. By the mid-eighteenth century, half the population of highland Bolivia was *forastero* (Sánchez-Albornoz 1978, 51–2; Wightman 1990). Colonial rule, then, transformed population distributions in the Andes almost beyond pre-Columbian recognition.

In Amazonia, the concentration of populations internally to regions came about primarily at the hands of the missions. It differed from the comparable process in the highlands, firstly in that the populations gathered together came from much larger hinterlands, and secondly in that the peoples relocated to missions were drawn from *different* ethno-linguistic groups. Hence, lowland missions played a role in ethnogenesis and linguistic change that was less apparent in the *reducciones* of the highlands. The role of missions in facilitating the spread of disease among native populations was either comparable to that of *reducciones*, or perhaps greater, depending on estimates for pre-colonial population densities. Meanwhile, the process whereby European colonization provoked long-distance migrations, from one region to another, operated in Amazonia primarily through 'flight migration', as peoples in closer proximity and more subject to European depredations fled the contact zone and migrated toward more isolated refugia. Flight migration brought about major changes in pre-Columbian population distributions in Amazonia. Since missions were established primarily along riverbanks, a specific process was that by which non-mission populations retreated into inter-fluvial regions, often regarded as less favourable territories for human settlement and subsistence.

The picture on the Andes–Amazonia frontier itself is complex. In some important work on this topic, Anne-Christine Taylor has argued that the 'physical continuities and economic links' that had prevailed across the frontier in Inca times were destroyed under the impact of early European raiding, settlement, and diseases. As a result, 'the old Inka *limes* turned into a sort of no-man's land … in the context of a parasitic frontier economy oscillating between peaceful trade and mutual plundering'. The frontier itself 'shrivelled and fossilized', as there developed a 'widening gap between the highlands and lowlands, and the expansion of the no-man's-land between them' (A.-C. Taylor 1999, 209, 216–17). This process developed more rapidly in some regions than others, and in Ecuador and the far north of Peru its onset was delayed until as late as c. 1600 by more extensive European settlement and colonization. By the latter period, nevertheless, there prevailed from north to south what Taylor presents essentially as a *new* frontier (the relevant sub-section of her essay is in part titled 'The Birth of a Frontier': A.-C. Taylor 1999, 208–19). Given the kinds of cultural attitudes towards Amazonians described by ethno-historians for the Incas, based on oppositions between civilization and savagery (Chapters 5.1 and 5.2), Taylor nevertheless also endorses the prevalence of essential continuities across Inca and Spanish times, such that the 'spatial, social, and economic split between highland and lowland peoples exacerbated an ethnic and cultural polarization that had already begun in the Inka period' (A.-C. Taylor 1999, 217). And while, in the north, her work perhaps shifts the establishment of the colonial frontier forward by several decades, it necessarily also supports the 'big picture' of a firm frontier prevailing between Andes and Amazonia during colonial times.

Taylor's arguments are also relevant to the question of the movement of people and goods between Andes and Amazonia during colonial times. Given the sharp decline and dispersal of the indigenous population, and the impact of the missions as outliers of Spanish Peru, it seems likely that such movement became less everyday after the Conquest. It also seems probable that communications across the frontier came to be based more on long-distance travel and less on mediated, down-the-line exchange. After the establishment of the missions, and excepting brief moments of peculiarly intense Andes–Amazonia interaction occurring during incidents such as the Juan Santos Atahualpa rebellion (for which see Chapter 5.4), cross-frontier population movements depended mainly on the incursions of friars, native auxiliaries, troops and also fugitives of different kinds from the highlands, while the transfer of goods rested on a limited exchange of tropical produce for highland imports. Lastly, the implication is that the latter exchanges took place more from Andes to Amazonia than in the reverse direction, motivated primarily by lowland demand for some specialized highland products. Native Amazonians themselves, meanwhile, had still less motive than Europeans or indigenous Andeans to cross the frontier, whether for trade, conquest or refuge, and to do so carried greater risks for them.

Conclusions

Virtually throughout the colonial period, the Andes–Amazonia frontier was a firm phenomenon. Spanish Peru – the dominant Andean polity to prevail during the three centuries following the European invasions – showed little interest and generated only a tenuous demographic and administrative presence in adjacent Amazonia. Even to the degree that it did maintain such a presence, this came about through limited support for the actions of partially autonomous, religiously motivated groups: the religious orders and their missionaries. And this support itself had its limits and might be withdrawn if circumstances so dictated, even at the risk of the missionizing endeavour itself.

From a historical perspective, what seems striking is that the relations of Spanish Peru with Amazonia and its peoples should have proven so similar, broadly speaking, to those of the Inca Empire – the immediately preceding hegemonic Andean polity. Though population densities and ethnic territories along the frontier may have undergone huge changes, relations between Andes and Amazonia (in particular the modest projection of power and population from the former to the latter) changed relatively little across the Conquest era. This seems clearly to suggest, then, that it was the *Andean* nature of both polities that determined the persistence and character of the frontier. Although as other chapters in this book make quite clear, debate remains vigorous as to the nature of the frontier during prehistory, there seems to be some consensus that it became firmer over time – starting from scant evidence for any significant divide in earliest prehistory, to much firmer evidence in late prehistory and the earliest historical centuries (see the Conclusion to this volume). The package of Andean civilization – intensive, temperate agriculture and animal husbandry, very high population densities, and urban civilization – coalesced only slowly, but it was already firmly established long before Europeans inherited and reshaped it. It was surely this package that differentiated Andes from Amazonia, and that thus sustained a relatively firm frontier, for several centuries after the arrival of Europeans in the New World.

5.4

A case study in Andes–Amazonia relations under colonial rule: The Juan Santos Atahualpa rebellion (1742–52)

Adrian J. Pearce

Introduction

An earlier contribution to this volume set out historical understandings of the nature of the Andes–Amazonia 'frontier' during the Spanish colonial period (Chapter 5.3). Its main argument was that this frontier displayed considerable substance or solidity, such that Spain's presence and influence in the Amazonian lowlands beyond the upper *montaña* was limited. That is not, of course, to say that there was no movement of peoples, languages or goods across the frontier; for there certainly was such movement. The general rule of a limited Spanish presence in Amazonia displayed an important exception, in the missions maintained primarily by friars of the Jesuit and Franciscan orders. These missions had a major demographic and cultural impact of their own, and provided a means by which limited communication between highlands and lowlands was maintained throughout the centuries following the conquest. For the most part, however, the footprint of Spain in the lowlands was weak and tenuous, while the missions themselves stood in somewhat awkward relation to the colonial state. Amazonia in no sense formed part of the colonial heartland, which lay firmly to the west, in the sierra and on the coast. Spain's support even for the missions was contingent, and it might be withdrawn if circumstances so dictated.

The present chapter provides concrete illustration of the key themes identified in its companion, to give a clearer idea of how the processes described there operated in practice. To do so, it looks at a major indigenous insurrection affecting the upper Amazon in the mid-eighteenth century: the rebellion of Juan Santos Atahualpa. This provides a good illustration of the cross-frontier dynamic during the colonial era, for at first glance, it appears to have marked a moment of peculiarly intense interaction and intervention between highlands and lowlands. On closer inspection, however, the rebellion only reinforces the sense that the colonial

Andes–Amazonia frontier was indeed a phenomenon of real substance. In the sections that follow, I first describe the rebellion itself in brief outline. I then offer an interpretation for what it meant for the broader issues discussed in this volume and for the nature of the Andes–Amazonia divide, particularly during the colonial era.

History

The Juan Santos Atahualpa rebellion took place in the central montaña: that is to say, in the region to the east of Tarma, beyond the Chanchamayo valley. This region is bounded or crossed by the rivers Apurimac, Ene, Perené, Pachitea, Tambo and the Alto Ucayali. It embraces the Gran Pajonal, a plateau of grassland and cloud forest rising to 2,000 metres above the surrounding lowlands and covering some 4,000 square miles. It is inhabited by a variety of indigenous peoples, including the Machiguenga, Piro, Cunibo, Cashibo, Amuesha and Asháninka (known during colonial times and until recently as the Campa). A unique feature, of some relevance to the events discussed in this chapter, is the Cerro de la Sal, near modern La Merced, with readily accessible surface deposits of salt. These deposits were exploited by the different groups of the region, who often travelled long distances to obtain salt for preserving foodstuffs (the classic ethno-historical and anthropological account is Varese 1968/2006).

The central montaña remained unoccupied and largely unexplored by Europeans until the early 1700s, several sixteenth- and seventeenth century incursions notwithstanding. The Gran Pajonal itself was barely known to Spaniards in Peru prior to the 1730s. But, at the hands of the charismatic Father Francisco de San Joseph, the Franciscan order from this time mounted a fresh missionizing drive focused on the region. A missionary college was founded as a base, at Santa Rosa de Ocopa in the Mantaro valley, and significant state funding was secured in support (Amich 1975). The Franciscan missions rapidly proliferated: by 1736, 24 stations had been established within the region or along the access routes from the highlands, with a native population in excess of 4,800 (Jones 2016, 331), and the number continued to grow thereafter. The friars established a mission at the Cerro de la Sal itself, and sought to control the supply of salt there. Projects were drawn up for a more extensive and effective colonization of the region. Europeans, then, with the backing of the colonial state, established a significant presence in the central lowlands for the first time.

This process was brought to an abrupt end by the rebellion of Juan Santos Atahualpa. Amid much myth-making and many obscurities, it seems clear that Juan Santos was a Quechua-speaking mestizo from Cuzco, and had studied with the Jesuits there. In May 1742 he arrived in the Gran Pajonal and sparked a rebellion that spread rapidly across the central montaña, uniting its peoples in a temporary multi-ethnic alliance. (It is speculated that frequent contact between different peoples converging on the Cerro de la Sal over many years facilitated this alliance.)

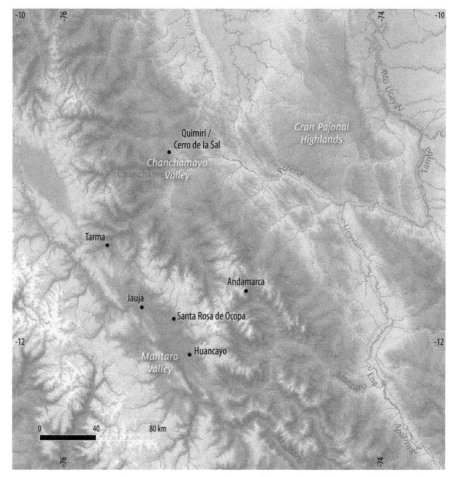

Figure 5.4.1 Map showing the region affected by the Juan Santos Atahualpa rebellion (1742–52). © Adrian J. Pearce and Paul Heggarty.

As a highlander, and given the fragmentary sources for his rebellion, the specific nature of Santos' appeal to lowland peoples remains obscure, but he clearly exploited resentment and fears arising from recent Spanish incursions and missionary activities. Within days, the indigenous population abandoned the missions en masse, and the Franciscans themselves were expelled entirely from the region (Castro Arenas 1973; see Loayza 1942, for most of the relevant primary sources). In 1752, Juan Santos' forces even left the lowlands and assaulted the highland town of Andamarca, occupying it for several days before they withdrew (Glave 2009).

The response of the Spanish state to the rebellion was at first its standard one in the face of indigenous uprisings, based on military suppression. A series of *entradas* or armed expeditions were launched, that sought to locate the rebels and crush the insurrection. A total of four such expeditions were organized, in 1742, 1743,

1746 and 1750. They began as local responses, staged with militia forces from the adjacent highland provinces of Tarma and Jauja, but then became formal military ventures made up of regular troops dispatched across the Andes from distant Lima. All these expeditions failed, however. For the most part, the rebels refused to come to battle, and simply evaded confrontation until the Spanish were obliged to withdraw from the region. But in 1743, 80 soldiers were left to guard a makeshift fort at Quimiri (the Cerro de la Sal settlement) after the larger force they accompanied withdrew to Tarma; they were then besieged by indigenous forces and were killed to the last man. In the face of these defeats, the viceroy of Peru in the late 1740s, the Count of Superunda, abandoned the offensive strategy in favour of a defensive one. He oversaw the construction of a string of forts along the upper montaña with the aim of containing and isolating the lowlands. Roving patrols guarded the frontier, at considerable expense to the royal coffers. Juan Santos' rebellion had proven strikingly successful: Europeans abandoned the central montaña, and would not begin to recolonize the region for well over a century, until long after the end of the colonial era.

Discussion

At first glance, the rebellion of Juan Santos Atahualpa seems to point to a remarkable fluidity and force of relations across any putative Andes–Amazonia frontier. Thus, we witness the missionizing and colonizing endeavour of the Franciscans, launched by Europeans from the highlands with the active backing of the Spanish Andean state. We note the role of Juan Santos himself, an Andean with some European education and religious culture, but who sparked a large-scale uprising among peoples of Amazonia. We might emphasize the projection of military force from the highlands into the lowlands, in the expeditions sent from Spanish Peru to extinguish the rebellion. And we might further note the more modest projection of the rebellion from lowlands to highlands – of which more in a moment – and even a brief military incursion of 'Amazonians' into the Andes, at Andamarca in 1752.

A closer look at this episode, however, points to very different conclusions. Historians of colonial Peru have tended to see Juan Santos' rebellion from an Andean perspective, and so to discuss it as part of Andean as much as Amazonian history. They have thus pondered the rebellion's significance for the Andes themselves, as much as for the central montaña, and have dwelt on evidence that seems to support such a significance. Evidence of this kind includes the titles assumed by the rebel himself, whose name was often extended to 'Juan Santos Atahualpa Apu Inca' (sometimes even with the addition of 'Jesus Sacramentado': Zarzar 1989). He is thus touted as an early expression of the 'Inca national movement' of the eighteenth century, that flourished most fully in the rebellion of Túpaq Amaru II some forty years later (Rowe 1954). Juan Santos directed much of his recorded rhetoric at a native Andean constituency and concerns, calling for the abolition of forced labour in silver mines and textile workshops – issues necessarily of scant relevance in the Amazonian lowlands. Some highland Indians and even Afro-Peruvians fled to join Juan Santos' movement, while he sought to build relations with caciques in adjacent Andean provinces; news of the rebel successes was apparently greeted with jubilation in Tarma (Varese 2006, 110–14). There was concern that other contemporary rebels in the Andes, notably during a rising at Huarochirí in Lima province in 1750, would link up with or receive support from Juan Santos (C. F. Walker 2008, 176). On these grounds, the distinguished historian Steve Stern has argued that the rebellion not only formed part of a broader 'Age of Andean Insurrection' in the mid-eighteenth century, but that it posed a real threat to Spanish rule in the Andes (Stern 1987). This interpretation has taken root in Peru, where Juan Santos is seen as a major early figure in national emancipation. His effigy adorns the *Panteón de los Próceres* in Lima, alongside other heroes of the independence wars.

Whatever the wider ethnic and social tensions in the Andes identified by Stern for this period, however, this interpretation is unconvincing, and has found little support among historians (see for example Jones 2016, 325). On the one hand, the real capacity of the rebellion to reach beyond its base in the montaña was frankly limited. The Andean rebels at Huarochirí waited in vain for assistance from Juan Santos, and their own insurrection was swiftly crushed by regular Spanish forces. Meanwhile, the rebellion's sole real projection of force into the highlands, at Andamarca, was not only of brief duration, but affected an exceptionally isolated town, of little economic or political significance. Contemporaries, writing from an Andean perspective, recorded those parts of Juan Santos' rhetoric and strategy that targeted his highland homeland. But the true causes of the rebellion necessarily lay within the Amazonian lowlands, and not the Andes. Juan Santos' genius, or perhaps his good fortune, was to exploit lowland anxieties and anger arising from the growing missionary presence in the region in recent years. It was this recent process, rather than the deeper grievances of native peoples in the highlands, that first provided fertile ground for the rebellion, and then supplied most of its militants. In this sense, Juan Santos himself was of only relative importance. While he disappeared from the historical record after 1752, rumours later circulated to the effect that the lowland indigenous people themselves eventually killed him, perhaps once the rebellion had triumphed and he had served his purpose.

In fact, Juan Santos' rebellion thrived precisely because it was based in the lowlands, in remote and densely forested regions far beyond the colonial heartland. On the one hand, this gave the rebels their crucial military advantage. On the other, it meant that Spanish interest in this region, or indeed concern at its loss, was necessarily limited. The four Spanish armed expeditions against the rebels met the same fate said to have greeted Inca armies in the lowlands centuries earlier: they failed to come to grips with an enemy that refused to commit to pitched battle and often simply took refuge deeper in the forest, while difficulties of movement and supply across exceptionally harsh terrain sapped their will, just as lowland diseases thinned out their numbers. The scale of the defeat was striking: the killing of the 80 men left to man the fort at Quimiri in 1743 marked the worst Spanish military loss at native hands in Peru since the conquest in the 1530s. Viceroy Superunda later wrote of the difficulties faced by campaigns in the lowlands:

> These expeditions, excessively costly and to little purpose, represent an intolerable burden on the provinces concerned … [The provinces] suffer irreparable harm, though not from the Savages. These are enemies who … never show their face, and mock the most gallant sally by fleeing before it; nature fights for them with the shelter it affords in impenetrable mountainous lands … To pursue them is more alike to hunting or stalking wild beasts than to conquering men. (Manso de Velasco 1983, 254)

For almost three centuries, from the 1530s to the 1810s, every indigenous rebellion that took place in the relatively open and accessible terrain of the Andean highlands and coast was crushed by Spanish arms. This was true of countless minor acts of desperate vengeance against local officials, as it was of the greatest of all the insurrections, the bloody civil war of the Túpaq Amaru rebellion (Walker 2014). Juan Santos' rebellion, by contrast, inflicted military defeat on the Spaniards and expelled them permanently from the central lowlands. But it did so precisely because it was not in truth an Andean rebellion at all, but rather an Amazonian one. In this sense, and Juan Santos' own leadership notwithstanding, it bore closer resemblance to other enduring native campaigns against Spain on the fringes of the empire, whether among the 'Araucanians' of southern Chile or the Chiriguanas in lowland Upper Peru (Bolivia) (for an overview see Weber 2005).

And neither did Juan Santos' success lie solely in the ability of Amazonian peoples to defeat or elude Spanish armed forces. For the fact was that Spain had little stake in the central montaña, and so little commitment to investing in its defence or recovery. Thus, it was not only that the rebellion was difficult to suppress in military terms; it was also that there was insufficient motive for Spanish Peru to persist in its attempt to subjugate lands that were figuratively as well as literally marginal to its economic and political core. The Franciscan presence in this region, as we have seen, was both a recent and a shallow one. As long as the missionary initiative appeared to prosper, Spaniards were willing to contemplate a deeper colonization. But in the face of the rebellion and the defeat of the expeditions dispatched against it, the entire enterprise was discarded with a rapidity that seems surprising unless the lack of real incentives to conquest and subjugation of the region is taken into account. Recent research on Juan Santos' rebellion even argues that tensions between the viceregal authorities and the Franciscan order in Peru, and particularly the missionary college of Santa Rosa de Ocopa, contributed to the abandonment of military attempts to subdue a rebellion that affected lands primarily of interest to the order rather than the colonial state (Jones 2016). This underscores both the contingent nature of state support for missions in Amazonia, and the degree to which the attention of Spanish Peru was focused 'inwards' on the Andes, rather than 'outwards' to Amazonia. Spain could never have tolerated a rebellion on such a scale in the colonial Andean heartland. But faced with one in the tropical lowlands to the east, it built a line of forts and fell back behind them – rebuilding in stone a frontier whose ecological and sociological foundations had been laid centuries before.

Conclusions

The rebellion of Juan Santos Atahualpa appeared to represent a moment of intense interaction between Andes and Amazonia. On closer inspection, however, it serves to illustrate the major points made earlier in the companion to this chapter, so that the colonial Andes–Amazonia frontier only emerges in sharpened perspective from this episode. I ended my earlier contribution by noting what seem to be striking parallels between Spanish colonial and Inca imperial interaction with and attitudes to the Amazon region (Chapter 5.3). This was a point not lost on the colonial officials who confronted the Juan Santos rebellion in the 1740s. In justifying his decision to abandon *entradas* against the lowland peoples and to retreat behind the new fortifications, viceroy Superunda noted that 'even the Incas did not take the trouble to add these vassals to their Empire' (Manso de Velasco 1983, 254). This comment followed the defeat of several armed expeditions against lowland peoples, embracing serious military reverses, and yet it was cast in the terms of contempt for Amazonians and perhaps a certain sympathy with the experience of the preceding imperial state in the Andes. Certainly, and though he is unlikely to have known it, Superunda replicated Inca policy when he fortified the upper montaña, throwing up a cordon protecting and isolating the highland world from the eastern lands below. In both cases, then, the Andean imperial writ ran as far as the upper montaña, that marked a distinct political and economic frontier with the lowlands of Amazonia beyond.

Conclusion. The Andes–Amazonia divide: Myth and reality

Adrian J. Pearce, David G. Beresford-Jones and Paul Heggarty

For most of the past five hundred years, if not longer, the human societies of the Andes and Amazonia have been regarded as displaying fundamental differences. Whether in their subsistence practices, population densities, degree of urbanization, broader social organization or the languages they spoke, the distinct character of the peoples of the two regions has been taken almost as a given. This cultural divide was naturalized as an inevitable outcome of the clear geographical and environmental contrasts between Andes and Amazonia, between temperate highlands and tropical lowlands, walled off from each other by the steep, humid and often impassable slopes of the eastern piedmont. The course of human history and the development of societies on either side of the piedmont, then, were at heart considered to have been determined by environment, and so to have remained essentially immutable over time. But recent revisionism, based on new findings and interpretations of the archaeology of Amazonia, in line with insights from anthropology, have critically revisited these long-standing, engrained assumptions. Indeed, new thinking has sought comprehensively to debunk the notion that there was much real substance to the Andes–Amazonia divide at all. Rather, that divide might be considered little more than a myth: a purely cultural construct, arising from colonial or post-colonial prejudices and preconceptions. It was this debate that stimulated us to convene a conference held in Leipzig in 2014, and subsequently to edit this volume.

We emphasized in our Introduction how, from an editorial standpoint, this book was not driven by theory. It set out from no fundamental presumption as to the nature or indeed the existence of any putative Andes–Amazonia divide. We also pointed out that, simplifying grossly, there may be a general tendency among Amazonianists to take a stance towards this question that is closer to anthropology, more concerned with connections, networks, and so on, and so more inherently 'anti-divide'. Andeanists, meanwhile, may have typically seen things more in terms of complex societies, power relations and so forth, and tend to be more 'pro-divide'. There are many exceptions to this rule, of course. But it will not have escaped the notice of attentive readers that all three editors of this book are Andeanists.

Nevertheless, neither in our invitations to participants in the Leipzig conference, nor in editing and assembling the book itself, did we favour any particular view over any other. Rather, we were interested primarily in the dedicated application of interdisciplinary study to what seemed to us among the most important topics in South American prehistory – and one with clear relevance to the intractable and controversial topic of environmental determinism, which applies everywhere, but perhaps nowhere more starkly than here (as we set out in our Introduction to this volume).

We have thus found surprising the degree to which so many of our diverse contributions continue to favour the reality of an Andes–Amazonia divide in later prehistory after all. This divide is manifest in two ways: in different characteristics (physiological or cultural) of the populations of the Andes or of Amazonia, and in the far lower degree of interaction between these two populations than is apparent internally to either. If the 'divide' is indeed a myth, then it is one that turns out still to hold a strange power over scholars working across numerous disciplines.

Yet, as many chapters in the book make clear, the differences between the human societies of the Andes and of Amazonia did not date from time immemorial. That is to say, the Andes–Amazonia divide did not derive from first human settlement, but arose in more recent times. The chapters collected in Part 2 are devoted to 'Deep Time', generally meaning the first half of the Holocene, while several contributors to other sections also make reference to this early period. Two points are apparent. Firstly, this is the least-known period of all, simply because the evidence available to any of the disciplines is poor. This is the inevitable product of greater time-depth: archaeological sites and source materials are more elusive, and the research dedicated to them also sometimes scantier (see Chapters 1.1, 2.1, 2.4 and 4.4). Secondly, however, in so far as the available evidence *can* shed light on our key concerns here, it gives little indication of any significant differentiation between Andes and Amazonia. Such contacts and influences as can be detected at these earliest times by archaeology, for example, went in multiple directions (Chapters 1.1, 2.1 and 3.7) and ranged across coast, highlands and eastern lowlands apparently indiscriminately (Chapter 2.4). Certainly, no predominant influence from Amazonia to Andes or vice versa is discernible in the archaeology of these times. Linguistics can add very little signal for this deepest timeframe (Chapter 2.3), although much later, when the earliest meaningful linguistic relations can be determined between the two regions, they too seem to present a 'balanced interaction' (Chapter 4.1). Only in genetics and cranial morphology is some differentiation apparent that might go back to founder populations and first settlement, though even here, majority opinion favours differentiation through later processes, again post-dating the Middle Holocene (Chapters 2.2, 3.2 and 3.3). On the other hand, one of the few chapters presenting primary (archaeological) data at these great time depths – Chapter 4.4 on early Holocene shell middens in the Llanos de Moxos – points to an *independent* process of cultural development in Amazonia for this earliest period.

From the Middle Holocene onwards, however, the picture changes, to develop in a clear and essentially novel direction. From this time, a divide does indeed become detectable to many of our specialists across the full range of disciplines, and a divide that then grew in substance and resolution into later prehistory, until it was unambiguous by the final centuries prior to the European invasions. Some of the most striking evidence for this divide is archaeological, and dates to the final millennium before European contact. We have seen that Wilkinson (Chapter 3.1), working on the piedmont region itself, argues for a divide between Andes and Amazonia that was not only increasingly pronounced over time, but constituted a 'stark reality' by Inca times. Wilkinson also appears to make among the strongest defences of the ecological foundations of the divide, when he suggests that the piedmont itself was permanently settled only within the last thousand years. Prümers (Chapter 4.3), meanwhile, working from the Amazonian perspective of the Llanos de Mojos in the same period, finds virtually no evidence whatever of Andean influence in this well-studied region, adjacent to the Altiplano. And Beresford-Jones and Machicado Murillo (Chapter 1.1) invoke the idea of convergent yet independent trajectories across the divide for this later period.

From genetics and cranial morphology, too, there seems strong evidence of differentiation that probably post-dates the Middle Holocene. Strauss (Chapter 2.2) concludes that cranial morphology indicates that the east–west division of South America imposed by the Andean cordillera 'is crucial to understanding the population structure' of the continent as a whole. For their part, Santos (Chapter 3.2) and Barbieri (Chapter 3.3) agree that in all major genetic studies, Central Andean populations appear as a distinctive group. All three authors discuss the various means by which differentiation might have come about, whether through different founder populations, subsequent stochastic drift, functional adaptation to high altitude, or developmental plasticity. Yet Santos emphasizes the consensus that the distinctive genetic pattern found in the Central Andes does not go back to different founder populations or other deep-time processes, but is likely to have developed only much later, again during the second half of the Holocene. Indeed, the latest analysis of ancient DNA (Nakatsuka et al. 2020) also suggests a population structure for the continent with early Holocene roots but which strongly correlates with geography since at least around 2000 BP. The languages of the Central Andes, too, are of a structural type very different to the languages of Amazonia, even if this opposition is, as Van Gijn and Muysken argue (Chapter 3.5), more complex and geographically incremental than previously thought.

Since the Andes–Amazonia divide detected by many authors grew in substance and resolution over time, it is unsurprising that the authors discussing the most recent periods should find among the clearest evidence for it. Both ethnohistorical chapters, by Tyuleneva (Chapter 5.1) and Bertazoni (Chapter 5.2), find attitudes of cultural superiority already entrenched in the Andes by Inca times, underpinning an already prevailing opposition between their own Andean civilization and a perceived Amazonian 'barbarism'. Bertazoni argues that Amazonia was nevertheless construed as an integral part of the Inca Empire, and in doing so provides a further clue as to the changing nature of Andes–Amazonia relations after the Spanish Conquest of the 1530s. Pearce (Chapters 5.3 and 5.4) shows that the divide between Andes and Amazonia was a thing of substance under Spanish rule, when abundant documentation leaves little room for doubt that the highlands and the coast constituted Spain's colonial heartlands, with Amazonia little more than a marginal marchland. And yet Bertazoni's last point hints at how much still did change with the European invasions, when the conceptual integration of Amazonia into the native Andean world was discarded by the Spanish, in favour of a still more radical divide setting the highlands (and coast) apart from the eastern lowlands. The Andes–Amazonia divide discussed by these authors was not simply a creation of Spanish colonialism, then, but Europeans did harden and sharpen it, nonetheless.

So if most of our authors see a divide developing between human societies in the Andes and Amazonia subsequent to the Middle Holocene, then what caused it? What was its nature? On this point, contributors tend to return to the 'usual suspects': more intense resource exploitation in the Andes, above all through the expansion of agriculture and irrigation from the (archaeological) Initial Period onwards (after 4000 BP), leading to higher population densities and greater sophistication in social and political organization. For Wilkinson (Chapter 3.1), to cite the key argument once more, these trends gave rise to 'contrasting regional systems with distinctive characteristics – a product of the expansion of imperial states in the highlands and of major linguistic-agricultural complexes in the lowlands'. For Santos (Chapter 3.2), as we have seen, the distinctive genetic profile of Andean populations can best be understood as the consequence of the degree of hierarchical organization of their societies: capable of co-opting labour and resources towards advanced agriculture, armies, and the road networks that fuelled and facilitated the movement of people and their genes around the region. In Amazonia, by contrast, differing degrees of dependence on agriculture, and more varied forms of social and cultural organization, led to different genetic outcomes.

Santos stands alone among our contributors in his willingness to go further, and to suggest an analogy between the human genetics of the Andes and the spread of agriculture and consequent mass movements of peoples, along the lines envisaged by some for the Neolithic transition in Europe. But he and Wilkinson are far from alone in concluding that, in contrast to deeper time periods, the predominant influence along and across the 'divide' in more recent times has been literally a top-down one, from Andes to Amazonia. For Wilkinson, the first permanent human settlement of the piedmont came in the form of colonization from the Andes. For his fellow archaeologist, Herrera, too, the period from 1000 BP witnessed an inversion of Andes–Amazonia relations in the Upper Marañón, with the advent of Andean hegemony there. But Barbieri (Chapter 3.3), in looking at the human genetics specifically of this same piedmont (or 'highland/lowland transitional environment') similarly notes that the predominant direction of gene-flow across the divide has been from the Andean highlands. And the linguists Van Gijn and Muysken (Chapter 3.5) also observe that contact influences between Andes and Amazonia 'have operated mostly in one direction, from the highland languages into the lowland ones'.

Of course, no monolithic view is presented by our 26 contributors, and there are dissenting voices. Dillehay, McCray and Netherly (Chapter 3.7) call for a whole-sale rethinking not only of relations between Andes and Amazonia, but also for taking the Pacific coast separately from the Andean 'co-tradition'. They further call for greater sensitivity to cultural and political dynamics at more local levels, both outside and in relation to broader geographical frames of reference. Among the most numerous voices to entertain significant connections across the divide are those of our linguistic contributors. While recognizing the cohesion of the (Central) Andean languages, Van Gijn and Muysken (Chapter 3.5) suggest that the true divide between these languages and those of Amazonia lies not along the piedmont itself, but rather further to the east, within Amazonia itself. Zariquiey (Chapter 4.2) disproves one outdated claim for a long-distance language relation-ship across the frontier, but only to advance a tentative hypothesis of a 'Southern Andes–Amazonia' linguistic convergence area instead, suggestive of wider contacts between languages on either side of the divide. And to archaeologists, it will be striking to read Adelaar's suggestion (Chapter 4.1) that Puquina, widely regarded by linguists as probably the primary language of ancient Tiwanaku on the Altiplano, may have originated in part in Amazonia. Tenuous as these associations may be, given how little language data survives on the long-extinct Puquina, many archae-ologists will find them beguiling, not least in view of the unexplored Tiwanaku archaeological record of Cochabamba. More generally, however, Adelaar's thesis suggests that the direction of influence was not unremittingly from the Andes to Amazonia over recent millennia.

By far the strongest dissenting voices, however, come from a single discipline, and one moreover that claims to take the widest perspective and to be best placed to integrate the findings of others into its single 'four-field' perspective. The two chapters by distinguished anthropologists, Hornborg (Chapter 1.4) and Zuidema (also an ethnohistorian: Chapter 1.5), take a view substantially different from that expressed in most other contributions. Basing himself on case studies from the sec-ond millennium BP or earlier, Hornborg detects a 'recurring pattern' of interaction between Andes and Amazonia that had major social and cultural impacts. Zuidema, too, finds evidence for an Andes–Amazonia culture area or co-tradition, but rather as the reflection of a deep-time cultural continuum stretching from the Andes all the way into central Brazil, and therefore not incongruent with the archaeological record, sparse though that is for such time-depths. Hornborg, meanwhile, further suggests that Amazonian polities may have been as densely populated, extensive and hierarchical in their social and political organization as those of the Andes, so that the very notion of an Andes–Amazonia divide is a myth or an illusion, gener-ated purely by European colonialism, exclusively since the Spanish conquest.

We should be clear here that Hornborg and (somewhat differently) Zuidema represent views held more widely within their discipline and indeed by many Amazonian archaeologists (Chapter 1.1). Participants in the Leipzig conference will recall Bruce Mannheim, a distinguished anthropologist and linguist, and an Andeanist to boot, rising from his chair to state that while he was glad that the conference was taking place, he also very much hoped that it would also be the *last* event on its theme that would ever need to be held. Anthropology, then, came more to bury the Andes–Amazonia divide than to legitimate it, much less to endorse it.

How are we to understand this position, in contrast to that assumed by most contributors from other disciplines? In part, the answer surely lies precisely in different 'ways of seeing' from one discipline to the next. Anthropology, with its focus on cultural and social relations and connections across vastly different geographical and chronological contexts, may be able to perceive such connections where other disciplines do not – or indeed, may take as connections phenomena not necessarily regarded as such by specialists from other fields. The different stance taken by anthropologists in this volume, then, may speak simply to the same diversity of disciplinary methodologies and approaches that provides the core rationale for this book.

Beyond this, however, the chapters by Hornborg and Zuidema do seem to pose challenges, on both sides of this *disciplinary* 'divide'. In presuming comparable populations, scales, and degrees of hierarchical organization for polities in the Andes and in Amazonia, Hornborg bases himself in no small part on the remarkable changes in perception of Amazonian prehistory that have unfolded from recent archaeological investigations and methodological innovations. And yet many archaeological contributors to this book, especially those who focus on later time periods, whether they write from an Andean or an Amazonian perspective, continue to find ample evidence to support the notion of difference in social organization and/or a real divide to either side of the eastern piedmont. This seems to us to support the view of Beresford-Jones and Machicado Murillo (Chapter 1.1), that it 'may be time to rein back on some of the recent hyperbole attending the intensity and chronology of human settlement in Amazonia and to rebalance, somewhat, the pendulum of archaeological perceptions'.

On the other hand, other disciplines cannot simply dismiss the findings of anthropology, of wide-ranging connections and cultural similarities between peoples of the Andes and of Amazonia. Some of Hornborg's evidence for relations and cultural connections across the divide is in fact challenged or controverted in other chapters here: the ostensibly Amazonian iconography at the early highland site of Chavín de Huántar, for example (see Chapter 2.4), or the supposedly common origins of raised field agriculture in the eastern lowlands and on the Altiplano (see Chapter 4.3). But other evidence finds no ready response, including anthropomorphic sculptures found both in southern Colombia and on the lower Amazon that are so similar as to suggest 'direct emulation', for Hornborg. Zuidema's discussion of striking similarities between the cultural systems of the Incas and of contemporary peoples living deep in Brazilian Amazonia, too, cries out for further exploration and explanation. And these authors' chapters and arguments are the more powerful for complementing each other across very different time frames. Zuidema deals with deep time; Hornborg primarily with the second millennium BP.

To conclude: the chapters in this volume were shaped by intense cross-disciplinary discussions, and though they take particular disciplinary standpoints, they were written with sensitivity to and with a view to informing other disciplines. The overall effect is one of independent verification and validation of findings, to the degree that most chapters, whatever their disciplinary perspective, point to similar conclusions. By late prehistory, the peoples of the Andes and Amazonia had distinct genetic heritages and spoke languages that respected a divide between the two regions, both in their origins and expansions and in their convergence towards broad structural types. This is surely suggestive of a separation and differentiation that had proceeded over millennia. Moreover, their artistic and architectural styles, manifest in ceramics, buildings or settlement planning, corresponded to different autochthonous traditions, with little mutual overlap. Several scholars in this volume also incline towards the view that in the Andes, population densities were higher, and social and political organization larger-scale and more complex. There is no consensus on this, although there is (ethnohistorical) evidence that the two populations did indeed view each other differently, and that Andeans saw themselves as culturally superior. In any case, contacts and communication *between* Andeans and Amazonians seem to have been very substantially more limited than among the different peoples *within* each group. This seems to hold true even though some flow of both people and goods certainly did cross the divide in prehistory. Indeed, in some cases, the *lack* of influence, and presumably even of much real communication, between Andes and Amazonia seems striking – the paradigm case being that of the Llanos de Mojos.

Some conspicuous similarities in aspects of the cultures of different peoples very far to either side of the eastern piedmont require explanation. We also recognize the dissenting voices among our contributors, as well as the simplification that comes with summarizing work of such range and complexity in just a few short paragraphs. Overall, however, we are confident that the Andes–Amazonia divide is more than simply the product of European colonialism or of scholarly blinkeredness. On the contrary, it formed part of the lived experience of peoples both of highlands and lowlands in prehistoric times. In reaching this conclusion, we are aware that we are controverting much of the recent thinking deriving from anthropology and (Amazonian) archaeology. But we will end by noting that we are the more confident in doing so, for basing our view on work deriving not from any single author, nor any single discipline, but from many.

Notes

1.1 Archaeology

1. Here by 'convergent' we mean the independent evolution of similar features in different lineages. For the avoidance of doubt, this is distinct to its meaning in linguistics (see Heggarty, Chapter 1.2, this volume).

1.4 Anthropology

1. However, pre-colonial lowland societies constructed extensive earthworks in various parts of Amazonia (Balée and Erickson 2006; Rostain 2013; Salazar 2008; Schaan 2012; Saunaluoma 2013).
2. The major exception is the account of friar Gaspar Carvajal (1934) of the voyage down the Amazon by Francisco de Orellana in 1542, which documents densely populated settlements along the river.
3. This understanding of Amazonia has until recently prevailed even in modern anthropology and archaeology (Meggers 1971).
4. The Inca, too, appear to have perceived the Amazonian lowlands as an inferior region populated by savage peoples (see Chapters 5.1 and 5.2, this volume).
5. Lévi-Strauss has discussed Andean–Amazonian mythological parallels in terms both of the influence of one region on the other (1973, 344–5) and of common and presumably ancient themes such as the 'rolling-head' theme, which occurs for example, among Pano-Tacana-speakers in the lowlands as well as in the Andean highlands (1978, 98). Another very widespread theme is the 'revolt of the objects', identified in Amazonia (Santos-Granero 2009, 3) as well as on ceramics from the Moche culture (AD 200–700) on the north coast of Peru (Quilter 1990).
6. In Descola's (2013) quadripartite scheme, animistic representations of the world posit similar 'interiorities' but dissimilar 'physicalities', whereas analogism represents both aspects as dissimilar.
7. The temple constructions at Chavín de Huántar may have been intentionally designed to enhance acoustic effects such as the sound of water rushing through the stone-lined galleries and canals (cf. Burger 1992, 143).
8. See Schaan, Ranzi and Damasceno Barbosa 2010, 66–7.
9. Note that the center of Tiwanaku, like Chavín de Huántar, thus occupied a position from which it could mediate trade between the Pacific coast and the tropical eastern lowlands.
10. The Middle Horizon expansion of Wari may in part have been geared to controlling trade with the lowlands along the Apurímac (Raymond 1988, 298; Wilkinson 2018). The expansion of Wari appears to have promoted the dispersal of Quechua over much of the central Andes (Heggarty and Beresford-Jones 2012).
11. Carvajal's (1934) account describes several such complex polities along the Amazon in 1542.

1.5 The Andes–Amazonia culture area

1. Editors' note: Tom Zuidema died on 2 March 2016, before he was able to take into account our editorial comments on his chapter and requests for clarification. For this reason, although we have lightly edited his text on stylistic grounds, we have otherwise left it as originally submitted. His original unedited manuscript can be obtained on request from the editors.

2.1 Initial east and west connections across South America

1. Acknowledgements: I wish to thank Paul Heggarty and David Beresford-Jones for inviting me to the Leipzig symposium on Andean and Amazonian linkages.

2.2 The Andes–Amazonia divide and human morphological diversification in South America

1. I gratefully acknowledge Paul Heggarty, David Beresford-Jones and Adrian Pearce, who invited me to take part in their 'Andes–Amazon' symposium (Leipzig 2014) and in this publication. FAPESP (17/16451-2) and CNPq (409474/2016-9 and 435980/2018-1) provided financial support. I dedicate this chapter to the inspiring work done by Hector Pucciarelli in South American anthropology.

3.1 How real is the Andes–Amazonia divide? An archaeological view from the eastern piedmont

1. For the sake of brevity, when referring to the Andes and Amazonia in this chapter I am in both cases excluding the coastal regions. The coasts add extra layers of variation and complexity that are beyond the scope of the current discussion.
2. Obviously, the piedmont continues into the Southern Cone, where the lands to the east are dominated not by tropical rainforest but by temperate grasslands. Given the present focus on the Andes–Amazonia divide, my usage of the term piedmont will therefore exclude areas south of the Tropic of Capricorn.
3. A few decades ago, the archaeological consensus would likely have been that the Andes was an environment naturally conducive to intensive agriculture, dense population aggregations and state formation – while Amazonia was inherently hostile to all these phenomena. This view has since proven to be an incorrect (or at least wildly exaggerated). Hierarchical 'chiefdoms' and substantial farming communities have been shown to exist in multiple areas of prehistoric Amazonia (see Heckenberger and Neves 2009; Chapters 1.1, 1.4 and 3.6).
4. LIP sites across the Andes are often sited on hilltops and ridges, which has been widely interpreted as reflecting concerns over defence. I tend to discount this interpretation in the case of the Amaybamba LIP sites, however. Firstly, unlike most LIP sites in the region they show no evidence of defensive structures (for example, perimeter walls or ditches); and secondly, they ignore many highly defensible hilltops and ridges that are closer to the valley floor, in favour of higher locations that are within the 2,150–2,700 m elevation zone.
5. As Lyon (1981, 8) has suggested, it is likely that the Incas perceived their exchanges with Amazonian groups as a form of tribute, while the Amazonians understood them more as gifts given between equals. Such differences in perception aside, the flow of goods between the highlands and lowlands was still markedly different from the formal labour extraction systems of the Andes.

3.2 Genetic diversity patterns in the Andes and Amazonia

1. I am grateful to Paul Heggarty, Adrian Pearce and David Beresford-Jones for putting together a group of scientists interested in pre-Columbian South American history during the 'Andes–Amazon' symposium held in Leipzig in 2014, and for inviting me to publish this chapter.

3.3 Genetic exchanges in the highland/lowland transitional environments of South America

1. The final dataset includes data from available publications (Mazières et al. 2008; Gayà-Vidal et al. 2011; Baca et al. 2012; Roewer et al. 2013; Sandoval, Lacerda et al. 2013; Sandoval et al. 2016; Barbieri et al. 2014, 2017; Mendisco et al. 2014; Purps et al. 2014; Cárdenas et al. 2015; Guevara et al. 2016; Di Corcia et al. 2017). Haplotypes for which data are missing for certain loci (mostly in the ancient DNA samples) were not discarded, and the missing values were simply ignored in the pairwise comparisons. Unstable loci DSY385a and b were excluded. Haplotype similarity was adjusted for the mutation rate for each locus as reported in the Y-STR haplotype reference database (website https://yhrd.org/) following Barbieri et al. (2017), using the Average Square Distance formula (ASD) (Goldstein and Pollock 1997). ASD is commonly used to calculate the divergence age between populations from their STR haplotypes and corresponds to the average variance divided by the mutation rate at each locus. For our purposes, we use ASD to approximate the divergence time between pairs of sequences, with greater confidence in the relative degree of similarity than in any exact divergence time estimates.

3.5 Highland–lowland relations: A linguistic view

1. The classification of languages on the basis of their grammatical (or typological) patterns is an alternative to other types of classifications, for example, in terms of language families. The advantage of typological data is that they allow for systematic comparison between languages even when it is not possible to establish any relationship of common descent in any language family tree. Moreover, given the fact that grammatical characteristics of languages can diffuse from one language to the other as the result of language contact, they are potentially indicative of past contact events.
2. One reviewer points out that much more work would be needed to establish this more conclusively, and this is certainly the case.
3. 'Linguistic areas' have been defined as social spaces (regions, countries, [sub-]continents) in which languages from different families have influenced each other significantly, leading to striking or remarkable structural resemblances across genealogical boundaries (Van Gijn and Muysken 2016). They are thus similar to 'culture areas' in anthropology. See Chapter 1.2, this volume.
4. This appears in contrast with what was said earlier about relative structural homogeneity of the western part of the continent. In fact, it may be said that there are many larger groupings which show structural resemblances and a number of specific languages, often isolates, with highly different profiles.
5. Andoa was not considered for this graph because it had too many unknowns.
6. Mosetén ends up relatively close to the Uru-Chipayan languages in the Andean cluster, with which it may have a shared history (see Zariquiey, this volume; Adelaar, this volume). We thank Paul Heggarty for pointing out this fact to us.
7. Yanesha' has developed a three-vowel system similar to the prototypical Andean vowel system, which is attributed to contact influence (Adelaar 2006).
8. One mid vowel /e/ is reconstructed for proto-Arawak, contrasting with high and low vowels (Aikhenvald 1999, 76).
9. Even though retroflex affricates have been reconstructed for Proto-Quechua, they are absent in the dialects surveyed here (Adelaar and Muysken 2004, 200–1).
10. The lower black dot in each distribution in Figure 3.5.9 refers to Huallaga Quechua.
11. Adstrate refers to a language variety spoken alongside the main language spoken, and superstrate to a socially dominant prestige language spoken alongside the main language.
12. In most Quechua varieties, the nominal and verbal paradigms are related, but not identical, for example [1sɢ] –y/-ni, [2sɢ] –yki/-nki, [3sɢ] –n/-n, [1pʟɪ] –nchik/-nchik.
13. Dryer and Haspelmath (2013a, 2013b) classifies Movima and Baure as VOA languages, but that is on the basis of older material. We have classified Movima as a VAO language on the basis of the interpretation of arguments in the direct voice (Haude 2006), Baure is analysed as a VAO language in Danielsen (2007, 332). We have classified Sirionó as an OAV language, following personal communication of Noé Gasparini, who currently works on the language.
14. Esther Matteson mentions that Yine 'has developed a decimal system of counting, this is rare among the languages of the Arawakan family' (https://tinyurl.com/yylnm5tb).
15. Possibly the numerals 6 and higher represent loans from Ayacucho Quechua, this is not entirely clear, however (Alexander-Bakkerus 2005, 177).

3.6 Rethinking the role of agriculture and language expansion for ancient Amazonians

1. I will use in this chapter the term 'family', instead of 'stock', to designate the different Tupían languages in order to keep them at the same hierarchical level as of the Arawak family.

4.1 Linguistic connections between the Altiplano region and the Amazonian lowlands

1. The dominance of Aymara in highland Bolivia as late as 1600 is demonstrated by a contemporary document showing the distribution of languages required for evangelization (Bouysse-Cassagne 1975); see also below.
2. Torero (1987, 353) observes that the name Uruquilla was also used in colonial sources for a population distinct from the Uros (alleged Uru-Chipaya speakers). The matter requires additional investigation.
3. The notation < … > is used here for expressions in colonial spelling with an uncertain phonetic interpretation.
4. In some colonial documents the language spoken in Moquegua is referred to as *Coli*, which may have been an alternative denomination for the local variety of Puquina (cf. Julien 1979).

5. The combination <ch> most likely represents an alveo-palatal affricate [č].
6. There is a first person plural form *señ/sin* 'we', 'our' that does not seem to have a correlate in Arawak.
7. Note that the feminine 3rd person possessive and subject agreement prefix for the Arawak family as a whole was reconstructed as **tʰu-* (Payne 1991, 376), which is closer to the Puquina form *chu* [ču] than any of the corresponding forms in Baure and Iñapari.
8. Loss of the gender distinction can also be observed in Amuesha, an Arawak language strongly influenced by an Andean environment (Adelaar 2006). By contrast, the (Andean) Chipaya language continues to distinguish grammatical gender.
9. The full form of this suffix is <qui> [ki].
10. The following abbreviations are used in this chapter: AG 'agentive (nominalization)', COP 'copula', DECL 'declarative', ERG 'ergative (case)', INT 'interrogative', INV 'inverse', PART 'past participle (nominalization)', 1st pers, etc. 'first person', etc.
11. Unfortunately, the extant Puquina data do not contain many cases (if any) of pronouns that are suffixed to nominal expressions other than those derived from verbs. Hence, the total picture remains incomplete.
12. <casara-> 'to marry', from Spanish *casada* 'married (of women)'.
13. Note that an element <quis>, which may be of Puquina origin, is found in the Inca month names.
14. The research leading to this chapter has received funding by the European Research Council under the European Union's Seventh Framework Programme (FP7/2007–2013)/ERC grant agreement no. 295918.

4.2 Hypothesized language relationships across the Andes–Amazonia divide: The cases of Uro, Pano-Takana and Mosetén

1. There is now, however, some scepticism as to this relationship. Fleck (2013, 23), for instance, claims that: 'a genetic Panoan-Takanan relationship has not yet been convincingly demonstrated'. Valenzuela and Zariquiey (2015) counter that by offering abundant linguistic evidence that such a relationship can indeed be convincingly demonstrated by rigorously applying the orthodox 'comparative method' of historical linguistics.

4.3 The Andes as seen from Mojos

1. Bustos Santelices (1976, 4; 1978); Céspedes (2014); Dougherty and Calandra (1982); Sanematsu (2011).
2. Bone was dated to 1341 ± 24 BP (KIA 31855), equivalent to cal AD 670–767 (2σ).
3. *Quipucamayos: Relación de la descendencia, gobierno y conquista de los incas* (1542), cited in Combès and Tyuleneva (2011, 209, Anexo 1).

4.4 The archaeological significance of shell middens in the Llanos de Moxos: Between the Andes and Amazonia

1. This work has been funded by the Swiss National Science Foundation (SNSF) grant no. P300P2_158459/1. We thank E. Canal Beeby, and the volume editors for helping to improve the manuscript. We thank the Bolivian Ministerio de Culturas y Turismo, the Gobernación del Beni, the Municipio of Trinidad, the staff of the Museo Etnoarqueológico 'Kenneth Lee', the local communities, and the *ganaderos* who supported our research efforts in the Llanos de Moxos.

5.1 The Amazonian Indians as viewed by three Andean chroniclers

1. In citing from the chronicles, instead of page numbers, folio numbers are used for the Guamán Poma and Pachacuti Yamqui texts, and chapter numbers for that of Garcilaso de la Vega, so as to facilitate reference to the numerous different editions.
2. '…cincuenta mil millones de indios…' – translator's note.

5.2 The place of Antisuyu in the discourse of Guamán Poma de Ayala

1. Some of the ethnic groups with which the Incas established relationships included the Machiguenga, Ashaninka, Yanesha, Yine (Piro) and Kaxinawá (Huni Kuin), among many others. The nature of these relations varied according to each group as well as to specific periods within Inca history (Santos-Granero 1992; Saignes 1985). Still nowadays one can find references about the Incas in the mythologies of several western Amazonian groups such as, for example, the Arawak speaking Ashaninka and the Pano speaking Kaxinawá (Pimenta 2009; Lagrou 2006).
2. All translations into English from the original Spanish in this chapter are those of the author.
3. Guamán Poma annotates other parts of his mapamundi, but only to offer names of places or people, not to give further information as in the case of Antisuyu.
4. *Otorongo* is jaguar in Quechua (Lara 1973). Achachi (from the Aymara), indicates patrilinear descent.
5. For a discussion on the relevance of the numbers 7 and 22 among South American Indians, see Brotherston (2006).
6. The association between warriors and birds (and its feathers) was an Andean tradition prevalent long before the advent of the Incas. Feathers also had a very special place in Inca society and the Antisuyu was probably the major supplier of feathers for the Inca Empire. As Tahuantinsuyu expanded over time, so did the demand for feathers. One of the reasons the conquest of the Antisuyu was so important for the Incas was likely the potential direct access to feathers as well as other desired items.

5.3 Colonial coda: The Andes–Amazonia frontier under Spanish rule

1. The Spanish Viceroyalty of Peru embraced modern Peru, Bolivia and Ecuador (and indeed most of the rest of Spanish South America) for most of the colonial period.
2. Some incentives were regionally specific: one of the anonymous readers of this chapter for UCL Press suggested that a further factor in Peru lay in 'the Spanish interest in assuming control of Inca royal coca estates, as a way of profiting from existing crop production'. I thank this reader for bringing this point to my attention.

References

Primary Sources and Works Published before 1900

Acosta, José de. 1590. *Historia natural y moral de las Indias*. Seville: Juan de León.

Albornoz, Cristóbal de. 1967. 'Instrucción para descubrir todas las guacas del Pirú y sus camayos y haziendas', *Journal de la Société des Américanistes* 56 (1): 7–39. [Originally written c. 1582].

Alcaya, Diego Felipe de. 2011 [originally published 1636]. 'Relación cierta…'. In *Paititi: Ensayos y Documentos* (Colección Scripta Autochtona 8), edited by Isabelle Combès and Vera Tyuleneva, Anexo 4, 240–51. Cochabamba: Editorial Itinerarios.

Amich, José. 1975. *Historia de las misiones del convento de Santa Rosa de Ocopa*, edited by Julián Heras. Lima: Milla Batres.

Armentia, N. 1886. *Diario del viaje al Madre de Dios*. La Paz.

Bertonio, Ludovico. 1984. *Vocabulario de la lengua aymara*, edited by Xavier Albó and Félix Layme. Cochabamba: Centro de Estudios de la Realidad Económica y Social.

Betanzos, Juan de. 1996 [originally published 1576]. *Narrative of the Incas*, translated and edited by Roland Hamilton and Dana Buchanan. Austin: University of Texas Press.

Cabello Valboa, Miguel. 1951 [originally published 1586]. *Miscelánea antártica: Una historia del Perú antiguo*. Lima: Universidad Nacional Mayor de San Marcos.

Capac Ayllu. 2004 [originally published 1569]. 'Memoria de las Provinçias que conquistó Topa Ynga Yupangui padre de Guaina Capac Ynga con sus hermanos'. In *Textos andinos: Corpus de textos khipu incaicos y coloniales*, edited by Martti Pärssinen and Jukka Kiviharju. Helsinki: Instituto Iberoamericano de Finlandia.

Carvajal, Gaspar. 1934. 'Discovery of the Orellana River'. In *The Discovery of the Amazon According to the Account of Friar Gaspar de Carvajal and Other Documents*, by José Toribio Medina; edited by H.C. Heaton; translated by Bertram T. Lee, 167–235. New York: American Geographical Society.

Cieza de León, Pedro. 1984 [originally published 1553]. *Obras completas, I: La crónica del Perú: Las guerras civiles peruanas*. Madrid: Instituto Gonzalo Fernández de Oviedo.

Cobo, Bernabé. 1964 [originally published 1636]. *Historia del nuevo mundo* (Biblioteca de Autores Españoles 92), edited by F. Mateos. Madrid: Atlas.

Cobo, Bernabé. 1998 [originally published 1653]. *History of the Inca Empire*, edited and translated by Roland Hamilton. Austin: University of Texas Press.

Garcilaso de la Vega, Inca. 1985 [originally published 1609]. *Comentarios reales de los Incas*. Caracas: Biblioteca Ayacucho.

Guamán Poma de Ayala, Felipe. 1936 [originally published 1615]. *Nueva corónica y buen gobierno*. Paris: Institut d'ethnologie.

Guamán Poma de Ayala, Felipe. 1980 [originally published 1615]. *El primer nueva corónica y buen gobierno*, edited by John V. Murra and Rolena Adorno; translated by Jorge L. Urioste. 3 vols. Mexico City: Siglo Veintiuno.

Guamán Poma de Ayala, Felipe. 1987 [originally published 1615]. *Nueva crónica y buen gobierno*, edited by John V. Murra and Rolena Adorno; translated by Jorge L. Urioste. 3 vols. Madrid: Historia 16.

Guamán Poma de Ayala, Felipe. 2008 [originally published 1615]. *Nueva corónica y buen gobierno*, edited by Franklin Pease; translated by Jan Szemiński. 2nd ed. 3 vols. Lima: Fondo de Cultura Económica.

Las Casas, Bartolomé de. 1967. *Apologética historia sumaria*, edited by Edmundo O'Gorman. Mexico City: Universidad Nacional Autonoma de Mexico.

Manso de Velasco, José A. 1983. *Relación y documentos de gobierno del virrey del Perú, José A. Manso de Velasco, Conde de Superunda (1745–1761)*, edited by Alfredo Moreno Cebrián. Madrid: Instituto Gonzalo Fernández de Oviedo.

Medina, José Toribio. 1934. *The Discovery of the Amazon According to the Account of Friar Gaspar de Carvajal and Other Documents*, edited by H.C. Heaton; translated by Bertram T. Lee. New York: American Geographical Society.

Oré, Luis Jerónimo de. 1607. *Rituale seu manuale peruanum*. Naples: Giacomo Carlino and Costantino Vitale.

Pachacuti Yamqui Salcamaygua, Joan de Santa Cruz. 1993 [originally published c. 1613]. *Relación de antigüedades deste reyno del Piru*, edited by Pierre Duviols and César Itier. Cusco: Centro de Estudios Regionales Andinos Bartolomé de las Casas.

Prescott, William H. 1847. *History of the Conquest of Peru, with a Preliminary View of the Civilization of the Incas*. London: Richard Bentley.

San Pedro, Juan de. 1992 [originally published 1560?]. *La persecución del demonio: Crónica de los primeros Agustinos en el norte del Perú*, edited by Eric E. Deeds. Málaga: Editorial Algazara.

Santo Tomás, Domingo de. 1995. *Grammatica o arte de la lengua general de los Indios de los Reynos del Perú*, edited by Rodolfo Cerrón-Palomino. Cusco: Centro de Estudios Regionales Andinos Bartolomé de las Casas.

Secondary Sources

Ackermann, Rebecca R. and James M. Cheverud. 2004. 'Detecting Genetic Drift versus Selection in Human Evolution', *Proceedings of the National Academy of Sciences of the United States of America* 101 (52): 17946–51.

Adelaar, Willem F.H. 1987. 'Comments on A.A. Torero, "Lenguas y pueblos altiplánicos en torno al siglo XVI"', *Revista Andina* 5 (2): 373–5.

Adelaar, Willem F.H. 1989. 'En pos de la lengua culle'. In *Temas de lingüística amerindia: Actas del Primer Congreso Nacional de Investigaciones Lingüístico-Filológicas*, edited by Rodolfo Cerrón-Palomino and Gustavo Politis, 83–105. Lima: CONCYTEC-GTZ.

Adelaar, Willem F.H. 2006. 'The Quechua Impact in Amuesha, an Arawak Language of the Peruvian Amazon'. In *Grammars in Contact: A Cross-Linguistic Typology*, edited by Alexandra Y. Aikhenvald and R.M.W. Dixon, 290–312. Oxford: Oxford University Press.

Adelaar, Willem F.H. 2008. 'Towards a Typological Profile of the Andean Languages'. In *Evidence and Counter-Evidence: Essays in Honour of Frederik Kortlandt, Volume 2: General Linguistics*, edited by A. Lubotsky, J. Schaeken and J. Wiedenhof, 23–33. Amsterdam: Rodopi.

Adelaar, Willem F.H. 2009. 'Inverse Markers in Andean Languages: A Comparative View'. In *The Linguistics of Endangered Languages: Contributions to Morphology and Morpho-Syntax*, edited by W.L. Wetzels, 171–85. Utrecht: Netherlands Graduate School of Linguistics.

Adelaar, Willem F.H. 2012a. 'Languages of the Middle Andes in Areal-Typological Perspective: Emphasis on Quechuan and Aymaran'. In *The Indigenous Languages of South America: A Comprehensive Guide*, edited by Lyle Campbell and Verónica Grondona, 575–624. Berlin: De Gruyter Mouton.

Adelaar, Willem F.H. 2012b. 'Modeling Convergence: Towards a Reconstruction of the History of Quechuan–Aymaran Interaction', *Lingua* 122 (5): 461–9.

Adelaar, Willem F.H. and Pieter C. Muysken. 2004. *The Languages of the Andes*. Cambridge: Cambridge University Press.

Adelaar, Willem F.H. and Simon C. van de Kerke. 2009. 'Puquina'. In *Lenguas de Bolivia, Volume 1: Ámbito andino*, edited by E.I. Crevels and P.C. Muysken, 125–46. La Paz: Plural.

Adorno, Rolena. 1988. *Guamán Poma: Writing and Resistance in Colonial Peru*. Austin: University of Texas Press.

Adorno, Rolena, Tom Cummins, Teresa Gisbert, Maarten van de Guchte, Mercedes López-Baralt and John V. Murra. 1992. *Guamán Poma de Ayala: The Colonial Art of an Andean Author*. New York: Americas Society.

Ahlfeld, F. and R.N. Wegner. 1931. 'Über die Herkunft der im Bereich altperuanischer Kulturen gefundenen Schmuckstücke aus Sodalith', *Zeitschrift für Ethnologie* 63 (5/6): 288–96.

Aikhenvald, Alexandra Y. 1999. 'The Arawak Language Family'. In *The Amazonian Languages*, edited by R.M.W. Dixon and Alexandra Y. Aikhenvald, 65–106. Cambridge: Cambridge University Press.

Albó, Xavier. 1995. *Bolivia plurilingüe: Guía para planificadores y educadores*. La Paz: CIPCA and UNICEF.

Alcais, A., L. Abel, C. David, M.E. Torrez, P. Flandre and J.P. Dedet. 1997. 'Risk Factors for Onset of Cutaneous and Mucocutaneous Leishmaniasis in Bolivia', *American Journal of Tropical Medicine and Hygiene* 57 (1): 79–84.

Aldenderfer, Mark S. 1998. *Montane Foragers: Asana and the South-Central Andean Archaic*. Iowa City: University of Iowa Press.

Alexander-Bakkerus, Astrid. 2005. *Eighteenth-Century Cholón*. Utrecht: Landelijk Onderzoekschool Taalwetenschap.

Alicea Ortiz, Neftalí. 1975a. *Análisis fonémico preliminar del idioma taushiro: Ejercicios y problemas de cálculo en taushiro y castellano*. Lima: Ministerio de Educación and Instituto Lingüístico de Verano.

Alicea Ortiz, Neftalí. 1975b. *Análisis preliminar de la gramática del idioma taushiro*. Lima: Ministerio de Educación and Instituto Lingüístico de Verano.

Alva, Walter. 1986. *Cerámica temprana en el valle de Jequetepeque, norte del Perú* (Materialien zur Allgemeinen und Vergleichenden Archäologie 32). Munich: C.H. Beck.

Alva, Walter. 1992. 'Orfebrería del Formativo'. In *Oro del Perú Antiguo*, edited by J.A. del Valle, 17–116. Lima: Banco del Crédito.

Alva Meneses, Ignacio. 2012. *Ventarrón y Collud: Origen y auge de la civilización en la costa norte del Perú.* Lima: Ministerio de Cultura.

Álvarez, P. 2002. 'Inventario de sitios arqueológicos del Parque Nacional y Área Natural de Manejo Integrado Madidi y su zona de influencia: Un diagnóstico preliminar'. Unpublished Manuscript. Wildlife Conservation Society.

Ammerman, Albert J. and L.L. Cavalli-Sforza. 1984. *The Neolithic Transition and the Genetics of Populations in Europe*. Princeton: Princeton University Press.

Anderson, David G. and J. Christopher Gillam. 2000. 'Paleoindian Colonization of the Americas: Implications from an Examination of Physiography, Demography, and Artifact Distribution', *American Antiquity* 65 (1): 43–66.

Anderson, David G. and Kenneth E. Sassaman. 2012. *Recent Developments in Southeastern Archaeology: From Colonization to Complexity*. Washington, DC: Society for American Archaeology Press.

Anderson, Lorrie and Mary Ruth Wise. 1963. 'Contrastive Features of Candoshi Clause Types'. In *Studies in Peruvian Indian Languages, I*, edited by Benjamin F. Elson, 67–102. Norman: Summer Institute of Linguistics of the University of Oklahoma.

Angenot-de-Lima, Geralda. 2002. 'Description phonologique, grammaticale et lexicale du Moré, langue Amazonienne de Bolivie et du Brésil'. PhD thesis, Leiden University.

Aparicio Vega, Manuel Jesús. 1999. *De Vilcabamba a Camisea: Historiografía de la Provincia de la Convención.* Cusco: Universidad Nacional de San Antonio Abad del Cusco.

Arellano López, Jorge. 2002. *Reconocimiento arqueológico de la cuenca del Río Orthon, Amazonía boliviana.* Quito: Museo Jacinto Jijón y Caamaño.

Arnold, Dean E. and Kenneth A. Prettol. 1988. 'Aboriginal Earthworks near the Mouth of the Beni, Bolivia', *Journal of Field Archaeology* 15 (4): 457–65.

Arroyo-Kalin, Manuel. 2010. 'The Amazonian Formative: Crop Domestication and Anthropogenic Soils', *Diversity* 2 (4): 473–504.

Arroyo-Kalin, Manuel. 2014. 'Amazonian Dark Earths: Geoarchaeology'. In *Encyclopedia of Global Archaeology*, edited by Claire Smith, 168–78. New York: Springer.

Assadourian, Carlos Sempat. 1994. '"La gran vejación y destruición de la tierra": Las guerras de sucesión y de conquista en el derrumbe de la población indígena del Perú'. In *Transiciones hacia el sistema colonial andino*, by Carlos Sempat Assadourian, 19–62. Lima: Instituto de Estudios Peruanos and El Colegio de México.

Azevedo, Soledad de, Ariadna Nocera, Carolina Paschetta, Lucía Castillo, Marina González and Rolando González-José. 2011. 'Evaluating Microevolutionary Models for the Early Settlement of the New World: The Importance of Recurrent Gene Flow with Asia', *American Journal of Physical Anthropology* 146 (4): 539–52.

Baca, Mateusz, Karolina Doan, Maciej Sobczyk, Anna Stankovic and Piotr Węgleński. 2012. 'Ancient DNA Reveals Kinship Burial Patterns of a Pre-Columbian Andean Community', *BMC Genetics* 13, Article 30: 1–11. Accessed 21 April 2020. https://doi.org/10.1186/1471-2156-13-30.

Bailliet, Graciela, and 11 others. 2009. 'Brief Communication: Restricted Geographic Distribution for Y-Q* Paragroup in South America', *American Journal of Physical Anthropology* 140 (3): 578–82.

Bakewell, Peter. 1984. *Miners of the Red Mountain: Indian Labor in Potosí, 1545–1650.* Albuquerque: University of New Mexico Press.

Balbo, Andrea, Marco Madella, Ivan Briz Godino and Myrian Álvarez. 2011. 'Shell Midden Research: An Interdisciplinary Agenda for the Quaternary and Social Sciences', *Quaternary International* 239 (1/2): 147–52.

Balée, William. 1989. 'The Culture of Amazonian Forests'. In *Resource Management in Amazonia: Indigenous and Folk Strategies*, edited by D.A. Posey and W. Balée, 1–21. New York: New York Botanical Garden.

Balée, William. 2013. 'An Estimate of Anthropogenesis'. In *Cultural Forests of the Amazon: A Historical Ecology of People and Their Landscapes*, by William Balée, 32–52. Tuscaloosa: University of Alabama Press.

Balée, William and Clark L. Erickson, eds. 2006. *Time and Complexity in Historical Ecology: Studies in the Neotropical Lowlands*. New York: Columbia University Press.

Barbieri, Chiara and 16 others. 2019. 'The Current Genomic Landscape of Western South America: Andes, Amazonia, and Pacific Coast', *Molecular Biology and Evolution* 36 (12): 2698–713. http://doi.org/10.1093/molbev/msz174.

Barbieri, Chiara, Paul Heggarty, Loredana Castrì, Donata Luiselli and Davide Pettener. 2011. 'Mitochondrial DNA Variability in the Titicaca Basin: Matches and Mismatches with Linguistics and Ethnohistory', *American Journal of Human Biology* 23 (1): 89–99. http://doi.org/10.1002/ajhb.21107.

Barbieri, Chiara, Paul Heggarty, Daniele Yang Yao, Gianmarco Ferri, Sara De Fanti, Stefania Sarno, Graziella Ciani, Alessio Boattini, Donata Luiselli and Davide Pettener. 2014. 'Between Andes and Amazon: The Genetic Profile of the Arawak-Speaking Yanesha', *American Journal of Physical Anthropology* 155 (4): 600–9. http://doi.org/10.1002/ajpa.22616.

Barbieri, Chiara and 11 others. 2017. 'Enclaves of Genetic Diversity Resisted Inca Impacts on Population History', *Scientific Reports* 7, Article 17411: 1–12. Accessed 21 April 2020. https://doi.org/10.1038/s41598-017-17728-w.

Barbujani, Guido, Arianna Magagni, Eric Minch and L. Luca Cavalli-Sforza. 1997. 'An Apportionment of Human DNA Diversity', *Proceedings of the National Academy of Sciences of the United States of America* 94 (9): 4516–19.

Barthlott, Wilhelm, Jens Mutke, Daud Rafiqpoor, Gerold Kier and Holger Kreft. 2005. 'Global Centers of Vascular Plant Diversity', *Nova Acta Leopoldina* 92 (342): 61–83.

Bass, William M. 1964. 'The Variation in Physical Types of the Prehistoric Plains Indians', *Plains Anthropologist* 9 (24): 65–145.

Basso, Ellen B. 2011. 'Amazonian Ritual Communication in Relation to Multilingual Social Networks'. In *Ethnicity in Ancient Amazonia: Reconstructing Past Identities from Archaeology, Linguistics, and Ethnohistory*, edited by Alf Hornborg and Jonathan D. Hill, 155–71. Boulder: University Press of Colorado.

Battaglia, Vincenza, Viola Grugni, Ugo Alessandro Perego, Norman Angerhofer, J. Edgar Gomez-Palmieri, Scott Ray Woodward, Alessandro Achilli, Natalie Myres, Antonio Torroni and Ornella Semino. 2013. 'The First Peopling of South America: New Evidence from Y-Chromosome Haplogroup Q', *PLoS One* 8 (8), Article e71390: 1–13. Accessed 21 April 2020. https://doi.org/10.1371/journal.pone.0071390.

Bauer, Brian S., Javier Fonseca Santa Cruz and Miriam Aráoz Silva. 2015. *Vilcabamba and the Archaeology of Inca Resistance*. Los Angeles: Cotsen Institute of Archaeology Press.

Beall, Cynthia M. 2014. 'Adaptation to High Altitude: Phenotypes and Genotypes', *Annual Review of Anthropology* 43: 251–72.

Beals, Kenneth L., Courtland L. Smith and Stephen M. Dodd. 1984. 'Brain Size, Cranial Morphology, Climate, and Time Machines', *Current Anthropology* 25 (3): 301–30.

Becker, Richard A., Allan R. Wilks, Ray Brownrigg, Thomas P. Minka and Alex Deckmyn. 2018. 'maps: Draw Geographical Maps'. Accessed 18 May 2020. https://CRAN.R-project.org/package=maps.

Bellwood, Peter. 2005. *First Farmers: The Origins of Agricultural Societies*. Malden, MA: Blackwell.

Bennett, W.C. 1936. 'Excavations in Bolivia', *Anthropological Papers of the American Museum of Natural History* 35 (4): 329–507.

Bennett, Wendell C. 1948. 'The Peruvian Co-Tradition', *Memoirs of the Society for American Archaeology* 4: 1–7.

Beresford-Jones, David. 2011. *The Lost Woodlands of Ancient Nasca: A Case-Study in Ecological and Cultural Collapse*. Oxford: Oxford University Press.

Beresford-Jones, David and Paul Heggarty. 2012a. 'Broadening Our Horizons: Towards an Interdisciplinary Prehistory of the Andes'. In *Archaeology and Language in the Andes: A Cross-Disciplinary Exploration of Prehistory*, edited by Paul Heggarty and David Beresford-Jones, 57–84. Oxford: Oxford University Press. http://doi.org/10.5871/bacad/9780197265031.003.0003.

Beresford-Jones, David and Paul Heggarty. 2012b. 'Introduction: Archaeology, Linguistics, and the Andean Past: A Much-Needed Conversation'. In *Archaeology and Language in the Andes: A Cross-Disciplinary Exploration of Prehistory*, edited by Paul Heggarty and David Beresford-Jones, 1–41. Oxford: Oxford University Press. http://fdslive.oup.com/www.oup.com/academic/pdf/13/9780197265031_prelim.pdf.

Beresford-Jones, David and 15 others. 2015. 'Re-Evaluating the Resource Potential of Lomas Fog Oasis Environments for Preceramic Hunter-Gatherers under Past ENSO Modes on the South Coast of Peru', *Quaternary Science Reviews* 129: 196–215. http://doi.org/10.1016/j.quascirev.2015.10.025.

Beresford-Jones, David and 10 others. 2018. 'Refining the Maritime Foundations of Andean Civilization: How Plant Fiber Technology Drove Social Complexity during the Preceramic Period', *Journal of Archaeological Method and Theory* 25: 393–425. https://doi.org/10.1007/s10816-017-9341-3.

Bernal, Valeria, S. Ivan Perez and Paula N. Gonzalez. 2006. 'Variation and Causal Factors of Craniofacial Robusticity in Patagonian Hunter-Gatherers from the Late Holocene', *American Journal of Human Biology* 18 (6): 748–65.

Bertazoni Martins, Cristiana. 2007a. 'Antisuyu: An Investigation of Inca Attitudes to Their Western Amazonian Territories'. PhD thesis, University of Essex.

Bertazoni, Cristiana. 2007b. 'Representations of Western Amazonian Indians on Inca Colonial Qeros', *Revista do Museu de Arqueologia e Etnologia* (São Paulo) 17: 321–31.

Bertazoni, Cristiana. 2014. '"Apu Ollantay": Inca Theatre as an Example of the Modes of Interaction between the Incas and Western Amazonian Societies', *Boletim do Museu Paraense Emílio Goeldi* 9 (1): 27–36.

Betti, Lia, François Balloux, William Amos, Tsunehiko Hanihara and Andrea Manica. 2009. 'Distance from Africa, Not Climate, Explains Within-Population Phenotypic Diversity in Humans', *Proceedings of the Royal Society B: Biological Sciences* 276: 809–14.

Bidou, Patrice. 1976. 'Les Fils de l'Anaconda Céleste (les Tatuyo): Étude de la structure socio-politique'. PhD thesis, University of Paris.

Birchall, Joshua. 2014a. 'Verbal Argument Marking Patterns in South American Languages'. In *The Native Languages of South America: Origins, Development, Typology*, edited by Loretta O'Connor and Pieter Muysken, 223–49. Cambridge: Cambridge University Press.

Birchall, Joshua. 2014b. 'Argument Realization in the Languages of South America'. PhD thesis, Radboud University Nijmegen.

Bird, Junius B., John Hyslop and Milica Dimitrijevic Skinner. 1985. *The Preceramic Excavations at the Huaca Prieta Chicama Valley, Peru* (Anthropological Papers of the American Museum of Natural History 62). New York: American Museum of Natural History.

Bisso-Machado, Rafael, Maria Cátira Bortolini and Francisco Mauro Salzano. 2012. 'Uniparental Genetic Markers in South Amerindians', *Genetics and Molecular Biology* 35 (2): 365–87.

Blench, Roger. 2012. 'The Role of Agriculture in Explaining the Diversity of Amerindian Languages'. In *The Past Ahead: Language, Culture, and Identity in the Neotropics*, edited by Christian Isendahl, 13–37. Uppsala: Uppsala University.

Blower, David. 2000. 'The Many Facets of Mullu: More Than Just a *Spondylus* Shell', *Andean Past* 6: 209–28.

Boas, Franz. 1912. *Changes in the Bodily Form of Descendants of Immigrants*. New York: Columbia University Press.

Bodner, Martin and 17 others. 2012. 'Rapid Coastal Spread of First Americans: Novel Insights from South America's Southern Cone Mitochondrial Genomes', *Genome Research* 22 (5): 811–20.

Bolnick, Deborah A., Beth A. Shook, Lyle Campbell and Ives Goddard. 2004. 'Problematic Use of Greenberg's Linguistic Classification of the Americas in Studies of Native American Genetic Variation', *American Journal of Human Genetics* 75 (3): 519–22.

Bolton, Herbert E. 1917. 'The Mission as a Frontier Institution in the Spanish-American Colonies', *American Historical Review* 23 (1): 42–61.

Bonilla, Victor D. 1968. *Siervos de Dios y amos de indios*. Bogotá: Ediciones Tercer Mundo.

Bonnier, Elisabeth 1997a. 'Morfología del espacio aldeano y su expresión cultural en los Andes centrales'. In *Arquitectura y civilización en los Andes prehispánicos*, edited by E. Bonnier and H. Bishof, 28–41. Mannheim: Reiss Museum and Sociedad Arqueológica Peruano-Alemana.

Bonnier, Elisabeth. 1997b. 'Preceramic Architecture in the Andes: The Mito Tradition'. In *Arquitectura y civilización en los Andes prehispánicos = Prehispanic Architecture and Civilization in the Andes*, edited by Elisabeth Bonnier and Henning Bischof, 120–44. Mannheim: Sociedad Arqueológica Peruano-Alemana.

Bonnier, Elisabeth and Henning Bischof, eds. 1997. *Arquitectura y civilización en los Andes prehispánicos = Prehispanic Architecture and Civilization in the Andes*. Mannheim: Sociedad Arqueológica Peruano-Alemana.

Bonnier, E. and C. Rozenberg. 1988. 'Du sanctuaire au hameau: À propos de la néolithisation dans la cordillère des Andes centrales', *L'Anthropologie* 92 (3): 983–96.

Boomert, A. 1987. 'Gifts of the Amazons: "Green Stone" Pendants and Beads as Items of Ceremonial Exchange in Amazonia and the Caribbean', *Antropologica* 67: 33–54.

Borman, M.B. 1962. 'Cofán Phonemes'. In *Studies in Ecuadorian Indian Languages, I*, edited by Benjamin Elson, 45–59. Norman: Summer Institute of Linguistics of the University of Oklahoma.

Borrero, Luis Alberto. 2015. 'Moving: Hunter-Gatherers and the Cultural Geography of South America', *Quaternary International* 363: 126–33.

Bortolini, Maria-Catira and 20 others. 2003. 'Y-Chromosome Evidence for Differing Ancient Demographic Histories in the Americas', *American Journal of Human Genetics* 73 (3): 524–39.

Bouysse-Cassagne, Thérèse. 1975. 'Pertenencia étnica, status económico y lenguas en Charcas a fines del siglo XVI'. In *Tasa de la Visita General de Francisco de Toledo*, edited by N.D. Cook, 312–28. Lima: Universidad Nacional Mayor de San Marcos.

Bowcock, Anne M., Judith R. Kidd, Joanna L. Mountain, Joan M. Hebert, Luciano Carotenuto, Kenneth K. Kidd and L. Luca Cavalli-Sforza. 1991. 'Drift, Admixture, and Selection in Human Evolution: A Study with DNA Polymorphisms', *Proceedings of the National Academy of Sciences of the United States of America* 88 (3): 839–43.

Bowern, Claire, Patience Epps, Russell Gray, Jane Hill, Keith Hunley, Patrick McConvell and Jason Zentz. 2011. 'Does Lateral Transmission Obscure Inheritance in Hunter-Gatherer Languages?', *PLoS One* 6 (9), Article e25195: 1–9. Accessed 28 April 2020. https://doi.org/10.1371/journal.pone.0025195.

Bray, Tamara L. 2003. 'To Dine Splendidly: Imperial Pottery, Commensal Politics, and the Inca State'. In *The Archaeology and Politics of Food and Feasting in Early States and Empires*, edited by Tamara L. Bray, 93–142. New York: Kluwer Academic.

Briceño Rosario, Jesús Gregorio. 2010. 'Las tradiciones líticas del Pleistoceno Tardío en la quebrada Santa María, costa norte del Perú: Una contribución al conocimiento de las puntas de proyectil paleoindias Cola de Pescado'. PhD thesis, Freie Universität Berlin.

Briceño, Jesús. 2011. 'Últimos descubrimientos del Paijanense en la parte alta de los valles de Chicama, Moche y Virú, norte del Perú: Nuevas perspectivas sobre los primeros cazadores-recolectores en los Andes de Sudamérica', *Boletín de Arqueología PUCP* 15: 165–203.

Briz Godino, Ivan, Myrian Álvarez, Andrea Balbo, Débora Zurro, Marco Madella, Ximena Villagrán and Charles French. 2011. 'Towards High-Resolution Shell Midden Archaeology: Experimental and Ethnoarchaeology in Tierra del Fuego (Argentina)', *Quaternary International* 239 (1/2): 125–34.

Brokaw, Galen. 2010. *A History of the Khipu*. Cambridge: Cambridge University Press.

Brotherston, Gordon. 1992. *Book of the Fourth World: Reading the Native Americas through Their Literature*. Cambridge: Cambridge University Press.

Brotherston, Gordon. 2006. 'The Legible Jaguar', *Journal of Latin American Cultural Studies* 15 (2): 159–69.

Browman, David L. 1975. 'Trade Patterns in the Central Highlands of Peru in the First Millennium BC', *World Archaeology* 6 (3): 322–9.

Browman, David L. 1978. 'Toward the Development of the Tiahuanaco (Tiwanaku) State'. In *Advances in Andean Archaeology*, edited by David L. Browman, 327–49. The Hague: Mouton.

Browman, David L. 1989. 'Origins and Development of Andean Pastoralism: An Overview of the Past 6000 Years'. In *The Walking Larder: Patterns of Domestication, Pastoralism, and Predation*, edited by Juliet Clutton-Brock, 256–68. London: Unwin Hyman.

Bruil, Martine. 2014. 'Clause-Typing and Evidentiality in Ecuadorian Siona'. PhD thesis, Leiden University.

Bryant, David and Vincent Moulton. 2004. 'Neighbor-Net: An Agglomerative Method for the Construction of Phylogenetic Networks', *Molecular Biology and Evolution* 21 (2): 255–65.

Bueno, Lucas, Adriana Schimdt Dias and James Steele. 2013. 'The Late Pleistocene/Early Holocene Archaeological Record in Brazil: A Geo-Referenced Database', *Quaternary International* 301: 74–93.

Burbridge, Rachel E., Francis E. Mayle and Timothy J. Killeen. 2004. 'Fifty-Thousand-Year Vegetation and Climate History of Noel Kempff Mercado National Park, Bolivian Amazon', *Quaternary Research* 61 (2): 215–30.

Burger, Joachim, Susanne Hummel, Bernd Hermann and Winifred Henke. 1999. 'DNA Preservation: A Microsatellite-DNA Study on Ancient Skeletal Remains', *Electrophoresis* 20 (8): 1722–8.

Burger, Richard L. 1984. *The Prehistoric Occupation of Chavin de Huántar, Peru*. Berkeley: University of California Press.

Burger, Richard L. 1985. 'Prehistoric Stylistic Change and Cultural Development at Huaricoto, Peru', *National Geographic Research* 1 (4): 505–34.

Burger, Richard L. 1992. *Chavin and the Origins of Andean Civilization*. London: Thames and Hudson.

Burger, Richard L. 2002. 'Letter from Peru: Andean Odyssey', *Archaeology* 55 (6). Accessed 2 June 2020. https://archive.archaeology.org/0211/abstracts/peru.html.

Burger, Richard L. and Lucy Salazar-Burger. 1985. 'The Early Ceremonial Center of Huaricoto'. In *Early Ceremonial Architecture in the Andes*, edited by Christopher B. Donnan, 111–38. Washington, DC: Dumbarton Oaks Research Library and Collection.

Burger, Richard L. and Lucy Salazar-Burger. 1986. 'Early Organizational Diversity in the Peruvian Highlands: Huaricoto and Kotosh'. In *Andean Archaeology: Papers in Memory of Clifford Evans*, edited by Ramiro Matos M., Solveig A. Turpin and Herbert H. Eling, 65–82. Los Angeles: Institute of Archaeology, University of California.

Bush, M.B., W.D. Gosling and P.A. Colinvaux. 2011. 'Climate and Vegetation Change in the Lowlands of the Amazon Basin'. In *Tropical Rainforest Responses to Climatic Change*, edited by Mark B. Bush, John R. Flenley and William D. Gosling, 61–84. 2nd ed. Berlin: Springer.

Bustamante, Carlos D., Esteban González Burchard and Francisco M. De La Vega. 2011. 'Genomics for the World', *Nature* 475: 163–5.

Bustos Santelices, Víctor. 1976. *Investigaciones arqueológicas en Trinidad, Departamento del Beni*. La Paz: Instituto Nacional de Arqueología.

Bustos Santelices, Víctor A. 1978. 'La arqueología de los Llanos del Beni, Bolivia'. Unpublished report. Documentos Internos 32/78. La Paz: Instituto Nacional de Arqueología.

Büttner, Thomas. 1983. *Las lenguas de los Andes centrales: Estudios sobre la clasificación genetica, areal y tipológica*. Madrid: Instituto de Cooperación Iberoamericana.

Byers, Alton C. 2000. 'Contemporary Landscape Change in the Huascarán National Park and Buffer Zone, Cordillera Blanca, Peru', *Mountain Research and Development* 20 (1): 52–63.

Cabana, Graciela S. and 22 others. 2014. 'Population Genetic Structure of Traditional Populations in the Peruvian Central Andes and Implications for South American Population History', *Human Biology* 86 (3): 147–65.

Caja, Consuelo and Walter Díaz. 2009. *Reconocimiento y registro del entorno territorial del Qhapaq Ñan, Volumen 4: El Qhapaq Ñan en la ruta del Chinchaysuyu entre Piás y Chachapoyas*. Lima: Instituto Nacional de Cultura.

Callegari-Jacques, Sidia M., Eduardo M. Tarazona-Santos, Robert H. Gilman, Phabiola Herrera, Lilia Cabrera, Sidney E.B. dos Santos, Luiza Morés, Mara H. Hutz and Francisco M. Salzano. 2011. 'Autosome STRs in Native South America: Testing Models of Association with Geography and Language', *American Journal of Physical Anthropology* 145 (3): 371–81.

Camino, Alejandro. 1977. 'Trueque, correrías e intercambios entre los Quechuas andinos y los Piro y Machiguenga de la montaña peruana', *Amazonía Peruana* 1 (2): 123–40.

Camino, Lupe. 1992. *Cerros, plantas y lagunas poderosas: La medicina al norte del Perú*. Piura: Centro de Investigación y Promoción del Campesinado.

Campbell, Lyle. 1988. 'Book Review – *Language in the Americas*, by Joseph H. Greenberg', *Language* 64 (3): 591–615. http://doi.org/10.2307/414535.

Campbell, Lyle. 1991. 'On So-Called Pan-Americanisms', *International Journal of American Linguistics* 57 (3): 394–9. http://doi.org/10.1086/ijal.57.3.3519725.

Campbell, Lyle. 1997. *American Indian Languages: The Historical Linguistics of Native America*. New York: Oxford University Press.

Campbell, Lyle and William J. Poser. 2008. *Language Classification: History and Method*. Cambridge: Cambridge University Press.

Cândido, Gláucia Vieira. 2004. 'Descrição Morfossintática da Língua Shanenawa (Pano)'. PhD thesis, Universidad Estadual de Campinas, São Paulo.

Capriles, José M. 2014. 'Mobile Communities and Pastoralist Landscapes during the Formative Period in the Central Altiplano of Bolivia', *Latin American Antiquity* 25 (1): 3–26.

Capriles, José M. and Juan Albarracin-Jordan. 2013. 'The Earliest Human Occupations in Bolivia: A Review of the Archaeological Evidence', *Quaternary International* 301: 46–59.

Capriles, José M. and 10 others. 2016. 'High-Altitude Adaptation and Late Pleistocene Foraging in the Bolivian Andes', *Journal of Archaeological Science: Reports* 6: 463–74.

Capriles, José M., Umberto Lombardo, Blaine Maley, Carlos Zuna, Heinz Veit and Douglas J. Kennett. 2019. 'Persistent Early to Middle Holocene Tropical Foraging in Southwestern Amazonia', *Science Advances* 5 (4), Article eaav5449: 1–10. Accessed 29 April 2020. https://doi.org/10.1126/sciadv.aav5449.

Cárdenas, Jorge Mario, Tanja Heinz, Jacobo Pardo-Seco, Vanesa Álvarez-Iglesias, Patricia Taboada-Echalar, Paula Sánchez-Diz, Ángel Carracedo and Antonio Salas. 2015. 'The Multiethnic Ancestry of Bolivians as Revealed by the Analysis of Y-Chromosome Markers', *Forensic Science International: Genetics* 14: 210–18.

Cárdenas-Arroyo, Felipe and Tamara L. Bray, eds. 1998. *Intercambio y comercio entre costa, Andes y selva: Arqueología y etnohistoria de Suramérica*. Santafé de Bogotá: Universidad de Los Andes.

Cardich, Augusto. 1994. 'Descubrimientos de un complejo precerámico en Cajamarca, Perú', *Revista del Museo de la Plata* 9 (74): 225–37.

Carlson, David S. and Dennis P. Van Gerven. 1977. 'Masticatory Function and Post-Pleistocene Evolution in Nubia', *American Journal of Physical Anthropology* 46 (3): 495–506.

Carneiro, Robert L. 1974. 'The Transition from Hunting to Horticulture in the Amazon Basin'. In *Man in Adaptation: The Cultural Present*, edited by Yehudi A. Cohen, 157–66. 2nd ed. Hawthorne, NY: Aldine de Gruyter.

Carson, E. Ann. 2006. 'Maximum Likelihood Estimation of Human Craniometric Heritabilities', *American Journal of Physical Anthropology* 131 (2): 169–80.

Carson, John Francis, Bronwen S. Whitney, Francis E. Mayle, José Iriarte, Heiko Prümers, J. Daniel Soto and Jennifer Watling. 2014. 'Environmental Impact of Geometric Earthwork Construction in Pre-Columbian Amazonia', *Proceedings of the National Academy of Sciences of the United States of America* 111 (29): 10497–502.

Carter, Benjamin P. 2011. '*Spondylus* in South American Prehistory'. In *Spondylus in Prehistory: New Data and Approaches: Contributions to the Archaeology of Shell Technologies* (BAR International Series 2216), edited by Fotis Ifantidis and Marianna Nikolaidou, 63–89. Oxford: Archaeopress.

Castro Arenas, Mario. 1973. *La rebelión de Juan Santos*. Lima: Carlos Milla Batres.

Cavalli-Sforza, Luca, Paolo Menozzi and Alberto Piazza. 1994. *The History and Geography of Human Genes*. Princeton: Princeton University Press.

Ccente Pinmeda, Elmer and Oscar Román Godines. 2006. *Reconocimiento y registro del entorno territorial del Qhapaq Ñan, Volumen 3: El Qhapaq Ñan en la ruta del Chinchaysuyu entre Huanucopampa y Conchucos*. Lima: Instituto Nacional de Cultura.

Cerrón-Palomino, Rodolfo. 1995. *La lengua de Naimlap: Reconstrucción y obsolescencia del Mochica*. Lima: Fondo Editorial de la Pontificia Universidad Católica del Perú.

Cerrón-Palomino, Rodolfo. 2000. *Lingüística aimara*. Cusco: Centro de Estudios Regionales Andinos Bartolomé de Las Casas.

Cerrón-Palomino, Rodolfo. 2003. *Lingüística quechua*. 2nd ed. Cusco: Centro de Estudios Regionales Andinos Bartolomé de las Casas.

Cerrón-Palomino, Rodolfo. 2006. *El chipaya o la lengua de los hombres del agua*. Lima: Fondo Editorial de la Pontificia Universidad Católica del Perú.

Cerrón-Palomino, Rodolfo. 2008. *Quechumara: Estructuras paralelas del quechua y del aimara*. 2nd ed. La Paz: Plural.

Cerrón-Palomino, Rodolfo. 2012. 'Unravelling the Enigma of the "Particular Language" of the Incas'. In *Archaeology and Language in the Andes: A Cross-Disciplinary Exploration of Prehistory*, edited by Paul Heggarty and David Beresford-Jones, 265–94. Oxford: Oxford University Press. http://doi.org/10.5871/bacad/9780197265031.003.0011.

Cerrón-Palomino, Rodolfo. 2013. *Las lenguas de los incas: El puquina, el aimara y el quechua*. Frankfurt am Main: Peter Lang.

Cerrón-Palomino, Rodolfo and Enrique Ballón Aguirre. 2011. *Chipaya: Léxico y etnotaxonomía*. Lima: Fondo Editorial de la Pontificia Universidad Católica del Perú and Radboud University Centre for Language Studies.

Cerrón-Palomino, Rodolfo, Jaime Barrientos Quispe and Sergio Cangahuala Castro. 2016. *El uro de la Bahía de Puno*. Lima: Pontificia Universidad Católica del Perú, Instituto Riva-Agüero.

Cerrón-Palomino, Rodolfo and Gustavo Solís Fonseca, eds. 1989. *Temas de lingüística Amerindia*. Lima: Consejo Nacional de Ciencia y Tecnología.

Céspedes P., Ricardo. 2014. 'Informe de prospección Proyecto "Moxos", Beni, Junio 1991', *Arqueoantropológicas* 4 (4): 197–208.

Chacaltana, Sofía, Elizabeth N. Arkush and Giancarlo Marcone. 2017. *Nuevas tendencias en el estudio de los caminos*. Lima: Ministerio de Cultura.

Chang, Will and Lev Michael. 2014. 'A Relaxed Admixture Model of Language Contact', *Language Dynamics and Change* 4 (1): 1–26.

Chapdelaine, Claude and Gérard Gagné. 2015. 'A Temple for the Dead at San Juanito, Lower Santa Valley, during the Initial Period'. In *Funerary Practices and Models in the Ancient Andes: The Return of the Living Dead*, edited by Peter Eeckhout and Lawrence S. Owens, 34–54. New York: Cambridge University Press.

Chauchat, Claude. 1992. *Préhistoire de la côte nord du Pérou: Le Paijanien de Cupisnique* (Cahiers du Quaternaire 18). Paris: Centre National de la Recherche Scientifique.

Chauchat, Claude and Jorge Zevallos Quiñones. 1979. 'Una punta en cola de pescado de la costa norte del Perú', *Ñawpa Pacha* 17 (1): 143–6.

Chávez-Velásquez, Amanda, Adriana Aguado-Martínez, Luis M. Ortega-Mora, Eva Casas-Astos, Enrique Serrano-Martínez, Gina Casas-Velásquez, Jose A. Ruiz-Santa-Quiteria and Gema Álvarez-García. 2014. '*Toxoplasma gondii* and *Neospora caninum* Seroprevalences in Domestic South American Camelids of the Peruvian Andes', *Tropical Animal Health and Production* 46 (7): 1141–7.

Chepstow-Lusty, Alex and Mark Winfield. 2000. 'Inca Agroforestry: Lessons from the Past', *Ambio* 29 (6): 322–8.

Cheverud, James M. 1988. 'A Comparison of Genetic and Phenotypic Correlations', *Evolution* 42 (5): 958–68.

Childe, V. Gordon. 1951. *Man Makes Himself*. London: Watts and Company.

Chirinos Rivera, Andrés. 2001. *Atlas lingüístico del Perú*. Cusco: Centro de Estudios Regionales Andinos Bartolomé de las Casas.

Chu Barrera, Alejandro. 2008. *Bandurria: Arena, mar y humedal en el surgimiento de la civilización andina*. Huacho: Proyecto Arqueológico Bandurria.

Church, Warren B. 1994. 'Early Occupations at Gran Pajaten, Peru', *Andean Past* 4: 281–318.

Church, Warren B. 1996. 'Prehistoric Cultural Development and Interregional Interaction in the Tropical Montane Forests of Peru'. PhD thesis, Yale University.

Church, Warren B. and Adriana von Hagen. 2008. 'Chachapoyas: Cultural Development at an Andean Cloud Forest Crossroads'. In *The Handbook of South American Archaeology*, edited by Helaine Silverman and William H. Isbell, 903–26. New York: Springer.

Claassen, Cheryl. 1998. *Shells*. Cambridge: Cambridge University Press.

Clapperton, C. 1993. *Quaternary Geology and Geomorphology of South America*. Amsterdam: Elsevier.

Clasby, Ryan and Jorge Meneses Bartra. 2012. 'Nuevas investigaciones en Huayurco: Resultados iniciales de las excavaciones de un sitio de la ceja de selva de los Andes peruanos', *Arqueología y Sociedad* 25: 303–26.

Clement, Charles R. 1999. '1492 and the Loss of Amazonian Crop Genetic Resources, II: Crop Biogeography at Contact', *Economic Botany* 53 (2): 203–16.

Clement, Charles R., Michelly de Cristo-Araújo, Geo Coppens d'Eeckenbrugge, Alessandro Alves Pereira and Doriane Picanço-Rodrigues. 2010. 'Origin and Domestication of Native Amazonian Crops', *Diversity* 2 (1): 72–106.

Clement, Charles R., William M. Denevan, Michael J. Heckenberger, André Braga Junqueira, Eduardo G. Neves, Wenceslau G. Teixeira and William I. Woods. 2015. 'The Domestication of Amazonia before European Conquest', *Proceedings of the Royal Society B: Biological Sciences* 282: 32–40.

Cole, Jeffrey A. 1985. *The Potosí Mita, 1573–1700: Compulsory Indian Labor in the Andes*. Stanford: Stanford University Press.

Cole, Peter. 1982. *Imbabura Quechua*. Amsterdam: North Holland Publishing Company.

Coler-Thayer, Matthew Lee. 2010. 'A Grammatical Description of Muylaq' Aymara'. PhD thesis, Vrije Universiteit Amsterdam.

Combès, Isabelle. 2008. 'Planchas, brazaletes y hachuelas: Las rutas prehispánicas del metal andino desde el Guapay hasta el Pantanal', *Revista Andina* 47: 53–82.

Combès, Isabelle. 2009. 'Saypurú: El misterio de la mina perdida, del Inca chiriguano y del dios mestizo', *Revista Andina* 48: 185–224.

Combès, Isabelle. 2010. *Diccionario étnico: Santa Cruz la Vieja y su entorno en el siglo XVI* (Scripta Autochtona 4). Cochabamba: Instituto Latinoamericano de Misionología.

Combès, Isabelle. 2011a. 'Candire, Condori y Condorillo: Presencdia incaica en la cordillera chiriguana'. In *Por donde hay soplo: Estudios amazónicos en los países andinos* (Actes et Mémoires de l'Institut Français d'Études Andines 29), edited by J.-P. Chaumeil, O. Espinosa de Rivero and M. Cornejo Chaparro, 271–93. Lima: Fondo Editorial PUCP, CAAAP and EREA-LESC.

Combès, Isabelle. 2011b. 'Pai Sumé, el Rey Blanco y el Paititi', *Anthropos* 106 (1): 99–114.

Combès, Isabelle. 2012. 'Mojos, Moxos y Moços'. Unpublished article.

Combès, Isabelle and Vera Tyuleneva, eds. 2011. *Paititi: Ensayos y documentos* (Scripta Autochtona 8). Cochabamba: Instituto Latinoamericano de Misionología.

Contreras, Daniel A. 2010. 'A Mito-Style Structure at Chavín de Huántar: Dating and Implications', *Latin American Antiquity* 21 (1): 3–21.

Contreras, Daniel A. 2011. 'How Far to Conchucos? A GIS Approach to Assessing the Implications of Exotic Materials at Chavín de Huántar', *World Archaeology* 43 (3): 380–97.

Contreras, W. 2007. *Afiche conmemorativo del Sesquicentenario de la llegada de los Colonos Autro-Alemanes a Pozuzo-Perú (1857–1859)*. Pozuzo: Asociación de Historia y Cultura de Pozuzo, Club Cultural de Prusia y Museo Schafferer. ESERGRAF Ediciones y servicios gráficos, RUC.

Cook, Noble David. 1981. *Demographic Collapse: Indian Peru, 1520–1620*. Cambridge: Cambridge University Press.

Coombs, David, Heidi Coombs and Robert Weber. 1976. *Gramática quechua: San Martín*. Lima: Ministerio de Educación.

Cordeiro, R.C., B. Turcq, K. Suguio, A. Oliveira da Silva, A. Sifeddine and C. Volkmer-Ribeiro. 2008. 'Holocene Fires in East Amazonia (Carajás), New Evidences, Chronology and Relation with Paleoclimate', *Global and Planetary Change* 61 (1/2): 49–62.

Córdoba, Lorena, Pilar M. Valenzuela and Diego Villar. 2012. 'Pano Meridional'. In *Las lenguas de Bolivia*, Vol. 2: *Amazonía*, edited by Mily Crevels and Pieter Muysken, 27–70. La Paz: Plural Editores.

Cordy-Collins, Alana. 1978. 'The Dual Divinity Concept in Chavín Art', *El Dorado* 3 (2): 1–31.

Coulter, J.K. 1972. 'Soil Management Systems'. In *Soils of the Humid Tropics*, 193–7. Washington, DC: National Academy of Sciences.

Covey, R. Alan. 2006. *How the Incas Built Their Heartland: State Formation and the Innovation of Imperial Strategies in the Sacred Valley, Peru*. Ann Arbor: University of Michigan Press.

Creamer, Winifred, Alvaro Ruiz and Jonathan Haas. 2007. 'Archaeological Investigation of Late Archaic Sites (3000–1800 BC) in the Pativilca Valley, Peru', *Fieldiana Anthropology* 40: 1–78.

Créqui-Montfort, Georges de and Paul Rivet. 1913. 'Linguistique bolivienne: La langue lapačú ou apolista', *Zeitschrift für Ethnologie* 45 (3): 512–31.

Créqui-Montfort, Georges de and Paul Rivet. 1921. 'La famille linguistique Takana (suite)', *Journal de la Société des Américanistes de Paris* 13 (2): 281–301.

Créqui-Montfort, Georges de and Paul Rivet. 1925. 'Linguistique bolivienne: La langue Uru ou Pukina', *Journal de la Société des Américanistes* 17: 211–44.

Créqui-Montfort, Georges de and Paul Rivet. 1926. 'Linguistique bolivienne: La langue Uru ou Pukina' [continuation: appendices 1–3], *Journal de la Société des Américanistes* 18: 111–39.

Créqui-Montfort, Georges de and Paul Rivet. 1927. 'Linguistique bolivienne: La langue Uru ou Pukina' [continuation: appendix 4], *Journal de la Société des Américanistes* 19, 57–116.

Crevels, Mily. 2012a. 'Itonama'. In *Las lenguas de Bolivia*, Vol. 2: *Amazonía*, edited by Mily Crevels and Pieter Muysken, 233–394. La Paz: Plural Editores.

Crevels, Mily. 2012b. 'Canichana'. In *Las lenguas de Bolivia*, Vol. 2: *Amazonía*, edited by Mily Crevels and Pieter Muysken, 415–49. La Paz: Plural Editores.

Crevels, Mily and Pieter Muysken. 2012. 'Cayubaba'. In *Las lenguas de Bolivia*, Vol. 2: *Amazonía*, edited by Mily Crevels and Pieter Muysken, 341–74. La Paz: Plural Editores.

Crevels, Mily and Hein van der Voort. 2008. 'The Guaporé-Mamoré Region as a Linguistic Area'. In *From Linguistic Areas to Areal Linguistics*, edited by Pieter Muysken, 151–79. Amsterdam: John Benjamins Publishing Company.

Cruxent, José María and Irving Rouse. 1958–9. *An Archaeological Chronology of Venezuela*. 2 vols. Washington, DC: Pan American Union.

Cruz, Pablo J. 2011. 'El brillo del Señor Sonriente: Miradas alternativas sobre las placas metálicas Surandinas', *Mundo de Antes* 6/7: 97–131.

Cruz, Pablo J. 2015. 'Fronteras difusas: Nuevas perspectivas en la relacion Andes-tierras bajas en tiempos del Inka'. In *Ocupacion Inka y dinamicas regionales en los Andes (Siglos XV–XVII)*, edited by C. Rivera Casanovas, 155–75. La Paz: IFEA and Plural Editores.

Cruz, Pablo and Ivan Guillot. 2009. *Terra Argéntea: Los reinos de metales prehispánicos en el cruce de la Historia y la Arqueología* (Surandino Monográfico 1). 1–19. Buenos Aires: PROHAL.

Cusihuamán Gutiérrez, Antonio. 2001. *Gramática quechua: Cuzco-Collao*. 2nd ed. Cusco: Centro de Estudios Regionales Andinos Bartolomé de las Casas.

Dahl, Östen. 2008. 'An Exercise in A Posteriori Language Sampling', *STUF: Sprachtypologie und Universalienforschung* 61 (3): 208–20.

Dahl, Östen, J. Christopher Gillam, David G. Anderson, José Iriarte and Silvia M. Copé. 2011. 'Linguistic Diversity Zones and Cartographic Modeling: GIS as a Method for Understanding the Prehistory of Lowland South America'. In *Ethnicity in Ancient Amazonia: Reconstructing Past Identities from Archaeology, Linguistics, and Ethnohistory*, edited by Alf Hornborg and Jonathan D. Hill, 211–24. Boulder: University Press of Colorado.

D'Altroy, Terence N. 2002. *The Incas*. Malden, MA: Blackwell.

D'Altroy, Terence N. 2015. *The Incas*. 2nd ed. Chichester: Wiley-Blackwell.

D'Altroy, Terence N. and Timothy K. Earle. 1985. 'Staple Finance, Wealth Finance, and Storage in the Inka Political Economy', *Current Anthropology* 26 (2): 187–206.

D'Altroy, Terence N. and Katharina Schreiber. 2004. 'Andean Empires'. In *Andean Archaeology*, edited by Helaine Silverman, 255–79. Malden, MA: Blackwell.

Danielsen, Swintha 2007. *Baure: An Arawak Language of Bolivia*. Leiden: CNWS Publications.

Dean, Carolyn. 2001. 'Andean Androgyny and the Making of Men'. In *Gender in Pre-Hispanic America: A Symposium at Dumbarton Oaks, 12 and 13 October 1996*, edited by Cecelia F. Klein and Jeffrey Quilter, 143–82. Washington, DC: Dumbarton Oaks Research Library and Collection.

Dediu, Dan and Stephen C. Levinson. 2012. 'Abstract Profiles of Structural Stability Point to Universal Tendencies, Family-Specific Factors, and Ancient Connections between Languages', *PLoS One* 7 (9), Article e45198: 1–15. Accessed 5 May 2020. https://doi.org/10.1371/journal.pone.0045198.

Delgado-Burbano, Miguel E. 2012. 'Dental and Craniofacial Diversity in the Northern Andes, and the Early Peopling of South America'. In *Southbound: Late Pleistocene Peopling of Latin America*, edited by Laura Miotti, Mónica Salemme, Nora Flegenheimer and Ted Goebel, 33–8. College Station: Texas A&M University.

Denevan, William M. 1966. *The Aboriginal Cultural Geography of the Llanos de Mojos of Bolivia*. Berkeley: University of California Press.

Denevan, William M., ed. 1976. *The Native Population of the Americas in 1492*. 2nd ed. Madison: University of Wisconsin Press.

Denevan, William M. 1992a. 'The Aboriginal Population of Amazonia'. In *The Native Population of the Americas in 1492*, edited by William M. Denevan, 205–34. 2nd ed. Madison: University of Wisconsin Press.

Denevan, William M. 1992b. 'The Pristine Myth: The Landscape of the Americas in 1492', *Annals of the Association of American Geographers* 82 (3): 369–85.

Denevan, William M. 2002. *Cultivated Landscapes of Native Amazonia and the Andes*. Oxford: Oxford University Press.

Denevan, William M. 2003. 'The Native Population of Amazonia in 1492 Reconsidered', *Revista de Indias* 63 (227): 175–87.

Derbyshire, Desmond C. 1987. 'Morphosyntactic Areal Characteristics of Amazonian Languages', *International Journal of American Linguistics* 53 (3): 311–26.

Derbyshire, Desmond C. and Geoffrey K. Pullum. 1986. 'Introduction'. In *Handbook of Amazonian Languages, Volume 1*, edited by Desmond C. Derbyshire and Geoffrey K. Pullum, 1–28. Berlin: Mouton de Gruyter.

Descola, Philippe. 2013. *Beyond Nature and Culture*, translated by Janet Lloyd. Chicago: University of Chicago Press.

Devor, E.J. 1987. 'Transmission of Human Craniofacial Dimensions', *Journal of Craniofacial Genetics and Developmental Biology* 7 (2): 95–106.

Diamond, Jared and Peter Bellwood. 2003. 'Farmers and Their Languages: The First Expansions', *Science* 300 (5619): 597–603. http://doi.org/10.1126/science.1078208.

Dickau, Ruth, Maria C. Bruno, José Iriarte, Heiko Prümers, Carla Jaimes Betancourt, Irene Holst and Francis E. Mayle. 2012. 'Diversity of Cultivars and Other Plant Resources Used at Habitation Sites in the Llanos de Mojos, Beni, Bolivia: Evidence from Macrobotanical Remains, Starch Grains, and Phytoliths', *Journal of Archaeological Science* 39 (2): 357–70.

Di Corcia, T., C. Sanchez Mellado, T.J. Davila Francia, G. Ferri, S. Sarno, D. Luiselli and O. Rickards. 2017. 'East of the Andes: The Genetic Profile of the Peruvian Amazon Populations', *American Journal of Physical Anthropology* 163 (2): 328–38.

Dietrich, Wolf. 1986. *El idioma chiriguano: Gramática, textos, vocabulario*. Madrid: Instituto de Cooperación Iberoamericana.

Dillehay, Thomas D. 2000. *The Settlement of the Americas: A New Prehistory*. New York: Basic Books.

Dillehay, Tom D. 2008. 'Profiles in Pleistocene History'. In *The Handbook of South American Archaeology*, edited by Helaine Silverman and William H. Isbell, 29–44. New York: Springer.

Dillehay, Tom D. 2009. 'Probing Deeper into First American Studies', *Proceedings of the National Academy of Sciences of the United States of America* 106 (4): 971–78.

Dillehay, Tom D., ed. 2011. *From Foraging to Farming in the Andes: New Perspectives on Food Production and Social Organization*. New York: Cambridge University Press.

Dillehay, Tom D. 2013. 'Economic Mobility, Exchange, and Order in the Andes'. In *Merchants, Markets, and Exchange in the Pre-Columbian World*, edited by K.G. Hirth and J. Pillsbury, 283–308. Washington, DC: Dumbarton Oaks Research Library and Collection.

Dillehay, Tom D. 2017. *Where the Land Meets the Sea: Fourteen Millennia of Human History at Huaca Prieta, Peru*. Austin: University of Texas Press.

Dillehay, Tom D. and 28 others. 2012. 'Chronology, Mound-Building and Environment at Huaca Prieta, Coastal Peru, from 13700 to 4000 Years Ago', *Antiquity* 86: 48–70.

Dillehay, Tom D., Herbert H. Eling and Jack Rossen. 2005. 'Preceramic Irrigation Canals in the Peruvian Andes', *Proceedings of the National Academy of Sciences of the United States of America* 102 (47): 17241–4.

Dillehay, Tom D. and Patricia J. Netherly. 1983. 'Exploring the Upper Zaña Valley in Peru: A Unique Tropical Forest Setting Offers Insights into the Andean Past', *Archaeology* 36 (4): 22–30.

Dillehay, Tom D., Patricia J. Netherly and Jack Rossen. 2011. 'Preceramic Mounds and Hillside Villages'. In *From Foraging to Farming in the Andes: New Perspectives on Food Production and Social Organization*, edited by Tom D. Dillehay, 135–62. New York: Cambridge University Press.

Dillehay, Tom D. and Lautaro Núñez. 1988. 'Camelids, Caravans, and Complex Societies in the South-Central Andes'. In *Recent Studies in Pre-Columbian Archaeology*, edited by Nicholas J. Saunders and Olivier de Montmollin, 603–34. Oxford: British Archaeological Papers.

Dillehay, Tom D., Jack Rossen, Thomas C. Andres and David E. Williams. 2007. 'Preceramic Adoption of Peanut, Squash, and Cotton in Northern Peru', *Science* 316 (5833): 1890–3.

Dillehay, Tom D., Verónica I. Williams and Calogero M. Santoro. 2006. 'Áreas periféricas y nucleares: Contextos de interacciones sociales complejas y multidireccionales', *Chungara: Revista de Antropología Chilena* 38 (2): 249–56.

Dixon, R.M.W. and Alexandra Y. Aikhenvald, eds. 1999. *The Amazonian Languages*. Cambridge: Cambridge University Press.

Dobyns, Henry F. 1966. 'Estimating Aboriginal American Population: An Appraisal of Techniques with a New Hemispheric Estimate', *Current Anthropology* 7 (4): 395–416.

Donnan, Christopher B., ed. 1985. *Early Ceremonial Architecture in the Andes*. Washington, DC: Dumbarton Oaks Research Library and Collection.

Dornelles, Cláudia L., Sandro L. Bonatto, Loreta B. De Freitas and Francisco M. Salzano. 2005. 'Is Haplogroup X Present in Extant South American Indians?', *American Journal of Physical Anthropology* 127 (4): 439–48.

Dougherty, Bernard and Horacio A. Calandra. 1982. 'Excavaciones arqueológicas en la Loma Alta de Casarabe, Llanos de Moxos, Departamento del Beni, Bolivia', *Relaciones de la Sociedad Argentina de Antropología* 14 (2): 9–48.

Dougherty, Bernard and Horacio A. Calandra. 1985a. 'Ambiente y arqueología en el Oriente Boliviano: La provincia Iténez del departamento Beni', *Relaciones de la Sociedad Argentina de Antropología* 16: 37–61.

Dougherty, Bernard and Horacio A. Calandra. 1985b. 'Archaeological Research in Northeastern Beni, Bolivia'. In *National Geographic Society Research Reports, Volume 21: 1980–1983*, 129–36.

Drew, David. 1984. 'The Cusichaca Project: Aspects of Archaeological Reconnaissance: The Lucumayo and Santa Teresa Valleys'. In *Current Archaeological Projects in the Central Andes: Some Approaches and Results* (BAR International Series 210), edited by A. Kendall, 345–65. Oxford: BAR.

Dryer, Matthew S. 2013. 'Order of Subject, Object and Verb'. In *The World Atlas of Language Structures Online*, edited by Matthew S. Dryer and Martin Haspelmath. Munich: Max Planck Digital Library. Accessed 20 May 2020. http://wals.info/chapter/81.

Dryer, Matthew S. and Martin Haspelmath, eds. 2013a. *The World Atlas of Language Structures*. Leipzig: Max Planck Institute for Evolutionary Anthropology.

Dryer, Matthew S. and Martin Haspelmath, eds. 2013b. *The World Atlas of Language Structures Online*. Munich: Max Planck Digital Library. Accessed 2 June 2020. https://wals.info/.

Dudley, Meredith. 2011. 'Ethnogenesis at the Interface of the Andes and the Amazon: Re-Examining Ethnicity in the Piedmont Region of Apolobamba, Bolivia'. In *Ethnicity in Ancient Amazonia: Reconstructing Past Identities from Archaeology, Linguistics, and Ethnohistory*, edited by Alf Hornborg and Jonathan D. Hill, 297–319. Boulder: University Press of Colorado.

Duff-Tripp, Martha. 1997. *Gramática del idioma yanesha' (amuesha)*. Lima: Ministerio de Educación and Instituto Lingüístico de Verano.

Dunn, Michael, Angela Terrill, Ger Reesink, Robert A. Foley and Stephen C. Levinson. 2005. 'Structural Phylogenetics and the Reconstruction of Ancient Language History', *Science* 309 (5743): 2072–5.

Eastman, Robert and Elizabeth Eastman. 1963. 'Iquito Syntax'. In *Studies in Peruvian Indian Languages, I*, edited by Benjamin F. Elson, 145–92. Norman: Summer Institute of Linguistics of the University of Oklahoma.

Echevarría, Gori Tumi. 2008. 'Excavaciones arqueológicas en la cuenca del Lago Rogoaguado, provincia de Yacuma (Beni, Bolivia)', *Estudios Amazónicos* 7: 87–150.

Eichstaedt, Christina A., Tiago Antão, Alexia Cardona, Luca Pagani, Toomas Kivisild and Maru Mormina. 2015. 'Genetic and Phenotypic Differentiation of an Andean Intermediate Altitude Population', *Physiological Reports* 3 (5), Article e12376: 1–15. Accessed 8 May 2020. https://doi.org/10.14814/phy2.12376.

Eichstaedt, Christina A., Tiago Antão, Luca Pagani, Alexia Cardona, Toomas Kivisild and Maru Mormina. 2014. 'The Andean Adaptive Toolkit to Counteract High Altitude Maladaptation: Genome-Wide and Phenotypic Analysis of the Collas', *PLoS One* 9 (3), Article e93314: 1–12. Accessed 8 May 2020. https://doi.org/10.1371/journal.pone.0093314.

Elera Arévalo, Carlos Gustavo. 1980. 'Investigaciones sobre patrones funerarios en el sitio formativo del Morro de Eten, valle de Lambayeque, norte del Perú'. Bachelor's thesis, Pontificia Universidad Católica del Perú.

Elliott, J.H. 1987a. 'Spain and America before 1700'. In *Colonial Spanish America*, edited by Leslie Bethell, 59–111. Cambridge: Cambridge University Press.

Elliott, J.H. 1987b. 'The Spanish Conquest'. In *Colonial Spanish America*, edited by Leslie Bethell, 1–58. Cambridge: Cambridge University Press.

Emkow, Carola. 2006. 'A Grammar of Araona, an Amazonian Language of Northwestern Bolivia'. PhD thesis, La Trobe University.

Emkow, Carola. 2012. 'Araona'. In *Las lenguas de Bolivia*, Vol. 2: *Amazonía*, edited by Mily Crevels and Pieter Muysken, 155–89. La Paz: Plural Editores.

Epps, Patience. 2009. 'Language Classification, Language Contact, and Amazonian Prehistory', *Language and Linguistics Compass* 3 (2): 581–606. http://doi.org/10.1111/j.1749-818X.2009.00126.x.

Epps, Patience. 2017. 'Subsistence Pattern and Contact-Driven Language Change', *Language Dynamics and Change* 7 (1): 47–101. http://doi.org/10.1163/22105832-00602004.

Epps, Patience and Lev Michael. 2017. 'The Areal Linguistics of Amazonia'. In *The Cambridge Handbook of Areal Linguistics*, edited by Raymond Hickey, 934–63. Cambridge: Cambridge University Press. http://doi.org/10.1017/9781107279872.034

Epps, Patience and Andrés Pablo Salanova. 2013. 'The Languages of Amazonia', *Tipití: Journal of the Society for the Anthropology of Lowland South America* 11 (1): 1–27.

Epps, Patience and Kristine Stenzel, eds. 2013. *Upper Rio Negro: Cultural and Linguistic Interaction in Northwestern Amazonia*. Rio de Janeiro: Museu Nacional and Museu do Índio – FUNAI.

Erickson, Clark L. 1980. 'Sistemas agrícolas prehispánicos en los Llanos de Mojos', *América Indígena* 60 (4): 731–55.

Erickson, Clark L. 2000a. 'An Artificial Landscape-Scale Fishery in the Bolivian Amazon', *Nature* 408: 190–3.

Erickson, Clark L. 2000b. 'Lomas de Ocupación en los Llanos de Moxos'. In *Arqueología de las Tierras Bajas*, edited by Alicia Durán Coirolo and Roberto Bracco Boksar, 207–26. Montevideo: Ministerio de Educación y Cultura, Comisión Nacional de Arqueología.

Erickson, Clark L. 2006. 'The Domesticated Landscapes of the Bolivian Amazon'. In *Time and Complexity in Historical Ecology: Studies in the Neotropical Lowlands*, edited by Willam Balée and Clark L. Erickson, 235–78. New York: Columbia University Press.

Erickson, Clark L. 2008. 'Amazonia: The Historical Ecology of a Domesticated Landscape'. In *The Handbook of South American Archaeology*, edited by Helaine Silverman and William H. Isbell, 157–83. New York: Springer.

Erickson, Clark L. 2010. 'The Transformation of Environment into Landscape: The Historical Ecology of Monumental Earthwork Construction in the Bolivian Amazon', *Diversity* 2 (4): 618–52.

Erickson, Clark L., Patricia Álvarez and Sergio Calla M. 2008. *Zanjas circundantes: Obras de tierra monumentales de Baures en la Amazonia Boliviana: Informe del trabajo de campo de la temporada 2007*. Proyecto Agro-Arqueológico del Beni.

Erickson, Clark L. and J. Faldín. 1978. 'Preliminary Report on the Archaeological Survey in the Llanos de Mojos, Bolivia, San Ignacio to San Borja'. Unpublished report, Documentos Internos 36/78. La Paz: Instituto Nacional de Arqueología.

Eriksen, Love. 2011. *Nature and Culture in Prehistoric Amazonia* (Lund Studies in Human Ecology 12). Lund: Lund University. Accessed 21 May 2020. https://lup.lub.lu.se/search/publication/1890748.

Espejo Nuñez, J. 1964. 'Sobre un nuevo fragmento de la Estela de Yauya', *Boletín del Museo Nacional de Arqueología y Antropología* 1: 2.

Espinoza Soriano, Waldemar. 1967. 'Los señoríos étnicos de Chachapoyas y la alianza hispano-chacha: Visitas, informaciones y memoriales inéditos de 1572–1574', *Revista Histórica* 30: 224–333.

Evans, Clifford and Betty J. Meggers. 1968. *Archaeological Investigations on the Rio Napo, Eastern Ecuador*. Washington, DC: Smithsonian Institution Press.

Fabian, Stephen Michael. 1992. *Space-Time of the Bororo of Brazil*. Gainesville: University Press of Florida.

Fabian, Stephen M. 1998. 'Waiting to Tie the Knot: Thoughts on Structural Similarities between Bororo and Inca', *Journal of the Steward Anthropological Society* 26 (1/2): 19–36.

Fabre, Alain. 1995. 'Lexical Similarities between Uru-Chipaya and Pano-Takanan Languages: Genetical Relationship or Areal Diffusion?', *Opción: Revista de Ciencias Humanas y Sociales* 11 (18): 45–73.

Fabre, Alain. 1998. *Manual de las lenguas indígenas sudamericanas II*. Munich: Lincom Europa.

Fagundes, Nelson J.R. and 12 others. 2008. 'Mitochondrial Population Genomics Supports a Single Pre-Clovis Origin with a Coastal Route for the Peopling of the Americas', *American Journal of Human Genetics* 82 (3): 583–92.

Fast Mowitz, Gerhard and Ruby Fast. 1981. *Introducción al idioma achuar*. Lima: Ministerio de Educación and Instituto Lingüístico de Verano.

Fast Mowitz, Gerhard, Ruby Warkentin de Fast and Daniel Fast Warkentin. 1996. *Diccionario achuar-shiwiar-castellano*. Lima: Ministerio de Educación and Instituto Lingüístico de Verano.

Faust, Norma and Eugene E. Loos. 2002. *Gramática del idioma yaminahua*. Lima: Ministerio de Educación and Instituto Lingüístico de Verano.

Fausto, Carlos and Eduardo G. Neves. 2018. 'Was There Ever a Neolithic in the Neotropics? Plant Familiarisation and Biodiversity in the Amazon', *Antiquity* 92 (366): 1604–18.

Fehren-Schmitz, Lars and 10 others. 2014. 'Climate Change Underlies Global Demographic, Genetic, and Cultural Transitions in Pre-Columbian Southern Peru', *Proceedings of the National Academy of Sciences of the United States of America* 111 (26): 9443–8. http://doi.org/10.1073/pnas.1403466111.

Fehren-Schmitz, Lars and 15 others. 2015. 'A Re-Appraisal of the Early Andean Human Remains from Lauricocha in Peru', *PloS One* 10 (6): e0127141. https://doi.org/10.1371/journal.pone.0127141

Fernandes Caromano, Caroline, Leandro Matthews Cascon, Eduardo Góes Neves and Rita Scheel-Ybert. 2013. 'Revealing Fires and Rich Diets: Macro- and Micro-Archaeobotanical Analysis at the Hatahara Site, Central Amazonia', *Tipití: Journal of the Society for the Anthropology of Lowland South America* 11 (2): 40–51.

Ferrié, Francis. 2018. *Apolobamba indígena*. Cochabamba: Instituto Latinoamericano de Misionología.

Fewkes, J. Walter. 1912. 'The Problems of the Unity or Plurality and the Probable Place of Origin of the American Aborigines', *American Anthropologist* 14 (1): 1–59.

Finucane, Brian C. 2009. 'Maize and Sociopolitical Complexity in the Ayacucho Valley, Peru', *Current Anthropology* 50 (4): 535–45.

Firestone, Homer L. 1965. *Description and Classification of Sirionó: A Tupí-Guaraní Language*. The Hague: Mouton.

Fischer, Rafael and Eva van Lier. 2011. 'Cofán Subordinate Clauses in a Typology of Subordination'. In *Subordination in Native South American Languages*, edited by Rik van Gijn, Katharina Haude and Pieter Muysken, 221–50. Amsterdam: John Benjamins Publishing Company.

Fleck, David W. 2013. *Panoan Languages and Linguistics* (Anthropological Papers of the American Museum of Natural History 99). New York: American Museum of Natural History.

Fonseca Santa Cruz, Javier and Brian S. Bauer. 2013. 'Dating the Wari Remains at Espíritu Pampa (Vilcabamba, Cusco)', *Andean Past* 11: 111–21.

Frank, Susana. 2008. *Pueblos originarios de América: Introducción*. Buenos Aires: Ediciones del Sol.

Freitas, Fábio O. and Patricia G. Bustamante. 2013. 'Amazonian Maize: Diversity, Spatial Distribution and Historical-Cultural Diffusion', *Tipití: Journal of the Society for the Anthropology of Lowland South America* 11 (2): 60–5.

Fretwell, Stephen D. and Henry L. Lucas. 1969. 'On Territorial Behavior and Other Factors Influencing Habitat Distribution in Birds', *Acta Biotheoretica* 19: 16–36.

Friedemann, Nina S. and Jaime Arocha. 1982. 'Sibundoyes e Ingas: Sabios en medicina y botánica'. In *Herederos del jaguar y la anaconda*, edited by Nina S. Friedemann and Jaime Arocha. Bogotá: Carlos Valencia editores.

Fung de Pineda, Rosa. 1988. 'The Late Preceramic and Initial Period'. In *Peruvian Prehistory: An Overview of Pre-Inca and Inca Society*, edited by Richard W. Keatinge, 67–96. Cambridge: Cambridge University Press.

Fuselli, Silvia, Eduardo Tarazona-Santos, Isabelle Dupanloup, Alonso Soto, Donata Luiselli and Davide Pettener. 2003. 'Mitochondrial DNA Diversity in South America and the Genetic History of Andean Highlanders', *Molecular Biology and Evolution* 20 (10): 1682–91.

Gade, Daniel W. 1979. 'Inca and Colonial Settlement, Coca Cultivation and Endemic Disease in the Tropical Forest', *Journal of Historical Geography* 5 (3): 263–79.

Gade, Daniel W. 1999. 'Valleys of Mystery on the Peruvian Jungle Margin and the Inca Coca Connection'. In *Nature and Culture in the Andes*, by Daniel W. Gade, 137–56. Madison: University of Wisconsin Press.

Gade, Daniel W. 2016. *Spell of the Urubamba: Anthropogeographical Essays on an Andean Valley in Space and Time*. Cham: Springer.

García Salazar, Gabriela Victoria. 1993. 'Asheninca-ucayali: Morfologia e fonologia'. Master's thesis, Universidade Federal de Santa Catarina.

Gasparini, Noé. 2012. 'Observations sociolinguistiques et esquisse de la phonologie du siriono: Langue tupi-guarani de Bolivie'. Master's thesis, Université Lumière Lyon 2.

Gassón, Rafael A. 2000. 'Quirípas and Mostacillas: The Evolution of Shell Beads as a Medium of Exchange in Northern South America', *Ethnohistory* 47 (3/4): 581–609.

Gayà-Vidal, Magdalena, Pedro Moral, Nancy Saenz-Ruales, Pascale Gerbault, Laure Tonasso, Mercedes Villena, René Vasquez, Claudio M. Bravi and Jean-Michel Dugoujon. 2011. 'MtDNA and Y-Chromosome Diversity in Aymaras and Quechuas from Bolivia: Different Stories and Special Genetic Traits of the Andean Altiplano Populations', *American Journal of Physical Anthropology* 145 (2): 215–30.

Gignoux, Christopher R., Brenna M. Henn and Joanna L. Mountain. 2011. 'Rapid, Global Demographic Expansions after the Origins of Agriculture', *Proceedings of the National Academy of Sciences of the United States of America* 108 (15): 6044–9.

Gilbert, M. Thomas P., Jonas Binladen, Webb Miller, Carsten Wiuf, Eske Willerslev, Hendrik Poinar, John E. Carlson, James H. Leebens-Mack and Stephan C. Schuster. 2007. 'Recharacterization of Ancient DNA Miscoding Lesions: Insights in the Era of Sequencing-by-Synthesis', *Nucleic Acids Research* 35 (1): 1–10.

Gil García, Francisco M. 2002. 'Acontecimientos y regularidades chullparias: Más allá de las tipologías: Reflexiones en torno a la construcción del paisaje chullpario', *Revista Española de Antropología Americana* 32: 207–41.

Girard, Victor. 1971. *Proto-Takanan Phonology*. Berkeley: University of California Press.

Glave, Luis Miguel. 2009. 'El Apu Ynga camina de nuevo: Juan Santos Atahualpa y el asalto de Andamarca en 1752', *Perspectivas Latinoamericanas* 6: 28–68.

Gnecchi-Ruscone, Guido Alberto and 20 others. 2019. 'Dissecting the Pre-Columbian Genomic Ancestry of Native Americans along the Andes–Amazonia Divide', *Molecular Biology and Evolution* 36 (6): 1254–69.

Gnecco, Cristóbal and Santiago Mora. 1997. 'Late Pleistocene/Early Holocene Tropical Forest Occupations at San Isidro and Peña Roja, Colombia', *Antiquity* 71 (273): 683–90.

Goddard, Ives. 1987. 'Book Review – *Language in the Americas*, by Joseph H. Greenberg', *Current Anthropology* 28 (5): 656–7. https://www.jstor.org/stable/2743361.

Goddard, Ives and L. Campbell. 1994. 'The History and Classification of American Indian Languages: What Are the Implications for the Peopling of the Americas?'. In *Method and Theory for Investigating the Peopling of the Americas*, edited by R. Bonnichsen and D.G. Steele, 189–207. Corvallis: Center for the Study of the First Americans, Oregon State University.

Goldstein, D.B. and D.D. Pollock. 1997. 'Launching Microsatellites: A Review of Mutation Processes and Methods of Phylogenetic Inference', *Journal of Heredity* 88 (5): 335–42.

Goldstein, Paul S. 2003. 'From Stew-Eaters to Maize-Drinkers: The Chicha Economy and the Tiwanaku Expansion'. In *The Archaeology and Politics of Food and Feasting in Early States and Empires*, edited by Tamara L. Bray, 143–72. New York: Kluwer Academic.

Golluscio, Lucía, Adriana Fraguas and Fresia Mellico. 2009. 'Mapudungun'. In *World Loanword Database*, edited by M. Haspelmath and U. Tadmor. Leipzig: Max Planck Institute for Evolutionary Anthropology.

Gomes, Graziela de Jesus. 2010. 'Aspectos morfossintaticos da lingua Huariapano (Pano)'. Master's thesis, Universidade Estadual de Campinas.

González, Hebe. 2015. 'El Chaco como área lingüística: Una evaluación de los rasgos fonológicos'. In *Language Contact and Documentation*, edited by B. Comrie and L. Golluscio, 165–203. Berlin: De Gruyter.

González-José, Rolando, Maria Cátira Bortolini, Fabrício R. Santos and Sandro L. Bonatto. 2008. 'The Peopling of America: Craniofacial Shape Variation on a Continental Scale and Its Interpretation from an Interdisciplinary View', *American Journal of Physical Anthropology* 137 (2): 175–87.

González-José, Rolando, Antonio González-Martín, Miquel Hernández, Héctor M. Pucciarelli, Marina Sardi, Alfonso Rosales and Silvina Van der Molen. 2003. 'Craniometric Evidence for Palaeoamerican Survival in Baja California', *Nature* 425: 62–5.

González-José, Rolando, Walter Neves, Marta Mirazón Lahr, Silvia González, Héctor Pucciarelli, Miquel Hernández Martínez and Gonzalo Correal. 2005a. 'Late Pleistocene/Holocene Craniofacial Morphology in Mesoamerican Paleoindians: Implications for the Peopling of the New World', *American Journal of Physical Anthropology* 128 (4): 772–80.

González-José, Rolando, Fernando Ramírez-Rozzi, Marina Sardi, Neus Martínez-Abadías, Miquel Hernández and Hector M. Pucciarelli. 2005b. 'Functional-Cranial Approach to the Influence of Economic Strategy on Skull Morphology', *American Journal of Physical Anthropology* 128 (4): 757–71.

Graf, Kelly E., Caroline V. Ketron and Michael R. Waters, eds. 2014. *Paleoamerican Odyssey*. College Station: Texas A&M University Press.

Granberry, Julian and Gary S. Vescelius. 2004. *Languages of the Pre-Columbian Antilles*. Tuscaloosa: University of Alabama Press.

Greenberg, Joseph H. 1960. 'The General Classification of Central and South American Languages'. In *Selected Papers of the 5th International Congress of Anthropological and Ethnographic Sciences (1956)*, edited by A. Wallace. Philadelphia: University of Pennsylvania Press.

Greenberg, Joseph H. 1987. *Language in the Americas*. Stanford: Stanford University Press.

Greenberg, Joseph H. 1996. 'In Defense of Amerind', *International Journal of American Linguistics* 62 (2): 131–64.

Greenberg, Joseph H., Christy G. Turner and Stephen L. Zegura. 1986. 'The Settlement of the Americas: A Comparison of the Linguistic, Dental, and Genetic Evidence', *Current Anthropology* 27 (5): 477–97.

Greenhill, Simon J., Chieh-Hsi Wu, Xia Hua, Michael Dunn, Stephen C. Levinson and Russell D. Gray. 2017. 'Evolutionary Dynamics of Language Systems'. *Proceedings of the National Academy of Sciences of the United States of America* 114 (42): E8822–9.

Gremillion, Kristen J., Loukas Barton and Dolores R. Piperno. 2014. 'Particularism and the Retreat from Theory in the Archaeology of Agricultural Origins', *Proceedings of the National Academy of Sciences of the United States of America* 111 (17): 6171–7.

Grieder, Terence. 1978. *The Art and Archaeology of Pashash*. Austin: University of Texas Press.

Grieder, Terence, and Alberto Bueno Mendoza. 1985. 'Ceremonial Architecture at La Galgada'. In *Early Ceremonial Architecture in the Andes: A Conference at Dumbarton Oaks, 8th to 10th October 1982*, edited by C. Donnan. Washington, DC: Dumbarton Oaks Research Library and Collection.

Grieder, Terence, Alberto Bueno Mendoza, C. Earle Smith and Robert M. Malina. 1988. *La Galgada, Peru: A Preceramic Culture in Transition*. Austin: University of Texas Press.

Guengerich, A. 2012. 'Proyecto Arqueológico Pueblo Chachapoya (PAPCHA) Sitio de Monte Viudo, Chachapoyas, Amazonas'. Unpublished report. Lima: Ministerio de Cultura.

Guevara, Evelyn K., Jukka U. Palo, Sonia Guillén and Antti Sajantila. 2016. 'MtDNA and Y-Chromosomal Diversity in the Chachapoya, a Population from the Northeast Peruvian Andes–Amazon Divide', *American Journal of Human Biology* 28 (6): 857–67.

Guffroy, Jean, ed. 1987. *Loja préhispanique: Recherches archéologiques dans les Andes méridionales de l'Equateur* (Synthèse 27). Paris: Editions Recherche sur les Civilisations.

Guffroy, Jean, ed. 1994. *Cerro Ñañañique: Un établissement monumental de la Période Formative, en limite de désert (Haut Piura, Pérou)*. Paris: ORSTOM.

Guffroy, Jean. 2008. 'Cultural Boundaries and Crossings: Ecuador and Peru'. In *The Handbook of South American Archaeology*, edited by Helaine Silverman and William H. Isbell, 889–902. New York: Springer.

Guglielmino-Matessi, C.R., P. Gluckman and L.L. Cavalli-Sforza. 1979. 'Climate and the Evolution of Skull Metrics in Man', *American Journal of Physical Anthropology* 50 (4): 549–64.

Guillaume, Antoine. 2008. *A Grammar of Cavineña*. Berlin: de Gruyter Mouton.

Guillaume, Antoine. 2012. 'Maropa (Reyesano)'. In *Las lenguas de Bolivia*, Vol. 2: *Amazonía*, edited by Mily Crevels and Pieter Muysken, 191–232. La Paz: Plural Editores.

Güldemann, Tom. 2018. 'Language Contact and Areal Linguistics in Africa'. In *The Languages and Linguistics of Africa*, edited by Tom Güldemann, 445–545. Berlin: De Gruyter Mouton.

Hagelberg, Erika, Michael Hofreiter and Christine Keyser. 2015. 'Ancient DNA: The First Three Decades', *Philosophical Transactions of the Royal Society B: Biological Sciences* 370 (1660), Article 20130371: 1–6. Accessed 10 May 2020. https://doi.org/10.1098/rstb.2013.0371.

Håkansson, N. Thomas and Mats Widgren, eds. 2014. *Landesque Capital: The Historical Ecology of Enduring Landscape Modifications*. Walnut Creek, CA: Left Coast Press.

Hammarström, Harald, Robert Forkel and Martin Haspelmath. 2019. *Glottolog 4.0*. Accessed 20 May 2020. http://glottolog.org

Hammarström, Harald, Robert Forkel, Martin Haspelmath and Sebastian Bank. 2015. *Glottolog 2.4*. Leipzig: Max Planck Institute for Evolutionary Anthropology.

Hanagarth, Werner. 1993. *Acerca de la geoecología de las sabanas del Beni en el noreste de Bolivia*. La Paz: Instituto de Ecología.

Hannss, Katja. 2008. *Uchumataqu: The Lost Language of the Urus of Bolivia: A Grammatical Description of the Language as Documented between 1894 and 1952*. Leiden: Research School of Asian, African and Amerindian Studies (CNWS).

Hannss, Katja. 2009. 'Uchumataqu (Uru)'. In *Las lenguas de Bolivia*, Vol. 1: *Ámbito andino*, edited by E.I. Crevels and P.C. Muysken, 79–115. La Paz: Plural Editores.

Hanson, Rebecca. 2010. 'A Grammar of Yine (Piro)'. PhD thesis, La Trobe University.

Hardman, Martha J. 1983. *Jaqaru: Compendio de estructura fonológica y morfológica*. Lima: Instituto de Estudios Peruanos and Instituto Indigenista Interamericano.

Hardman, M.J. 2000. *Jaqaru*. Munich: Lincom Europa.

Hardman, M.J. 2001. *Aymara*. Munich: Lincom Europa.

Harris, Daniel N. and 17 others. 2018. 'Evolutionary Genomic Dynamics of Peruvians before, during, and after the Inca Empire', *Proceedings of the National Academy of Sciences of the United States of America* 115 (28): E6526–35.

Harris, David. 2002. 'The Expansion Capacity of Early Agricultural Systems: A Comparative Perspective on the Spread of Agriculture'. In *Examining the Farming/Language Dispersal Hypothesis*, edited by Peter Bellwood and Colin Renfrew, 31–9. Cambridge: McDonald Institute for Archaeological Research.

Harvati, Katerina and Timothy D. Weaver. 2006. 'Human Cranial Anatomy and the Differential Preservation of Population History and Climate Signatures', *Anatomical Record: Advances in Integrative Anatomy and Evolutionary Biology* 288 (12): 1225–33.

Hastings, Charles M. 1987. 'Implications of Andean Verticality in the Evolution of Political Complexity: A View from the Margins'. In *The Origins and Development of the Andean State*, edited by Jonathan Haas, Shelia Pozorski and Thomas Pozorski, 145–57. Cambridge: Cambridge University Press.

Hastorf, Christine A. 1987. 'Archaeological Evidence of Coca (*Erythroxylum coca*, Erythroxylaceae) in the Upper Mantaro Valley, Peru', *Economic Botany* 41 (2): 292–301.

Hastorf, Christine A. 2003. 'Community with the Ancestors: Ceremonies and Social Memory in the Middle Formative at Chiripa, Bolivia', *Journal of Anthropological Archaeology* 22 (4): 305–32.

Hastorf, Christine A. 2006. 'Domesticated Food and Society in Early Coastal Peru'. In *Time and Complexity in Historical Ecology: Studies in the Neotropical Lowlands*, edited by Willam Balée and Clark L. Erickson, 87–126. New York: Columbia University Press.

Haude, Katharina. 2006. 'A Grammar of Movima'. PhD thesis, Radboud University Nijmegen.

Hawkes, J.G. 1990. *The Potato: Evolution, Biodiversity, and Genetic Resources*. Washington, DC: Smithsonian Institution Press.

Haynie, Hannah, Claire Bowern, Patience Epps, Jane Hill and Patrick McConvell. 2014. 'Wanderwörter in Languages of the Americas and Australia', *Ampersand* 1: 1–18. http://doi.org/10.1016/j.amper.2014.10.001.

Hebsgaard, Martin B., Matthew J. Phillips and Eske Willerslev. 2005. 'Geologically Ancient DNA: Fact or Artefact?', *Trends in Microbiology* 13 (5): 212–20.

Heckenberger, Michael Joseph. 1996. 'War and Peace in the Shadow of Empire: Sociopolitical Change in the Upper Xingu of Southeastern Amazonia, AD 1400–2000'. PhD thesis, University of Pittsburgh.

Heckenberger, Michael J. 2002. 'Rethinking the Arawakan Diaspora: Hierarchy, Regionality, and the Amazonian Formative'. In *Comparative Arawakan Histories: Rethinking Language Family and Culture Area in Amazonia*, edited by Jonathan D. Hill and Fernando Santos-Granero, 99–122. Urbana: University of Illinois Press.

Heckenberger, Michael J. 2003. 'The Enigma of the Great Cities: Body and State in Amazonia', *Tipití: Journal of the Society for the Anthropology of Lowland South America* 1 (1): 27–58.

Heckenberger, Michael J. 2005. 'Social Dynamics before Europe'. In *The Ecology of Power: Culture, Place, and Personhood in the Southern Amazon, AD 1000–2000*, by Michael J. Heckenberger, 113–42. New York: Routledge.

Heckenberger, Michael J. 2008. 'Amazonian Mosaics: Identity, Interaction, and Integration in the Tropical Forest'. In *The Handbook of South American Archaeology*, edited by Helaine Silverman and William H. Isbell, 941–62. New York: Springer.

Heckenberger, Michael J. 2009. 'Lost Garden Cities: Pre-Columbian Life in the Amazon', *Scientific American* 301 (4): 64–71.

Heckenberger, Michael. 2011. 'Deep History, Cultural Identities, and Ethnogenesis in the Southern Amazon'. In *Ethnicity in Ancient Amazonia: Reconstructing Past Identities from Archaeology, Linguistics, and Ethnohistory*, edited by Alf Hornborg and Jonathan D. Hill, 57–74. Boulder: University Press of Colorado.

Heckenberger, Michael J., J. Christian Russell, Joshua R. Toney and Morgan J. Schmidt. 2007. 'The Legacy of Cultural Landscapes in the Brazilian Amazon: Implications for Biodiversity', *Philosophical Transactions of the Royal Society B: Biological Sciences* 362 (1478): 197–208.

Heckenberger, Michael and Eduardo Góes Neves. 2009. 'Amazonian Archaeology', *Annual Review of Anthropology* 38: 251–66.

Heckenberger, Michael J., Afukaka Kuikuro, Urissapá Tabata Kuikuro, J. Christian Russell, Morgan Schmidt, Carlos Fausto and Bruna Franchetto. 2003. 'Amazonia 1492: Pristine Forest or Cultural Parkland?', *Science* 301 (5640): 1710–14.

Heckenberger, Michael J., James B. Petersen and Eduardo Góes Neves. 1999. 'Village Size and Permanence in Amazonia: Two Archaeological Examples from Brazil', *Latin American Antiquity* 10 (4): 353–76.

Heckenberger, Michael J., J. Christian Russell, Carlos Fausto, Joshua R. Toney, Morgan J. Schmidt, Edithe Pereira, Bruna Franchetto and Afukaka Kuikuro. 2008. 'Pre-Columbian Urbanism, Anthropogenic Landscapes, and the Future of the Amazon', *Science* 321 (5893): 1214–17.

Heggarty, Paul. 2007. 'Linguistics for Archaeologists: Principles, Methods and the Case of the Incas', *Cambridge Archaeological Journal* 17 (3): 311–40. http://doi.org/10.1017/S095977430700039X.

Heggarty, Paul. 2008. 'Linguistics for Archaeologists: A Case-study in the Andes', *Cambridge Archaeological Journal* 18 (1): 35–56. https://doi.org/10.1017/S0959774308000036

Heggarty, Paul. 2014. 'Prehistory by Bayesian Phylogenetics? The State of the Art on Indo-European Origins', *Antiquity* 88 (340): 566–77. http://doi.org/10.1017/S0003598X00101188.

Heggarty, Paul. 2015. 'Prehistory through Language and Archaeology'. In *The Routledge Handbook of Historical Linguistics*, edited by Claire Bowern and Bethwyn Evans, 598–626. London: Routledge. OpenAccess at: https://www.routledgehandbooks.com/doi/10.4324/9781315794013.ch28.

Heggarty, Paul. 2017. 'Towards a (Pre)history of Linguistic Convergence Areas: Correlates in Genetics, Archaeology, History and Geography', *Mémoires de la Société de Linguistique de Paris* 24: 135–78.

Heggarty, Paul and David Beresford-Jones. 2010. 'Agriculture and Language Dispersals: Limitations, Refinements, and an Andean Exception?', *Current Anthropology* 51 (2): 163–91. http://doi.org/10.1086/650533.

Heggarty, Paul and David Beresford-Jones, eds. 2012. *Archaeology and Language in the Andes: A Cross-Disciplinary Exploration of Prehistory*. Oxford: Oxford University Press. http://doi.org/10.5871/bacad/9780197265031.001.0001.

Heggarty, P. and C. Renfrew. 2014a. 'Introduction: Languages'. In *The Cambridge World Prehistory*, edited by C. Renfrew and P. Bahn, 19–44. Cambridge: Cambridge University Press.

Heggarty, P. and C. Renfrew. 2014b. 'The Americas: Languages'. In *The Cambridge World Prehistory*, edited by C. Renfrew and P. Bahn, 1316–43. Cambridge: Cambridge University Press.

Helberg Chávez, Heinrich Albert. 1984. 'Skizze einer Grammatik des Amarakaeri'. PhD thesis, Eberhard Karls Universität Tübingen.

Hemming, John. 1995. *Red Gold: The Conquest of the Brazilian Indians*. London: Papermac.

Hemming, John. 2008. *Tree of Rivers: The Story of the Amazon*. London: Thames and Hudson.

Hermenegildo, Tiago, Tamsin C. O'Connell, Vera L.C. Guapindaia and Eduardo G. Neves. 2017. 'New Evidence for Subsistence Strategies of Late Pre-Colonial Societies of the Mouth of the Amazon Based on Carbon and Nitrogen Isotopic Data', *Quaternary International* 448: 139–49.

Herrera Wassilowsky, Alexander. 1998. 'Acerca de un tercer fragmento de la Estela de Yauya', *Baessler-Archiv* 46: 231–53.

Herrera Wassilowsky, Alexander. 2003. 'La Serpiente de Oro y los Inkas: La ocupación Inka en el Alto Marañón y el puerto balsero de Pogtán', *Boletín de Arqueología PUCP* 7: 189–215.

Herrera Wassilowsky, Alexander. 2005. 'Las kancha circulares: Espacios de interacción social en la sierra norte del Perú', *Boletín de Arqueología PUCP* 9: 233–55.

Herrera Wassilowsky, Alexander. 2006. 'Territorio e Identidad: Apuntes para una modelo de la complejidad social andina'. In *Complejidad social en la arqueología y antropología de la Sierra de Ancash: Trabajos de la primera y segunda Mesa Redonda de Arqueología de la Sierra de Ancash*, edited by Alexander Herrera, Carolina Orsini and Kevin Lane, 3–18. Milan: Civiche Raccolte d'Arte Applicata del Castello Sforzesco.

Herrera Wassilowsky, Alexander. 2016. 'Multilingualism on the North Coast of Peru: An Archaeological Perspective on Quingnam, Muchik, and Quechua Toponyms from the Nepeña Valley and Its Headwaters', *Indiana* 33 (1): 161–76.

Herrera Wassilowsky, Alexander. In preparation A. *Water, Ancestors and Memory in an Andean Landscape,* Vol. 1: *Archaeological Investigations in the Callejón de Huaylas and the Western Escarpment of the Cordillera Negra (Ancash, Peru).*

Herrera Wassilowsky, Alexander. In preparation B. *Water, Ancestors and Memory in an Andean Landscape,* Vol. 2: *Archaeological Investigations in the Conchucos Region (Ancash, Peru).*

Herrera Wassilowsky, Alexander. In preparation C. 'Investigations at Gotushjirka'. In *Water, Ancestors and Memory in an Andean Landscape,* Vol. 2: *Archaeological Investigations in the Conchucos Region (Ancash, Peru).*

Herrera Wassilowsky, Alexander, Carolina Orsini and Kevin Lane, eds. 2006. *Complejidad social en la arqueología y antropología de la Sierra de Ancash: Trabajos de la primera y segunda Mesa Redonda de Arqueología de la Sierra de Ancash.* Milan: Civiche Raccolte d'Arte Applicata del Castello Sforzesco.

Herzog, Tamar. 2015. *Frontiers of Possession: Spain and Portugal in Europe and the Americas.* Cambridge, MA: Harvard University Press.

Hilbert, Lautaro, Eduardo Góes Neves, Francisco Pugliese, Bronwen S. Whitney, Myrtle Shock, Elizabeth Veasey, Carlos Augusto Zimpel and José Iriarte. 2017. 'Evidence for Mid-Holocene Rice Domestication in the Americas', *Nature Ecology and Evolution* 1 (11): 1693–8. https://doi.org/10.1038/s41559-017-0322-4

Hill, Jonathan D. and Fernando Santos-Granero, eds. 2002. *Comparative Arawakan Histories: Rethinking Language Family and Culture Area in Amazonia.* Urbana: University of Illinois Press.

Hocquenghem, Anne Marie. 1990. *Los Guayacundos de Caxas y la sierra piurana: Siglos XV y XVI.* Lima: Centro de Investigación y Promoción del Campesinado.

Holdridge, L.R. 1967. *Life Zone Ecology.* San Jose: Tropical Sciences Center.

Hoopes, John W. 1994. 'Ford Revisited: A Critical Review of the Chronology and Relationships of the Earliest Ceramic Complexes in the New World, 6000–1500 BC', *Journal of World Prehistory* 8: 1–49.

Hornborg, Alf. 1990. 'Highland and Lowland Conceptions of Social Space in South America: Some Ethnoarchaeological Affinities', *Folk* 32: 61–92.

Hornborg, Alf. 2005. 'Ethnogenesis, Regional Integration, and Ecology in Prehistoric Amazonia: Toward a System Perspective', *Current Anthropology* 46 (4): 589–620.

Hornborg, Alf. 2014. 'Political Economy, Ethnogenesis, and Language Dispersals in the Prehispanic Andes: A World-System Perspective', *American Anthropologist* 116 (4): 810–23.

Hornborg, Alf. 2015. 'The Political Economy of Technofetishism: Agency, Amazonian Ontologies, and Global Magic', *HAU: Journal of Ethnographic Theory* 5 (1): 35–57.

Hornborg, Alf and Love Eriksen. 2011. 'An Attempt to Understand Panoan Ethnogenesis in Relation to Long-Term Patterns and Transformations of Regional Interaction in Western Amazonia'. In *Ethnicity in Ancient Amazonia: Reconstructing Past Identities from Archaeology, Linguistics, and Ethnohistory*, edited by Alf Hornborg and Jonathan D. Hill, 129–51. Boulder: University Press of Colorado.

Hornborg, Alf and Jonathan D. Hill, eds. 2011. *Ethnicity in Ancient Amazonia: Reconstructing Past Identities from Archaeology, Linguistics, and Ethnohistory.* Boulder: University Press of Colorado.

Howard, George D. 1947. *Prehistoric Ceramic Styles of Lowland South America, Their Distribution and History* (Yale University Publications in Anthropology 37). New Haven: Yale University Press.

Howard, Rosaleen. 2011. 'The Quechua Language in the Andes Today: Between Statistics, the State, and Daily Life'. In *History and Language in the Andes*, edited by Paul Heggarty and Adrian J. Pearce, 189–213. New York: Palgrave Macmillan. http://doi.org/10.1057/9780230370579

Howells, W.W. 1989. *Skull Shapes and the Map: Craniometric Analyses in the Dispersion of Modern Homo* (Papers of the Peabody Museum of Archaeology and Ethnology 79). Cambridge, MA: Peabody Museum of Archaeology and Ethnology.

Hubbe, Mark, Tsunehiko Hanihara and Katerina Harvati. 2009. 'Climate Signatures in the Morphological Differentiation of Worldwide Modern Human Populations', *Anatomical Record: Advances in Integrative Anatomy and Evolutionary Biology* 292 (11): 1720–33.

Hubbe, Mark, Walter A. Neves, João Paulo V. Atui, Castor Cartelle and Miya A. Pereira da Silva. 2004. 'A New Early Human Skeleton from Brazil: Support for the "Two Main Biological Components Model" for the Settlement of the Americas', *Current Research in the Pleistocene* 21: 77–81.

Hubbe, Mark, Walter A. Neves, Heleno Licurgo do Amaral and Niéde Guidon. 2007. 'Brief Communication: "Zuzu" Strikes Again – Morphological Affinities of the Early Holocene Human Skeleton from Toca dos Coqueiros, Piauí, Brazil', *American Journal of Physical Anthropology* 134 (2): 285–91.

Hubbe, Mark, Mercedes Okumura, Danilo V. Bernardo and Walter A. Neves. 2014. 'Cranial Morphological Diversity of Early, Middle, and Late Holocene Brazilian Groups: Implications for Human Dispersion in Brazil', *American Journal of Physical Anthropology* 155 (4): 546–58.

Hudjashov, Georgi and 10 others. 2007. 'Revealing the Prehistoric Settlement of Australia by Y Chromosome and mtDNA Analysis', *Proceedings of the National Academy of Sciences of the United States of America* 104 (21): 8726–30.

Hugh-Jones, Christine. 1979. *From the Milk River: Spatial and Temporal Processes in Northwest Amazonia*. Cambridge: Cambridge University Press.

Hummel, Susanne. 2003. *Ancient DNA Typing: Methods, Strategies and Applications*. Berlin: Springer.

Hünemeier, Tábita and 10 others. 2012a. 'Cultural Diversification Promotes Rapid Phenotypic Evolution in Xávante Indians', *Proceedings of the National Academy of Sciences of the United States of America* 109 (1): 73–7.

Hünemeier, Tábita and 14 others. 2012b. 'Evolutionary Responses to a Constructed Niche: Ancient Mesoamericans as a Model of Gene-Culture Coevolution', *PLoS One* 7 (6), Article e38862: 1–10. Accessed 12 May 2020. https://doi.org/10.1371/journal.pone.0038862.

Hunley, K.L., G.S. Cabana, D.A. Merriwether and J.C. Long. 2007. 'A Formal Test of Linguistic and Genetic Coevolution in Native Central and South America', *American Journal of Physical Anthropology* 132 (4): 622–31.

Hyde, Sylvia. 1980. *Diccionario amahuaca*. Yarinacocha: Instituto Lingüístico de Verano.

Ibarra Asencios, Bebel, ed. 2003. *Arqueología de la Sierra de Ancash: Propuestas y perspectivas*. Lima: Instituto Cultural Rvna.

Inokuchi, Kinya. 2008. 'La arquitectura de Kuntur Wasi: Secuencia constructiva y cronología de un centro ceremonial del Período Formativo', *Boletín de Arqueología PUCP* 12: 219–47.

Inokuchi, Kinya. 2010. 'La arquitectura de Kuntur Wasi: Secuencia constructiva y cronología de un centro ceremonial del Período Formativo'. In *El Período Formativo: Enfoques y evidencias recientes: Cincuenta años de la Misión Arqueológica Japonesa y su vigencia, I*, edited by Peter Kaulicke and Yoshio Onuki, 219–47. Lima: Pontificia Universidad Católica del Perú.

INRENA-PNUD. 1995. *Estudio de reconocimiento del uso del recurso hídrico por los diferentes sectores productivos en el Perú: Convenio, INRENA, PNUD-DDSMS*. Lima: Instituto Nacional de Recursos Naturales.

Iriarte, José. 2009. 'Narrowing the Gap: Exploring the Diversity of Early Food-Production Economies in the Americas', *Current Anthropology* 50 (5): 677–80. http://doi.org/10.1086/605493.

Iriarte, José, Bruno Glaser, Jennifer Watling, Adam Wainwright, Jago Jonathan Birk, Delphine Renard, Stéphen Rostain and Doyle McKey. 2010. 'Late Holocene Neotropical Agricultural Landscapes: Phytolith and Stable Carbon Isotope Analysis of Raised Fields from French Guianan Coastal Savannahs', *Journal of Archaeological Science* 37 (12): 2984–94.

Iriarte, José, Irene Holst, Oscar Marozzi, Claudia Listopad, Eduardo Alonso, Andrés Rinderknecht and Juan Montaña. 2004. 'Evidence for Cultivar Adoption and Emerging Complexity during the Mid-Holocene in the La Plata Basin', *Nature* 432: 614–17. https://doi.org/10.1038/nature02983.

Isbell, William H. 1988. 'City and State in Middle Horizon Huari'. In *Peruvian Prehistory: An Overview of Pre-Inca and Inca Society*, edited by Richard W. Keatinge, 164–89. Cambridge: Cambridge University Press.

Isbell, William H. 1989. 'Honcopampa: Was it a Huari Administrative Centre?'. In *The Nature of Huari: A Reappraisal of the Middle Horizon Period in Peru*, edited by R. Czwarno, F.M. Meddens and A. Morgan (BAR International Series). Oxford: BAR.

Isbell, William H. 1997. *Mummies and Mortuary Monuments: A Postprocessual Prehistory of Central Andean Social Organization*. Austin: University of Texas Press.

Isbell, William H. 2004. 'Mortuary Preferences: A Wari Culture Case Study from Middle Horizon Peru', *Latin American Antiquity* 15 (1): 3–32.

Isbell, W. and H. Silverman. 2008. 'Regional Patterns'. In *Andean Archaeology III: North and South*, edited by W. Isbell and H. Silverman. New York: Springer.

Isendahl, Christian. 2011. 'The Domestication and Early Spread of Manioc (*Manihot esculenta* Crantz): A Brief Synthesis', *Latin American Antiquity* 22 (4): 452–68.

Itier, César. 2016. 'La formación del quechua ayacuchano, un proceso inca y colonial', *Bulletin de l'Institut Français d'Études Andines* 45 (2): 307–26.

Izumi, Seiichi, Pedro José Cuculiza and Chiaki Kano. 1972. *Excavations at Shillacoto, Huánuco, Peru*. Tokyo: University of Tokyo.

Izumi, Seiichi and Toshihiko Sono. 1963. *Andes 2: Excavations at Kotosh, Peru, 1960*. Tokyo: Kadokawa.

Izumi, Seiichi and Kazuo Terada. 1972. *Andes 4: Excavations at Kotosh, Peru, 1963 and 1966*. Tokyo: University of Tokyo Press.

Jackson, Jean E. 1983. *The Fish People: Linguistic Exogamy and Tukanoan Identity in Northwest Amazonia*. Cambridge: Cambridge University Press.

Jaimes Betancourt, Carla. 2004. 'Secuencia Cerámica del Corte 1 de la Loma Mendoza'. Tésis de Licenciatura, Universidad Mayor de San Andrés, La Paz.

Jaimes Betancourt, Carla. 2011. 'Hecho en Mojos: Mil años de alfarería en la Loma Salvatierra'. In *Anales de la XXIV Reunión Anual de Etnología*, Vol. 1, 79–96. La Paz: MUSEF.

Jaimes Betancourt, Carla. 2012a. *La cerámica de la Loma Salvatierra: Beni-Bolivia*. La Paz: Plural Editores.

Jaimes Betancourt, Carla. 2012b. 'La cerámica de dos montículos habitacionales en el área de Casarabe, Llanos de Moxos'. In *The Past Ahead: Language, Culture, and Identity in the Neotropics*, edited by Christian Isendahl, 161–84. Uppsala: Uppsala University.

Jaimes Betancourt, Carla. 2013. 'Diversidad cultural en los Llanos de Mojos'. In *Arqueología Amazónica*, edited by F. Valdez. Quito: Abya-Yala.

Jaimes Betancourt, Carla. 2014. 'Unidad en la diversidad: Implicaciones de la variabilidad cerámica de la región del Iténez, Bolivia'. In *Antes de Orellana: Actas del 3er Encuentro Internacional de Arqueología Amazónica*, edited by Stéphen Rostain, 281–90. Quito: IFEA, FLACSO and Embajada de EEAA.

Jaimes Betancourt, Carla. 2016. 'Dos fases cerámicas de la cronología ocupacional de las zanjas de la provincial Iténez: Beni, Bolivia'. In *Cerâmicas arqueológicas da Amazônia: Rumo a uma nova síntese*, edited by Cristiana Barreto, Helena Pinto Lima and Carla Jaimes Betancourt, 435–47. Belém: IPHAN – Ministério da Cultura / Museu Paraense Emilio Goeldi.

Jaimes Betancourt, Carla and Heiko Prümers. 2015. 'La Fase Jasiaquiri: Una ocupación de los siglos IV–VI en la provincial Iténez, Llanos de Mojos, Bolivia'. In *En el corazón de América del Sur 3: Arqueología de las tierras bajas de Bolivia y zonas limítrofes*, edited by Sonia Alconini and Carla Jaimes Betancourt, 17–40. Santa Cruz de la Sierra: Biblioteca del Museo de Historia, Universidad Autónoma Gabriel René Moreno.

Jamieson, Ross W. 2005. 'Colonialism, Social Archaeology and *Lo Andino*: Historical Archaeology in the Andes', *World Archaeology* 37 (3): 352–72.

Jantz, R.L. and Douglas W. Owsley. 2001. 'Variation among Early North American Crania', *American Journal of Physical Anthropology* 114 (2): 146–55.

Janusek, John Wayne. 2008. *Ancient Tiwanaku*. New York: Cambridge University Press.

Johnson, Allen W. and Timothy Earle. 2000. *The Evolution of Human Societies: From Foraging Group to Agrarian State*. 2nd ed. Stanford: Stanford University Press.

Johnson, Orville E. and Stephen H. Levinsohn. 1990. *Gramatica secoya*. Quito: Instituto Lingüístico de Verano.

Jones, Cameron D. 2016. 'The Evolution of Spanish Governance during the Early Bourbon Period in Peru: The Juan Santos Atahualpa Rebellion and the Missionaries of Ocopa', *The Americas* 73 (3): 325–48.

Jordan, Peter and Marek Zvelebil, eds. 2009. *Ceramics before Farming: The Dispersal of Pottery among Prehistoric Eurasian Hunter-Gatherers*. Walnut Creek, CA: Left Coast Press.

Josselin de Jong, J.P.B. de. 1983. 'The Malay Archipelago as a Field of Ethnological Study [1935]'. In *Structural Anthropology in the Netherlands: A Reader*, edited by P.E. de Josselin de Jong, Dordrecht: Foris.

Jota, Marilza S. and 14 others 2011. 'A New Subhaplogroup of Native American Y-Chromosomes from the Andes', *American Journal of Physical Anthropology* 146 (4): 553–9.

Julien, Catherine Jean. 1979. 'Koli: A Language Spoken on the Peruvian Coast', *Andean Perspective Newsletter* 3: 5–11.

Julien, Catherine J. 1983. *Hatunqolla: A View of Inca Rule from the Lake Titicaca Region* (University of California Publications in Anthropology 15). Berkeley: University of California Press.

Kamen, Henry. 1997. *Philip of Spain*. New Haven: Yale University Press.

Kano, Chiaki. 1979. *The Origins of the Chavin Culture* (Pre-Columbian Art and Archaeology 22). Washington, DC: Dumbarton Oaks.

Karafet, Tatiana M., Fernando L. Mendez, Monica B. Meilerman, Peter A. Underhill, Stephen L. Zegura and Michael F. Hammer. 2008. 'New Binary Polymorphisms Reshape and Increase Resolution of the Human Y Chromosomal Haplogroup Tree', *Genome Research* 18 (5): 830–8.

Kaufman, T. and V. Golla. 2000. 'Language Groupings in the New World: Their Reliability and Usability in Cross-Disciplinary Studies'. In *America Past, America Present: Genes and Languages in the Americas and Beyond*, edited by C. Renfrew, 47–57. Cambridge: McDonald Institute for Archaeological Research.

Kaulicke, Peter. 1982. 'Keramik der frühen Initialperidose aus Pandanche, Dpto. Cajamarca, Peru', *Beiträge zur Allgemeinen und Vergleichenden Archäologie* 2 (1981): 363–89.

Kaulicke, Peter. 1994. *Los orígenes de la civilización Andina: Arqueología del Perú*. Lima: Editorial Brasa.

Kaulicke, Peter. 1998. 'El Período Formativo de Piura'. In *Perspectivas regionales del Período Formativo en el Perú*, edited by Peter Kaulicke, 19–36. Lima: Pontificia Universidad Católica del Perú.

Kaulicke, Peter. 2010a. 'Algunas reflexiones sobre lenguas y sociedades en el Período Formativo centroandino', *Boletín de Arqueología PUCP* 14: 123–39.

Kaulicke, Peter. 2010b. *Las cronologías del Formativo: 50 años de investigaciones japonesas en perspectiva*. Lima: Pontificia Universidad Católica del Perú.

Kaulicke, Peter. 2011. 'Algunas reflexiones sobre lenguas y sociedades en el Período Formativo centroandino'. In *Lenguas y sociedades en el Antiguo Perú: Hacia un enfoque interdisciplinario*, edited by Peter Kaulicke, Rodolfo Cerrón-Palomino, Paul Heggarty and David Beresford-Jones, 123–39. Lima: Pontificia Universidad Católica del Perú.

Kaulicke, Peter, ed. 2019a. *Historia económica del antiguo Perú*. Lima: Banco Central de Reserva del Perú and Instituto de Estudios Peruanos.

Kaulicke, Peter. 2019b. 'Las economías tempranas (ca. 13,000 a 500 AC)'. In *Historia económica del antigo Perú*, edited by Peter Kaulicke, 47–153. Lima: Banco Central de Reserva del Perú and Instituto de Estudios Peruanos.

Kendall, Ann. 1984. 'Archaeological Investigations of the Late Intermediate Period and Late Horizon Period at Cusichaca, Peru'. In *Current Archaeological Projects in the Central Andes: Some Approaches and Results* (BAR International Series 210), edited by A. Kendall, 247–90. Oxford: BAR.

Kennett, Douglas J., B. Lynn Ingram, John R. Southon and Karen Wise. 2002. 'Differences in 14C Age between Stratigraphically Associated Charcoal and Marine Shell from the Archaic Period Site of Kilometer 4, Southern Peru: Old Wood or Old Water?', *Radiocarbon* 44 (1): 53–8.

Kerke, Simon van de. 2009. 'Leko'. In *Las lenguas de Bolivia,* Vol. 1: *Ámbito andino*, edited by Mily Crevels and Pieter Muysken, 287–332. La Paz: Plural Editores.

Kerke, Simon van de and Pieter Muysken. 2014. 'The Andean Matrix'. In *The Native Languages of South America: Origins, Development, Typology*, edited by Loretta O'Connor and Pieter Muysken, 126–51. Cambridge: Cambridge University Press.

Key, Mary Ritchie. 1968. *Comparative Tacanan Phonology, with Cavineña Phonology and Notes on Pano-Tacanan Relationships*. The Hague: Mouton.

Keyeux, Genoveva, Clemencia Rodas, Nancy Gelvez and Dee Carter. 2002. 'Possible Migration Routes into South America Deduced from Mitochondrial DNA Studies in Colombian Amerindian Populations', *Human Biology* 74 (2): 211–33.

Killick, Evan. 2009. 'Ashéninka Amity: A Study of Social Relations in an Amazonian Society', *Journal of the Royal Anthropological Institute* 15 (4): 701–18.

Kipnis, Renato. 1998. 'Early Hunter-Gatherers in the Americas: Perspectives from Central Brazil', *Antiquity* 72 (277): 581–92.

Kirsanow, Karola and Joachim Burger. 2012. 'Ancient Human DNA', *Annals of Anatomy* 194 (1): 121–32.

Kistler, Logan and 16 others. 2018. 'Multiproxy Evidence Highlights a Complex Evolutionary Legacy of Maize in South America', *Science* 362 (6420): 1309–13.

Klein, Cecelia F. and Jeffrey Quilter, eds. 2001. *Gender in Pre-Hispanic America: A Symposium at Dumbarton Oaks, 12 and 13 October 1996*. Washington, DC: Dumbarton Oaks Research Library and Collection.

Knight, Alan. 2002. *Mexico: The Colonial Era*. Cambridge: Cambridge University Press.

Kojan, David Joshua. 2002. 'Cultural Identity and Historical Narratives of the Bolivian Eastern Andes: An Archaeological Study'. PhD thesis, University of California, Berkeley.

Konigsberg, Lyle W. 1990. 'Analysis of Prehistoric Biological Variation under a Model of Isolation by Geographic and Temporal Distance', *Human Biology* 62 (1): 49–70.

Konigsberg, Lyle W. and Stephen D. Ousley. 1995. 'Multivariate Quantitative Genetics of Anthropometric Traits from the Boas Data', *Human Biology* 67 (3): 481–98.

Koschmieder, Klaus. 2012. *Jucusbamba: Investigaciones arqueológicas y motivos Chachapoya en el norte de la Provincia de Luya, Departamento Amazonas, Perú*. Lima: Tarea Asociación Gráfica Educativa.

Kracke, Waud H., ed. 1993. *Leadership in Lowland South America* (South American Indian Studies). Bennington, VT: Bennington College.

Krasnoukhova, Olga Vladimirovna. 2012. 'The Noun Phrase in the Languages of South America'. PhD thesis, Radboud University Nijmegen.

Krasnoukhova, Olga. 2014. 'The Noun Phrase: Focus on Demonstratives, Redrawing the Semantic Map'. In *The Native Languages of South America: Origins, Development, Typology*, edited by Loretta O'Connor and PieterMuysken, 250–73. Cambridge: Cambridge University Press.

Kundu, Sharbadeb and Sankar Kumar Ghosh. 2015. 'Trend of Different Molecular Markers in the Last Decades for Studying Human Migrations', *Gene* 556 (2): 81–90.

Lagrou, Elsje. 2006. 'Laughing at Power and the Power of Laughing in Cashinahua Narrative and Performance', *Tipití: Journal of the Society for the Anthropology of Lowland South America* 4 (1/2): 33–56.

Landerman, Peter. 1973. *Vocabulario quechua del Pastaza*. Yarinacocha: Instituto Lingüístico de Verano.

Langstroth Plotkin, Roberto. 1996. 'Forest Islands in an Amazonian Savanna of Northeastern Bolivia'. PhD thesis, University of Wisconsin-Madison.

Lanning, Edward P. 1963. 'Ceramic Sequence for Piura and Chira Coast, North Peru', *University of California Publications in Archaeology and Ethnology* 46 (2): 135–284.

Lanning, Edward P. 1967. *Peru before the Incas*. Englewood Cliffs, NJ: Prentice Hall.

Lara, Jesús. 1973. *Mitos, leyendas y cuentos de los Quechuas*. La Paz: Editorial Los Amigos del Libro.

Lara, Jesús. 1978. *Diccionario qhëshwa–castellano, castellano–qhëshwa*. 2nd ed. La Paz: Editorial Los Amigos del Libro.

Latcham, Richard. 1928. *La Prehistoria de Chile*. Santiago: Sociedad Impresora y Litografia Universo.

Lathrap, Donald W. 1968a. 'Aboriginal Occupations and Changes in the River Channel on the Central Ucayali, Peru', *American Antiquity* 33 (1): 62–79.

Lathrap, D. 1968b. 'The "Hunting" Economies of the Tropical Forest Zone of South America: An Attempt at Historical Perspective'. In *Man the Hunter*, edited by R.B. Lee and I. DeVore, 23–9. Chicago: Aldine.

Lathrap, Donald W. 1970. *The Upper Amazon*. New York: Praeger.

Lathrap, Donald W. 1971. 'The Tropical Forest and the Cultural Context of Chavín'. In *Dumbarton Oaks Conference on Chavín*, edited by Elizabeth P. Benson, 73–100. Washington, DC: Dumbarton Oaks.

Lathrap, Donald W. 1973. 'The Antiquity and Importance of Long-Distance Trade Relationships in the Moist Tropics of Pre-Columbian South America', *World Archaeology* 5 (2): 170–86.

Lathrap, D.W. 1974. 'The Moist Tropics, the Arid Lands, and the Appearance of Great Art Styles in the New World'. In *Art and Environment in Native North America* (Museums of Texas Tech University Special Publications 7), edited by M.E. King and I. Traylor. Lubbock: Texas Tech University Press.

Lathrap, D. 1977. 'Our Father the Cayman, Our Mother the Gourd: Spinden Revisited, or a Unitary Model for Emergence of Agriculture in the New World'. In *Origins of Agriculture*, edited by C.E. Reed, 713–51. The Hague: Mouton.

Latorre, Claudio, Ricardo De Pol-Holz, Chris Carter and Calogero M. Santoro. 2017. 'Using Archaeological Shell Middens as a Proxy for Past Local Coastal Upwelling in Northern Chile', *Quaternary International* 427 (A): 128–36.

Lau, George F. 2010. 'House Forms and Recuay Culture: Residential Compounds at Yayno (Ancash, Peru), a Fortified Hilltop Town, AD 400–800', *Journal of Anthropological Archaeology* 29 (3): 327–51.

Lavallée, Danièle. 2000. *The First South Americans: The Peopling of a Continent from the Earliest Evidence to High Culture*, translated by Paul G. Bahn. Salt Lake City: University of Utah Press.

Lee, Vincent R. 2000. *Forgotten Vilcabamba: Final Stronghold of the Incas*. Wilson, WY: Sixpac Manco Publications.

Lefebvre, Claire and Pieter Muysken. 1988. *Mixed Categories: Nominalizations in Quechua*. Dordrecht: Kluwer Academic.

Lehmann, Johannes, Dirse C. Kern, Bruno Glaser and William I. Woods, eds. 2003. *Amazonian Dark Earths: Origin, Properties, Management*. Dordrecht: Kluwer Academic.

Lehmann, Walter. 1929. 'Vocabulario de la lengua Uro sacado en el pueblecito de Hanko Hake o sea Uru eru'itu. 13. Oktober 1929'. Unpublished manuscript. Berlin: Ibero-Amerikanisches Institut.

León Canales, Elmo Arturo. 2007. *Orígenes humanos en los Andes del Perú*. Lima: Universidad de San Martín de Porres.

León Gómez, Miguel. 2003. 'Espacio geográfico y organización social de los grupos éticos del Callejón de Conchucos'. In *Arqueología de Ancash: Propuestas y perspectivas*, edited by Bebel Ibarra, 457–66. Lima: Instituto Cultural Runa.

León Gómez, Miguel. 2018. *Entre quebradas y montañas: Una historia regional de Conchucos, siglos XVI–XX*. Lima: Tarea.

Levillier, Roberto. 1976. *El Paititi, El Dorado y las Amazonas*. Buenos Aires: Emecé Editores.

LeVine, Terry Y. 1979. 'Prehistoric Political and Economic Change in Highland Peru: An Ethnohistorical Study of the Mantaro Valley'. Master's thesis, University of California, Los Angeles.

Levis, Carolina and 154 others. 2017. 'Persistent Effects of Pre-Columbian Plant Domestication on Amazonian Forest Composition', *Science* 355 (6328): 925–31.

Lévi-Strauss, Claude. 1958. 'Les Organisations Dualistes Existent-Elles?'. In *Anthropologie Structurale*, edited by Claude Lévi-Strauss, 147–82. Paris: Plon.

Lévi-Strauss, Claude. 1973. *From Honey to Ashes*, translated by John Weightman and Doreen Weightman. New York: Harper and Row.

Lévi-Strauss, Claude. 1978. *The Origin of Table Manners*, translated by John Weightman and Doreen Weightman. New York: Harper and Row.

Lewis, Cecil M. and 10 others. 2007. 'Mitochondrial DNA and the Peopling of South America', *Human Biology* 79 (2): 159–78.

Lewis, Cecil M., Raúl Y. Tito, Beatriz Lizárraga and Anne C. Stone. 2005. 'Land, Language, and Loci: mtDNA in Native Americans and the Genetic History of Peru', *American Journal of Physical Anthropology* 127 (3): 351–60.

Lewontin, R.C. 1972. 'The Apportionment of Human Diversity'. In *Evolutionary Biology, Volume 6*, edited by Theodosius Dobzhansky, Max K. Hecht and William C. Steere, 381–98. New York: Appleton-Century-Crofts.

Lindahl, Tomas. 1993. 'Instability and Decay of the Primary Structure of DNA', *Nature* 362: 709–15.

Lindo, John and 13 others. 2018. 'The Genetic Prehistory of the Andean Highlands 7000 Years BP through European Contact', *Science Advances* 4 (11), Article eaau4921: 1–10. Accessed 12 May 2020. https://doi.org/10.1126/sciadv.aau4921.

Linz, Bodo and 15 others. 2007. 'An African Origin for the Intimate Association between Humans and *Helicobacter pylori*', *Nature* 445: 915–18.

Liu, Hua, Franck Prugnolle, Andrea Manica and François Balloux. 2006. 'A Geographically Explicit Genetic Model of Worldwide Human-Settlement History', *American Journal of Human Genetics* 79 (2): 230–7.

Livi Bacci, Massimo. 2008. *Conquest: The Destruction of the American Indios*, translated by Carl Ipsen. Cambridge: Polity Press.

Llamas, Bastien and 30 others. 2016. 'Ancient Mitochondrial DNA Provides High-Resolution Time Scale of the Peopling of the Americas', *Science Advances* 2 (4), Article e1501385: 1–10. Accessed 12 May 2020. https://doi.org/10.1126/sciadv.1501385.

Loayza, Francisco A. 1942. *Juan Santos, el invencible*. Lima: Editorial D. Miranda.

Lodeho, Laure. 2012. 'Les premiers peuplements du nord du Pérou: L'apport de la technologie lithique à la définition des ensembles culturels et de leurs relations, à la fin du Pléistocène et à l'Holocène ancien et moyen'. PhD thesis, Université Paris 1.

Lombardo, Umberto. 2014. 'Neotectonics, Flooding Patterns and Landscape Evolution in Southern Amazonia', *Earth Surface Dynamics* 2 (2): 493–511.

Lombardo, Umberto, Elisa Canal-Beeby and Heinz Veit. 2011. 'Eco-Archaeological Regions in the Bolivian Amazon: An Overview of Pre-Columbian Earthworks Linking Them to Their Environmental Settings', *Geographica Helvetica* 66 (3): 173–82.

Lombardo, Umberto and José M. Capriles. 2013. *Informe de Temporada 2012*. La Paz: Unidad de Arqueología y Museos, Ministerio de Culturas y Turismo.

Lombardo, Umberto, Sebastian Denier and Heinz Veit. 2015. 'Soil Properties and Pre-Columbian Settlement Patterns in the Monumental Mounds Region of the Llanos de Moxos, Bolivian Amazon', *SOIL* 1 (1): 65–81.

Lombardo, Umberto, José Iriarte, Lautaro Hilbert, Javier Ruiz-Pérez, José M. Capriles and Heinz Veit. 2020. 'Early Holocene Crop Cultivation and Landscape Modification in Amazonia'. *Nature* 581: 190–3. http://doi.org/10.1038/s41586-020-2162-7.

Lombardo, Umberto, Jan-Hendrik May and Heinz Veit. 2012. 'Mid- to Late-Holocene Fluvial Activity behind Pre-Columbian Social Complexity in the Southwestern Amazon Basin', *The Holocene* 22 (9): 1035–45.

Lombardo, Umberto and Heiko Prümers. 2010. 'Pre-Columbian Human Occupation Patterns in the Eastern Plains of the Llanos de Moxos, Bolivian Amazonia', *Journal of Archaeological Science* 37 (8): 1875–85.

Lombardo, Umberto, Leonor Rodrigues and Heinz Veit. 2018. 'Alluvial Plain Dynamics and Human Occupation in SW Amazonia during the Holocene: A Paleosol-Based Reconstruction', *Quaternary Science Reviews* 180: 30–41.

Lombardo, Umberto, Katherine Szabo, José M. Capriles, Jan-Hendrik May, Wulf Amelung, Rainer Hutterer, Eva Lehndorff, Anna Plotzki and Heinz Veit. 2013. 'Early and Middle Holocene Hunter-Gatherer Occupations in Western Amazonia: The Hidden Shell Middens', *PLoS One* 8 (8), Article e72746: 1–14. Accessed 13 May 2020. https://doi.org/10.1371/journal.pone.0072746.

Lombardo, Umberto and Heinz Veit. 2014. 'The Origin of Oriented Lakes: Evidence from the Bolivian Amazon', *Geomorphology* 204: 502–9.

Loos, Eugene Emil. 1969. *The Phonology of Capanahua and its Grammatical Basis*. Norman: Summer Institute of Linguistics of the University of Oklahoma.

Loos, Eugene and Betty Loos. 2003. *Diccionario capanahua–castellano*. 2nd ed. Lima: Instituto Lingüístico de Verano.

Lorandi, Ana María. 2005. *Spanish King of the Incas: The Epic Life of Pedro Bohorques*, translated by Ann de León. Pittsburgh: University of Pittsburgh Press.

Lorandi, Ana María and Roxana Boixadós. 1988. 'Etnohistoria de los valles Calchaquíes en los siglos XVI y XVII', *Runa: Archivo para las Ciencias del Hombre* 17/18: 263–419.

Lothrop, S.K. 1941. 'Gold Ornaments of Chavin Style from Chongoyape, Peru', *American Antiquity* 6 (3): 250–62.

Lounsbury, Floyd G. 1986. 'Some Aspects of the Inka Kinship System'. In *Anthropological History of Andean Polities*, edited by Nathan Wachtel, John V. Murra and Jacques Revel, 121–36. Cambridge and Paris: Cambridge University Press and Editions de la Maison des Sciences de l'Homme.

Lourdeau, Antoine. 2015. 'Lithic Technology and Prehistoric Settlement in Central and Northeast Brazil: Definition and Spatial Distribution of the Itaparica Technocomplex', *PaleoAmerica* 1 (1): 52–67.

Lowie, Robert H. 1948. 'The Tropical Forests: An Introduction'. In *Handbook of South American Indians,* Vol. 3 (Bureau of American Ethnology Bulletin 143), edited by J.H. Steward, 1–56. Washington, DC: Bureau of American Ethnology.

Luiselli, Donata, Lucia Simoni, Eduardo Tarazona-Santos, Santiago Pastor and Davide Pettener. 2000. 'Genetic Structure of Quechua-Speakers of Central Andes and Geographic Patterns of Gene Frequencies in South Amerindian Populations', *American Journal of Physical Anthropology* 113 (1): 5–17.

Lumbreras, Luis G. 1974. *The Peoples and Cultures of Ancient Peru*, translated by Betty J. Meggers. Washington, DC: Smithsonian Institution Press.

Lumbreras, Luis Guillermo. 1993. *Chavín de Huántar: Excavaciones en la Galería de las Ofrendas* (Materialien zur Allgemeinen und Vergleichenden Archäologie 51). Mainz am Rhein: Philipp von Zabern.

Lumbreras, Luis Guillermo. 2004. 'The Qhapac Nan Museums Network', *Museum International* 56 (3): 111–17.

Luteyn, James J. and Steven S. Churchill. 2000. 'Vegetation of the Tropical Andes: An Overview'. In *Imperfect Balance: Landscape Transformations in the Pre-Columbian Americas*, edited by David L. Lentz. New York: Columbia University Press.

Lynch, John. 2012. *New Worlds: A Religious History of Latin America*. New Haven: Yale University Press.

Lynch, Michael and Bruce Walsh. 1998. *Genetics and Analysis of Quantitative Traits*. Sunderland, MA: Sinauer Associates.

Lynch, Thomas F. 1973. 'Harvest Timing, Transhumance, and the Process of Domestication', *American Anthrolopogist* 75 (5): 1254–9.

Lyon, Patricia J. 1981. 'An Imaginary Frontier: Prehistoric Highland-Lowland Interchange in the Southern Peruvian Andes'. In *Networks of the Past: Regional Interaction in Archaeology*, edited by Peter D. Francis, Francois J. Kense and Philip G. Duke, 3–18. Calgary: University of Calgary.

Maezumi, S. Yoshi, Daiana Alves, Mark Robinson, Jonas Gregorio de Souza, Carolina Levis, Robert L. Barnett, Edemar Almeida de Oliveira, Dunia Urrego, Denise Schaan and José Iriarte. 2018. 'The Legacy of 4,500 Years of Polyculture Agroforestry in the Eastern Amazon', *Nature Plants* 4: 540–7.

Magalhães, Marcos Pereira. 2018. *A humanidade e a Amazônia: 11 mil anos de evolução histórica em Carajás*. Belém: Museu Paraense Emílio Goeldi.

Maggard, Greg J. 2011. 'Las ocupaciones humanas del Pleistoceno Final y el Holoceno Temprano en la costa norte del Perú', *Boletín de Arqueología PUCP* 15: 121–43.

Maggard, Greg J. 2013. 'Las ocupaciones humanas del Pleistoceno Final y el Holoceno Temprano en la costa norte del Perú'. In *Tradiciones andinas tempranas: Cultura, tecnología y medioambiente*, edited by Peter Kaulicke and Tom D. Dillehay, 121–43. Lima: Pontificia Universidad Católica del Perú.

Maggard, Greg and Tom D. Dillehay. 2011. 'El Palto Phase (13800–9800 BP)'. In *From Foraging to Farming in the Andes: New Perspectives on Food Production and Social Organization*, edited by Tom D. Dillehay, 77–94. New York: Cambridge University Press.

Maldonado, Blanca, Heiko Prümers and Ernst Pernicka. 2010. 'The Metal Artifacts from Loma Salvatierra, Bolivia'. In *Archäometrie und Denkmalpflege* (Metalla Sonderheft 3), edited by O. Hahn, A. Hauptmann, D. Modarressi-Tehrani and M. Prange, 110–12. Bochum: Deutsches Bergbau-Museum.

Manica, Andrea, William Amos, François Balloux and Tsunehiko Hanihara. 2007. 'The Effect of Ancient Population Bottlenecks on Human Phenotypic Variation', *Nature* 448: 346–8.

Manica, Andrea, Franck Prugnolle and François Balloux. 2005. 'Geography is a Better Determinant of Human Genetic Differentiation than Ethnicity', *Human Genetics* 118: 366–71.

Mann, Charles C. 2008. 'Ancient Earthmovers of the Amazon', *Science* 321 (5893): 1148–52.

Mannheim, Bruce. 1991. *The Language of the Inka since the European Invasion*. Austin: University of Texas Press.

Mantha, Alexis. 2006. 'Late Prehispanic Social Complexity in the Rapayán Valley, Upper Marañón Drainage, Central Andes of Peru'. In *Complejidad social en la arqueología y antropología de la Sierra de Ancash*, edited by Alexander Herrera, Carolina Orsini and Kevin Lane. Milan: Civiche Raccolte d'Arte Applicata del Castello Sforzesco.

Mantha, Alexis. 2013. 'Shifting Territorialities under the Inka Empire: The Case of the Rapayán Valley in the Central Andean Highlands', *Archeological Papers of the American Anthropological Association* 22 (1): 164–88.

Mantha, Alexis and Hernando Malca Cardoza. 2017. 'Excavaciones en el complejo arqueológico de Rapayán (Ancash, Perú): Resultados e interpretaciones', *Indiana* 34 (1): 95–127.

Mao, Xianyun and 11 others. 2007. 'A Genomewide Admixture Mapping Panel for Hispanic/Latino Populations', *American Journal of Human Genetics* 80 (6): 1171–8.

Marcos, Jorge G. 2015. *Un sitio llamado Real Alto*. Quito: Universidad Internacional del Ecuador.

Marks, A.W. 2012. 'Evidence for Language Contact in the Numeral Systems of Quechuan, Aymaran, Cavineña, and Chipaya'. In *Proceedings of the 15th Annual Workshop on American Indigenous Languages (April 27–28th, 2012)* (Santa Barbara Papers in Linguistics 23), edited by E. Hoey and D. Wdzenczny, 1–22. Santa Barbara, CA: UCSB.

Marquet, Pablo A., Calogero M. Santoro, Claudio Latorre, Vivien G. Standen, Sebastián R. Abades, Marcelo M. Rivadeneira, Bernardo Arriaza and Michael E. Hochberg. 2012. 'Emergence of Social Complexity among Coastal Hunter-Gatherers in the Atacama Desert of Northern Chile', *Proceedings of the National Academy of Sciences of the United States of America* 109 (37): 14754–60.

Martínez-Abadías, Neus, Mireia Esparza, Torstein Sjøvold, Rolando González-José, Mauro Santos and Miquel Hernández. 2009. 'Heritability of Human Cranial Dimensions: Comparing the Evolvability of Different Cranial Regions', *Journal of Anatomy* 214 (1): 19–35.

Matisoff, James A. 1990. 'On Megalocomparison', *Language* 66 (1): 106–20.

Matisoff, James A. 1991. 'Sino-Tibetan Linguistics: Present State and Future Prospects', *Annual Review of Anthropology* 20: 469–504.

Matos M., Ramiro, Solveig A. Turpin and Herbert H. Eling, eds. 1986. *Andean Archaeology: Papers in Memory of Clifford Evans*. Los Angeles: Institute of Archaeology, University of California.

Matras, Yaron. 2011. 'Explaining Convergence and the Formation of Linguistic Areas'. In *Geographical Typology and Linguistic Areas: With Special Reference to Africa*, edited by O. Hieda, C. König and H. Nakagawa, 143–60. Amsterdam: John Benjamins.

Mayer, Enrique. 2002. *The Articulated Peasant: Household Economies in the Andes*. Boulder, CO: Westview Press.

Mayle, Francis E., Rachel Burbridge and Timothy J. Killeen. 2000. 'Millennial-Scale Dynamics of Southern Amazonian Rain Forests', *Science* 290 (5500): 2291–4.

Mayle, Francis E., Robert P. Langstroth, Rosie A. Fisher and Patrick Meir. 2006. 'Long-Term Forest-Savannah Dynamics in the Bolivian Amazon: Implications for Conservation', *Philosophical Transactions of the Royal Society B: Biological Sciences* 362 (1478): 291–307.

Mayle, Francis E. and Mitchell J. Power. 2008. 'Impact of a Drier Early–Mid-Holocene Climate upon Amazonian Forests', *Philosophical Transactions of the Royal Society B: Biological Sciences* 363 (1498): 1829–38.

Mazières, S. and 10 others. 2008. 'Uniparental (mtDNA, Y-Chromosome) Polymorphisms in French Guiana and Two Related Populations: Implications for the Region's Colonization', *Annals of Human Genetics* 72 (1): 145–56.

McEwan, Colin. 2001. 'Axiality and Access to Invisible Worlds'. In *Unknown Amazon: Culture in Nature in Ancient Brazil*, edited by Colin McEwan, Cristiana Barreto and Eduardo Neves, 176–97. London: British Museum Press.

McEwan, Colin, Cristiana Barreto and Eduardo Neves, eds. 2001. *Unknown Amazon: Culture in Nature in Ancient Brazil*. London: British Museum Press.

McKey, D. and 10 others 2014. 'New Approaches to Pre-Columbian Raised-Field Agriculture: Ecology of Seasonally Flooded Savannas, and Living Raised Fields in Africa, as Windows on the Past and the Future'. In *Amazonía: Memorias de las conferencias magistrales del 3er Encuentro Internacional de Arqueología Amazónica*, 91–136. Quito: MCCTH/SENESCYT/3EIAA.

McKey, Doyle and Stéphen Rostain. 2016. 'Farming Technology in Amazonia'. In *Encyclopaedia of the History of Science, Technology, and Medicine in Non-Western Cultures*, edited by Helaine Selin,. 3rd ed. Dordrecht: Springer.

McMahon, April M.S. and Robert McMahon. 1995. 'Linguistics, Genetics and Archaeology: Internal and External Evidence in the Amerind Controversy', *Transactions of the Philological Society* 93 (2): 125–225. https://doi.org/10.1111/j.1467-968X.1995.tb00438.x.

McMichael, C.H., D.R. Piperno, M.B. Bush, M.R. Silman, A.R. Zimmerman, M.F. Raczka and L.C. Lobato. 2012. 'Sparse Pre-Columbian Human Habitation in Western Amazonia', *Science* 336 (6087): 1429–31.

Meggers, Betty J. 1954. 'Environmental Limitation on the Development of Culture', *American Anthropologist* 56 (5): 801–24.

Meggers, Betty. 1957. 'Environment and Culture in the Amazon Basin: An Appraisal of the Theory of Environmental Determinism'. In *Studies in Human Ecology*, edited by Angel Palerm, 71–89. Washington, DC: Anthropological Society and the General Secretariat of the Organization of American States.

Meggers, Betty J. 1971. *Amazonia: Man and Culture in a Counterfeit Paradise*. Chicago: Aldine.

Meggers, Betty J. 1977. 'Vegetational Fluctuation and Prehistoric Cultural Adaptation in Amazonia: Some Tentative Correlations', *World Archaeology* 8 (3): 287–303.

Meggers, Betty J. 1997. 'La cerámica temprana en América del Sur: ¿Invención independiente o difusión?', *Revista de Arqueología Americana* 13: 7–40.

Meggers, Betty J. 2001. 'The Mystery of the Marajoara: An Ecological Solution', *Amazoniana* 16 (3/4): 421–40.

Meggers, Betty J. and Clifford Evans. 1957. *Archaeological Investigations at the Mouth of the Amazon* (Bureau of American Ethnology Bulletin 167). Washington, DC: Smithsonian Institution.

Meggers, Betty and Clifford Evans. 1961. 'An Experimental Formulation of Horizon Styles in the Tropical Forest Area of South America'. In *Essays in Pre-Columbian Art and Archaeology*, edited by S. Lothrop, 372–88. Cambridge, MA: Harvard University Press.

Meggers, Betty and Eurico Miller. 2003. 'Hunter-Gatherers in Amazonia during the Pleistocene–Holocene Transition'. In *Under the Canopy: The Archaeology of Tropical Rain Forests*, edited by Julio Mercader, 291–316. New Brunswick, NJ: Rutgers University Press.

Meltzer, David J. 2009. *First Peoples in a New World: Colonizing Ice Age America*. Berkeley: University of California Press.

Mendisco, Fanny, Christine Keyser, Veronica Seldes, Clara Rivolta, Pablo Mercolli, Pablo Cruz, Axel E. Nielsen, Eric Crubezy and Bertrand Ludes. 2014. 'Genetic Diversity of a Late Prehispanic Group of the Quebrada de Humahuaca, Northwestern Argentina', *Annals of Human Genetics* 78 (5): 367–80.

Menéndez, Lumila, Valeria Bernal, Paula Novellino and S. Ivan Perez. 2014. 'Effect of Bite Force and Diet Composition on Craniofacial Diversification of Southern South American Human Populations', *American Journal of Physical Anthropology* 155 (1): 114–27.

Menghin, Oswald. 1962. *Estudios de Prehistoria Araucana* (Studia praehistorica 2). Buenos Aires: Centro Argentino de Estudios Prehistóricos.

Mercader, Julia and 12 others. 2018. 'Exaggerated Expectations in Ancient Starch Research and the Need for New Taphonomic and Authenticity Criteria', *Facets* 3: 777–98. https://doi.org/10.1139/facets-2017-0126.

Mercier H., Juan Marcos. 1979. *Nosotros los Napu-Runas: Napu Runapa Rimay: Mitos e historia*. Iquitos: Publicaciones CETA.

Métraux, Alfred. 1935. 'Civilización material de los indios uru-chipaya de Carangas (Bolivia)', *Revista del Instituto de Etnología de la Universidad Nacional de Tucumán* 3: 85–129.

Métraux, Alfred. 1936. 'Les indiens uro-čipaya de Carangas (suite)', *Journal de la Société des Américanistes* 28 (2): 337–94.

Métraux, Alfred. 1959. 'The Revolution of the Ax', *Diogenes* 25: 28–40.

Michael, Lev. 2008. 'Nanti Evidential Practice: Language, Knowledge, and Social Action in an Amazonian Society'. PhD thesis, University of Texas at Austin.

Michael, Lev, Christine Beier, Karina Sullón, Stephanie Farmer, Greg Finley and Michael Roswell. 2009. *Una breve descripción del idioma Muniche*. Austin, TX: Cabeceras Aid Project.

Michael, Lev, Will Chang and Tammy Stark. 2014. 'Exploring Phonological Areality in the Circum-Andean Region Using a Naive Bayes Classifier', *Language Dynamics and Change* 4 (1): 27–86.

Michael, Lev, Stephanie Farmer, Gregory Finley, Christine Beier and Karina Sullón Acosta. 2013. 'A Sketch of Muniche Segmental and Prosodic Phonology', *International Journal of American Linguistics* 79 (3): 307–47.

Michael, Lev and Zachary O'Hagan. 2016. *A Linguistic Analysis of Old Omagua Ecclesiastical Texts* (Cadernos do Etnolingüística – Série Monografias 4). Cadernos do Etnolingüística.

Michel López, Marcos Rodolfo. 1993. 'Prospección arqueológica de San Ignacio de Moxos, Provincia Moxos, Departamento de Beni, Bolivia'. Tésis de Licenciatura, Universidad Mayor de San Andrés, La Paz.

Michel López, Marcos and Carlos Lémuz Aguirre. 1992. 'Influencia barrancoide en el bajo Maniqui', *Nuevos Aportes: Revista de Antropología* 1 (1): 51–65.

Mihas, Elena. 2010. 'Essentials of Ashéninka Perené Grammar'. PhD thesis, University of Wisconsin-Milwaukee.

Miller, E.T. 2009. 'Pesquisas arqueológicas no Pantanal do Guaporé: A sequência seriada da cerâmica da Fase Bacabal'. In *Arqueologia Interpretativa: O Método Quantitativo para Estabelecimento de Sequências Cerâmicas: Estudos de caso*, edited by Betty J. Meggers, 103–17. Porto Nacional: Universidade Estadual do Tocantins.

Molinié, Antoinette. 2004. 'The Resurrection of the Inca: The Role of Indian Representations in the Invention of the Peruvian Nation', *History and Anthropology* 15 (3): 233–50.

Moraes, Claide de Paula. 2015. 'O determinismo agrícola na arqueologia amazônica', *Estudos Avançados* 29 (83): 25–43.

Morales, D. 1979. *El dios felino en Pacopampa*. Lima: Universidad Nacional Mayor de San Marcos, Seminario de Historia Rural Andina.

Morales, Daniel. 1998 'Investigaciones arqueológicas en Pacopampa, Departamento de Cajamarca', *Boletín de Arqueología PUCP* 2: 113–26.

Morales, Daniel. 1999. 'Investigaciones arqueológicas en Pacopampa, Departamento de Cajamarca'. In *Perspectivas regionales del Período Formativo en el Perú*, edited by Peter Kaulicke, 113–26. Lima: Pontificia Universidad Católica del Perú.

Morales, Daniel. 2011. 'La arqueología en la Amazonía peruana y sus relaciones con el área andina'. In *Por donde hay soplo: Estudios amazónicos en los países andinos*, edited by Jean-Pierre Chaumeil, Oscar Espinoza and Manuel Cornejo, 137–60. Lima: IFEA, CAAAP, EREA-LESC.

More Cahuapaza, Alexander, Paolo Villegas Ogoña and Mónica Alzamora Torres. 2014. *Piura: Áreas prioritarias para la conservación de la biodiversidad*. Lima: Naturaleza y Cultura Internacional (NCI).

Moreno-Mayar, J. Víctor, Ben A. Potter and 16 others. 2018. 'Terminal Pleistocene Alaskan Genome Reveals First Founding Population of Native Americans', *Nature* 553: 203–7.

Moreno-Mayar, J. Víctor, Lasse Vinner and 52 others. 2018. 'Early Human Dispersals within the Americas', *Science* 362 (6419): 1–11. Accessed 14 May 2020. https://doi.org/10.1126/science.aav2621.

Morris, Craig. 1979. 'Maize Beer in the Economics, Politics and Religion of the Inca Empire'. In *Fermented Foods in Nutrition*, edited by C. Gastineau, W. Darby and T. Turner, 21–34. New York: Academic Press.

Morris, Douglas W. and Shomen Mukherjee. 2006. 'Simulated and Human Metapopulations Created by Habitat Selection', *Evolutionary Ecology Research* 8: 1263–75.

Moseley, Michael Edward. 1974. *The Maritime Foundations of Andean Civilization*. Menlo Park, CA: Cummings.

Moseley, Michael E. 1992. *The Incas and Their Ancestors: The Archaeology of Peru*. London: Thames and Hudson.

Mousseau, Timothy A. and Derek A. Roff. 1987. 'Natural Selection and Heritability of Fitness Components', *Heredity* 59 (2): 181–97.

Mujica Pinilla, R. 1992. 'Los Ángeles de la Conquista y las Plumas del Sol'. In *Ángeles Apócrifos en la América Virreinal*, edited by R. Mujica Pinilla, 235–305. Lima: Fondo de Cultura Económica.

Mumford, Jeremy Ravi. 2012. *Vertical Empire: The General Resettlement of Indians in the Colonial Andes*. Durham, NC: Duke University Press.

Murra, John. 1972. 'El "control vertical" de un máximo de pisos ecológicos en la economía de las sociedades andinas'. In *Visita de la Provincia de Leon de Huánuco en 1562*, edited by John Murra, 427–76. Huánuco: Universidad Nacional Hermilio Valdizan.

Murra, John. 1978. 'Los límites y limitaciones del "archipiélago vertical" en los Andes', *Avances* 1: 75–80.

Murra, John. 1985. 'The Limits and Limitations of the "Vertical Archipielago" in the Andes'. In *Andean Ecology and Civilization: An Interdisciplinary Perspective on Andean Ecological Complementarity*, edited by S. Masuda, I. Shimada and C. Morris, 15–20. Tokyo: Tokyo University Press.

Muysken, Pieter. 2009. 'Kallawaya'. In *Las lenguas de Bolivia*, Vol. 1: *Ámbito andino*, edited by Mily Crevels and Pieter Muysken, 147–67. La Paz: Plural Editores.

Muysken, Pieter. 2010. 'Scenarios for Language Contact'. In *The Handbook of Language Contact*, edited by Raymond Hickey, 265–81. Oxford: Wiley-Blackwell.

Muysken, Pieter. 2012a. 'Contacts between Indigenous Languages in South America'. In *Handbook of South American Historical Linguistics*, edited by Veronica Grondona and Lyle Campbell, 235–58. Berlin: Mouton de Gruyter.

Muysken, Pieter. 2012b. 'Modelling the Quechua–Aymara Relationship: Sociolinguistic Scenarios and Possible Archaeological Evidence'. In *Archaeology and Language in the Andes: A Cross-Disciplinary Exploration of Prehistory*, edited by Paul Heggarty and David Beresford-Jones, 83–107. Oxford: Oxford University Press. http://doi.org/10.5871/bacad/9780197265031.003.0004.

Muysken, Pieter and 11 others. 2014a. 'The Languages of South America: Deep Families, Areal Relationships, and Language Contact'. In *The Native Languages of South America: Origins, Development, Typology*, edited by Loretta O'Connor and Pieter Muysken, 299–322. Cambridge: Cambridge University Press.

Muysken, Pieter and 9 others. 2014b. *South American Indigenous Language Structures (SAILS) Online*. Leipzig: Max Planck Institute for Evolutionary Anthropology. Accessed 2 June. https://sails.clld.org/.

Nakatsuka, Nathan and 49 others. 2020. 'A Paleogenomic Reconstruction of the Deep Population History of the Andes', *CELL* 181 (5): 1131–45.e21.

Narváez, Alfredo, ed. 2007. *Arqueología de Yanacocha: Nuevos aportes para la historia de Cajamarca, I*. Lima: Yanacocha.

Narváez Vargas, L.A. 2013. 'Kuélap: Centro del poder politico religioso de los Chachapoyas'. In *Los Chachapoyas*, edited by Federico Kauffmann Doig, 87–160. Lima: Banco de Crédito del Perú.

National Research Council. 1989. *Lost Crops of the Incas: Little-Known Plants of the Andes with Promise for Worldwide Cultivation*. Washington, DC: National Academy Press.

Navarro, Manuel. 1903. *Vocabulario castellano-quechua-pano con sus gramáticas quechua y pana*. Lima: Imprenta del Estado.

Neel, James V. and Francisco M. Salzano. 1967. 'Further Studies on the Xavante Indians: Some Hypotheses-Generalizations Resulting from These Studies', *American Journal of Human Genetics* 19 (4): 554–74.

Neel, J.V., F.M. Salzano, P.C. Junqueira, F. Keiter and D. Maybury-Lewis. 1964. 'Studies on the Xavante Indians of the Brazilian Mato Grosso', *American Journal of Human Genetics* 16 (1): 52–140.

Netherly, Patricia J. 1977. 'Local Level Lords on the North Coast of Peru'. PhD thesis, Cornell University.

Netherly, Patricia J. 2011a. 'An Overview of Climate in Northern South America from the Late Pleistocene to the Mid-Holocene'. In *From Foraging to Farming in the Andes: New Perspectives on Food Production and Social Organization*, edited by Tom D. Dillehay, 76–99. New York: Cambridge University Press.

Netherly, Patricia J. 2011b. 'Pleistocene and Holocene Environments from the Zaña to the Chicama Valleys 25,000 to 6,000 Years Ago'. In *From Foraging to Farming in the Andes: New Perspectives on Food Production and Social Organization*, edited by Tom D. Dillehay, 43–76. New York: Cambridge University Press.

Nettle, Daniel. 1999. 'Linguistic Diversity of the Americas Can Be Reconciled with a Recent Colonization', *Proceedings of the National Academy of Sciences of the United States of America* 96 (6): 3325–9.

Neumann, Georg K. 1942. 'The Origin of the Prairid Physical Type of American Indian', *Papers of the Michigan Academy of Science, Arts, and Letters* 27: 539–42.

Neumann, Georg K. 1952. 'Archaeology and Race in the American Indian'. In *Archaeology of Eastern United States*, edited by J.B. Griffin, 13–34. Chicago: Chicago University Press.

Neves, Eduardo G. 1998. 'Paths in Dark Waters: Archaeology as Indigenous History in the Upper Rio Negro Basin, Northwest Amazon'. PhD thesis, Indiana University.

Neves, Eduardo G. 2001. 'Indigenous Historical Trajectories in the Upper Rio Negro Basin'. In *Unknown Amazon: Culture in Nature in Ancient Brazil*, edited by Colin McEwan, Cristiana Barreto and Eduardo Goés Neves, 251–82. London: British Museum Press.

Neves, Eduardo G. 2008. 'Ecology, Ceramic Chronology and Distribution, Long-term History, and Political Change in the Amazonian Floodplain'. In *The Handbook of South American Archaeology*, edited by Helaine Silverman and William H. Isbell, 359–79. New York: Springer.

Neves, Eduardo G. 2013. 'Was Agriculture a Key Productive Activity in Pre-Colonial Amazonia? The Stable Productive Basis for Social Equality in the Central Amazon'. In *Human–Environment Interactions: Current and Future Directions*, edited by Eduardo S.Brondízio and Emilio F.Moran, 371–88. Dordrecht Springer.

Neves, Eduardo G. and Michael J. Heckenberger. 2019. 'The Call of the Wild: Rethinking Food Production in Ancient Amazonia', *Annual Review of Anthropology* 48: 371–88.

Neves, Eduardo G. and James B. Petersen. 2006. 'Political Economy and Pre-Columbian Landscape Transformations in Central Amazonia'. In *Time and Complexity in Historical Ecology: Studies in the Neotropical Lowlands*, edited by Willam Balée and Clark L. Erickson, 279–310. New York: Columbia University Press.

Neves, Eduardo G., James B. Petersen, Robert N. Bartone and Claudio A. Da Silva. 2003. 'Historical and Socio-Cultural Origins of Amazonian Dark Earths'. In *Amazonian Dark Earths: Origin, Properties, Management.*, 29–50. Dordrecht: Kluwer Academic.

Neves, Walter A., Max Blum and Lyvia Kozameh. 1999. 'Were the Fuegians Relicts of a Paleoindian Nonspecialized Morphology in the Americas?', *Current Research in the Pleistocene* 16: 90–2.

Neves, Walter A. and Mark Hubbe. 2005. 'Cranial Morphology of Early Americans from Lagoa Santa, Brazil: Implications for the Settlement of the New World', *Proceedings of the National Academy of Sciences of the United States of America* 102 (51): 18309–14.

Neves, Walter A., Mark Hubbe and Gonzalo Correal. 2007. 'Human Skeletal Remains from Sabana de Bogotá, Colombia: A Case of Paleoamerican Morphology Late Survival in South America?', *American Journal of Physical Anthropology* 133 (4): 1080–98.

Neves, Walter A., Mark Hubbe, Maria Mercedes M. Okumura, Rolando González-José, Levy Figuti, Sabine Eggers and Paulo Antonio Dantas De Blasis. 2005. 'A New Early Holocene Human Skeleton from Brazil: Implications for the Settlement of the New World', *Journal of Human Evolution* 48 (4): 403–14.

Neves, Walter A., Mark Hubbe and Luís Beethoven Piló. 2007. 'Early Holocene Human Skeletal Remains from Sumidouro Cave, Lagoa Santa, Brazil: History of Discoveries, Geological and Chronological Context, and Comparative Cranial Morphology', *Journal of Human Evolution* 52 (1): 16–30.

Neves, Walter A., Mark Hubbe, Pedro A. M. Ribeiro and Danilo V. Bernardo. 2004. 'Afinidades morfológicas de três crânios associados à Tradição Umbu: Uma análise exploratória multivariada', *Revista do CEPA* 28 (39): 159–85.

Neves, Walter Alves, André Prous, Rolando González-José, Renato Kipnis and Joseph Powell. 2003. 'Early Holocene Human Skeletal Remains from Santana do Riacho, Brazil: Implications for the Settlement of the New World', *Journal of Human Evolution* 45 (1): 19–42.

Nichols, Johanna. 1990. 'Linguistic Diversity and the First Settlement of the New World', *Language* 66 (3): 475–521.

Nichols, Johanna. 1992. *Linguistic Diversity in Space and Time*. Chicago: University of Chicago Press.

Nielsen, Axel E. 2001. 'Evolucion social en Quebrada de Humahuaca (AD 700–1536)'. In *Historia Argentina Prehispanica*, edited by Eduardo E. Berberian and Axel E. Nielsen, 171–264. Cordoba (Argentina): Brujas.

Nielsen, Axel E. 2009. 'Pastoralism and the Non-Pastoral World in the Late Pre-Columbian History of the Southern Andes (1000–1535)', *Nomadic Peoples* 13 (2): 17–35.

Nimuendajú, Curt. 1946. *The Eastern Timbira* (University of California Publications in American Archaeology and Ethnology 41), edited and translated by Robert Lowie. Berkeley: University of California Press.

Nir, Amnon. 2008. 'Anca Uallo Chanca: ¿Mito o Historia?', *Iberoamérica Global* 1 (2): 23–33.

Nordenskiöld, Erland. 1910. 'Archäologische Forschungen im Bolivianischen Flachland', *Zeitschrift für Ethnologie* 42 (5): 806–22.

Nordenskiöld, Erland. 1913. 'Urnengräber und Mounds im bolivianischen Flachland', *Baessler-Archiv* 3 (6): 205–55.

Nordenskiöld, Erland. 1917. 'Die östliche Ausbreitung der Tiahuanacokultur in Bolivien und ihr Verhältnis zur Aruakkultur in Mojos', *Zeitschrift für Ethnologie* 49 (1): 10–20.

Nuckolls, Janis B. 2001. 'Ideophones in Pastaza Quechua'. In *Ideophones*, edited by F. Voeltz, K. Erhard and Christa Kilian-Hatz, 271–85. Amsterdam: John Benjamins.

Nuckolls, Janis B. 2010. *Lessons from a Quechua Strongwoman: Ideophony, Dialogue, and Perspective*. Tucson: University of Arizona Press.

Núñez, Lautaro and Tom D. Dillehay. 1979. *Movilidad giratoria, armonía social y desarrollo en los Andes Meridionales: Patrones de tráfico e interacción económica*. Antofagasta: Universidad Catolica del Norte.

Núñez, Lautaro and Tom D. Dillehay. 1995. *Movilidad giratoria, armonía social y desarrollo en los Andes Meridionales: Patrones de tráfico e interacción económica*. 2nd ed. Antofagasta: Universidad Catolica del Norte.

Oberem, U. 1974. 'Trade and Trade Goods in the Ecuadorian Montaña'. In *Native South Americans: Ethnology of the Least Known Continent*, edited by Patricia J. Lyon; translated by Alegonda M. Schokkenbroek, 346–57. Boston: Little, Brown.

Oberem, Udo. 1980. *Los Quijos, historia de la transculturación de un grupo indígena en el Oriente Ecuatoriano*. Otavalo: Instituto Otavaleño de Antropología.

O'Fallon, Brendan D. and Lars Fehren-Schmitz. 2011. 'Native Americans Experienced a Strong Population Bottleneck Coincident with European Contact', *Proceedings of the National Academy of Sciences of the United States of America* 108 (51): 20444–8.

Olawsky, Knut J. 2006. *A Grammar of Urarina*. Berlin: de Gruyter Mouton.

Olivera, Quirino. 1998. 'Evidencias arqueológicas del Periodo Formativo en la cuenca baja del río Utcubamba y Chinchipe', *Boletín de Arqueología PUCP* 2: 105–12.

Olivera, Quirino. 2014. *Arqueología Alto Amazónica: Los orígenes de la civilización en el Perú*. Lima: Industria Gráfica.

Olsen, Kenneth M. 2004. 'SNPs, SSRs and Inferences on Cassava's Origin', *Plant Molecular Biology* 56 (4): 517–26.

Olsen, Kenneth M. and Barbara A. Schaal. 2001. 'Microsatellite Variation in Cassava (*Manihot esculenta*, Euphorbiaceae) and Its Wild Relatives: Further Evidence for a Southern Amazonian Origin of Domestication', *American Journal of Botany* 88 (1): 131–42.

Olson, Ronald D. 1965. 'Mayan Affinities with Chipaya of Bolivia II: Cognates', *International Journal of American Linguistics* 31 (1): 29–38.

Olza Zubiri, Jesús, Conchita Nuni de Chapi and Juan Tube. 2004. *Gramática moja-ignaciana (morfosintaxis)*. Cochabamba: Editorial Verbo Divino.

Onuki, Yoshio, ed. 1995. *Kuntur Wasi y Cerro Blanco: Dos sitios del Formativo en el Norte del Perú*. Tokyo: Hokusen-sha.

Orellana Halkyer, Nancy, Macarena Fuentes-Guajardo, José M. Capriles and Francisco Rothhammer. 2014. 'En torno al poblamiento de los Andes Sur-Centrales y su vinculación con la Amazonía', *Interciencia* 39 (8): 586–90.

Osborn, Henry. 1948. 'Amahuaca Phonemes', *International Journal of American Linguistics* 14 (3): 188–90.

Ossio, Juan M. 2015. 'Ages of the World in the Andes'. In *The Measure and Meaning of Time in Mesoamerica and the Andes*, edited by Anthony F. Aveni, 211–37. Washington, DC: Dumbarton Oaks Research Library and Collection.

Ott, Willis and Rebecca B. Ott. 1983. *Diccionario ignaciano y castellano, con apuntes gramáticales*. Cochabamba: Instituto Lingüístico de Verano.

Ottaviano, John and Ida Ottaviano. 1965. 'Tacana'. In *Gramáticas estructurales de lenguas bolivianas 3*, edited by E. Matteson, 309–417. Riberalta: Instituto Lingüístico de Verano.

Overall, Simon. 2007. 'A Grammar of Aguaruna'. PhD thesis, La Trobe University.

Oyuela-Caycedo, Augusto. 1995. 'Rock versus Clay: The Evolution of Pottery Technology in the Case of San Jacinto 1, Colombia'. In *The Emergence of Pottery: Technology and Innovation in Ancient Societies*, edited by William Barnett and John Hoopes, 133–44.

Oyuela-Caycedo, Augusto and Renée M. Bonzani. 2005. *San Jacinto 1: A Historical Ecological Approach to an Archaic Site in Colombia*. Tuscaloosa: University of Alabama Press.

Pääbo, Svante, Hendrik Poinar, David Serre, Viviane Jaenicke-Després, Juliane Hebler, Nadin Rohland, Melanie Kuch, Johannes Krause, Linda Vigilant and Michael Hofreiter. 2004. 'Genetic Analyses from Ancient DNA', *Annual Review of Genetics* 38: 645–79. https://doi.org/10.1146/annurev.genet.37.110801.143214.

Pache, Matthias, Søren Wichmann and Mikhail Zhivlov. 2016. 'Words for "Dog" as a Diagnostic of Language Contact in the Americas'. In *Language Contact and Change in the Americas: Studies in Honor of Marianne Mithun*, edited by Andrea L. Berez-Kroeker, Diane M. Hintz and Carmen Jany, 385–409. Amsterdam: John Benjamins.

Pakendorf, Brigitte and Mark Stoneking. 2005. 'Mitochondrial DNA and Human Evolution', *Annual Review of Genomics and Human Genetics* 6: 165–83.

Parker, Stephen G. 1995. *Datos de la lengua iñapari*. Yarinacocha: Ministerio de Educación and Instituto Lingüístico de Verano.

Parker, Steve. 2010. *Chamicuro Data: Exhaustive List (Datos del chamicuro: lista exhaustiva): Language and Culture Documentation and Description*. Arlington, TX: SIL Publications.

Pärssinen, Martti. 1992. *Tawantinsuyu: The Inca State and its Political Organization*. Helsinki: Suomen Historiallinen Seura.

Pärssinen, Martti and Antti Korpisaari, eds. 2003. *Western Amazonia – Amazônia Ocidental: Multidisciplinary Studies on Ancient Expansionistic Movements, Fortifications and Sedentary Life* (Renvall Institute Publications 14). Helsinki: Renvall Institute for Area and Cultural Studies.

Pärssinen, Martti, Denise Schaan and Alceu Ranzi. 2009. 'Pre-Columbian Geometric Earthworks in the Upper Purús: A Complex Society in Western Amazonia', *Antiquity* 83: 1084–95.

Pärssinen, Martti, Ari Siiriäinen and Antti Korpisaari. 2003. 'Fortifications Related to the Inca Expansion'. In *Western Amazonia – Amazônia Ocidental: Multidisciplinary Studies on Ancient Expansionistic Movements, Fortifications and Sedentary Life*, edited by Martti Pärssinen and Antti Korpisaari, 29–72. (Renvall Institute Publications 14). Helsinki: Renvall Institute for Area and Cultural Studies.

Paschetta, Carolina, Soledad de Azevedo, Lucía Castillo, Neus Martínez-Abadías, Miquel Hernández, Daniel E. Lieberman and Rolando González-José. 2010. 'The Influence of Masticatory Loading on Craniofacial Morphology: A Test Case across Technological Transitions in the Ohio Valley', *American Journal of Physical Anthropology* 141 (2): 297–314.

Patiño, Diógenes. n.d. *Investigaciones de arqueologia de rescate: El altiplano nariñense, el valle de Sibundoy y la ceja de montaña andina en el Putumayo*. Popayán: Instituto Vallecaucano de Investigaciones Científicas.

Patiño, Diógenes. 2016. 'El altiplano nariñense en la arqueología del sur de Colombia'. Unpublished manuscript. https://www.academia.edu/28648283.

Paulsen, Allison C. 1974. 'The Thorny Oyster and the Voice of God: *Spondylus* and *Strombus* in Andean Prehistory', *American Antiquity* 39 (4): 597–607.

Payne, David L. 1981. *The Phonology and Morphology of Axininca Campa*. Dallas: Summer Institute of Linguistics and University of Texas at Arlington.

Payne, David L. 1991. 'A Classification of Maipuran (Arawakan) Languages Based on Shared Lexical Retentions'. In *Handbook of Amazonian languages, Volume 3*, edited by Desmond C. Derbyshire and Geoffrey K. Pullum, 355–499. Berlin: de Gruyter Mouton.

Payne, Doris. 1985. 'Aspects of the Grammar of Yagua: A Typological Perspective'. PhD thesis, University of California, Los Angeles.

Payne, Doris. 1986. 'Basic Constituent Order in Yagua Clauses: Implications for Word Order Universals'. In *Handbook of Amazonian Languages, Volume 1*, edited by Desmond C. Derbyshire and Geoffrey K. Pullum, 440–65. Berlin: de Gruyter Mouton.

Payne, Doris. 1990. 'Morphological Characteristics of Amazonian Languages'. In *Amazonian Linguistics: Studies in Lowland South American Languages*, edited by Doris Payne, 213–41. Austin: University of Texas Press.

Payne, Doris. 2001. 'Book Review – The Amazonian Languages, edited by R.M.W. Dixon and Alexandra Aikhenvald', *Language* 77 (3): 594–8.

Payne, Judith K. 1989. *Lecciones para el aprendizaje del idioma ashéninca*. Yarinacocha: Ministerio de Educación and Instituto Lingüístico de Verano.

Pearce, Adrian J. 2001. 'The Peruvian Population Census of 1725–1740', *Latin American Research Review* 36 (3): 69–104. https://www.jstor.org/stable/2692121.

Pearce, Adrian J. and Paul Heggarty. 2011. '"Mining the Data" on the Huancayo–Huancavelica Quechua Frontier'. In *History and Language in the Andes*, edited by Paul Heggarty and Adrian J. Pearce, 87–109. New York: Palgrave Macmillan. http://doi.org/10.1057/9780230370579.

Pearsall, D.M. 2003. 'Plant Food Resources of the Ecuadorian Formative: An Overview and Comparison to the Central Andes'. In *Archaeology of Formative Ecuador*, edited by J.S. Raymond and R. Burger, 213–57. Washington, DC: Dumbarton Oaks.

Peeke, M. Catherine. 1973. *Preliminary Grammar of Auca*. Norman: Summer Institute of Linguistics of the University of Oklahoma.

Peeke, Catherine. 1991. *Bosquejo gramatical del záparo*, revised by Mary Ruth Wise and Stephen H. Levinsohn. Quito: Instituto Lingüístico de Verano.

Peeke, Catherine and Mary Sargent. 1959. *Pronombres personales en shimigae*. Quito: Ministerio de Educación and Instituto Lingüístico de Verano, Universidad de Oklahoma.

Peeri, D. 1998. 'Marine Animals and Monsters in Maritime Cartography from the 15th–17th Centuries', *CMS News*, Report 24–25, Haifa: University of Haifa Center for Maritime Studies.

Perego, Ugo A. and 15 others. 2009. 'Distinctive Paleo-Indian Migration Routes from Beringia Marked by Two Rare mtDNA Haplogroups', *Current Biology* 19 (1): 1–8.

Perego, Ugo A. and 20 others. 2010. 'The Initial Peopling of the Americas: A Growing Number of Founding Mitochondrial Genomes from Beringia', *Genome Research* 20 (9): 1174–9.

Perego, Ugo A., Hovirag Lancioni, Maribel Tribaldos, Norman Angerhofer, Jayne E. Ekins, Anna Olivieri, Scott R. Woodward, Juan Miguel Pascale, Richard Cooke, Jorge Motta and Alessandro Achilli. 2012. 'Decrypting the Mitochondrial Gene Pool of Modern Panamanians', *PLoS One* 7 (6), Article e38337: 1–10. Accessed 16 May 2020. https://doi.org/10.1371/journal.pone.0038337.

Perez, S. Ivan, Valeria Bernal, Paula N. Gonzalez, Marina Sardi and Gustavo G. Politis. 2009. 'Discrepancy between Cranial and DNA Data of Early Americans: Implications for American Peopling', *PLoS One* 4 (5), Article e5746: 1–11. Accessed 16 May 2020. https://doi.org/10.1371/journal.pone.0005746.

Perez, S. Ivan, Verónica Lema, José Alexandre Felizola Diniz-Filho, Valeria Bernal, Paula N. Gonzalez, Diego Gobbo and Héctor M. Pucciarelli. 2011. 'The Role of Diet and Temperature in Shaping Cranial Diversification of South American Human Populations: An Approach Based on Spatial Regression and Divergence Rate Tests', *Journal of Biogeography* 38 (1): 148–63.

Perez, S. Ivan and Leandro R. Monteiro. 2009. 'Nonrandom Factors in Modern Human Morphological Diversification: A Study of Craniofacial Variation in Southern South American Populations', *Evolution* 63 (4): 978–93.

Pérez Calderón, Ismael. 1994. 'Monumentos arqueológicos de Santiago de Chuco, La Libertad', *Boletín de Lima* 91–6: 225–75.

Peters, Charles M. 2000. 'Precolumbian Silviculture and Indigenous Management of Neotropical Forests'. In *Imperfect Balance: Landscape Transformations in the Precolumbian Americas*, edited by David L. Lentz, 203–23. New York: Columbia University Press.

Pickersgill, Barbara. 2007. 'Domestication of Plants in the Americas: Insights from Mendelian and Molecular Genetics', *Annals of Botany* 100 (5): 925–40.

Pickrell, Joseph K. and David Reich. 2014. 'Toward a New History and Geography of Human Genes Informed by Ancient DNA', *Trends in Genetics* 30 (9): 377–89.

Pillsbury, Joanne. 1996. 'The Thorny Oyster and the Origins of Empire: Implications of Recently Uncovered *Spondylus* Imagery from Chan Chan, Peru', *Latin American Antiquity* 7 (4): 313–40.

Pimenta, José. 2009. 'Parceiros de troca, parceiros de projetos: Ayompari e suas variações entre Ashaninka do Alto Juruá'. In *Faces da Indianidade*, edited by Maria I. Smiljanic, José Pimenta and Stephen Grant Baines, 101–26 Curtiba: Nexo Design.

Pinhasi, Ron and 18 others. 2015. 'Optimal Ancient DNA Yields from the Inner Ear Part of the Human Petrous Bone', *PLoS One* 10 (6), Article e0129102: 1–13. Accessed 16 May 2020. https://doi.org/10.1371/journal.pone.0129102.

Piperno, Dolores R. 2007. 'Prehistoric Human Occupation and Impacts on Neotropical Forest Landscapes during the Late Pleistocene and Early/Middle Holocene'. In *Tropical Rainforest Responses to Climatic Change*, edited by Mark B. Bush and John R. Flenley, 193–218. Berlin: Springer.

Piperno, Dolores R. 2011a. 'The Origins of Plant Cultivation and Domestication in the New World Tropics: Patterns, Process, and New Developments', *Current Anthropology* 52 (Supplement 4): S453–70.

Piperno, Dolores. 2011b. 'Northern Peruvian Early and Middle Preceramic Agriculture in Central and South American Contexts'. In *From Foraging to Farming in the Andes: New Perspectives on Food Production and Social Organization*, edited by Tom D. Dillehay, 275–84. New York: Cambridge University Press.

Piperno, Dolores R. and Tom D. Dillehay. 2008. 'Starch Grains on Human Teeth Reveal Early Broad Crop Diet in Northern Peru', *Proceedings of the National Academy of Sciences of the Unites States of America* 105 (50): 19622–7.

Piperno, Dolores R., Crystal McMichael and Mark B. Bush. 2015. 'Amazonia and the Anthropocene: What Was the Spatial Extent and Intensity of Human Landscape Modification in the Amazon Basin at the End of Prehistory?', *The Holocene* 25 (10): 1588–97.

Piperno, Dolores R., Crystal McMichael and Mark B. Bush. 2017. 'Further Evidence for Localized, Short-Term Anthropogenic Forest Alterations across Pre-Columbian Amazonia', *Proceedings of the National Academy of Sciences of the United States of America* 114 (21): E4118–19.

Piperno, Dolores R. and Deborah M. Pearsall. 1998. *The Origins of Agriculture in the Lowland Neotropics*. San Diego: Academic Press.

Plaza, Pedro. 2009. 'Quechua'. In *Las lenguas de Bolivia*, Vol. 1: *Ámbito andino*, edited by Mily Crevels and Pieter Muysken, 215–84. La Paz: Plural Editores.

Plowman, Timothy. 1985. 'Coca Chewing and the Botanical Origins of Coca (*Erythroxylum* spp.) in South America'. In *Coca and Cocaine: Effects on People and Policy in Latin America*, edited by Deborah Pacini and Christine Franquemont, 5–34. Ithaca, NY: Cultural Survival.

Ponce Sanginés, Carlos. 1981. *Tiwanaku: Espacio, tiempo y cultura: Ensayo de síntesis arqueológica*. 4th ed. La Paz: Editorial Los Amigos del Libro.

Ponce Sanginés, Carlos. 1994. 'Noticia adicional sobre el pectoral antemencionado de Las Piedras (Riberalta)', *Pumapunku Año* 3 (7): 89–99.

Posnansky, Arthur. 1957. *Tihuanacu: La cuna del hombre americano*, Vols. 3–4. La Paz: Ministerio de Educación.

Posth, Cosimo and 71 others. 2018. 'Reconstructing the Deep Population History of Central and South America', *Cell* 175 (5): 1185–97. https://doi.org/10.1016/j.cell.2018.10.027

Powell, Adam, Stephen Shennan and Mark G. Thomas. 2009. 'Late Pleistocene Demography and the Appearance of Modern Human Behavior', *Science* 324 (5932): 1298–301.

Powell, Joseph F. 2005. *The First Americans: Race, Evolution, and the Origin of Native Americans*. Cambridge: Cambridge University Press.

Priest, Perry N. and Anne Priest. 1965. 'Sirionó'. In *Gramáticas estructurales de lenguas bolivianas 1*, edited by E. Matteson, 281–373. Riberalta: Instituto Lingüístico de Verano.

Programa Qhapaq Ñan. 2009. *El Qhapaq Ñan en la ruta del Chinchaysuyu entre Punpu y Pallasca*. Lima: Instituto Nacional de Cultura.

Prugnolle, Franck, Andrea Manica and François Balloux. 2005. 'Geography Predicts Neutral Genetic Diversity of Human Populations', *Current Biology* 15 (5): 159–60.

Prümers, Heiko. 2004. 'Hügel umgeben von "schönen Monstern": Ausgrabungen in der Loma Mendoza (Bolivien)'. In *Expeditionen in Vergessene Welten: 25 Jahre archäologische Forschungen in Amerika, Afrika und Asien* (AVA-Forschungen 10), edited by Markus Reindel, 47–78. Bonn: Linden-Soft.

Prümers, Heiko. 2007. '¿"Charlatanocracia" en Mojos? Investigaciones arqueológicas en la Loma Salvatierra, Beni, Bolivia', *Boletín de Arqueología PUCP* 11: 103–16.

Prümers, Heiko. 2009. '¿"Charlatanocracia" en Moxos?'. In *Procesos y expresiones de poder, identidad y orden tempranos en Sudamérica: Segunda parte*, edited by Peter Kaulicke and Tom D. Dillehay, 103–16. Lima: Fondo Editorial de la Pontificia Universidad Católica del Perú..

Prümers, Heiko. 2012. 'El Proyecto Lomas de Casarabe: Investigaciones arqueológicas en los Llanos de Mojos, Bolivia'. In *The Past Ahead: Language, Culture, and Identity in the Neotropics*, edited by Christian Isendahl, 139–59. Uppsala: Uppsala University.

Prümers, Heiko. 2013. 'Volver a los sitios – el Proyecto Boliviano-Alemán en Mojos'. In *"Para quê serve o conhecimento se eu não posso dividi-lo?" = "Was nützt alles Wissen, wenn man es nicht teilen kann?": Gedenkschrift für Erwin Heinrich Frank* (Estudios Indiana 5), edited by Birgit Krekeler, Eva König, Stefan Neumann and Hans-Dieter Ölschleger, 375–96. Berlin: Ibero Amerikanisches Institut.

Prümers, Heiko. 2014. 'Sitios Prehispánicos con Zanjas en Bella Vista, Provincia Iténez, Bolivia'. In *Amazonia: Memorias del 3er Encuentro Internacional de Arqueologia Amazonica*, edited by Stéphen Rostain, 73–89. Quito: Ministerio Coordinador de Conocimiento y Talento Humano e IKIAM.

Prümers, Heiko, ed. 2015. *Loma Mendoza. Las excavaciones del Instituto Alemán de Arqueología y de la Dirección Nacional de Arqueología en los años 1999–2002*. La Paz: Plural.

Prümers, Heiko and Carla Jaimes Betancourt. 2014a. '100 años de investigación arqueológica en los Llanos de Mojos', *Arqueoantropológicas* 4 (4): 11–53.

Prümers, Heiko and Carla Jaimes Betancourt. 2014b. 'Die frühen Siedler von Jasiaquiri (Bolivien)', *Zeitschrift für Archäologie Außereuropäischer Kulturen* 6: 309–32.

Prümers, Heiko and Carla Jaimes Betancourt. 2017. 'Die Phase Equijebe in Jasiaquiri und Urnengräber am Guaporé', *Zeitschrift für Archäologie Außereuropäischer Kulturen* 7: 357–72.

Pucciarelli, Héctor M., Walter A. Neves, Rolando González-José, Marina L. Sardi, Fernando Ramírez Rozzi, Adelaida Struck and Mary Y. Bonilla. 2006. 'East–West Cranial Differentiation in Pre-Columbian Human Populations of South America', *HOMO: Journal of Comparative Human Biology* 57 (2): 133–50.

Pucciarelli, Héctor M., S. Ivan Perez and Gustavo G. Politis. 2010. 'Early Holocene Human Remains from the Argentinean Pampas: Additional Evidence for Distinctive Cranial Morphology of Early South Americans', *American Journal of Physical Anthropology* 143 (2): 298–305.

Pugliese, Francisco Antonio, Carlos Augusto Zimpel Neto and Eduardo Góes Neves. 2019. 'What Do Amazonian Shellmounds Tell Us about the Long-Term Indigenous History of South America?'. In *Encyclopedia of Global Archaeology*, edited by Claire Smith. Cham: Springer. Accessed 21 May 2020. https://doi.org/10.1007/978-3-319-51726-1_3030-2.

Purps, Josephine and 162 others. 2014. 'A Global Analysis of Y-Chromosomal Haplotype Diversity for 23 STR Loci', *Forensic Science International: Genetics* 12: 12–23. https://doi.org/10.1016/j.fsigen.2014.04.008

Quesada C., Félix. 1976. *Gramática quechua: Cajamarca-Cañaris*. Lima: IEP.

Quilter, Jeffrey. 1990. 'The Moche Revolt of the Objects', *Latin American Antiquity* 1 (1): 42–65.

Quilter, Jeffrey. 2014. *The Ancient Central Andes*. London: Routledge.

Quilter, Jeffrey, Bernardino Ojeda E., Deborah M. Pearsall, Daniel H. Sandweiss, John G. Jones and Elizabeth S. Wing. 1991. 'Subsistence Economy of El Paraíso, an Early Peruvian Site', *Science* 251 (4991): 277–83.

Radding, Cynthia. 2005. *Landscapes of Power and Identity: Comparative Histories in the Sonoran Desert and the Forests of Amazonia from Colony to Republic*. Durham, NC: Duke University Press.

Rademaker, Kurt, Gregory Hodgins, Katherine Moore, Sonia Zarrillo, Christopher Miller, Gordon R.M. Bromley, Peter Leach, David A. Reid, Willy Yépez Álvarez and Daniel H. Sandweiss. 2014. 'Paleoindian Settlement of the High-Altitude Peruvian Andes', *Science* 346 (6208): 466–9. http://doi.org/10.1126/science.1258260.

Raghavan, Mannasa and 100 others. 2015. 'Genomic Evidence for the Pleistocene and Recent Population History of Native Americans', *Science* 349 (6250), Article aab3884: 1–10. Accessed 16 May 2020. https://doi.org/10.1126/science.aab3884.

Ramachandran, Sohini, Omkar Deshpande, Charles C. Roseman, Noah A. Rosenberg, Marcus W. Feldman and L. Luca Cavalli-Sforza. 2005. 'Support from the Relationship of Genetic and Geographic Distance in Human Populations for a Serial Founder Effect Originating in Africa', *Proceedings of the National Academy of Sciences of the United States of America* 102 (44): 15942–7.

Ramallo, Virginia, Rafael Bisso-Machado, Claudio Bravi, Michael D. Coble, Francisco M. Salzano, Tábita Hünemeier and Maria Cátira Bortolini. 2013. 'Demographic Expansions in South America: Enlightening a Complex Scenario with Genetic and Linguistic Data', *American Journal of Physical Anthropology* 150 (3): 453–63.

Ramírez de Jara, M.C. 1996. *Frontera fluida entre Andes, Piedemonte y Selva: El caso del Valle de Sibundoy, siglos XVI–XVIII*. Bogotá: Instituto colombiano de cultura hispánica.

Raposo-do-Amaral, C.M., H. Krieger, P.H. Cabello and B. Beiguelman. 1989. 'Heritability of Quantitative Orbital Traits', *Human Biology* 61 (4): 551–7.

Rasmussen, Morten and 41 others. 2014. 'The Genome of a Late Pleistocene Human from a Clovis Burial Site in Western Montana', *Nature* 506: 225–9.

Rasmussen, Morten and 18 others. 2015. 'The Ancestry and Affiliations of Kennewick Man', *Nature* 523: 455–8.

Raymond, J. Scott. 1976. 'Late Prehistoric and Historic Settlements in the Upper Montana of Peru', *Calgary University Archaeological Association Annual Conference Proceedings* 6: 205–14.

Raymond, J. Scott. 1988. 'A View from the Tropical Forest'. In *Peruvian Prehistory: An Overview of Pre-Inca and Inca Society*, edited by Richard W. Keatinge, 279–300. Cambridge: Cambridge University Press.

Reeve, Mary-Elizabeth. 1994. 'Regional Interaction in the Western Amazon: The Early Colonial Encounter and the Jesuit Years: 1538–1767', *Ethnohistory* 41 (1): 106–38.

Regueiro, Maria, Joseph Alvarez, Diane Rowold and Rene J. Herrera. 2013. 'On the Origins, Rapid Expansion and Genetic Diversity of Native Americans from Hunting-Gatherers to Agriculturalists', *American Journal of Physical Anthropology* 150 (3): 333–48.

Reich, David and 63 others. 2012. 'Reconstructing Native American Population History', *Nature* 488: 370–4. https://doi.org/10.1038/nature11258

Reichel-Dolmatoff, Gerardo. 1972. 'The Feline Motif in Prehistoric San Agustín Sculpture'. In *The Cult of the Feline: A Conference in Pre-Columbian Iconography*, edited by Elizabeth P. Benson, 51–64. Washington, DC: Dumbarton Oaks.

Reichlen, Henry and Paule Reichlen. 1949. 'Recherches archéologiques dans les Andes de Cajamarca', *Journal de la Société des Américanistes* 38: 137–74.

Reichlen, Henry and Paule Reichlen. 1950. 'Recherches archéologiques dans les Andes du Haute Utcubamba', *Journal de la Société des Américanistes* 39: 219–46.

Relethford, John H. 1994. 'Craniometric Variation among Modern Human Populations', *American Journal of Physical Anthropology* 95 (1): 53–62.

Relethford, John H. 2002. 'Apportionment of Global Human Genetic Diversity Based on Craniometrics and Skin Color', *American Journal of Physical Anthropology* 118 (4): 393–8.

Relethford, John H. 2004. 'Boas and Beyond: Migration and Craniometric Variation', *American Journal of Human Biology* 16 (4): 379–86.

Relethford, John H. and John Blangero. 1990. 'Detection of Differential Gene Flow from Patterns of Quantitative Variation', *Human Biology* 62 (1): 5–25.

Relethford, John H., Michael H. Crawford and John Blangero. 1997. 'Genetic Drift and Gene Flow in Post-Famine Ireland', *Human Biology* 69 (4): 443–65.

Relethford, John H. and Henry C. Harpending. 1994. 'Craniometric Variation, Genetic Theory, and Modern Human Origins', *American Journal of Physical Anthropology* 95 (3): 249–70.

Renard-Casevitz, France-Marie. 1981. 'Las fronteras de las conquistas en el siglo XVI en la Montaña Meridional del Perú', *Boletín del Instituto Francés de Estudios Andinos* 10 (3/4): 113–40.

Renard-Casevitz, France-Marie, Thierry Saignes and Anne-Christine Taylor-Descola. 1986. *L'Inca, l'Espagnol et les Sauvages*. Paris: Éditions Recherche sur les Civilisations.

Renard-Casevitz, France-Marie, Thierry Saignes and Anne-Christine Taylor. 1988. *Al este de los Andes: Relaciones entre las sociedades amazónicas entre los siglos XV y XVII*. Lima: Instituto Francés de Estudios Andinos.

Renaud, Gabriel, Viviane Slon, Ana T. Duggan and Janet Kelso. 2015. 'Schmutzi: Estimation of Contamination and Endogenous Mitochondrial Consensus Calling for Ancient DNA', *Genome Biology* 16, Article 224: 1–18. Accessed 16 May 2020. https://doi.org/10.1186/s13059-015-0776-0.

Renfrew, Colin. 1987. *Archaeology and Language: The Puzzle of Indo-European Origins*. London: Jonathan Cape.

Restall, Matthew and Kris Lane. 2011. *Latin America in Colonial Times*. New York: Cambridge University Press.

Reynel, Carlos, R. Toby Pennington and Tiina Särkinen. 2013. *Cómo se formó la diversidad ecológica del Perú*. Lima: Jesús Bellido.

Rich, Rolland G. 1999. *Diccionario Arabela–Castellano* (Serie Lingüística Peruana 49). Lima: Instituto Lingüístico de Verano.

Richards, M.B., V.A. Macaulay, H.-J. Bandelt and B.C. Sykes. 1998. 'Phylogeography of Mitochondrial DNA in Western Europe', *Annals of Human Genetics* 62 (3): 241–60.

Rival, Laura M. 2002. *Trekking through History: The Huaorani of Amazonian Ecuador*. New York: Columbia University Press.

Rivera, M. 1974. 'Una hipotesis sobre movimientos poblacionales altiplánicos y trans-altiplánicos a las costas del norte de Chile', *Chungara* 5: 7–31.

Rivet, Paul. 1910. 'Sur quelques dialectes Pano peu connus', *Journal de la Société des Américanistes* 7: 221–42.

Rodrigues, Aryon Dall'Igna. 2000. 'Panorama das línguas indígenas da Amazônia'. In *As Línguas Amazônicas Hoje*, edited by F. Queixalós and O. Renault-Lescure, 15–28. São Paulo: Instituto Socioambiental, Museu Parense Emílio Goeldi.

Rodrigues, Aryon Dall'Igna. 2005. 'Sobre as línguas indígenas e sua pesquisa no Brasil', *Ciencia e Cultura* 57 (2): 35–8.

Rodrigues, Aryon Dall'Igna. 2009. 'A Case of Affinity Among Tupí, Karíb, and Macro-Jê'. *Revista Brasileira de Linguística Antropológica* 1 (1): 137–62. http://doi.org/10.26512/rbla.v1i1.12289

Rodriguez-Delfin, Luis A., Verónica E. Rubin-de-Celis and Marco A. Zago. 2001. 'Genetic Diversity in an Andean Population from Peru and Regional Migration Patterns of Amerindians in South America: Data from Y Chromosome and Mitochondrial DNA', *Human Heredity* 51 (1/2): 97–106.

Rodriguez Kembel, Silvia and John W. Rick. 2004. 'Building Authority at Chavín de Huántar: Models of Social Organization and Development in the Initial Period and Early Horizon'. In *Andean Archaeology*, edited by Helaine Silverman, 51–76. Malden, MA: Blackwell.

Roe, Peter G. 1974. *A Further Exploration of the Rowe Chavín Seriation and Its Implications for North Central Coast Chronology*. Washington, DC: Dumbarton Oaks.

Roewer, Lutz and 30 others. 2013. 'Continent-Wide Decoupling of Y-Chromosomal Genetic Variation from Language and Geography in Native South Americans', *PLoS Genetics* 9 (4), Article e1003460: 1–16. Accessed 16 May 2020. https://doi.org/10.1371/journal.pgen.1003460.

Rojas, Pedro. 1969. 'La Huaca Huayurco, Jaen, Cajamarca', *Boletín del Seminario de Arqueología* 4: 48–56.

Rojas Berscia, Luis Miguel. 2015. *Shawi Sketch Grammar*. Manuscript. Nijmegen: Radboud University.

Roos, Robert F. de. 1994. 'La historia del "Disco del Beni"', *Pumapunku* 3 (7): 81–8.

Roosevelt, Anna. 1989. 'Resource Management in Amazonia before the Conquest: Beyond Ethnographic Projection'. In *Resource Management in Amazonia: Indigenous and Folk Strategies*, edited by D.A. Posey and W. Balée, 30–62. New York: New York Botanical Garden.

Roosevelt, Anna Curtenius. 1991. *Moundbuilders of the Amazon: Geophysical Archaeology on Marajo Island, Brazil*. San Diego: Academic Press.

Roosevelt, Anna Curtenius. 1995. 'Early Pottery in the Amazon: Twenty Years of Scholarly Obscurity'. In *The Emergence of Pottery: Technology and Innovation in Ancient Societies*, edited by William Barnett and John W. Hoopes, 115–31. Washington, DC: Smithsonian Institution Press.

Roosevelt, Anna Curtenius. 2013. 'The Amazon and the Anthropocene: 13,000 Years of Human Influence in a Tropical Rainforest', *Anthropocene* 4: 69–87.

Roosevelt, Anna Curtenius. 2017. 'Method and Theory of Early Farming: The Orinoco and Caribbean Coasts of South America', *Earth Science Research* 6 (1): 1–42.

Roosevelt, Anna Curtenius, J. Douglas and L. Brown. 2002. 'The Migrations and Adaptions of the First Americans Clovis and Pre-Clovis Viewed from South America'. In *The First Americans: The Pleistocene Colonization of the New World*, edited by N.G. Jablonski, 159–235. San Francisco: University of California Press.

Roosevelt, Anna Curtenius, R.A. Housley, M. Imazio da Silveira, S. Maranca and R. Johnson. 1991. 'Eighth Millennium Pottery from a Prehistoric Shell Midden in the Brazilian Amazon', *Science* 254 (5038): 1621–4.

Roosevelt, Anna Curtenius and 16 others. 1996. 'Paleoindian Cave Dwellers in the Amazon: The Peopling of the Americas', *Science* 272 (5260): 373–84.

Rose, Françoise. 2014. 'Mojeño Trinitario'. In *Las lenguas de Bolivia,* Vol. 3: *Oriente*, edited by Mily Crevels and Pieter Muysken, 59–97. La Paz: Plural.

Roseman, Charles C. 2004. 'Detecting Interregionally Diversifying Natural Selection on Modern Human Cranial Form by Using Matched Molecular and Morphometric Data', *Proceedings of the National Academy of Sciences of the United States of America* 101 (35): 12824–9.

Roseman, Charles C. and Timothy D. Weaver. 2004. 'Multivariate Apportionment of Global Human Craniometric Diversity', *American Journal of Physical Anthropology* 125 (3): 257–63.

Roseman, Charles C. and Timothy D. Weaver. 2007. 'Molecules versus Morphology? Not for the Human Cranium', *Bioessays* 29 (12): 1185–8. https://doi.org/10.1002/bies.20678

Rosenberg, Noah A., Jonathan K. Pritchard, James L. Weber, Howard M. Cann, Kenneth K. Kidd, Lev A. Zhivotovsky and Marcus W. Feldman. 2002. 'Genetic Structure of Human Populations', *Science* 298 (5602): 2381–5.

Ross, Ann H., Douglas H. Ubelaker and Anthony B. Falsetti. 2002. 'Craniometric Variation in the Americas', *Human Biology* 74 (6): 807–18.

Ross, Ann H., Douglas H. Ubelaker and Sonia Guillén. 2008. 'Craniometric Patterning within Ancient Peru', *Latin American Antiquity* 19 (2): 158–66.

Rossen, Jack. 2011. 'Preceramic Plant Gathering, Gardening, and Farming'. In *From Foraging to Farming in the Andes: New Perspectives on Food Production and Social Organization*, edited by Tom D. Dillehay, 177–92. New York: Cambridge University Press.

Rostain, Stéphen. 2008. 'Agricultural Earthworks on the French Guiana Coast'. In *The Handbook of South American Archaeology*, edited by Helaine Silverman and William H. Isbell, 217–33. New York: Springer.

Rostain, Stéphen. 2013. *Islands in the Rainforest: Landscape Management in Pre-Columbian Amazonia*, translated by Michelle Eliott. Walnut Creek, CA: Left Coast Press.

Rostworowski de Diez Canseco, María. 1991. 'Las Macroetnías en el ámbito andino', *Allpanchis* 22 (35/36): 3–23.

Rostworowski de Diez Canseco, María. 1993. *Ensayos de historia Andina: Elites, etnías, recursos*. Lima: Instituto de Estudios Peruanos.

Rostworowski de Diez Canseco, María. 1999. *Historia del Tahuantinsuyu*. 2nd ed. Lima: Instituto de Estudios Peruanos.

Rothhammer, Francisco and Tom D. Dillehay. 2009. 'The Late Pleistocene Colonization of South America: An Interdisciplinary Perspective', *Annals of Human Genetics* 73 (5): 540–9.

Rothhammer, Francisco and Claudio Silva. 1990. 'Craniometrical Variation among South American Prehistoric Populations: Climatic, Altitudinal, Chronological, and Geographic Contributions', *American Journal of Physical Anthropology* 82 (1): 9–17.

Rowe, John H. 1954. 'El movimiento nacional Inca del siglo XVIII', *Revista Universitaria* (Cuzco) 7: 17–47.

Rowe, John H. 1960. 'Cultural Unity and Diversification in Peruvian Archaeology'. In *Men and Cultures*, edited by A. Wallace. Philadelphia: University of Pennsylvania Press.

Rowe, John H. 1967. 'An Interpretation of Radiocarbon Measurements on Archaeological Samples from Peru'. In *Peruvian Archaeology: Selected Readings*, edited by John H. Rowe and D. Menzel. Palo Alto, CA: Peek.

Rowley-Conwy, Peter and Robert Layton. 2011. 'Foraging and Farming as Niche Construction: Stable and Unstable Adaptations', *Philosophical Transactions of the Royal Society B: Biological Sciences* 366 (1566): 849–62.

Ruiz Barcellos, Jorge Luis. 2011. '"Chachapuya" y "purum": Identidad y simbolización ancestral de una sociedad tardía en el departamento de amazonas', *Arqueología y Sociedad* 23: 1–22.

Ruiz Estrada, A. 2009. *La Alfarería de Kuelap: Tradición y Cambio* (Tesis 04). Lima: Avqi Ediciones.

Ruiz-Narváez, Edward A., Fabricio R. Santos, Denise R. Carvalho-Silva, Jorge Azofeifa, Ramiro Barrantes and Sergio D.J. Pena. 2005. 'Genetic Variation of the Y Chromosome in Chibcha-Speaking Amerindians of Costa Rica and Panama', *Human Biology* 77 (1): 71–91.

Ruppert, Hans. 1982. 'Zur Verbreitung und Herkunft von Türkis und Sodalith in präkolumbischen Kulturen der Kordilleren', *Baessler-Archiv* 30: 69–124.

Ruppert, Hans. 1983. 'Geochemische Untersuchungen an Türkis und Sodalith aus Lagerstätten und Präkolumbischen Kulturen der Kordilleren', *Berliner Beiträge zur Archäometrie* 8: 101–210.

Saad, George. 2012. 'A Grammar Sketch of Shuar, with a Focus on the Verb Phrase'. Master's thesis, Radboud University Nijmegen.

Saignes, T. 1985. *Los Andes Orientales: Historia de un Olvido*. Lima: Instituto Francés de Estudios Andinos.

Saint, Rachel and Kenneth L. Pike. 1962. 'Auca Phonemics'. In *Studies in Ecuadorian Indian Languages, I*, edited by Benjamin Elson, 2–30. Norman: Summer Institute of Linguistics of the University of Oklahoma.

Saintenoy, Thibault. 2016. 'Arqueología de Las Llaqtas del Valle del Apurímac: Contribución al Estudio de la Territorialidad de las Comunidades Aldeanas Serranas en los Andes Prehispánicos', *Chungará* 48 (2): 147–72.

Saint Pierre, Michelle de, Claudio M. Bravi, Josefina M.B. Motti, Noriyuki Fuku, Masashi Tanaka, Elena Llop, Sandro L. Bonatto and Mauricio Moraga. 2012a. 'An Alternative Model for the Early Peopling of Southern South America Revealed by Analyses of Three Mitochondrial DNA Haplogroups', *PLoS One* 7 (9), Article e43486: 1–12. Accessed 17 May 2020. https://doi.org/10.1371/journal.pone.0043486.

Saint Pierre, Michelle de and 14 others. 2012b. 'Arrival of Paleo-Indians to the Southern Cone of South America: New Clues from Mitogenomes', *PLoS One* 7 (12), Article e51311: 1–9. Accessed 17 May 2020. https://doi.org/10.1371/journal.pone.0051311.

Sakel, Jeanette. 2004. *A Grammar of Mosetén*. Berlin: de Gruyter Mouton.

Salazar, Ernesto. 2008. 'Pre-Columbian Mound Complexes in the Upano River Valley, Lowland Ecuador'. In *The Handbook of South American Archaeology*, edited by Helaine Silverman and William H. Isbell, 263–78. New York: Springer.

Salazar-Burger and Richard L. Burger. 1996. 'Cupisnique'. In *Andean Art at Dumbarton Oaks 1*, edited by Elizabeth H. Boone, 87–100. Washington, DC: Dumbarton Oaks Research Library and Collection.

Salomon, Frank. 1985. 'The Dynamic Potential of the Complementarity Concept'. In *Andean Ecology and Civilization: An Interdisciplinary Perspective on Andean Ecological Complementarity*, edited by Shozo Masuda, Izumi Shimada and Craig Morris, 511–31. Tokyo: Tokyo University Press.

Salomon, Frank. 1986. *Native Lords of Quito in the Age of the Incas: The Political Economy of North Andean Chiefdoms*. Cambridge: Cambridge University Press.

Salomon, Frank. 1987. 'A North Andean Status Trader Complex under Inka Rule', *Ethnohistory* 34 (1): 63–77.

Salomon, Frank and George L. Urioste. 1991. *The Huarochirí Manuscript: A Testament of Ancient and Colonial Andean Religion*. Austin: University of Texas Press.

Salzano, Francisco M. and Sidia M. Callegari-Jacques. 1988. *South American Indians: A Case Study in Evolution*. Oxford: Clarendon Press.

Samaniego, Lorenzo. 2007. *Punkurí: Proyecto cultural*. Chimbote: Gráfica Reyes.

Sánchez-Albornoz, Nicolás, 1978. *Indios y tributos en el Alto Perú*. Lima: Instituto de Estudios Peruanos.

Sandoval, José Raul, Daniela R. Lacerda and 9 others. 2013a. 'The Genetic History of Indigenous Populations of the Peruvian and Bolivian Altiplano: The Legacy of the Uros', *PLoS One* 8 (9), Article e73006: 1–11. Accessed 17 May 2020. https://doi.org/10.1371/journal.pone.0073006.

Sandoval, José Raul, Alberto Salazar-Granara, Oscar Acosta, Wilder Castillo-Herrera, Ricardo Fujita, Sergio D.J. Pena and Fabrício R. Santos. 2013b. 'Tracing the genomic ancestry of Peruvians reveals a major legacy of pre-Columbian ancestors', *Journal of Human Genetics*, 58: 627–34. https://doi.org/10.1038/jhg.2013.73

Sandoval, José Raul and 10 others. 2016. 'The Genetic History of Peruvian Quechua-Lamistas and Chankas: Uniparental DNA Patterns among Autochthonous Amazonian and Andean Populations', *Annals of Human Genetics* 80 (2): 88–101. https://doi.org/10.1111/ahg.12145

Sanematsu, Katsuyoshi, ed. 2006. 'The Project Mojos 2005 Report'. Unpublished manuscript. Tokyo: Rikkyo University.

Sanematsu, Katsuyoshi. 2011. 'The Archaeology of the Bolivian Amazon: An Excavation of the Loma Chocolatalito and the Religion and World View of Ancient Mojos Society', *Language, Culture, and Communication: Journal of the College of Intercultural Communication* 3: 43–71.

Santos, Fabrício R., Arpita Pandya, Chris Tyler-Smith, Sérgio D.J. Pena, Moses Schanfield, William R. Leonard, Ludmila Osipova, Michael H. Crawford and R. John Mitchell. 1999. 'The Central Siberian Origin for Native American Y Chromosomes', *American Journal of Human Genetics* 64 (2): 619–28.

Santos-Granero, Fernando. 1992. *Etnohistoria de la Alta Amazonía: Siglos XVI–XVIII*. Quito: Editora Abya-Yala.

Santos-Granero, Fernando. 2002. 'The Arawakan Matrix: Ethos, Language, and History in Native South America'. In *Comparative Arawakan Histories: Rethinking Language Family and Culture Area in Amazonia*, edited by Jonathan David Hill and Fernando Santos-Granero, 25–50. Urbana: University of Illinois Press.

Santos-Granero, Fernando. 2005. 'Las fronteras son creadas para ser transgredidas: Magia, historia y política de la antigua divisoria entre Andes y Amazonía en el Peru', *Histórica* 29 (1): 107–48.

Santos-Granero, Fernando. 2009. 'Introduction: Amerindian Constructional Views of the World'. In *The Occult Life of Things: Native Amazonian Theories of Materiality and Personhood*, edited by Fernando Santos-Granero, 1–29. Tucson: University of Arizona Press.

Sardi, Marina L., Fernando Ramírez Rozzi, Rolando González-José and Héctor M. Pucciarelli. 2005. 'South Amerindian Craniofacial Morphology: Diversity and Implications for Amerindian Evolution', *American Journal of Physical Anthropology* 128 (4): 747–56.

Sauer, Carl Ortwin. 1952. *Agricultural Origins and Dispersals: The Domestication of Animals and Foodstuffs*. Washington, DC: American Geogphysical Union.

Saunaluoma, Sanna. 2012. 'Geometric Earthworks in the State of Acre, Brazil: Excavations at the Fazenda Atlântica and Quinauá Sites', *Latin American Antiquity* 23 (4): 565–83.

Saunaluoma, Sanna. 2013. 'Pre-Columbian Earthwork Sites in the Frontier Region between Brazil and Bolivia, Southwestern Amazon'. PhD thesis, University of Helsinki.

Saunaluoma, Sanna, Martti Pärssinen and Denise Schaan. 2018. 'Diversity of Pre-Colonial Earthworks in the Brazilian State of Acre, Southwestern Amazonia', *Journal of Field Archaeology* 43 (5): 362–79.

Saunaluoma, Sanna and Denise Schaan. 2012. 'Monumentality in Western Amazonian Formative Societies: Geometric Ditched Enclosures in the Brazilian State of Acre', *Antiqua* 2, Article e1: 1–11. Accessed 21 May 2020. https://doi.org/10.4081/antiqua.2012.e1.

Saunders, Nicholas J. 1998a. 'Introduction: Icons of Power'. In *Icons of Power: Feline Symbolism in the Americas*, edited by Nicholas J. Saunders, 1–11. London: Routledge.

Saunders, Nicholas J. 1998b. 'Architecture of Symbolism: The Feline Image'. In *Icons of Power: Feline Symbolism in the Americas*, edited by Nicholas J. Saunders, 12–52. London: Routledge.

Schaan, Denise P. 2001. 'Into the Labyrinths of Marajoara Pottery: Status and Cultural Identity in Prehistoric Amazonia'. In *Unknown Amazon*, edited by Colin McEwan, Cristiana Barreto and Eduardo G. Neves, 108–33. London: British Museum Press.

Schaan, Denise P. 2008. 'The Nonagricultural Chiefdoms of Marajó Island'. In *The Handbook of South American Archaeology*, edited by Helaine Silverman and William H. Isbell, 339–57. New York: Springer.

Schaan, Denise P. 2012. *Sacred Geographies of Ancient Amazonia: Historical Ecology of Social Complexity*. Walnut Creek, CA: Left Coast Press.

Schaan, Denise P., Miriam Bueno, Alceu Ranzi, Antonia Barbosa, Arlan Silva, Edegar Casagrande, Allana Rodrigues, Alessandra Dantas and Ivandra Rampanelli. 2010. 'Construindo paisagens como espaços sociais: O caso dos geoglifos do Acre', *Revista de Arqueologia* 23 (1): 30–41.

Schaan, Denise P., Martti Pärssinen, Alceu Ranzi and Jacó César Piccoli. 2007. 'Geoglifos da Amazônia Ocidental: Evidência de complexidade social entre povos da terra firme', *Revista de Arqueologia* 20: 67–82.

Schaan, Denise P., Alceu Ranzi and Antonia Damasceno Barbosa. 2010. *Geoglifos: Paisagens da Amazônia Ocidental*. Rio Branco: GKNORONHA.

Schaedel, Richard P. 1985. 'Coast-Highland Interrelationships and Ethnic Groups in Northern Peru (500 BC–AD 1980)'. In *Andean Ecology and Civilization: An Interdisciplinary Perspective on Andean Ecological Complementarity*, edited by Shozo Masuda, Izumi Shimada and Craig Morris, 443–74. Tokyo: University of Tokyo Press.

Schjellerup, Inge. 1997. 'Incas and Spaniards in the Conquest of the Chachapoyas: Archaeological and Ethnohistorical Research in the North-Eastern Andes of Peru'. PhD thesis, University of Gothenburg.

Schjellerup, Inge. 2003. *Los valles olvidados: Pasado y presente en la utilización de recursos en la Ceja de Selva, Perú = The Forgotten Valleys: Past and Present in the Utilization of Resources in the Ceja de Selva, Peru*. Copenhagen: National Museum of Denmark.

Schmidt Dias, Adriana and Lucas Bueno. 2014. 'The Initial Colonization of South America Eastern Lowlands: Brazilian Archaeology Contributions to Settlement of the America Models'. In *Paleoamerican Odyssey*, edited by Kelly E. Graf, Caroline V. Ketron and Michael R. Waters, 339–58. College Station: Texas A&M University Press.

Schmitz, Pedro Ignácio, Jairo Henrique Rogge, André Osorio Rosa, Marcus Vinicius Beber and Ellen Augusta Valer de Freitas. 2009. 'Aterros da tradição pantanal nas fazendas Sagrado Coração de Jesus e Bodoquena, Corumbá, MS', *Pesquisas: Antropologia* 67: 321–73.

Schurr, Theodore G. 2004. 'The Peopling of the New World: Perspectives from Molecular Anthropology', *Annual Review of Anthropology* 33: 551–83.

Scliar, Marilia O. and 14 others. 2014. 'Bayesian Inferences Suggest that Amazon Yunga Natives Diverged from Andeans Less than 5000 ybp: Implications for South American Prehistory', *BMC Evolutionary Biology* 14, Article 174: 1–8. Accessed 17 May 2020. https://doi.org/10.1186/s12862-014-0174-3.

Scliar, Marilia O., Giordano B. Soares-Souza, Juliana Chevitarese, Livia Lemos, Wagner C.S. Magalhães, Nelson J. Fagundes, Sandro L. Bonatto, Meredith Yeager, Stephen J. Chanock and Eduardo Tarazona-Santos. 2012. 'The Population Genetics of Quechuas, the Largest Native South American Group: Autosomal Sequences, SNPs, and Microsatellites Evidence High Level of Diversity', *American Journal of Physical Anthropology* 147 (3): 443–51. http://doi.org/10.1002/ajpa.22013.

Seki, Yuji, Juan Pablo Villanueva, Masato Sakai, Diana Alemán, Mauro Ordóñez, Walter Tosso, Araceli Espinoza, Kinya Inokuchi and Daniel Morales. 2008. 'Nuevas evidencias del sitio arqueológico de Pacopampa, en la sierra norte del Perú', *Boletín de Arqueología PUCP* 12: 69–95.

Seki, Yuji and 8 others. 2010. 'Nuevas evidencias del sitio arqueológico de Pacopampa, en la sierra norte del Perú'. In *El Período Formativo: Enfoques y evidencias recientes: Cincuenta años de la Misión Arqueológica Japonesa y su vigencia, I*, edited by Peter Kaulicke and Yoshio Onuki, 69–95. Lima: Pontificia Universidad Católica del Perú.

Serre, David and Svante Pääbo. 2004. 'Evidence for Gradients of Human Genetic Diversity within and among Continents', *Genome Research* 14 (9): 1679–85.

Shady, Ruth. 1971. 'Bagua, una secuencia del Período Formativo en la cuenca inferior de Bagua'. Bachelor's thesis, Universidad Nacional Mayor de San Marcos.

Shady, Ruth. 1974. 'Investigaciones arqueológicas en la Cuenca del Utcubamba'. Paper presented at the 41st International Congress of Americanists, Mexico, 579–89.

Shady Solís, Ruth. 1987. 'Tradición y cambio en las sociedades formativas de Bagua, Amazonas, Perú', *Revista Andina* 5 (2): 457–87.

Shady, Ruth. 1999. 'Sociedades formativas de Bagua-Jaen y sus relaciones andinas y amazónicas'. In *Formativo Sudamericano*, edited by Paulina Ledergerber-Crespo, 201–16. Quito: Abya-Yala.

Shady Solis, Ruth and Carlos Leyva, eds. 2003. *La Ciudad Sagrada del Caral-Supe: Los origenes de la civilizacion Andina y la formacion del estado pristino en el antiguo Peru*. Lima: Instituto Nacional de Cultura.

Shady, Ruth and Hermilio Rosas. 1979. 'El Complejo Bagua y el sistema de establecimientos durante el Formativo en la sierra norte del Perú', *Ñawpa Pacha* 17 (1): 109–42.

Shaver, Harold. 1996. *Diccionario nomatsiguenga–castellano, castellano–nomatsiguenga*. Lima: Ministerio de Educación and Instituto Lingüístico de Verano.

Shell, Olive. 1965. 'Pano Reconstruction'. PhD thesis, University of Pennsylvania.

Sherratt, Andrew. 1981. *Plough and Pastoralism: Aspects of the Secondary Products Revolution*. Cambridge: Cambridge University Press.

Sherratt, Andrew. 1983. 'The Secondary Exploitation of Animals in the Old World', *World Archaeology* 15 (1): 90–104.

Sherwood, Richard J., Dana L. Duren, Ellen W. Demerath, Stefan A. Czerwinski, Roger M. Siervogel and Bradford Towne. 2008. 'Quantitative Genetics of Modern Human Cranial Variation', *Journal of Human Evolution* 54 (6): 909–14.

Shimada, Izumi. 1982. 'Horizontal Archipelago and Coast–Highland Interaction in North Peru: Archaeological Models', *Senri Ethnological Studies* 10: 137–210.

Shimada, Izumi. 1985. 'Introduction'. In *Andean Ecology and Civilization: An Interdisciplinary Perspective on Andean Ecological Complementarity*, edited by Shozo Masuda, Izumi Shimada and Craig Morris, xi–xxxii. Tokyo: Tokyo University Press.

Shimada, Izumi. 1999. 'The Evolution of Andean Diversity: Regional Formations (500 BCE–CE 600)'. In *The Cambridge History of the Native Peoples of the Americas*, Vol. 3: *South America, Part 1*, edited by Frank Salomon and Stuart B. Schwartz, 350–517. Cambridge: Cambridge University Press.

Shimada, Izumi, Carlos Elera and Melody J. Shimada. 1983. 'Excavaciones efectuadas en el centro ceremonial de Huaca Lucía-Chólope del Horizonte Temprano, Batán Grande, costa norte del Perú', *Arqueológicas* 19 (1979–1981): 109–210.

Shock, Myrtle, Claide de Paula Moraes, Jaqueline da Silva Belletti, Márjorie Lima, Francini Medeiros da Silva, Lígia Trombetta Lima, Mariana Franco Cassino and Angela Maria Araújo de Lima. 2014. 'Initial Contributions of Charred Plant Remains from Archaeological Sites in the Amazon to Reconstructions of Historical Ecology'. In *Antes de Orellana: Actas del 3er Encuentro Internacional de Arqueología Amazónica*, edited by Stéphen Rostain, 291–96. Quito: IFEA, FLACSO. Accessed 3 June 2020. https://www.academia.edu/download/35137201/2014_Antes_de_Orellanas_Actas_3EIAA_1.pdf.

Siiriäinen, Ari and Antti Korpisaari, eds. 2002. *Reports of the Finish-Bolivian Archaeological Project in the Bolivian Amazon*. Helsinki: University of Helsinki.

Siiriäinen, Ari and Antti Korpisaari, eds. 2003. *Reports of the Finnish-Bolivian Archaeological Project in the Bolivian Amazon, II*. Helsinki: University of Helsinki.

Siiriäinen, Ari and Martti Pärssinen. 2001. 'The Amazonian Interest of the Inca State (Tawantinsuyu)', *Baessler-Archiv* 49: 45–78.

Silveira, Maura Imázio da, Elisangela Regina de Oliveira, Dirse Clara Kern, Marcondes Lima da Costa and Suyanne Flávia Santos Rodrigues. 2011. 'O sítio Jabuti, em Bragança, Pará, no cenário arqueológico do litoral amazônico', *Boletim do Museu Paraense Emílio Goeldi: Ciências Humanas* 6 (2): 335–45.

Simons, Gary F. and Charles D. Fennig, eds. 2018. *Ethnologue: Languages of the World*. 21st ed. Dallas: SIL International.

Siveroni, Viviana. 2006. 'Mi casa es tu templo: Una visión alternativa de la arquitectura de la tradición Kotosh', *Arqueología y Sociedad* 17: 121–48.

Skar, Sarah Lund. 1994. *Lives Together – Worlds Apart: Quechua Colonization in Jungle and City*. Oslo: Scandinavian University Press.

Skoglund, Pontus, Swapan Mallick, Maria Cátira Bortolini, Niru Chennagiri, Tábita Hünemeier, Maria Luiza Petzl-Erler, Francisco Mauro Salzano, Nick Patterson and David Reich. 2015. 'Genetic Evidence for Two Founding Populations of the Americas', *Nature* 525: 104–8. http://doi.org/10.1038/nature14895.

Skoglund, Pontus, Bernd H. Northoff, Michael V. Shunkov, Anatoli P. Derevianko, Svante Pääbo, Johannes Krause and Mattias Jakobsson. 2014. 'Separating Endogenous Ancient DNA from Modern Day Contamination in a Siberian Neandertal', *Proceedings of the National Academy of Sciences of the United States of America* 111 (6): 2229–34.

Skoglund, Pontus and David Reich. 2016. 'A Genomic View of the Peopling of the Americas', *Current Opinion in Genetics and Development* 41: 27–35. https://doi.org/10.1016/j.gde.2016.06.016.

Smith, Michael E., Gary M. Feinman, Robert D. Drennan, Timothy Earle and Ian Morris. 2012. 'Archaeology as a Social Science', *Proceedings of the National Academy of Sciences of the United States of America* 109 (20): 7617–21.

Snell, Betty E. 1978. *Machiguenga: Fonología y vocabulario breve*. Pucallpa: Instituto Lingüístico del Verano.

Snell, Betty E. 1998. *Pequeño diccionario machiguenga–castellano*. Lima: Instituto Lingüístico de Verano.

Sombroek, Wim G. 1966. *Amazon Soils: A Reconnaissance of the Soils of the Brazilian Amazon Region*. Wageningen: Centre for Agricultural Publications and Documentation.

Sparing-Chávez, Margarethe. 2012. *Aspects of Amahuaca Grammar: An Endangered Language of the Amazon Basin*. Dallas: SIL International.

Sparks, Corey S. and Richard L. Jantz. 2002. 'A Reassessment of Human Cranial Plasticity: Boas Revisited', *Proceedings of the National Academy of Sciences of the United States of America* 99 (23): 14636–39.

Stackelbeck, Kary and Tom D. Dillehay. 2011. 'Tierra Blanca Phase (7800–5000 BP)'. In *From Foraging to Farming in the Andes: New Perspectives on Food Production and Social Organization*, edited by Tom D. Dillehay, 117–34. New York: Cambridge University Press.

Stahl, Peter W. 2004. 'Archaeology: Greater Expectations', *Nature* 432: 561–2.

Stahl, Peter W. 2005. 'An Exploratory Osteological Study of the Muscovy Duck (*Cairina moschata*) (Aves: Anatidae) with Implications for Neotropical Archaeology', *Journal of Archaeological Science* 32 (6): 915–29.

Stahl, Peter W. 2008. 'Animal Domestication in South America'. In *The Handbook of South American Archaeology*, edited by Helaine Silverman and William H. Isbell, 121–30. New York: Springer.

Stahl, Peter W. 2015. 'Interpreting Interfluvial Landscape Transformations in the Pre-Columbian Amazon', *The Holocene* 25 (10): 1598–603.

Stahl, Peter W., Michael C. Muse and Florencio Delgado-Espinoza. 2006. 'New Evidence for Pre-Columbian Muscovy Duck *Cairina moschata* from Ecuador', *Ibis* 148 (4): 657–63.

Stanish, Charles. 2001. 'The Origin of State Societies in South America', *Annual Review of Anthropology* 30: 41–64.

Stark, Louisa R. 1972. 'Machaj-Juyai: Secret Language of the Callahuayas', *Papers in Andean Linguistics* 1 (2): 199–218.

Stern, Steve J. 1987. 'The Age of Andean Insurrection, 1742–1782: A Reappraisal'. In *Resistance, Rebellion, and Consciousness in the Andean Peasant World, 18th to 20th Centuries*, edited by Steve J. Stern, 34–93. Madison: University of Wisconsin Press.

Stern, Steve J. 1993. *Peru's Indian Peoples and the Challenge of Spanish Conquest: Huamanga to 1640*. 2nd ed. Madison: University of Wisconsin Press.

Steward, Julian H., ed. 1946. *Handbook of South American Indians, Volume 2: The Andean Civilizations*. Washington, DC: Smithsonian Institution.

Steward, Julian H., ed. 1948. *Handbook of South American Indians, Volume 3: The Tropical Forest Tribes*. Washington, DC: Smithsonian Institution.

Steward, Julian H., ed. 1963. *Handbook of South American Indians*. New York: Cooper Square Publishers.

Steward, Julian H. and Louis C. Faron. 1959. *Native Peoples of South America*. New York: McGraw-Hill.

Stothert, Karen E., Dolores R. Piperno and Thomas C. Andres. 2003. 'Terminal Pleistocene/Early Holocene Human Adaptation in Coastal Ecuador: The Las Vegas Evidence', *Quaternary International* 109/110: 23–43.

Strauss, André, Mark Hubbe, Walter A. Neves, Danilo V. Bernardo and João Paulo V. Atuí. 2015. 'The Cranial Morphology of the Botocudo Indians, Brazil', *American Journal of Physical Anthropology* 157 (2): 202–16.

Suárez, Jorge A. 1969. 'Moseten and Pano-Tacanan', *Anthropological Linguistics* 11 (9): 255–66.

Suárez, Jorge A. 1977. 'La posición lingüística del mosetén, del panotacana y del arahuaco', *Anales de Antropología* 14 (1): 243–255.

Suárez, Rafael. 2015. 'The Paleoamerican Occupation of the Plains of Uruguay: Technology, Adaptations, and Mobility', *PaleoAmerica* 1 (1): 88–104.

Sunquist, Mel and Fiona Sunquist. 2002. *Wild Cats of the World*. Chicago: University of Chicago Press.

Swadesh, Morris. 1959. *Mapas de clasificación lingüística de México y las Américas* (Cuadernos del Instituto de Historia 51; Serie Antropológica 8). México City: Universidad Nacional Autónoma de México.

Swift, Kenneth E. 1988. *Morfología del caquinte (Arawak preandino)*. Yarinacocha: Ministerio de Educación and Instituto Lingüístico de Verano.

Tarazona-Santos, Eduardo, Denise R. Carvalho-Silva, Davide Pettener, Donata Luiselli, Gian Franco De Stefano, Cristina Martinez Labarga, Olga Rickards, Chris Tyler-Smith, Sérgio D.J. Pena and Fabrício R. Santos. 2001.

'Genetic Differentiation in South Amerindians is Related to Environmental and Cultural diversity: Evidence from the Y Chromosome', *American Journal of Human Genetics* 68 (6): 1485–96.

Tarazona-Santos, Eduardo and Fabrício R. Santos. 2002. 'The Peopling of the Americas: A Second Major Migration?', *American Journal of Human Genetics* 70 (5): 1377–80.

Taylor, Anne-Christine. 1992. 'História Pós-Colombiana da Alta Amazônia'. In *História dos Índios no Brasil*, edited by Manuela Carneiro da Cunha, 213–38. São Paulo: Companhia das Letras.

Taylor, Anne-Christine. 1999. 'The Western Margins of Amazonia from the Early Sixteenth to the Early Nineteenth Century'. In *The Cambridge History of the Native Peoples of the Americas*, Vol. 3: *South America, Part 2*, edited by Frank Salomon and Stuart B. Schwartz, 188–256. Cambridge: Cambridge University Press.

Taylor, Gérald. 1999. *Ritos y Tradiciones de Huarochirí* (Travaux de l'Institut Français d'Études Andines 116), edited and translated by Gerald Taylor. 2nd ed. Lima: Instituto Francés de Estudios Andinos, Banco Central de Reserva del Perú and Universidad Particular Ricardo Palma.

Tellenbach, Michael. 1998. *Chavín: Investigaciones acerca del desarrollo cultural Centro-Andino en las épocas Ofrendas y Chavín-Tardío*. Andes (Boletín de la Misión Arqueológica Andina 2). Warsaw: University of Warsaw, Polish Society for Latin American Studies.

Tello, J.C. 1923. 'Wira-Kocha', *Inca* 1: 93–320; 583–606.

Tello, J.C. 1960. *Chavín, cultura matriz de la civilización andina: Con revisión de Toribio Mejía Xesspe*. Lima: Impr. de la Universidad de San Marcos.

Ter Steege, Hans and 119 others. 2013. 'Hyperdominance in the Amazonian Tree Flora', *Science* 342 (6156), Article 1243092: 1–9. Accessed 17 May 2020. https://doi.org/10.1126/science.1243092.

Thomason, Sarah G. 2001. *Language Contact: An Introduction*. Edinburgh: Edinburgh University Press.

Thomason, Sarah G. and Terrence Kaufman. 1988. *Language Contact, Creolization, and Genetic Linguistics*. Berkeley: University of California Press.

Thompson, Donald E. 1980. 'The Precolumbian and Colonial Heritage of Rapayán', *Archaeology* 33 (2): 44–51.

Thompson, Donald E. 1983. 'Buildings Are for People: Speculations on the Aesthetics and Cultural Impact of Structures and Their Arrangement'. In *Prehistoric Settlement Patterns: Essays in Honor of Gordon R. Willey*, edited by Egon Z. Vogt and Richard M. Leventhal, Cambridge, MA: Peabody Museum.

Thornton, Russell. 2005. 'Native American Demographic and Tribal Survival into the Twenty-First Century', *American Studies* 46 (3/4): 23–38.

Thurner, Mark. 1997. *From Two Republics to One Divided: Contradictions of Postcolonial Nationmaking in Andean Peru*. Durham, NC: Duke University Press.

Tobar, Maria Elena. 1995. 'Modo, aspecto y tiempo en Cofán'. PhD thesis, Universidad de los Andes.

Topic, John. 1992. 'La Huacas de Huamachuco: Precisiones en torno a una Imágen Indígena de un Paisaje Andino'. In *La Persecución del Demonio: Crónica de los Primeros Agustinos en el Norte del Perú*, edited by E.E. Deeds. Málaga: Editorial Algazara.

Topic, John. 1998. 'Ethnogenesis in Huamachuco', *Andean Past* 5: 109–27.

Topic, John, Theresa Topic and Alfredo Melly Cava. 2002. 'Catequil: The Archaeology, Ethnohistory, and Ethnography of a Major Provincial Huaca'. In *Andean Archaeology I: Variations in Sociopolitical Organization*, edited by William H. Isbell and Helaine Silverman, 303–37. New York: Plenum Press.

Torero, Alfredo. 1964. 'Los dialectos quechuas', *Anales científicos de la Universidad Agraria* 2 (4): 446–78.

Torero, Alfredo. 1970. 'Lingüística e historia de la Sociedad Andina', *Anales Científicos de la Universidad Agraria* 8 (3/4): 231–64.

Torero, Alfredo. 1972. 'Lingüística e historia de la sociedad andina'. In *El reto del multilingüismo en el Perú*, edited by Alberto Escobar, 51–106. Lima: Instituto de Estudios Peruanos. https://repositorio.iep.org.pe/bitstream/IEP/661/2/peruproblema9.pdf

Torero, Alfredo. 1984. 'El comercio lejano y la difusión del quechua: El caso de Ecuador', *Revista Andina* 2 (2): 367–402.

Torero, Alfredo. 1987. 'Lenguas y pueblos altiplánicos en torno al siglo XVI', *Revista Andina* 5 (2): 329–405.

Torero, Alfredo. 1989. 'Areas toponímicas e idiomas en la sierra norte peruana: Un trabajo de recuperación lingüística', *Revista Andina* 7 (1): 217–57.

Torero, Alfredo. 1992. 'Acerca de la familia lingüística uruquilla (Uru-Chipaya)', *Revista Andina* 10 (1): 171–91.

Torero, Alfredo. 2002. *Idiomas de los Andes: Lingüística e Historia*. Lima: Editorial Horizonte and Institut Français d'Études Andines.

Torres, Constantino Manuel. 1987. *The Iconography of South American Snuff Trays and Related Paraphernalia*. Gothenburg: Göteborgs Etnografiska Museum.

Torroni, Antonio, Alessandro Achilli, Vincent Macaulay, Martin Richards, Hans-Jürgen Bandelt. 2006. 'Harvesting the Fruit of the Human mtDNA Tree', *Trends in Genetics* 22 (6): 339–45.

Torroni, Antonio, Theodore G. Schurr, Margaret F. Cabell, Michael D. Brown, James V. Neel, Merethe Larsen, David G. Smith, Carlos M. Vullo and Douglas C. Wallace. 1993. 'Asian Affinities and Continental Radiation of the Four Founding Native American mtDNAs', *American Journal of Human Genetics* 53 (3): 563–90.

Tyuleneva, Vera. 2007. 'La tierra del Paititi y el Lago Rogoaguado', *Estudios Amazónicos* 4 (6): 97–154.

Tyuleneva, Vera. 2010. *Cuatro viajes a la Amazonía Boliviana*. La Paz: Zeus.

Tyuleneva, Vera. 2011. 'El Paititi y las expediciones incas en la selva al este del Cusco'. In *Paititi: Ensayos y documentos* (Serie Scripta Autochtona 8), edited by Isabelle Combès and Vera Tyuleneva, 7–22. Cochabamba: Instituto Latinoamericano de Misionología – Editorial Itinerarios.

Tyuleneva, Vera. 2012. 'El Paititi en la geografía histórica'. PhD thesis, Pontificia Universidad Católica del Perú.

Tyuleneva, Vera. 2015. *Buscando Ayavirezamo: Nuevos datos sobre la historia de Apolobamba*. La Paz: FOBOMADE.

Underhill, Peter A. and Toomas Kivisild. 2007. 'Use of Y Chromosome and Mitochondrial DNA Population Structure in Tracing Human Migrations', *Annual Review of Genetics* 41: 539–64.

Underhill, P.A., G. Passarino, A.A. Lin, P. Shen, M. Mirazón Lahr, R.A. Foley, P.J. Oefner and L.L. Cavalli-Sforza. 2001. 'The Phylogeography of Y Chromosome Binary Haplotypes and the Origins of Modern Human Populations', *Annals of Human Genetics* 65 (1): 43–62.

Urrego, Dunia H., Mark B. Bush, Miles R. Silman, Alexander Y. Correa-Metrio, Marie-Pierre Ledru, Francis E. Mayle, Gina Paduano and Bryan G. Valencia. 2009. 'Millennial-Scale Ecological Changes in Tropical South America since the Last Glacial Maximum'. In *Past Climate Variability in South America and Surrounding Regions*, edited by Francoise Vimeux, Florence Sylvestre and Myriam Khodri, 283–300. Dordrecht: Springer.

Urrego, Dunia H., Mark B. Bush, Miles R. Silman, Brittany A. Niccum, Paulina De La Rosa, Crystal H. McMichael, Stephen Hagen and Michael Palace. 2013. 'Holocene Fires, Forest Stability and Human Occupation in South-Western Amazonia', *Journal of Biogeography* 40 (3): 521–33.

Urton, Gary. 1996. 'R. Tom Zuidema, Dutch Structuralism, and the Application of the "Leiden Orientation" to Andean Studies', *Journal of the Steward Anthropological Society* 24 (1/2): 1–36.

Urton, Gary. 1999. *Inca Myths*. London: British Museum Press.

Urton, Gary. 2003. *Signs of the Inka Khipu: Binary Coding in the Andean Knotted-String Records*. Austin: University of Texas Press.

Urton, Gary. 2012. 'The Herder–Cultivator Relationship as a Paradigm for Archaeological Origins, Linguistic Dispersals and the Evolution of Record-Keeping in the Andes'. In *Archaeology and Language in the Andes: A Cross-Disciplinary Exploration of Prehistory*, edited by Paul Heggarty and David Beresford-Jones, 321–43. Oxford: Oxford University Press. http://doi.org/10.5871/bacad/9780197265031.003.0013.

Uzendoski, Michael A. 2004. 'Manioc Beer and Meat: Value, Reproduction and Cosmic Substance among the Napo Runa of the Ecuadorian Amazon', *Journal of the Royal Anthropological Institute* 10 (4): 883–902.

Valdez, Francisco. 2008. 'Inter-Zonal Relationships in Ecuador'. In *The Handbook of South American Archaeology*, edited by Helaine Silverman and William H. Isbell, 865–88. New York: Springer.

Valdez, Francisco. 2014. 'Investigaciones arqueológicas en Palanda, Santa Ana-La Florida (Ecuador)'. In *Arqueología Alto Amazónica: Los orígenes de la civilización en el Perú*, edited by Quirino Olivera Núñez, 222–45. Lima: Apus Graph Ediciones.

Valdez, Francisco, Jean Guffroy, Geoffroy de Saulieu, Julio Hurtado and Alexandra Yepes. 2005. 'Découverte d'un site cérémoniel formatif sur le versant oriental des Andes', *Comptes Rendus Palevol* 4 (4): 369–74.

Valenzuela, Pilar M. 2003. 'Transitivity in Shipibo-Konibo Grammar'. PhD thesis, University of Oregon.

Valenzuela, Pilar. 2012. *Voces Shiwilu: 400 Años de resistencia lingüística en Jeberos*. Lima: Fondo Editorial Pontificia Universidad Católica del Perú.

Valenzuela, Pilar and Antoine Guillaume. 2017. 'Estudios sincrónicos y diacrónicos sobre lenguas Pano y Takana: Una introducción', *Amerindia* 39 (1): 1–49.

Valenzuela, Pilar and Roberto Zariquiey. 2015. 'In Defense of the Pano-Takana Hypothesis'. Unpublished manuscript.

Vallejos Yopán, Rosa. 2010. 'A Grammar of Kokama-Kokamilla'. PhD thesis, University of Oregon.

Van Gijn, Rik. 2006. 'A Grammar of Yurakaré'. PhD thesis, Radboud University Nijmegen.

Van Gijn, Rik. 2012. 'Switch-Attention (aka Switch-Reference) in South-American Temporal Clauses: Facilitating Oral Transmission', *Linguistic Discovery* 10 (1): 112–27.

Van Gijn, Rik. 2014a. 'The Andean Foothills and Adjacent Amazonian Fringe'. In *The Native Languages of South America: Origins, Development, Typology*, edited by Loretta O'Connor and Pieter Muysken, 102–25. Cambridge: Cambridge University Press.

Van Gijn, Rik. 2014b. 'Subordination Strategies in South America: Nominalization'. In *The Native Languages of South America: Origins, Development, Typology*, edited by Loretta O'Connor and Pieter Muysken, 274–96. Cambridge: Cambridge University Press.

Van Gijn, Rik. 2016. 'Switch Reference in Western South America'. In *Switch Reference 2.0*, edited by Rik Van Gijn and Jeremy Hammond, 153–26. Amsterdam: John Benjamins.

Van Gijn, Rik. 2019. 'Case Markers as Subordinators in South American Indigenous Languages'. In *Nominalization in Languages of the Americas*, edited by Roberto Zariquiey, Masayoshi Shibatani and David W. Fleck, 197–247. Amsterdam: John Benjamins Publishing Company.

Van Gijn, Rik, Harald Hammarström, Simon van de Kerke, Olga Krasnoukhova and Pieter Muysken. 2017. 'Linguistic Areas, Linguistic Convergence and River Systems in South America'. In *The Cambridge Handbook of Areal Linguistics*, edited by Raymond Hickey, 964–96. Cambridge: Cambridge University Press. http://doi.org/10.1017/9781107279872.034

Van Gijn, Rik and Pieter Muysken. 2016. 'Linguistic Areas', *Oxford Bibliographies*. Accessed 17 May 2020. https://doi.org/10.1093/obo/9780199772810-0133.

Van Wouden, Franciscus Antonius Evert 1935. *Sociale structuurtypen in de Groote Oost*. Leiden: J. Ginsberg.

Van Wouden, Franciscus Antonius Evert 1956. 'Locale groepen en dubbele afstamming in Kodi, West Sumba', *Bijdragen tot de Taal-, Land-, en Volkenkunde* 112 (2): 204–46.

Van Wouden, Franciscus Antonius Evert 1968. *Types of Social Structure in Eastern Indonesia*. The Hague: Nijhoff.

Van Wouden, Franciscus Antonius Evert. 1983. 'Local Groups and Double Descent in Kodi, West Sumba [1956]'. In *Structural Anthropology in the Netherlands: A Reader*, edited by P. E. de Josselin de Jong. Dordrecht: Foris.

Varela, Héctor Hugo and José Alberto Cocilovo. 2007. 'Phenotypic, Maximum Genetic, and Special Environmental Variability in Prehistoric Human Populations', *American Journal of Physical Anthropology* 132 (1): 17–24.

Varese, Stefano. 2006 [1st ed. published 1968]. *La sal de los cerros: Resistencia y utopía an la Amazonía peruana*. 4th ed. Lima: Fondo Editorial del Congreso del Perú.

Vásquez, Víctor and Teresa Rosales Tham. 2014. 'Restos de fauna y vegetales de Huaca Ventarrón: Unidad III–X'. In *Ventarrón y Collud: Origen y auge de la civilización en la costa norte del Perú*, edited by Ignacio Alva, 251–72. Lima: Ministerio de Cultura.

Vavilov, N.I. 1992. *Origin and Geography of Cultivated Plants*, translated by Doris Löve. Cambridge: Cambridge University Press.

Vigouroux, Yves, Jeffrey C. Glaubitz, Yoshihiro Matsuoka, Major M. Goodman, Jesús Sánchez G. and John Doebley. 2008. 'Population Structure and Genetic Diversity of New World Maize Races Assessed by DNA Microsatellites', *American Journal of Botany* 95 (10): 1240–53.

Villafañe, Lucrecia. 2004. 'Gramática Yuki'. PhD thesis , Radboud University Nijmegen.

Viveiros de Castro, Eduardo. 1996. 'Images of Nature and Society in Amazonian Ethnology', *Annual Review of Anthropology* 25: 179–200.

Von den Driesch, A. and R. Hutterer. 2012. 'Mazamas, Patos criollos y anguilas de lodo: Restos de subsidencia del asentamiento precolombino "Loma Salvatierra", Llanos de Mojos, Bolivia', *Zeitschrift für Archäologie Außereuropäischer Kulturen* 4: 341–67.

Von Kaupp, Robert and Octavio Fernández Carrasco. 2010. *Vilcabamba desconocida: exploraciones 1997–2003*. Cusco: Gráfica Rivera.

Vuillermet, Marine. 2012. 'A Grammar of Ese Ejja, a Takanan Language of the Bolvian Amazon'. PhD thesis, Université Lumière Lyon 2.

Wachtel, Nathan. 1973. 'Pensamiento salvaje y aculturación: El espacio y el tiempo en Felipe Guamán Poma de Ayala y el Inca Garcilaso de la Vega'. In *Sociedad e ideologia: Ensayos de historia y antropologia Andinas* by Nathan Wachtel, 165–218. Lima: Instituto de Estudios Peruanos.

Wachtel, Nathan. 1986. 'Men of the Water: The Uru Problem (XVI and XVII Centuries)'. In *Anthropological History of Andean Polities*, edited by John V. Murra, Nathan Wachtel and Jacques Revel. Cambridge: Cambridge University Press.

Wagner, Gustavo, Klaus Hilbert, Dione Bandeira, Maria Cristina Tenório and Maria Mercedes Okumura. 2011. 'Sambaquis (Shell Mounds) of the Brazilian Coast', *Quaternary International* 239 (1/2): 51–60.

Walker, Charles F. 2008. *Shaky Colonialism: The 1746 Earthquake-Tsunami in Lima, Peru, and Its Long Aftermath*. Durham, NC: Duke University Press.

Walker, Charles F. 2014. *The Tupac Amaru Rebellion*. Cambridge, MA: Harvard University Press.

Walker, Harry. 2012. 'Demonic Trade: Debt, Materiality, and Agency in Amazonia', *Journal of the Royal Anthropological Institute* 18 (1): 140–59.

Walker, John Hamilton. 1999. 'Agricultural Change in the Bolivian Amazon'. PhD thesis, University of Pennsylvania.

Walker, John Hamilton. 2004. *Agricultural Change in the Bolivian Amazon – Cambio Agrícola en la Amazonía Boliviana* (Memoirs in Latin American Archaeology 13). Pittsburgh: University of Pittsburgh Latin American Archaeology Publications and Trinidad (Bolivia): Fundación Kenneth Lee.

Walker, John H. 2008a. 'Pre-Columbian Ring Ditches along the Yacuma and Rapulo Rivers, Beni, Bolivia: A Preliminary Review', *Journal of Field Archaeology* 33 (4): 413–27.

Walker, John H. 2008b. 'The Llanos de Mojos'. In *The Handbook of South American Archaeology*, edited by Helaine Silverman and William H. Isbell, 927–39. New York: Springer.

Walker, John H. 2011a. 'Amazonian Dark Earth and Ring Ditches in the Central Llanos de Mojos, Bolivia', *Culture, Agriculture, Food and Environment* 33 (1): 2–14.

Walker, John H. 2011b. 'Ceramic Assemblages and Landscape in the Mid-1st Millennium Llanos de Mojos, Beni, Bolivia', *Journal of Field Archaeology* 36 (2): 119–31.

Walker, John H. 2012. 'Recent Landscape Archaeology in South America', *Journal of Archaeological Research* 20 (4): 309–55.

Walker, John H. 2018. *Island, River, and Field: Landscape Archaeology in the Llanos de Mojos*. Albuquerque: University of New Mexico Press.

Walker, Robert S. and Lincoln A. Ribeiro. 2011. 'Bayesian Phylogeography of the Arawak Expansion in Lowland South America', *Proceedings of the Royal Society B: Biological Sciences* 278 (1718): 2562–7. http://doi.org/10.1098/rspb.2010.2579.

Wall, Jeffrey D., Rong Jiang, Christopher Gignoux, Gary K. Chen, Celeste Eng, Scott Huntsman and Paul Marjoram. 2011. 'Genetic Variation in Native Americans, Inferred from Latino SNP and Resequencing Data', *Molecular Biology and Evolution* 28 (8): 2231–7.

Wang, Sijia and 26 others. 2007. 'Genetic Variation and Population Structure in Native Americans', *PLoS Genetics* 3 (11): 2049–67.

Wassén, S. Henry, ed. 1972. *A Medicine-Man's Implements and Plants in a Tiahuanacoid Tomb in Highland Bolivia*. Gothenburg: Göteborgs Etnografiska Museum.

Waters, Michael R. and Thomas W. Stafford. 2014. 'The First Americans: A Review of the Evidence for the Late-Pleistocene Peopling of the Americas'. In *Paleoamerican Odyssey*, edited by Kelly E. Graf, Caroline V. Ketron and Michael R. Waters, 541–60. College Station: Texas A&M University Press.

Watling, Jennifer, José Iriarte, Francis E. Mayle, Denise Schaan, Luiz C.R. Pessenda, Neil J. Loader, F. Alayne Street-Perrott, Ruth E. Dickau, Antonia Damasceno and Alceu Ranzi. 2017. 'Impact of Pre-Columbian "Geoglyph" Builders on Amazonian Forests', *Proceedings of the National Academy of Sciences of the United States of America* 114 (8): 1868–73.

Watling, Jennifer, Myrtle P. Shock, Guilherme Z. Mongeló, Fernando O. Almeida, Thiago Kater, Paulo E. De Oliveira and Eduardo G. Neves. 2018. 'Direct Archaeological Evidence for Southwestern Amazonia as an Early Plant Domestication and Food Production Centre', *PLoS One* 13 (7), Article e0199868: 1–28. Accessed 17 May 2020. https://doi.org/10.1371/journal.pone.0199868.

Weber, David John. 1989. *A Grammar of Huallaga (Huánuco) Quechua*. Berkeley: University of California Press.

Weber, David J. 2005. *Bárbaros: Spaniards and Their Savages in the Age of Enlightenment*. New Haven: Yale University Press.

Weng, Chengyu, Mark B. Bush, Jason H. Curtis, Alan L. Kolata, Tom D. Dillehay and Michael W. Binford. 2006. 'Deglaciation and Holocene Climate Change in the Western Peruvian Andes', *Quaternary Research* 66 (1): 87–96.

Whitney, Bronwen S., Francis E. Mayle, Surangi W. Punyasena, Katharine A. Fitzpatrick, Michael J. Burn, René Guillen, Ezequiel Chavez, David Mann, R. Toby Pennington and Sarah E. Metcalfe. 2011. 'A 45 kyr Palaeoclimate Record from the Lowland Interior of Tropical South America', *Palaeogeography, Palaeoclimatology, Palaeoecology* 307 (1–4): 177–92.

Wightman, Ann M. 1990. *Indigenous Migration and Social Change: The Forasteros of Cuzco, 1570–1720*. Durham, NC: Duke University Press.

Wilder, Jason A., Sarah B. Kingan, Zahra Mobasher, Maya Metni Pilkington and Michael F. Hammer. 2004. 'Global Patterns of Human Mitochondrial DNA and Y-Chromosome Structure Are Not Influenced by Higher Migration Rates of Females versus Males', *Nature Genetics* 36: 1122–5.

Wilkinson, Darryl. 2013. 'Politics, Infrastructure and Non-Human Subjects: The Inka Occupation of the Amaybamba Cloud Forests'. PhD thesis, Columbia University.

Wilkinson, Darryl. 2018. 'The Influence of Amazonia on State Formation in the Ancient Andes', *Antiquity* 92 (365): 1362–76.

Willerslev, Eske and Alan Cooper. 2005. 'Ancient DNA', *Proceedings of the Royal Society B: Biological Sciences* 272 (1558): 3–16.

Willey, Gordon R. and Philip Phillips. 1958. *Method and Theory in American Archaeology*. Chicago: University of Chicago Press.

Williams, Caroline A. 2004. *Between Resistance and Adaptation: Indigenous Peoples and the Colonisation of the Chocó, 1510–1753*. Liverpool: Liverpool University Press.

Williams-Blangero, S. and J. Blangero. 1989. 'Anthropometric Variation and the Genetic Structure of the Jirels of Nepal', *Human Biology* 61 (1): 1–12.

Williams-Blangero, S. and J. Blangero. 1990. 'Effects of Population Structure on Within-Group Variation in the Jirels of Nepal', *Human Biology* 62 (1): 131–46.

Wise, Mary Ruth. 2014. 'Rastros desconcertantes de contactos entre idiomas y culturas a lo largo de los contrafuertes orientales de los Andes del Perú'. In *Estudios sobre lenguas Andinas y Amazónicas: Homenaje a Rodolfo Cerrón-Palomino*, edited by Willem E.H. Adelaar, Pilar Valenzuela Bismarck and Roberto Zariquiey Biondi, 305–26. Lima: Fondo Editorial, Universidad Católica del Perú.

Wistrand-Robinson, Lila. 1991. 'Uto-Aztecan Affinities with Panoan of Peru I: Correspondences'. In *Language Change in South American Indian Languages*, edited by Mary Ritchie Key, 243–76. Philadelphia: University of Pennsylvania Press.

Wood, Jacquelyn L.A., Defne Tezel, Destin Joyal and Dylan J. Fraser. 2015. 'Population Size is Weakly Related to Quantitative Genetic Variation and Trait Differentiation in a Stream Fish', *Evolution* 69 (9): 2303–18.

Woods, William I., Wenceslau G. Teixeira, Johannes Lehmann, Christoph Steiner, Antoinette WinklerPrins and Lilian Rebellato, eds. 2009. *Amazonian Dark Earths: Wim Sombroek's Vision*. Dordrecht: Springer.

Yamamoto, Atsushi. 2008. 'Ingatambo: Un sitio estratégico de contacto interregional en la zona norte del Perú', *Boletín de Arqueología PUCP* 12: 25–51.

Yamamoto, Atsushi. 2010. 'Ingatambo: Un sitio estratégico de contacto interregional en la zona norte del Perú'. In *El Período Formativo: Enfoques y evidencias recientes: Cincuenta años de la Misión Arqueológica Japonesa y su vigencia, I*, edited by Peter Kaulicke and Yoshio Onuki, 219–47. Lima: Pontificia Universidad Católica del Perú.

Yamamoto, Atsushi. 2012. 'Las rutas interregionales en el Período Formativo para el norte del Perú y el sur del Ecuador: Una perspectiva desde el sitio Ingatambo, valle de Huancabamba', *Arqueología y Sociedad* 25: 9–34.

Yang, Ning Ning and 25 others. 2010. 'Contrasting Patterns of Nuclear and mtDNA Diversity in Native American Populations', *Annals of Human Genetics* 74 (6): 525–38.

Y-Chromosome Consortium. 2002. 'A nomenclature system for the tree of human Y-chromosomal binary haplo-groups'. *Genome Research* 12, 339–48. https://doi.org/10.1101/gr.217602

Zariquiey Biondi, Roberto. 2011. 'A Grammar of Kashibo-Kakataibo'. PhD thesis, La Trobe University.

Zarzar, Alonso. 1989. *"Apo Capac Huayna, Jesús Sacramentado": Mito, utopía y milenarismo en el pensamiento de Juan Santos Atahualpa*. Lima: Centro Amazónico de Antropología y Aplicación Práctica.

Zeder, Melinda A. 2015. 'Core Questions in Domestication Research', *Proceedings of the National Academy of Sciences of the United States of America* 112 (11): 3191–8.

Zeidler, James A. 1988. 'Feline Imagery, Stone Mortars, and Formative Period Interaction Spheres in the Northern Andean Area', *Journal of Latin American Lore* 14 (2): 243–83.

Zihlmann, N. 2016. 'Shell Middens in the Llanos de Moxos: A Quantitative Approach'. Master's thesis, University of Bern.

Zubrow, Ezra B.W. 2005. 'Prehistoric Space: An Archaeological Perspective', *Journal of World Anthropology: Occasional Papers* 2 (1): 1–42.

Zuidema, R. Tom. 1964. *The Ceque System of Cuzco: The Social Organization of the Capital of the Inca*. Leiden: E.J. Brill.

Zuidema, R. Tom. 1965. 'American Social Systems and Their Mutual Similarity', *Bijdragen tot de Taal-, Land-, en Volkenkunde* 121 (1): 103–19.

Zuidema, R. Tom. 1966. 'El calendario Inca'. In *XXXVI Congreso Internacional de Americanistas, España, 1964: Actas y memorias*, Vol. 2, edited by Alfredo Jiménez Núñez, 25–30. Seville: ECESA.

Zuidema, R. Tom. 1977. 'The Inca Kinship System: A New Theoretical View'. In *Andean Kinship and Marriage* (Special Publication of the American Anthropological Association 7), edited by Ralph Bolton and Enrique Mayer, 240–81. Washington, DC: American Anthropological Association.

Zuidema, R. Tom. 1983. 'Hierarchy and Space in Incaic Social Organization', *Ethnohistory* 30 (2): 49–75.

Zuidema, R. Tom. 1990. *Inca Civilization in Cuzco*, translated by Jean-Jacques Decoster. Austin: University of Texas Press.

Zuidema, R. Tom. 1991. 'Guamán Poma and the Art of Empire: Towards an Iconography of Inca Royal Dress'. In *Transatlantic Encounters: Europeans and Andeans in the Sixteenth Century*, edited by Kenneth J. Andrien and Rolena Adorno, 151–202. Berkeley: University of California Press.

Zuidema, R. Tom. 1992. 'El encuentro de los calendarios Andino y Español'. In *Los Conquistados: 1492 y la población indígena de las Américas*, edited by Heraclio Bonilla, 287–316. Quito: Tercer Mundo editores, FLACSO.

Zuidema, R. Tom. 1995. *El sistema de Ceques del Cuzco: La organización social de la capital de los Incas: Con nuevo ensayo preliminar*. Lima: Pontificia Universidad Católica del Perú, Fondo Editorial.

Zuidema, R. Tom. 2011. *El calendario Inca: Tiempo y espacio en la organización ritual del Cuzco: La idea del pasado*. Lima: Fondo Editorial del Congreso del Perú and Fondo Editorial Pontificia Universidad Católica del Perú.

Zuidema, R. Tom. 2013. 'Les Moitiés de Cuzco et la Mémoire Inca'. In *Au miroir de l'anthropologie histo-rique: Mélanges offerts à Nathan Wachtel*, edited by Juan Carlos Garavaglia, Jacques Poloni-Simard and Gilles Rivière, 119–34. Rennes: Presses Universitaires de Rennes.

Zuidema, R. Tom. 2014. 'Andean Calendrical Knowledge in the Royal Tunics Called TARCO HUALLCA: Inca, Huari and Tiahuanaco Tunics Read as Fourfold Almanacs'. In *Textiles Technical Pracrice and Power in the Andes*, edited by Denise Arnold and Penelope Dransart, 83–106. London: Archetype.

Zuloaga Rada, Marina. 2012. *La conquista negociada: Guarangas, autoridades locales e imperio en Huaylas, Perú (1532–1610)*. Lima: Instituto de Estudios Peruanos and Instituto Francés de Estudios Andinos.

Index

CPSIA information can be obtained
at www.ICGtesting.com
Printed in the USA
BVHW022115200621
609777BV00031B/449